PENGUIN BOOKS

VIETNAM VOICES

John Clark Pratt served for twenty years in the United States Air Force, retiring in 1974 with the rank of lieutenant colonel. During his years of service, he was both a jet instructor pilot and professor of English at the U.S. Air Force Academy. During his tour in Southeast Asia, he commanded the Thailand detachment of Project CHECO (Contemporary Historical Examination of Combat Operations), and it was in Thailand that he wrote four book-length analyses of air operations in the war, flew 101 combat hours in nine different kinds of aircraft, and supervised the microfilming of documents relative to the war. He has written or edited five books: the Viking Critical Library Edition of *One Flew over the Cuckoo's Nest* (also published by Penguin Books); *The Laotian Fragments,* a Vietnam War novel; *The Meaning of Modern Poetry; John Steinbeck;* and (with Victor Neufeldt) *George Eliot's "Middlemarch" Notebooks.* The recipient of a Ph.D. from Princeton University, he has taught American literature in Thailand, Portugal, and the Soviet Union. Mr. Pratt was for five years chairman of the English Department at Colorado State University, where he is at present professor of English.

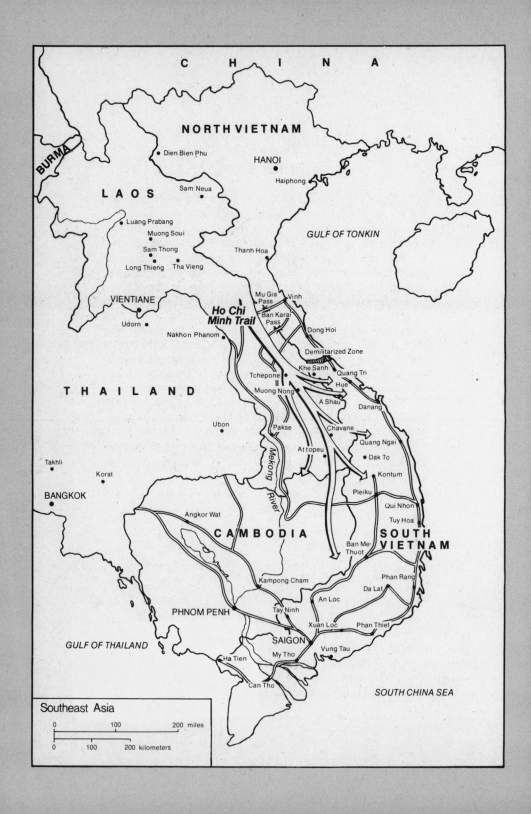

CHINA

NORTH VIETNAM

Dien Bien Phu •   HANOI •

• Sam Neua   Haiphong •

LAOS

Luang Prabang •
Muong Soui •   GULF OF TONKIN
Sam Thong •
Long Thieng • Tha Vieng •   Thanh Hoa •

VIENTIANE •   Mu Gia   Vinh •
                     Pass
Udorn •   *Ho Chi*   Ban Karai
          Minh Trail Pass   Dong Hoi •

Nakhon Phanom •   Demilitarized Zone

THAILAND   Tchepone •   Khe Sanh •   Quang Tri •
                  Muong Nong •   Hue •
                         A Shau •
          Ubon •   Chavane •   Danang •
               Pakse •   Quang Ngai •
                         Attopeu •   Dak To •
Takhli •   Kontum •
Korat •
                         Pleiku •
BANGKOK •   Qui Nhon •

          Angkor Wat •   Tuy Hoa •

          CAMBODIA   SOUTH
                         VIETNAM
                    Ban Me
                    Thuot •
                         Phan Rang •
          Kampong Cham •   Da Lat •
                         An Loc •
PHNOM PENH •   Tay Ninh •
                    Xuan Loc • Phan Thiet •
GULF OF THAILAND   SAIGON •
               My Tho •   Vung Tau •
     • Ha Tien
          Can Tho •   SOUTH CHINA SEA

Mekong River

BURMA

Southeast Asia

0   100   200 miles
0   100   200 kilometers

VIETNAM VOICES

PERSPECTIVES ON THE WAR YEARS 1941–1982

Compiled by
JOHN CLARK PRATT

PENGUIN BOOKS

To those who have written
and to those who would learn
the truth about war in Southeast Asia

PENGUIN BOOKS

Viking Penguin Inc., 40 West 23rd Street,
New York, New York 10010, U.S.A.
Penguin Books Ltd, Harmondsworth,
Middlesex, England
Penguin Books Australia Ltd, Ringwood,
Victoria, Australia
Penguin Books Canada Limited, 2801 John Street,
Markham, Ontario, Canada L3R 1B4
Penguin Books (N.Z.) Ltd, 182–190 Wairau Road,
Auckland 10, New Zealand

First published in the United States of America
in simultaneous hardcover and paperback editions
by Viking Penguin Inc. 1984
Published simultaneously in Canada

Copyright © John Clark Pratt, 1984
All rights reserved

LIBRARY OF CONGRESS CATALOGING IN PUBLICATION DATA
Main entry under title:
Vietnam voices.
  Bibliography: p.
  1. Vietnamese Conflict, 1961–1975. 2. Indochina—
History—1945–   . I. Pratt, John Clark.
[DS557.7.V566 1984b] 959.704'3 84-11172
ISBN 0 14 00.6359 5

Printed in the United States of America by
R.R. Donnelley & Sons Company, Harrisonburg, Virginia
Set in Times Roman
Maps by Christine Goodman
Designed by Sharen DuGoff Egana

Pages 707–708 constitute an extension of this copyright page.

PREFACE

When those who were there remember the Vietnam War, what they think about most are sights, sounds, smells, and feelings. The nighttime beauty of someone else's firefight, the red dust, leeches, women in au dais, rain, *Playboy* centerfolds, GI mustaches, stewardesses on contract flights over and back, scuffed combat boots, body bags, charts and graphs, the Vietnamese children—all these images are part of what they still *see*. Those children—the memory of their high-pitched voices selling everything from "boo-coo cold" Coca-Cola to their sisters—as well as the other sounds: the *whop-whop-whop* of helicopters, the shouted word "incoming," the thump and crunch of artillery, the silence of guard duty on the perimeter, the grating rasp of Saigon motorscooters, the hollow voices of family on an overseas telephone connection, the ever-present crowing of roosters, and the music—live, taped, or on Armed Forces Radio. Mainly hard rock, yes, but also such tunes as "The Windmills of Your Mind," "San Francisco," and, as pronounced by the numerous Filipina or Vietnamese songstresses, "The Gleen Gleen Glass of Home." Never forgotten, too, are the smells of cordite, of death, of a local Vietnamese restaurant, of jet fuel, of the rivers and klongs, of garlic on a woman's breath, of clean clothes and sheets after days in the field, and of high-grade dope. The remembered feelings? Hatred, shame, exultation, satisfaction, fear, horror, and relief—especially when boarding that last flight back to "the world." Often short-lived, however, relief was usually followed by shocked sadness immediately after one's return. As one GI put it: "I didn't come home; I just came back. Home had changed so much that I didn't recognize it. And no one recognized me, either."

No single volume can re-create the whole Vietnam War, but in *Vietnam Voices* I have tried as best I can to answer the ongoing requests to "tell it like it was." None of the many chronologically arranged selections attempts to be definitive; instead, each entry is representative of a larger element and is, I hope, at least true. To many readers, for instance, the selections from works of fiction may seem more "real" than those that should be taken as fact. Only by reading all genres, I believe, can one begin to experience the panorama created by hundreds of differing perspectives of the war. I think that all the views are here: those of the generals, the privates, the draftees, the "lifers," the pilots, the sailors, the presidents, the secretaries of state, the politicians, the North Vietnamese, the South Vietnamese, the Laotians, the CIA agents, the journalists, the protestors, the Cambodians, the POWs, and the families who waited at home. Any omitted perspective, I think, was just not written down.

Vietnam Voices should have been 3,000 pages (my first compilation was much longer), but the intention here is to present the war in an apprehendable form. So large is the body of published and archival Vietnam War literature that the sheer number of available pages boggles well-intentioned chroniclers and readers alike. Also inhibiting is point of view: most of the published works so obviously mirror their authors' personal persuasions that many open-minded readers may be offended. *Vietnam Voices* attempts to be objective, and even though some readers may object to the space given either to the protestors or to the truly heroic exploits of some military men or to the views of the North Vietnamese and Viet Cong (who were, after all, fighting for their country, too), I hope that each perspective has been given enough voice so as not to omit any important aspect of the Vietnam experience.

Regardless, the Southeast Asian war (which included Laos, Cambodia, and Thailand) *must* be understood if nations are not to re-create it in other parts of the world. To believe merely that the United States voluntarily lost the war is hardly enough; what must also be recognized is how this major nation-building attempt in three Asian countries began, developed, and was progressively abandoned amid conflicting claims of victory and loss. Could what the United States was trying to accomplish ever have succeeded at all? Can democratic institutions be imposed from outside on historically autocratic societies? Answers to these and many other questions are possible only if one knows what the Vietnam War really was. *Vietnam Voices* is designed to provide a comprehensive introduction to such a search for understanding.

One of the issues that pervades this book is of course the question of nationhood, but there are also many others: the effects of individual personalities (on all sides); professional versus inducted military men; the morality of human actions (especially in combat); the role of the press; high-level political jealousies and infighting; the question of how much "truth" to reveal; the definition of national goals; the responsibility of the individual conscience; the question of "face"; and the conduct of the war itself. Also evident throughout is the dehumanization of contemporary speech (KBA—"killed by air," "gook" and "dink," and "funny bomb"). Featured as well are the media, with characters as diverse as Walter Cronkite and John Wayne, the latter of whose legend not only influenced the conduct of the war but perhaps more importantly had already helped to create the romantic attitudes toward war that would be so abruptly shattered by the disillusioning reality of combat in Vietnam.

Finally, to state that the whole experience was indeed tragic has become commonplace—but more intriguing, I think, is that in its origins, development, conduct, and denouement, the Vietnam War fits models of literary tragedy provided by Aristotle, Seneca, Shakespeare, and Hegel. Not only just one of the many ironies, the war seen as classic tragedy brings once again into question the basic difference between "life" and "art." Accordingly, much like Shakespeare's later editors, I have created none of the text, but what I have done is indicate Scene and Act divisions at moments of obvious action shifts. Whether one reads *Vietnam Voices* as history, political science, theatre, or Victorian novel, this book presents aspects of the entire war as a drama in which the dialogue is created only by the players themselves. As such, *Vietnam Voices* is truly their story—and yours.

> —John Clark Pratt
> (Vietnam, Laos, Thailand, 1969–70)

ACKNOWLEDGMENTS

No work such as this one could have been completed alone. In addition to thanking the authors whose works I used, as well as those whose writing I could not include, I would like to acknowledge the following people who provided me with invaluable assistance and advice: Joseph W. Angell; Donald Barrett, Librarian, U.S. Air Force Academy; Lieutenant Colonel Mark Berent; Joy Bonnett, USMC Historical Center; Professor Martin Bucco; Tom and Nancy Buchanan; Merritt Clifton; Vince Demma, Center for Military History; Bill Ehrhart; Al Goldberg, Historian, Department of Defense; Wilson Hurley, artist; Colonel Frederick T. Kiley; Edward Lansdale; Ed Marolda, U.S. Naval Historical Center; Bob Perea; Professor Gareth Porter; Colonel Al Preyss; the Raven FACS; Colonel Jack Schlight, Office of Air Force History; Neil Shropshire; Jack Shulimson, USMC Historical Center; Professor Charles Smith; Lieutenant Colonel Eric Solander, U.S. Air Force Office of Public Affairs; and Professor Rosemary Whitaker.

Special thanks must go to Dan Weaver of Viking Penguin, who fought fights for and with the manuscript, and to Viking Penguin's Alan Williams, who has believed in this book almost as long as I have. To John Newman, Special Collections Librarian at Colorado State University, I owe gratitude not only for logistical support and desk space, but also for his rumored comments that I was not what they would think of as a "usual" colonel.

Finally, love and appreciation to my daughter, Pamela, who helped me wrestle the rough draft into shape, and to my wife, Dory, who welcomed me back from that long year in Vietnam, never dreaming that my doing this book would require the emotional equivalent of another complete combat tour, this time with her along.

CONTENTS

LIST OF MAPS

PROLOGUE

1941–May 1955

Peace is a casualty of war

—GI latrine graffito, Saigon

"We don't have twelve years' experience in this country.
We have one year's experience twelve times."
—John Paul Vann, American adviser,
shortly before his death in 1972

"I think that the foreign policy of every country and indeed of the
superpowers should have two levels: (1) which I would call the short-
term goal and (2) the long-term goals. When I look at American
foreign policy, or western foreign policy, I don't see the long-term
goal. I see only short-term goals, and that's why you are always losers
in your conflicts with the Soviet Union. . . . Do you remember that
Shakespeare line in 'As You Like It,' when the character called Jack
enters and says, 'The world is a stage. People come and go out.' I
don't remember it exactly. Everybody has his entrances and his exits.
International politics is also such a scene in my opinion. At every
period there is a play going on. The play which is going on since
World War II has in it two superstars, two superpowers, several
co-stars, which are the industrial countries, and a lot of extras of
people who have no real part."
—Fereydoum Hoveyda,
former Iranian ambassador to the United Nations

"We have a saying we used in Vietnam, that
we finally found out why there are two crew
members in the F-4. One is to fly the
airplane and one is to carry the briefcase full
of the rules of engagement."
—General John D. LaVelle,
Commander, Seventh Air Force

"Perhaps to have been born is the
fundamental crime."
—Bill Tremblay

A young American woman, Cathy Gigante, remembers what it was to grow up during the Vietnam War.

When I Was Young

When I was young, things were different. The sky was a bluer shade of blue when the sun shined. Summer was short and winter, beautiful. Spring, abrupt and full of flowers. Autumn was a bundle of leaves. And time crawled by slowly, hesitantly, as if on its knees. . . .

And there was a war going on all during my childhood, but I did not know it then. It did not really register. A president was shot and then his brother, but they were just words to me, just names, like Vietnam and Kent State and Martin Luther King were named. I was a child. I knew nothing of war.

I watched cartoons. I paged through thin picture books with pretty, lacy drawings. I played 'Princess' and 'Hide and Seek.' I played 'House' and jumped rope. That is what I did when the world was bleeding.

And the world watched newsreels, read papers scattered with photographs of the dead, the mangled and those who were alive. Men fought the war in a place across the sea. Women cried. The brown children there were shot and bombed and sprayed with fire. I just played. I knew nothing of war. . . .

It was a slow realization. It built up over the years, tiny fragments upon segments, segments upon bigger pieces of knowledge. I saw photographs. I read the captions under them in the newspapers. I saw a girl as old as myself running naked down a road, her mouth thrown open in a scream that I could almost hear. I saw a little boy even younger than me carrying his dog tightly in his arms as he ran. I saw the American soldiers, weary and thin, slight forms against the backdrop of jungle. I saw the faces, all of the faces, saw the fear and the dirt smeared across them. And I saw the dead.

But it was all still quite unreal to me, so far away, like a bump in a crater on the moon. Vietnam was like a John Wayne movie, or a story in a book. It was like make-believe: I could see it, yet I could not feel it. It did not touch me. It did not frighten me. Going to the dentist and to school were the only things I held any fear for. . . .

And when Nixon was running for president, my cousin Gary told me that Nixon would cut the school week down to three days. I still don't know where he dug that one up but I wanted Nixon to win. Badly. But after he was elected, I found that Gary was wrong. Everyone was wrong. Nixon wasn't the one.

I read 'Little Women.' I read books about a girl named Beany who had freckles that she was always trying to get rid of. I did not read the newspapers, only the funnies, but every so often I would stumble across a stark black-and-white photograph in the first few pages.

In school, the girls were wearing silverish bracelets that hugged their wrists. I didn't have one, but I wanted one. They had names and numbers stamped into the surface in little black print. They were worn for the soldiers who were prisoners of war in Vietnam. But on the arms of sixth graders, they were only ornaments, charms. To the girls, they were bracelets. We did not understand that the thin bands of metal were not pieces of jewelry, but were symbols. We did not grasp the point, only misused it. We were young.

I began to grow taller, even taller than some of the boys in my class. I began to shave my legs and to wear a flat, elastic brassiere, though I wasn't quite ready for either. But when I began to lay my Ken doll on top of Barbie and made them move around in their stiff, plastic nakedness, I knew that I was growing up.

The war was maturing also. On the news, they said that it would end soon, but we had heard that many times over the years.

School was the same. I sat towards the back of the class, in my tense, cross-fingered nervousness, hoping that Sister Patrick Maureen would not call on me, and if she did, I prayed that I would, Please God!, know the answer. The girls wore their bracelets. The boys lifted our pleated skirts with the windowpoles when Sister Patrick left the room. Life went on as usual. The war went on also.

I don't remember the moment the war ended; it was a quiet sort of finish. I just remember the lists of names in the newspapers. I remember pictures and words, but nothing specific. I remember that after a while the girls stopped wearing their bracelets.

Now I read books about the war, books by men who have had pieces of their bodies blown off or who were crippled severely, books by other men who were tortured. There are television programs and movies. I can see the Kennedys murdered over and over again on film, and can even look at still frames of the step-by-step assassination process, in black-and-white or living color. I can witness the 1960s or early 1970s in print or in pictures, yet it is difficult to believe that I was a child growing up through all of it. I was never told what war was. I never thought that people really bled and hurt and died. I was not only blind, but deaf and dumb as well. I was tucked neatly inside of a dark cocoon of silence, wrapped up tightly and held there.

And when I think back, I feel very foolish. When I sit and study all that was going on and consider how ignorant and unaffected I was by everything, I feel almost embarrassed. I was young at the time and I doubt if anything I could have known or done would have made any difference, yet I hardly knew that there was a war raging. I did not really know the meaning of the word. I did not even know what Vietnam was exactly, or how it began, and now that unknowingness seems almost like a brand of disrespect, like laughing at a funeral. I went on as if nothing were happening, and people were dying for me. Did they die to keep me living in my sheltered, childish ignorance, or in hopes that the war would disrupt my peaceful life and cause me to see?

Nevertheless, I just played games and went to school. That is what I did when the world was bleeding.

The sky is a faded hue, even when the sun is shining. The ground is sometimes shaky under my feet. The seasons all seem to melt into each other and then the cycle is repeated. And time goes by quickly, as if jogging. Now I read the newspapers and examine all of the photographs closely. Now I am aware.

Now I am afraid.[1]

An American president also remembers.

President Ronald Reagan's News Conference of April 1982

"If I recall correctly, when France gave up Indochina as a colony, the leading nations of the world met in Geneva in regard to helping those colonies become independent nations. And since North and South Vietnam had been previous to colonization two separate countries, provisions were made that these two countries could by a vote of all their people together decide whether they wanted to be one country or not. . . ."

"And there wasn't anything surreptitious about it, but when Ho Chi Minh refused to participate in such an election and there was provision that the peoples of both countries could cross the border and live in the other country if they wanted to, and when they began leaving by the thousands and thousands from North Vietnam to live in South Vietnam, Ho Chi Minh closed the border and again violated that part of the agreement. . . ."

"And openly, our country sent military advisers there to help a country which had been a colony have such things as a national security force, an army if you might say, or a military, to defend itself. And they were doing this, I recall correctly, also in civilian clothes, no weapons, until they began being blown up where they lived, in walking down the street by people riding by on bicycles and throwing pipe bombs at them, and then they were permitted to carry side arms or wear uniforms . . ."

"But it was totally a program until John F. Kennedy, when these attacks and forays became so great, that John F. Kennedy authorized the sending in of a division of marines, that was the first move toward combat moves in Vietnam . . ."

Here is the way the Vietnam War really was.

1941   Living in exile in the southern Chinese village of Chingsi, Ho Chi Minh forms the Vietnam Doc Lap Dong Minh, the "League for Independence of Vietnam." During the next few years, Ho and his anti-Japanese Viet Minh guerrillas are trained and supported by a U.S. OSS (Office of Strategic Services) unit code-named "Deer Team."

1945   **6 August**—Atomic bomb dropped on Hiroshima. **9 August**—Atomic bomb dropped on Nagasaki. **10 August**—World War II ends with Japan's surrender. **25 August**—With members of U.S. "Deer Team" present, Ho Chi Minh announces independence for the Democratic Republic of Vietnam (DRV) as a "republic" within the French Union. **26 August**—Ho Chi Minh enters Hanoi. During the next few months, Chinese and French troops disarm occupying Japanese soldiers north of Vietnam's 16th parallel; British forces do the same in the South and free interned French army. **23 September**—French forces overthrow Ho Chi Minh's DRV government in Saigon. British concur with France's claim to sovereignty. Promising to withdraw from the North, France opens negotiations with Ho Chi Minh on DRV's "status." United States issues statement that expresses no policy for or against French control, but the United States "assumes that the French claim to have the support of the people [will be] borne out by future events."

1946   **20 November**—Fighting breaks out between Viet Minh and French in Haiphong, leading to French occupation of that city. **20 December**—Ho Chi Minh declares that the Viet Minh are at war with France and takes his followers to the jungles and hills. French Indochina War begins.

The first significant U.S. policy statement toward Indochina shows an attempt to resist what is seen to be Communist expansion, while at the same time to promote Vietnamese independence and self-government without antagonizing France, the major U.S. continental European ally.

Executive Secretariat Files
Department of State Policy Statement on Indochina
September 27, 1948

A. OBJECTIVES

The immediate objective of US policy in Indochina is to assist in a solution of the present impasse which will be mutually satisfactory to the French and the Vietnamese peoples, which will result in the termination of the present hostilities, and which will be within the framework of US security.

Our long-term objectives are: (1) to eliminate so far as possible Communist influence in Indochina and to see installed a self-governing nationalist state which will be friendly to the US and which, commensurate with the capacity of the peoples involved, will be patterned upon our conception of a democratic state as opposed to the totalitarian state which would

evolve inevitably from Communist domination; (2) to foster the association of the peoples of Indochina with the western powers, particularly
with France with whose customs, language and laws they are familiar, to
the end that those peoples will prefer freely to cooperate with the western
powers culturally, economically and politically; (3) to raise the standard
of living so that the peoples of Indochina will be less receptive to totalitarian influences and will have an incentive to work productively and thus
contribute to a better balanced world economy; and (4) to prevent undue
Chinese penetration and subsequent influence in Indochina so that the
peoples of Indochina will not be hampered in their natural developments
by the pressure of an alien people and alien interests. . . .[2]

1949   Chinese Communists overthrow Chiang Kai-shek's Nationalists,
who flee to Formosa. French establish Bao Dai (former emperor of
Annam) as Vietnam's chief of state and sign agreement with royal
government of Laos that maintains French control in "Associated
States."

Having agreed at Yalta to Soviet control over formerly independent East-
ern European countries, the U.S. government becomes alarmed at the
possibility of the Chinese Communist expansion in Asia. This cable to
Saigon from the U.S. secretary of state, Dean Acheson, shows the birth of
the "domino theory" that will determine subsequent U.S. foreign policy.

Outgoing Telegram
Department of State

MAY 10, 1949

AMCONSUL: SAIGON, INDOCHINA

ASSUMPTION URTEL 141 DEPT DESIRES SUCCESS BAODAI EXPERIMENT ENTIRELY
CORRECT. SINCE APPEARS BE NO OTHER ALTERNATIVE TO ESTAB COMMIE PAT-
TERN VIETNAM. DEPT CONSIDERS NO EFFORT SHLD BE SPARED BY FR[ENCH],
OTHER WESTERN POWERS, AND NON-COMMIE ASIAN NATIONS TO ASSURE EXPERI-
MENT BEST CHANCE SUCCEEDING.

AT PROPER TIME AND UNDER PROPER CIRCUMSTANCES DEPT WILL BE PREPARED
DO ITS PART BY EXTENDING RECOGNITION BAODAI GOVT AND BY EXPLORING
POSSIBILITY OF COMPLYING WITH ANY REQUEST BY SUCH GOVT FOR US ARMS
AND ECON ASSISTANCE. MUST BE UNDERSTOOD HOWEVER AID PROGRAM THIS
NATURE WLD REQUIRE CONGRESSIONAL APPROVAL. SINCE US CLD HOWEVER
SCARCELY AFFORD BACKING GOVT WHICH WLD HAVE COLOR AND BE LIKELY
SUFFER FATE OF PUPPET REGIME IT MUST FIRST BE CLEAR FR WILL OFFER ALL
NECESSARY CONCESSIONS TO MAKE BAODAI SOLUTION ATTRACTIVE TO NATION-

ALISTS. THIS IS STEP OF WHICH FR THEMSELVES MUST SEE URGENT NECESSITY
VIEW POSSIBLY SHORT TIME REMAINING BEFORE COMMIE SUCCESSES CHINA FELT
INDOCHINA. MOREOVER, BAODAI GOVT MUST THROUGH OWN OFFER DEMON-
STRATE CAPACITY ORGANIZE AND CONDUCT AFFAIRS WISELY SO TO ENSURE
MAXIMUM OPPORTUNITY OBTAINING REQUISITE POPULAR SUPPORT INASMUCH AS
GOVT CREATED INDOCHINA ANALOGOUS KOUMINTANG WLD BE FOREDOOMED
FAILURE. . . .

Acheson[3]

1950 **18 January**—Government of People's Republic of China (PRC)
recognizes Ho Chi Minh's Democratic Republic of Vietnam (DRV).
30 January—U.S.S.R. recognizes DRV. **7 February**—United States
recognizes Bao Dai as head of the State of Vietnam in Saigon.

---

*In Washington, as Senator Joseph R. McCarthy's strident denunciation of
alleged Communist influence becomes louder, U.S. policy toward Indochina reflects a growing concern.*

Report by the National Security Council
on the Position of the United States
with Respect to Indochina

27 February 1950

THE PROBLEM

1. To undertake a determination of all practicable United States measures to protect its security in Indochina and to prevent the expansion of
communist aggression in that area.

ANALYSIS

2. It is recognized that the threat of communist aggression against
Indochina is only one phase of anticipated communist plans to seize all of
Southeast Asia. It is understood that Burma is weak internally and could
be invaded without strong opposition or even that the Government of
Burma could be subverted. However, Indochina is the area most immediately threatened. It is also the only area adjacent to communist China
which contains a large European army, which along with native troops is
now in armed conflict with the forces of communist aggression. A decision to contain communist expansion at the border of Indochina must be
considered as a part of a wider study to prevent communist aggression
into other parts of Southeast Asia.

3. A large segment of the Indochinese nationalist movement was seized
in 1945 by Ho Chi Minh, a Vietnamese who under various aliases has
served as a communist agent for thirty years. He has attracted non-
communist as well as communist elements to his support. In 1946, he

attempted, but failed to secure French agreement to his recognition as the head of a government of Vietnam. Since then he has directed a guerrilla army in raids against French installations and lines of communication. French forces which have been attempting to restore law and order found themselves pitted against a determined adversary who manufactures effective arms locally, who received supplies of arms from outside sources, who maintained no capital or permanent headquarters and who was, and is able, to disrupt and harass almost any area within Vietnam (Tonkin, Annam and Cochinchina) at will.

4. The United States has, since the Japanese surrender, pointed out to the French Government that the legitimate nationalist aspirations of the people of Indochina must be satisfied, and that a return to the prewar colonial rule is not possible. The Department of State has pointed out to the French Government that it was and is necessary to establish and support governments in Indochina particularly in Vietnam, under leaders who are capable of attracting to their causes the non-communist nationalist followers who had drifted to the Ho Chi Minh communist movement in the absence of any non-communist nationalist movement around which to plan their aspirations. . . .

7. The newly formed States of Vietnam, Laos and Cambodia do not as yet have sufficient political stability nor military power to prevent the infiltration into their areas of Ho Chi Minh's forces. The French Armed Forces, while apparently effectively utilized at the present time, can do little more than to maintain the status quo. Their strength of some 140,000 does, however, represent an army in being and the only military bulwark in that area against the further expansion of communist aggression from either internal or external forces.

8. The presence of Chinese Communist troops along the border of Indochina makes it possible for arms, material and troops to move freely from Communist China to the northern Tonkin area now controlled by Ho Chi Minh. There is already evidence of movement of arms.

9. In the present state of affairs, it is doubtful that the combined native Indochinese and French troops can successfully contain Ho's forces should they be strengthened by either Chinese Communist troops crossing the border, or Communist-supplied arms and material in quantity from outside Indochina strengthening Ho's forces.

CONCLUSIONS

10. It is important to United States security interests that all practicable measures be taken to prevent further communist expansion in Southeast Asia. Indochina is a key area of Southeast Asia and is under immediate threat.

11. The neighboring countries of Thailand and Burma could be expected to fall under Communist domination if Indochina were controlled by a Communist-dominated government. The balance of Southeast Asia would then be in grave hazard.

12. Accordingly, the Departments of State and Defense should prepare as a matter of priority a program of all practicable measures designed to protect United States security interests in Indochina.[4]

1950 **6 March**—As one of the National Security Council recommended "practicable measures," a U.S. investigatory mission is sent to Saigon. **1 May**—President Truman authorizes $10,000,000 for military aid to France. **30 May**—The first U.S. Economic Mission (USECOM) is established in Saigon. **25 June**—North Korea invades South Korea. Korean War begins. **4 July**—Under a mandate from the United Nations, U.S. armed forces arrive in Korea. **10 October**—U.S. Military Assistance and Advisory Group (MAAG) is established in Saigon. **26 October**—Victorious U.N. forces control all of Korea. **November**—Communist Chinese forces enter Korean War; U.N. forces are routed and forced to retreat far south. **23 December**—United States signs mutual defense agreement with France, South Vietnam, Cambodia, and Laos.

Regardless of their political orientation, most analysts recognize the long-term changes that are taking place in Asia. In 1951 Asian historian Robert Payne writes about them in Red Storm over Asia.

The woods are burning, boy; there's a big fire going on all around.
—ARTHUR MILLER, *Death of a Salesman*

This book is concerned with the Communist march across Asia, chiefly during the years 1948–1950. . . . During those three years, the most significant events in Asia were the Communist conquest of China, the extension of the influence of the government of the Indonesian Republic over the majority of the islands of the Indies, and the war in Korea: in all these events Communism played a major part, and so they are studied here at some length. . . .

Anyone looking at the map of Asia where the Communist-occupied territories are marked in red sees a vast red thundercloud from which a few drops of scalding rain are descending. There are drops in India and Pakistan, in Iran, in Burma and Malaya; there are large splashes in the Philippines and in Indochina. A thundercloud cannot be contained. It must pass on or be broken up, or it must change into some other kind of cloud altogether. The very shape of the thundercloud is something that should be studied carefully. What is clear is that unless radical measures are taken, the raindrops will become a flood.

The thundercloud has been gathering for a long time, and before it is finally dissipated, if it is ever dissipated, we can expect more raindrops to fall. . . .

The revolt of Asia began, on the whole, slowly and cautiously. The Communists were not a force to be reckoned with outside China, because the nationalists had stolen their thunder and because most of the Communist parties had lost whatever prestige they once possessed by cooperating with the colonial powers against a common enemy. But once the influence of the colonial powers began to be withdrawn, there was a vacuum. The Communists attempted to regain, and sometimes succeeded in regaining, their former authority, and there followed a sharp struggle between the Communists and Socialists for power. Asia was left without a moral code. The old religions, the old customary laws, the old feudalism, the carefully endowed pretexts by which certain castes were allowed to rule, all these became suspect. It was not that the revolutionaries had overthrown the past, for the past remained, the old traditions giving color to the revolutionary movements, but the absence of any defined principles or any certain aim once their independence was established allowed gravitation toward a state where there were no principles. An almost nihilistic opportunism became inevitable in all the countries where a moderate "third force" either failed to take power or found itself with no means of exerting its power. The countries which had felt the pressure of colonialism most severely became the most anarchistic. If the massacres in the communal disputes in India did not arise solely as the result of the peculiar social system which the British had imposed on India, at least they arose partly as the consequence of Great Britain's failure to impose a moral code applicable to the conquerors and the conquered alike. In Korea and Burma the long history of postwar violence had its origins in the violent traditions of the past, but the violence we have known in recent history springs very largely from the explosion which occurs when colonialism is removed. The Burmese, trained to an acquiescent Buddhism, and the Koreans, trained in Shintoism, were violent in the same way and for the same reasons: they possessed no aims, no certain direction, no mythology, no code by which the relations between individuals could be ruled. As a consequence, their pent-up energies exploded very often into a savage nihilism. Since no one was traditionally empowered to rule, everyone could rule. Since no one was entitled to wealth, everyone was entitled to wealth. Since the old laws were clearly in abeyance, everyone was entitled to do as he pleased. . . .

What, then, should be done? One thing is quite clear: the sending of arms to Indochina to aid the French garrisons without a complete revision of the agreement of March 8, 1949, is a counsel of despair, for the arms cannot be put to effective use unless there is a close understanding between the government and the peasant partisans who fight on the side of the French. What is needed, far more than armaments, is the expansion of the social arm of America until it reaches the villages of Asia. It is not enough that there should be American information centers in the large towns, though such centers have been opened in Hanoi, Saigon, and Vientiane, the capital of Laos. What is far more necessary is that there should be in America an understanding of the forces which move the Indochinese peasants, and a real understanding of their demands, and the kind of government which they, rather than the French, are prepared to accept. It will have to be a government in which the peasants are represented on the highest levels. The danger lies in the possibility that the French, once in possession of American arms, will be even less inclined to listen to the legitimate claims of the peasants; it is significant that it was only when they were assured of American guns in a continuous stream that Bao Dai's government introduced extraordinary powers providing for automatic capital punishment in cases of sabotage. The law allowed the premier, Thanh Van Huu, to take powers by decree "to allow him to act rapidly and effectively against terrorists, saboteurs, and their accomplices." These new measures allowed the government to set up special courts empowered to try and execute terrorists within forty-eight hours, but the word "terrorist" could be extended to include anyone accused by an informer of participating in, or collaborating with, Viet-Minh. In effect, these measures, which were devised by a special ministerial commission working in secret to avoid assassination attempts, deprived the Indochinese of any vestige of habeas corpus. It was significant that the French waited five years before they gave informers these high and dangerous powers: the law was signed by Bao Dai as chief of state as late as June 8, 1950. Henceforward any accused political prisoner could be imprisoned without trial for an indefinite period, or he could be shot after no more than a cursory examination.

It is unlikely that the rigidity of the French military government will lessen with the arrival of American military and economic aid. Many politically conscious Indochinese have seen in the increasing influence of America in their affairs a hope of a greater independence. The French themselves have accepted American aid only because the drain on their own resources has been such as to strangle their advance, and they have demonstrated a kind of casual, secretive bitterness in the way in which they have been compelled to seek help from others. They point out that they do not do this of their own choosing, and they refuse to accept advice on how to deal with the Indochinese peasant, saying that they have had nearly a hundred years of experience in Indochina, whereas American advisers have been present on the scene for only a few weeks.

The crucial peril, therefore, does not lie in the intentions of Mao Tse-tung or in the physical power of Viet-Minh. It lies in the absence of any real intention to create a social revolution in the south. As long as merchants in Saigon and Hanoi can make vast fortunes, as long as the government encourages the smoking of opium by making opium a state monopoly, as long as the casinos flourish, as long as the peasants are unrepresented in an authoritarian government, there can be no hope of a social revolution under French auspices; and as long as Viet-Minh alone carries through the social revolution in the territory where it operates, the success of Viet-Minh is assured.[5]

In the early 1950s, British reporter and author Graham Greene is living in Saigon. His novel The Quiet American *(1956) presents the relationship between a middle-aged British correspondent, Thomas Fowler, and a young American, Alden Pyle, who is a member of the newly established American Economic Mission to the Bao Dai government.*

The morning Pyle arrived in the square by the Continental I had seen enough of my American colleagues of the Press, big, noisy, boyish and middle-aged, full of sour cracks against the French, who were, when all was said, fighting this war. Periodically, after an engagement had been tidily finished and the casualties removed from the scene, they would be summoned to Hanoi, nearly four hours' flight away, addressed by the Commander-in-Chief, lodged for one night in a Press Camp where they boasted that the barman was the best in Indo-China, flown over the late battlefield, at a height of 3,000 feet (the limit of a heavy machine-gun's range) and then delivered safely and noisily back, like a school-treat, to the Continental Hotel in Saigon.

Pyle was quiet, he seemed modest, sometimes that first day I had to lean forward to catch what he was saying. And he was very, very serious. Several times he seemed to shrink up within himself at the noise of the American Press on the terrace above—the terrace which was popularly believed to be safer from hand-grenades. But he criticized nobody. . . .

With his gangly legs and his crew-cut and his wide campus gaze he seemed incapable of harm. The tables on the street were most of them full. 'Do you mind?' he had asked with serious courtesy. 'My name's Pyle. I'm new here,' and he had folded himself around a chair and ordered a beer. Then he looked quickly up into the hard noon glare.

'Was that a grenade?' he asked with excitement and hope.

'Most likely the exhaust of a car,' I said, and was suddenly sorry for his disappointment. One forgets so quickly one's own youth: once I was interested myself in what for want of a better term they called news. But grenades had staled on me; they were something listed on the back page of the local paper—so many last night in Saigon, so many in Cholon: they never made the European Press. Up the street came the lovely flat figures—the white silk trousers, the long tight jackets in pink and mauve patterns slit up the thigh. I watched them with the nostalgia I knew I would feel when I had left these regions for ever. 'They are lovely, aren't they?' I said over my beer, and Pyle cast them a cursory glance as they went up the rue Catinat.

'Oh, sure,' he said indifferently: he was a serious type. 'The Minister's very concerned about these grenades. It would be very awkward, he says, if there was an incident—with one of us, I mean.'

'With one of you? Yes, I suppose that would be serious. Congress wouldn't like it.' Why does one want to tease the innocent? Perhaps only ten days ago he had been walking back across the Common in Boston, his arms full of the books he had been reading in advance on the Far East and the problems of China. He didn't even hear what I said; he was absorbed already in the dilemmas of Democracy and the responsibilities of the West; he was determined—I learnt that very soon—to do good, not to any individual person but to a country, a continent, a world. . . .

'Have you read York Harding?' he asked.

'No. No, I don't think so. What did he write?'

He gazed at a milk-bar across the street and said dreamily, 'That looks like a soda-fountain.' I wondered what depth of homesickness lay behind his odd choice of what to observe in a scene so unfamiliar. But hadn't I on my first walk up the rue Catinat noticed first the shop with the Guerlain perfume and comforted myself with the thought that, after all, Europe was only distant thirty hours? He looked reluctantly away from the milk-bar and said, 'York wrote a book called *The Advance of Red China*. It's a very profound book.'

'I haven't read it. Do you know him?'

He nodded solemnly and lapsed into silence. But he broke it again a moment later to modify the impression he had given. 'I don't know him well,' he said. 'I guess I only met him twice.' I liked him for that—to consider it was boasting to claim acquaintance with—what was his name?—York Harding. I was to learn later that he had an enormous respect for what he called serious writers. That term excluded novelists, poets and dramatists unless they had what he called a contemporary theme, and even then it was better to read the straight stuff as you got it from York. . . .

I began, while he watched me intently like a prize pupil, by explaining the situation in the north, in Tonkin, where the French in those days were hanging on to the delta of the Red River, which contained Hanoi and the only northern port, Haiphong. Here most of the rice was grown, and when the harvest was ready the annual battle for the rice always began.

'That's the north,' I said. 'The French may hold, poor devils, if the Chinese don't come to help the Vietminh. A war of jungle and mountain and marsh, paddy fields where you wade shoulder-high and the enemy simply disappear, bury their arms, put on peasant dress. But you can rot comfortably in the damp in Hanoi. They don't throw bombs there. God knows why. You could call it a regular war.'

'And here in the south?'

'The French control the main roads until seven in the evening: they control the watch towers after that, and the towns—part of them. That doesn't mean you are safe, or there wouldn't be iron grilles in front of the restaurants.'

How often I had explained all this before. I was a record always turned on for the benefit of newcomers—the visiting Member of Parliament, the new British Minister. Sometimes I would wake up in the night saying, 'Take the case of the Caodaists.' Or the Hoa-Haos or the Binh Xuyen, all the private armies who sold their services for money or revenge.

Strangers found them picturesque, but there is nothing picturesque in treachery and distrust.

'And now,' I said, 'there's General Thé. He was Caodaist Chief of Staff, but he's taken to the hills to fight both sides, the French, the Communists . . .'

'York,' Pyle said, 'wrote that what the East needed was a Third Force.' Perhaps I should have seen that fanatic gleam, the quick response to a phrase, the magic sound of figures: Fifth Column, Third Force, Seventh Day. I might have saved all of us a lot of trouble, even Pyle, if I had realized the direction of that indefatigable young brain. But I left him with arid bones of background and took my daily walk up and down the rue Catinat. He would have to learn for himself the real background that held you as a smell does: the gold of the rice-fields under a flat late sun: the fishers' fragile cranes hovering over the fields like mosquitoes: the cups of tea on an old abbot's platform, with his bed and his commercial calendars, his buckets and broken cups and the junk of a lifetime washed up around his chair: the mollusc hats of the girls repairing the road where a mine had burst: the gold and the young green and the bright dresses of the south, and in the north the deep browns and the black clothes and the circle of enemy mountains and the drone of planes.

Having become personally involved in supplying munitions to General Thé's "Third Force," Pyle later reveals his attitude to Fowler.

'You know so much now, it won't hurt to tell you a bit more. I saw Thé this afternoon.'

'Saw him? Is he in Saigon? I suppose he came to see how his bomb worked.'

'That's in confidence, Thomas. I dealt with him very severely.' He spoke like the captain of a school-team who has found one of his boys breaking his training. All the same I asked him with a certain hope, 'Have you thrown him over?'

'I told him that if he made another uncontrolled demonstration we would have no more to do with him.'

'But haven't you finished with him already, Pyle?' I pushed impatiently at his dog which was nosing around my ankles.

'I can't. (Sit down, Duke.) In the long run he's the only hope we have. If he came to power with our help, we could rely on him . . .'

'How many people have to die before you realize . . . ?' But I could tell that it was a hopeless argument.

'Realize what, Thomas?'

'That there's no such thing as gratitude in politics.'

'At least they won't hate us like they hate the French.'

'Are you sure? Sometimes we have a kind of love for our enemies and sometimes we feel hate for our friends.'

'You talk like a European, Thomas. These people aren't complicated.'

'Is that what you've learned in a few months? You'll be calling them childlike next.'

'Well—in a way.' . . .

Later, Fowler goes to see a Saigon businessman whom he suspects is a member of an anti-Thé faction.

Mr Heng himself came cordially forward and ushered me into a little inner room lined with the black carved uncomfortable chairs you find in every Chinese ante-room, unused, unwelcoming. But I had the sense that on this occasion the chairs had been employed, for there were five little tea-cups on the table, and two were not empty. 'I have interrupted a meeting,' I said.

'A matter of business,' Mr Heng said evasively, 'of no importance. I am always glad to see you, Mr Fowler.'

'I've come from the Place Garnier,' I said.

'I thought that was it.'

'You've heard . . .'

'Someone telephoned to me. It was thought best that I keep away from Mr Chou's for a while. The police will be very active today.'

'But you had nothing to do with it.'

'It is the business of the police to find a culprit.'

'It was Pyle again,' I said.

'Yes.'

'It was a terrible thing to do.'

'General Thé is not a very controlled character.'

'And bombs aren't for boys from Boston. Who is Pyle's chief, Heng?'

'I have the impression that Mr Pyle is very much his own master.'

'What is he? O.S.S.?'

'The initial letters are not very important. I think now they are different.'

'What can I do, Heng? He's got to be stopped.'

'You can publish the truth. Or perhaps you cannot?'

'My paper's not interested in General Thé. They are only interested in your people, Heng.' . . .

After dinner I sat and waited for Pyle in my room over the rue Catinat; he had said, 'I'll be with you at latest by ten,' and when midnight struck I couldn't stay quiet any longer and went down into the street. A lot of old women in black trousers squatted on the landing: it was February and I suppose too hot for them in bed. One trishaw driver pedalled slowly by towards the river-front and I could see lamps burning where they had disembarked the new American planes. There was no sign of Pyle anywhere in the long street.

Of course, I told myself, he might have been detained for some reason at the American Legation, but surely in that case he would have telephoned to the restaurant—he was very meticulous about small courtesies. I turned to go indoors when I saw a girl waiting in the next doorway. I couldn't see her face, only the white silk trousers and the long flowered robe, but I knew her for all that. She had so often waited for me to come home at just this place and hour.

'Phuong,' I said—which means Phoenix, but nothing nowadays is fabulous and nothing rises from its ashes. I knew before she had time to tell me that she was waiting for Pyle too. 'He isn't here.'

After being informed of Pyle's murder, Fowler meets another employee of the American embassy.

The Economic Attaché was standing by his Packard when I came out, trying to explain something to his driver. He was a stout middle-aged man with an exaggerated bottom and a face that looked as if it never needed a razor. He called out, 'Fowler. Could you explain to this darned driver . . . ?'

I explained.

He said, 'But that's just what I told him, but he always pretends not to understand French.'

'It may be a matter of accent.'

'I was three years in Paris. My accent's good enough for one of these darned Vietnamese.'

'The voice of Democracy,' I said.

'What's that?'

'I expect it's a book by York Harding.'

'I don't get you.' He took a suspicious look at the box I carried. 'What've you got there?' he said.

'Two pairs of white silk trousers, two silk robes, some girl's underpants—three pairs, I think. All home products. No American aid.'

'Have you been up there?' he asked.

'Yes.'

'You heard the news?'

'Yes.'

'It's a terrible thing,' he said, 'terrible.'

'I expect the Minister's very disturbed.'

'I should say. He's with the High Commissioner now, and he's asked for an interview with the President.' He put his hand on my arm and walked me away from the cars. 'You knew young Pyle well, didn't you? I can't get over a thing like that happening to him. I knew his father. Professor Harold C. Pyle—you'll have heard of him?'

'No.'

'He's the world authority on underwater erosion. Didn't you see his picture on the cover of *Time* the other month?'

'Oh, I think I remember. A crumbling cliff in the background and gold-rimmed glasses in the foreground.'

'That's him. I had to draft the cable home. It was terrible. I loved that boy like he was my son.'

'That makes you closely related to his father.'

He turned his wet brown eyes on me. He said, 'What's getting you? That's not the way to talk when a fine young fellow . . .'

'I'm sorry,' I said. 'Death takes people in different ways.' Perhaps he had really loved Pyle. 'What did you say in your cable?' I asked.

He replied seriously and literally, ' "Grieved to report your son died a soldier's death in cause of Democracy." The Minister signed it.'

'A soldier's death,' I said. 'Mightn't that prove a bit confusing? I mean to the folks at home. The Economic Aid Mission doesn't sound like the Army. Do you get Purple Hearts?'

He said in a low voice, tense with ambiguity, 'He had special duties.'

'Oh yes, we all guessed that.'

'He didn't talk, did he?'

'Oh no,' I said, and Vigot's phrase came back to me, 'He was a very quiet American.'

'Have you any hunch,' he asked, 'why they killed him? and who?'

Suddenly I was angry; I was tired of the whole pack of them with their private stores of Coca-Cola and their portable hospitals and their too wide cars and their not quite latest guns. I said, 'Yes. They killed him because he was too innocent to live. He was young and ignorant and silly and he got involved. He had no more of a notion than any of you what the whole affair's about, and you gave him money and York Harding's books on the East and said, "Go ahead. Win the East for Democracy." He never saw anything he hadn't heard in a lecture-hall, and his writers and his lecturers made a fool of him. When he saw a dead body he couldn't see the wounds. A Red menace, a soldier of democracy.'

'I thought you were his friend,' he said in a tone of reproach.

'I *was* his friend. I'd have liked to see him reading the Sunday supplements at home and following the baseball. I'd have liked to see him safe with a standardized American girl who subscribed to the Book Club.'

He cleared his throat with embarrassment. 'Of course,' he said, 'I'd forgotten that unfortunate business. I was quite on your side, Fowler. He behaved very badly. I don't mind telling you I had a long talk with him about the girl. You see, I had the advantage of knowing Professor and Mrs Pyle.'

I . . . walked away. . . . and when I looked back at him he was watching me with pained perplexity: an eternal brother who didn't understand.[6]

1951 **31 March**—In Korea, the 38th parallel is regained by U.N. forces. **11 April**—U.N. Commander-in-Chief Douglas MacArthur is relieved of duty by President Truman when MacArthur advocates extending the war to Chinese territory. **10 July**—Negotiations between U.N. and North Korean representatives begin.

During the Korean truce negotiations, fighting continues, and the United States further increases its involvement throughout Southeast Asia.

**Statement of Policy
by the National Security Council
on United States Objectives and Courses of Action
with Respect to Southeast Asia**

25 June 1952

OBJECTIVE

1. To prevent the countries of Southeast Asia from passing into the communist orbit, and to assist them to develop the will and ability to resist communism from within and without and to contribute to the strengthening of the free world. . . .

COURSES OF ACTION

Southeast Asia

7. With respect to Southeast Asia, the United States should:

a. Strengthen propaganda and cultural activities, as appropriate, in relation to the area to foster increased alignment of the people with the free world.

b. Continue, as appropriate, programs of economic and technical assistance designed to strengthen the indigenous non-communist governments of the area.

c. Encourage the countries of Southeast Asia to restore and expand their commerce with each other and with the rest of the free world, and stimulate the flow of the raw material resources of the area to the free world.

d. Seek agreement with other nations, including at least France, the UK, Australia and New Zealand, for a joint warning to Communist China regarding the grave consequences of Chinese aggression against Southeast Asia, the issuance of such a warning to be contingent upon the prior agreement of France and the UK to participate in the courses of action set forth in paragraphs 10*c,* 12, 14*f* (1) and (2), and 15*c* (1) and (2), and such others as are determined as a result of prior trilateral consultation, in the event such a warning is ignored.

e. Seek UK and French agreement in principle that a naval blockade of Communist China should be included in the minimum courses of action set forth in paragraph 10*c* below.

f. Continue to encourage and support closer cooperation among the countries of Southeast Asia, and between those countries and the United States, Great Britain, France, the Philippines, Australia, New Zealand, South Asia and Japan.

g. Strengthen, as appropriate, covert operations designed to assist in the achievement of U.S. objectives in Southeast Asia.

h. Continue activities and operations designed to encourage the overseas Chinese communities in Southeast Asia to organize and activate anti-communist groups and activities within their own communities, to resist the effects of parallel pro-communist groups and activities and, generally, to increase their orientation toward the free world.

i. Take measures to promote the coordinated defense of the area, and encourage and support the spirit of resistance among the peoples of Southeast Asia to Chinese Communist aggression and to the encroachments of local communists.

j. Make clear to the American people the importance of Southeast Asia to the security of the United States so that they may be prepared for any of the courses of action proposed herein.[7]

1952   **1 November**—The United States explodes the first hydrogen bomb.
1953   **20 January**—Dwight D. Eisenhower inaugurated president of the United States. **5 March**—Joseph Stalin dies. **13 April**—Viet Minh and Lao Liberation forces seize Sam Neua province in northwest Laos from French. Pathet Lao (Communist) government formed. **May**—United States sends six C-119 civilian transport aircraft and pilots to assist French against Viet Minh/Pathet Lao. **19 June**— Convicted atomic spies Julius and Ethel Rosenberg executed for having passed information to the U.S.S.R.

The day after the Rosenbergs' execution, U.S. Air Force Colonel Edward Geary Lansdale leaves the Philippines for his first official visit to Saigon. During the next fifteen years, Lansdale will become significantly involved in all American policy and actions in Vietnam. His autobiography, In the Midst of Wars, *presents an unclassified version of his experiences.*

On June 20, 1953, with progress in the Philippines going well, I was able to accept an invitation to join a small U.S. group headed by General John W. "Iron Mike" O'Daniel which stopped at Clark AFB en route to Indochina. In Saigon the group was to meet with French General Henri Navarre, for any counseling he wished and to examine his needs for resources. Navarre arrived in Saigon shortly before we did, assuming command over all the forces fighting the Communist Vietminh guerrillas in the Associated States of Vietnam, Cambodia, and Laos. The visit of about six weeks gave me a unique introduction to the affairs of Indochina, at the height of French power, in a savage war that had been going on since 1946.

Some of the French officials had demurred about my last-minute inclusion in the O'Daniel mission (apparently they saw me as a dangerous revolutionary), but General Navarre welcomed me graciously. He was devising details for a grand plan for winning the war and asked me for thoughts on unconventional operations, such as intelligence, psychological warfare, counter-guerrilla maquis, and pacification. He agreed that I required a firsthand look, so I traveled throughout the three Associated States visiting headquarters, combat areas, training camps, and local political groups involved in pacification. I had only a smattering of French so I relied heavily on interpreters, sign-language, and a pocket dictionary. The people were strikingly different from the Filipinos, but the guerrilla methods of the Communists were all too familiar. . . .

The majority of the Vietnamese, still hungering for independence, had no side to join. They were opposed to both the Communist Vietminh and the French. As the war raged around their families and homes, they gave lip service to whichever side was locally dominant, in order to stay alive. When French Union forces ravaged the countryside trying to destroy the Vietminh guerrillas, the resentful people joined the Vietminh to get revenge. Later, when the French increased measures of Vietnamese self-rule and promised an independent Vietnam, nationalists started joining the fight against the Vietminh in ever-mounting numbers. By the time I visited Vietnam in 1953, millions of Vietnamese had taken a definite stand against the Vietminh.

I was amazed at the hundreds of forts I saw in Vietnam, ranging from big complexes of bunkers and trench systems to little *Beau Geste* movie set forts that housed a squad, a platoon, or a company. Totally unlike the Philippine Army's campaign against the Huks, most of the French Union forces were manning static defense positions. Frequently, most of the countryside had been left to the enemy. There was a Vietnamese Army and large forces of local Vietnamese militia, both with a liberal sprinkling of French soldiery to train, advise, administer, and even command them. The Vietnamese civil administration reflected this same mixture. There were French administrators and advisers throughout the governmental structure. It struck me that French paternalism was turning over the controls of self-rule too slowly and grudgingly to the Vietnamese to generate any enthusiasm among Vietnamese nationalists. I didn't see how Navarre was going to win, unless he made radical changes to get the Vietnamese nationalists much more deeply involved. They needed something worth risking their lives for. I said as much. French officials reacted as though they thought I was going to undertake radical changes myself and appeared glad when I left Indochina.

Plain arithmetic was pertinent to any scrutiny of the struggle in Indochina. The best estimates I could get from French officers and neutral observers put Vietminh strength at somewhere between 300,000 and 400,000 men. (Oddly enough, General Vo nguyen Giap who commanded the Vietminh was equally offhand about numbers in his writings later, speaking of "hundreds of thousands.") From captured documents and other evidence, I deduced conservatively that there were about 335,000 men in the Vietminh regular army and in its local militia, and perhaps a million civilians helping them actively, including villagers impressed into forced labor as porters of supplies. Against them were arrayed some 433,000 men of the French "Forces d'Extrême-Orient": 233,000 in the French Expeditionary Force of 177,000 regulars and 56,000 *supplétifs* (native militia in the French command) and 199,500 men in the Associated States Forces (of which the Vietnamese Army had over 100,000, a big growth over its start in 1949). Whatever the true figure of the enemy's strength, the numbers were too close to a one-to-one ratio for conventional forces to have any realistic hope of defeating guerrilla forces. Even imaginative unconventional campaigns required a better ratio. In Malaya it took 65,000 troops and police to defeat 8,000 guerrillas. In the Philippines it was 50,000 troops and constabulary against 15,000 guerrillas.

Some memories of my Indochina visit have stuck with me. There was the hasty trip to a foreign legion outpost on the Plaine des Jarres in Laos to observe a sudden Vietminh invasion of the area—only to discover that the Communist invasion had been called off when the French preclusively bought up the opium crop in the region and thus denied it to the enemy. (Ever since, I have noted wryly how Communist military forces of the North Vietnamese or Pathet Lao become most active in that region every year at opium harvest time. The opium now pays for many of their battalions and divisions.) There was General Navarre briefing us about his plan for moving troops into the countryside against the enemy, apparently talking from notes hidden within the palm of his left hand; I wondered if the notes had been written on a postage stamp. There was a formal call on Norodom Sihanouk in Phnom Penh, the king turned prince, who had given up the throne shortly before to become prime minister of Cambodia. It was the only time I ever met this plump playboy. (Years later, he made a movie in which he as the hero bested a villainous American spy who was a caricature of me. Evidently he loved fantasy.) Also, there were the stories told me by French volunteers who formed maquis, or guerrilla bands, among the mountain tribes of how Chinese Communist divisions had gone into border provinces of North Vietnam to "pacify" the region by denuding it of every living human being. (I couldn't get into the area to verify the stories at firsthand, but I noted that several years later the Chinese Communists reportedly pacified Eastern Tibet in identical fashion.)

I left Saigon eager to get back to the more soluble problems of the Philippines. I had little notion that I ever would see the troubled people of Indochina again.[8]

1953 **27 July**—Korean armistice. South Korean President Syngman Rhee refuses to sign but agrees to support terms. **12 August**—U.S.S.R. explodes its first hydrogen bomb.

1954 **13 March**—Viet Minh forces begin ground assaults on Dien Bien Phu, the battle that will be the last major engagement of the French

Indochina War. The United States turns down a French request for overt military intervention. **7 April**—At a news conference, President Eisenhower makes this statement: "You have a row of dominoes set up; you knock over the first one, and what will happen to the last one is that it will go over very quickly. So you have a beginning of a disintegration that would have the most profound influences."

Most senior military and diplomatic officials write end-of-tour reports and are debriefed upon completing an assignment. Here are excerpts from one such debriefing, conducted as the French position at Dien Bien Phu is becoming increasingly hopeless. General Trapnall has just returned from Saigon.

The following are comments made by Major General Thomas J. H. Trapnall, Junior, former Chief of the Military Assistance Advisory Group (MAAG) Indochina, at his debriefing, 3 May 1954.

GENERAL

The battle of Indochina is an armed revolution which is now in its eighth year. It is a savage conflict fought in a fantastic country in which the battle may be waged one day in waist-deep muddy rice paddies or later in an impenetrable mountainous jungle. The sun saps the vitality of friend and foe alike, but particularly the European soldier. Torrential monsoon rains turn the delta battleground into a vast swamp which no conventional vehicle can successfully negotiate. It is a war of many paradoxes—

Where there is no popular will to win on the part of the Vietnamese.

Where the leader of the Rebels is more popular than the Vietnamese Chief of State.

Where a sizeable French army is composed of relatively few Frenchmen.

Where the partners of the Associated States regard each other as more dangerous than the enemy.

Where a large segment of the population seeks to expel the French at any price, possibly at the cost of extinction as a new nation.

This is a war which has no easy and immediate solution, a politico-military chess game in which the players sit thousands of miles distant—in Paris, Washington, Peiping, and Moscow. . . .

POLITICAL ASPECTS

A strictly military solution to the war in Indochina is not possible. Military operations are too closely bound to concurrent political problems, and most of the military decisions concerning tactics and strategy have their origin in the politics of the situation here. The governments of the three Associated States are comparatively weak, and are almost as insistent upon complete autonomy from France as they are on liberation from the Communists. It is doubtful if the ordinary people understand the issues at stake between the rebel and Associated States objectives. It probably appears to them that they are being ground between the two political groups, one of which seeks to achieve autonomy by Communist methods. The other by political evolution. They are not aware of the dangers of domination by Communism nor of the difference between democracy and the Communist People's Government as we understand it.

The French have a tremendous investment in Indochina and have made great strides in bringing the advantages of Western civilization to the people. Yet the French are not wanted. Colonialism is still the chief argument against the French and with some substance. The natives are still considered as second-rate people and the French have only made concessions reluctantly and when forced to do so. There is a lack of camaraderie between the native soldier and officer and the French. Separate messes are maintained, due in some measure to the difference in dietary preference, but also due to this lack of friendly association in a common cause.

The Viet Minh, on the other hand, are fighting a clever war of attrition, without chance of a major military victory, but apparently feeling that time is working in their favor and that French and U.S. public opinion will force eventual favorable negotiation.

PSYCHOLOGICAL ASPECTS
In 1949 the French, in a search for Nationalist support against Ho Chi Minh, recognized Bao Dai, playboy scion of the ancient Annamite emperors as Chief of State of Viet Nam which was given its independence within the framework of the French Union. Bao Dai is popularly believed to be very pro-French, and most of the people have a luke-warm feeling toward the Government which they feel is not earnestly working for their complete independence from France. The French promise independence, but only reluctantly give concessions.

The key to this problem is a strong and effective Nationalist army with the support of the Populist [sic] behind it. When the people have confidence in their government and in its ability, through the Nationalist army, to give them the protection from Communist terrorism which is necessary for business and commerce, then complete victory will be in sight.

THE U.S. CONTRIBUTION TO THE WAR IN INDOCHINA
The U.S. has greatly contributed to the success of the French in holding Indochina from the beginning. In January 1951, material was rushed from the docks of Haiphong to the battlefield of Vinh Yen, then being fought under the personal direction of Marshall De Lattre himself. Since then, delivery of aid has kept pace with changing French needs, often on a crash basis, down to the present heroic defense of Dien Bien Phu. U.S. aid has consisted of budgetary support, furnishing of end items, military hardware, and of technical training teams. The magnitude and range of this contribution is shown by the following very few examples. All of these figures are as of 31 March this year.

a. 785 million dollars has been allocated for the budgetary support of the French Expeditionary Force and the Vietnamese Army. This will assist in meeting budgetary requirements for pay, food, and allowances for these troops.

b. Under MDA Programs, a total of more than 784 millions of dollars has been programmed for the years 1950–54. Of this, more than 440 million dollars worth of military end items have been received.

c. To date, 31 March 1954, 441 ships have delivered a total of 478 thousands of long tons of MDA equipment to Indochina. . . .

CONCLUSION

I recommend that . . . full-scale U.S. training mission be established with the Associated States forces to achieve an effective training base by Spring of 1956. That the French overwhelm the enemy in the interim is a vital concurrent requirement, and, again, this objective must be achieved by governmental agreement, with the U.S. insisting that the French Government establish military victory as a primary objective and so instruct the field commander, who may then be relieved of his anxieties regarding casualties and indifferent political and moral support from France.

In conclusion, I reaffirm my opinion that victory in Indochina is an international rather than a local matter, and essentially political as well as military.[9]

1954 **7 May**—The French garrison of Dien Bien Phu surrenders to the Viet Minh. **8 May**—Peace talks begin in Geneva between the French and the Viet Minh.

Later, in Desmond Meiring's novel The Brinkman, *a Frenchman remembers his war.*

Jean-Philippe sat and looked back over his coffee and his brandy under the tree in the quiet garden, totally and discourteously blind to the attentive and strikingly beautiful girl who sat beside him, and to that explosive yet graceful bust which normally would effortlessly and exclusively and mesmerically have riveted his attention, even against the collapse of empires and the fall of kings.

Blind, he thought.

But how could you have known until the end that you had played a fool's game for eight years? It had certainly seemed a game in Saigon at the start. In the élite paratroop battalions the actions were sometimes surprisingly sharp, though most often when you arrived it was already too late, and there were only the burned or mutilated bodies and the charred villages and the great whispering treetops of the jungle (even then subconsciously you always knew that the trees, the jungle, were naturally on the side of the Viet Minh).

When you found the peasants in the rice fields they were always as patently innocent as their own scimitar-horned and vast-barreled and enormously powerful water buffalo, lethargic and domesticated, and known to become violent and charge only against Europeans, whose smell they disliked. The men and women and children, if that was the season, worked in the paddy calf-deep or knee-deep in the water. They moved slowly forward in lines, bending with practiced suppleness, their legs straight and apart. The performance could seem religious, for, when the paratroopers were there, they did not talk at all. They did not even look up at them. Clearly they hoped that by ignoring them completely they could dismiss them from existence. When the paratroopers finally hauled some ancient from the lines he invariably knew nothing. Certainly, there had been other soldiers there. Vietnamese, yes, but strangers. Of course they knew that the village's pro-French headman and three of his councilors had been murdered, and their homes burned. It was very sad. In which direction had the Vietnamese soldiers gone? Naturally, they had gone back into the jungle. It was where they had come from, wasn't it?

Often the ancient would smile widely during the interrogation, not at all through bravado, or because he thought the ceremony particularly amusing. It was a nervous tic, a Vietnamese characteristic too often misunderstood by Europeans, to smile hilariously when most terrified. This apart, the man would stand composed, in his great conical shading hat, whose curves were rather like those of the roofs of his temples, of his sculpture, of his writing, impossibly alien.

In your leaves in Saigon you haunted the bars in groups in the Rue Catinat or you gambled or danced in Cholon, or you slept with the pliant and vibrant and murmuring *métisses* or Vietnamese, with their tiny breasts and waists and buttocks, and their lustrous floods of hair, animals groomed for love for a thousand years. It was that kind of war at the start, office hours only. But the warnings were already there, the mounting rhythm of assassinations in the city, unceasing and methodical, the acute sense of being out of step with time when some *colon* or older officer, bored in a bar, suggested the diversion of going out again to *casser du Ngac,* to break some peasants.

One morning you woke in some army post in the bush in the center of an invisible enemy that struck at will, and you knew finally and completely that this was no longer a minor military exercise against a ragged band of communist extremists, which was the official French line right up to the end, but that virtually the entire country and its people were against you. The discovery was permanent and not good for the morale. It reduced you to the splendid isolation of a mercenary in a last outpost, valiantly brandishing an outmoded military ethic in the void, heroically defending a distant and divided and largely disinterested government, and consistently beaten by professionals and the facts. You were like some thundering knight in armor facing farcically up to a good shot with a bazooka. The romantic myth could not really be expected to survive after quite so many defeats, the loss of the whole string of garrisons on the northeastern frontier with China in 1950, the liquidation of the Hoa-Binh pocket over the next two years, the retreat from North Laos in 1953 with the loss of five battalions. All the defeats up to Dien Bien Phu.

There was no myth left after that. Dien Bien Phu suggested that the Viet Minh, in that terrain, probably had the best infantry in the world, among the best generals, the best logistic support, and the best fifth-column preparation. Who would have guessed that Giap and the other Viet Minh generals would take their model from the Germans under Kesselring in North Italy and the Russians about Stalingrad, and bring their heavy guns down from the heights about Dien Bien Phu and dig them right in, beautifully camouflaged against aviation, in strong points in the saucer plain within easy and lethal range of the French camp? Or that for every fighting-man in Giap's twelve-thousand-man divisions round Dien Bien Phu probably twice as many men and women supplied him in monstrous single unending antlike columns through the jungle tracks, up from the delta, quite invisible from the air? Who could have thought that so everyday and triumphantly respectable a thing as a bicycle could be so militarily decisive?—and of course that was why there had been so fantastically many thefts of bicycles in Hanoi and the main towns before Dien Bien Phu—for a man or woman pushing a bicycle could travel the narrowest path, carrying on it fifty or a hundred kilos of rice or shells or parts of a disassembled howitzer. Or that, a year before Dien Bien Phu, the Viet Minh already controlled at least two-thirds of the whole Red River delta area, which was laughably supposed to be France's secure base area between the battleground and the sea?

Jean-Philippe had always been amused by the way that the mind generally totally ignored the vast historical importance of such cataclysms when it recalled them afterwards, and identified them instead by frivolously minor images. Thus, for him, Dien Bien Phu and the subsequent death marches were symbolized not by the big tragic things, the exhaustion and the casualties and the appalling hunger and the mercilessly impersonal cruelty, but quite simply by a composite image of the farcically tiny Viet Minh. He found that frankly embarrassing. The defeat could not possibly have been quite so humiliating if by comparison the French troops had not seemed such hulking great brutes of men.

On the fifty-fourth day of the fighting Jean-Philippe commanded his battalion, then composed of forty-three men. The last attack came at nine at night, under parachute flares. It was pure surrealism. There was even a grotesque breathless toylike beauty about it. The small, frail, agile men who floated within their overlarge uniforms, swarmed up the last slope again, diligently chanting their *Tien-len, Doc-lap, Tien-len, Doc-lap,* forward to independence, and died in heaps. Three hung like insects, their arms outstretched and fighting it, on the last rolls of barbed wire. The last bursts from the machine-gun section on Jean-Philippe's right killed them pointlessly, but they jerked sharply and their uniforms flapped again loyally when the Viets slung a bamboo Bangalore torpedo under the wire next to them and exploded it. When the attackers were near enough Jean-Philippe threw his last two grenades and settled back in his slit trench to wait for the sudden and total and ominously final silence.[10]

On 1 June 1954, Colonel Lansdale arrives back in Saigon to head the newly formed U.S. Saigon Military Mission (SMM). Often operating independently from the formally constituted MAAG (Military Assistance and Advisory Group) and embassy staff, the CIA-run SMM functions as explained in these excerpts from the top-secret operational report written by Colonel Lansdale himself.

II. MISSION

The Saigon Military Mission (SMM) was born in a Washington policy meeting early in 1954, when Dien Bien Phu was still holding out against the encircling Vietminh. The SMM was to enter into Vietnam quietly and assist the Vietnamese, rather than the French, in unconventional warfare. The French were to be kept as friendly allies in the process, as far as possible.

The broad mission for the team was to undertake paramilitary operations against the enemy and to wage political-psychological warfare. Later, after Geneva, the mission was modified to prepare the means for undertaking paramilitary operations in Communist areas rather than to wage unconventional warfare. . . .

III. HIGHLIGHTS OF THE YEAR

a. *Early Days*

The Saigon Military Mission (SMM) started on 1 June 1954, when its Chief, Colonel Edward G. Lansdale, USAF, arrived in Saigon with a small box of files and clothes and a borrowed typewriter, courtesy of an SA-16 flight set up for him by the 13th Air Force at Clark AFB. Lt-General John O'Daniel and Embassy Chargé Rob McClintock had arranged for his appointment as Assistant Air Attache, since it was improper for U.S. officers at MAAG at that time to have advisory conferences with Vietnamese officers. Ambassador Heath had concurred already. There was no desk space for an office, no vehicle, no safe for files. He roomed with General O'Daniel, later moved to a small house rented by MAAG. Secret communications with Washington were provided through the Saigon station of CIA.

There was deepening gloom in Vietnam. Dien Bien Phu had fallen. The French were capitulating to the Vietminh at Geneva. The first night in Saigon, Vietminh saboteurs blew up large ammunition dumps at the airport, rocking Saigon throughout the night. General O'Daniel and Charge McClintock agreed that it was time to start taking positive action.

O'Daniel paved the way for a quick first-hand survey of the situation throughout the country. McClintock paved the way for contacts with Vietnamese political leaders. Our Chief's reputation from the Philippines had preceded him. Hundreds of Vietnamese acquaintanceships were made quickly.

Working in close cooperation with George Hellyer, USIS Chief, a new psychological warfare campaign was devised for the Vietnamese Army and for the government in Hanoi. Shortly after, a refresher course in combat psywar was constructed and Vietnamese Army personnel were rushed through it. A similar course was initiated for the Ministry of Information. Rumor campaigns were added to the tactics and tried out in Hanoi. It was almost too late.

The first rumor campaign was to be a carefully planted story of a Chinese Communist regiment in Tonkin taking reprisals against a Vietminh village whose girls the Chinese had raped, recalling Chinese Nationalist troop behavior in 1945 and confirming Vietnamese fears of Chinese occupation under Vietminh rule; the story was to be planted by soldiers of the Vietnamese Armed Psywar Company in Hanoi dressed in civilian clothes. The troops received their instructions silently, dressed in civilian clothes, went on the mission, and failed to return. They had deserted to the Vietminh. Weeks later, Tonkinese told an excited story of the misbehavior of the Chinese Divisions in Vietminh territory. Investigated, it turned out to be the old rumor campaign, with Vietnamese embellishments. . . .[11]

1954   26 June—Bao Dai appoints Ngo Dinh Diem as premier of South Vietnam. **7 July**—Ngo Dinh Diem arrives in Saigon.

Ho Chi Minh's mid-1954 policy, as well as his attitude toward foreigners in Vietnam, appear in this document released in translation by the Democratic Republic of Vietnam.

Report by Ho Chi Minh to the Sixth Plenum of the Party Central Committee, July 15, 1954

The Vietnamese, Cambodian and Lao peoples are united and their resistance grows ever more vigorous. Our guerilla forces in South, Central and North Viet Nam not only have stood firm but have grown ever stronger. From the Border Campaign to the Hoa Binh, Tay Bac and other campaigns, our regular forces have recorded repeated successes. These victories plus the major one at Dien Bien Phu have brought about an important change in the situation. The fiasco of the Navarre plan has led to the collapse of the Laniel-Bidault cabinet and the shrinking of French-occupied zones.

We owe our successes to the correct policy of our Party and Government, the heroism of our armed forces and people, and the support of the fraternal countries and the world's people. Our successes also belong to the world movement for peace and democracy.

Besides military successes, initial ones have also been scored on the antifeudal front. The former have had a good effect on the mobilization of the masses to implement our land policy and the latter, on our struggle against imperialism. Our successes inspire our people and the peoples of the world and reinforce our diplomatic position at Geneva; they have compelled our enemy to enter into talks with us. Compared with what Bollaert put forward in 1947, France's attitude at present has noticeably changed. Thus, since the start of the resistance, our posture has grown stronger and the enemy's weaker. But we should bear in mind that this should be understood in a relative, not absolute, sense. We must guard against subjectiveness and not underrate our enemy. Our successes have awakened the American imperialists. After the Dien Bien Phu campaign, the latter's intentions and plan for intervention have also undergone changes aimed at protracting and internationalizing the Indochina war, sabotaging the Geneva Conference, and ousting the French by every means, in order to occupy Viet Nam, Cambodia and Laos, enslave the peoples of these countries and create further tension in the world.

Therefore, the *US imperialists* not only are the enemy of the world's people but are becoming the *main and direct enemy of the Vietnamese, Cambodian and Lao peoples.* . . .

At present the situation has changed; so have our tasks and consequently so should our policy and slogans. Up to now we have concentrated our efforts on wiping out the forces of the French imperialist aggressors. But now the French are having talks with us while the American imperialists are becoming our main and direct enemy; so our spearhead must be directed at the latter. Until peace is restored, we shall keep fighting the French; but the brunt of our attack and that of the world's peoples should be focused on the United States. US policy is to expand and internationalize the Indochina war. Ours is to struggle for peace and oppose the US war policy. For some nine years now, our Party has made clear its programme: Complete independence for Viet Nam, Cambodia and Laos, which must be freed from the French yoke; to refuse to recognize the French Union, drive out all French troops from Indochina, destroy the puppet administrations and armed forces, confiscate all properties of the imperialists and the traitors, launch a drive for the reduction of land rents and interest rates as a step towards agrarian reform, bring democracy to the whole nation, and carry our war of resistance through to final victory. This programme has won many successes. It is a correct one.

However, in the new situation we cannot maintain the old programme. Our previous motto was "Resistance to the end." At present, we must put forward a new one: "Peace, Unity, Independence, Democracy". . . .

Peace calls for an end to the war; and to end the war one must agree on a cease-fire. A cease-fire requires regrouping zones, that is, enemy troops should be regrouped in a zone with a view to their gradual withdrawal, and ours in another. We must secure a vast area where we would have ample means for building, consolidating and developing our forces so as to exert influence over other regions and thereby advance towards reunification. The setting up of regrouping zones does not mean partition of the country; it is a temporary measure leading to reunification. Owing to the delimitation and exchange of zones, some previously free areas will be temporarily occupied by the enemy; their inhabitants will be dissatisfied; some people might fall prey to discouragement and to enemy deception. We should make it clear to our compatriots that the trials they are going to endure for the sake of the interests of the whole country, for the sake of our long-range interests, will be a cause for glory and will earn them the gratitude of the whole nation. We should keep everyone free from pessimism and negativism and urge all to continue a vigorous struggle for the complete withdrawal of French forces and for independence.

To set up regrouping zones as a step towards peace, to hold nationwide elections to achieve national reunification, such is our policy. The aims of our war of resistance and independence, unity, democracy and peace. The very restoration of peace is aimed at serving the cause of reunification, independence and democracy. The new situation requires a new policy for securing new successes.

At any juncture, peace or war, we must firmly hold the initiative, show foresight and be in full readiness.[12]

At the same time, Colonel Lansdale is getting to know Saigon.

In the South, I became acquainted with the sects, unaware that they were soon to involve me in deadly drama. Two of the sects, the Hoa Hao and the Cao Dai, were indigenous religions with a million or so adherents each and with their main centers in the agrarian provinces west of Saigon. The third sect, the Binh Xuyen, was a social organization numbering tens of thousands in the Saigon-Cholon metropolitan area, whose leaders had won control of the criminal underworld. I was struck by the medieval warlord image all three sects conveyed. Each had its own armed forces complete with generals and battalions, its own political parties, and definite territories which it dominated. Nearly all the sect forces were in the pay of the French Army as *supplétifs* (militia). The one exception was a dissident Cao Dai group of guerrillas under Trinh minh Thé, who held a territory near the Cambodian border; they fought both the French and the Communists. When I expressed interest in visiting them, French officers told me to have nothing to do with such "monsters."

My first guide in trips to the sect territories was every bit as colorful as the sect leaders we saw. He was Colonel Jean Leroy, leader of a Catholic guerrilla group called the Unités Mobiles de Défense des Chrétientés. Short, wiry, and intense, he apparently combined the most forceful characteristics of his French father and Vietnamese mother. Meeting him at his house in Saigon, I noticed the fortress look of the place with its barbed wire barriers, the sandbagged machine gun positions in the yard, and heavily armed troops at every vantage point. Leroy explained blithely that he had moved recently into Saigon, had liked the house, and had forcibly ejected the family that owned it. Now the owners were showing up at the house with lawyers and police to get it back—and Leroy was daring them to start a fight for the house if they had the guts to do so.

In the capital city itself, I bumped into one more piece of Vietnamese reality. I had heard stories from French and Vietnamese acquaintances that Bao Dai had run short of funds for his fun and games on the Riviera and had sold the position of chief of police for Saigon-Cholon to the boss of the underworld, "Bay" Vien (General Le van Vien), for forty-four million piastres (then about $1.25 million U.S. at the official rate). Bay Vien commanded the Binh Xuyen sect forces, levied a take on commercial traffic into and out of the city, and ran the city's gambling casinos, houses of prostitution, and opium trade. This sordid transaction was made possible by the final initialing on June 4, 1954, of the Franco-Vietnamese treaty giving Vietnam the independence from France that had been announced the year before. Legally, as the chief of state of an independent nation, Bao Dai could act as he pleased. The sellout of the police to the boss gangster came close to killing off the infant country in the following months. I saw some of the first fruits of this deal in an incident I will long remember.

It happened one night when I was in my room at the BOQ attempting to read local French newspapers with the aid of a translator's dictionary. I heard the telephone ringing in the hall a few doors from my room. It kept on ringing and I finally got up and answered it. "Allo! Allo! Allo!" I shouted into the instrument in the manner worthy of the temperamental local telephone system. From the instrument gushed an excited American female voice, in accents of the Deep South, asking, "What are all these strange soldiers doing shooting around the house?" Baffled, I started asking questions. I learned that three American girls, secretaries at the American embassy, were living in a small house a few blocks away. At the moment, all of them were hiding under beds, from which position the telephoning was being done. In the background, I could hear a burst of submachine gun fire and then the boom of an explosion. The voice on the telephone said there seemed to be a battle going on in their yard and in the street in front of their house. "Y'all come over and help us. You hear?" I drove right over.

A company of troops in the green berets of the Binh Xuyen were in combat posture along the street and in the yard. The target of their bursts of submachine gun fire was a two-story house just behind the bungalow where the American girls lived. A hand grenade came sailing out of an upper window and landed in the street, causing a wild scramble for safety among the attackers. After seeing that the girls were safe and cautioning them to stay put behind the protection of the bungalow's walls, I sought out the Binh Xuyen commander. I finally translated the gist of his words. He was trying to arrest somebody inside the house. We must have been observed talking, for with that, a voice shouted out of the house that the people inside would only surrender to the French officer, not the Binh Xuyen! I looked around. Not a French officer in sight. Evidently I must be lucky Pierre. After laborious talk in my atrocious French, arrangements finally were made. The Binh Xuyen withdrew and let me take custody of the prisoners, a man, his wife, and two children. From their hurried pleas, I made out the words "military" and "army," so I put them in my car and took them to General Hinh's house in Cholon. They were clearly glad to arrive safely at the Vietnamese Army commander's home.

It was then that I learned the cause of the wild scene at the girls' bungalow. Having come into possession of the police in the capital city, the Binh Xuyen were setting out to rid the police force of all those members who had been too effective in fighting crime. The good cops were being cleaned out. The man I had rescued was a Sûreté detective. General Hinh and the Vietnamese Army gave safe haven to him and to scores of other experienced detectives and policemen by establishing a new intelligence and investigative organization, the Military Security Service or MSS, and by enrolling these highly qualified refugees in it. The highest-ranking Vietnamese in the Sûreté under the French, Mai huu Xuan, was one of the refugees and was made a general in the Vietnamese Army and put in command of MSS.

What was most memorable about this event was not the formation of a new military organization but the way a man had defended his home and family by using hand grenades. I tucked it away in my mind as something useful to know. A man could stay safe behind walls and keep a company of troops at bay with hand grenades tossed through windows or doors. From then on, I kept a supply of grenades in my own living quarters.[13]

The Final Declaration of the Geneva Conference on Indochina is signed by neither the United States nor the Bao Dai government. The United States issues a "response," which promises "to refrain from the threat or use of force to disturb" the provisions but states that the required elections should be held under supervision of the United Nations. This position is to become the major public justification for South Vietnam's refusal, with U.S. support, to agree to elections under paragraph 7 of the Declaration.

Geneva Conference
Indo-China

21 July 1954: Original: French

Final Declaration, dated the 21st July, 1954, of the Geneva Conference on the problem of restoring peace in Indo-China, in which the representatives of Cambodia, the Democratic Republic of Viet-Nam, France, Laos, the People's Republic of China, the State of Viet-Nam, the Union of Soviet Socialist Republics, the United Kingdom, and the United States of America took part.

1. The Conference takes note of the agreements ending hostilities in Cambodia, Laos and Viet-Nam and organizing international control and the supervision of the execution of the provisions of these agreements.

2. The Conference expresses satisfaction at the ending of hostilities in Cambodia, Laos and Viet-Nam; the Conference expresses its conviction that the execution of the provisions set out in the present declaration and in the agreements on the cessation of hostilities will permit Cambodia, Laos, and Viet-Nam henceforth to play their part, in full independence and sovereignty, in the peaceful community of nations.

3. The Conference takes note of the declarations made by the Governments of Cambodia and of Laos of their intention to adopt measures permitting all citizens to take their place in the national community, in particular by participating in the next general elections, which, in conformity with the constitution of each of these countries, shall take place in the course of the year 1955, by secret ballot and in conditions of respect for fundamental freedoms.

4. The Conference takes note of the clauses in the agreement on the cessation of hostilities in Viet-Nam prohibiting the introduction into Viet-Nam of foreign troops and military personnel as well as of all kinds of arms and munitions. The Conference also takes note of the declarations made by the Governments of Cambodia and Laos of their resolution not to request foreign aid, whether in war material, in personnel or in instructors except for the purpose of the effective defence of their territory and, in the case of Laos, to the extent defined by the agreements on the cessation of hostilities in Laos.

5. The Conference takes note of the clauses in the agreement on the cessation of hostilities in Viet-Nam to the effect that no military base under the control of a foreign State may be established in the regrouping zones of the two parties, the latter having the obligation to see that the zones allotted to them shall not constitute part of any military alliance and shall not be utilized for the resumption of hostilities or in the service of an aggressive policy. The Conference also takes note of the declarations of the Governments of Cambodia and Laos to the effect that they will not join in any agreement with other States if this agreement includes the obligation to participate in a military alliance not in conformity with the principles of the Charter of the United Nations or, in the case of Laos, with the principles of the agreement on the cessation of hostilities in Laos or, so long as their security is not threatened, the obligation to establish bases on Cambodian or Laotian territory for the military forces of foreign Powers.

6. The Conference recognizes that the essential purpose of the agreement relating to Viet-Nam is to settle military questions with a view to ending hostilities and that the military demarcation line is provisional and

should not in any way be interpreted as constituting a political or territorial boundary. The Conference expresses its conviction that the execution of the provisions set out in the present declaration and in the agreement on the cessation of hostilities creates the necessary basis for the achievement in the near future of a political settlement in Viet-Nam.

7. The Conference declares that, so far as Viet-Nam is concerned, the settlement of political problems, affected on the basis of respect for the principles of independence, unity and territorial integrity, shall permit the Viet-Namese people to enjoy the fundamental freedoms, guaranteed by democratic institutions established as a result of free general elections by secret ballot. In order to ensure that sufficient progress in the restoration of peace has been made, and that all the necessary conditions obtain for free expression of the national will, general elections shall be held in July 1956, under the supervision of an international commission composed of representatives of the Member States of the International Supervisory Commission, referred to in the agreement on the cessation of hostilities. Consultations will be held on this subject between the competent representative authorities of the two zones from 20 July 1955 onwards.

8. The provisions of the agreements on the cessation of hostilities intended to ensure the protection of individuals and of property must be most strictly applied and must, in particular, allow everyone in Viet-Nam to decide freely in which zone he wishes to live.

9. The competent representative authorities of the Northern and Southern zones of Viet-Nam, as well as the authorities of Laos and Cambodia, must not permit any individual or collective reprisals against persons who have collaborated in any way with one of the parties during the war, or against members of such persons' families.

10. The Conference takes note of the declaration of the Government of the French Republic to the effect that it is ready to withdraw its troops from the territory of Cambodia, Laos, and Viet-Nam, at the requests of the Governments concerned and within periods which shall be fixed by agreement between the parties except in the cases where, by agreement between the two parties, a certain number of French troops shall remain at specified points and for a specified time.

11. The Conference takes note of the declaration of the French Government to the effect that for the settlement of all the problems connected with the reestablishment and consolidation of peace in Cambodia, Laos and Viet-Nam, the French Government will proceed from the principle of respect for the independence and sovereignty, unity, and territorial integrity of Cambodia, Laos and Viet-Nam.

12. In their relations with Cambodia, Laos and Viet-Nam, each member of the Geneva Conference undertakes to respect the sovereignty, the independence, the unity and the territorial integrity of the above-mentioned states, and to refrain from any interference in their internal affairs.

13. The members of the Conference agree to consult one another on any question which may be referred to them by the International Super-

visory Commission, in order to study such measures as may prove necessary to ensure that the agreements on the cessation of hostilities in Cambodia, Laos and Viet-Nam are respected.[14]

In Saigon, Colonel Lansdale comments on the Geneva accords.

A separate declaration was made at Geneva that kept the people of
Vietnam in mind. It added a further period to the timetable. The representatives of Cambodia, the Democratic Republic of Vietnam, France,
Laos, the People's Republic of China, the State of Vietnam, the United
Kingdom, and the United States of America took part. This declaration
"recognized" the military demarcation line as temporary and stated that
the people of Vietnam would choose their own future in general elections
to be held in July 1956. This future was described as one in which the
Vietnamese people were "to enjoy the fundamental freedoms, guaranteed by democratic institutions established as a result of free general
elections by secret ballot." Prior to these elections, Vietnamese citizens
could decide in which zone they preferred to live, the Communist zone or
the Bao Dai-French zone. . . .

After studying the Geneva documents, I concluded that a number of us
in Vietnam had been sentenced to hard labor for the next two years.
There were masses of people living in North Vietnam who would want to
take advantage of the Geneva-given chance to move out before the Communists took over. They would not only need help in making the move,
but ideally ought to be provided with a way of making a fresh start in the
free South. Long stays in refugee camps would be as demoralizing and
vitiating to these Vietnamese as such stays had been to refugees in Europe and the Middle East. If Vietnam actually was becoming independent
from France, it was going to need the vigorous participation of every
citizen to make a success of the non-Communist part of the new nation
before the proposed plebiscite was held in 1956. Not only that, but who
would want to forsake his family home for a long journey to a new
existence in a camp? I saw that part of the hard labor ahead would have
to include providing for the care and transportation of a great mass of
migrants and then finding the means for farmers to start new farms,
fishermen to move into new fishing grounds, artisans to locate new industrial employment. It would be a gigantic undertaking.[15]

*In Hanoi, on 28 July 1954, a group of French journalists prepare to evacu-
ate the city. Jean Larteguy, reporter and author of* Yellow Fever *and other
works about Southeast Asia, is living in Hanoi and Saigon during this
period.*

Jérôme got to the Press Camp shortly before the midday meal. On the
balcony he caught sight of Rovignon, a huge hairy man, standing with his
hands on his hips and yelling:

'What the hell have you done with my pants?'

With his nose in the air and his mouth wide open, a boy was scuttling about the garden.

'Wait a bit, sir . . . always in a hurry, sir, no good.'

'You're going to get a boot in the arse. Where are my pants?'

The boy, who delighted in the journalist's outbursts of temper, was now clucking like a broody hen.

Rovignon had a shaven pate and a massive neck, which made him look like an all-in wrestler who was out of training.

He made as though to step down, the boy pretended to take to his heels, and they both burst out laughing.

Jérôme was quite fond of Rovignon because he was conscientious, efficient, and believed in his mission as a press correspondent. He hailed him; Rovignon caught sight of him and greeted him with warmth.

'Hello, Jérôme! So you too have turned up for Hanoi's funeral? I'll join you in the bar in five minutes.'

At the end of the meal the Squid [another journalist] produced from his pocket a leaflet which had been distributed to the French troops on the night of the cease-fire and handed it to Jérôme:

'Have you seen this?'

> 'Officers, non-commissioned officers, French and foreign soldiers of the Expeditionary Force:
> 'Soon you will be embarking for your beloved country. There'll be no more fighting for you, but we nationalists of Vietnam are still faced with the task of barring the way to the Red Peril. We shall do nothing against you. Behave as we do, remain our friends and give us as many arms and as much ammunition as you can.
>
> The National Resistance Front'

Jérôme read the pamphlet three times. He visualised Lê dictating it in his harsh voice to an obtuse typist who watched him with that particularly stupid expression the Vietnamese assume when they do not quite understand something.

Raising his head, he saw that the Squid was waiting for his reactions and he realised he too was thinking of Tuan-Van-Lê.

'What are the nationalist movements doing?' he asked.

Rovignon shrugged his shoulders and poured himself out some wine. The Squid chuckled with satisfaction:

'They're doing nothing.'

With his mouth wide open he waited, then went on in the same rapid tone, without stressing one word more than another.

'They've all left for Saigon with their families, their furniture and their servants, pinching what they could from the tills of the various offices for which they were responsible.'

'And this leaflet?'

'It was printed by a small group of maniacs. These fellows will all get themselves bumped off if they persist in their fun and games. In addition to the Vietminh secret police which has been at work in Hanoi for some time, they're up against the French Sûreté, who aren't keen on law and order being disturbed, and the Vietnamese Sûreté who are after their blood . . . because they hold them responsible for one or two murders, including that of the Governor of the North. . . .'

'Who's behind them?'

'The Americans perhaps . . . one of their countless services, or maybe the Kuomintang . . . but it comes to the same thing. Perhaps no one.'[16]

At the same time, as seen in M. J. Bosse's novel The Journey of Tao Kim Nam, *a young North Vietnamese man considers his situation under the terms of the July declaration.*

Two months ago he would have given no thought to safety. The planting was done, and he was wondering if he might find a girl who could take the place of his first woman. He had shown little interest in the news of the French and Vietminh War, which had been raging five years, and when he heard a rumor that the Vietminh had won that war, he shrugged his shoulders and quoted an old proverb.

"When the water rises, the fish eats the ant. When the water drops, the ant eats the fish." He spat some betel juice on the dusty earth and looked solemnly at the listening men. "It is all the same." . . .

And so two months ago a green bereted soldier had come into the village. At the top of his voice he read a paper: Ba Lang was freed that instant from the French. After waving a red flag and drinking too much chumchum, he disappeared. For three days the village waited. Then the Vietminh came in force.

To begin with, the leader, *le Commissaire,* made speeches. A great new country would rise from the wasted land, he said. With enthusiasm he described battles that the Vietminh had won from the French. He sounded like old men bragging of their youth. The battles he described were as glorious sounding as tales of a time when farmers wore jewels and no man hated another. . . . Enlightened, he said, was what men became when each had as much as his neighbor. Enlightenment was what people must have to be happy. He told the villagers not to worry, they would soon have it. That afternoon some paper banners were strung up in the square. THE LAND BELONGS TO THE PEOPLE WHO WORK IT said the banners. And so the next day the Commissar talked to Nam, and so the day after that Nam heard his field hands whispering as he passed by.

Nam was resigned. If land were taken from him, what could he do? Man could no more change fate than he could change the course of the sun. Life was hard, and harder when [a] new government came along. Nam recalled the words of his father: Patience outlasts government. And Nam remembered how the village had endured occupation before, when the Japanese had come.[17]

On 8 August General "Iron Mike" O'Daniel, Chief of MAAG, Saigon, cables Secretary of State John Foster Dulles. This message summarizes the intentions of the United States in its future relations with South Vietnam.

FROM: SAIGON

TO: SECRETARY OF STATE

REC'D: AUGUST 8, 1954
2:28 P.M.

PRIORITY

FROM CHMAAG SAIGON TO DEPTAR INFO SECDEF, SECSTATE, JCS, CINCPAC, AM-EMBASSY SAIGON

HAVE PREPARED STUDY HERE OUR POINT OF VIEW US PART FUTURE VIETNAM INCLUDING ESTIMATE SITUATION AND CONCEPT OPERATION IN SUBSTANCE FOL-LOWING:

MISSION: ESTABLISH POLITICAL, PSYCHOLOGICAL, MILITARY, ECONOMIC COURSES ACTION FOR ADOPTION BY US TO INSURE FREE VIETNAM SURVIVAL AS NATION. DEVELOP VIETNAM AS EFFECTIVE BARRIER CONTINUED COMMUNIST EXPANSION AS NATION. . . .

FOLLOWING TASKS BE ACCOMPLISHED:

A. POLITICAL, PSYCHOLOGICAL. US TO USE ITS OWN INTERPRETATION OF THE FRENCH VIETNAM CEASE-FIRE AGREEMENT TO PROVIDE ALL POSSIBLE FREEDOM RELATIONS WITH VIETNAM. US MUST UNDERTAKE MAJOR POLITICAL PSYCHO-LOGICAL ACTION RE FRANCE, SE ASIA AND VIETNAM. BY AGREEMENTS US AS-SUME DOMINANT ROLE COOPERATION WITH FRANCE AND VIETNAM TO DEVELOP STRONG VIABLE US POLITICAL PSYCHOLOGICAL ACTIONS RE SE ASIA. PRODUCE STRONG POSITIVE SUPPORT FROM NATIONS HAVING PRIMARY INTEREST SE ASIA. DEVELOP STRONG DEMOCRATIC STATE ORIENTED TOWARD WEST BY PERSUADING GOVERNMENT VIETNAM TO ANNOUNCE COMPLETE INDEPENDENCE, AND FOR FRENCH TO ANNOUNCE DATE OF WITHDRAWAL FRENCH FORCES AND DATE VIET-NAM BECOMES ENTIRELY FREE. . . .

WE BELIEVE SUCH PLAN LAST RESORT SOLUTION ON SALVAGING REMAINING VIETNAM AND OFFER IT FOR CONSIDERATION IN FORMULATION US POLICY FOR SE ASIA. AMBASSADOR CONCURS. AMBASSADOR GENERALLY CONCURS WITH OBJEC-TIVES ABOVE OUTLINE AND WITH MY ANALYSIS SITUATION. HE APPROVES ENTIRE REPORT AS A TIMELY, USEFUL INITIAL PLAN, ALTHOUGH HE HAS RESERVATION AS TO SOME OF METHODS PROPOSED, AS HE DOUBTS NECESSITY OF US TO BECOME QUITE SO FAR INVOLVED IN OPERATION OF THIS GOVERNMENT EXCEPT ON MILI-TARY TRAINING SIDE. COMMENT: I FEEL THIS IS WAR IN EVERY SENSE. WARTIME METHODS, THEREFORE, ARE IN ORDER ALL FIELDS UNTIL EMERGENCY PASSED.[18]

As Ho Chi Minh has expressed his distrust of American "imperialists," so does the United States distrust not only the Communists but the French as well. This excerpt from the National Security Council's mid-1954 "State-ment of Policy . . . in the Far East," distributed shortly after the July Geneva accords, establishes the future U.S. role.

INDOCHINA: POLITICAL AND COVERT ACTION.

a. Make every possible effort, not openly inconsistent with the U.S. position as to the armistice agreements, to defeat Communist subversion and influence, to maintain and support friendly non-Communist governments in Cambodia and Laos, to maintain a friendly non-Communist South Vietnam, and to prevent a Communist victory through all-Vietnam elections.

b. Urge that the French promptly recognize and deal with Cambodia, Laos and free Vietnam as independent sovereign nations.

c. Strengthen U.S. representation and deal directly, wherever advantageous to the U.S., with the governments of Cambodia, Laos and free Vietnam.

d. Working through the French only insofar as necessary, assist Cambodia, Laos and free Vietnam to maintain (1) military forces necessary for internal security and (2) economic conditions conducive to the maintenance and strength of non-Communist regimes and comparing favorably with those in adjacent Communist areas.

e. Aid emigration from North Vietnam and resettlement of peoples unwilling to remain under Communist rule.

f. Exploit available means to make more difficult the control by the Viet Minh of North Vietnam.

g. Exploit available means to prevent North Vietnam from becoming permanently incorporated in the Soviet bloc, using as feasible and desirable consular relations and non-strategic trade.

h. Conduct covert operations on a large and effective scale in support of the foregoing policies.[19]

Some of the "political and covert" actions are described in the SMM (Saigon Military Mission) report.

AUGUST 1954

An agreement had been reached that the personnel ceiling of U.S. military personnel with MAAG would be frozen at the number present in Vietnam on the date of the cease-fire, under the terms of the Geneva Agreement. In South Vietnam this deadline was to be 11 August. It meant that SMM might have only two members present, unless action were taken. General O'Daniel agreed to the addition of ten SMM men under MAAG cover, plus any others in the Defense pipeline who arrived before the deadline. A call for help went out. Ten officers in Korea, Japan, and Okinawa were selected and were rushed to Vietnam.

SMM had one small MAAG house. Negotiations were started for other housing, but the new members of the team arrived before housing was ready and were crammed three and four to a hotel room for the first days. Meetings were held to assess the new members' abilities. None had had political-psychological warfare experience. Most were experienced in paramilitary and clandestine intelligence operations. Plans were made quickly, for time was running out in the north; already the Vietminh had started taking over secret control of Hanoi and other areas of Tonkin still held by French forces.

Major Conein was given responsibility for developing a paramilitary organization in the north, to be in position when the Vietminh took over. . . . [His] team was moved north immediately as part of the MAAG staff working on the refugee problem. The team had headquarters in Hanoi, with a branch in Haiphong. Among cover duties, this team supervised the refugee flow for the Hanoi airlift organized by the French. One day, as a CAT C-46 finished loading, they saw a small child standing on the ground below the loading door. They shouted for the pilot to wait, picked the child up and shoved him into the aircraft, which then promptly taxied out for its takeoff in the constant air shuttle. A Vietnamese man and woman ran up to the team, asking what they had done with their small boy, whom they'd brought out to say goodbye to relatives. The chagrined team explained, finally talked the parents into going south to Free Vietnam, put them in the next aircraft to catch up with their son in Saigon. . . .

A second paramilitary team was formed to explore possibilities of organizing resistance against the Vietminh from bases in the south. This team consisted of Army Lt-Col Raymond Wittmayer, Army Major Fred Allen, and Army Lt Edward Williams. The latter was our only experienced counter-espionage officer and undertook double duties, including working with revolutionary political groups. Major Allen eventually was able to mount a Vietnamese paramilitary effort in Tonkin from the south, barely beating the Vietminh shutdown in Haiphong as his teams went in, trained and equipped for their assigned missions.

Navy Lt Edward Bain and Marine Captain Richard Smith were assigned as the support group for SMM. Actually, support for an effort such as SMM is a major operation in itself, running the gamut from the usual administrative and personnel functions to the intricate business of clandestine air, maritime, and land supply of paramilitary materiel. In effect, they became our official smugglers as well as paymasters, housing officers, transportation officers, warehousemen, file clerks, and mess officers. The work load was such that other team members frequently pitched in and helped.

SEPTEMBER 1954

Highly-placed officials from Washington visited Saigon and, in private conversations, indicated that current estimates led to the conclusion that Vietnam probably would have to be written off as a loss. We admitted that prospects were gloomy, but were positive that there was still a fighting chance.

On 8 September, SMM officers visited Secretary of State for Defense Chan and walked into a tense situation in his office. Chan had just arrested Lt-Col Lan (G-6 of the Vietnamese Army) and Capt Giai (G-5 of the Army). Armed guards filled the room. We were told what had happened and assured that everything was all right by all three principals. Later, we discovered that Chan was alone and that the guards were Lt-Col Lan's commandos. Lan was charged with political terrorism (by his "action" squads) and Giai with anti-Diem propaganda (using G-5 leaflet, rumor, and broadcast facilities).

The arrest of Lan and Giai, who simply refused to consider themselves arrested, and of Lt Minh, officer in charge of the Army radio station which was guarded by Army troops, brought into the open a plot by the Army Chief of Staff, General Hinh, to overthrow the government. Hinh had hinted at such a plot to his American friends, using a silver cigarette box given him by Egypt's Naguib to carry the hint. SMM became thoroughly involved in the tense controversy which followed, due to our Chief's closeness to both President Diem and General Hinh. He had met the latter in the Philippines in 1952, was a friend of both Hinh's wife and favorite mistress. (The mistress was a pupil in a small English class conducted for mistresses of important personages, at their request. . . .)

While various U.S. officials including General O'Daniel and Foreign Service Officer Frank [name illegible] participated in U.S. attempts to heal the split between the President and his Army, Ambassador Heath asked us to make a major effort to end the controversy. This effort strained relations with Diem and never was successful, but did dampen Army enthusiasm for the plot. At one moment, when there was likelihood of an attack by armored vehicles on the Presidential Palace, SMM told Hinh bluntly that U.S. support most probably would stop in such an event. At the same time a group from the Presidential Guards asked for tactical advice on how to stop armored vehicles with the only weapons available to the Guards: carbines, rifles, and hand grenades. The advice, on tank traps and destruction with improvised weapons, must have sounded grim. The following morning, when the attack was to take place, we visited the Palace; not a guard was left on the grounds; President Diem was alone upstairs, calmly getting his work done.

As a result of the Hinh trouble, Diem started looking around for troops upon whom he could count. Some Tonkinese militia, refugees from the north, were assembled in Saigon close to the Palace. But they were insufficient for what he needed. Diem made an agreement with General Trinh Minh Thé, leader of some 3,000 Cao Dai dissidents in the vicinity of Tayninh, to give General Thé some needed financial support; The was to give armed support to the government if necessary and to provide a safe haven for the government if it had to flee. Thé's guerrillas, known as the Lien Minh, were strongly nationalist and were still fighting the Vietminh and the French. At Ambassador Heath's request, the U.S. secretly furnished Diem with funds for Thé, through the SMM. Shortly afterwards, an invitation came from The to visit him. Ambassador Heath approved the visit. . . .

The northern SMM team under Conein had organized a paramilitary group, (which we will disguise by the Vietnamese name of Binh) through the Northern Dai Viets, a political party with loyalties to Bao Dai. The group was to be trained and supported by the U.S. as patriotic Vietnamese, to come eventually under government control when the government was ready for such activities. Thirteen Binhs were quietly exfiltrated through the port of Haiphong, under the direction of Lt Andrews, and taken on the first stage of the journey to their training area by a U.S. Navy ship. This was the first of a series of helpful actions by Task Force 98, commanded by Admiral Sabin.

Another paramilitary group for Tonkin operations was being developed in Saigon through General Nguyen Van Vy. In September this group started shaping up fast, and the project was given to Major Allen. (We will give this group the Vietnamese name of Hao). . . .

Towards the end of the month, it was learned that the largest printing establishment in the north intended to remain in Hanoi and do business with the Vietminh. An attempt was made by SMM to destroy the modern presses, but Vietminh security agents already had moved into the plant and frustrated the attempt. This operation was under a Vietnamese patriot whom we shall call Trieu; his case officer was Capt Arundel. Earlier in the month they had engineered a black psywar strike in Hanoi: leaflets signed by the Vietminh instructing Tonkinese on how to behave for the Vietminh takeover of the Hanoi region in early October, including items about property, money reform, and a three-day holiday of workers upon takeover. The day following the distribution of these leaflets, refugee registration tripled. Two days later Vietminh currency was worth half the value prior to the leaflets. The Vietminh took to the radio to denounce the leaflets; the leaflets were so authentic in appearance that even most of the rank and file Vietminh were sure that the radio denunciations were a French trick.

The Hanoi psywar strike had other consequences. Binh had enlisted a high police official of Hanoi as part of his team, to effect the release from jail of any team members if arrested. The official at the last moment decided to assist in the leaflet distribution personally. Police officers spotted him, chased his vehicle through the empty Hanoi streets of early morning, finally opened fire on him and caught him. He was the only member of the group caught. He was held in prison as a Vietminh agent.[20]

M. J. Bosse describes one of the refugees from North Vietnam in his novel. Having walked to Haiphong, Tao Kim Nam boards a crowded American ship for transportation to Saigon.

In the blaze of noon, when belowdecks was metal hot, many old men sat topside, and one or another would talk. The rest would smoke bamboo pipes or chew betel or munch a little ball of rice saved from the morning meal. To be with old men was to be safe, was what Nam thought, but he did not join them the first day. The first afternoon, after the giving of gifts, he stood again at the rail and gazed eastward at the empty, colorless horizon, or westward where, with the haze lifting, he could see white dunes of sand between rocky headlands on the shore, and beyond them a line of mountains, so swathed in clouds they seemed to dissolve into the sky.

Behind him sat the old men in a circle, and children, racing awkwardly through the deck throng, always managed to avoid the forbidden territory where those old men, puffing, seemed to suck up what air was above them.

Behind him Nam could hear them recalling their violent youths, when women ran from them; then complaining of the youth of today, who either joined the murderous Vietminh or hid behind Americans. They liked nothing but their own youths. They hated everyone, even the nationalists in whom they would put their trust in Saigon. Behind Nam they made a sound of the wind's constancy, a sound that comforted him, recalling to him the sound of the elders of Ba Lang, when they too had sat in circles in the dust, with the wind to their backs, and in the surety of their days had cursed everyone. . . .

The second day the black market was in full progress. From the evidence of clothing, the black-market men were former members of the army. Since that army had been so badly beaten by the Vietminh, perhaps these ex-members of it vented their hatred upon the refugees because they could no longer get satisfaction in battle. At any rate, they worked with ruthless efficiency.

For one or two piastres they bought rice from people; then when the people became hungry, having sold not eaten their rice, the black-market men sold the rice back to them at great cost. Or, and this is what the black marketeers favored, the people could exchange their packs of cigarettes for rice. Without violence the operation began, and without violence it continued into the second morning. But by noon there were rumors of a change. People said it was better to sell whatever the ex-army men wanted you to sell, either rice or tobacco, and get yourself a piastre, than refuse and have them push you back into the shadows behind the bunks, where they could get what they wanted anyway, without you getting a thing in return.

By evening the black marketeers were bolder. This was because the Americans did not seem to understand what was happening. The sailors did not cull out the voice of threat from the voice of domestic squabbling, and did not interpret a dig in the ribs as more than a horseplay of boredom.

And so a few dozen men filled sack after sack with food and tobacco, while many of the two thousand people went hungry, and their neighbors watched helplessly. . . . Not long after that, before Nam was asleep, a priest came through and stopped to talk to the whispering men. Nam heard what the priest said. Do nothing, he said, but wait for the Americans to punish them.

The next day that was the ship rumor—let the army men have what they want, because they won't have it long; the Americans will punish them.[21]

1954   **8 September**—One of many U.S.-sponsored mutual defense alliances, the Southeast Asia Treaty Organization, is formalized. Member states of Great Britain, France, Australia, New Zealand, the Philippines, Thailand, and Pakistan approve a protocol, which includes "Cambodia, . . . Laos, and the free territory under the jurisdiction of the State of Vietnam." **23 October**—President Eisenhower authorizes direct U.S. aid to Prime Minister Diem's government, thus bypassing the French.

Colonel Lansdale's SMM (Saigon Military Mission) report chronicles the events of the last few months of 1954.

OCTOBER 1954

Hanoi was evacuated on 9 October. The northern SMM team left with the last French troops, disturbed by what they had seen of the grim efficiency of the Vietminh in their takeover, the contrast between the silent march of the victorious Vietminh troops in their tennis shoes and the clanking armor of the well-equipped French whose western tactics and equipment had failed aginst the Communist military-political-economic campaign.

The northern team had spent the last days of Hanoi in contaminating the oil supply of the bus company for a gradual wreckage of engines in the buses, in taking the first actions for delayed sabotage of the railroad (which required teamwork with a CIA special technical team in Japan who performed their part brilliantly), and in writing detailed notes of potential targets for future paramilitary operations (U.S. adherence to the Geneva Agreement prevented SMM from carrying out the active sabotage it desired to do against the power plant, water facilities, harbor, and bridge). The team had a bad moment when contaminating the oil. They had to work quickly at night, in an enclosed storage room. Fumes from the contaminant came close to knocking them out. Dizzy and weak-kneed, they masked their faces with handkerchiefs and completed the job.

Meanwhile, Polish and Russian ships had arrived in the south to transport southern Vietminh to Tonkin under the Geneva Agreement. This offered the opportunity for another black psywar strike. A leaflet was developed by Binh with the help of Capt Arundel, attributed to the Vietminh Resistance Committee. Among other items, it reassured the

Vietminh they would be kept safe below decks from imperialist air and submarine attacks, and requested that warm clothing be brought; the warm clothing item would be coupled with a verbal rumor campaign that Vietminh were being sent into China as railroad laborers.

SMM had been busily developing G-5 of the Vietnamese Army for such psywar efforts. Under Arundel's direction, the First Armed Propaganda Company printed the leaflets and distributed them, by soldiers in civilian clothes who penetrated into southern Vietminh zones on foot. (Distribution in Camau was made while columnist Joseph Alsop was on his visit there which led to his sensational, gloomy articles later; our soldier "Vietminh" failed in an attempt to get the leaflet into Alsop's hands in Camau; Alsop was never told this story). Intelligence reports and other later reports revealed that village and delegation committees complained about "deportation" to the north, after distribution of the leaflet. . . .

Contention between Diem and Hinh had become murderous. . . . Finally, we learned that Hinh was close to action; he had selected 26 October as the morning for an attack on the Presidential Palace. Hinh was counting heavily on Lt-Col Lan's special forces and on Captain Giai who was running Hinh's secret headquarters at Hinh's home. We invited these two officers to visit the Philippines, on the pretext that we were making an official trip, could take them along and open the way for them to see some inner workings of the fight against Filipino Communists which they probably would never see otherwise. Hinh reluctantly turned down his own invitation; he had had a memorable time of it on his last visit to Manila in 1952. Lt-Col Lan was a French agent and the temptation to see behind-the-scenes was too much. He and Giai accompanied SMM officers on the MAAG C-47 which General O'Daniel instantly made available for the operation. 26 October was spent in the Philippines. The attack on the palace didn't come off.

NOVEMBER 1954

General Lawton Collins arrived as Ambassador on 8 November. . . .

Collins, in his first press conference, made it plain that the U.S. was supporting President Diem. The new Ambassador applied pressure on General Hinh and on 29 November Hinh left for Paris. His other key conspirators followed.

Part of the SMM team became involved in staff work to back up the energetic campaign to save Vietnam which Collins pushed forward. Some SMM members were scattered around the Pacific, accompanying Vietnamese for secret training, obtaining and shipping supplies to be smuggled into north Vietnam and hidden there. In the Philippines, more support was being constructed to help SMM, in expediting the flow of supplies, and in creating Freedom Company, a non-profit Philippines corporation backed by President Magsaysay, which would supply Filipinos experienced in fighting the Communist Huks to help in Vietnam (or elsewhere). . . .

On 23 November, twenty-one selected Vietnamese agents and two cooks of our Hao paramilitary group were put aboard a Navy ship in the Saigon River, in daylight. They appeared as coolies, joined the coolie and refugee throng moving on and off ship, and disappeared one by one. It was brilliantly planned and executed, agents being picked up from unobtrusive assemly points throughout the metropolis. Lt Andrews made the plans and carried out the movement under the supervision of Major Allen. The ship took the Hao agents, in compartmented groups, to an overseas point, the first stage in a movement to a secret training area.

DECEMBER 1954

Discussions between the U.S., Vietnamese and French had reached a point where it appeared that a military training mission using U.S. officers was in the immediate offing. General O'Daniel had a U.S.-French planning group working on the problem, under Col Rosson. One paper they were developing was a plan for pacification of Vietminh and dissident areas; this paper was passed to SMM for its assistance with the drafting. SMM wrote much of the paper, changing the concept from the old rigid police controls of all areas to some of our concepts of winning over the population and instituting a classification of areas by the amount of trouble in each, the amount of control required, and fixing responsibilities between civil and military authorities. With a few changes, this was issued by President Diem on 31 December as the National Security Action (Pacification) Directive. . . .

There was still much disquiet in Vietnam, particularly among anti-Communist political groups who were not included in the government. SMM officers were contacted by a number of such groups who felt that they "would have to commit suicide in 1956" (the 1956 plebiscite promised in the 1954 Geneva agreement), when the Vietminh would surely take over against so weak a government. One group of farmers and militia in the south was talked out of migrating to Madagascar by SMM and staying on their farms. A number of these groups asked SMM for help in training personnel for eventual guerrilla warfare if the Vietminh won. Persons such as the then Minister of Defense and Trinh Minh The were among those loyal to the government who also requested such help. It was decided that a more basic guerrilla training program might be undertaken for such groups than was available at the secret training site to which we had sent the Binh and Hao groups. Plans were made with Major Bohanan and Mr. John C. Wachtel in the Philippines for a solution of this problem; the United States backed the development, through them, of a small Freedom Company training camp in a hidden valley on the Clark AFB reservation.

Till and Peg Durdin of the N.Y. Times, Hank Lieberman of the N.Y. Times, Homer Bigart of the N.Y. Herald-Tribune, John Mecklin of Life-Time [sic], and John Roderick of Associated Press, have been warm friends of SMM and worked hard to penetrate the fabric of French propaganda and give the U.S. an objective account of events in Vietnam. The group met with us at times to analyze objectives and motives of propaganda known to them, meeting at their own request as U.S. citizens. These mature and responsible news correspondents performed a valuable service for their country.[22]

1954   **2 December**—Senator Joseph R. McCarthy is censured by the U.S. Senate for improper conduct in his investigation of alleged Communists.

As will happen with increasing frequency, journalists in Saigon observe and write impressions that vary widely from officially released information. Quite a few write fiction too. In The Ugly American, *Vietnam becomes the country of Sarkhan, and Colonel Lansdale is portrayed as Colonel Hillandale, the "Six–Foot Swami," an astrologer and palmist. Here the colonel is briefing the American ambassador.*

"Well, sir," said Colonel Hillandale, "first I have to give you some background. Every person and every nation has a key which will open their hearts. If you use the right key, you can maneuver any person or any nation any way you want.

"The key to Sarkhan—and to several other nations in Southeast Asia— is palmistry and astrology. All you have to do to learn this is to walk along the streets and look at the occult establishments. The men who operate them are called doctors, and they're respected. There are chairs of palmistry and astrology in every Sarkhanese University, and the Prime Minister himself has a Ph.D. in Occult Science.

"There are many things which we don't know much about in the United States which are held in high regard by the Asians, and in which they have developed a genuine skill. Palmistry and astrology are among these.

"The Sarkhanese officials wouldn't make a major decision without consulting a doctor of the occult. Shortly after I arrived a well-known astrologer announced that on the eighteenth a 'big man' would die in Sarkhan. Well, sir, on the seventeenth almost every important official in Sarkhan flew to Rangoon so as to be out of the country on that fateful day. Even the King and the Prime Minister went away. They make no bones about it—they believe.

"It so happens that palmistry and astrology are hobbies of mine; I studied them when I was in China. It was immediately clear to me that I had knowledge which would be helpful in furthering U.S. interests out here.

"When I asked to read palms at the Philippine Ambassador's dinner, it was a God-given opportunity. All of the Sarkhanese brass except the King were present. . . .

"Well, the Prime Minister asked me to read his palm. Naturally I was familiar with his background, and I described it to him. Everyone is always amazed if you can tell him intimate details about his youth.

"Then I told His Excellency that he was planning a six-months' trip around the world, and he damned near jumped out of his underwear.

"Of course you haven't heard about it, sir. No one in your embassy knows what the score is until it explodes in his face—if you'll pardon me for being frank. But about a week ago I was passing the Prime Minister's residence and I saw the servants airing the furniture in the back and putting cotton covers on it. All it took was a little discreet questioning to find out that His Excellency was making a trip around the world. Then I found out from the airline when he was going and who would accompany him. This was a closely-guarded secret."

"What did His Excellency say when you told him he was making a trip?"

"He was surprised, and then he asked me why he was making the trip. Well, I know what the political situation is here; and I told him that two men, both old friends of his, were fighting for power under him, and he didn't know which one to pick. So he was delaying the decision by making a trip around the world."

"Then what did he say?"

"He walked up and down the room for a few minutes, sweating like a Westerner, and then he asked me what the men's names were. I told him I couldn't tell that from his hand, and that I was too new here in Sarkhan to be familiar with officials' names. But I could describe the men from looking at his palm. And I did. I told him one was small, emaciated, and had liver trouble. The other was big and red-faced.

"He paced and sweat some more; then he sat down with a groan and asked me which of the two he should have killed."

Ambassador MacWhite jumped up. "My God, you were speaking of General Saugh and General Bhakal."

"Yes, sir."

"What did you tell him?"

"I didn't know what our policy was, so I advised him that it would be a mistake to kill either; and that a man who was as devout a Buddhist as he is shouldn't even have asked the question. I further suggested that a smarter thing to do would be to send *them* out of the country for about six months instead of his going."

"You did! My God, they announced not an hour ago that Saugh is going to America as Special Ambassador Plenipotentiary, and that Bhakal is going to Russia with the same title. They're leaving next week."[23]

1955   12 February—United States assumes all training of South Vietnamese military.

Although the early months of 1955 seem outwardly calm, the various factions within South Vietnam's tenuous coalition government continue to plot against the official government as well as each other, as Colonel Lansdale recounts.

I met with Generals Thé and Phuong, two of the sect military leaders, once again. They told me that the United Sects Front was about to issue an ultimatum to Diem, demanding that he give them the choice spots in the government and the major say in how the government was run. Diem could continue to preside as a straw man. The ultimatum must be complied with in five days. If Diem refused, the sect armed forces would make a show of strength, and force him to give in. I told Thé and Phuong that, if they were ever to withdraw honorably from the front, the time for doing so was at hand. Their withdrawal might give pause to the others who were rushing into actions that would wreck the progress being made in Vietnam. The two generals said that the greatest bar to withdrawal was what the Cao Dai Pope could do about Phuong's position as chief of the Cao Dai military forces. Maybe I was right, though, about its being time to act. How about our meeting again that night? I agreed.

I saw Ambassador Collins and told him what was afoot, noting that time for studying the problem had run out. The threat of a show of force by private sect armies against the government was a challenge that Diem would rise to meet. He was a scrapper. Moreover, the Vietnamese Army would support him. Its officers had little use for the sect armies. Despite rumors to the contrary, I was sure that the Vietnamese Army would fight in a showdown. The United Sects Front was on a collision course leading to a civil war, unless its leaders could be persuaded to act rationally. A firm stand by Generals Thé and Phuong might initiate a pause in which cooler heads could prevail. It was time for fast, positive action.

Collins told me to see what I could do with Thé and Phuong that night, and to keep him advised. I stayed up most of the night talking with the two generals at Phuong's Saigon residence, through Joe Redick as interpreter. They had decided firmly to quit the front, so our talk was on how best to do this and still keep their positions of strength and use them for constructive ends. I had telephoned Collins about their decision. He asked me to bring them by his house in the morning. I remarked that they would be rather tired in the morning, but a private meeting in which he congratulated them for their resolve might be useful in bucking them up.

In the morning Thé, Phuong, Redick, and I drove to the residence of Collins, bushed from the long night of talk and in need of showers, clean clothes, and breakfast. I assured them that it would be just a brief and friendly call, and then we could all be on our way again. I was surprised, when we entered, to find that Collins had his own special staff of political, economic, and information experts with him. As we sat down with the two sect generals, I sharing a couch with Collins and Redick seated on a footstool next to the generals to act as interpreter, the bevy of American experts pulled up chairs in a semicircle around us, put large notepads in their laps, took out pens and pencils, and sat poised, apparently ready to record every precious word for posterity.

Collins started the proceedings by telling his visitors how shocked he was as a military man over the disloyal behavior of the two generals toward their government. I stopped Redick as he dutifully started to translate this and pleaded with Collins to congratulate the generals for their decision to remain *loyal* to the government. This led to a fervent argument between Collins and me, while the two sect generals sat there puzzled, watching the scene and unable to understand the English we were speaking. I pointed out that, as Collins had suggested, I had invited Generals Thé and Phuong for a private meeting with him. Instead, there was a group sitting with pads and pencils who might be taken for journalists by his guests. The least that might be done was to explain who the note-takers were. Beyond that, I urged that he simply offer his congratulations on their commitment to be loyal; they shouldn't be scolded. Collins merely repeated his original remarks in a louder voice, adding that he was trying to prevent bloodshed.

Obviously the meeting was getting nowhere, and I was afraid that Thé and Phuong might catch the import of his words, become angry, and let their ire overrule their decision to pull out of the front. A clash between the sects and the government would then become a certainty. It was hardly the way to avoid bloodshed. So I forced a smile, stood up, and motioned the two generals to come along with me. I explained to Collins that I would give them breakfast and tell them that he had lauded their decision. We left.

After breakfast Thé and Phuong went to the meeting of the front where the ultimatum to Diem was to be decided upon. The two generals voiced their objections to the ultimatum and then resigned from the front, making it plain that they also were speaking for the armed forces under their command. They left the front meeting in an uproar. When I heard this news, I saw Collins and told him what had happened. By that time he and his staff were at the luncheon table. We had a bit of uproar among ourselves, too, about the way the early-morning meeting at the residence had gone. I know that I didn't endear myself to the others by my contribution to the conversation about the morning confrontation. I was grateful, however, that the headlong rush of the sects toward violence had received a check. I urged that whatever action the Americans and French were to take with Diem to resolve the sect problem be done promptly. The respite given by the courageous stand of Thé and Phuong might prove to be fleeting.

The respite was indeed all too brief. Those remaining in the front decided to go ahead with their scheme without the backing of Thé and Phuong and their forces. The front sent the ultimatum to Diem on March 22, telling him that he had until March 27 to agree to it, "or else." Diem

mastered his temper and coolly offered to negotiate with the front
leaders, saying that he had some proposals of his own wherein all good
patriots could participate with him in constructing something more solid
and lasting for the benefit of the country. The offer to negotiate was
refused. The Binh Xuyen positioned mortars for a bombardment of the
palace if Diem refused to accept the ultimatum.[24]

*Jean Larteguy fictionalizes the events of late April as follows: for Trinh-
Sat, read Thé; President Dinh-Thu is Diem; Colonel Teryman
(Terre=land) is Lansdale. The scene is the presidential palace on April 25,
1955.*

The President was seated on the edge of his chair, with his hands folded
on his knees. He sat motionless in this uncomfortable position, senile and
at the same time childish. His small hands were chubby, his face impassive and his motionless eyes as black and glinting as anthracite.

Colonel Teryman had grey, closely cropped hair, a hooked nose and
thin lips. He was wearing a light drill uniform with an open collar and
because of a certain stiffness in his bearing he looked like a Prussian
officer. Anger made him clench his heavy jaws. With fresh arguments he
was trying once again to persuade the President, who was as soft as wax,
to attack the Binh-Xuyens forthwith. Colonel Kim, who commanded the
three parachute battalions which had been transferred from Tonkin, had
been waiting for two hours in the antechamber for the decision for which
he was hoping. . . .

'If we strike hard and immediately,' Teryman insisted, 'the Emperor
will be taken by surprise and, from Cannes, won't be able to intervene.
The High Commissioner won't have time to refer the matter to Paris and
will therefore have to accept the situation.

'Once South Vietnam is rid of her pirates, she'll figure as a proper State
in the eyes of the world and, after making the other sects toe the line and
disbanding their private armies, she'll be able to devote all her energies to
the struggle against communism.'

To underline his argument, Colonel Teryman kept thumping a flimsy
table with his fists, thereby annoying the President who rose to his feet.

'I am going to pray,' he said.

Leaving Teryman disconcerted, he went through a narrow door into
his oratory and fell on his knees. He immersed himself in a dialogue
with the god he had invented, a god of prejudice and fury, who maintained the ancient hierarchies, demanded endless prayers and accepted
only men who were pure and had never touched a woman, that creature
of corruption. . . .

The American was now taking to task the second brother, the professor, who had a disproportionately long face in relation to his shortness of
stature. . . .

'If I'm not given an immediate assurance that the day after tomorrow

morning the troops that are still loyal to the President will attack the
Binh-Xuyens, I shall never set foot in this palace again. I shall go back to
Washington and notify the State Department that it would be a mistake
to support your government any longer.'

'My brother is praying.'

'Go and wake him up. He's not praying, he's sleeping.'

The President had fallen asleep on his prie-dieu with a benign smile on
his face. His brother shook him by the shoulder:

'We must come to a decision.'

'Tomorrow.'

'No, now. Colonel Teryman's going to leave us in the lurch, which
would be serious. The colonel's our only support. The American Ambassador is abandoning us and siding with the French.'

'Do what you like but leave me alone.'

Dinh-Tac re-emerged from the oratory and solemnly announced to
Teryman:

'My brother the President has prayed and reflected at great length and
has decided that we shall attack the Binh-Xuyens the day after tomorrow
morning.'

Teryman lit a cigarette and inhaled the smoke. If the attempt failed the
President would claim that the decision to attack the Binh-Xuyens had
been imposed on him by force. This was the trick he always played and
Teryman was used to it. All the politicians with whom he had dealt were
cowards. . . .

As he drove back to his villa Colonel Teryman kept thinking of Trinh-
Sat, that harsh pitiless man who had the makings of a dictator. And what
South Vietnam needed was a dictatorship.

But the word offended the worthy American conscience. So he had
been saddled with this laughing-stock of a president who was always
surrounded by his family, this mandarin steeped in piety and incapable of
taking a decision.

But Lionel Teryman was keeping Trinh-Sat in reserve. It was his secret
card in the event of the President abandoning him and coming to some
agreement with the French.

On arriving home the colonel felt tired. He poured himself out a
whisky and water and lay down under the fan.

The wound in his thigh was hurting him. To thank him for having
brought him to power, the head of an inconsistent medieval little state
had tried to have him assassinated.

In Paris, in the Ministry for the Associated States, there was a file on
Teryman. But it was extremely incomplete, for it was based on press
cuttings combined with a few garbled reports and padded out with pieces
of Intelligence Service gossip.

The American was represented as a new Lawrence of Arabia, of questionable sexual habits since he was not known to have any woman in his
life, brutal, uncouth and violently anti-French.

Teryman was by no means averse to women but, in order to be accepted by the President, he practised self-imposed chastity.

He was neither a remarkable Intelligence agent nor a specialist in political action, but a masterly stage manager. He could get hold of the most bigoted old scoundrel, the most inexperienced novice and, out of a gang leader, make a president of the republic; out of an odious and tyrannical old fogey, an all-powerful dictator.

The Americans had staked four hundred million dollars on President Dinh-Tu. They were prodigal but were anxious to guarantee their stakes. So they had entrusted Teryman with the task of imposing him on the masses. But the State Department distrusted the colonel and kept him under observation, for he was capable at any moment of reversing his policy without even notifying his superiors should the brief he had been given cease to please him.[25]

Colonel Lansdale sees the conflict from his own perspective.

Battle for Saigon

I spent the morning of April 28 at my office. . . .

At noon a telephone call from Doc Lap Palace asked if I would please come and see Diem right away. Joe Redick and I set out for the palace by the shortest route. Approaching Place Khai-Dinh, a traffic circle where five boulevards and streets meet, I noticed something amiss. Bicyclists were bumping into each other and falling in the street. Cars were stopping, their doors popping open and spewing passengers onto the pavement where they lay huddled. At first glance it looked like a massive slapstick scene. I slowed down, amazed. Then I heard the machine gun fire, a sound that had been muffled by the houses along the street. It was so unexpected an event in the heavy traffic that it seemed to take me forever to link the dropping of people onto the ground with the firing of machine guns. When I caught on, I stopped the car. Redick and I dropped flat on the pavement with the others.

The firing died away after several minutes. We got back into the car and drove past the scramble of stilled traffic at the circle. Seeing us on the move, people started getting to their feet again, apparently shaken but unhurt. The firing must have been over our heads. In the spacious public park behind the palace, I noticed that something new had been added: batteries of artillery with Vietnamese Army crews camped around the guns. They looked incongruous among the tennis courts, playgrounds, bridle paths, and beds of brilliant flowers beneath the tall tropical trees.

Diem was pacing up and down the long second-story porch of the palace's eastern portico when we arrived. Instead of going inside to his office, as was customary, we stood on the porch and talked. Diem had received word from Washington just before telephoning me. It had been reported to him that Ambassador Collins had obtained President Eisen-

hower's approval for a change of U.S. policy toward Vietnam. Diem was
to be "dumped" in favor of a coalition government. Was this report true?
Diem looked at me intently as he asked this. I said firmly that I didn't
believe the report. Collins had assured me before his departure that the
U.S. would support Diem, despite any rumors to the contrary. Diem
refused to tell me the source of his information. I said that I would.
initiate a check with Washington by radio to make doubly sure of what
I'd just told him. Since it was midnight in Washington on the other side of
the world, it would be hours before a reply could be expected from top
U.S. officials.

Diem relaxed a little at my reassurances. He said there had been reports of shooting in the streets all over town, and I described what had
happened on our way to see him. Diem thought the Binh Xuyen probably
were working themselves up toward an action to break the truce. He
grinned impishly and added that he had some new tactical intelligence
about the Binh Xuyen. Their mortars had been freshly sighted in on the
palace. The very spot on the porch where we were standing was the exact
target for an 81-mm. mortar acquired by the Binh Xuyen during the
truce. We might get blown up even as we stood there talking to each
other.

I asked Diem about the Binh Xuyen chief of staff, who was to come
over to the nationalist side, Colonel Thai hoang Minh. Diem said arrangements had been made to pass Colonel Minh and his four battalions
(which were then near Go Cong south of Saigon) through the lines,
where they would be integrated into the national army. Minh had said
that his own troops and six Binh Xuyen battalions of "Sûreté assault
troops" were practically at swords' points. One platoon loyal to Minh was
in the Rue Catinat area, in the French security zone close to Doc Lap
Palace.

We left after I had suggested to Diem that he get off the porch if it was
indeed to be the target of 81-mm. mortar shells "at any moment." I drove
to my house on Duy Tan, about eight blocks from the palace. There was
scarcely any traffic on the streets. It was a little past one o'clock in the
afternoon, and all sensible people in Saigon were at home for lunch and
siesta. Just as I was turning into the driveway at my house, there came a
series of loud explosions from the direction of the palace. Obviously, the
attack on the palace had started. When I entered my house, the telephone was ringing.

It was Ngo dinh Diem calling me. His voice sounded calm, unperturbed. I asked if he was all right. Yes, he told me; he was calling
General Ely and had arranged with the switchboard for me to hear the
conversation as a witness. Before I could ask further questions, Ely came
on the line. I did my best to follow the conversation, which was in French
(later verifying it with Redick and Diem). Diem told Ely that Doc Lap
Palace was under fire from the Binh Xuyen and he wanted Ely to know
that this hostile action broke the truce. Ely said that he couldn't hear any

sounds of an attack on the palace at his house. (He lived about half the distance from the palace as my house, where the explosions were a loud din in the midday air. I wondered if Ely could be inside a closed room, perhaps with an air-conditioner drowning out the sound of close-by artillery explosions. Was this possible?)

Diem seemed surprised that Ely couldn't hear the shelling. Just then, there came a great *wha-a-am* over the telephone. A long pause. Diem came back on the line, his voice a bit shaky. He asked if Ely had heard *that!* A shell had exploded against the wall of the bedroom from where Diem was speaking. He wanted Ely to understand that Diem hadn't broken the truce. The Binh Xuyen had. Diem was giving orders immediately to the Vietnamese Army to fight back. Ely started to say something, but Diem broke in to state that he had informed Ely of the facts and was taking action. He hung up. . . .

It was late afternoon. . . . Dense clouds of smoke darkened the sky above Cholon, where a large section of the city was burning, and each side claimed the other had set it. The fire raged virtually unchecked, since firemen couldn't get through the combat lines. Thousands of people ran through the streets from their burning homes, seeking safety but trying to avoid the strong points where infantry fighting raged. The Vietnamese Army and government workers were opening temporary shelters for these refugees in schoolhouses in an attempt to organize care for them, although many spent the night in the streets. I learned later that a hundred people had died in the fire, another five hundred known casualties went to hospitals, and many thousands were left homeless. More than a square mile of the most densely populated section of the city had been burned out.

I stopped by the big house on Rue Taberd where most of my team lived. Burned-out and shell-shattered vehicles gave the street outside a junkyard look, and a crumpled sedan lay across the front steps, blocking the door. I climbed over a wall to get in. Everyone and everything inside was intact. I asked Major Fred Allen of the team, who knew General Nguyen van Vy quite well, to try to see Vy or to find out what he was doing. Vy reportedly was carrying out Bao Dai's orders. Our embassy officials had told me that Vy had come to Saigon from Dalat with one battalion of Imperial Guards and had taken over the command of the Vietnamese Army, presumably to stop the counterattack against the Binh Xuyen. Allen made fruitless attempts, but Vy, though in town, wouldn't or couldn't see him. Later, Vietnamese Army officers told me that Vy was issuing orders as a commander, but that nobody was obeying them. They added that Vy had unsuccessfully attempted to relieve Big Minh of command over the troops fighting against the Binh Xuyen in the city, in order to replace him with one of Vy's officers.

After dark, in savage nighttime battles, the army stormed Binh Xuyen strongholds at the Grand Monde gambling casino and at the Petrus Ky High School, both in Cholon. General Phuong of the Cao Dai stopped by to tell me about the Petrus Ky attack, saying that some Frenchmen had been captured there along with the Binh Xuyen. (The next day, Diem confirmed this report about Frenchmen at Petrus Ky, giving me the names of those then being held by the Vietnamese Army. Later, he reported that a total of thirty-seven Frenchmen eventually had been found at Petrus Ky, some of whom admitted they were members of a *colon* militia organization.)

Late that night I heard from Washington. There were blunt words for me: my radio message had contained statements at variance with other information being received; if it was true that Diem was alive, was still the head of the government, and actually was being supported by the national army as I claimed, then I should get my statements confirmed by the senior U.S. officials on the scene. Tiredly, I wondered how I was going to get some of these Americans to see what was under their noses. I fell asleep thinking about it. . . .

The next day:

At the palace I walked in on a conference between Diem and a group of Vietnamese Army officers. General Ty and Colonel Don were among them, as were both of the top commanders in the battle against the Binh Xuyen, Little Minh and Big Minh. They were jubilant. The army had crossed the Arroyo Chinois in Cholon and the Binh Xuyen were on the run. Wasn't I going to congratulate them? I told them hell no, not yet. While they were all standing around praising each other, their attack across the canal at the river was getting clobbered because they wouldn't give it artillery support.

I reminded them, as they knew, that I was under strict orders not to give them any commands. However, my orders didn't forbid me telling them a story. Now hear this! Once upon a time some Vietnamese Army commanders were drinking tea together with their boss and telling him how wonderful they were when they should have been moving one of the artillery batteries from Doc Lap Palace, or from in front of the chief of staff's home, or from the General Staff headquarters courtyard, and used that artillery to support Trinh minh Thé at Tan-Thuan-Dong bridge. His unit was the only one on the entire front coming up against big guns protected by armor plating. It also was the only unit without artillery support. The military commanders were about to be condemned by the people, who would become savage when they heard this. Right now, I was damned mad and was waiting for my listeners to finish the story for me.

There was a stunned silence when I stopped. Diem broke it by telling Little Minh to get artillery over to Trinh minh Thé right away. Little Minh hurried off and the others started leaving. I congratulated them on the crossing of the Arroyo Chinois. They looked at me a bit dubiously. I had been very angry when I had interrupted their meeting. I assured them again that I was happy over their success so far. The battle was still far from won, however, and it was no time to start relaxing.

Diem asked me to stay on and talk with him. We went to a small sitting room furnished with a couch and some heavy chairs positioned too far from each other for easy conversation, so I suggested that we sit together on the couch. Diem opened the conversation by saying that he had never seen me as angry as I had been just now. After all, Trinh minh Thé was a military man and would have to take his chances along with others in battle. I shouldn't become so concerned about his affairs. Even though Trinh minh Thé was a friend, he was just one of the many Vietnamese patriots who were my friends and was perhaps not as well educated or as experienced as some of the others. I told Diem to stop this line of talk. It was leading to a point where he might say something that would make me angry all over again. Trinh minh Thé had given Diem his support when men with more education and experience had hung back. Right now, he was out risking his neck for Diem. His sort of friendship was worth more than all the fair-weather friends put together. Furthermore, somebody had been criminally stupid in putting Thé's guerrilla troops, who were neither well enough trained nor well enough equipped, into a formal assault with no fire support. It was a lousy use of guerrilla capabilities.

Diem changed the subject. He told me, in detail and at great length, about all the revolutionary activities then afoot among Vietnamese nationalists. He gave me thumbnail biographies of a number of the leaders. These had been active in the 4th International agitation. Those had been with the Vietminh as political cadre. Still others had been discredited in this, that, or another activity which had failed. Diem, seeing my interest, delivered a monologue about revolutionary Vietnamese personalities for over two hours. As he talked, evening came to Saigon. The lights went on inside the palace. I reminded Diem that he had things to do, and so did I. I was starting to say goodbye when his brother Nhu came into the room.

Nhu walked right up to where we were sitting on the couch and stood silently for a few moments, just looking at us. Finally, he said softly, "Trinh minh Thé has been killed. At the bridge. I've just heard and thought you should know." The news hit me hard. I was scarcely listening as Nhu explained that he had checked carefully for details before coming in to inform us. He was sorry to say it, but the news seemed to be true. Trinh minh Thé had been struck behind the ear, apparently by a rifle bullet. From the angle at which he was hit, the rifleman had been behind and above Thé. The troops there were saying that it must have been a sniper. There was talk about a French sniper from the nearby French defense positions.

Nhu left the room. Diem and I sat wordless on the couch. I rose to leave, to be alone with my grief. I turned to Diem and told him, "We have lost a true friend." I couldn't trust myself to say more. Diem looked at my face and started crying. Great sobs racked his body. I sat down again and held him in my arms. He asked me brokenly to forgive him for the way he had talked about Trinh minh Thé a little earlier. I told him there really was nothing to forgive, but he must always remember. True comrades were rare. He must never turn away from the unselfish ones who served freedom. We sat there quietly after that until he regained control. Then I left for my house. The tears made it hard for me to see as I drove.[26]

With Diem now firmly in control, the Frenchmen in Jean Larteguy's Yellow Fever *look forward to the future.*

Then Julien ambled past the shop-windows in the Rue Catinat, followed two pretty half-caste girls who were traipsing down the street, and suddenly wondered under what regime Vietnam was living. It was no longer a monarchy since the Emperor had lost his authority; perhaps a republic of the presidential type . . . but the Revolutionary Committee continued to function and the President seemed relegated to a secondary role. He asked himself another question: Who had won? The President, the Americans, the Vietminhs?

Meetings were announced at every street corner, the Vietnamese flags above the public buildings had doubled in extent.

Throughout the day Julien kept wandering about the town and when, in the evening, at Luthier-Verneuil's dinner, he made his appearance dressed in white, easy-mannered and ironical, with a lock of fair hair falling over his forehead, he appeared to the financier's guests like Fantasio at the beginning of a feast.

He had had a scented bath, his silk shirt caressed his skin, the ice tinkled merrily in his glass. He savoured the pleasure of imagining himself rich, of finding, in the eyes of the young women with their daring dresses, a promise and, in the eyes of the men, the regret at not having his youth and sparkle. He felt he could go to any lengths. These company directors, these bank managers, this admiral, these two colonels, their wives and their daughters, were his benevolent accomplices.

Luthier-Verneuil asked him:

'What did you see in Saigon?'

'I looked for a republic but couldn't find one.'

He had spoken fairly loudly and all heads were turned towards him. He felt he could risk putting on his little act.

'I was walking past the Town Hall at ten o'clock and the Emperor almost crashed down on my head; they were throwing his portrait out of the window. On the balcony everyone was laughing and applauding. It was 1789 all over again, but in the local manner: a nice little revolution without anyone being hurt: a revolution by patronage. The Swiss Guards, in this case the Binh-Xuyens, had disbanded at the first cannon shot and withdrawn across the arroyo; the Emperor was in Cannes and was in no danger of being beheaded like Capet; Robespierre-Trinh-Sat, instead of being guillotined, had died on the field of battle. The Bastille was a mere bridge, but, instead of Latude, twenty million piastres were found there. Badges of rank were falling on every shoulder. I hear that at the Palais Norodom . . . I mean the Palais de l'Indépendance . . . a nice little republic was being prepared under the direction of the little President. I drove over there in a taxi.

'Five hundred and fifty delegates from all over the country were to vote on an extremely important motion. Lined up in two rows I came across the usual mixture of bearded elders in black trousers and black robes, intellectuals from Hué with grave faces and perfect manners and, here and there, a few worthy *nhaqués* who had been collected at random in the street and were wondering what on earth they were doing under the President's chandeliers. The new-born republic is sure to be a good little girl, obedient to her parents and full of reverence.

'The ballot papers are checked and rechecked; refreshments are served; but it's impossible to come to an agreement. The delegates of the South declare that the ballot papers of the delegates of the North and Centre are fakes; the delegates of the Centre accuse those of the South of being colonialists; and everyone accuses those of the North of being Vietminhs.

'But all this takes place without a voice being raised in anger, with any amount of bowing and scraping. The meeting is postponed until tomorrow. No republic.

'I just have time to rush to the Town Hall where the Revolutionary Committee is holding a meeting.

'Barely three hundred people are assembled in the square outside with a few banners: "Down with the colonialists and their plots"; "Down with the intention of managing the country's affairs from abroad." The last one is very long and the people carrying it are unable to co-ordinate their movements; it bobs up and down, sways from side to side and finally collapses on the ground. A man on the balcony keeps screaming into a microphone but no one pays any attention. He tries to strike up the revolutionary hymn, but as he's the only one who knows it, since he's just composed it, his little solo is drowned in private conversations which continue all round me. A shower of rain sends everyone scuttling for shelter. A republic cannot be born in a rainstorm. That's well known!

'I go upstairs into the Council Chamber of the Town Hall. There I see a number of worthy idlers, some of those perpetual students, habitués of the Quartier Latin, who've just turned up. They're all Trotskyists, Existentialists, or Federalists. There are no more Vietminhs, they've all disappeared, leaving these jovial fanatics in pledge. I have a drink and a chat with them; I see the moment coming when I'm going to be part of an anticolonialist committee. They all vote, so do I. I suddenly ask one of them why the Revolutionary Committee indulges in such violent anti-French propaganda.

' "It's to annoy the President," he tells me. "He started off with anticolonialist slogans; we've got to shout louder than him."

'I soon feel a headache coming on, so off I go to the Vietnamese officers. They're extremely pleasant and offer me whisky. It's Lê-Dao's whisky; they've looted his entire stock. I ask them whether they're soon going to proclaim the republic.

' "There's plenty of time," says General Tranh. "We've got to sort things out first. We've also got to have an Assembly to elect the President. But if it elected someone else instead of him, he'd be obliged to dissolve it, which would create a bad effect. It's a military man we need at the head of Vietnam in these critical times."

' "Then why not make the President a general?"

'He doesn't like my suggestion. He turns his back on me. I'm given no more whisky.

'So I go off to the Caodists, not Trinh-Sat's but the real ones: the partisans of Pope Pham-Cong-Tac. Glass in hand, they're all celebrating the "disincarnation" of Trinh-Sat who was beginning to irritate them. I ask them:

' "What about this republic?"

'The pope blinks.

' "We shall have to replace the Emperor," he says, "with a spiritual power which will be above parties."

'I see what he wants: in place of the President, Cao-Dai, the Supreme Being, who would correspond with his ministers through mediums and the Magic Basket. . . .

'The Americans would also like to give birth to a nice friendly little republic, but they're wondering how much it will cost. The French don't agree; they feel that republicanism is not for export and want to keep the monopoly of it for Metropolitan France. Then I met Ndiem, a friend of mine who's in the Ministry of National Economy. I asked him what he thought of it. He told me:

' "Personally, I don't give a damn, but I'd very much like someone to pay my salary. It's now two months since I drew any pay."

'Yet I should have liked to discover a little republic! . . . I'll try again tomorrow.'

Everyone found Julien's account extremely funny. He was asked to call on the admiral and the banker. The young woman seated on his left clamped her leg against his; the one on his right did likewise. His glass kept being refilled. . . .

'The only one missing is Colonel Lionel Teryman,' the Squid observed. 'I wonder what's happened to that fellow?'

Bernot grunted in his chair:

'The little President asked for him back. From what Vernier tells me, the colonel is bored stiff because he can't find anyone "suitable" to put up against the man who's employing him. So he spends his time planning referendums, rigged elections and an agrarian reform, which will put the whole country up in arms. But he's fallen foul of Hoang, the big chief of all the police forces. Elections are held, say, at Cholon, and Teryman arranges for 92 per cent of the votes to be in favour of the President.

Hoang sees to it that the final figure is 110 per cent, and the American colonel then gets it in the neck from everyone, including the President, / who would willingly accept 100 per cent but no more.

'Good old Hoang! He loves having a good time, so you're quite liable to see him at your dinner here next year.'

'What about the President and his brothers,' Rovignon asked, 'how much longer do you give them?'

The Squid, who was as resentful as an old priest and had never forgiven the President for expelling him, allowing him no more than forty-eight hours to pack up and leave, announced in his flat voice which belied the gleam in his dark eyes:

'We'll get them in the end . . . next year or the year after. They'll come begging us to help them to escape from oblivion with an article or even a paragraph. We'll keep them waiting on the telephone and we'll fail to turn up at the meetings we've arranged with them. They'll be nothing more than shades, exiles incapable of adapting themselves to a new life and who keep chewing over their memories. They're the new White Russians of Paris; so they may as well learn to drive a taxi.'[27]

The Americans in Vietnam, however, are interested in more significant matters, as seen in this State Department cable from Saigon.

Department of State

FROM: SAIGON
TO: SECRETARY OF STATE
NO: 5074, MAY 5, 9 P.M. (SECTION FOUR OF FOUR)
NIACT
SENT DEPARTMENT 5074, REPEATED INFORMATION NIACT PARIS 1305

CONCLUSIONS:

A. IT WOULD APPEAR TO ME THAT THE ESSENTIAL STEPS IN RECONSTITUTION OF JOINT AMERICAN-FRENCH APPROACH TO SITUATION IN VIETNAM SHOULD BE AS FOLLOWS:

(1) DIEM GOVERNMENT SHOULD BE FULLY SUPPORTED IN BRINGING TO A FINAL AND QUICK SOLUTION ITS CONFLICT WITH THE BINH XUYEN.

(A) THIS WILL REQUIRE ON PART OF FRENCH, NOT ONLY IN PARIS BUT MORE IMPORTANTLY IN SAIGON, THAT GENUINE ASSISTANCE RATHER THAN PASSIVE SELF-OBSTRUCTION BE OFFERED TO VIETNAMESE GOVERNMENT AND ARMED FORCES.

(B) SPECIFICALLY, GENERAL ELY SHOULD BE DIRECTED TAKE ACTIVE STEPS TO PERSUADE BINH XUYEN TO WITHDRAW THEIR FORCES FROM THREE POLICE POSTS REMAINING WITHIN FRENCH SECURITY ZONE IN SAIGON, OR IF BINH XUYEN REFUSE, THEN TO PERMIT VIETNAM ARMED FORCES TO REDUCE THESE POSTS WITH MINIMUM OF CASUALTIES.

(C) ALL ECHELONS OF FRENCH BUREAUCRACY, INCLUDING ARMED FORCES, SHOULD BE INSTRUCTED TO DESIST FROM AGITATING AGAINST DIEM GOVERNMENT.

(D) OFFICIAL PRESSURE, BOTH IN PARIS AND SAIGON, SHOULD BE BROUGHT UPON RADIO FRANCE-ASIA, A SEMI-GOVERNMENTAL INSTITUTION, TO CEASE ITS ATTACKS ON DIEM GOVERNMENT.

(E) SUCH STEPS AS MAY BE POSSIBLE SHOULD BE TAKEN TO PERSUADE FRENCH PRESSMEN TO CEASE THEIR ATTACKS, PARTICULARLY IN SAIGON.

(F) FRENCH GARRISON IN SAIGON-CHOLON SHOULD BE REDUCED WITHOUT DELAY.

(G) THERE SHOULD BE A PUBLIC ANNOUNCEMENT BY APPROPRIATE FRENCH AUTHORITIES OF THEIR FULL SUPPORT OF DIEM GOVERNMENT IN PRESENT CONFLICT WITH BINH XUYEN. POSSIBLE TO ASSIST ORGANIZATION AND TRAINING OF ESSENTIAL LOGISTICAL SERVICES OF VIETNAMESE ARMED FORCES SO AS TO MAKE THEM AS INDEPENDENT AS POSSIBLE OF FEC. THIS IS UNDER WAY IN ACCORDANCE WITH MY INSTRUCTIONS TO MAAG.

(2) AS SOON AS CURRENT CRISIS IS OVER, DECISIVE EFFORT MUST BE MADE TO PERSUADE OR OTHERWISE FORCE DIEM TO REORGANIZE HIS GOVERNMENT AND TO ESTABLISH A CABINET COMPETENT TO IMPLEMENT BROAD PROGRAMS OF REFORM COVERED BY THE COLLINS-ELY SEVEN-POINT PROGRAM, PLUS A PROGRAM FOR INTEGRATION OF SECTS INTO NORMAL LIFE OF VIETNAM.

(3) IF, AFTER REASONABLE FURTHER PERIOD OF TRIAL, DIEM IS UNABLE TO CONSTITUTE A GOVERNMENT CAPABLE OF IMPLEMENTING THESE PROGRAMS, US SHOULD JOIN WITH FRANCE AND BAO DAI IN ASSISTING LIBERAL VIETNAMESE NATIONALISTS TO ESTABLISH A COMPETENT GOVERNMENT.

B. I RECOGNIZE THAT GENERAL ELY MAY IRREVOCABLY BE OPPOSED TO SUPPORTING ANY DIEM GOVERNMENT. IF THIS SHOULD PROVE TO BE TRUE, I WOULD SUGGEST WE URGE FAURE GOVERNMENT TO REPLACE HIM, PREFERABLY WITH MAN OF CALIBER OF DEVINAT, OR PERHAPS GEORGES-NIACT. AT SAME TIME, IT WOULD PROBABLY BE NECESSARY TO REPLACE GENERAL JACQUAT (WHO HAS INCURRED VIOLENT ANIMOSITY OF VIETNAMESE DURING BINH XUYEN AFFAIRS) WITH MAN LIKE GENERAL COGNY.

C. REFERENCE STEP (3) ABOVE, I RECOGNIZE ALSO THAT IT MAY BE POLITICALLY DIFFICULT TO WITHDRAW US SUPPORT FROM DIEM EVEN IF TRIAL PROVES IS CAPABLE OF ESTABLISHING AN EFFECTIVE GOVERNMENT. I STILL FEEL THAT EVEN IF DIEM MANAGES SUPPRESS BINH XUYEN, THIS WILL NOT CHANGE HIS OWN BASIC INCAPACITY TO MANAGE THE AFFAIRS OF GOVERNMENT. HIS PRESENT SUCCESSES MAY EVEN MAKE IT HARDER FOR US TO PERSUADE DIEM TO TAKE COMPETENT MEN INTO GOVERNMENT, TO DECENTRALIZE AUTHORITY TO HIS MINISTERS, AND TO ESTABLISH SOUND PROCEDURES FOR THE IMPLEMENTATION OF REFORM PROGRAMS. I AM STILL CONVINCED DIEM DOES NOT HAVE KNACK OF HANDLING MEN NOR THE EXECUTIVE CAPACITY TRULY TO UNIFY THE

COUNTRY AND ESTABLISH AN EFFECTIVE GOVERNMENT. IF THIS SHOULD BE-
COME EVIDENT, WE SHOULD EITHER WITHDRAW FROM VIETNAM BECAUSE OUR
MONEY WILL BE WASTED, OR WE SHOULD TAKE SUCH STEPS AS CAN LEGITI-
MATELY BE TAKEN TO SECURE AN EFFECTIVE NEW PREMIER.

D. THROUGHOUT ALL THIS I FEEL WE MUST KEEP OUR EYES CLEARLY ON OUR
MAIN OBJECTIVE IN VIETNAM, I.E., TO ASSIST IN SAVING THIS COUNTRY FROM
COMMUNISM. NO MATTER WHO HEADS THE GOVERNMENT HERE, FREE VIETNAM
WILL NOT BE SAVED UNLESS SOUND POLITICAL, ECONOMIC AND MILITARY PRO-
GRAMS ARE PROMPTLY AND EFFECTIVELY PUT INTO ACTION. THIS WILL REQUIRE
WHOLEHEARTED AGREEMENT AND COORDINATION BETWEEN VIETNAMESE,
AMERICANS AND FRENCH. DIFFICULT AS THIS MAY BE TO ACHIEVE, IT IS POSSI-
BLE, IN MY JUDGMENT. IF THIS TRIPARTITE APPROACH IS NOT SECURE, WE
SHOULD WITHDRAW FROM VIETNAM.

Kidder[28]

ACT I

May 1955–November 1963

AS I SLIDE DOWN THE
BANISTER OF LIFE
I'LL ALWAYS REMEMBER
VIETNAM AS A SPLINTER
IN MY ASS

—GI latrine graffito, Saigon

Colonel Lansdale describes the aftermath of the struggle.

Saigon presented a battered and frowzy look to passengers arriving aboard airliners on May 10. Coming in, the planes flew above the remnants of the Binh Xuyen fleeing down river, the battle wreckage of buildings, the clutter of French tanks and troops along the streets, and vast patches of charred and blackened ruins in Cholon districts where the great fire had raged. Among the arrivals that day was George Frederick Reinhardt, the new American ambassador. A career foreign service officer, he replaced the president's special envoy, J. Lawton Collins. Clearly, the United States was giving up its attempt at a quick and simplistic fix of Vietnam's complex problems, through a powerful lieutenant of the U.S. chief executive, in favor of a more conventional approach through professional diplomacy.[1]

A week later, the policy that will direct Ambassador Reinhardt's "conventional approach" is drafted in Washington.

Draft Statement and National Security Council Staff Study on U.S. Policy on All-Vietnam Elections
May 17, 1955

GENERAL CONSIDERATIONS

1. It is U.S. policy to maintain a friendly non-Communist Free Vietnam: to assist Free Vietnam to maintain (a) military forces necessary for internal security, and (b) economic conditions conducive to the maintenance of the strength of the non-Communist regime; and to prevent a Communist victory through all-Vietnam elections.

2. Free Vietnamese strength is essential to any effective approach to the election problem. If Free Vietnam is to cope adequately with national elections it will have to be strong enough to deter or defeat Vietminh insurrections in its territory, to impose and sustain order in its territory, and to win a free election limited to its own zone and held under its own auspices and control. Otherwise, the Vietminh can take over through internal insurrections or the Government of Free Vietnam will be so weak that it will find it difficult even to give lip service to the idea of national unification through elections, or to insist on adequate conditions for free elections.

3. U.S. policy toward all-Vietnam elections should be predicated on the assumption that there is a possibility of assisting Free Vietnam to achieve

the degree of strength described above. If it becomes clear that Free Vietnam cannot achieve such strength, U.S. policy toward Free Vietnam should be reviewed.

4. U.S. policy must also protect against a Communist take-over of Free Vietnam, even if the Communists were able to win elections under safeguards in North Vietnam. On the other hand, U.S. policy should be prepared to take advantage of the unlikely possibility that North Vietnam might be freed through elections.[2]

Two months later Ho Chi Minh sends a letter to the Saigon government.

Message from Ho Chi Minh and Foreign Minister Pham Van Dong to RVN Chief of State Bao Dai and Prime Minister Ngo Dinh Diem
July 19, 1955

The holding on schedule of the consultative conference by the competent authorities of the North and South is of great importance, and has a bearing not only on the prospect of the unity of our country but also on the loyal implementation of the Geneva Agreements, and the consolidation of peace in Indo-China and in the world.

Following the June 6, 1955 declaration by the Government of the Democratic Republic of Viet-nam, Sai-gon Radio on July 16, 1955, made known the "position of the Government of the State of Viet-nam on the problem of general elections for the unification of the national territory." The statement mentioned general elections and reunification but did not touch upon a very important and most realistic issue, that of the meeting of the competent representative authorities of the two zones, of the holding of the consultative conference on the question of general elections and reunification, as provided for by the Geneva Agreements. Moreover there were in the statement things which are untrue and which would not help to create a favourable climate for the convening of the consultative conference.

Our compatriots from the South to the North, irrespective of classes, creeds and political affiliations have deeply at heart the reunification of the country, and are looking forward to the early convening of the consultative conference and to its good outcome. All the countries responsible for the guarantee of the implementation of the Geneva Agreements and in general all the peace-loving countries in the world are anxious to see that the consultative conference will be held and yield good results and that the reunification of our country will be achieved.

The Government of the Democratic Republic of Viet-nam proposes that you appoint your representatives and that they and ours hold the consultative conference from July 20, 1955 onwards, as provided for by the Geneva Agreements, at a place agreeable to both sides, on the Vietnamese territory, in order to discuss the problem of reunification of our country by means of free general elections all over Viet-nam.[3]

Rather than reply, Prime Minister Diem issues the following declaration.

Declaration of the Government
of the State of Vietnam on Reunification
August 9, 1955

In the last July 1955 broadcast, the Vietnamese national Government has made it clear its position towards the problem of territorial unity.

The Government does not consider itself bound in any respect by the Geneva Agreements which it did not sign.

Once more, the Government reasserts that in any circumstance, it places national interests above all, being resolved to achieve at all cost the obvious aim it is pursuing and eventually to achieve national unity, peace and freedom.

The Viet-Minh leaders have had a note dated July 19 transmitted to the Government, in which they asked for the convening of a consultative conference on general elections. This is just a propaganda move aimed at making the people believe that they are the champions of our territorial unity. Everyone still remembers that last year at Geneva, the Vietnamese Communists boisterously advocated the partition of our territory and asked for an economically self-sufficient area whereas the delegation of the State of Viet-nam proposed an armistice without any partition, not even provisional, with a view to safeguarding the sacred rights of the Vietnamese national and territorial unity, national independence and individual freedom. As the Vietnamese delegation states, the Vietnamese Government then stood for the fulfillment of national aspirations by the means which have been given back to Viet-nam by the French solemn recognition of the independence and sovereignty of Viet-nam, as a legal, independent state.

The policy of the Government remains unchanged. Confronted with the partition of the country, which is contrary to the will of the entire people, the Government will see to it that everybody throughout the country may live free from fear, and completely free from all totalitarian oppression. As a champion of justice, of genuine democracy, the Government always holds that the principles of free general election is a peaceful and democratic means only if, first of all, the freedom to live and freedom of vote is sufficiently guaranteed.

In this connection, nothing constructive can be contemplated in the present situation in the North where, under the rule of the Vietnamese Communists, the citizens do not enjoy democratic freedoms and fundamental human rights.[4]

1955 September—Announcement from Hanoi of the formation of the Communist "Fatherland Front" in South Vietnam.

Devoting most of his attention to the consolidation of his power, Prime Minister Diem depends heavily upon advice from Colonel Lansdale.

I explained to Diem that the only acceptable, viable way to bring about the drastic change that he and the MNR had in mind would be through suffrage, a free expression of the people's will through the ballot box. If Diem was so sure that the people were about to explode unless there was a change, he should let them say so by a vote. The results would be recognized throughout the world, since there was wide acceptance of the principle of the people's ultimate sovereignty.

Further, a plebiscite designed only to let the people choose a new chief of state at this point wasn't enough. Since Bao Dai had stepped down from emperor to chief of state, Vietnam had been governing itself through a mishmash of laws and decrees that stemmed largely from its days of colonial rule. Some of them were clearly outmoded in a nation that now was independent. If the people were to be given the say in electing their leadership, the people would want the process to continue and to grow. That meant a whole new set of rules, embodied in a consti-tution. Even North Vietnam had such a constitution. In an electoral contest between the old customs under Bao Dai and something new under Diem, Diem would have to spell out what that something new was. At the very least, he would have to link his candidacy with a mandate for the creation of a constitution written by representatives chosen by the people. He would have to set a definite date for an election of representa-tives to a Constitutional Assembly, meanwhile—if the people chose him over Bao Dai—holding office as a public trust until the Constitution came into being, at which time he would have to abide by it.

This conversation took place late in September. It left Diem in a very thoughtful mood. Several days later, Diem showed in his conversation with me that he had accepted the idea of a popular election. He was already planning how it could be held throughout the country in a single day.

On October 6, 1955, Diem announced a referendum to be held on October 23 to let the people decide who should be chief of state, Bao Dai or Ngo dinh Diem with his pledge of initiating constitutional government. The voters would be given two ballots, one bearing the name and picture of Bao Dai, the other the name and picture of Ngo dinh Diem. The voter would cast the ballot of his preference and discard the other. I urged Diem to use a good photograph of Bao Dai on these ballots, since I was sure that Diem would use a good one of himself. Also, I cautioned him against a possible stuffing of the ballot box by the MNR, since he and the electorate would have to believe fully in the validity of the vote results in case he won and set about constructing a new political system. Cheating would be building the future on a false foundation and this would mean that whatever he did next would be short-lived. He must look ahead to the needs of still unborn generations if he was running for the position of "father of his country," which would be the import of the referendum.[5]

1955   23 October—Although immediately declared "illegal" by Bao Dai, who is living in France, the national "referendum" gives Diem 5,721,735 votes to Bao Dai's 63,017. **26 October**—Ngo Dinh Diem declares South Vietnam a republic, with himself as president. **28 October**—U.S. MAAG (Military Assistance and Advisory Group) Indochina renamed MAAG Vietnam. Official MAAG strength: 348 U.S. personnel. In addition, there are USECOM advisers and a number of Michigan State University police science experts training internal security forces.

1956   January—Diem's forces take control of Tay Ninh city, principal Cao Dai stronghold. Internal opposition from the established sects has been crushed. **2 February**—Some 350 additional Americans are authorized for TERM (Temporary Equipment Recovery Mission), to reclaim U.S. military equipment remaining in Vietnam. The ICC (International Control Commission) offers no "formal objection" by 2–1 (Poland) vote.

In Washington, Colonel Lansdale participates in policy discussions.

In my meeting with the Dulles brothers early in 1956, I asked the secretary of state to use his influence with the U.S. military to get me transferred from Vietnam, just as he evidently had used it to have me sent there in 1954. I told him that my days for constructive work there seemed to be ending anyhow, thanks to U.S. policy restrictions. My request appeared to surprise him. He told me flatly that there was much more work with which I could help in Vietnam. He brought up the subject of the 1956 plebiscite as proposed at the 1954 Geneva Conference. I surely wanted to stay in Vietnam and see my friends there through whatever problems and perils the plebiscite would bring, didn't I? I should stay in Vietnam at least through 1956.

I wondered if I had heard correctly. The 1956 plebiscite? I said I doubted there would be any plebiscite; too much had happened since the conference at Geneva. He said that of course there would be a plebiscite and asked me to explain my doubts. I reminded him of Diem's refusal, in 1955, to meet with Hanoi's Communist leaders on the subject and noted that there had been no change in his attitude since. Moreover, if the U.S. did some official arm-twisting and forced Diem into meeting the Hanoi officials to arrange a plebiscite, another obstacle probably would arise. The Communist officials who had waged a successful war against the French were terrible bunglers at running a government. Their stock with the public in North Vietnam was so abysmally low that they wouldn't dare put it to a vote, let alone chance a contest against Diem, whose popularity was at a peak. (Diem's landslide victory over Bao Dai at the polls wasn't lost on Hanoi's leaders.) I felt certain that the Communist leaders, while declaiming loudly about holding a plebiscite, would do everything they could to postpone it.

When pressed for the reasons behind these conclusions about the probable attitude of Hanoi officials, I told the Dulles brothers what I had heard from refugees and travelers from North Vietnam. The Communist land reform program had been carried out in too radical a fashion, too abruptly, with even small family farms taken away from the owners and handed over not to the poor, but to village ne'er-do-wells, beggars, and the indolent. Apparently the thought was that when they failed at farming, the farms then could be impounded by the state as idle land and be made into collectivized state farms. Rural sections of North Vietnam were in revolt, especially in Ho chi Minh's home province of Nghe An where troops had been called in to reestablish governmental control. On Soviet advice, the Politburo had suspended the land reform program and had publicly censured the officials in charge of the program, but the agrarian population was still seething against the government.

Another Communist agrarian measure had disillusioned the North Vietnamese population further, particularly in the Red River region where the majority lived. Wanting to make up the deficit in rice production, the Hanoi government had followed Chinese advice and denuded the hills of trees in order to plant upland rice. With the natural cover gone, the water rushed off the hills when the rains came, bringing unprecedented floods and misery to the lowlands. On top of earning all this resentment in the rural areas, the Hanoi regime had also managed to be maladroit with its most prized asset, the youth. Revolt was stirring at the University of Hanoi, where students were demanding relief from the heavy input of political indoctrination in all their lectures. Students complained that their instructors skimped even highly technical subjects in favor of long dissertations on dialectical materialism. Much the same thing was happening in the high schools of North Vietnam. Its most promising youth were finding fault with the regime.

For these reasons I felt that the Communist leaders in Hanoi would discreetly inform the Soviets (co-sponsors of the 1954 Geneva accords) to go slow on pressing for a plebiscite in any meeting with the British (the other Geneva co-sponsor). None of this ruled out the possibility of a Communist adventure into South Vietnam, overt or covert; traditionally, making trouble in a neighbor's land can divert attention from trouble at home. In Vietnam there would be powerful motivations for the rice-deficit North to gain control of the rice-surplus South. All I was saying was that I was sure the Communist leaders knew that they couldn't win this goal via the ballot box.

My argument about whether or not the plebiscite would be held had no discernible effect on the length of my tour of duty in Vietnam. I returned to Saigon "for the rest of the year." Thus I was in Vietnam when the next action about the plebiscite took place in London in April 1956. On April 11 representatives of the nations sponsoring the 1954 Geneva Conference, Lord Reading for the United Kingdom and Gromyko for the Soviet Union, agreed that the proposed plebiscite was unfeasible under prevailing conditions in Vietnam and therefore wouldn't be held.[6]

A few months later in Washington, as noted in The Pentagon Papers, *the "American Friends of Vietnam" hold a meeting.*

On June 1, 1956, a prestigious group of citizens assembled in Washington as the "American Friends of Vietnam." They heard Senator John F. Kennedy characterize Vietnam as:

"(1) . . . the cornerstone of the Free World in Southeast Asia, the keystone in the arch, the finger in the dike. . . . The fundamental tenets of this nation's foreign policy, in short, depend in considerable measure upon a strong and free Vietnamese nation.

"(2) . . . Vietnam represents a proving ground of democracy in Asia . . . the alternative to Communist dictatorship. If this democratic experiment fails, if some one million refugees have fled the totalitarianism of the North only to find neither freedom nor security in the South, then weakness, not strength, will characterize the meaning of democracy in the minds of still more Asians.

"(3) . . . Vietnam represents a test of American responsibility and determination in Asia. If we are not the parents of little Vietnam, then surely we are the godparents. . . . If it falls victim to any of the perils that threaten its existence . . . our prestige in Asia will sink to a new low.

"(4) . . . The key position of Vietnam in Southeast Asia . . . makes inevitable the involvement of this nation's security in any new outbreak of trouble."[7]

What later becomes known as the U.S. "rollback" policy is adopted in September.

National Security Council: Statement of Policy on U.S. Policy in Mainland Southeast Asia September 5, 1956

VIET NAM

54. Assist Free Viet Nam to develop a strong, stable and constitutional government to enable Free Viet Nam to assert an increasingly attractive contrast to conditions in the present Communist zone.

55. Work toward the weakening of the Communists in peaceful reunification of a free and independent Viet Nam under anti-Communist leadership.

56. Support the position of the Government of Free Viet Nam that all-Viet Nam elections may take place only after it is satisfied that genuinely free elections can be held throughout both zones of Viet Nam.

57. Assist Free Viet Nam to build up indigenous armed forces, includ-

ing independent logistical and administrative services, which will be capable of assuring internal security and of providing limited initial resistance to attack by the Viet Minh.

58. Encourage Vietnamese military planning for defense against external aggression along lines consistent with U.S. planning concepts based upon approved U.S. policy, and discreetly manifest in other ways U.S. interest in assisting Free Viet Nam, in accordance with the SEATO Treaty, to defend itself against external aggression.

VI. SUPPLEMENTARY STATEMENT OF POLICY ON THE SPECIAL SITUATION IN NORTH VIET NAM

65. Treat the Viet Minh as not constituting a legitimate government, and discourage other non-Communist states from developing or maintaining relations with the Viet Minh regime.

66. Prevent the Viet Minh from expanding their political influence and territorial control in Free Viet Nam and Southeast Asia.

67. Deter the Viet Minh from attacking or subverting Free Viet Nam or Laos.

68. Probe weaknesses of the Viet Minh and exploit them internally and internationally whenever possible.

69. Exploit nationalist sentiment within North Viet Nam as a means of weakening and disrupting Sino-Soviet domination.

70. Assist the Government of Viet Nam to undertake programs of political, economic and psychological warfare against Viet Minh Communists.

71. Apply, as necessary to achieve U.S. objectives, restrictions on U.S. exports and shipping and on foreign assets similar to those already in effect for Communist China and North Korea.[8]

1956 **1 September**—United States begins to train ARVN (Army of the Republic of Vietnam), first in Vietnam, later in the Philippines and in the United States. **23 October**—Hungarian uprising against Communist government. Russians invade and put down rebellion.

1957 **31 May**—French terminate all military training in Vietnam. United States assumes total military advisory role. **24 June**—U.S. Army 1st Special Forces Group (Okinawa) team sent to Nha Trang to train South Vietnamese. **4 October**—Bombs explode in Saigon at U.S. MAAG and U.S.I.S. (United States Information Agency) buildings. The thirteen people wounded are the first announced American casualties in Vietnam.

On 18 November in Moscow, Mao Tse-tung addresses representatives of the Communist and Workers' Parties of the Socialist countries. His speech, excerpted here, has great impact on U.S. policy.

"East Wind Over the West Wind"

In 1946 when Chiang Kai-shek launched his attacks against us, many of our comrades and people throughout the country were very much worried: Could the war be won? I myself was also worried about this. But of one thing we were confident. At that time an American journalist named Anna Louise Strong came to Yenan. We discussed many questions in our talks, including Chiang Kai-shek, Hitler, Japan, the United States, the atom bomb, etc. I said that all the reputedly powerful reactionaries were merely paper tigers. The reason was that they were divorced from the people. You see, wasn't Hitler a paper tiger? Wasn't Hitler overthrown? I also said that the tsar was a paper tiger, the Chinese emperor was a paper tiger, Japanese imperialism was a paper tiger. You see they were all down and out. U.S. imperialism has not yet fallen and it has the atom bomb. I believe it will also fall. It is also a paper tiger. . . .

I am of the opinion that the international situation has now reached a new turning point. There are two winds in the world today: the East wind and the West wind. There is a Chinese saying: "Either the East wind prevails over the West wind or the West wind prevails over the East wind." I think the characteristic of the situation today is the East wind prevailing over the West wind. That is to say, the socialist forces are overwhelmingly superior to the imperialist forces.[9]

1958 **31 May**—With activation of TERM (Temporary Equipment Recovery Mission), there are now 792 Americans assigned to MAAG/TERM, plus 555 USECOM (U.S. Economic Mission) advisers.
23 August—People's Republic of China renews attacks against Nationalist Chinese offshore islands of Quemoy and Ma-tsu.

Late in the year that historian Gareth Porter calls "the most difficult postwar year for the revolution in the South" because of the "heavier" and "more successful . . . repression by the Diem government," Vietnamese Communist Party policy is expressed from Hanoi as follows.

Lao Dong Party Directive for the South:
"Situation and Tasks for 1959"
Late 1958

3) Because the enemy is determined to strengthen the apparatus of repression and war provocation by increasing its forces and its reactionary character in a number of villages and to use that apparatus to attack us, and because the people's movement under the leadership of our Party is not yet strong enough to hold back their bloody hand, during the past period, the enemy has caused heavier losses for our Party and people's

movement than in previous years. They have carried out their schemes to a relatively greater degree, especially in plundering sweeps, despite the fact that the struggle movement of the people opposing them is more advanced than in previous years. . . .

7) The Path and line of struggle of the Party in the South has been relatively understood from the top to the bottom. Liaison has been relatively healthy and improved. Party cells have been consolidated in a relatively well-rounded manner, and there is more of a spirit of secrecy. The quality and quantity of the Party action has been strengthened, the organization of the Party section is relatively more stable and solid. Because of that, despite the enemy's cruel terror and repression (which has caused the Party a significant number of losses) our Party section still survives, is strengthened and developing, and is leading the masses' struggle on to many accomplishments. . . . The widespread, dominant ideological error in the Party section is: a rightist desire for peace, due to assessing the enemy too highly and ourselves too low, and due to standpoints whose preparation has not been thorough. It is shown in the struggle movement every day in the tendency toward reformism, not daring to mobilize the masses to struggle or going over to individual assassination, punishing traitors in a disorderly manner, expecting armed uprising or attacking the enemy carelessly, and lacking determination to overcome difficulties and hardships in their work. There is also leftist deviation, of devoting all the forces to armed struggle and general uprising (Tay Ninh).

II. TASKS FOR 59
We have analyzed the comparison of forces between us and the enemy during the recent period and at present. In the next period, how will the comparison of forces develop?

The U.S.-Diem government losses in the comparison of forces in the world and in the country will change more unfavorably for them every day (this will be discussed when we study it).

That situation creates contradictions between the U.S.-Diem government and people's strata in the South which are constantly deepening, creating favorable conditions for the revolutionary struggle movement to become stronger and broader every day and to cause the internal contradictions of the enemy, created by the dictatorial, fascist, family-ruled U.S. colony to further increase every day. Given their natural decline, U.S.-Diem will definitely step up their country-stealing and country-selling policies which were described above.

Having no further doubts, U.S.-Diem will do everything possible to terrorize, repress the masses' movement and our Party section more violently, hoping to save their situation of isolation and decline.

Therefore, they will still create many difficulties for us, and they will be able to achieve a certain part of their schemes. Our Party section must see ahead and try to overcome them in order to guide the mass movement steadily forward to hinder the enemy.

Based on the above situation between the enemy and ourselves now and the changes about to take place, we can see that the . . . tasks have not changed, but the forms and the level of the struggle movement in the near future must be broader, stronger, and more decisive.[10]

1959   1 January—Cuban Revolution. Fidel Castro takes power. **January**— In Hanoi, the DRV government decides in early 1959 to authorize the use of armed force in the South and begins actively to direct the insurgency.

Based upon interviews and captured documents, an account of the methods of DRV training and infiltration is documented by The Pentagon Papers.

Most of the physically fit Southerners had been placed in the North Vietnam Army (NVA) where they acquired military training and discipline, and political indoctrination—the 305th, 324th, 325th, 330th, and 338th NVA Divisions were filled with Southerners, and remained so until 1959, when infiltration started on a large scale. Those Southerners with non-military professional skills were placed in DRV civilian society where they could be useful. But all, no matter where placed, were apparently watched to assess their reliability, and eventually selected for return to the South by DRV authorities. Civilians were urged to "volunteer" to return, soldiers were ordered to do so. Almost all were pleased to comply, not only because it meant a return to family and land of birth, but because few liked North Vietnam, and because they had heard of the sufferings inflicted upon their people by the GVN, and wanted to "liberate" them from Diem and the Americans. The chosen were then sent to special training centers—the most important of which for the interviewed regroupees was at Xuan Mai—where they attended courses of several weeks to several months, depending on their background. The emphasis—about two-thirds of instructional time—was on political indoctrination. Themes included an impending victory in the South, to be followed by "peace, neutrality, and reunification." They were taught that after infiltration, they were to approach uncommitted Southerners, by stressing the land reform policy of the Viet Cong, by urging families to call back sons serving in ARVN, and by castigating the agroville-strategic hamlet program of the GVN. One propaganda specialist related that he was instructed to press three programs: political struggle, armed struggle, and "military proselyting" (*vinh van*)—the latter again aimed at sapping the will of ARVN to fight, and causing desertions.

Following training, the regroupees were formed into units of 40 to 400 for the trip south. A few were infiltrated by sea, but the majority were taken by truck through North Vietnam to Laos, and thence walked south on foot. The journey took at least two and one-half months; most reported the trails were well organized, with camps built at intervals, and guides available at each camp to conduct arrivals on the next leg of their trip. Strict camouflage discipline was observed, and conversations with camp attendants or guide personnel was forbidden. On arrival at their destinations in South Vietnam, they were smoothly integrated into local Viet Cong organizations. (Little subsequent friction was reported by the regroupees between themselves and the Viet Cong, but some southern VC recruited in the late Fifties or early Sixties, the "winter cadres," have . . . expressed animosity toward the "autumn cadres," as the regroupees were called.)

From all indications, the early infiltration was quite small scale, involving no more than a few hundred persons in all. There are no reports indicating DRV preparations of an apparatus to handle large-scale, systematic movements of people and supplies before 1958. Early in that year, according to one prisoner, Montagnards from Quang Tri and Thua Thien Provinces began to receive training in North Vietnam in the establishment and operation of way-stations and guide systems in Laos and South Vietnam; the prisoner left North Vietnam in March, 1959 with a group of other cadre to organize tribesmen for those missions. He testified that thereafter he made several inspection trips along the routes to check on the building of troop shelters in the encampments. Several other POW have disclosed that in early 1959 they were chosen to man "special border-crossing teams" for moving drugs, food, and other materiel across the DMZ into Quang Tri and Thua Thien. In April, 1959, a prisoner reported that the Lao Dong Party Central Committee directed the forming of a headquarters to control this effort, which came into being on May 5, 1959, as the 559th Transportation Group, directly subordinate to Party headquarters. Another prisoner served with the 70th Battalion of the 559th Group, which was formed in 1959 and sent into southern Laos. The 70th Battalion received weapons, ammunition, mail, and supplies from Hanoi and transported them to another organization in charge of distribution to insurgent units. The 70th Battalion was in charge of 20 way-stations, furnished escorts for infiltrating groups from North to South Vietnam, and transported sick and wounded personnel from Thua Thien Province back to North Vietnam. While the 559th Group was being deployed on land, other prisoners reported that the 603d Battalion was formed in June, 1959, to manage maritime infiltration into South Vietnam. [During 1959, this study concludes, 4582 confirmed North Vietnamese-trained soldiers infiltrated south.][11]

As their Communist counterparts in South Vietnam have done, Pathet Lao guerrillas increase their attacks against royal government forces in Laos. A CIA study comments on this development.

Conclusions

1. We believe that the Communist resumption of guerrilla warfare in Laos was primarily a reaction to a stronger anti-Communist posture by the Laotian Government and to recent US initiatives in support of Laos.

We consider that it was undertaken mainly to protect the Communist apparatus in Laos and to improve Communist prospects for gaining control of the country.

2. The Communists probably believed: (a) that guerrilla warfare offered some prospects—at low risk—of promoting Communist objectives in Laos even if the Laotian Government received substantial moral and material support from the outside; and (b) that military forces which the West would be likely to commit inside Laos would be indecisive against the flexible Communist guerrilla tactics.

3. We estimate that the Communists intend to keep the risks and the costs of their action on a low level and they are not likely in the near future to resort to large-scale guerrilla activity, at least so long as the UN fact-finding mission is in Laos.

4. Most uncommitted and anti-Communist countries would probably support Western intervention in Laos if they were convinced that the Laotian Government's position was grave and that there was direct Communist Bloc support of the Laotian rebels. In that event, they would prefer that such action be taken under UN auspices.

5. Hanoi and Peiping have warned that any foreign military intervention in Laos would be considered as a direct threat to their national security. However, depending partly on the scale and nature of the military move, the Communist military reaction to the Western intervention, whether under UN, SEATO, or US auspices, initially would probably take the form of further covert North Vietnamese intervention rather than overt invasion. There probably would be less effort than at present to camouflage this intervention. This Communist action might, in the first instance, be limited to seizing substantial territory in Laos—such as Sam Neua and Phong Saly provinces—which we believe they could do under existing conditions with an augmentation of present guerrilla forces, and then using this situation for political bargaining purposes. The Communists would probably be prepared to accept a prolonged and unresolved struggle, particularly if the country were geographically divided. If non-Asian forces were committed in Laos, the likelihood of an overt Communist invasion would increase.[12]

In mid-1959 the National Security Council drafts a revision of U.S. policy toward Vietnam and the "associated" states of Laos and Cambodia.

c. Through the Mutual Assistance Program (MAP) and other measures, support the maintenance of free Asian military forces which are (1) capable of maintaining internal security and of identifying and delaying Communist aggression and which (2) together with U.S. and other allied military power and acting in a manner most responsive to broad U.S. interests are capable of coping with, and thereby deterring, any type of Communist aggression.

d. Provide MAP aid to those free Far Eastern countries where it is needed to maintain national independence and where it will be effectively utilized in consonance with U.S. interests.

  e. In the event of Communist overt armed attack or imminent threat of such attack against any country in the area not covered by a security treaty to which the United States is party, the menace to U.S. security interests would be so grave as to justify the President in requesting authority from Congress to take necessary action to deal with the situation, including the use of U.S. armed forces, if appropriate and feasible. In any event, the United States should consider the advisability of taking the issue before the United Nations.

  f. If requested by a legitimate local government which required assistance to defeat local Communist subversion or rebellion not constituting armed attack, the United States should view such a situation so gravely that, in addition to giving all possible covert and overt support within the Executive Branch authority, the President should at once consider requesting Congressional authority to take appropriate action, which might if necessary and feasible, include the use of U.S. military forces either locally or against the external source of such subversion or rebellion.[13]

1959 8 July—Viet Cong forces attack Bien Hoa air base. Two U.S. advisers are killed.

At the same time, a series of articles by correspondent Albert M. Colegrove for the Scripps-Howard newspapers causes the first major congressional and public interest in Vietnam. Colegrove charges that there is waste and fraud in the American aid program, as well as cliquish high living among the American community in Saigon. Various members of the American diplomatic community are called on to testify before committees of both the House and Senate, and the hearings begin on 30 July, 1959.

[SENATOR CAPEHART]. I think one of the first questions I would like to ask is: Are there a lot of Communist sympathizers in Saigon and in Vietnam that stir up a lot of trouble?
MR. DURBROW [Elbridge Durbrow, U.S. ambassador to Saigon, 1957–61]. No, sir; I do not think there are a lot of them, but there definitely are some. There are trained Communist cadres, however.

  The best estimate we can make is that there probably are perhaps 3,000 in the country. Some of them were left there at the time of the population transfer, the refugee movements of 1954–55; others have infiltrated into the country and they are active. And as I stated yesterday, they have to hide out in the jungles, in the forests, and in the swamps because the Government is going at them as diligently as they can. These Communists have been able to sneak out and make attacks on individuals and different posts. . . .

SENATOR MANSFELD. Now, Mr. Durbrow, in the opening statements at this hearing we have had a picture drawn of some very significant changes in the situation in Vietnam since 1955.

We know, for example, that in that year the survival of a free Vietnam and a free Vietnamese Government was still in grave doubt; was that a correct statement?

MR. DURBROW. Quite correct.

SENATOR MANSFIELD. The stability of the government was threatened by the Binh Xuyen, by dissident political religious sects such as the Hoa Hao and the Cao Dai.

There was a very substantial armed Communist Vietminh underground in the south; is that correct?

MR. DURBROW. Not only in the south, sir; they were concentrated down there, but they were all over the country, the Communists, in particular.

The sects were in the southwest basically, and in Saigon, but as far as the Binh Xuyen is concerned, they were primarily in the Saigon-Cholon area.

SENATOR MANSFIELD. Yes.

There was little real military strength to resist a Vietminh invasion from the north had it come about at that time?

MR. DURBROW. Very little, sir.

SENATOR MANSFIELD. South Vietnam was a war-prostrated area with very extensive devastation?

MR. DURBROW. Quite correct. There is still evidence of that, sir.

SENATOR MANSFIELD. There were hundreds of thousands of refugees from the north waiting to be resettled, the figure being somewhere between 600,000, the official figure, and 1 million?

MR. DURBROW. Correct.

SENATOR MANSFIELD. These conditions have changed in significant degree in the past 4 years, have they not?

MR. DURBROW. Very much so.

SENATOR MANSFIELD. And there is a far greater degree of internal stability and security in Vietnam than there was in 1955?

MR. DURBROW. Very definitely.

SENATOR MANSFIELD. I should like to read into the record at this point a statement by Maj. Gen. Samuel L. Myers, former Deputy Chief of MAAG in Vietnam. General Myers stated on April 17 of this year, and I quote:

> The Binh Xuyen group was completely eliminated as a menace. The Cao
> Dai group was pacified or reoriented through political means to a point
> where it ceased to be any considerable obstacle. The Hoa Hao had been
> reduced to a handful of the diehards still holding out against the Govern-
> ment and still conducting extremely limited armed raids and assassina-
> tions. The Vietminh guerrillas, although constantly reinforced by men and
> weapons from outside south Vietnam, were gradually nibbled away until
> they ceased to be a major menace to the Government. In fact, estimates

at the time of my departure indicated that there was a very limited number of hostile individuals under arms in the country. Two territorial regiments, reinforced occasionally by one or two regular army regiments,
were able to cope with their depredations.

That would indicate a far greater degree of internal stability in Vietnam
than that which existed 4 years ago; would it not?
MR. DURBROW. Yes, sir.
SENATOR MANSFIELD. I read further from Major General Myers' statement.
Speaking of the Vietnamese armed forces, he says, and I quote:

> They are now able to maintain internal security and have reached the
> point where that responsibility could be turned over to the civilian
> agencies. If there should be renewed aggression from the north on the
> part of the Vietminh, they can give a really good account of themselves.
> There are many Vietnamese who are even more optimistic than that state-
> ment implies and feel that they have the capability of counterattack.

That statement would indicate, would it not, considerable reduction of
the danger of invasion from the north as it existed 4 years ago, or at least
a far greater capacity to cope with it; would it not?
MR. DURBROW. I would say the latter, sir.
SENATOR MANSFIELD. A far greater capacity to cope with it?
MR. DURBROW. Because there are still Communists around, the danger is
always there, ever present. But the possibility of countering it is much
greater than it was before.[14]

1959   30 August—Second election held in South Vietnam. Although a
few opposition candidates are elected, President Diem refuses to
allow them to take their seats.

---

*To "counter the danger" in Laos, in 1960 the United States sends Special
Forces advisers there, too. Benjamin Schemmer's* The Raid *describes their
arrival.*

Early in 1960, [Army Special Forces officer Don] Blackburn got word to
organize a clandestine group to go to Laos for six months to train a
Laotian army. The CIA had originally been assigned the mission, but it
wasn't working. Blackburn picked Simons to recruit a new force. They
were code-named "White Star" teams. Simons took 107 men to Laos.
Before they left, he told them all, "You are going to lose your manhood.
Some dumb sonovabitch from the jungle is going to tick you off. But
you're going to keep your mouth shut and take it."
Simons and his men left Fort Bragg in July; when they arrived in Laos,
no one could tell him whom he was supposed to train or what to train
them for. But there was so much ferment in the country, so much military

activity from North Vietnamese cross border operations, and so little
muscle in Laos's military force (it was mainly a palace guard) that some
kind of army was obviously needed. Simons decided to build one. When
the government wouldn't recruit any volunteers, Simons kidnapped them.
His men roamed all over the country, impressing thousands of Meo
tribesmen uprooted by the turmoil in their land. He put them in compounds behind barbed wire, fed them, clothed them—and gradually
taught them to soldier. They were eager to learn; life had a purpose and
they were even being paid. Bull Simons kidnapped 12 battalions of "volunteers," and they proved to be such tough opposition that North Vietnam soon lost much of its appetite for the cross border raids that had torn
Laos apart and almost toppled its government. When Simons' six-month
tour of duty was up, he brought every member of his White Star teams
back to the States alive. One of his deputies on that mission later recalled: "I would follow Bull Simons to hell and back for the sheer joy of
being with him on the visit."[15]

*At the same time, in South Vietnam an article in a Lao Dong (Communist
Party) internal journal in the South defines the policy for the use of armed
force to achieve a "general uprising" but not yet to begin a "guerrilla war."*

Article in a Lao Dong Party Internal Journal in the South
February 1960

*In order to fulfill the task before them, what path must the Vietnamese
people in general and people of the Southern zone in particular, take to
defeat the U.S.-Diem government and establish a People's Democratic
coalition government in the South?*

The path of Vietnamese revolution in the South at present is the path
of general uprising to seize political power. General uprising to seize
political power is the fundamental path of development of the Vietnamese revolution in the South. General uprising to overthrow the My
Diem government, seize political power and return it to the hands of the
people is the objective and line of the struggle of the whole Party and
people at present. Therefore all facets of activities must be actively carried out, and prepared in all respects in accord with that objective and
line. If we are separated from that in objective and line in daily activities,
we will make big mistakes in regard to the general line.

The line of the Vietnamese revolution in the South of general uprising
to seize political power is the only correct line, is precise and very appropriate to the present situation. . . .

*To be correct how must we conceptualize the path of general uprising to
seize political power.*

The path of general uprising to seize political power is the path of
long-term political struggle combined with armed struggle. . . .

How must we conceive of the armed struggle?

The concept of armed struggle at present is armed struggle according to the line of general uprising to seize political power and not armed struggle as during the period of resistance war in which we took the countryside to surround the cities and finally liberated cities. Armed struggle at the present time is not guerrilla war, nor is it protracted interzonal warfare, fighting to liberate area and establish a government as during the resistance period.

Armed struggle at the present time means the whole people armed for self-defense and propaganda. If we wish to achieve the whole people armed and propagandizing, we must rely on the political forces of the masses, rely on the organized masses and on that basis arm the masses with the main factor being arms for the people. The people must get their own arms, in order to defend themselves, oppose and annihilate puppet personnel, militia, security agents, spies, and cruel and stubborn landlords in order to protect their rights and their homes, preserve the country and keep their own land. They must not passively sit and wait but must stand up and liberate themselves. But on the other hand, the people must also have armed self-defense units in order to join with the people and help the people destroy the stubborn and cruel group within the government and army of U.S.-Diem and with the forces of the entire people, make the U.S.-Diem army disintegrate in terms of morale and organization.[16]

1960   17 March—DRV protests that U.S. MAAG, Saigon, is turning the South into a U.S. military base.

As had happened earlier in the North, Communist cadres in the South have apparently taken the policy of "armed struggle" too literally.

Letter from the Party Committee for South Vietnam to Party Chapters March 28, 1960

However, in the past, a number of our Party Headquarters have committed a number of errors, some of which are very serious.

Along with the achievements . . . a number of Party Headquarters have committed errors, some of which are critical.

With regard to the implementation [of policies], the most critical error concerns the self-defense armed forces in a number of areas which did not implement correctly the lines of the Party, whose attacks spilled on to targets that were not the most vital, and which have punished a number of elements that we do not, as yet, have to punish. They have also warned and threatened village officials and spies in an indiscriminate manner.

In a number of areas, the leading organs have gone as far as getting into rash adventures: dissolving [local] administrative machinery, guiding the people to tear up their ID Cards, pushing a number to commit provacative actions, such as taking over posts, setting fire to village offices, cutting down trees, digging up roads, setting up obstacles, etc.—generally speaking, thereby destroying the legal status of the people [vis-à-vis the enemy government].

There are areas where orders were issued forbidding boats and cars to pass through, forbidding rice mills belonging to the capitalists to operate, forcing the people to mill their own rice, etc., thus hindering the work of the people. . . .

With regard to the policy concerning the front, a number of our comrades have failed to implement the policy and strategy of the Party correctly. In some areas, the term "traitors" was given too broad a definition and made to include even those who, to make a living, have had to work for the enemy. In some areas, no distinction was made in the treatment of the landlords, and all the landlords were lumped together as direct enemies of the revolution, without due regard to their political stand, and without distinguishing cruel landlords from other landlords.

With regard to the enemy soldiers, these comrades did not pay enough attention to propagandizing them about our policy—instead they relied too much on threats, and thereby frightened these soldiers. These comrades have failed to see the need for us to win the sympathy of these soldiers, to isolate the reactionaries, sow dissension to a high degree within the ranks of the government of the South, and direct [our strength] against the Americans and Diem. To the point that, in the areas where former local officials, spies and reactionaries—frightened by the present situation—went looking for our comrades to beg forgiveness, our comrades and the people either were indifferent and did not try to win them over to our side, or drove them away.

At present, generally speaking many areas are concentrating too heavily on building up and organizing armed self-defense, and on directing armed activities, and are neglecting the task of pushing ahead and leading the political struggle movement of the people.[17]

1960 **5 May**—U.S. MAAG, Vietnam, increased from 357 to 685, in addition to the 350 assigned to TERM (Temporary Equipment Recovery Mission). Many are U.S. Army Special Forces advisers. **10 August**—In Laos, Captain Kong Le ousts U.S.-supported Rightist General Phoumi Nosavan. **November**—Senator John F. Kennedy narrowly defeats Vice-President Richard M. Nixon in presidential election.

Having been in Saigon for over a year, William Colby (later appointed director of the CIA) is promoted, as he explains in his memoir, Honorable Men.

My chief was transferred to a new assignment and I was named to succeed him as CIA chief of station. It occurred at a moment when we were still furiously debating which of the many recommended policies the United States ought to pursue in Vietnam, and while each agency was still pretty much allowed to try its own thing, MAAG was energetically training and supplying the South Vietnam Army to engage in large-scale maneuvers so that it would be well prepared to fight a Korean-type war. The State Department officers in the embassy were busily engaged with the conducted political disputes in Saigon. AID was immersed in its elaborate programs for administrative, economic and social reforms. And none of it was working to set the Communists back. Day by day the situation continued to deteriorate.

The Viet Cong were making gains everywhere, establishing their authority in more and more of the countryside and denying it to the government and its programs. And all our intelligence reports revealed that their forces were growing—both through increased infiltration from the North and the recruitment of villagers in the South.

To make matters worse, [on 11 November] a coup attempt was launched against Diem, led by a disaffected parachute colonel, who believed that Diem wasn't fighting the Communists aggressively enough. A number of the anti-Diem opposition politicians in Saigon joined him to provide a political element, and for a day and a half Diem was besieged in his Palace while the rebel paratroopers surrounded it. Because of the proximity of our residence, the Colby family got their baptism of fire on that occasion. Bullets whined through our windows, and I barricaded Barbara and the children in a hall on the top floor. Some hours later, the situation had quieted and I could get down to the embassy, where the Ambassador needed all hands and heads. By midafternoon we alerted Barbara that it would be a good idea to take advantage of the lull and leave the premises while it was still daylight, in case there might be another fight that night. She gathered the children, collected a small assortment of hand baggage and proceeded to the nearest American neighbors in a direction away from the Palace.

For several hours, nearly a full day really, it wasn't clear which way the coup would go, whether or not Diem could survive it, and the United States embassy took a hands-off stance. CIA officers, however, were in touch with all the factions involved, from the Palace to the military coup leader, to the political committee led by Diem's opponent, Pham Quang Dan, and our radio net kept us up on every minute's move. At one point Nhu sent me a message, asking that I attend a conference between the contestants at the Palace gate to warrant the safety of both sides. But by the time it took place Diem had rallied troops from outside Saigon, including the 7th Division under Nguyen Van Thieu, and the parachutist colonel fled to Cambodia in a plane he obtained from Air Force Transport Commander Nguyen Cao Ky. Dr. Dan and most of the politicians were arrested, but one showed up a day later on the doorstep of the CIA officer who had been with him during the coup, pleading for help to avoid Diem's retribution, which he feared would be harsh. CIA's loyalty to its sources was at stake, so I had him hidden for several days in a house temporarily empty as a result of some CIA personnel transfers, and later arranged a courier flight abroad onto which he was loaded in a mail sack, to be passed through CIA's covert channels for resettlement in Europe.[18]

1960   16 December—In Laos, Phoumi Nosavan regains control of government. Kong Le and his battalion join the Pathet Lao.

The DRV decides to take action in Laos, as The Pentagon Papers *notes.*

It was not, however, until December, 1960, that the DRV announced to foreign diplomats resident in Hanoi its decision to intervene in Laos; during 1961 the DRV presence in Laos was transformed from a semi-covert MAAG-like undertaking to an operational theater. Beginning in December, 1960, and throughout 1961 and early 1962, Soviet aircraft flew 2,000 to 3,000 sorties from the DRV to Laos, delivering more than 3,000 tons of supplies to communist forces, which expanded their territory to hold the northern half of the country. Ethnic North Vietnamese appeared in Pathet Lao formations, and Kong Le himself admitted that NVA officers and soldiers were serving as "technicians" with his paratroops. North Vietnamese from NVA formations were captured by RLG forces and captured documents substantiated the presence of entire NVA units.[19]

In Saigon, CIA Station Chief Colby is able to implement some of his ideas.

The Communists added to the pressure; in December [1960] they established the National Liberation Front as the political framework for their fight against South Vietnam's government, in effect a clear declaration of revolution if not war. It was in this atmosphere, then, that I decided to experiment with an idea we in CIA had about how that revolution should be combated.

The idea had grown up among several of us. There was Gilbert Layton, a gruff, straightforward paramilitary specialist who had arrived in Vietnam in an Army colonel's uniform to manage our program helping the Vietnamese Special Forces develop operations against the North. He had run across a young man I will call Ben (because he is presently with the CIA), who at that time, however, was a member of the International Voluntary Service, a precursor of the Peace Corps, which, I must emphasize, had absolutely no connection with CIA. Ben was working with the Rhade tribe of Montagnards in the region around Ban Me Thuot in the Highland Plateau, had learned its language and culture, and was concerned by the growing Communist guerrilla strength in the area. Layton and he came up with a scheme by which the Rhade villages could defend themselves against the Communists. They asked if CIA could get the villagers weapons so that they would not have to depend on the Vietnamese Army units in the area, which were never there when needed and whose idea of how to defend them was to conduct great "sweeps" through the region before which the Communist forces simply vanished. CIA certainly could help; in fact it was the only American agency with the flexibility that could respond to such a local request directly and did not have to set up a complex program through Vietnamese government channels, which might or might not pass the material to the place it was needed.

But there were some problems. The Vietnamese government was worried about the Montagnards. In 1958 there had been a movement among them advocating their autonomy, rather than their assimilation, as sought by the Vietnamese, and the Communists were actively promising them that sort of tribal autonomy. So I believed it essential that CIA's help be put in a political framework. Layton and I came up with the idea of combining the self-defense concept with economic and social improvement for the villages that joined the program, and furthermore recommended that the Vietnamese Special Forces be in charge of the effort, with Americans in a supporting role only. In order that CIA not be thought to be developing its own private army, we turned to the U.S. Army Special Forces to provide the tactical training needed. And we called on the regular medical, educational, and other developmental agencies of the Vietnamese government, supported by AID (with some direct CIA supplies to break through bottlenecks), for the economic- and social-improvement part. With this joint approach we had no problem securing approval from the American Country Team, nor from Desmond FitzGerald at CIA headquarters at home, who understood immediately the importance of combining security, economic and social features into one program. But the real question was whether the government would permit it, and the answer to that lay with Nhu and Diem.

My weekly sessions with Nhu by now had covered the entire history of his and Diem's rise to power, and we had moved on to discuss matters that clearly revealed the differences between Diem's essentially administrative and military approach and Nhu's own belief in the need for a political answer to the Communist challenge. I made no secret of my sympathy with his view, and as a result he and his subordinates were convinced that my only objective was to help strengthen them against the Communists and that I was willing to respect their authority and leadership in the effort, whether they accepted my ideas totally or not. So when I outlined my plan for an experiment in the small Montagnard community of Buon Enao outside Ban Me Thuot, to be undertaken in collaboration with the Vietnamese Special Forces and in coordination with the local authorities, Nhu quickly agreed. He understood the essentially political aim of a project to get villagers to participate in their own self-defense and social and economic improvement, and saw it as a means of building a new political base for the Vietnamese Government.

Once Nhu approved, and assured me that he would obtain Diem's approval as well, Ben (who left the IVS and was put on our payroll) sat down and talked with the village elders at Buon Enao about enlisting the village in an effort to improve both its security and its welfare, and doing it for themselves with some help from the Vietnamese and Americans rather than depending on the administrative and military authorities in Ban Me Thuot. They cautiously agreed, and Ben and a small group of Vietnamese and American Special Forces personnel moved to the village and began to train the local young men and women in a program of defense and development. Trenches were dug in which the families could hide during an attack; a basic sanitation survey was conducted to separate the water supply from sewage; the log houses were dusted with DDT; a small stock of carbines was delivered, and the young men were trained to use them on patrol and in defense positions; some of the girls were taught simple first aid; and an emergency radio contact was set up with a nearby military center to pass the word if an attack occurred. While a Vietnamese flag was run up over the village, the political message of the program was deliberately downplayed; the interests of the village itself and not the Saigon regime was the main theme.

It worked. The villagers enthusiastically joined in the various activities, and a sense of confidence grew. We had deliberately chosen a village in a comparatively safe area, to permit it to build some strength before coming under pressure. But neighboring villages quickly heard of the activities in the best word-of-mouth tradition and sent their leaders to inquire how they could join the program. Thus the strategic principle developed by Marshal Lyautey in Morocco almost a century before was applied, and the "ink spot" grew. As more and more villages were included, it became clear that something more was needed than individual centers protecting themselves. So, from among the young men trained in the different villages, groups were chosen to serve as "strike forces," patrolling the empty territory between population centers and reinforcing any community that came under attack. But the principle was one of defense; the strategy was to gradually expand the area and people defended, to exclude the Communist organizers and guerrillas from both. The approach was the opposite of the traditional military. There was no stress on attacking the enemy; indeed, the ideal was for him quietly to fade away in the face of this program, or even to abandon the Communists and join the newly self-sufficient and confident communities participating in it.

Nhu was impressed. On one of the first trips he had ever made to the countryside (other than those to the hill palace at Dalat), he came to Buon Enao to see for himself and, as a result, approved the expansion of the program not only in the Highland area, but to a number of other villages along the coast and in the Delta as well. The initial villages in those areas were generally Catholic, to reassure Diem that we would not be arming Communists, and the priest-leader of one told me of discussion at an annual diocesan retreat in which the priests talked about the comparative effectiveness of the American carbine versus the Russian AK-47.

CIA's experiment spread with such rapidity that I decided to give it a name, Citizens' Irregular Defense Groups, to clarify to the U.S. Special Forces units that implemented it, under CIA's over-all control, that it was a citizens' and not a military operation, that its objective was defense rather than offense, and that it should be kept irregular to meet the different needs of the different communities in which it was being carried out. But as it expanded—30,000 weapons were eventually distributed—it raised qualms in military circles about its lack of coordination with the regular military forces and their operations, and the familiar cry for a single chain of command (military, of course) began to be heard. Meanwhile, in our weekly conversations, Nhu became more and more enthusiastic over the political revolution he could see as the result of the program, starting at the local community level, building upward and gradually replacing the French-trained bureaucracy and urban elite with a new, uniquely Vietnamese society and leadership. It was, he said, what Ho had accomplished with his Vietnamese brand of Communism but what Diem had not with his non-Communist nationalism. The seed of his "Strategic Hamlet" campaign had been planted. . . .

As press and Washington attention to Vietnam grew, a steady stream of visitors from the United States came to inspect our efforts. And in January 1961 a special one arrived, to whom I paid particular attention.

John F. Kennedy had, of course, just been elected President and was developing policies he would use to "pay any price, bear any burden, meet any hardship, support any friend, oppose any foe to assure the survival and success of liberty," as he was to pledge in his Inaugural Address. And the visitor he sent out to Vietnam to help him in this was the "Ugly American," Ed Lansdale, who had returned to the Pentagon after his service in CIA. I understood that his fertile imagination and his deep knowledge of Southeast Asia had been enlisted by the new administration to help it determine what it should do in Vietnam. I had never met him. But I knew from the lore of the Far East Division of his brilliant work with Magsaysay in the Philippines and in Vietnam during the anarchy of 1954, and I was determined that he understand the essentially political nature of the operations I was carrying out in the countryside and the importance of not diverging into a purely military or urban political approach. CIA headquarters was suspicious that his assignment represented a Pentagon move to assume authority over the Agency's activities in Vietnam, and some in the Pentagon feared that he was about to be named as Kennedy's ambassador to Vietnam, with an inevitable conflict with the regular military ranks of MAAG. But I welcomed the chance to make my case about the real nature of the war at a level where it might have some effect, and I knew that Lansdale was enough of a political thinker to appreciate it.

Lansdale didn't know me, either, and our first session together, at which I gathered the senior officers of the station to discuss the situation and explain our programs to him, was a shambles. He obviously thought he was being subjected to some form of shell game and said hardly a word during the whole evening. But he did go out into the countryside to take a look at what we were doing, and he did talk to Vietnamese. And so he did learn that the station's activities were both welcome and effective and came away with the conclusion that I hoped he would: that the conflict was essentially a guerrilla war and that the military approach was not the answer.[20]

1961   6 January—In Moscow, Soviet Chairman Nikita Khrushchev delivers a speech that promises worldwide U.S.S.R. support for "wars of national liberation."

General Lansdale reports to the secretary of defense on his visit to Vietnam.

Memorandum for Secretary of Defense
Deputy Secretary of Defense

FROM: Brig Gen Lansdale, OSO/OSD
SUBJ: Vietnam

As desired by you, I visited Vietnam 2–14 January 1961. After twelve days of intensive looking and listening over some old familiar ground, I have come to the following personal convictions:

a. 1961 promises to be a fateful year for Vietnam.

b. The Communist Viet Cong hope to win back Vietnam south of the 17th Parallel this year, if at all possible, and are much further along towards accomplishing this objective than I had realized from reading the reports received in Washington.

c. The free Vietnamese, and their government, probably will be able to do no more than postpone eventual defeat—unless they find a Vietnamese way of mobilizing their total resources and then utilizing them with spirit.

d. The U.S. team in Vietnam will be unable to help the Vietnamese with real effectiveness, unless the U.S. system of their operation is changed sufficiently to free these Americans to do the job that needs doing, and unless they do it with sensitive understanding and wisdom.

e. If Free Vietnam is won by the Communists, the remainder of Southeast Asia will be easy pickings for our enemy, because the toughest local force on our side will be gone. A Communist victory also would be a major blow to U.S. prestige and influence, not only in Asia but throughout the world, since the world believes that Vietnam has remained free only through U.S. help. Such a victory would tell leaders of other govern-ments that it doesn't pay to be a friend of the U.S., and would be an even more marked lesson than Laos.

f. Vietnam can be kept free, but it will require a changed U.S. atti-tude, plenty of hard work and patience, and a new spirit by the Viet-namese. The Viet Cong have been pushing too hard militarily to get their roots down firmly and can be defeated by an inspired and deter-mined effort.

g. Ngo Dinh Diem is still the only Vietnamese with executive ability and the required determination to be an effective President. I believe there will be another attempt to get rid of him soon, unless the U.S. makes it clear that we are backing him as the elected top man. If the 11 November coup had been successful, I believe that a number of highly selfish and mediocre people would be squabbling among themselves for power while the Communists took over. The Communists will be more alert to exploit the next coup attempt. At present, most Vietnamese oppositionists believe that the U.S. would look favorably upon a success-ful coup.

h. Vietnam has progressed faster in material things than it has spiritu-ally. The people have more possessions but are starting to lose the will to protect their liberty. There is a big lesson here to be learned about the U.S. aid program which needs some most serious study.

RECOMMENDATIONS

Before I left Saigon, I discussed my impressions with Ambassador Dur-brow who was most gracious towards me during the visit. Included in these impressions was my feeling that many of the Americans in Saigon perhaps subconciously believed in defeat, probably had spent too much time and energy on the political situation in Saigon instead of on the very real Viet Cong menace, and were in need of some bolstering up by the Chief of Mission. In this feeling of defeat, I would have to except the Chief of MAAG and the local CIA Chief who believe we can win. Am-bassador Durbrow told me of the memo he had issued to all Americans in Saigon after the 11 November coup attempt. I said this was a good move, but much more than writing a paper was needed. . . .

So, what should we do about it? I have a concrete recommendation. We need an American in Saigon who can work with real skill, with great sensitivity to Vietnamese feelings, and with a fine sense of the dangerous limits of Vietnamese national security in a time of emergency. This un-usual American should be given the task of creating an opposition party which would coalesce the majority of the opposition into one organiza-tion, of helping this new party adopt a platform which contains sound ideas for building national entities which the Vietnamese people would find worth defending against the Communists, and of strongly influencing it to play the role of loyal opposition while President Diem is in power and the nation is in such great danger. . . .

The Viet Cong crowded a lot of action into the year 1960. They infiltrated thousands of armed forces into South Vietnam, recruited local levies of military territorials and guerrillas, and undertook large scale guerrilla and terroristic operations. In so doing, they neglected doing sound political work at the grass roots level and broke one of Mao Tse Tung's cardinal rules. Many people in the south now under their thumb are unhappy about it, but too terrified to act against these new rulers. The Viet Cong apparently have been working hard recently to rectify this error, and now have political cadres in the field. We still have a chance of beating them if we can give the people some fighting chance of gaining security and some political basis of action.[21]

Although he had visited Laos on an earlier trip, General Lansdale has no recommendations about U.S. policy toward this country. In an official report, however, Laotian General Oudone Sananikone describes the situation there.

As of the first week of January, 1961, the Plaine des Jarres belonged to the Pathet Lao and the Viet Minh.

Such was the confused political situation and the poor security situation in Laos when I received a message from a friend telling me that it was now safe for me to return to Vientiane. I landed in Vientiane . . . in early January 1961 and immediately reported to General Phoumi Nosavan. I told him that I could be of more use to the country and the army if I were relieved of my somewhat useless attache assignment and given some active, more important functions to perform. General Nosavan just looked at me and said nothing. It was clear to me that because I had been in Kong Le's custody, had taken no active role in the counter-*coup*, had been out of the country during the fight for Vientiane, and furthermore, was not from Savannakhet, General Nosavan did not fully trust me.

I spent the rest of the day renewing contacts with my fellow officers in the Army staff and visited the fresh battlefields around the city where the heavy fighting had taken place three weeks or so earlier. I also visited an American friend, who happened to work for the CIA and who exercised some influence with General Nosavan. I told this friend that I had returned with the hope that I would be given a useful assignment, perhaps a command.

The next day I was summoned to headquarters and ordered to relieve Kouprasith Abhay as commander of the 15th Mobile Group which at that time was fighting Kong Le at Vang Vieng, on Route 13 about 75 miles north of Vientiane. I was very pleased with these orders and although I could never prove it, I believe that my American friend was instrumental in securing this command for me.

The 15th Mobile Group was a light infantry regimental combat team composed of three very understrength rifle battalions, an armored platoon of light tanks, an artillery battery (105-mm howitzers), an engineer company and a small administration and logistic element. My orders were to push Kong Le and his allied Pathet Lao force north to Sala Phou Khoun where the road forks; Route 13 continues north to Luang Prabang, while Route 7 leads east to Muong Soui, the Plain des Jarres and eventually to North Vietnam at Barthelemy Pass.

While my 15th Mobile Group pushed north, Brig. General Kham Khong was to advance with his larger mobile group from Paksane north along Route 4 to Muong Soui, then to attack Sala Phou Koun along Route 7 from the east. The Americans in Vientiane and the NLA staff were making wagers on which task force would be the first to reach Sala Phou Koun. The overwhelming odds favored Kham Khong, according to the bettors in Vientiane. Another task force was to attack south along Route 13 from Luang Prabang. This was GM 11 with three BIs and a battery of 105-mm howitzers.

I utilized three days following my appointment to command of GM 15 to gathering a small staff—a chief of staff, an operations officer, and an intelligence officer—in Vientiane, and then drove north to relieve Colonel Abhay. With two reinforced companies as security, I rode at the head of the column in an AM-20. This was an armored command car; it had an open hatch—no turret. We bivouaced at Hine Heup, on the Nam Lik river that night, about one-third of the distance to Sala Phou Koun. The forward elements of the GM were fighting north of Muong Kassy at this time, still well short of Sala Phou Koun. The GM command post was at Vang Vieng, between Hine Heup and Kassey, but Colonel Abhay had already flown back to Vientiane.

The next morning our small convoy started north for Vang Vieng. As we approached a curve in the road only five kilometers out of Hine Heup, I saw that a potential ambush site lay just ahead. I ordered full speed to my AM-20 driver and we roared around the curve—and through an ambush. The enemy fire was late and inaccurate and we made it through with light damage. Only five or so kilometers farther on, the episode was repeated but the damage was a little greater. My intelligence officer soon decided he enjoyed life in Vientiane a little more than the excitement of Route 13 and he disappeared.

In any event, I took command at Vang Vieng and was soon able to advance my command post to Muong Kassy.

The fighting was heavy during the weeks I held this command. It was during this campaign that I first became aware of a new form of American involvement in the war; the White Star teams. As I visited my forward combat elements I saw some foreigners among them. As I asked around no one could tell me who they were except that they were Americans who helped with air support and intelligence. When I asked my headquarters for an explanation I was told that these were the White Star teams. It was not until later that I discovered the teams were made up of U.S. Army Special Forces officers and NCOs. In fact, one of these officers, Captain Moon, was killed in action during this fight along Route

13; I later saw a memorial to the 7th Special Forces at Fort Bragg on which Captain Moon's name was listed. During this period I had almost no contact with the White Star teams because they were always in the forward area, never at my headquarters. . . .

While in Vientiane General Nosavan asked me to be his military adviser in the ministry of defense. It was here that I learned a little more about the White Star program. The first U.S. Army Special Forces teams had been deployed in July 1959. By the time of the Kong Le *coup* of August 1960, U.S. Army Special Forces teams were training NLA officers and men in weapons, maintenance and specialist courses at all the regional training centers. In January 1961, the French withdrew entirely from the training activity and U.S. Army Special Forces teams began to be assigned to NLA units in the field, giving advice on combat operations. . . . I also found that there were many more of these teams working in Region II than in Region V. It was in the Second Region that the White Star teams were working with the Meo people of Xiang Khoang and Samneua, assisting and supporting Colonel Vang Pao, who with this American support, was becoming the dominant leader in the region. Although Colonel Vang Pao's troops initially were as much a part of the National Lao Army as I was, they received special treatment from the Americans because they operated in this strategic zone in the highlands along the North Vietnam frontier. Quite without the knowledge or approval of the NLA staff, the White Star teams also organized and trained Meo units outside the structure of the NLA, using cadre and troops pulled from the NLA. Gradually, six or seven regular NLA Meo battalions were drawn down to near skeleton strength as their personnel disappeared into the new irregular battalions. Since the NLA headquarters was not aware of what was happening, it continued to pay the NLA Meo battalions according to their original strength reports. Meanwhile, the Americans were also paying the irregular battalions they were forming. Consequently, the Meo irregulars were receiving double pay. The Meo had also received special attention from the French during their administration in Laos and they had earned the reputation of tough, strong campaigners, well suited to the arduous life in their steep, rugged homeland.

With American logistic support and White Star training and combat assistance, the Meo units of Colonel Vang Pao developed into the most combat effective elements of the NLA. This, and the fact that they operated in a zone critical to the plans and operations of the Communists, meant that they attracted major efforts by the North Vietnamese to destroy them, but although these efforts continued throughout the war, Vang Pao's troops were never subdued.[22]

Toward the end of January 1961, outgoing President Eisenhower meets with President-elect John F. Kennedy on the eve of his inauguration. The main subject, according to Presidential Adviser Clark Clifford in The Pentagon Papers, *is Laos.*

Secretary Herter stated, with President Eisenhower's approval, that we should continue every effort to make a political settlement in Laos. He added, however, that if such efforts were fruitless, then the United States must intervene in concert with our allies. If we were unable to persuade our allies, then we must go it alone.

At this point, President Eisenhower said with considerable emotion that Laos was the key to the entire area of Southeast Asia. He said that if we permitted Laos to fall, then we would have to write off all the area. He stated that we must not permit a Communist take-over. He reiterated that we should make every effort to persuade member nations of SEATO or the ICC to accept the burden with us to defend the freedom of Laos.

As he concluded these remarks, President Eisenhower stated it was imperative that Laos be defended. He said that the United States should accept this task with our allies, if we could persuade them, and alone if we could not. He added that "our unilateral intervention would be our last desperate hope" in the event we were unable to prevail upon the other signatories to join us.

At one time it was hoped that perhaps some type of arrangment could be made with Kong Le. This had proved fruitless, however, and President Eisenhower said "he was a lost soul and wholly irretrievable."

Commenting upon President Eisenhower's statement that we would have to go to the support of Laos alone if we could not persuade others to proceed with us, President-elect Kennedy asked the question as to how long it would take to put an American division into Laos. Secretary Gates replied that it would take from twelve to seventeen days but that some of that time could be saved if American forces, then in the Pacific, could be utilized. Secretary Gates added that the American forces were in excellent shape and that modernization of the Army was making good progress.[23]

Ten days after President Kennedy is inaugurated, the following statement is released by Hanoi.

On January 29, 1961, Hanoi Radio broadcast in English to Europe and Asia its first announcement concerning the NLF:

A "National Front for the Liberation of South Vietnam" was recently formed in South Vietnam by various forces opposing the fascist Ngo Dinh Diem regime. . . . The National Front for the Liberation of South Vietnam calls on the entire people to unite and heroically rise up and struggle with the following program of action:

'1. To overthrow the disguised colonial regime of the imperialists and the dictatorial administration, and to form a national and democratic coalition administration.

'2. To carry out a broad and progressive democracy, promulgate the freedom of expression, of the press, of belief, reunion, association and of movement and other democratic freedoms; to carry out general amnesty of political detainees, dissolve the concentration camps dubbed "prosperity zones" and "resettlement centers," abolish the fascist law 10-59 and other anti-democratic laws.

'3. Abolish the economic monopoly of the United States and its henchmen, protect homemade products, encourage the home industry, expand agriculture, and build an independent and sovereign economy; to provide jobs to unemployed people, increase wages for workers, armymen, and office employees; to abolish arbitrary fines and apply an equitable and rational tax system; to help forced evacuees from North Vietnam who now desire to rejoin their native places; and to provide jobs to those who want to remain.

'4. To carry out land rent reduction, guarantee the peasants' right to till their present plots of land, and redistribute communal land in preparation for land reform.

'5. To eliminate the U.S.-style culture of enslavement and depravation; to build a national and progressive culture and education, eliminate illiteracy, open more schools, and carry out reform in the educational and examination system.

'6. To abolish the system of American military advisers, eliminate foreign military bases in Vietnam, and to build a national army defending the fatherland and the people.'[24]

At the same time, fighting in Laos intensifies, and President Kennedy is faced with his first major crisis. Arthur Schlesinger will later report:

The problem now, in Kennedy's judgment, was to make Moscow understand the choice it confronted: cease-fire and neutralization on the one hand; American intervention on the other. On March 23 his press conference took place against the unusual background of three maps of Laos illustrating the progress of communist encroachment. The Soviet Union, he said, had flown more than 1000 sorties into the battle area since December. There could be no peaceful solution without "a cessation of the present armed attacks by externally supported Communists." If the attacks do not stop, "those who support a genuinely neutral Laos will have to consider their response." As for the United States, no one should doubt its objective. "If in the past there has been any possible ground for misunderstanding of our desire for a truly neutral Laos, there should be none now." Nor should anyone doubt our resolution. "The security of all of southeast Asia will be endangered if Laos loses its neutral independence. Its own safety runs with the safety of us all—in real neutrality observed by all. . . . I know that every American will want his country to honor its obligations to the point that freedom and security of the free world and ourselves may be achieved."

His tone was grave; and he backed it up with military and diplomatic action. The Seventh Fleet moved into the South China Sea, combat troops were alerted in Okinawa, and 500 Marines with helicopters moved

into Thailand across the Mekong River from Vientiane. In Japan 2000
Marines performing as extras for the film "Marine, Let's Go!" vanished
from the set. On the diplomatic front Kennedy asked Nehru to support a
cease-fire, which the Indian Prime Minister promptly did; and he arranged a quick meeting with Prime Minister Macmillan, then in the
Caribbean, at Key West, where Macmillan reluctantly agreed that, if
limited intervention along the Mekong became necessary, Britain would
support it. Dean Rusk went to a SEATO conference at Bangkok on
March 27 and secured troop pledges from Thailand, Pakistan and the
Philippines, though French opposition prevented the organization as a
whole from promising any thing more specific than "appropriate" measures. In Washington the President saw Gromyko at the White House,
took him to a bench in the Rose Garden and, observing that too many
wars had arisen from miscalculation, said that Moscow must not misjudge
the American determination to stop aggression in Southeast Asia. Chip
Bohlen told me that night that Gromyko was "serious" this time, as he
had not been in his talk with Rusk nine days earlier; obviously he had
new instructions. The sense of acute tension over Laos appeared to be
subsiding. For his part Khrushchev had no desire to send Russian troops
to fight in the jungles of Laos and even less to set off a nuclear war.
Moreover, he could console himself, and hopefully the Pathet Lao, with
the thought which had already occurred to Kennedy and which Khrushchev put to Llewellyn Thompson in an expansive moment: "Why take
risks over Laos? It will fall into our laps like a ripe apple." After weigh-
ing these various factors, Khrushchev on April 1 expressed readiness in
principle to consider the British proposal.

THE HUNDREDTH DAY

Kennedy had won his first objective. But Khrushchev was at first unwilling to call for a cease-fire as the condition of an international conference. For more than three weeks the British and the Russians debated
this point. It is not clear whether Khrushchev was stalling because he
wanted time to explain his policy to the Pathet Lao and the Chinese or
because he wanted to give the neutralist and communist forces the chance
to occupy as much of Laos as they could: probably for both reasons.
Certainly the Pathet Lao and Kong Le continued to make new gains and
the Phoumi regime to show new weaknesses.

The fighting in these weeks made it more clear than ever that cease-fire
would mean little if Laos lacked a government strong and stable enough
to deal with the Pathet Lao. Kennedy had come early to doubt the
briefings he received about the virtues of General Phoumi. In February,
David Ormsby Gore, now a Member of Parliament and an Under Secretary of State in the Foreign Office, stopped by in Washington and, speaking with the bluntness of an old friend, offered a caustic picture of American policy in Laos. The United States, he said, had done its best to
destroy Souvanna Phouma, who represented the best hope of a non-

communist Laos, and instead was backing a crooked, right-wing gang; the impression of Washington always rushing about to prop up corrupt dictators in Asia could not have happy consequences.

Then late in March Averell Harriman, on his first assignment as roving ambassador, arranged to see Souvanna Phouma in New Delhi. He did this without authorization from Washington. Accustomed to the informality of Franklin D. Roosevelt's diplomacy, when he would go off on the most delicate missions with a few lines of general guidance, he was not yet used to the postwar State Department and its habit of tethering envoys with pages of minute and comprehensive instruction. His talk with the Laotian prince was friendly. Souvanna said that the people of Laos did not wish to be communist and that Laos could be saved from communism, but that time was running out. He proposed the establishment of a coalition government, including the Pathet Lao, and the guarantee of Laotian neutrality by the fourteen-nation conference. He felt that, with the support of 90 per cent of the people, he had the authority to unite his country.

Harriman was favorably impressed. In addition, he had known Winthrop Brown from wartime days in London and had more confidence in Brown's estimate of Souvanna than in the State Department's inevitable judgment that the beleaguered prince was practically a communist. Washington, or at the least the White House, found Averell's testimony weighty. He was, after all, the most experienced and distinguished of American diplomats. Only his age had disqualified him from consideration as Secretary of State. He had spent much of his life in dealing with the Russians—ever since he had bargained with Trotsky over mining concessions in the twenties. During the Second World War he had worked with Roosevelt, Churchill and Stalin and attended nearly all the wartime conferences. He had served as ambassador to Moscow and London. He had run the Marshall Plan in Europe and had been Truman's national security adviser during the Korean War. In all these years he had not succumbed to illusions either about communism or about the anticommunist crusade.

His world trip had shown him the brilliance of the hopes excited by the new President. Convinced that America had not had such potentialities of world influence since the days of F.D.R., he bounded back to Washington filled with energy, purpose and ideas, looking years younger than he had in his last melancholy days as a New York politician. I remember his coming shortly after his return to a farewell dinner I gave for Ken Galbraith, who was about to depart on his new assignment as Ambassador to India. Harriman, in the highest of spirits, talked everyone down, especially the guest of honor; this last, of course, was no inconsiderable feat. When Harriman reported to the White House, he delighted Kennedy, who had known him in his political rather than his diplomatic role, with his freedom and vigor of mind in foreign matters, his realism of judgment and his unconcealed contempt for received opinion. The President concluded that Washington ought to take a new look at Souvanna, and the prince was encouraged to add the United States to his world tour. Souvanna scheduled his Washington visit for April 19–20 but then canceled it when Rusk said he had a speaking engagement in Georgia and could not receive him. Snubbed again, as he thought, Souvanna returned to Moscow.

In the end Rusk did not keep his Georgia engagement, for this was the week of the Bay of Pigs. On Thursday, April 20, Kennedy, determined not to permit restraint in Cuba to be construed as irresolution everywhere, transformed the corps of American military advisers in Laos, who up to this point had wandered about in civilian clothes, into a Military Assistance and Advisory Group, authorizing them to put on uniforms and accompany the Laotian troops. Later that day, when Nixon saw the President and urged an invasion of Cuba, he also urged "a commitment of American air power" to Laos. According to Nixon's recollection, Kennedy replied, "I just don't think we ought to get involved in Laos, particularly where we might find ourselves fighting millions of Chinese troops in the jungles. In any event, I don't see how we can make any move in Laos, which is 5000 miles away, if we don't make a move in Cuba, which is only 90 miles away."

On April 24 the Russians finally agreed on the cease-fire appeal. They were perhaps impressed by the introduction of MAAG and undoubtedly swayed by the intervention of Nehru. (The Indian leader had been skeptical about the American desire for neutralization until Galbraith assured him that Americans were practical men and did not set military value on the Lao, "who do not believe in getting killed like the civilized races.") The next day the Laotian government gratefully accepted the call. So did Souvanna, still on his travels, and even Souphanouvong. But fighting did not cease; and, according to reports reaching Washington on Wednesday, April 26, the Pathet Lao were attacking in force, as if to overrun the country before the cease-fire could take effect. On Thursday the National Security Council held a long and confused session. Walt Rostow has told me that it was the worst White House meeting he attended in the entire Kennedy administration.

Rostow and the Laos task force, supported by Harriman who was now on a trip of inspection in Laos, still urged a limited commitment of American troops to the Mekong valley. But the Joint Chiefs, chastened by the Bay of Pigs, declined to guarantee the success of the military operation, even with the 60,000 men they had recommended a month before. The participants in the meeting found it hard to make out what the Chiefs were trying to say. Indeed, the military were so divided that Vice-President Johnson finally proposed that they put their views in writing in order to clarify their differences. The President, it is said, later received seven different memoranda, from the four Chiefs of Staff and three service secretaries. (It was about this time that a group of foreign students visited the White House and the President, introduced to a young lady from Laos, remarked, "Has anyone asked your advice yet?")[25]

During the Laotian crisis, CIA Station Chief William Colby flies from Saigon to Washington to participate in the drafting of a new program for Vietnam, as described in Honorable Men.

Lansdale's message did get through to the new administration, even if he was torpedoed as ambassador. In April I was called to Washington to participate in an interdepartmental "task force" drawing up a "program of action for Vietnam" for the new President. And a number of my ideas were included in it: the need to provide MAAG support and advice to the territorial forces as well as the Army, to press the economic-development program in the countryside, to expand intelligence operations in both South and North Vietnam, to carry forward CIA's program of village defense and to support the growth of "independent or quasi-independent organizations of political, syndical or professional character" (a reference to my Rome experience to be gradually applied in Vietnam). In the process I also met our new ambassador, Frederick Nolting, and had a chance to put some of my ideas to him as well. The President approved the program, which mercifully had almost none of the State Department's favorite rhetoric about "reforms."[26]

1961   11 May—Vice-President Lyndon Johnson visits Vietnam, then India and Pakistan. **11 May**—An additional 400 Special Forces troops plus 100 "advisers" arrive in Vietnam.

In Saigon in August, Ambassador Gilpatrick writes an "aide-memoire" to President Diem, a letter that includes the following paragraph on the U.S. advisory role.

I mentioned earlier that U.S. advisors are now authorized to accompany ARVN units on operations down to battalion and separate company level. This is a significant improvement over the former arrangement, when advisors were not authorized to accompany units into operational areas except in exceptional circumstances. While I feel that this is a major step forward in the more effective utilization of MAAG advisors, I am concerned that this forward looking authorization is not being fully implemented. The implementing directive (RVNAF Memorandum, Number 563/TTM/P3/1, dated 5 May 1961) reserves the decisions as to whether or not MAAG advisors are permitted to accompany units, largely to ARVN field commanders—based on their estimate of "security limits imposed by battlefield conditions." While I recognize and concur in the concern of the GVN at all levels regarding the security of U.S. military personnel, I feel that ARVN commanders are often over zealous in their desire to insure the one hundred percent security of MAAG advisors in operational areas—a condition which cannot be attained under current circumstances. Of course, I do not wish advisors to engage in actual combat except in self defense. However, I feel that lack of absolute security measures should not preclude them from performing their mission. In the future, I am hopeful that ARVN commanders will avail themselves more frequently of the professional competence available to them through MAAG advisory assistance in both the planning and conduct of tactical operations.[27]

In October the following directive is issued in Washington.

National Security Action Memorandum No. 104

The White House
Washington (October 13, 1961)

TO: The Secretary of State
      The Secretary of Defense
      The Director of Central Intelligence

SUBJECT: Southeast Asia

The President on October 11, 1961, directed that the following actions be taken:

1. Make preparations for the publication of the white paper on North Vietnamese aggression against South Viet Nam which is now being drafted in the Department of State.

2. Develop plans for possible action in the Viet Nam ICC based upon the white paper, preliminary to possible action under paragraph 3 below.

3. Develop plans for presentation of the Viet Nam case in the United Nations.

4. Subject to agreement with the Government of Viet Nam which is now being sought, introduce the Air Force Jungle Jim Squadron into Viet Nam for the initial purpose of training Vietnamese forces.

5. Initiate guerrilla ground action, including use of U.S. advisers if necessary, against Communist aerial resupply missions in the Tchepone area [of Laos].

6. General Taylor should undertake a mission to Saigon to explore ways in which assistance of all types might be more effective.

The President also agreed that certain other actions developed by the Task Force and concurred in by the agencies concerned, but which do not require specific Presidential approval, should be undertaken on an urgent basis.

McGeorge Bundy[28]

Simultaneously, the Viet Cong Central Office for South Vietnam (COSVN) reassesses its own policies and procedures for the struggle against the Diem government.

The Character of the Present Period, and Our Tasks and Line of Action

1) The development of the situation shows that the Southern revolution has entered a high tide with characteristics and possibilities of development which the Central Committee has judged as follows:

". . . The period of temporary stabilization of the U.S.-Diem regime has passed and the period of continuous crisis and serious decline has begun."

". . . The forms of limited guerrilla war and partial uprisings have appeared, the period of prolonged political crisis has begun; those forms of active guerrilla warfare have opened a revolutionary high tide and develop more strongly everyday. Through that process, the enemy's forces and government will continue to disintegrate, the revolutionary forces will be rapidly built and developed and forms of revolutionary government will appear in localities everywhere. A general all-sided crisis of the U.S.-Diem regime will appear, and a general offensive and general uprising of the people will break out, overthrow the U.S.-Diem regime and liberate the South. Also during that process, the enemy will experience increasingly deep internal contradictions and the revolutionary movement will rise higher everyday. Coups or military revolts could occur, in which the revolution must seize the opportune moment in order to turn it into a situation favorable to the revolution. At the same time, the possibility of armed intervention by bringing troops of U.S. imperialism and its lackeys into the South by whatever forms and in whatever scope is also a complex problem which we must follow and find ways to limit, guard against and be prepared to cope with in a timely fashion.

Clearly the high tide situation has not yet entered into the general offensive and uprising but only opens a period of partial uprising and partial offensive and expands more and more to hasten the process of the enemy's disintegration, develop our forces, and fundamentally change the relationship of forces between the enemy and ourselves; that is the process of creating ripe conditions for a general offensive and general uprising. . . ."

2) Based on the characteristics and possibilities for development of the present revolutionary period, the Central Committee has presented the following tasks and line of action:

"The immediate revolutionary task in the South is to endeavor to rapidly build up our forces in both political and military aspects, concentrate the vast revolutionary forces in the National Liberation Front, launch a powerful political struggle movement of the masses, actively annihilate the enemy's manpower, preserve and develop our forces, make the enemy's government and forces fall apart on an ever broadening scale; advance to become master of the mountain and jungle, win the whole lowlands and strive to build bases and push the political struggle in the cities, create conditions and grasp every opportune movement to overthrow the U.S.-Diem government and liberate the South.

"Promote the political struggle further while pushing armed struggle up till it is equal with political struggle, attack the enemy in both political and military aspects. . . . Depending on the relationship of forces between the enemy and ourselves, and depending on the concrete situation in each region, put forward appropriate lines for action and forms of struggle, taking military struggle as primary in the mountainous region, with the task of annihilating the enemy's manpower in order to expand our base areas and build our forces. In the plains region political and military struggle can be on the same level, and depending on the concrete situation in each place in the plans, aim at striking a balance between the two forms of struggle, and in the degree of wearing down and annihilating the enemy's manpower. In the cities, take political struggle as primary, including both legal and illegal forms."[29]

In Smith Hempstone's novel A Tract of Time, *American CIA adviser Harry Coltart and a Montagnard village chief discuss the problems of resisting the Communist movement toward a "general uprising."*

Harry propped the Browning against the bank of the watercourse and sank gratefully to his knees, gasping for breath. He slumped back against the bank, conscious of the cloud of gnats attracted by the sweat on his face, and filled his lungs with air. Yé squatted on his heels, oblivious to the insects, tracing cabalistic designs in the sand with the butt of his burp gun. The two men averted their gaze from one another, conscious of the thing which lay between them, wounding their thoughts. The American was the first to speak. . . .

"The Viets are your enemies, Yé."

"Why, Erohé, tell me why?"

"Because they are Communists. Because they will enslave you. Because they will steal your land and make cattle of you. You know all this." As he enumerated each point, Harry unbent a finger from his clenched fist and when he had finished held the three fingers close to Yé's face, as if to force the truth on the chief through the physical proximity of his hand. Yé wrinkled his brow and studied the designs he had etched in the sand, as if hoping to find there the answers to the questions which afflicted him.

"Communists? We do not know what this means. Your words may be true but we do not know it. What we do know is that the *Yoane,* the yellow Annamese of the plains, have been our enemies since these hills were young. The Vietcong come from the north, from the mountains. From that direction we have not been threatened since the time of the men you call Mongols. And who amongst us can remember that time?"

"I speak the truth. The Viets . . ."

"We do not know it, Erohé. What we do know is that you are a *Boc,* a high-nose from beyond the bitter water, whose home is not this place, while many of the Vietcong are of our blood. You serve the *Yoane*, who always have been our enemies. These things we know. And for this . . ."

"But you know . . ."

Yé raised his hand and Harry fell silent.

"And for this reason," Yé continued, "many believe that the Koho should not fight the Vietcong. But come," he added, rising to his feet, "soon the sun will be high. It is better to travel now and to talk later."

Yé sniffed the air and listened intently for a minute, his head cocked to one side and his forefinger to his lips. Satisfied, he nodded to the American, slung his burp gun and set off down the dry watercourse. . . .

What Yé had said, Harry knew, was the kernel of the whole problem of organizing the hill tribes, the montagnards as the French called them, to resist the Vietcong. And Englehardt,* in his methodical, professorial fashion, had convinced him that it was essential that the hill tribes should be persuaded to fight. As Englehardt said, what the newspapers persisted in calling "the Ho Chi Minh trail"—as if it were a turnpike instead of a huge tract of broken country through which literally hundreds of trails wandered—funneled through the core of the montagnard country. Over these trails from North Vietnam through the Koho hills to the Mekong delta came much of importance to the Vietcong in their struggle against the Diem regime. Nobody from Englehardt on down pretended that the Vietcong would collapse if the supply routes through the montagnard country were cut. The rebellion already was self-sustaining, despite the pap that State fed to reporters like John McWhorter for daily regurgitation to their readers. That was a point that troubled Harry. He half suspected that there could be no American victory in Vietnam and he disliked persuading primitive tribesmen to commit themselves to a losing game. How was it Englehardt had put it? That there was a difference between losing and not winning? Yes. His hulking, gray-faced superior had suggested that a condition of permanent stalemate might be possible and desirable. It was one of the good things about working for Englehardt. He had the reputation for being not only an honorable, intelligent man but a patient one, one willing to talk through a problem until a logical, ethical solution presented itself. . . .

What we've got to do, Harry thought, is to recreate the circumstances of the twelfth century, when the montagnards fought with the Vietnamese against the Hindu Chams. But that was a long time ago. Hemmed into their barren hills by a circle of Annamese forts, the only lowlanders with whom the hill tribes had come in contact in recent centuries were tax collectors, Annamese soldiers living off the land, and the occasional trader. Nor had the French helped much. Out of a curious blend of imperial necessity and sentimental attachment, they had administered the montagnards separately from the rest of Indochina, thus reinforcing the hill tribes' inherent sense of isolation and antagonism toward the Anna-

*CIA Station Chief, Saigon.

mese of the plains. The past provided at best a shaky foundation, Harry thought as he swung along in Yé's footsteps, for building a pro-Diem movement among the montagnards. But it had to be and it was his job to build that alliance with gold, promises, and, if necessary, threats. That, as Englehardt would have put it, was the name of the game.

And yet Harry knew that the little brown man in front of him was no fool. Yé would do what seemed to him best for his people and Harry respected him for that. That was what he himself wanted for them, too, he guessed.[30]

In November President Kennedy receives this hurried message from the ambassador to India, John Kenneth Galbraith, who has visited Vietnam. His "full and . . . close analysis" later provides more detailed justification for the following views.

TO DIRECTOR, CIA, FROM BANGKOK, 20 NOVEMBER 1961
FOR THE PRESIDENT FROM AMBASSADOR GALBRAITH

I HAVE JUST COMPLETED THREE INTENSIVE DAYS IN SAIGON WHICH, WITH CINCPAC [COMMANDER-IN-CHIEF, PACIFIC] TALKS, GIVES ME A MUCH BETTER FEELING FOR THIS TANGLED SITUATION. TOMORROW NIGHT I AM SENDING YOU A FULL AND, I TRUST RATHER CLOSE ANALYSIS WHICH I PRAY YOU READ AT AVERAGE SPEED. THAT CONCERNS OUR LONGER COURSE BUT MEANWHILE I MUST REGISTER CONCLUSIONS ON TWO OR THREE MATTERS ON WHICH ACTION MAY BE PENDING AND I ADD A GENERAL THOUGHT OR TWO.

(1) THERE IS SCARCELY THE SLIGHTEST PRACTICAL CHANCE THAT THE ADMINISTRATIVE AND POLITICAL REFORMS NOW BEING PRESSED UPON DIEM WILL RESULT IN REAL CHANGE. THEY RECKON WITHOUT DEEPER POLITICAL REALITIES AND INSECURITIES OF HIS POSITION AND THE NATURE OF POLITICIANS OF THIS AGE. HE WILL PROMISE BUT HE WILL NOT PERFORM BECAUSE IT IS MOST UNLIKELY THAT HE CAN PERFORM. ACCORDINGLY, IT IS IMPORTANT THAT IN EXCHANGE OF LETTERS WHICH I SUPPOSE NOW TO BE INEVITABLE THAT OUR PROPOSED AID BE GEARED TO DEMONSTRATE ACTION NOT PROMISES. THIS MAY SLIGHTLY INCREASE THE EFFECT. BUT MOSTLY IT WILL KEEP US FROM WHAT OTHERWISE WILL BE A PURELY ONE-SIDED COMMITMENT TO DIEM. IN THE ABSENCE OF FUNDAMENTAL REFORM, THE HELP WE ARE NOW PROPOSING WILL NOT SAVE THE SITUATION.

(2) IN MY JUDGEMENT, IN THE IMMEDIATE SITUATION THERE SHOULD BE NO, REPEAT NO, CHANGE IN EITHER POLITICAL OR MAAG LEADERSHIP. POLITICAL LEADERSHIP IS USING ACCUMULATED CAPITAL TO GET WHATEVER SLIGHT ADMINISTRATIVE AND POLITICAL IMPROVEMENT MAY RESULT FROM THIS INITIATIVE. MAAG CHANGE WOULD, IN MY JUDGEMENT, SET BACK WHATEVER SLIGHT CHANCE THERE IS FOR MILITARY REFORMS AND SENSIBLE COUNTER-INSURGENCY ACTION.

(3) WHILE SITUATION IS INDUBITABLY BAD, MILITARY ASPECTS SEEM TO ME OUT OF PERSPECTIVE. A COMPARATIVELY WELL-EQUIPPED ARMY WITH PARA-

MILITARY FORMATIONS NUMBERING A QUARTER MILLION MEN IS FACING A MAXI-
MUM OF FIFTEEN TO EIGHTEEN THOUSAND LIGHTLY ARMED MEN. IF THIS WERE
EQUALITY, THE UNITED STATES WOULD HARDLY BE SAFE AGAINST THE SIOUX. I
KNOW THE THEORIES ABOUT THIS KIND OF WARFARE.

(4) THE FOREGOING, AMONG OTHER THINGS, LEADS ME TO BELIEVE THAT YOUR
DECISION AGAINST TROOP COMMITMENT WAS WHOLLY SOUND AND WITH FULL
DISCOUNT FOR MY HIGH THRESHOLD ON THIS MATTER. DECISIVE MILITARY FAC-
TOR IS NOT MANPOWER OR EVEN CONFIDENCE BUT BAD ORGANIZATION, INCOM-
PETENT USE AND DEPLOYMENT OF FORCES, INABILITY TO PROTECT TERRITORY
ONCE CLEARED, AND PROBABLY POOR POLITICAL BASE. AMERICAN FORCES
WOULD NOT CORRECT THIS. THEIR INABILITY TO DO SO WOULD CREATE A
WORSE CRISIS OF CONFIDENCE AS THIS BECAME EVIDENT.

(5) I NOTE THAT PROBLEM OF CONFIDENCE IS PARTLY OUR MAKING. THERE IS A
FASHIONABLE TENDENCY, THOUGH NOT BY MOST SENIOR MILITARY AND DIPLO-
MATIC FIGURES, TO DEPICT YOUR DECISION OF LAST SPRING ON LAOS AS A
DISASTER WITHOUT ANY REFERENCE TO ALTERNATIVES AVAILABLE. THIS FLOWS
OVER TO LOCAL COMMUNITY. WORD SHOULD BE PASSED DOWN THAT WHEN WE
MAKE THE BEST OF BAD ALTERNATIVES SECOND GUESSING OF THIS SORT DOES
NO SERVICE.

(6) AS I WILL ARGUE, THERE IS NO SOLUTION THAT DOES NOT INVOLVE A
CHANGE OF GOVERNMENT. TO SAY THERE IS NO ALTERNATIVE IS NONSENSE FOR
THERE NEVER HAS SEEMED TO BE WHERE ONE MAN HAS DOMINATED THE
SCENE. SO WHILE WE MUST PLAY OUT THE INEFFECTIVE AND HOPELESS COURSE
ON WHICH WE ARE LAUNCHED FOR A LITTLE WHILE, WE MUST LOOK AHEAD
VERY SOON TO A NEW GOVERNMENT. ON THIS MORE LATER. GIVEN AN EVEN
MODERATELY EFFECTIVE GOVERNMENT AND PUTTING THE RELATIVE MILITARY
POWER INTO PERSPECTIVE, I CAN'T HELP THINKING THAT THE INSURGENCY
MIGHT VERY SOON BE SETTLED.[31]

*Ten days later President Kennedy approves what is to become one of the
most controversial operations of the Southeast Asia conflict. The president
also reserves "execution" authorization to "Washington."*

National Security Action Memorandum No. 115

*The White House
Washington (November 30, 1961)*

TO: The Secretary of State
      The Secretary of Defense

SUBJECT: Defoliant Operations in Viet Nam

The President has approved the recommendation of the Secretary of
State and the Deputy Secretary of Defense to participate in a selective
and carefully controlled joint program of defoliant operations in Viet

Nam starting with the clearance of key routes and proceeding thereafter to food denial only if the most careful basis of resettlement and alternative food supply has been created. Operations in Zone D and the border areas shall not be undertaken until there are realistic possibilities of immediate military exploitation.

The President further agreed that there should be careful prior consideration and authorization by Washington of any plans developed by CINCPAC and the country team under this authority before such plans are executed.

McGeorge Bundy[32]

1961 **31 December**—U.S. military personnel attached to MAAG (Military Assistance and Advisory Group), Saigon, now number 2,067. Total U.S. military personnel in South Vietnam: 3,200. U.S. casualties to date: 11 killed; 3 wounded (DOD/OASD [Department of Defense/Office of Assistant Secretary of Defense] 27 Mar 75).

1962 **9 January**—MAAG, Saigon, personnel strength is now 2,646. **18 January**—With Chairman Khrushchev's speech in mind, President Kennedy redefines the Southeast Asia conflict: "subversive insurgency ('wars of liberation') is a major form of politico-military conflict equal in importance to conventional warfare" (NSAM 124). **February**—Two South Vietnamese T-28 aircraft bomb Diem's presidential palace in an attempt at either a coup or an assassination.

On 11 June the main character of Smith Hempstone's A Tract of Time *has been called down from his Montagnard village for consultations. Harry Coltart, a CIA adviser, is having dinner in Saigon with John McWhorter, a newsman.*

McWhorter shoved his plate aside, scrambled to his feet, and threw his soggy napkin on his chair.

"Get the bill will you, Harry?" he shouted over his shoulder, "this may be important."

Harry called for the bill and paid it, McWhorter leaning against the wall, his right hand pressing against the free ear, shutting out the sound of a siren wailing somewhere. He hung up suddenly, motioned to Harry to come, and ran for the street, shouting for a taxi. Harry clattered down the gangway, the planks swaying under his weight, to find McWhorter opening the door of a cab.

"What is it?" he demanded. "What's going on?"

"Get in. Tell you then."

Harry clambered into the cab, the weight of McWhorter's body forcing him against the opposite door. It was stiflingly hot, the street white with glare from the river.

"Chua Xa Loi," McWhorter shouted to the driver, "and step on it." The reporter threw himself back into the seat as the taxi lurched forward, the driver leaning on the horn. "It's about to happen," he said.

"What? What's happening?"

"The Buddhists. It's a helluva story."

"What are you talking about?" Harry asked.

"Wait and see."

The Catinat, as the taxi approached the pagoda, was solid with bodies. Traffic was hopelessly snarled, horns blaring and hooting, and beyond them the imperative cry of the claxons. A truck tried to force its way through the mob but stalled. As the terrfied driver tried to get out, the mob rocked the truck and finally turned it on its side. Somehow the mob got the driver up above their heads and passed him, bobbing like a beachball, from hand to hand, tearing at his clothes. Finally, naked and bloody, he disappeared from sight. Riot police, their wicker shields held high in front of their faces, their teeth clenched, flailed at the mob with their bamboo truncheons, trying to force a passage through the wall of human flesh. Those in front tried to give way before the blows, clawing at those behind them in their effort to escape. From the crowd came a low moan, the cry of an animal in pain. As they forced their way out of the cab, McWhorter tossing a handful of small bills over the driver's shoulder onto the front seat, a woman lost her footing and fell screaming under the feet of the mob, the cries of her agony eaten by the hoarse rumbling of the rabble. The police phalanx hacked its way toward them and hands tore at Harry's clothes, ripping his coat.

"Get . . . out of . . . here," he shouted at McWhorter.

"The wall," the reporter screamed, "get to the wall."

The two Americans fought their way onto the pavement and hurled themselves into a doorway. The police phalanx, unable to break through, changed directions, probing for a weak point, and pressed forward away from them and to the left, the truncheons whirling, the shields held high, the blows unheard in the din. Over the heads of the crowd, Harry could see tear gas cannisters shaped like ice cream containers wobbling in uncertain flight. And in answer, a rain of cobblestones rattled off the wicker shields of the police. They'll fire soon, Harry thought, soon the police will fire.

"This way," McWhorter shouted, "follow me."

He put his shoulder down and forced his way out onto the pavement again, "La presse," he bellowed, "j'suis journaliste americain."

A squat Annamese in an open-necked shirt fought his way to McWhorter's side and shouted something in his ear. The reporter shouted back. Harry could hear nothing but the animal cries of the mob. There was no chance to go back. He followed McWhorter and the Annamese, using his elbows and knees, cursing himself for his stupidity. This had nothing to do with him.

Finally they broke through the mob. On the cobblestones in front of the pagoda, a triple circle of Buddhist bonzes, their monks' robes angry orange in the afternoon sun, stood with their arms linked. Within the circle, in the middle of the street, sat an old bonze, his sticklike legs crossed beneath him, his shaven head splotched with liver patches, his eyes vacant and fixed on something Harry could not see. The crowd surged backward and forward against the triple chain of monks, giving off an odor strange to him. It had the richness of rancid butter mixed with something animal and sexual and, at the same time, pure and exalted. It was borne on the moans of the mob, was a part of it. Two monks tipped a container of liquid over the old bonze, turning his saffron robe to deep brown, and the pungent smell of gasoline pressed against Harry's nostrils, the odor growing with his dawning horror.

"No, no," he shouted, trying to force his way through the wall of orange robes, his hands slipping off bare, sweating shoulders, his fingernails gouging greasy flesh. But the wall would not yield and he found himself pinned breathlessly against the slippery shoulder of a young monk by the pressure of the crowd. The seated monk turned his head toward him. . . .

Suddenly the old bonze erupted into a pillar of flame, the puff of flames and heat forcing back the crowd, from the throat of which came a new and greater moan that was half a shout of triumph, half a cry of fear, and with it came the terrible, sweet smell of burning flesh, the scent of madness. The old bonze did not move. No sound came from him. His mouth formed a black hole, as in a Goya sketch, frozen in surprise or exaltation. The flames licked thirstily around him, consuming his robe, eating the withered flesh, leaving only a charred scarecrow. Slowly, as if in resignation, the blackened shape tipped, the sticks of its legs still crossed, the palms of the hands together in the contemplative position, the black hole of the mouth frozen open, and the ruined body fell over onto its side in a flutter of ashes. The crowd howled in its frenzy and, far away, Harry could see the truncheons rising and falling rhythmically, flailing the living flesh, pressing toward the oily smoke which hung in a single wisp over the circle of monks.

"A camera, God if I only had a camera!" McWhorter shouted.

Harry was suddenly, explosively ill on the sweating shoulder of the monk against whom he pressed. With all the force left in his spent nervous system, Harry drove his doubled fist hard into the stomach of the bonze, pushing the surprised eyes away from him with the heel of his other hand, his hand sliding off a shoulder drenched in his own vomit.[33]

1962   **30 June**—There are now 5,576 U.S. servicemen in Vietnam.
           23 July—Secretary of Defense McNamara orders a "planned

withdrawal" study, with a target date of 1965 for complete "phase-out" of U.S. military forces.

The same day the Geneva Agreements on the neutralization of Laos are signed.

At Geneva on 23 July 1962, a new political settlement was reached. As of that period, U.S. intelligence reported 12 NVA battalions in Laos, some 6,000 strong. In addition, 3,000 NVA personnel were serving with PL units.

The Geneva Agreement on Laos of 1962 consisted of joint declaration by the several nations concerned with Indochina—including the U.S., the DRV, and the GVN—agreeing that Laos would be neutralized:

> All foreign regular and irregular troops, foreign paramilitary formations and foreign military personnel shall be withdrawn from Laos . . . the introduction of foreign regular and irregular troops, foreign para-military formations and foreign military personnel into Laos of armaments, munitions, and war materiel generally, except such quantities as the Royal Government of Laos may consider necessary for the national defense of Laos, is prohibited . . .

In concert with the Pathet Lao, the DRV circumvented these agreements. Although measures were taken to conceal DRV presence and ostensibly to withdraw DRV forces—40 North Vietnamese were removed under ICC [International Control Commission] observation—U.S. intelligence obtained good evidence, including a number of eye witness statements, that the bulk of the NVA forces remained in Laos; U.S. estimates placed NVA strength in Laos in early 1963 at 4,000 troops in 8 battalions, plus 2,000 Pathet Lao advisors.

In any event, . . . the DRV could look upon its Laotian enterprise as successful in substantially expanding its sphere of influence in Laos, to include control over the territory adjacent to South Vietnam over which passed its "Ho Chi Minh Trail" of infiltration. Eventually the enterprise brought about withdrawal of the U.S. military presence from Laos, per the Geneva Agreement of 1962. If the Vientiane government, braced with broad U.S. aid, surprised the DRV with its resiliency, it at least proved unable to challenge the Pathet Lao—and DRV—gains. Whatever the DRV longer term goal in Laos, reunification of Vietnam seemed thereafter to take priority over further extension in Laos.[34]

In mid-1962 a freelance American correspondent named Miranda Pickerel arrives in Laos, as depicted in Pamela Sanders' novel Miranda.

Vientiane became my base. I acquired an apartment of sorts, a second-hand Honda motorcycle, and a fat old Vietnamese maid named Hooey.

At the outset I had three "strings": *The New York Times,* the *Daily Express,* and *Time-Life.* Later I picked up the *Daily Telegraph.*

Van Sweldt had given me the *Times* stringership on the condition that I get the *Time-Life* job as well. "Because *they* pay," he explained. "You can't possibly live off the *Times.*" Since the *Times* paid me fifty dollars a month retainer plus lineage, and since my stories usually ran to five lines on page thirty-two, Van Sweldt clearly had logic on his side. But I kept the string, partly because it forced me to stay abreast of the daily news, and mostly because the paper's prestige carried weight. (The Lao leaders had become psychologically dependent on the *Times* for news of their own country. During the newspaper blackout in New York that year, all activity ceased in Laos and Prince Souvanna Phouma was heard to inquire anxiously about a settlement of the printers' strike. We began to believe what we had suspected all along—that had there been no correspondents in Laos, nothing would have occurred there.) . . .

As a French colonial backwater, Vientiane had been dreaming along for decades. The languid, lackadaisical ambience verged on the somnambulistic. It made one sleepy just to get out of bed in the morning.

"*Bau penh yanh,*" the Lao said about everything. "Never mind."

In the last two years, however, an infusion of Americans and American cash had given this world capital village a frontier atmosphere. Bars and brothels sprang up—the OK Corral, the Dixie, the White Rose, the Casbah & Grill, the Turkey Farm—most of them located on a carabao track known, wishfully, as "the Strip." A gambling casino opened under the aegis of the chief of police. On the road to Wattay airport was a California-style "motel" with a swimming pool, owned by a CIA-funded airline called Bird & Sons.

Curious flowers of Progress blossomed—a single traffic light was installed—but the rest of the town remained as atavistically tacky as ever. Ramshackle storefronts sagged and warped in the rain; slatted wooden sidewalks buckled in the sun. Here and there stood government *bureaux*—the Ministry of Posts, the Ministry of Information and Propaganda—all painted French Colonial Piss. The pervasive aura of tranquility within these offices was churchlike. No papers rustled, no secretaries stirred, no typewriters clacked, no telephones jangled offensively. The only working telephones in the entire country were at the American Embassy. (Others used shortwave radios.) Interspersed among the ministries and embassies—of which there were a good many, Laos having recognized absolutely everyone—were noodle parlors, opium dens, dancehalls, Indian moneychangers, Vietnamese jewelry shops, Chinese and Corsican restaurants, a French *lycée,* a French hospital, a USIS library, an American military and aid compound (USOM), a hundred neighborhood *wats* where chickens and pigeons pecked in the dirt courtyards, two *salons de beauté* and two outdoor markets (morning and evening). Along the river and on the fringes of town were crumbling villas and weedy gardens choked with coral vine. The rest was rice paddies.

Pickerel goes to an embassy cocktail party.

When Van Sweldt introduced Sturgis Lee, he said with heavy stress, "Riddle works for the political *research* section in the American Embassy," by which I was given to understand that Sturgis Lee worked for the Central Intelligence Agency. In fact, having heard about him in Bangkok, I already knew that. So did everyone else.

Sturgis Lee was the youngest son of the oldest family in Roanoke, Virginia. He was thirty-two, stood well over six feet, weighed well over two hundred pounds, and had the sort of large flat-backed head that babies have. His hair was pale blond, his face round, his cheeks bright pink. His slightly protuberant eyes looked like Wedgwood saucers. Sartorially, Sturgis Lee was something of an iconoclast. On this particular afternoon, he was wearing a white sharkskin suit, a candy-striped shirt, a plaid pink and chartreuse Thai silk waistcoat, a green and white polka-dot tie, and white buck saddle shoes without socks. In his breast pocket was a voluminous red silk paisley handkerchief; from his buttonhole drooped some sort of enormous weed, perhaps a kind of wild morning glory. On his watch fob he wore a miniature jade Buddha, a tiger's claw, an ivory toothpick, a mandala given him by the Dalai Lama, the key to his Honda motorcycle, the toebone of St. Charles Borromeo encased in glass, a gold cigar-cutter, a *kha* amulet, a pair of stainless steel nail clippers, and a large rotten molar that had once graced the mouth of his favorite chestnut mare. On his left wrist he wore a *Montagnard* bracelet and some filthy knotted *baci* strings; on his right were three rubber bands. Beside him on the floor lay a wide-brimmed panama straw hat with a blue bandana round the crown and a silver-handled mahogany walking stick, which contained a flacon of Tillamore Dew Irish whiskey. . . .

In August, to my relief, *Time* sent me to Vietnam to cover for the Saigon stringer, Fred Hall, who was taking a two-week holiday in the Cameron Highlands. I stayed at the Continental Palace, a splendid old hotel with sagging beds, high ceilings, overhead fans, and antique plumbing. On the ground floor was the very popular open-air terrace bar known as "the Continental Shelf." American officers sat there now, like the French Foreign Legionnaires before them, drinking Ba-Mi-Ba *bière* and watching the girls waft by in their shimmering *ao dais*. The streetwalkers gathered on the sidewalk outside the hotel at five o'clock, just as they had during the French-Indochina war. Urchins peddled newspapers, black market chewing gum, secondhand paperback novels, or their sisters.

It was late afternoon when I checked into the hotel. Hall had left his cable card, some background files, and a list of names and telephone numbers of people who might be helpful. The first name on the list, underlined, was that of Steve Zimmerman, the *New York Times* correspondent. I called him and he invited me to have dinner with him at a Chinese restaurant in Cholon called the Diamond.

"What are your plans?" he asked, leaning forward to contemplate a heaping platter of hot spiced crab.

"I'm not sure. I suppose the first thing I ought to do is check in with MACV."

"Forget the PIOs." Zimmerman picked out a crab leg and crunched into it with gusto. "Of course you've got to check in—just in case," he grinned, "you get shot or captured. But steer clear of them after that. They'll just give you the old runaround—shuffle you off to some damned strategic hamlet."

Zimmerman looked like a studious lumberjack. He was six feet three, large-boned, with long feet and big hands. He had a large jutting nose, a prognathic jaw, and black hair cropped short and brushed forward onto his forehead in the current Ivy style. His movements were quick for a large man; he walked with loping strides and spoke rapidly with a modified Harvard inflection, sporadically punctuating his speech by pushing his horn-rimmed glasses back against the bridge of his nose. He was twenty-eight, enthusiastic, and ingenuous.

"Goddamnn," he would say, stopping suddenly in the middle of the street, "I just can't believe my luck. My first assignment overseas and look"—he waved his arm expansively and laughed with disbelief—"just look where I am." He was in love with everything—with the girls, the great restaurants, the city, the war, and, most of all, with his work. And with himself too. But it wasn't offensive; more of an incredulous delight in his own fate. He was the best reporter covering the best story on the best war for the best newspaper. And in a profession often characterized by pettiness and backbiting, Zimmerman was astonishingly unselfish. There was no story he would not share, no tip he would not pass on, no one he would not help. There was nothing small about him.

"The trick here," he said to me on that first night, "is to get out of Saigon. The farther out in the field you are, the looser the control, the greater the mobility, the easier it is to talk to people, and the more you learn. The reverse is equally true. The closer you are to Saigon, the more you'll be lied to. As far as the American Embassy and MACV are concerned, *we're* the enemy, not the VC. Nolting has been holding Diem's hand for so long he's begun to think like him. He and General Harkins are telling Washington that we're winning the war, that Diem is the savior of the people, and that everything is rosy. The fact is we're losing the war, Diem has got to go, and the entire system is rotten. We say that, and that makes us traitors. Meanwhile, Americans are starting to die in a war that most people in the States don't know is being fought. Hell, they don't even know where Vietnam is—they think it's in Hawaii."[35]

One of the first narratives about the conduct of the war, Richard Tregaskis's Vietnam Diary *provides readers with an encyclopedic panorama of people, places, and events in Vietnam during the fall of 1962.*

Tuesday, October 9, Over the Pacific
This is going to war, modern style—and comfortably thus far. I've been able to hitch a ride with a group of brass, heading down to Vietnam.

Most of these generals and colonels (and one ambassador) came up to Hawaii four days ago in this same aircraft, a big Boeing 707 model. ("Military model" means that it is a transport, freighter-style, with no windows—an aerial submarine, they say—a view of the outer world being cut off in the name of military austerity and functionalism. But inside there are reasonably comfortable seats.)

The brass came up for a conference with Defense Secretary Robert S. McNamara and staff (who jetted down from Washington, D.C., to meet them and the Pacific commander, Adm. Harry D. Felt). The conference lasted one day (yesterday)—one of a series, held every few months: the highest American command comes out to the Pacific to meet with the field commanders and deliberate on ways to win our running battle with the Communists in the hottest of the hot-war areas and our only shooting war—Vietnam.

Last night, the conference over and plans made for the conduct of the war against the Vietnam Reds for the next few weeks and months, Secretary McNamara and his staff roared off for Washington.

Today, at 12:30 P.M., the Southeast Asia military commanders took off in our big aerial submarine for Saigon and Bangkok. On board are Gen. Paul D. Harkins, chief of U.S. Military Assistance Command, Vietnam (USMACV), the U.S. Ambassadors to Vietnam and Thailand, the chiefs of a half-dozen military sections in Vietnam (some hush-hush, like the Special Forces), and some plain hitchhikers like me trying to get to Vietnam on various assignments.

I was lucky enough to find a seat, my over-all objective being to get a firsthand, eyewitness look at the strange, off-beat, new-style war in which we find ourselves engaged in the miserable little jungle country called Vietnam, which our nation's leaders have decided is pivotal and critical in our Asian struggle with Communism. I am lucky to have military orders appropriate to my mission of writing a book about the war in Vietnam, and thus ride with such a distinguished array of brass—but within a few days I expect to be with people at the opposite end of the military scale, people who are engaged in combat against the Communist Viet Cong (VC). . . .

I asked Gen. Harkins' public information (PI) chief, Lt. Col. Jim Smith, to introduce me to Frederick E. Nolting, Jr., the U.S. Ambassador to Vietnam. The Ambassador, a mild-voiced man of 48 with the gentle demeanor of a scholar, explained the mechanism of the strange war in Vietnam. But what he said was quite aggressive. He gestured with clenched hands:

"There are two fists to our effort. There is the [Vietnamese government] striking force: trained and supplied by us—and most especially provided with mobility (the helicopters)—and supplied with intelligence, which will put them in a position to find out where the hard core of the

VC is and isolate them—and we have been doing this with increasing success.

"While one fist is attacking, the other is pacifying through the 'strategic hamlet' program, the clear-and-hold operation." He was referring to the Vietnamese government program, supported by the Americans to the tune of hundreds of millions of dollars, of fencing in and protecting newly freed villages—cleared, that is, of VC's—and making the villages, and the farming families in them, strong enough to resist further VC attacks.

I knew from my military sources in Hawaii that Secretary McNamara has always been one of the strongest champions of the strategic hamlet program in Vietnam as the most important method of driving out the Communists—and keeping them out. McNamara is supposed to have practically forced this new program through and made sure that the first strategic hamlets were built.

"The aim and result today," Ambassador Nolting went on, "is to cut the VC off from their resources—that is, the *people*—and gradually to isolate them. It's somewhat similar to Malaya [the 10-year-long British campaign against the Communist insurgents in the Malay territories, where villagers were removed from Communist territory and resettled in new strong points where they could live in peace and be protected by military forces]. But the system in Malaya was to move people to new locations. Here, the system is to give them their needs and the incentive for defending themselves."

I asked the Ambassador how far we have progressed with his two-fisted program for clearing out the VC and holding the territory.

"It's too early to say it's over the hump. But certainly the VC are somewhat worried about it. I think they're somewhat in a quandary about what to do."

When I asked about the strength of the enemy in the country, he answered quite precisely: "About 60 to 65 per cent of the population are estimated controlled by the government, 15 or 20 per cent noncommitted, and about 15 to 20 per cent controlled by the VC." . . .

I went back to my seat and talked to a spy type heading back to Vietnam to go on with his secretive work. Matter of fact, he is what you might call the head spy for operations in Vietnam, a large, well-spoken, engaging man with a good sense of humor and an immense dedication to and enthusiasm for his job.

Like Ambasador Nolting, he seemed to feel that there was reason for optimism about the progress of our war against the VC, because our side is clearing and holding new pieces of Vietnam. "But we've got a lot to learn. We've never fought a guerrilla war on a national basis before. . . . We have to take the people away from the VC because they [the people] are the greatest single weapon . . . the first way of taking people away is by training and arming them. You don't take people away from the VC with high-flown slogans in Saigon, but . . . by having defenders in place. In addition, we are trying to do socio-economic things that are needed."

He said he was worried about the status of supposedly neutral Laos on Vietnam's western flank. It's well known that Russian planes are flying troops and supplies into Laos from Hanoi in North Vietnam, in violation of the Geneva agreement, which supposedly established Laos as a neutral.

"Do you think the Commies are concentrating their major effort on building up their position in Laos, and moving a lot of new strength into Vietnam from there?" I asked.

He didn't answer directly. "Laos will be a big blow if it goes . . . Laos is the strategic center of Southeast Asia, the key to Southeast Asia." But, he went on, "we are getting in some good licks against the Vietnamese Communists in the meantime, . . . and with our help, Ngo Dinh Diem may be able to get the VC really on the run before the Russians and Chinese build up too much strength in Laos.[36]

After meeting U.S. Marine lieutenant Kenneth Babbs, later to become known as author Ken Kesey's friend and bus driver, Tregaskis describes him as a "formidable specimen . . . about six-feet-four," with a "horrendous mustache" and wearing a long sheath knife, a "side arm," and a "bullet-studded bandolier." In a letter, Babbs reflects on his tour of duty.

Our squadron was the second one to go into SVN as a complete unit. The first unit was the Marine chopper squadron stationed at the time in Okinawa. They were in SVN a few months, then their year-long overseas tour expired. It was my squadron's turn for far east duty and we knew we'd be relieving the squadron in SVN. Technically we were advisors. Our job was to haul supplies in and out of outposts; evacuate wounded; and carry ARVN on heliborne operations. We weren't supposed to participate in the fighting. But when we started taking on fire, we knew we had to be ready to protect ourselves, and we started arming our choppers, which were essentially flying trucks.

At first, the VC were frightened by the choppers, but word must have gotten around quickly how vulnerable the machines were. We couldn't armor plate because the weight would lower our payload. There's so many cables and hoses running the rotor gear box, a rifle slug could knock us out of action. Lose hydraulic oil or lubricating oil, temperatures went up and we'd have to sit down quickly. So, as our tour continued, instead of running, the VC stayed and fired back . . . leading to that scene recorded for *Life* by Larry Burrows of the squadron that replaced us. They took a lot of damage when they went in on a strike. Lost some planes and pilots and crew chiefs. That was late '64 or early '65.

As the heat increased, the problem of when and where to fire back became acute. The hawks in the squadron wanted to shoot, any chance they got. The doves said defense only. The C.O. had to continually upgrade shoot-back policy. . . . Which would prevail, an attitude of nuke the gook, or what the hell we wanta mess these people and this country up for? 'Course, when the bullets are flying past his ear, even the tamest dove tends to ruffle his feathers a bit, and this then is what the pro-war or anti-war sentiment always comes down to: you can have any philosophical attitude of war you want, but none of it means diddly until the moment you have to decide whether to pull that trigger or not, and what you're aiming at, at the time. That's the moment every man who's ever been there never forgets. War becomes a collective account of those millions of individual decisions . . . and I'm not saying anything pro or con . . . just that every guy (and gal too, today) should know that it's the possible situation awaiting, should he be faced with military duty. . . .

One of my stories, for instance, is designed to show the way the squadron camaraderie was breaking down the longer we stayed in Vietnam (another theme, the same as *Heart of Darkness* . . . we went over there to civilize them and ended up getting barbarized).

Yep, we went in like boy scouts and came out like Hell's Angels.[37]

In the Philippines, regular U.S. Army units are alerted and deployed to South Vietnam as "advisers." James Crumley's novel One to Count Cadence *concerns the first formal U.S. troop movements into Vietnam.*

The company formation at 1300, for reasons of national security, was held in the mess hall. The Filipino KPs had been herded out to the volley-ball court, the louvers closed, and armed guards posted at every exit. The blackboard set up behind Saunders announced in small but clear letters: TOP SECRET. We were verbally reminded of the classification of the forthcoming talk, then it began.

It amounted, simply, to Vietnam for the 721st Communication Security Detachment, except that we became, in name only, the 1945th Communication Training Detachment (Provisional). Our assignment in the Republic of the Philippines was over, and our duties would be handled by Filipino operators now, ops that we would train as training for the time when we would begin training South Vietnamese ops. That time would come after we had set up a mobile det[atchment] in Vietnam. But still things weren't simple.

Because of the political implications of snooping on one's own army in a country where the army is in almost constant stages of revolt against the government, Diem had demanded the highest sort of security for our operation. "We will not," Saunders said, "be used as an arm of the political police," but no one had suggested that we would. For reasons of national security, Vietnamese, South, our Det would have to be located, not in Saigon where lovely chicks paraded in *au dais,* but the south of the central highlands, west by southwest of Nha Trang in the foothills of the Lang Bian mountains, hopefully out of the way of both the Vietcong and the bulk of the South Vietnamese generals. We would also travel to Vietnam in civilian clothes, but our old uniforms would be waiting for us at the new Det.

The major burden of perimeter defense would fall on three reinforced companies of provincial militia (and their families), but due to lack of training and weapons, etc. (the "etc.," patriotism, I assumed), we would have to be ready to be responsible for our own defense. We were going to soldier as well as clerk, for a change.

Our present operations closed as of this day, and one month of intensive training would begin immediately. Basic combat infantryman training in the mornings, working in the new vans, training Filipino ops, listening to tapes of South Vietnamese army tapes, and learning new net operations in the afternoons.

"Remember," Saunders said at the end, "that even though we are advisers in this no-war war, we have the right to fight back if attacked, and if we aren't mentally and physically ready to fight back, a bunch of you are going to find yourselves dead. If you want to stay alive: get ready." If he expected a Hollywood cheer, his face didn't show any disappointment when he didn't get it. "And I'll be kicking asses and taking names to be sure you do get ready." He smiled at the Head Moles, out of their holes for today, but they didn't smile back. They didn't go to Vietnam either, or to Hill 527, which was all I saw of Vietnam.

Comments as we left:

Novotny: Sorry, man, I'm too short to go.

Cagle: Reenlist, stupid.

Quinn: Big rumble tonight. Kick some ass, huh, Frankie?

Franklin: I'm a lover, not a fighter. I got a purple heart for the clap to prove it.

Haddad: My God, it'll cost me a fortune to go, a fortune, my God.

Peterson: Geez. . . .

Levenson and Collins: . . . (Nothing, because they both, like Novotny, had less than a month to go before their discharges.)

Morning: Fucking America off again to make the world safe for General Motors and AT&T. Tattletales to political spies in one easy step.

Quinn: I got lighter fluid and a lighter, mother, if you want to file your stinking protest right here in the hall.

Peterson: Geez. . . .

Krummel: Knock it off, you idiots.

Morning: You're sick, Quinn, sick.

Haddad: Wonder if the chaplain would understand my situation.

Krummel: Knock it off.

Quinn: I ain't a coward, and I ain't a Commie, and I ain't so sick I can't bust you up in the middle, Morning.

Cagle: Save your verbal enemas for the enemy, you guys.

Someone: Ah, shit, who gives a good goddamn?

Krummel: (whispering) I do.

Morning: (shouting) Me, mother-fucker. I fucking won't go.

Someone: Ah, shit.

But then it was time to go.

We flew to Saigon at night, then were hustled into an empty hangar with all our equipment, including the four vans. For twenty-four hours we lounged in our cheap civilian suits provided by the government, ate cold C-rations, slept on piles of barracks bags, and used five-gallon buckets for latrines while Saunders tried to find the trucks which were to carry us to the new Det. Our tribulations were just beginning.

When the trucks came, they were driven in one end of the hangar, loaded, then driven out the other end. The vans were to go next, but two of them wouldn't start, so we spent another six hours without barracks bags to lie on, without cold C-rations to gag on, but we still had the clammy cans to shit in, and one Lister bag of tepid water which seemed to have absorbed the stink from our bodies and the bitterness of the constant bitching from the men.

But then it was time to go, again.

We were loaded in trucks whose beds were covered with sandbags, then laced tightly shut, locked in our own stink. I assigned myself to my old Trick's truck, since I was in charge of assigning NCOs to keep the men from getting out of the trucks. While doing this, I noticed that the lead truck in the convoy pushed a heavy trailer arrangement in front of it like a cowcatcher in front of a train. A mine-catcher, I supposed, but I kept my suppositions to myself. The sandbagged floors and the company of ARVN troops riding shotgun in armored personnel carriers had already started talk, thought about death. But, as usual, dying was going to seem the easy part.

Sixteen men secured in the coarse, heavy heat, the constant sift of the sand, and the stench of each other and the tarstink of the canvas isn't a Sunday afternoon drive. Piss calls were infrequent, and we ate more cold C-rations and drank more water tasting of tin and dirt and last week's wash. Uncomfortable trip but uneventful, we drove through the first night, the next day, and that evening. Men slept, but a rough, fitful sleep as they tried to rest on the sandbags, or lean against the ribs, or each other. When the feeble light creeping through the canvas belied the raging sun above, some of them tried to play cards, but sandy dust and sweaty fingers chewed all the spots from the deck. Others tried to read, but raw-rimmed eyes couldn't follow the leaping, bounding words. Most sat silent in the grime of their bodies and in the blackness of their thoughts, wondering about the sandbags and wishing for the heft of a weapon in their hands. We all cursed—bitterly, without jokes—at everything, until the curses became as much a sound of the trip as the random rattling of the truck. Even asleep, each bump, each rut, each chuck hole drew forth epithets from sleepy mouths which never noted words passing.

But when the cowcatcher caught a mine and the convoy slammed to a halt, no one said a word. A single drawn breath robbed the truck of air, and we gasped like dying men. One man farted, another belched. Stomachs grumbled, guts contracted and growled in protest.

A few rounds were fired in front, then steady chatter and little pops as if from toy guns, then silence again. The Trick tried to climb out of the

truck over me, Franklin leading the way, shouting that he had to pee. I
pushed him back into the crowd, kept pushing until they all were down,
faces hugging the sandbags. Fear rose like a visible cloud from the huddled bodies, but I made them stay, while I dropped out the back and
crouched under the truck. Inside, Franklin groaned, trying to hold his
bladder, and Quinn shouted not to pee on him, but no one laughed, not
even Quinn.

The road, a track through a jungled forest, was gray in the light from a
moon as big and bright as a searchlight. *No one ambushes by moonlight,* I
thought, never thinking that those who would would do it in a way I
wasn't ready for yet. Murmurs, shrouded by canvas, seemed to fill the
space between the darkened trucks. Bodyless voices swept on a ghostly
wind, turned, then turned back, till they seemed my voice drifting away
from me. For an instant I was drunk with fear, and I knew the only way I
could control it was to do something, but there was nothing to do but
hold my bladder, keep my peace, and wait. Someone ran down the road
toward me, stopping at each truck, then angry, frightened whispers sawed
the night like the alarm cries of huge insects. Tetrick ran flatfooted like
an old cop chasing a young pickpocket, but an old cop who firmly intended to catch that pickpocket. I stood, whispered an order to stay down
inside the truck, then stepped out to meet him, already feeling better.

"What's up?" I asked, my tone calmer than I expected.

"Nothing," he said. "Just a mine. No real damage, but it will take
about half an hour to get the truck going again."

"Who fired?"

"Nervous fingers. One ARVN squad ran into another. One dead, four
wounded, and lucky at that. Idiots," he said. "Let the troops out for piss
call or they will be pissing all over themselves. Tell 'em, for God's sake,
stay on the road; the ditches may be mined." But as he said this, two
squads of ARVN troops ran past in both ditches heading toward the rear
of the convoy.

"Guess not," I said. As I looked, I saw a white track disappearing
quickly in the forest, a trail. "But I guess we're lucky."

"Keep 'em on the road anyway. Then get down to the weapons truck—
first one in front of the vans—and get yours. Okay?" he asked, then ran
off without an answer, his feet slapping against the dry road.

"Okay, you old ladies," I said, unlacing the canvas, "pull down your
bloomers, and come out to pee-pee. Trouble's all over, but stay on the
road. Novotny, keep them on the road." As I trotted away, I heard
Franklin's voice, high and loud with relief, "Sgt. Krummel, Quinn tried
to rape me while I was laying down," and Quinn's answer, "And I
woulda, if you hadn't been shaking like a twelve-year-old virgin," and
then his raw laughter. "Knock it off," I shouted over my shoulder, not
even hoping that they would.

Coming back, I tried to be casual, carrying the Armalite by its handle
like a suitcase, four grenades bagging the thin pockets of the civilian suit,

two full clips sticking out of my back pockets like fifths of cheap whiskey. Morning commented, of course, "Mamma Krummel back to protect his little brood," but I laughed at him. He expected push-ups and an ass-chewing, and grumbled. "It wasn't a joke," and I said, "Yes, I don't think so either." We smoked and talked quietly, our talk like the chatter from behind the other trucks, relaxed, confident, safe, but this cool babble couldn't cover the raw grunt and moan which slipped out of the forest to the right. No one spoke, then everyone, but the metallic clang of a round snapping into the Armalite stopped the noise. I sent Cagle for Tetrick, Morning to the truck cab for a flashlight, and the men into the opposite ditch, then gave Novotny two of the grenades.

Quinn's tooth flashed in the moonlight as he said, "Frankie, Frankie? Where you at, you ugly bastard."

One of the new men mumbled that he had been seen drifting down the moonlit trail. I gave Quinn the third grenade, then Morning the last when he came back with the flashlight.

"Five yards apart on me," I said. "Quinn last. No light yet. Morning behind me. Let's go," I said, then stepped off down the trail.

The trail seemed twice as white as I moved between the dark walls of foliage, following the faint trail of sharp prints made by new shoes in the dust, then the wavering serpentine track where he had peed as he strolled. The trail bent to the left, and as I cautiously slipped around the corner, I didn't need Morning's flash to see.

Malayan Gates, they call them, a bamboo pole tied to a tree beside the trail, a bamboo pole with three or four twelve-inch bamboo stakes lashed to its end, then bent away from the trail and tied to another tree and a trip wire. Franklin hadn't finished, and urine still dripped into the black pool at his feet where he knelt, his grey face turned back toward me, one arm pegged to his stomach where he had been holding himself, and the points of the stakes gleamed out of his back two inches about his belt. His eyes were wide and alive when I first saw him, but before I could move, they were wide, white and dead in his face. A muscle spasm gripped his mouth, and a rumbling, sputtering release from the large bowel mocked the prayer his mouth seemed to form, but his eyes were dead in his face. Morning quietly said "Jesus Christ" behind me. Novotny, stricken, mumbled "Told him to stay on the road. Told him . . . Told him . . . Told . . ." Quinn dropped his grenade and started to run. I laid the butt of the rifle into his stomach as he reached my side, laid it harder than I should have, but a rage clutched at my muscles, and I wouldn't have been surprised if I had started firing into Franklin's offending body. Quinn dropped to his knees and gagged.

"Take him back," I said, my voice colder than I could remember it ever being. "Take the son of a bitch back." I slapped Morning's shoulder and pushed Novotny. Their eyes came back to me from Franklin, then they started to stumble toward him. "No, you bastards, no! Quinn! Quinn! Take him back. Take the son of a bitch back." . . .

"Told him, told him to stay, stay on the road," Novotny gasped as we carried the surprising load, too light for man, too heavy for whatever it was.

"You told him; he didn't; forget it."

"Don't know how," was all he answered.

The troops, officers, non-coms and all, here is the first loss, forgot the standing orders against bunching up, bunched like cattle in the rain, lowing, and chewing their fearful lips.

"You?" Capt. Saunders said to Tetrick. Saunders stood among the troops, but they moved away when he spoke. He moved back among them.

Tetrick's head gleamed in the moonlight and his words were half lost under a dropped face. "Too tired," he said "Krummel, Krummel will."

Sure, sure, Krummel will. Yes, Krummel, savior of his brood, mother-hen to the world and that miscarriage in the poncho. Fuck yes, Krummel will!

I stripped back the poncho, and waited until the sight stuck in every mind, then said, not too loud but loud enough:

"Not much to send home to Mamma, is it?"

No one misunderstood. Now we were ready.[38]

1962 October—The Cuban missile crisis. Russians introduce medium-range ballistic missiles into Cuba; President Kennedy puts U.S. forces on worldwide alert and "quarantines" Cuba; Chairman Khrushchev withdraws missiles but gains pledge that United States will not invade the island.

Lieutenant Babbs keeps a journal, as will many Americans after him. From the combat zone, events "back in the world" take on a different perspective.

Even a big thing like the Kennedy-Khrushchev Cuba missile standoff escapes our attention. The same flavor pervades that news as it does all others. Unreal. A message from a foreign planet, via one of the prominent Science Fiction writers.

Lieutenant Cochran, squadron comic, has a positive slant: "Nuclear shit hit the atomic fan and we're in the safest place. No one's going to nuke Nam." . . .

At Soc Trang, South Vietnam, the short, dry, end-of-monsoons season whispers in on a hot wind. The usual three and four days of steady rain recede to a single afternoon's shower of hard fast duration. The nights are clear, and a breeze, not enough to ward off the mosquitoes, ripples the tent flaps. The morning sun bakes the asphalt runway and the water from yesterday's shower steams and condenses. . . .

The hot season reaches its zenith—three and four months of unrelenting heat—and the war that was stalled and mildewed picks up its tempo. VC are on the move. They pop out of canals and mangrove swamps to hit an outpost, capture guns and radios, disappear into the brush. ARVN plays hide and seek, tries to catch the attack before it happens, like an angry housewife stomping at an erratic cockroach before it makes the refuge between the baseboard and floor. . . .

Conversation overheard in the three-holer: Someday it will be over and we'll retire to that big outhouse in the sky where the fixtures are solid brass, the flushers never rust, the paper is always soft, and the stools are all pleasant. . . .

Our refrigerator in the tent is stocked with beer and mix. The R-4-D makes a weekly booze run to Saigon. I've acquired the gin and tonic habit. Very colonial. We barter across the fence with Vietnamese for French cheese and English crackers. In the evenings, back from our resupply runs, we gather on the porch, mix drinks in our metal mess gear cups, prepare hors d'oeuvres, have a pleasant chat before staggering to chow: char-broiled steaks. . . .

We operate to maximum: mechs work all night to have twelve to twenty choppers out every day, flying dawn to dusk, setting records for hours flown, passengers hauled, tons of cargo carried. Pride busting: doing more for less.

The Delta is flat, well-suited for helicopter operations. Even during the rainy season, while the ground is flooded, there is no great problem in setting a helicopter down in the two-foot-deep water.

Up north, around Da Nang, the terrain is mountainous, jungle, rain forests, trees three hundred feet high, clearings infrequent, and the land controlled by the VC. The Army is still flying the obsolete twin-rotor bananas, same engine as our H-34s, but they can't carry as heavy a load. The birds are mechanical monsters. Crews don't work all night to keep them flying. Different place, different pace.

Inscrutability. Dragging on and on. We the people are here because orders say so. What we get out of it depends on what we're looking for. For some, air medals, badges of glory, but no gory—please. For others, the warriors, war! A poor war admittedly but the only one we got. For Washington, a testing ground for tactics and weapons. For Saigon, an accumulation of American money and supplies. At a remote outpost, plenty of beer and rice magically dropped from the skies in a magnificent green whirlybird, splendid in its tricks and capers, delightful to watch and touch, particularly the amazing giants who make it perform.

In spite of the rain, the mud, the rumors, the hours of flying, the feeling it is pretty much wasted effort, it is an interesting experience and at times fun.

Y'know, the thing that's interesting about Vietnam is there's nothing on the line for us. Not as if we're fighting for our soil, our homes, our families, against a foreign invader.

Nope, we're here to assist the SVN against invasion from the NVN, but there's no invasion so far and who can tell the difference between a SVN and a NVN unless it's in an accent and habits of living in a slightly different climate and terrain like the diff between a Yankee trader and a southern farmer in the good old U S of A.

So I guess it's a matter of governments. We prop up theirs with ours but what's in it for us other than the usual tirades 'gainst the inroads of bogeyman Communism? . . . mus' be more to it . . . like say, Hiltons on the beachfront. Off shore oil wells in the South China Sea. Opium poppy farms in the highlands . . . big buck ball games and troops the expend-able pawns . . . or how about inordinate pride as the reason?

What the U.S. backs, the U.S. will make damned sure wins . . . the prestige race . . . convince rest of doubting world we are number one . . . not Russia . . . ideologies and ideas holding nations in bondage of war to prove they're right, by God! Fer, din't ya know, we're on His side so whatever we do's gotta succeed, right?

Time will tell, but looks to me like we're pissing our goodies into a sinkhole . . . and there's no bottom.[39]

Because of the secrecy and the political sensitivity of the American pres-ence, Rules of Engagement (ROE) are strict. According to one U.S. Ma-rine Corps history:

COMUSMACV, in Directive Number 62 of 24 November [1962], im-posed certain operational restrictions upon various categories of U.S. aircraft in SVN. The directive stated that the general aviation mission of all deployed U.S. aviation units was to provide training and support to the RVNAF in its counterinsurgency effort. Because of varied aircraft configurations and missions capabilities, mission types are defined as:

a. *Non-Operational:*
   (1) Training: Training flights are those carried out to transition Viet-namese or U.S. pilots into new aircraft, and for tactical upgrading and instruction of pilots and crews to develop better tactics and techniques, to include accelerated combat crew training under combat conditions.
   (2) Support: Typical missions are administrative, liaison, ferry, courier, logistics, flight proficiency, air rescue and maintenance test.
b. *Operational:*
   (1) Combat: Combat missions are always accomplished utilizing armed aircraft. Such missions include close air support, interdiction, escort, air cover, armed reconnaissance and air defense.
   (2) Combat Support: Combat support missions may be carried out with either armed or unarmed aircraft. Such missions include airborne forward air control, artillery adjustment, combat support liaison/observation, re-connaissance, aerial communications relay, airborne guide, defoliation, flare drop, airborne/airfield assault, airborne resupply and airborne com-

mand post. Psywar broadcast and leaflet drop will not be conducted except under unusual circumstances. . . .

GENERAL POLICY

a. In South Vietnam all operational missions flown by U.S. personnel and/or aircraft are classified as combat support. As a general policy, no missions will be undertaken utilizing U.S. personnel and/or aircraft unless it is beyond the capability of the Vietnamese Air Force (because of lack of training, equipment, etc.) to perform the mission. Efforts will be intensified to provide the necessary training for GVN personnel so that the VNAF can perform all required missions at the earliest possible time.[40]

Providing an overview, Assistant Secretary of State Roger Hilsman describes his perception of events at the end of 1962.

Another related sign was a slight stiffening in Viet Cong resistance, a return, really, of their old aggressiveness. Like the French, the American military kept hoping that the Viet Cong would someday, someplace, stand and fight, although they knew full well that guerrillas avoid pitched battle except at times and places that they are convinced that they can win. This was why a seemingly insignificant incident in early October was worrisome to the men in the field—and, as it happened because of President Diem's reaction to it, this particular incident was much more significant than even the men in the field realized at the time. Elements of the Seventh Division, stationed in the delta in the region around the town of My Tho, were on a routine sweep, when suddenly one of the Viet Cong units chose to turn and fight. It wiped out a whole platoon of Rangers, among the best troops the government had.

As a sign of stiffening Viet Cong resistance, the incident was bad. But it had even longer-range repercussions when President Diem heard about it. For a few days later, Diem called the Seventh Division commander to Saigon and rebuked him for his high rate of casualties and, intentionally or not, discouraged him from undertaking too many offensive operations.

No one knows what Diem's reasons for this action were. It could be argued that he sensed that defeating the guerrillas would be a long, slow process and that it would be better to husband the strength of the government forces rather than dissipate it in too much American "gung ho" offensive-mindedness. The basic idea of the strategic hamlet program was consistent with a slow approach in its stress on the "oil blot" principle.* But he never raised this question with either General Harkins or Ambassador Nolting, who did not learn of Diem's "go slow" instructions until much, much later. And this gives credibility to the rival explanation, which a few of the military advisers in the field adopted as well as most of

---

*The current U.S. theory that pacified areas would spread out from a central point. [Ed.]

the American press, particularly David Halberstam of the New York *Times* and Neil Sheehan of the United Press International.

THE PRESS VIEW

Halberstam and Sheehan started with the conviction that the struggle against the guerrillas could not be won with Ngo Dinh Diem and his regime. Diem, they felt, was an unpopular dictator, hearing and believing nothing but what his baleful brother, Ngo Dinh Nhu, and Madame Nhu told him. Because of its unpopularity, the regime adopted more and more repressive measures, and this made it inefficient as well. Province chiefs, corps commanders, division and regimental commanders, and even battalion commanders, were promoted, according to this thesis, not because of their effectiveness as soldiers but as a result of personal loyalty to the Ngos. This made for inefficient, cowardly leadership—it led, the argument concluded, to "political" generals who would not fight and who falsified the records.

Halberstam and Sheehan made friends with Lieutenant Colonel John Paul Vann, senior American adviser to the Seventh Division, an energetic, idealistic, dynamic officer with strong convictions about the need for a more aggressive and efficient conduct of the war and a willingness, in order to achieve it, to tread on the toes of either his Vietnamese counterparts or his own American superiors. The town of My Tho and the Seventh Division heaquarters were only forty kilometers by road from Saigon—a quick and easy drive—and Vann became a major source for Halberstam and Sheehan and served as their litmus paper to test the progress of the "shooting war." In the weeks following Diem's admonition to the Seventh Division commander, Colonel Vann—and through him Halberstam and Sheehan—became convinced that the Seventh Division was conducting operations against places that intelligence indicated were *free* of Viet Cong. This would inflate General Harkins' statistics on offensive operations, but avoid casualties. And when operations were mounted against areas where the Viet Cong really were, Vann and the newsmen were also convinced, the battle plans left a gap through which the Viet Cong might escape—again as a device for keeping government casualties low.

The evidence to support this interpretation of what was happening in the fall of 1962 in Vietnam is laid out in Halberstam's book, *The Making of a Quagmire.* In it, for example, he argues that in the end the helicopters did more harm than good, for they permitted the government forces to conduct operations on regular "office hours"—out in the field in the morning and back at base by cocktail hour. But Colonel Vann and the two or three other military advisers who were convinced that the "shooting war" was not going well were not able to convince the American military headquarters in Saigon of the merit of their view, nor were Halberstam and Sheehan doing much better in gaining adherents in Washington. Neither did very well, that is, until the battle of Ap Bac, which was a village near My Tho.

THE BATTLE OF AP BAC

Regular troops and conventional tactics are not effective against the guerrilla, and the more they are used the more frustration mounts. As late as October 1964, for example, a senior military spokesman in Saigon, speaking of ambushes, said, "Our fervent hope is that they'll stick their neck out with about six battalions around here some day and try to hold something, because as of that time, they've had it. . . . The VC are excellent at ambushes, but that's kind of a coward's way of fighting the war . . ."

The trouble, of course, is that if the guerrilla knows his job he will avoid a set-piece battle unless the cards are stacked in his favor. Very occasionally, however, a trap will work, and the guerrilla will be forced into a set-piece battle. This is what happened at Ap Bac.

Good intelligence was received in the last few days of December 1962 that a battalion of Viet Cong numbering about two hundred men were at the little village of Ap Bac. The government plan called for landing one battalion of regular forces by helicopter just north of the village to pin the Viet Cong down, while two battalions of civil guard troops would come up on foot from the south. Air and artillery support were also available, but most important of all was a company of armored and amphibious personnel carriers mounting a fifty caliber machine gun and recoilless rifles. Called 113s, these vehicles were the nearest thing to a tank in Vietnam, and their role at Ap Bac was to assault the Viet Cong position from the west. There was also a reserve force standing by with helicopters to fly them to whatever spot they were needed as the battle developed.

The first of the government battalions was landed without much trouble—the Viet Cong held their fire to avoid giving away their positions, while they probed for a way out to the south. Their probe met the first of the civil guard battalions, and they shifted their probe to the west. Here they ran into the second civil guard battalion and apparently saw the armored personnel carriers coming up still farther to the west. So the Viet Cong commander decided to return to the prepared positions at Ap Bac and give battle—"It is better," he wrote in his after-action report, which was later captured, "to stand and die than run and be slaughtered."

Back in their foxholes, the Viet Cong quickly pinned down the government troops advancing from the north through the flat paddy fields. The government commander and Colonel Vann then decided to land the reserve force by helicopter just west of the village. The Viet Cong had a clear field of fire on the helicopters as they came in with their troops. Five helicopters were shot down, three Americans were killed along with a large number of the Vietnamese troops as they left the helicopters and spread out toward the village.

Urgent orders went to the armored 113s to attack and relieve the situation—but the commander, whom Halberstam in his account calls a "key Diem appointee," refused to take his vehicles through the network of canals and paddy fields. The American adviser to the 113 unit finally scouted a route through the paddy fields himself, but it took the force four hours to cover it, although they took only fifteen minutes coming back over the same route. And when they finally did get to the scene of the battle, they still hung back, firing their machine guns and recoilless rifles blind, crouched down behind the armor.

The two civil guard battalions to the south came under the command of the province chief, rather than the Seventh Division—an arrangement, Halberstam says, that Diem and Nhu used in order to play province chiefs and division commanders off against each other. In any case, this particular province chief refused several requests to attack and relieve the two regular battalions. One of the civil guard battalion commanders, in fact, saw the opportunity in front of him and himself requested permission to attack. But the province chief insisted that his troops were there to form a blocking position, not to attack.

That night the Viet Cong slipped away, carrying their own dead, but leaving behind the government casualties—sixty-one dead and over one hundred wounded. It was a stunning defeat for the government forces. They had outnumbered the Viet Cong at least four to one. They had the mobility of helicopters. They had the superior firepower of artillery. They had support from the air. They had the awesome might of the armored personnel carriers. Yet they had been badly beaten.

What Colonel Vann and Halberstam had been saying about the inefficiency, bad leadership, and lack of aggressiveness of the government forces seemed to be confirmed—if not their conclusion that the cause of it all was the corruption and unpopularity of the Diem regime. The Diem government, naturally, tried to put the battle in the most optimistic light by arguing that the Viet Cong had suffered even more heavily than the government. It disgusted the American reporters that the American military headquarters did not deny this interpretation. It disgusted them even more when American headquarters actually seemed to agree with that interpretation. Then, a few days later, General Harkins himself called Ap Bac a "Vietnamese victory," because it had "taken the objective"—and their disgust was complete. . . .

All this was worsened by ineptness on the part of both the embassy and the American military headquarters in the way they handled the press. Ambassador Nolting argued with the press, usually accepting Diem's side of a controversy, and rarely if ever gave them a story. General Harkins gave the appearance of distrusting them. He refused, for example, to give American newsmen advance notice of operations because of the danger of leaks to the Viet Cong—a position which seemed to question the reporters' patriotism. In general, the attitude among high American military officers made the reporters feel that they were expected to write just what the military wanted them to write. The reporters frequently cited the remark Admiral Felt, Commander in Chief in the Pacific, made on first meeting Neil Sheehan—"So you're Sheehan. Why don't you get on the team?"

But even with the most skillful and sympathetic treatment, relations with the press would still have been troubled, for the government and the press had fundamentally different interests. The United States Government, for example, had introduced aircraft with the "Farmgate" units that were not provided for under the Geneva agreements and had increased the number of American advisers far past the six hundred permitted under those agreements. The American government believed that these moves were fully justified by the fact that it was the North Vietnamese that had started the guerrilla aggression in South Vietnam in violation of the Geneva agreements, but at the same time the American government did not want what they were doing highly publicized. The interest of the American press on the other hand—even their duty, as they saw it—was to inform the American public fully on what their government was doing. And I must confess that my own instincts in this case were on the side of the reporters. In March of 1962, after returning from my second trip to Vietnam, what seemed to me most urgently in need of revision was the policy of trying to keep "Farmgate" and the extent of American Air Force participation secret. We in the State Department had made too much of the political costs of a violation of the Geneva accords that was in truth fully justified by Communist aggression, and the President had made too much of adverse press reaction. In this early period, at least, it was a fair criticism to say that, whereas Eisenhower had read the newspapers too little, Kennedy was reading them too much.

In late November 1962, American reporters had been excluded by the Vietnamese Government from an operation that had involved forty-five American helicopters, the largest so far on the grounds, they later said, that they were afraid one might be killed. This made the reporters angry and what made them even angrier was that the American mission took it lying down. But this had now been corrected—American reporters could go where American soldiers went—so the reporters with whom I met had no complaints about the co-operativeness of the American authorities. As for the Vietnamese authorities things had not improved, but the reporters seemed to feel that recently, at least, the mission had supported the newsmen better than they had in the past. As for the war, they seemed to agree that the influx of military aid and helicopters had helped—but most of them emphatically did not agree that the optimism of Harkins and the American military headquarters was justified. One reporter, Charles Mohr, told me something that seemed particularly significant—that from the beginning of his tour in Vietnam he had driven regularly the forty miles to My Tho, in the Seventh Division area, but that the road was no longer safe. Mohr felt that the basic trouble was that the Ngo family, and particularly Nhu, were unalterably hostile to the United States. The only difference of opinion between us was that it seemed to me that our objective was not to be liked, but to get a job done.

So once again the judgment was mixed. Most of the reporters in Vietnam could agree both that Diem had obvious and serious flaws and that he also had impressive strengths. But they differed on whether it would be strengths or weaknesses that tipped the balance in the struggle with the Communists.[41]

1962 **31 December**—U.S. casualties to date: 42 KIA; 81 WIA (DOD/ OASD 27 Mar 75). Total U.S. military strength: 11,300 (DOD/ OASD 19 Mar 74).
1963 **5 February**—The American press reports the "first [U.S.] heli- copter . . . shot down by the enemy."

In April the CIA reports to the secretary of defense on the situation in Vietnam.

PROSPECTS IN SOUTH VIETNAM

A. We believe that Communist progress has been blunted and that the situation is improving. Strengthened South Vietnamese capabilities and effectiveness, and particularly US involvement, are causing the Viet Cong increased difficulty, although there are as yet no persuasive indications that the Communists have been grievously hurt. . . .

B. We believe the Communists will continue to wage a war of attrition, hoping for some break in the situation which will lead to victory. They evidently hope that a combination of military pressure and political dete- rioration will in time create favorable circumstances either for delivering a *coup de grâce* or for a political settlement which will enable them to continue the struggle on more favorable terms. We believe it unlikely, especially in view of the open US commitment, that the North Viet- namese regime will either resort to overt military attack or introduce acknowledged North Vietnamese military units into the south in an effort to win a quick victory. . . .

C. Assuming no great increase in external support to the Viet Cong, changes and improvements which have occurred during the past year now indicate that the Viet Cong can be contained militarily and that further progress can be made in expanding the area of government control and in creating greater security in the countryside.[42]

In Vietnam, however, some Americans feel less optimistic. The main char- acter in Charles Larson's novel The Chinese Game *is a U.S. Army captain named Belgard. Wounded, he is being evacuated to Saigon.*

"You know what's wrong with this fouled-up hemorrhoid of a war?" the pilot demanded. "There's no ruttin' villains."

The icy air lay like a plastic sheet on Belgard's lungs; he could no longer feel anything at all in his injured leg. He had been given the seat next to the pilot out of deference to his rank, but Grainger, crouched behind and between them, could at least stretch full length when the cramp in his haunch became unbearable.

"You think about that," the pilot shouted over the engine noise. On his egg-bald head he wore a shapeless stocking cap, lovingly knitted for him, he had declared, by an eight-year-old Hong Kong whore named Deborah. "Who do we hiss? Ho? Come on, for Christ's sake, the old gentleman's a patriot and an underdog, and any red-blooded American who'd hiss an underdog has got to be a pretty dangerous pervert, Captain, now you *know* that. So who? Kennedy? Kennedy inherited the mess from Eisenhower. Eisenhower? Bite your *tongue!* The Cong's trying to unite his tortured land. The G.I.'s trying to honor a commitment. We're all being pulled hither and yon, Captain—hither, thither, and yon."

"Like puppets," said Grainger.

"Like fouled-up bloody puppets."

Smoke from hundreds of jungle fires drifted along the shattered canyons and mingled with the seasonal haze to half hide the toothy peaks alongside them. The Montagnards were preparing their hills for rice and poppies. "There'll be a way out," Belgard said.

"Of this war?" shouted the pilot. "Never. We'll all be frozen with our hands around each other's throats. We'll all die cold and surprised, but we'll die."

"I don't agree."

"Captain, this isn't a nineteen forty-three movie. Don Ameche isn't going to win the girl. The girl's going to be decapitated in an air raid, and a defective gun's going to blow up in Don Ameche's face, and the last word everybody hears won't be 'love,' it'll be 'kill.' "

"If that's the script the audience buys, it isn't the producer who's sick, it's the audience."

"That may be—"

"And if that's the movie I'm seeing, Lieutenant, I'll walk out."

"That's the movie you're *in*, Captain."

"I can still walk out."

"Have you tried?"[43]

The movielike quality of the increasingly violent situation is also evident in the following events described by Nguyen Cao Ky, who is a South Vietnamese Air Force (VNAF) lieutenant colonel.

Roughly eleven million of the country's fifteen million people were Buddhists but only about one in four of them—about four million—were practicing followers of the Buddha. As a Catholic who at one time had been intended for the priesthood, Diem had spent much of his time in Catholic retreats in the United States before his return to government in Vietnam. The million Catholic refugees who crossed the 17th parallel from North Vietnam at the time of partition were among his strongest supporters. They established themselves in Catholic communities, principally in central Vietnam, which was also the stronghold of Buddhism. Soon the Buddhists became envious, claiming that the newly arrived Catholics were being allotted the most fertile land and receiving the biggest grants for schools and hospitals.

The friction between Buddhists and Catholics came to a head in 1963 in Hue, traditional seat of Buddhism in Vietnam, when rival celebrations clashed. The Buddhists were celebrating the anniversary of the Buddha's birth; the Catholics were commemorating the anniversary of the consecration of the Archbishop of Hue. The Catholics were allowed to fly the Vatican flag and parade sacred objects; the Buddhists were refused permission to do the same.

On May 8, the Buddha's birthday, Buddhists converged outside the radio station in Hue. When ordered to disperse they refused. Fire hoses and tear gas failed to drive them away. On Nhu's orders Major Dang Sy, deputy chief of the province and a Catholic, ordered live ammunition and grenades to be issued. Nine Buddhists died, killed by Sy's forces according to the Buddhist leaders, by Communist grenades according to Nhu.

The fuse was lit. In Saigon a saffron-robed priest had himself soaked in gasoline and then committed sacrificial suicide by fire at a busy road junction. Six more were to follow his example. The dramatic newsreel and press pictures went around the world and the world was horrified. Students in Saigon and Hue, not notably militant before, took to the streets in demonstrations. Diem acceded to certain Buddhist demands, including their right to fly flags, but Nhu called him a coward for these concessions.

It was at this moment that Madame Nhu uttered the words that made her one of the most despised women of our age, when she cried, "I would clap my hands at seeing another monk barbecue show."[44]

On the surface, the situation in Laos appears much calmer than in Vietnam. Robin Moore's novel The Green Berets *documents what is going on there.*

The United States officially withdrew its military assistance from Laos as a result of the Geneva accords which in theory neutralized the country in October of 1962. Fortunately, a few highly placed Americans were wise enough to realize that the Communists might not abide by the agreements they had signed and the Communist Pathet Lao with the assistance of their Uncle Ho in North Vietnam would again try to take over Laos.

With the Royal Laotian Army torn by political dissension and hardly a match for a determined Communist drive, attention turned to one group of fighting men who in the opinion of the U.S. Central Intelligence Agency, which was then in charge of Special Forces activities in Laos, would make the effort to stand up against the Pathet Lao and North Vietnamese Viet

Cong troops, or Viet Minh as they are still called in Laos—the hardy Meo tribesmen. A product of different ethnic origins from the torpid Laotians, they would fight bravely for their mountaintop homes. They would also, when properly led and supplied, carry on guerrilla warfare against the Communists. Thus, it was Meos who were trained and armed by Special Forces teams to resist Communist aggression.

One of the most successful Special Forces officers to work with the Meo tribesmen had been Major Bernard Arklin. Operating under the control of the CIA, Arklin's Special Forces team equipped and trained a large group of Meo tribesmen who took a heavy toll of Pathet Lao lives and equipment in 1962, when the Communists pushed through the jungles toward Vientiane, the capital of Laos, unopposed by the fleeing Royal Laotian troops.

With the end of official military assistance, the Central Intelligence Agency decided that Arklin was one of the men they needed to covertly keep the Meos in readiness to resist any possible Communist attacks in violation of the Geneva convention.

Arklin had just become reacquainted with his wife and three children back at Fort Bragg and was beginning to develop a taste for normal home life when he received orders sending him on detached service with the CIA in Thailand.

In Bangkok, Arklin began to feel his first excitement—and a sense of impending accomplishment—over the opportunity of rejoining the Meo tribesmen at the eastern approaches to the strategic Plain of Jars. This time he would not be wearing a uniform, but would dress as did his charges—in camouflage suits, miscellaneous clothing and the native loin-cloth. The only thing that distressed Arklin was that he could neither send nor receive mail. Methuan, his CIA control, would typewrite inconsequential letters to Arklin's wife above the endearments and signatures previously signed by Arklin on a large number of blank pieces of stationery to keep her from wondering what had happened to him.

In mid-June of 1963 Major Arklin took off from a small airstrip in the north of Thailand on the Laos border. He was equipped with a powerful radio transmitter, a medical kit (Arklin had been crosstrained as a medic) and as many weapons and boxes of ammunition as could be crowded into the single-engine plane. It was Arklin's third trip from the control base in Thailand to his Meo headquarters. This time he would be staying.[45]

In Vietnam, however, the situation has reached a crisis point. Nguyen Cao Ky remembers:

According to Nhu, the Buddhists were merely seeking publicity and were influenced by Communists. Dying for a cause did not make it just, he declared, and determined to teach the Buddhists a lesson. On August 21, 1963, he acted ferociously. Using white-uniformed Special Forces and combat police—largely paid for by American money—he stormed the Xa Loi and other venerated Buddhist pagodas throughout the country. In all, 1,400 men, mostly monks, were dragged to jails where they were beaten, half starved, sometimes subjected to electric shock torture. The American embassy was horrified, and taken completely by surprise. This was no accident. To make sure the Americans could not interfere during the long hours of the night, Nhu's men cut all the phone wires to the embassy.

That was the night of the pagodas. The following evening Henry Cabot Lodge arrived as American ambassador, succeeding Ambassador Frederick Nolting. That was the week when finally the Americans decided to get rid of their protégé, not by ordering Diem out of office, which would smack of colonialism (and would have outraged the Vietnamese) but by the simpler method of backing a group of generals who had long been planning a coup.[46]

On the day of his arrival in Saigon, (24 August 1963) Ambassador Lodge receives this message from Secretary of State Dean Rusk.

IT IS NOW CLEAR THAT WHETHER MILITARY PROPOSED MARTIAL LAW OR WHETHER NHU TRICKED THEM INTO IT, NHU TOOK ADVANTAGE OF ITS IMPOSITION TO SMASH PAGODAS WITH POLICE AND TUNG'S SPECIAL FORCES LOYAL TO HIM, THUS PLACING ONUS ON MILITARY IN EYES OF WORLD AND VIETNAMESE PEOPLE. ALSO CLEAR THAT NHU HAS MANEUVERED HIMSELF INTO COMMANDING POSITION.

US GOVERNMENT CANNOT TOLERATE SITUATION IN WHICH POWER LIES IN NHU'S HANDS. DIEM MUST BE GIVEN CHANCE TO RID HIMSELF OF NHU AND HIS COTERIE AND REPLACE THEM WITH BEST MILITARY AND POLITICAL PERSONALITIES AVAILABLE.

IF, IN SPITE OF ALL OF YOUR EFFORTS, DIEM REMAINS OBDURATE AND REFUSES, THEN WE MUST FACE THE POSSIBILITY THAT DIEM HIMSELF CANNOT BE PRESERVED. . . .

AMBASSADOR AND COUNTRY TEAM SHOULD URGENTLY EXAMINE ALL POSSIBLE ALTERNATIVE LEADERSHIP AND MAKE DETAILED PLANS AS TO HOW WE MIGHT BRING ABOUT DIEM'S REPLACEMENT IF THIS SHOULD BECOME NECESSARY.

ASSUME YOU WILL CONSULT WITH GENERAL HARKINS RE ANY PRECAUTIONS NECESSARY PROTECT AMERICAN PERSONNEL DURING CRISIS PERIOD.

YOU WILL UNDERSTAND THAT WE CANNOT FROM WASHINGTON GIVE YOU DETAILED INSTRUCTIONS AS TO HOW THIS OPERATION SHOULD PROCEED, BUT YOU WILL ALSO KNOW WE WILL BACK YOU TO THE HILT ON ACTIONS YOU TAKE TO ACHIEVE OUR OBJECTIVES.

NEEDLESS TO SAY WE HAVE HELD KNOWLEDGE OF THIS TELEGRAM TO MINIMUM ESSENTIAL PEOPLE AND ASSUME YOU WILL TAKE SIMILAR PRECAUTIONS TO PREVENT PREMATURE LEAKS.[47]

The next day Ambassador Lodge replies to Rusk and Assistant Secretary of State Roger Hilsman.

BELIEVE THAT CHANCES OF DIEM'S MEETING OUR DEMANDS ARE VIRTUALLY NIL. AT SAME TIME, BY MAKING THEM WE GIVE NHU CHANCE TO FORESTALL OR BLOCK ACTION BY MILITARY. RISK, WE BELIEVE, IS NOT WORTH TAKING, WITH NHU IN CONTROL COMBAT FORCES SAIGON.

THEREFORE, PROPOSE WE GO STRAIGHT TO GENERALS WITH OUR DEMANDS, WITHOUT INFORMING DIEM. WOULD TELL THEM WE PREPARED HAVE DIEM WITHOUT NHUS BUT IT IS IN EFFECT UP TO THEM WHETHER TO KEEP HIM. WOULD ALSO INSIST GENERALS TAKE STEPS TO RELEASE BUDDHIST LEADERS AND CARRY OUT JUNE 16 AGREEMENT.

REQUEST IMMEDIATE MODIFICATION INSTRUCTIONS. HOWEVER, DO NOT PROPOSE MOVE UNTIL WE ARE SATISFIED WITH E AND E PLANS [Escape and Evasion]. HARKINS CONCURS. I PRESENT CREDENTIALS PRESIDENT DIEM TOMORROW 11 A.M.[48]

A few days later (29 August) Ambassador Lodge cables Rusk in Washington.

WE ARE LAUNCHED ON A COURSE FROM WHICH THERE IS NO RESPECTABLE TURNING BACK: THE OVERTHROW OF THE DIEM GOVERNMENT. THERE IS NO TURNING BACK IN PART BECAUSE U.S. PRESTIGE IS ALREADY PUBLICLY COMMITTED TO THIS END IN LARGE MEASURE AND WILL BECOME MORE SO AS THE FACTS LEAK OUT. IN A MORE FUNDAMENTAL SENSE, THERE IS NO TURNING BACK BECAUSE THERE IS NO POSSIBILITY, IN MY VIEW, THAT THE WAR CAN BE WON UNDER A DIEM ADMINISTRATION, STILL LESS THAT DIEM OR ANY MEMBER OF THE FAMILY CAN GOVERN THE COUNTRY IN A WAY TO GAIN THE SUPPORT OF THE PEOPLE WHO COUNT, I.E., THE EDUCATED CLASS IN AND OUT OF GOVERNMENT SERVICE, CIVIL AND MILITARY—NOT TO MENTION THE AMERICAN PEOPLE. IN THE LAST FEW MONTHS (AND ESPECIALLY DAYS) THEY HAVE IN FACT POSITIVELY ALIENATED THESE PEOPLE TO AN INCALCULABLE DEGREE. SO THAT I AM PERSONALLY IN FULL AGREEMENT WITH THE POLICY WHICH I WAS INSTRUCTED TO CARRY OUT BY LAST SUNDAY'S TELEGRAM.

2. THE CHANCE OF BRINGING OFF A GENERALS' COUP DEPENDS ON THEM TO SOME EXTENT, BUT IT DEPENDS AT LEAST AS MUCH ON US.

3. WE SHOULD PROCEED TO MAKE ALL-OUT EFFORT TO GET GENERALS TO MOVE PROMPTLY. TO DO SO WE SHOULD HAVE AUTHORITY TO DO FOLLOWING:

(A) THAT GEN. HARKINS REPEAT TO GENERALS PERSONALLY MESSAGE PREVIOUSLY TRANSMITTED BY CAS[*] OFFICERS. THIS SHOULD ESTABLISH THEIR AUTHENTICITY. GEN. HARKINS SHOULD HAVE ORDER ON THIS.

*Controlled American Source: code name for CIA.

(B) IF NEVERTHELESS GENERALS INSIST ON PUBLIC STATEMENT THAT ALL U.S. AID TO VN THROUGH DIEM REGIME HAS BEEN STOPPED, WE WOULD AGREE, ON EXPRESS UNDERSTANDING THAT GENERALS WILL HAVE STARTED AT SAME TIME. (WE WOULD SEEK PERSUADE GENERALS THAT IT WOULD BE BETTER TO HOLD THIS CARD FOR USE IN EVENT OF STALEMATE. WE HOPE IT WILL NOT BE NECESSARY TO DO THIS AT ALL.)

(C) VNESE GENERALS DOUBT THAT WE HAVE THE WILL POWER, COURAGE, AND DETERMINATION TO SEE THIS THING THROUGH. THEY ARE HAUNTED BY THE IDEA THAT WE WILL RUN OUT ON THEM EVEN THOUGH WE HAVE TOLD THEM PURSUANT TO INSTRUCTIONS, THAT THE GAME HAD STARTED. . . .

6. I REALIZE THAT THIS COURSE INVOLVES A VERY SUBSTANTIAL RISK OF LOSING VN. IT ALSO INVOLVES SOME ADDITIONAL RISK TO AMERICAN LIVES. I WOULD NEVER PROPOSE IT IF I FELT THERE WAS A REASONABLE CHANCE OF HOLDING VN WITH DIEM. . . .

8. . . . GEN. HARKINS THINKS THAT I SHOULD ASK DIEM TO GET RID OF THE NHUS BEFORE STARTING THE GENERALS' ACTION. BUT I BELIEVE THAT SUCH A STEP HAS NO CHANCE OF GETTING THE DESIRED RESULT AND WOULD HAVE THE VERY SERIOUS EFFECT OF BEING REGARDED BY THE GENERALS AS A SIGN OF AMERICAN INDECISION AND DELAY. I BELIEVE THIS IS A RISK WHICH WE SHOULD NOT RUN. THE GENERALS DISTRUST US TOO MUCH ALREADY. ANOTHER POINT IS THAT DIEM WOULD CERTAINLY ASK FOR TIME TO CONSIDER SUCH A FAR-REACHING REQUEST. THIS WOULD GIVE THE BALL TO NHU.

9. WITH THE EXCEPTION OF PAR. 8 ABOVE GEN. HARKINS CONCURS IN THIS TELEGRAM.[49]

On 12 September President Kennedy holds a press conference.

Q. "Mr. President, in view of the prevailing confusion, is it possible to state today just what this Government's policy is toward the current government of South Viet-Nam?
THE PRESIDENT: "I think I have stated what my view is and we are for those things and those policies which help win the war there. That is why some 25,000 Americans have traveled 10,000 miles to participate in that struggle. What helps to win the war, we support; what interferes with the war effort, we oppose. I have already made it clear that any action by either government which may handicap the winning of the war is inconsistent with our policy or our objectives. This is the test which I think every agency and official of the United States Government must apply to all of our actions, and we shall be applying that test in various ways in the coming months, although I do not think it desirable to state all of our views at this time. I think they will be made more clear as time goes on.

"But we have a very simple policy in that area, I think. In some ways I think the Vietnamese people and ourselves agree; we want the war to be won, the Communists to be contained, and the Americans to go home.

That is our policy. I am sure it is the policy of the people of Viet-Nam. But we are not there to see a war lost, and we will follow the policy which I have indicated today of advancing those causes and issues which help win the war."[50]

Three weeks later President Kennedy orders General Maxwell Taylor and Secretary McNamara to visit Vietnam and assess the situation. Their conclusions follow.

Memorandum for the President

2 October 1963

MILITARY SITUATION AND TRENDS

The test of the military situation is whether the GVN is succeeding in widening its area of effective control of the population and the countryside. This is difficult to measure, and cannot be stated simply in terms of the number of strategic hamlets built or the number of roads that can now be travelled without escort. Nor can the overall situation be gauged solely in terms of the extent of GVN offensive action, relative weapon losses and defections, VC strength figures, or other measures of military performance. All of these factors are important and must be taken into account; however, a great deal of judgment is required in their interpretation. . . .

INDICATORS

	JUNE	JULY	AUGUST	SEPTEMBER (ESTIMATED)	MONTH AVERAGE YEAR AGO
No. of government initiated:					
Small operations	851	781	733	906	490
Large operations	125	163	166	141	71
Viet Cong Killed	1,896	1,918	1,685	2,034	2,000
GVN Killed	413	521	410	525	431
GVN Weapons Lost	590	780	720	802	390
VC Weapons Captured	390	375	430	400	450
Viet Cong Military Defectors	420	310	220	519	90
Viet Cong Initiated Incidents of all Types	1,310	1,380	1,375	1,675	1,660
Viet Cong Attacks	410	410	385	467	410
Estimated Viet Cong Strength					
Hard Core	21,000	21,000	21,000	21,000	22,000
Irregular	85,000	82,000	76,000	70,000	98,000

CONCLUSIONS

1. The military campaign has made great progress and continues to progress.

2. There are serious political tensions in Saigon (and perhaps elsewhere in South Vietnam) where the Diem-Nhu government is becoming increasingly unpopular.

3. There is no solid evidence of the possibility of a successful coup, although assassination of Diem or Nhu is always a possibility.

4. Although some, and perhaps an increasing number, of GVN military officers are becoming hostile to the government, they are more hostile to the Viet Cong than to the government and at least for the near future they will continue to perform their military duties.

5. Further repressive actions by Diem and Nhu could change the present favorable military trends. On the other hand, a return to more moderate methods of control and administration, unlikely though it may be, would substantially mitigate the political crisis.

6. It is not clear that pressures exerted by the U.S. will move Diem and Nhu toward moderation. Indeed, pressures may increase their obduracy. But unless such pressures are exerted, they are almost certain to continue past patterns of behavior. . . .

Recent days have been characterized by reports of greater Viet Cong activity, countrywide, coupled with evidence of improved weaponry in their hands. Some U.S. advisors, as well as some Vietnamese, view this increased activity as a logical reaction to the steadily growing strategic hamlet program, which they believe is progressively separating the Viet Cong from the rural population and from their sources of food and reinforcements. Others view it as a delayed effort to capitalize upon the political trouble. All agree that it reflects a continuing capability for offensive action.[51]

On 22 October the State Department compiles its own statistics, which present quite a different picture than those of the 2 October McNamara report.

Department of State Bureau of Intelligence and Research

RFE-90, October 22, 1963

TO: The Secretary
FROM: INR—Thomas L. Hughes
SUBJECT: *Statistics on the War Effort in South Vietnam Show Unfavorable Trends*

This report reviews the more significant statistics on the Communist insurgency in South Vietnam as indicators of trends in the military situation since July 1963.

ABSTRACT
Statistics on the insurgency in South Vietnam, although neither thoroughly
trustworthy nor entirely satisfactory as criteria, indicate an unfavorable
shift in the military balance. Since July 1963, the trend in Viet Cong casualties, weapons losses, and defections has been downward while the number
of Viet Cong armed attacks and other incidents has been upward. Comparison with earlier periods suggests that the military position of the government of Vietnam may have been set back to the point it occupied six
months to a year ago. These trends coincide in time with the sharp deterioration of the political situation. At the same time, even without the Buddhist issue and the attending government crisis, it is possible that the Diem
regime would have been unable to maintain the favorable trends of previous periods in the face of the accelerated Viet Cong effort.

STATISTICS AS INDICATORS
Statistics, in general, are only partial and not entirely satisfactory indica-
tors of progress in the total counterinsurgency effort in South Vietnam.
First, some statistics are incomplete, as for example, those relating to
Viet Cong attacks against strategic hamlets and desertions within the
South Vietnamese military and security services. Second, all statistics are
acquired largely if not entirely from official South Vietnamese sources.
As such, their validity must, to some degree at least, remain questionable, even though the efforts of the United States military and civilian
advisers have improved the quality of this data during the past year. . . .
Third, there are several other important indicators which are extremely
difficult, if not impossible, to handle statistically. These include: morale
and efficiency within the bureaucracy and the armed services, the degree
of locally acquired or volunteered intelligence, popular attitudes toward
the Viet Cong and the government, and the status and impact of the
government's political, social, and economic activities in support of the
strategic hamlet program. Nonetheless, statistics touch on some significant aspects of the military situation and provide a guide at least to trends
in the fighting.[52]

*Messages of 25 October and 30 October detail the plans for the impending
coup, as well as some of the communications problems. Ambassador
Lodge has been publicly scheduled to leave Saigon on a trip.*

Cablegram from Ambassador Lodge to McGeorge Bundy
Oct. 25, 1963

1. I APPRECIATE THE CONCERN EXPRESSED BY YOU IN REF. A RELATIVE TO THE
GEN. DON/CONEIN RELATIONSHIP, AND ALSO THE PRESENT LACK OF FIRM INTEL-
LIGENCE ON THE DETAILS OF THE GENERAL'S PLOT. I HOPE THAT REF. B WILL
ASSIST IN CLEARING UP SOME OF THE DOUBTS RELATIVE TO GENERAL'S PLANS,
AND I AM HOPEFUL THAT THE DETAILED PLANS PROMISED FOR TWO DAYS
BEFORE THE COUP ATTEMPT WILL CLEAR UP ANY REMAINING DOUBTS.

I. STATISTICAL TRENDS, 1962–1963

	JANUARY 1–JUNE 30, 1962	JULY 1–DECEMBER 30, 1962 (AND % OF CHANGE)	JANUARY 1–JUNE 30, 1963 (AND % OF CHANGE)	JULY 1–SEPTEMBER 18, 1963*	% OF PREVIOUS PERIOD
1. Viet Cong Incidents (total)	10,481	8,595 (−18%)	6,847 (−20%)	3,777	55%
2. Viet Cong Armed Attacks (total)	3,024	2,441 (−19%)	1,941 (−20%)	1,067	55%
Company-size and larger	156	63 (−40%)	72 (+14%)	34	47%
3. Viet Cong Casualties (total)	13,755	17,338 (+26%)	13,944 (−20%)	6,425	46%
4. GVN Casualties (total)	6,036	6,846 (+13%)	8,056 (+18%)	4,220	52%

	JANUARY–APRIL 1962	MAY–AUGUST 1962	SEPTEMBER–DECEMBER 1962	JANUARY–APRIL 1963	MAY–AUGUST 1963 (AND % OF CHANGE)	THRU SEPTEMBER 18, 1963 (AND % OF PREVIOUS PERIOD)
5. Viet Cong Weapons Losses	1,202	1,526	1,806	1,917	1,703 (−11%)	335 (20%)
GVN Weapons Losses	1,777	1,884	1,534	1,974	2,260 (+15%)	644 (28%)
6. Viet Cong Defections**				1,178	1,307 (+10%)	107 (8%)

1962 Total: 1,956

*Although only 42% of this period has elapsed, the statistics in this column are already 46%–55% of the total figures for the previous six-month period, as shown in the last column.

**This excludes "Chieu Hoi" returnees which have totalled 13,664 through August 1963 but which have declined sharply since July 1963.[52]

2. CAS HAS BEEN PUNCTILIOUS IN CARRYING OUT MY INSTRUCTIONS. I HAVE PERSONALLY APPROVED EACH MEETING BETWEEN GEN. DON AND CONEIN WHO HAS CARRIED OUT MY ORDERS IN EACH INSTANCE EXPLICITLY. WHILE I SHARE YOUR CONCERN ABOUT THE CONTINUED INVOLVEMENT OF CONEIN IN THIS MATTER, A SUITABLE SUBSTITUTE FOR CONEIN AS THE PRINCIPAL CONTACT IS NOT PRESENTLY AVAILABLE. CONEIN, AS YOU KNOW, IS A FRIEND OF SOME EIGHTEEN YEARS' STANDING WITH GEN. DON, AND GENERAL DON HAS EX-PRESSED EXTREME RELUCTANCE TO DEAL WITH ANYONE ELSE. I DO NOT BE-LIEVE THE INVOLVEMENT OF ANOTHER AMERICAN IN CLOSE CONTACT WITH THE GENERALS WOULD BE PRODUCTIVE. WE ARE, HOWEVER, CONSIDERING THE FEA-SIBILITY OF A PLAN FOR THE INTRODUCTION OF AN ADDITIONAL OFFICER AS A CUT-OUT BETWEEN CONEIN AND A DESIGNEE OF GEN. DON FOR COMMUNICA-TION PURPOSES ONLY. THIS OFFICER IS COMPLETELY UNWITTING OF ANY DE-TAILS OF PAST OR PRESENT COUP ACTIVITIES AND WILL REMAIN SO.

3. WITH REFERENCE TO GEN. HARKINS' COMMENT TO GEN. DON WHICH DON REPORTS TO HAVE REFERRED TO A PRESIDENTIAL DIRECTIVE AND THE PROPOSAL FOR A MEETING WITH ME, THIS MAY HAVE SERVED THE USEFUL PURPOSE OF ALLAYING THE GENERAL'S FEARS AS TO OUR INTEREST. IF THIS WERE A PROVO-CATION, THE GVN COULD HAVE ASSUMED AND MANUFACTURED ANY VARIATIONS OF THE SAME THEME. AS A PRECAUTIONARY MEASURE, HOWEVER, I OF COURSE REFUSED TO SEE GEN. DON. AS TO THE LACK OF INFORMATION AS TO GENERAL DON'S REAL BACKING, AND THE LACK OF EVIDENCE THAT ANY REAL CAPABILI-TIES FOR ACTION HAVE BEEN DEVELOPED, REF. B PROVIDES ONLY PART OF THE ANSWER. I FEEL SURE THAT THE RELUCTANCE OF THE GENERALS TO PROVIDE THE U.S. WITH FULL DETAILS OF THEIR PLANS AT THIS TIME, IS A REFLECTION OF THEIR OWN SENSE OF SECURITY AND A LACK OF CONFIDENCE THAT IN THE LARGE AMERICAN COMMUNITY PRESENT IN SAIGON THEIR PLANS WILL NOT BE PREMATURELY REVEALED.[53]

Not everyone in Saigon agrees, however. Using military instead of CIA channels, General Harkins cables General Maxwell Taylor, chairman of the Joint Chiefs of Staff.

Cablegram from General Harkins in Saigon to General Taylor
Oct. 30, 1963

YOUR JCS 4188-63 ARRIVED AS I WAS IN THE PROCESS OF DRAFTING ONE FOR YOU ALONG THE SAME LINES. I SHARE YOUR CONCERN. I HAVE NOT AS YET SEEN SAIGON 768. I SENT TO THE EMBASSY FOR A COPY AT 0830 THIS MORN-ING—AS OF NOW 1100—THE EMBASSY HAS NOT RELEASED IT. ALSO CINCPAC 0-300040Z INFO JCS CAME AS A SURPRISE TO ME AS I AM UNAWARE OF ANY CHANGE IN LOCAL SITUATION WHICH INDICATES NECESSITY FOR ACTIONS DI-RECTED. PERHAPS I'LL FIND THE ANSWER IN SAIGON 768. OR PERHAPS ACTIONS DIRECTED IN CINCPAC 300040Z ARE PRECAUTIONARY IN LIGHT OF GEN. DON'S STATEMENT REPORTED IN CAS 1925 THAT A COUP WOULD TAKE PLACE IN ANY CASE NOT LATER THAN 2 NOVEMBER.[54]

Nevertheless, plans for the impending coup continue.

Cablegram from McGeorge Bundy to Ambassador Lodge
Oct. 30, 1963

1. YOUR 2023, 2040, 2041 AND 2043 EXAMINED WITH CARE AT HIGHEST LEVELS HERE. YOU SHOULD PROMPTLY DISCUSS THIS REPLY AND ASSOCIATED MESSAGES WITH HARKINS WHOSE RESPONSIBILITIES TOWARD ANY COUP ARE VERY HEAVY ESPECIALLY AFTER YOU LEAVE. . . . THEY GIVE MUCH CLEARER PICTURE GROUP'S ALLEGED PLANS AND ALSO INDICATE CHANCES OF ACTION WITH OR WITHOUT OUR APPROVAL NOW SO SIGNIFICANT THAT WE SHOULD URGENTLY CONSIDER OUR ATTITUDE AND CONTINGENCY PLANS. WE NOTE PAR-TICULARLY DON'S CURIOSITY YOUR DEPARTURE AND HIS INSISTENCE CONEIN BE AVAILABLE FROM WEDNESDAY NIGHT ON, WHICH SUGGESTS DATE MIGHT BE AS EARLY AS THURSDAY.

2. BELIEVE OUR ATTITUDE TO COUP GROUP CAN STILL HAVE DECISIVE EFFECT ON ITS DECISIONS. WE BELIEVE THAT WHAT WE SAY TO COUP GROUP CAN PRODUCE DELAY OF COUP AND THAT BETRAYAL OF COUP PLANS TO DIEM IS NOT REPEAT NOT OUR ONLY WAY OF STOPPING COUP. WE THEREFORE NEED UR-GENTLY OUR COMBINED ASSESSMENT WITH HARKINS AND CAS (INCLUDING THEIR SEPARATE COMMENTS IF THEY DESIRE). WE CONCERNED THAT OUR LINE-UP OF FORCES IN SAIGON (BEING CABLED IN NEXT MESSAGE) INDICATES APPROXIMATELY EQUAL BALANCE OF FORCES, WITH SUBSTANTIAL POSSIBILTY SERIOUS AND PROLONGED FIGHTING OR EVEN DEFEAT. EITHER OF THESE COULD BE SERIOUS OR EVEN DISASTROUS FOR U.S. INTERESTS, SO THAT WE MUST HAVE ASSURANCE BALANCE OF FORCES CLEARLY FAVORABLE. . . .

10. WE REITERATE BURDEN OF PROOF MUST BE ON COUP GROUP TO SHOW A SUBSTANTIAL POSSIBILITY OF QUICK SUCCESS; OTHERWISE, WE SHOULD DISCOUR-AGE THEM FROM PROCEEDING SINCE A MISCALCULATION COULD RESULT IN JEOPARDIZING U.S. POSITION IN SOUTHEAST ASIA.[55]

Immediately, Lodge replies to Bundy (30 October):

1. WE MUST, OF COURSE, GET BEST POSSIBLE ESTIMATE OF CHANCE OF COUP'S SUCCESS AND THIS ESTIMATE MUST COLOR OUR THINKING, BUT DO NOT THINK WE HAVE THE POWER TO DELAY OR DISCOURAGE A COUP. DON HAS MADE IT CLEAR MANY TIMES THAT THIS IS A VIETNAMESE AFFAIR. IT IS THEORETICALLY POSSIBLE FOR US TO TURN OVER THE INFORMATION WHICH HAS BEEN GIVEN TO US IN CONFIDENCE TO DIEM AND THIS WOULD UNDOUBTEDLY STOP THE COUP AND WOULD MAKE TRAITORS OUT OF US. FOR PRACTICAL PURPOSES THEREFORE I WOULD SAY THAT WE HAVE VERY LITTLE INFLUENCE ON WHICH IS ESSEN-TIALLY A VIETNAMESE AFFAIR. IN ADDITION, THIS WOULD PLACE THE HEADS OF THE GENERALS, THEIR CIVILIAN SUPPORTERS, AND LOWER MILITARY OFFICERS ON THE SPOT, THEREBY SACRIFICING A SIGNIFICANT PORTION OF THE CIVILIAN AND MILITARY LEADERSHIP NEEDED TO CARRY THE WAR AGAINST THE VC TO ITS SUCCESSFUL CONCLUSION. AFTER OUR EFFORTS NOT TO DISCOURAGE A COUP

AND THIS CHANGE OF HEART, WE WOULD FORECLOSE ANY POSSIBILITY OF CHANGE OF THE GVN FOR THE BETTER. DIEM/NHU HAVE DISPLAYED NO INTENTIONS TO DATE OF A DESIRE TO CHANGE THE TRADITIONAL METHODS OF CONTROL THROUGH POLICE ACTION OR TAKE ANY REPEAT ANY ACTIONS WHICH WOULD UNDERMINE THE POWER POSITION OR SOLIDARITY OF THE NGO FAMILY. THIS, DESPITE OUR HEAVY PRESSURES DIRECTED DEPTEL 534. IF YOUR ATTEMPT TO THWART THIS COUP WERE SUCCESSFUL, WHICH WE DOUBT, IT IS OUR FIRM ESTIMATE THAT YOUNGER OFFICERS, SMALL GROUPS OF MILITARY, WOULD THEN ENGAGE IN AN ABORTIVE ACTION CREATING CHAOS IDEALLY SUITED TO VC OBJECTIVES.

2. WHILE WE WILL ATTEMPT A COMBINED ASSESSMENT IN A FOLLOWING MESSAGE, TIME HAS NOT YET PERMITTED SUBSTANTIVE EXAMINATION OF THIS MATTER WITH GENERAL HARKINS. MY GENERAL VIEW IS THAT THE U.S. IS TRYING TO BRING THIS MEDIEVAL COUNTRY INTO THE 20TH CENTURY AND THAT WE HAVE MADE CONSIDERABLE PROGRESS IN MILITARY AND ECONOMIC WAYS BUT TO GAIN VICTORY WE MUST ALSO BRING THEM INTO THE 20TH CENTURY POLITICALLY AND THAT CAN ONLY BE DONE BY EITHER A THOROUGHGOING CHANGE IN THE BEHAVIOR OF THE PRESENT GOVERNMENT OR BY ANOTHER GOVERNMENT. THE VIET CONG PROBLEM IS PARTLY MILITARY BUT IT IS ALSO PARTLY PSYCHOLOGICAL AND POLITICAL.

3. WITH RESPECT TO PARAGRAPH 3 REF., I BELIEVE THAT WE SHOULD CONTINUE OUR PRESENT POSITION OF KEEPING HANDS OFF BUT CONTINUE TO MONITOR AND PRESS FOR MORE DETAILED INFORMATION. CAS HAS BEEN ANALYZING POTENTIAL COUP FORCES FOR SOME TIME AND IT IS THEIR ESTIMATE THAT THE GENERALS HAVE PROBABLY FIGURED THEIR CHANCES PRETTY CLOSELY AND PROBABLY ALSO EXPECT THAT ONCE THEY BEGIN TO MOVE, NOT ONLY PLANNED UNITS, BUT OTHER UNITS WILL JOIN THEM. WE BELIEVE THAT VIETNAM'S BEST GENERALS ARE INVOLVED IN DIRECTING THIS EFFORT. IF THEY CAN'T PULL IT OFF, IT IS DOUBTFUL OTHER MILITARY LEADERSHIP COULD DO SO SUCCESSFULLY. IT IS UNDERSTANDABLE THAT THE GENERALS WOULD BE RETICENT TO REVEAL FULL DETAILS OF THEIR PLAN FOR FEAR OF LEAKS TO THE GVN. . . .

11. AS TO REQUESTS FROM THE GENERALS, THEY MAY WELL HAVE NEED OF FUNDS AT THE LAST MOMENT WITH WHICH TO BUY OFF POTENTIAL OPPOSITION. TO THE EXTENT THAT THESE FUNDS CAN BE PASSED DISCREETLY, I BELIEVE WE SHOULD FURNISH THEM; PROVIDED WE ARE CONVINCED THAT THE PROPOSED COUP IS SUFFICIENTLY WELL ORGANIZED TO HAVE A GOOD CHANCE OF SUCCESS. IF THEY ARE SUCCESSFUL, THEY WILL UNDOUBTEDLY ASK FOR PROMPT RECOGNITION AND SOME ASSURANCE THAT MILITARY AND ECONOMIC AID WILL CONTINUE AT NORMAL LEVEL. WE SHOULD BE PREPARED TO MAKE THESE STATEMENTS IF THE ISSUE IS CLEAR-CUT PREDICATING OUR POSITION ON THE PRESIDENT'S STATED DESIRE TO CONTINUE THE WAR AGINST THE VC TO FINAL VICTORY. VOA MIGHT BE AN IMPORTANT MEANS OF DISSEMINATING THIS MESSAGE. SHOULD THE COUP FAIL, WE WILL HAVE TO PICK UP THE PIECES AS BEST WE CAN AT THAT

TIME. WE HAVE A COMMITMENT TO THE GENERALS FROM THE AUGUST EPI-
SODE TO ATTEMPT TO HELP IN THE EVACUATION OF THEIR DEPENDENTS. WE
SHOULD TRY TO LIVE UP TO THIS IF CONDITIONS WILL PERMIT. AMERICAN
COMPLICITY WILL UNDOUBTEDLY BE CHARGED AND THERE MIGHT BE SOME
ACTS TAKEN AGAINST SPECIFIC PERSONALITIES WHICH WE SHOULD ANTICIPATE
AND MAKE PROVISION AGAINST AS BEST WE CAN. SHOULD THE COUP PROVE
INDECISIVE AND A PROTRACTED STRUGGLE IS IN PROGRESS, WE SHOULD PROBA-
BLY OFFER OUR GOOD OFFICES TO HELP RESOLVE THE ISSUE IN THE INTEREST
OF THE WAR AGAINST THE VC. THIS MIGHT HOLD SOME BENEFIT IN TERMS OF
CONCESSIONS BY GVN. WE WILL NATURALLY INCUR SOME OPPROBRIUM FROM
BOTH SIDES IN OUR ROLE AS MEDIATOR. HOWEVER, THIS OPPROBRIUM WOULD
PROBABLY BE LESS DISTASTEFUL THAN A DEADLOCK WHICH WOULD OPEN THE
DOOR TO THE VC. WE CONSIDER SUCH A DEADLOCK AS THE LEAST LIKELY
POSSIBILITY OF THE THREE.

12. AS REGARDS YOUR PARA. 10, I DO NOT KNOW WHAT MORE PROOF CAN BE
OFFERED THAN THE FACT THESE MEN ARE OBVIOUSLY PREPARED TO RISK THEIR
LIVES AND THAT THEY WANT NOTHING FOR THEMSELVES. IF I AM ANY JUDGE
OF HUMAN NATURE, DON'S FACE EXPRESSED OF SINCERITY AND DETERMINATION
ON THE MORNING THAT I SPOKE TO HIM. HEARTILY AGREE THAT A MISCALCULA-
TION COULD JEOPARDIZE POSITION IN SOUTHEAST ASIA. WE ALSO RUN TREMEN-
DOUS RISKS BY DOING NOTHING.

IF WE WERE CONVINCED THAT THE COUP WAS GOING TO FAIL, WE WOULD, OF
COURSE, DO EVERYTHING WE COULD TO STOP IT.

13. GEN. HARKINS HAS READ THIS AND DOES NOT CONCUR.[56]

Bundy wires back:

CAS 79407, 30 Oct '63 from Bundy to Lodge

1. OUR READING YOUR THOUGHTFUL 2063 LEADS US TO BELIEVE A SIGNIFICANT
DIFFERENCE OF SHADING MAY EXIST ON ONE CRUCIAL POINT (SEE NEXT PARA.)
AND ON ONE OR TWO LESSER MATTERS EASILY CLARIFIED.

2. WE DO NOT ACCEPT AS A BASIS FOR U.S. POLICY THAT WE HAVE NO POWER
TO DELAY OR DISCOURAGE A COUP. IN YOUR PARAGRAPH 12 YOU SAY THAT IF
YOU WERE CONVINCED THAT THE COUP WAS GOING TO FAIL YOU WOULD OF
COURSE DO EVERYTHING YOU COULD TO STOP IT. WE BELIEVE THAT ON THIS
SAME BASIS YOU SHOULD TAKE ACTION TO PERSUADE COUP LEADERS TO STOP OR
DELAY ANY OPERATION WHICH, IN YOUR BEST JUDGMENT, DOES NOT CLEARLY
GIVE HIGH PROSPECT OF SUCCESS. WE HAVE NOT CONSIDERED ANY BETRAYAL
OF GENERALS TO DIEM, AND OUR 79109 EXPLICITLY REJECTS THAT COURSE. WE
RECOGNIZE THE DANGER OF APPEARING HOSTILE TO GENERALS, BUT WE BE-
LIEVE THAT OUR OWN POSITION SHOULD BE ON AS FIRM GROUND AS POSSIBLE,
HENCE WE CANNOT LIMIT OURSELVES TO PROPOSITION IMPLIED IN YOUR MES-
SAGE THAT ONLY CONVICTION OF CERTAIN FAILURE JUSTIFIES INTERVENTION.

WE BELIEVE THAT YOUR STANDARD FOR INTERVENTION SHOULD BE THAT STATED ABOVE.

3. THEREFORE, IF YOU SHOULD CONCLUDE THAT THERE IS NOT CLEARLY A HIGH PROSPECT OF SUCCESS, YOU SHOULD COMMUNICATE THIS DOUBT TO GENERALS IN A WAY CALCULATED TO PERSUADE THEM TO DESIST AT LEAST UNTIL CHANCES ARE BETTER. IN SUCH A COMMUNICATION YOU SHOULD USE THE WEIGHT OF U.S. BEST ADVICE AND EXPLICITLY REJECT ANY IMPLICATION THAT WE OPPOSE THE EFFORT OF THE GENERALS BECAUSE OF PREFERENCE FOR PRESENT REGIME. WE RECOGNIZE NEED TO BEAR IN MIND GENERALS' INTERPRETATION OF U.S. ROLE IN 1960 COUP ATTEMPT, AND YOUR AGENT SHOULD MAINTAIN CLEAR DISTINCTION BETWEEN STRONG AND HONEST ADVICE GIVEN AS A FRIEND AND ANY OPPOSITION TO THEIR OBJECTIVES.

4. WE CONTINUE TO BE DEEPLY INTERESTED IN UP-TO-THE-MINUTE ASSESSMENT OF PROSPECTS AND ARE SENDING THIS BEFORE REPLY TO OUR CAS 79126. WE WANT CONTINUOUS EXCHANGE LATEST ASSESSMENTS ON THIS TOPIC.

5. TO CLARIFY OUR INTENT, PARAGRAPH 7 OF OUR 79109 IS RESCINDED AND WE RESTATE OUR DESIRES AS FOLLOWS:

A. WHILE YOU ARE IN SAIGON YOU WILL BE CHIEF OF COUNTRY TEAM IN ALL CIRCUMSTANCES AND OUR ONLY INSTRUCTION IS THAT WE ARE SURE IT WILL HELP TO HAVE HARKINS FULLY INFORMED AT ALL STAGES AND TO USE ADVICE FROM BOTH HIM AND SMITH IN FRAMING GUIDANCE FOR COUP CONTACTS AND ASSESSMENT. WE CONTINUE TO BE CONCERNED THAT NEITHER CONEIN NOR ANY OTHER REPORTING SOURCE IS GETTING THE CLARITY WE WOULD LIKE WITH RESPECT TO ALIGNMENT OF FORCES AND LEVEL OF DETERMINATION AMONG GENERALS.

B. WHEN YOU LEAVE SAIGON AND BEFORE THERE IS A COUP, TRUEHART WILL BE CHIEF OF THE COUNTRY TEAM. OUR ONLY MODIFICATION OF EXISTING PROCEDURES IS THAT IN THIS CIRCUMSTANCE WE WISH ALL INSTRUCTION TO CONEIN TO BE CONDUCTED IN IMMEDIATE CONSULTATION WITH HARKINS AND SMITH SO THAT ALL THREE KNOW WHAT IS SOLD IN CONEIN. ANY DISAGREEMENT AMONG THE THREE ON SUCH INSTRUCTION SHOULD BE REPORTED TO WASHINGTON AND HELD FOR OUR RESOLUTION, WHEN TIME PERMITS.

C. IF YOU HAVE LEFT AND A COUP OCCURS, WE BELIEVE THAT EMERGENCY SITUATION REQUIRES, PENDING YOUR RETURN, THAT DIRECTION OF COUNTRY TEAM BE VESTED IN MOST SENIOR OFFICER WITH EXPERIENCE OF MILITARY DECISIONS, AND THE OFFICER IN OUR VIEW IS HARKINS. WE DO *NOT* INTEND THAT THIS SWITCH IN FINAL RESPONSIBILITY SHOULD BE PUBLICIZED IN ANY WAY, AND HARKINS WILL OF COURSE BE GUIDED IN BASIC POSTURE BY OUR INSTRUCTIONS, WHICH FOLLOW IN PARAGRAPH 6. WE DO NOT BELIEVE THAT THIS SWITCH WILL HAVE THE EFFECT SUGGESTED IN YOUR PARAGRAPH 8.

6. THIS PARAGRAPH CONTAINS OUR PRESENT STANDING INSTRUCTIONS FOR U.S. POSTURE IN THE EVENT OF A COUP.

A. U.S. AUTHORITIES WILL REJECT APPEALS FOR DIRECT INTERVENTION FROM EITHER SIDE, AND U.S.-CONTROLLED AIRCRAFT AND OTHER RESOURCES WILL NOT BE COMMITTED BETWEEN THE BATTLE LINES OR IN SUPPORT OF EITHER SIDE, WITHOUT AUTHORIZATION FROM WASHINGTON.

B. IN EVENT OF INDECISIVE CONTEST, U.S. AUTHORITIES MAY IN THEIR DISCRETION AGREE TO PERFORM ANY ACTS AGREEABLE TO BOTH SIDES, SUCH AS REMOVAL OF KEY PERSONALITIES OR RELAY OF INFORMATION. IN SUCH ACTIONS, HOWEVER, U.S. AUTHORITIES WILL STRENUOUSLY AVOID APPEARANCE OF PRESSURE ON EITHER SIDE. IT IS NOT IN THE INTEREST OF USG TO BE OR APPEAR TO BE EITHER INSTRUMENT OF EXISTING GOVERNMENT OR INSTRUMENT OF COUP.

C. IN THE EVENT OF IMMINENT OR ACTUAL FAILURE OF COUP, U.S. AUTHORITIES MAY AFFORD ASYLUM IN THEIR DISCRETION TO THOSE TO WHOM THERE IS ANY EXPRESS OR IMPLIED OBLIGATION OF THIS SORT. WE BELIEVE HOWEVER THAT IN SUCH A CASE IT WOULD BE IN OUR INTEREST AND PROBABLY IN INTEREST OF THOSE SEEKING ASYLUM THAT THEY SEEK PROTECTION OF OTHER EMBASSIES IN ADDITION TO OUR OWN. THIS POINT SHOULD BE MADE STRONGLY IF NEED ARISES.

D. BUT ONCE A COUP UNDER RESPONSIBLE LEADERSHIP HAS BEGUN, AND WITHIN THESE RESTRICTIONS, IT IS IN THE INTEREST OF THE U.S. GOVERNMENT THAT IT SHOULD SUCCEED.[57]

In Saigon, as seen in Thomas Fleming's novel Officers' Wives, *some of the U.S. Army advisers have brought their families with them for the duration of their tours. On the night of 31 October, Lieutenant Colonel Adam Thayer and his wife, Honor, have bickered over her dislike of being in Saigon and Adam's preoccupation with his opposition to "the way the Army [is] fighting the war."*

The next morning Honor felt like her bones were made of lead. She dimly remembered Adam getting up. He said something about staying in the house. She drifted down into a shallow doze.

BLAM BLAM BLAM. A series of explosions rattled the windows of the house. Little Matt started screaming outside the bedroom door. Honor ran to him in her nightgown. "Mommy, it's the Viet Cong," he howled. "They're shooting in the street."

BLAM BLAM BLAM. More explosions. Cannon fire. Then the rattle of smaller guns. My God, it was the coup. They were shelling the presidential palace, only five or six blocks away. She reeled to a window. Heat waves shimmered in the moist air. The villa's gate was open and Pookie was out in the street. Was the child insane? Honor rushed downstairs to the front door. "Pookie," she screamed. "Are you tryin' to get killed? Get back in here."

Pookie paid no attention to her. She gazed down the street toward the boulevard. "Oh wow, tanks," she yelled. "They're throwing in tanks. This is terrific."

"Get in the house this instant."

The telephone rang. It was Amy Rosser, who lived four doors away. "Have you got a weapon?" she said.

"You mean a gun? No."

"You better come up here. I've got a forty-five and six hand grenades."

"I'll be there in two minutes."

"Don't use the street. There's a gate at the back of each garden. We leave them unlocked in case we have to fight from house to house."

Appalling. Adam had told her Alexandre Dumas was one of the safest streets in Saigon. Honor flung on a Hawaiian muumuu and a pair of go-aheads and shepherded Matt and Pookie through the four gates to the rear of the Rosser garden. Amy was waiting for her at the back door of the house, a big Army .45 in her hand. Honor felt frightened just by the sight of it. "Do you know how to shoot that?" she said.

"Of course," Amy said.

"Show us," Pookie said.

"Now is not the time to waste ammunition," Amy replied. "My God, she looks like Adam, doesn't she?"

"The very image. Do you think they'll come after us?"

"Not deliberately. But they're great looters. We might see a few of them."

On the boulevard the cannon and small arms rose to a new crescendo. Amy led them into the living room, where her chubby six-year-old, Grace, was peering out a window. "Would anyone like a drink?" Amy said. The children opted for Cokes. Honor said a bloody mary would help. Amy went out to the kitchen to get the refreshments. Some heavy guns started firing at the head of the street, less than a block away. The house rattled with the concussions. Matt started to cry again. Pookie and Grace held their ears. . . .

About four o'clock, the gunfire picked up again. A minute later, Matt yelled, "Viet Cong," and dove to the floor. Amy grabbed the .45 from the card table and snarled, "Upstairs." They scrambled for the stairs with Matt in the lead. Amy crouched on the landing, both hands aiming the gun at the front door, which swung open to reveal George Rosser carrying an automatic rifle.

"Jesus Christ," Amy gasped. She whirled on Matt. "Don't you know an American officer when you see one? You're not very bright for nine."

Matt burst into tears again. George reported that President Diem and his brother still refused to surrender. They had also rejected an offer of sanctuary in the American Embassy. But they had no hope of winning. Fourteen South Vietnamese generals and seven colonels had denounced them over the national radio.

George kept shaking his head. "I can't understand how Washington could treat us this way," he said. "We look like fools. The President, McNamara, the Ambassador, everyone's in on this thing but us."

"Us?" Honor said.

"MACV," Amy said bitterly. "The Army. The whole thing is disgraceful."

"Isn't Pete Burke on staff there? He knew about it last night," Honor said. "A reporter friend came in and told us just before we sat down to dinner."

Amy exchanged a grim look with George. "Do you still have doubts?"

"I guess not," George said.

Adam showed up about an hour later. He was in a very cheerful mood. He had been watching the fight around the palace. They were knocking out the President's tanks, one by one. It was only a question of time, he said. They started talking about the Vietnamese general in command of the coup. George said he was an idiot. Amy said his wife was a bigger idiot. George said Vietnam was going to be a mess if Adam and his friends thought a dodo like that could run the country. Adam said he would be good enough for the time being. They wanted somebody dumb, who would let them reorganize the war. . . .

"Tong Thong fini," Mrs. Truc . . . said when she came to work on the morning of November 2, 1963. Translation: President Diem is finished. Mrs. Truc drew her finger across her throat and produced one of her rare smiles. Joanna did not reciprocate. She was too tired. A night of gunfire had not been conducive to sleep. By this time she had no faith whatsoever that removing Diem would improve American prospects in Vietnam.

Pete had departed for MACV headquarters at dawn, leaving Bruce Lindstrom in command of defending the apartment house. Pete was not foolish enough to entrust Lindstrom or anyone else with a gun. He had acquired a supply of tear-gas grenades and gas masks. If a mob attacked the building, they were to flood the lower floors with gas and retreat to the roof, where helicopters could rescue them.

But no mob attacked, although the firing had ceased around 6 A.M., and Saigon's streets slowly filled with people. About noon, Pete returned, accompanied by Carl Springer. Pete looked inordinately gloomy and Carl had lost much of his usual effervescence. "Diem and his brother are dead," Pete said. "They shot them after they surrendered. Pretty crummy."

"The jerks," Carl Springer said. "Don't they realize how bad that's going to look in the U.S.?"

Pete had been losing patience with Carl for several weeks. Their friendship, begun in Quang Ngai Province, had been rooted in the mutual admiration for the risks they were both ready to take, Pete to lead his men, Carl to get his story.

"This isn't a goddamn publicity contest, Carl. It's a war," Pete said.

Springer listened uneasily while Pete told Joanna and the Lindstroms that the President and his brother had escaped from the besieged palace through a secret tunnel and taken refuge in the house of a wealthy friend in Cholon, the Chinese section of Saigon. The rebel generals had discovered their hideout and the Ngos fled to a nearby church, where they surrendered. En route to Army headquarters in an armored car, they were shot at point-blank range.

"What a mess," Joanna said.

"They just murdered them in cold blood?" Karen Lindstrom asked, wide-eyed.

"They had it coming to them," Carl Springer said. "They murdered a lot of innocent people in the last ten years."

"They were fighting a war, Carl. Innocent people get killed in every war. Haven't you ever read a history book? Or a newspaper, when we were in Korea and you were what—twelve years old?"

"When are you going to stop trying to sell that Korea bullshit?" Springer said.

"When are you going to stop encouraging people to murder our friends?"

Joanna sympathized with Pete's anger but she recoiled from his ruthless assertion of war's brutality. She had been recoiling—even fleeing—from Vietnam for months now. Ever since she had looked out the window of her apartment and seen a man sitting in the lotus position, the traditional Buddhist posture for meditation, in the center of a whirling column of flame. From that moment, she had begun yearning for some way to escape the human cauldron of Vietnam. Throughout the blazing summer and fall, Saigon had been a maelstrom of riots and rumors. Pete had become more and more baffled and dismayed by the divided, indecisive policy of the American government, the drift toward persuading the ARVN generals to revolt against Diem, without taking the U.S. Army, the ARVN's advisers, into the plot. Now it had ended exactly the way Pete had predicted it would end, with Diem and his brother dead. President Kennedy and Henry Cabot Lodge must have known it would end that way. Pete, a mere lieutenant colonel, had known it. Where did this knowledge leave those who were here to bear the burdens, meet the hardships, in defense of freedom? Were they accomplices or victims? Joanna tried not to think about it.[58]

Following the murder of Diem on 2 November, the political situation in South Vietnam becomes unstable and confusing. The Burkes and the Rossers express the way many Americans actually feel.

Three weeks later. It is three weeks later. Three weeks of watching Pete argue with Carl Springer, with Adam, with Tony and Clara Emerson, repeating to all of them his relentless soldier's conviction. "The coup was a mistake. We're all going to pay for it before this thing's over."

In memory the words hang there in the moist Saigon air like a swarm of deadly insects or death-bearing helicopters, descending on those optimistic young American faces. Not even Lieutenant Colonel Burke himself, a massive image of American military strength, realized how fearsome his prophecy was. He never dreamt it was not in his power to shield those he loved from the enemy that was waiting in the Iron Triangle, the A Shau Valley, War Zone C.

Cissie comes running out of her bedroom and climbs on Pete's lap to say good night. "Give me a bounce, Daddy," she says. Pete flips her a foot in the air with a flick of his leg and she giggles in glorious glee. He kisses her and gives her a squeeze that makes her squeal. She loves him to rough her up. Around them, drinks in hand, the other Americans in their apartment house continue their chatter.

"Big Minh is a leader. He just hasn't been given a chance."

"They should have elections and choose a civilian government."

"They won't do that until the generals make their fortunes."

"Root out corruption."

"Counterinsurgency."

"Meaningful negotiations."

"Liberation front."

"Military solution."

"Tran Van Huong."

"Tran Van Don."

What was happening? Time has stopped, fixed in that miasma of ideological and military platitudes and incomprehensible Vietnamese names, like the unreal stars of a planetarium. Names words emotions swirling around the father and daughter in the worn wing chair. The heart, that unstable organ, begins to fragment like an abandoned space capsule reentering the atmosphere of earth.

But time never really stops. Let us be precise about time. Let us admit its relentless supremacy. It is three weeks and one day later. It is three o'clock on the morning of November 24. President Diem and his brother have been in their graves for twenty-two days. For three weeks and one day the Americans have watched Saigon slide into sleazy sneering corruption while the Vietnamese generals, Diem's murderers, quarreled in the Gia Long Palace and Carl Springer and Tony Emerson pontificated and Pete grew more and more gloomy. The ARVN war effort had stopped, he said, fumbled to a halt, and the VC were building in strength everywhere.

At a dinner party earlier that night Adam told everyone President Kennedy would act to fill the vacuum, you could always depend on the Kennedys to act, they were men of action, they would carry the war North, they would make Ho Chi Minh squirm.

It is 3 A.M. and the telephone is ringing in the Burke apartment on Le Van Duyet Street and Lieutenant Colonel Burke is answering it in his usual style: "Burke here." Joanna lies awake beside him, staring into the night. Nothing unusual about it. Most Army wives had insomnia in Saigon. It was their heroism, their defiance of death's first cousin, darkness.

"What?" gasps Lieutenant Colonel Burke. "Are you sure?"

A pause while the voice of the duty officer at MACV replies.

"I'll be there in ten minutes."

"What's wrong?"

"The President's been shot."

That was when Joanna began distrusting time. For a moment she thought it had unreeled, they were back three weeks and any moment there would be a blast of gunfire from Tu Do Street as the tanks attacked the Gia Long Palace.

"What President?" she said.

"Jesus Christ. We've only got one. Kennedy."

"Who shot him?"

"I don't know. We're going to Condition One around the world. It could be World War III. They want us at headquarters. No matter what happens don't leave the apartment. If things go sour, I'll get you out of here."

"Where did it happen?"

"In Dallas."

He had his khakis on, he was lacing his shoes.

"Should I tell the kids?"

"Why not? He's dead. It's confirmed."

She really meant, should I tell myself? Can I admit this has happened? She was back on the beach at Mo Ka Lei hearing those star-shining words, feeling them reach across six thousand miles to illuminate her American heart, displacing her negative otherworldish Catholic faith with a nobler, more human credo. There was no other word for it, *credo,* in its root Latin meaning. *I pledge my heart.* She had pledged it, Pete had pledged it that night at Mo Ka Lei three years ago.

Here in Saigon she had watched the pledge become soiled, mutilated. Adam had appeared to tell her that the words were simply part of the Kennedy game, and they were all players willy-nilly, with winning the only meaning. But death, Adam had said nothing about death. Wasn't death the crucial difference between life and a game? Death and love. There were no games that could control them.

What if the game included God, after all? Did John F. Kennedy die because he was guilty of the murders of President Diem and his brother? It was hard for any American in Saigon on November 24, 1963, not to wonder, to at least try to read that possibility into history's blurred message. It became another ingredient in Joanna's growing demoralization.

The next morning, dazed from lack of sleep, Joanna tried to answer Tom's bewildered questions, only to be confused all over again by further events in Dallas, above all the murder of the assassin, Lee Harvey Oswald.

Joanna was almost grateful to be distracted from the macabre public theater of Dallas by a totally unexpected visitor: Thui Dat. She stood hesitantly in the doorway, her eyes red-rimmed, her lips trembling. The white ao-dai, the gleaming black hair, the perfect features of her delicate oval face, were consumed in grief. "I have come to seek Peter's—Colonel Burke's—help in saving my husband," she said.

"Pete should be home in an hour or so," Joanna said. "Come in. Let me get you some coffee."

Joanna made some instant coffee. When she returned to the living room, she found Thui weeping. "Excuse me," she said. "I am so miserable. My husband has been arrested by the generals who led the coup. He is here in Saigon awaiting trial. It is all my doing. I urged him to scorn the men who came to him with proposals to betray the President. Even though some were from your embassy. I told him I could not live with a man who dishonored his oath of loyalty. Now they are going to kill him."

"No," Joanna said. The word was automatic, involuntary. After she said it she realized her utter helplessness, her ignorance of what was happening around her. She was as exposed as this woman to the history that was engulfing them.

"I am ashamed to burden you at such a time. When you are no doubt as shocked by the murder of your President as I was at the death of President Diem. Do you think Kennedy was the victim of traitorous generals in your American Army?"

"No!" Joanna said. "Such a thing is—really quite impossible."

Thui heard the words as a rebuke. She nodded sadly. "You mean such things occur only in wretched countries like Vietnam," she said. "You are no doubt correct."[59]

Lieutenant Colonel Ky, who has been part of the coup and who will shortly be promoted and become commander of the South Vietnamese Air Force, remembers the days following the coup in a chapter in Twenty Years and Twenty Days. *This chapter is titled "Diem: the CIA Backs Our Coup."*

Washington did not immediately recognize the new government of Big Minh which they had quietly helped to engineer, but not because of the murders. Apparently Secretary of State Dean Rusk believed that a delay in official recognition of Big Minh would help to stifle possible world criticism of American interference and the idea that Big Minh and the other generals were American puppets.

The point was rammed home by Ambassador Lodge, as I discovered when a friend in America sent me a copy of *The New York Times,* in which Lodge insisted during an interview that "We never participated in the planning. We never gave any advice. We had nothing whatever to do with it [the coup]. We were punctilious in drawing that line."

It was all nonsense, of course. The United States was deeply involved and the plot, it can be assumed, had the blessing of President Kennedy, who insisted that a plane be placed at Diem's disposal to fly him out of Vietnam. An extremist took the law into his own hands and Diem died, just as another extremist took the law into *his* hands less than three weeks later when President Kennedy was assassinated.[60]

1963   31 December

	TOTAL	NET CHANGE
U.S. military personnel assigned in Vietnam	16,300	+ 5,000

U.S. casualties	YEAR	TO DATE (cumulative)
Killed in action	78	120
Wounded in action	411	492

(Source: DOD/OASD)

ACT II

December 1963–January 1968

"We'll bring peace to this land
if we have to kill them ALL."
—General Custer

This is a War of the Unwilling
Led by the Unqualified
Dying for the Ungrateful

—GI latrine graffiti, Saigon

Immediately after the coup, the U.S. secretary of defense assesses the situation.

Memorandum for the Record, December 21, 1963

The military government may be an improvement over the Diem-Nhu regime, but this is not as yet established and the future of the war remains in doubt.

The Viet Cong are receiving substantial support from North Vietnam and possibly elsewhere, and this support can be increased. Stopping this by sealing the borders, the extensive waterways, and the long coast line is difficult, if not impossible.

The VC appeal to the people of South Vietnam on political grounds has been effective, gained recruits for their armed forces, and neutralized resistance.

The ability of the GVN to reverse this trend remains to be proven. Much depends on the ability of the MRC [Military Revolutionary Council] to deploy their forces and pursue the conflict in a manner which will ensure the security of the people and provide them desired freedom, privileges, and some tangible benefits.

The lack of an outstanding individual to lead and absence of administrative experience with the MRC are ominous indicators.

The political stability of the new government under the MRC is subject to serious doubt. Conflicts of ambition, jealousy, differences of opinion over policy matters are all possible, could develop serious schisms, precipitate further dissensions and coup attempts all of which will affect the war effort against the VC.

Overcoming the VC movement by the GVN is formidable and difficult, but not impossible. The problems can be intensified by continuing increased support from NVN and political failures by the MRC. Hence, in my judgment, there are more reasons to doubt the future of the effort under present programs and moderate extensions to existing programs (i.e., harassing sabotage against NVN, border crossings, etc.;) than there are reasons to be optimistic about the future of our cause in South Vietnam.[1]

To some Americans, however, there are also "ominous indicators" in their own government's policies. A satirical play, MacBird, *based on Shakespeare's* Macbeth *(among other literary antecedents), parodies an early Lyndon Johnson news conference. President MacBird is speaking:*

This land will be a garden carefully pruned.
We'll lop off any branch that looks too tall,
That seems to grow too lofty or too fast.
And any weed that springs up on our soil,
To choke the plants I've neatly set in rows,
Gets plucked up root and all, by me, MacBird—
And this I do for you, my wholesome flowers.
I see a garden blooming undisturbed
Where all the buds are even in their rows.
An ordered garden, sweet with unity,
That is my dream; my Smooth Society.

Applause from REPORTERS *which finally dies down.*

I thank you, gentlemen. Next question, please.

REPORTER:
Your majesty, how do you plan to deal
With rebel groups which thrive in Viet Land?

MAC BIRD:
What rebel groups? Where is this Viet Land?
Who gave them folks permission to rebel?
Lord MacNamara, valiant chief of war,
What is this place I've just been asked about?

MAC NAMARA:
It's way off to the East, eight thousand miles.
A little land we're trying to subdue.

MAC BIRD:
What crap is this "we're *trying* to subdue"?
Since when do we permit an open challenge
To all the world's security and peace?
Rip out those Reds! Destroy them, root and branch!
Deploy whatever force you think we need!
Eradicate this noxious, spreading weed!

MAC NAMARA:
Your word is my command. Your will is done.
That land will be subdued ere set of sun.

Exit MAC NAMARA. MAC BIRD *turns back to press.*

MAC BIRD:
Gentlemen, I thank you all for coming.
You're now dismissed.

ALL:
Thank *you,* your majesty.

REPORTERS *begin to file out. Handshakes; cameras removed, etc. A small cluster gathers.*

1ST REPORTER:
What a shit!

2ND REPORTER:
I guess you've heard the rumors.

1ST REPORTER:
Rumors, hell! I heard him here today.

3RD REPORTER:
The world is gonna be his private garden.
Defoliating weeds and lopping branches.[2]

In Vietnam, according to a Lao Dong (Communist) Party document, captured later, the Viet Cong are also mapping strategy.

Resolution of the Ninth Conference of the Lao Dong Party Central Committee, December 1963

We must and have the capability to check and defeat the enemy in his "special war." This capability will increase if we are determined to fight the U.S. imperialists and their henchmen, if we have a clever strategem, and know how to exploit the contradictions in the enemy's internal organizations, contradictions between the U.S. imperialists and the other imperialists, especially the French imperialists, contradictions between the U.S. and their henchmen in South Viet-Nam and the bourgeois ruling clique in Southeast Asia. In this way, we can cause difficulties for the U.S. in using the aggressive force of the Southeast Asia bloc to escalate the war in South Viet-Nam. Additionally, we must develop the movement against the U.S. aggressors, and gain the support of the people of the world (especially those of the socialist countries, and countries in Asia, Africa, and Latin America) for the South Viet-Nam Revolution. This Revolution is conducted on three fronts: the political, military and diplomatic fronts; the diplomatic front is designed to isolate the enemy in the international arena and gain the backing of the entire world.

However, we must always be vigilant and prepared to cope with the U.S. if she takes the risk of turning the war in South Viet-Nam into a limited war. The possibility that a limited war in South Viet-Nam would turn into a world war is almost nonexistent because the purpose and significance of this war cannot generate conditions leading to a world war.

In the framework of the "special war," there are two possibilities:

—First, the Americans would carry on the war at the present or slightly higher level.

—Second, the Americans would intensify the war by bringing in troops many times larger [than the present number] or both American troops and troops from the Southeast Asian aggressive bloc will intervene in the war. . . .

If the U.S. imperialists send more troops to Viet-Nam to save the situation after suffering a series of failures, *the Revolution in Viet-Nam will meet more difficulties, the struggle will be stronger and harder but it will certainly succeed in attaining the final victory*. With 800,000 well trained troops, the French imperialists could not defeat the 12 million courageous Algerians and finally had to give independence and freedom to them. For the same reason, the U.S. imperialists cannot win over 14 million Vietnamese people in the South who have taken arms to fight the imperialists for almost 20 years, and who, with all the compatriots throughout the country, have defeated the hundreds of thousands of troops of the French expeditionary force. Now the South Vietnamese people show themselves capable of beating the enemy in any situation. They certainly have the determination, talents, strength and patience to crush any U.S. imperialists' schemes and plans, and finally to force them to withdraw from Viet-Nam as the French imperialists did.

There is the possibly that the South Viet-Nam Revolution must go through a transitional period which entails complex forms and methods of struggling before it attains the final victory. The reunification of the country must be carried out step by step. In the present national democratic revolutionary phase in South Viet-Nam, *we must strive to attain victory step by step and gradually push back the enemy before reaching the General Offensive and Uprising to win complete victory*. However, we may pass through a transitional period before we attain complete victory. In any case, we must encourage the entire Party, people, and army to attain the maximum victory, and we should not have a hesitating attitude or to pause at the transitional period. If we are highly determined to win and prepared to face any situation, the final victory will certainly be in the hands of our people.[3]

Shortly after the beginning of 1964, according to The Pentagon Papers, *President Johnson approves a new plan for covert operations against North Vietnam.*

The covert program was spawned in May of 1963, when the JCS directed CINCPAC to prepare a plan for GVN "hit and run" operations against NVN. These operations were to be "non-attributable" and carried out "with U.S. military materiel, training and advisory assistance." Approved by the JCS on 9 September as CINCPAC OPLAN 34-63, the plan was discussed during the Vietnam policy conference at Honolulu, 20 November 1963. Here a decision was made to develop a combined COMUS-MACV-CAS, Saigon plan for a 12-month program of covert operations. Instructions forwarded by the JCS on 26 November specifically requested provision for: "(1) harassment; (2) diversion; (3) political pressure; (4) capture of prisoners; (5) physical destruction; (6) acquisition of intelli-

gence; (7) generation of intelligence; and (8) diversion of DRV resources." Further, that the plan provide for "selected actions of graduated scope and intensity to include commando type coastal raids." To this
guidance was added that given by President Johnson to the effect that
"planning should include . . . estimates of such factors as: (1) resulting
damage to NVN; (2) the plausibility of denial; (3) possible NVN retaliation; and (4) other international reaction." The MACV-CAS plan, designated OPLAN 34A, and providing for "a spectrum of capabilities for
RVNAF to execute against NVN," was forwarded by CINCPAC on 19
December 1963.

The idea of putting direct pressure on North Vietnam met prompt
receptivity on the part of President Johnson. According to then Assistant
Secretary of State, Roger Hilsman, it was just a few days before the
military-CIA submission that State Department Counselor, Walt Rostow
passed to the President "a well-reasoned case for a gradual escalation."
Rostow was well-known as an advocate of taking direct measures against
the external sources of guerrilla support, having hammered away at this
theme since he first presented it at Fort Bragg in April 1961. In any
event, on 21 December, President Johnson directed that an interdepartmental committee study the MACV-CAS plan to select from it those least
risk [sic]." This committee, under the chairmanship of Major General
Krulak, USMC, completed its study on 2 January 1964 and submitted its
report for review by the principal officials of its various member agencies.
The report recommended the 3-phase approach and the variety of Phase I
operations described earlier. President Johnson approved the committee's
recommendations on 16 January and directed that the initial 4-month
phase of the program be implemented beginning 1 February.

In view of program performance and later decisions, the conceptualiza-
tion underlying the program of covert operations against North Vietnam is
particularly significant. JCS objectives for the initial CINCPAC formulation
were to increase the cost to the DRV of its role in the South Vietnamese
insurgency. The catalogue of operations submitted from Saigon was intended to "convince the DRV leadership that they should cease to support
insurgent activities in the RVN and Laos." Although, in its forwarding
letter, CINCPAC expressed doubt that all but a few of the 2062 separate
operations detailed by MACV-CAS could have that kind of effect. In his
view, only air attacks and a few other "punitive or attritional" operations
had any probability of success in achieving the stated objectives.[4]

1964   **January**—General William C. Westmoreland is assigned to U.S. Mili-
tary Assistance Command, Vietnam (MACV), Saigon. **30 January**—
Military coup in Saigon. Major General Nguyen Khanh ousts Major
General Duong Van Minh. **1 February**—Covert operations against
North Vietnam under OPLAN 34A begin.

In early March Scripps-Howard reporter Jim G. Lucas records his impressions of the war.

March 6, Can Tho

To understand anything at all about this strange little war, it helps to examine some of the organization problems.

For one thing, the command structure—ours and the Vietnamese—is grotesque. Like Topsy, it just growed.

On our part, we have MACV (Military Assistance Command, Viet Nam) headed by Gen. Paul Harkins. Harkins also is MACT (Military Assistance Command, Thailand).

Then we have MAAG (Military Advisory Assistance Group) headed by Maj. Gen. Charles Timmes. MAAG has been here since the early 1950's. It controls the advisory teams.

Then there is a Support Command, headed by Brig. Gen. Joe Stilwell, Jr. It controls the operating troops, such as the helicopter crews. Theoretically they are here to support the Vietnamese. In practice they are fighting a war.

On top of all this, we have a "country team" headed by Ambassador Henry Cabot Lodge, who is a major general in the Army Reserve.

Men in the field often work for all three commands. They must submit reports to all three. The paper work is horrendous. There are rumors that Lt. Gen. William C. Westmoreland will abolish MACV or MAAG when he succeeds Harkins. The troops devoutly hope this is true. Westmoreland is now Harkins' deputy.

The Vietnamese have four categories of troops in the field, some working for the Ministry of Defense, others for the Ministry of Interior.

At the lowest level there is the hamlet militia. They work in squads. They have, at most, one automatic weapon. If they are paid at all it is by the people they protect. Usually it is in rice.

Next there is the Self Defense Corps. It is organized in platoons, and slightly better armed. Its men are paid $9 a month.

Third echelon is the Civil Guard. Roughly it compares with our National Guard. It is organized into companies. Its men draw $12 a month.

Finally there is the ARVIN (Army of the Republic of Viet Nam). It is organized into regiments, divisions and corps. Its men are much better paid. They have fairly modern weapons.

On top of this there is the Vietnamese JGS (Joint General Staff), comparable to our Joint Chiefs of Staff. And to add to the confusion, the province chiefs (governors) are majors, and the district chiefs under them captains and first lieutenants. Each has his own troops. Each province chief has a U.S. Army major as his adviser.

Though the ARVIN is better paid and better armed, it is the Civil Guard that bears the brunt of the war. The average ARVIN battalion goes two weeks without making contact with the Viet Cong. An average Civil Guard company is fighting two days out of three.

There are reasons for this contrast. The Civil Guard is smaller (company-size units). It has less fire power; no artillery. Its men are sketchily trained. It does not have enough good officers, consequently it is not so well led.

But the big reason the Guard sees more action is psychological, and the Viet Cong are canny enough to exploit that. A Civil Guard company is a local unit. These boys grew up in the province where they're stationed. Everybody knows them.

If the Viet Cong can chew up a Civil Guard company, they effectively assert their rule over that area. A man joins the Civil Guard one week, and they bring his body home the next. That night the Viet Cong slip in and tell his widow, "We killed your man because he opposed us."

The message soon gets home. It makes no difference if an ARVIN battalion sweeps through the next week and kills 20 Communists while taking no losses—the villagers remember the local boys who died. The ARVIN soldiers are strangers.

It's a curious war, with all sorts of interlocking factors.

March 9, Can Tho
The 15,500 U.S. military personnel in Viet Nam are divided into two camps—the "Hawks" and the "Doves."

The Hawks believe this war should be fought as a war. Their solution to South Viet Nam's problem is to kill the Viet Cong.

The Doves believe this war is different. They say it can be won only by winning the people. They believe in something called "civic action."

The Doves call the Hawks "military minds."

The Hawks call the Doves "Peace Corps types," or "State Department boys."

The dividing line is hard to define. Often, West Point classmates of the same rank are in opposite camps. It depends largely on their assignment and their experience.

Those who work most intimately with the Vietnamese are inclined to be Doves. Those with the least contact are more often Hawks.

They do have a common goal: to win the war. They agree on some points; for instance, that we must win the people. They agree we are not doing that now.

To win the people, the Hawks say, you eliminate the Viet Cong. The average Vietnamese gives his allegiance to whoever controls his hamlet. He isn't concerned with ideology; he wants security. Kill the Viet Cong, replace him, and you have the people. It's that simple.

The Doves say we first must convince the people, by our deeds, that ours is the right side—that democracy works, that we are genuinely interested in them. This is "civic action." That's why we send unarmed medical teams into enemy country to give cholera shots.

We sometimes get bogged down in details. Recently I sat in on a meeting in which AID and MAAG (military advisory) people argued all morning whether to pay members of teams sent out to teach democracy 30 or 45 cents a day. (AID held out for 30 cents.) The issue still has not been resolved, and the program is stalemated.

Because we send our best officers and men to Viet Nam, how to win this war is debated endlessly. Many young lieutenants and captains have written monographs on the subject. I have read a half-dozen.

One captain recently was duty officer from midnight until dawn. Barring an attack (which did not materialize), he had nothing to do but keep awake. He used this time to put his thoughts on paper. Later he sent the paper up through channels.

Among other things, he said we are going to be involved here for at least 20 years, and the American people should be so informed. He (a Dove) also proposed gradually replacing our advisers with Nationalist Chinese. He pointed out we have trained their army well, but it has nothing to do so it can't remain good indefinitely. Send it to South Viet Nam, he said.

He suggested, too, that trading with the enemy be made a treasonable offense. Some foreign-owned companies, including American, operate with impunity in Viet Cong areas. They are widely believed to pay tribute.

One American officer says the enemy collects a tax on every gallon of aviation fuel. Two U.S. oil companies have filling stations in Viet Cong country. They have never been hit.

An article of faith with the Hawks is total mobilization. They say South Viet Nam is not mobilized, that it is still fighting a "part-time, peace-time, humanitarian war." They say you could raise another division from the boys walking the streets in Can Tho, or among the cab drivers in Saigon.

There are two Vietnamese divisions in the Mekong Delta; we need at least six, they contend.

The Doves say 100 divisions wouldn't do it.

The Hawks also want to deny the Viet Cong their privileged sanctuary in North Viet Nam. Bomb Hanoi, they say. Infiltrate North Viet Nam as the Commies have infiltrated the South.

Special Forces officers want to operate in the U-Minh forest, where no one but Viet Cong ever goes. Sure, we'd have casualties, they say. We might even lose whole units. But taking risks is part of our job. So far, they are forbidden to go.

Nonsense, the Doves say. We've tried infiltrating the North. And 85 per cent of our infiltrators were rounded up and shot within 24 hours. To make that idea practical, we must be able to command the similar loyalty from the South Viet Nam people. That, they insist, calls for more "civic action."[5]

At about this time the following parody is written, showing various perspectives on army Special Forces personnel.

The Special Forces Soldier

as seen by:

MACV HQ	A drunken, brawling, jeep stealing, woman corrupting, liar with a star sapphire Seiko watch and a demo knife.
HIMSELF	A tall, handsome, highly trained professional killer, female idol, sapphire ring wearing, demo knife carrying gentleman who is always on time due to the reliability of his Seiko watch.
HIS WIFE	A stinking member of the family who comes through Fort Bragg once a month with a rucksack full of dirty clothes and a hard-on.
COMMANDER	A fine speciman of a drunken, brawling, jeep stealing, woman corrputing, liar with a star sapphire ring, Seiko watch and a demo knife.
DEPARTMENT OF THE ARMY	An over-paid, overranked, tax burden that is indespensable because he has volunteered to go anywhere, do anything as long as he can booze it up, brawl, steal jeeps, corrupt women, lie, wear a star sapphire ring, Seiko watch, and carry a demo knife.[6]

In Laos, notes The Pentagon Papers, *increased military activity is now authorized.*

On 17 March, Ambassador Lodge reported a long conversation between General Khanh and a Laotian representative, with Souvanna's permission, at which a working agreement between military forces of the two governments was obtained. Khanh and Phoumi Nousavan, Laotian rightist military commander, arranged to resume diplomatic relations between the two countries during that week and came to other more specific agreements as follows:

> 1. Laotians agreed to allow South Vietnam to have free passage in Southern Laos, to create a combined Laotian-Vietnamese staff to use all the bases including Tchepone, and to conduct bombardment with unmarked T-28 planes (in the areas where FAR [Phoumi's] forces were engaged).
> 2. The 10-kilometer limit on hot pursuit is abrogated; commando raids and sabotage can be undertaken without limit by combined Laotian and South Vietnamese units; South Vietnamese officers will serve the Laotian units to provide added leadership.

Previously, President Johnson had indicated approval of cross-border ground penetrations into Laos "along any lines which can be worked out between Khanh and Phoumi with Souvanna's endorsement." Although asking Secretaries Rusk and McNamara to develop a joint recommendation concerning U.S. participation in air strikes within Laos, the President went on to state a position consonant with that of the State-ISA view:

My first thought is that it is important to seek support from Souvanna Phouma and to build a stronger case before we take action which might have only limited military effect and could trigger wider Communist action in Laos.[7]

President Johnson communicates his views to Ambassador Lodge in Saigon.

20 March 1964

FM: State 1484 (The Secretary)
TO: Saigon

For Ambassador Lodge from the President

We have studied your 1776 and I am asking State to have Bill Bundy make sure that you get out latest planning documents on ways of applying pressure and power against the North. I understand that some of this was discussed with you by McNamara mission in Saigon, but as plans are refined it would be helpful to have your detailed comments. As we agreed in our previous messages to each other, judgment is reserved for the present on overt military action in view of the consensus from Saigon conversations of McNamara mission with General Khanh and you on judgment that movement against the North at the present would be premature. We have share [*sic*] General Khanh's judgment that the immediate and essential task is to strengthen the southern base. For this reason our planning for action against the North is on a contingency basis at present, and immediate problem in this area is to develop the strongest possible military and political base for possible later action. There is additional international reason for avoiding immediate overt action in that we expect a showdown between the Chinese and Soviet Communist parties soon and action against the North will be more practicable after than before a showdown. But if at any time you feel that more immediate action is urgent, I count on you to let me know specifically the reasons for such action, together with your recommendations for its size and shape.[8]

1964   25 April—General William Westmoreland becomes Commander, U.S. Military Assistance Command, Vietnam (COMUSMACV).

In The Green Berets, *CIA adviser Bernard Arklin, after a peaceful spring in Laos, has reestablished his working relationship with the Meo tribesmen.*

The Laotians paid no attention to the Viet Cong Communists from North Vietnam who openly used the country as a sanctuary for organizing their forces and infiltrating South Vietnam. The VC, after all, only caused trouble to the South Vietnamese. And most Western diplomatic missions in Vientiane enjoyed, to the full, the amenities the city offered, secure in the apparently peaceful intentions of the Pathet Lao.

But not a member of the Meo tribe doubted that the Communists would soon be on the march again. As a result, Arklin had no trouble convincing his charges that they must be constantly ready to meet and kill the Pathets. Pay Dang, in fact, frequently expressed the consensus of Meo opinion when he said they should launch a surprise attack on the Pathet with their new weapons. That way they might be able to kill more than 100 and lose few men themselves.

Arklin tried to explain the Geneva convention: How the Pathet, neutralists, and rightists had promised to live together in harmony, and all foreigners had promised to cease military aid to any of the three factions making up the government. How it was not the way of democratic countries to anticipate Communist aggressive designs and attack first. The entire concept of not attacking first was beyond the realistic Meos' comprehension.

As Arklin's patrols and agents reported a steady flow of Communist troops and equipment traveling south unmolested along a trail only thirty-five or forty miles away, it was difficult to resist Pay Dang's coaxing that they take a company and ambush a Communist column. The montagnards were getting anxious to kill their hated enemies. Arklin had to permit more frequent animal sacrifices and drinking parties to hold in check his tribesmen's blood lust, inflamed by the profusion of new weapons and their ability to use them well.

The Communists were quietly biding their time; Arklin wished they would attack and get it over with. He was constantly worried that some of the Meos might disobey his orders and stage a raid on a Pathet Lao village. Meanwhile U-10 flights kept him supplied and brought in more arms.

By March, 1964, the weapons room contained enough heavy and light weapons and ammunition for battalion operations. Arklin had more than 400 men. They were paid monthly in Laotian currency flown in to him. Morale was high and the men were honed to a keen fighting edge when the first signs of militancy on the part of the Pathets was reported by a patrol.

In April Communist military units were processing only twenty miles away to the North and then marching south to Pathet Lao headquarters at Khang Khay. Arklin radioed this information to control and requested permission to ambush the columns of Communists now moving along trails, within striking range of the strongly fortified Meo village.

Permission was refused, pending the Pathet showing their hand more openly, but during the first week of May a message arrived that control would be at the airstrip the next morning. Arklin took an entire company with him to meet the plane.

Two U-10's landed and the Meo carriers ran across the field to unload. It was a less-than-jolly Frank Methuan who stepped from the ship. Arklin noticed his control's mood at once.

"What's the matter, Frank? I'm the one that should be looking like a six-week case of the ass."

"You look like the sorriest major I ever saw," the CIA man snapped.

Abashed, Arklin realized that unconsciously he may well have been letting himself go. In spite of all his precautions he had somehow contracted dysentery, which had taken its toll physically, to say nothing of reducing his desire to preserve military neatness at all times.

"I'm sorry, Frank. Guess I *have* been kind of careless lately. Not that it ever mattered to you before."

"Oh, Christ. I'm sorry, Bernie. I wish I was up here with you instead of fighting the Saigon-Bangkok-Pentagon-State Department war."

"What's it all about?"

"There's been a big flap between Military Assistance Command and the rest of the country team in Vietnam and Thailand."

"That sort of Olympian struggle never gets down to my level," Arklin said. "At least not when I'm out here with a bunch of restless montagnards."

"Well, it's getting down to you and your montagnards. For one thing all Special Forces in Vietnam now come directly under Military Assistance Command. They're trying to streamline things—they think. But what it comes down to is that a lot of Special Forces and our Combined Studies Group programs are being run by conventional army generals."

"This one too? In Laos?"

"They haven't gotten around to Laos yet. It may be a while, since the orthodox types running this crazy war don't like to admit to themselves that Americans are violating treaties—even though if we didn't the Commies would take this dinky little country that happens to be so strategically located any week they wanted."

"That's going to change a lot of things. From what you say, conventional officers sitting in comfortable offices will be writing the efficiency reports on Special Forces officers out in the field who are trying to outfight and outsmart the Viet Cong with their hands tied behind their backs."

"That's exactly what happened on May 1st."

"And my little operation? Are we going to piss all over the Meos again, take their weapons away like we did before and leave them to be butchered by the Pathet Lao?"

"Not as long as the Agency is running the show."

"We'll keep running it. We're ready to go. We have been for six months."

"You'll be getting action, plenty of it, soon. There's been a half-assed *coup d'état* in Vientiane. Nothing much. A new right-wing general has taken over control of the government temporarily. But this is all it takes to give the Communists an excuse to start moving into Vientiane."

Methuan pointed across the entrance to the flat Plain of Jars below them to the east. "General Kong Le has a few thousand troops over there which are all that's standing between the Communists and his Head-quarters at Vang Vieng. If the Pathet can roll into Vang Vieng they'll be fifty easy miles from Vientiane and taking over Laos. Your job is to do everything you can to harass and slow down the Pathets. We won't be able to give you direct orders. All we can do is tell you they're rolling. The rest is up to you."[9]

1964   17 May—In Laos, Pathet Lao/NVA forces open offensive on the Plaine des Jarres. **21 May**—Souvanna Phouma grants permission for U.S. Air Force "low-level reconnaissance" flights over Laos. **19 July**—In Vietnam, General Khanh and Air Vice Marshall Nguyen Cao Ky publicly call for extended out-of-country opera-tions including a "march north" into North Vietnam. The United States does not concur.

In July South Vietnamese naval forces (PTFs) carry out Operation 34A raids and commando landings against islands off the North Vietnamese coast. Simultaneously, U.S. Navy destroyers are conducting electronic intelligence-gathering patrols code-named "DeSoto" in international waters off North Vietnam. On 1 August Radio Hanoi broadcasts a protest to the commando raids.

At 2340 hours on 30 July, the Americans and their henchmen in South Vietnam sent two warships to bombard Hon Ngu Island off Qua Hoi Hoi, Nghe An Province. This island is four kilometers from the coast. At the same time, another warship was sent to bombard Hon Me island off Ba Lang, Thanh Hoa Province. This island is 12 kilometers from the coast.

These acts of the Americans and the southern administration constitute a gross violation of the sovereignty and territorial integrity of the DRV, an extremely serious violation of the 1954 Geneva agreements on Viet-nam, and a shameless provocation toward North Vietnam. Obviously, these are not individual acts, but are part of the premeditated common plan of the Americans and their henchmen to carry out schemes to inten-sify the provocative and destructive acts against the DRV while striving to step up their aggressive war in South Vietnam.

The VPA strongly protests the above-mentioned bombardments of these two islands by the warships of the Americans and their henchmen and urges the ICC to adopt effective measures to force the Americans and the southern administration to stop immediately their extremely dan-gerous and provocative acts and to respect and properly implement the 1954 Geneva agreements on Vietnam.[10]

During the next three days incidents occur that determine U.S. policy toward Southeast Asia for the next ten years. The Pentagon Papers *contains a summary of the Gulf of Tonkin incidents.*

THE FIRST INCIDENT

What happened in the Gulf? . . . U.S.S. *Maddox* commenced the second DE SOTO Patrol on 31 July. On the prior night South Vietnamese coastal patrol forces [PTFs] made a midnight attack, including an amphibious "commando" raid, on Hon Me and Hon Nieu Islands, about 19° N. latitude. At the time of this attack, U.S.S. *Maddox* was 120–130 miles away just heading into waters off North Vietnam. On 2 August, having reached the northernmost point on its patrol track and having headed South, the destroyer was intercepted by three North Vietnamese patrol boats. Apparently, these boats and a fleet of junks had moved into the area near the island to search for the attacking force and had mistaken *Maddox* for a South Vietnamese escort vessel. (Approximately eleven hours earlier, while on a northerly heading, *Maddox* had altered course to avoid the junk concentration shown on her radar: about six hours after that—now headed South—*Maddox* had altered her course to the southeast to avoid the junks a second time.) When the PT boats began their high-speed run at her, at a distance of approximately 10 miles, the destroyer was 28 miles from the coast and heading farther into international waters. Two of the boats closed to within 5,000 yards, launching one torpedo each. As they approached, *Maddox* fired on the boats with her 5-inch batteries and altered course to avoid the torpedoes, which were observed passing the starboard side at a distance of 100 to 200 yards. The third boat moved up abeam of the destroyer and took a direct 5-inch hit; it managed to launch a torpedo which failed to run. All three PT boats fired 50-caliber machine guns at *Maddox* as they made their firing runs, and a bullet fragment was recovered from the destroyer's superstructure. The attacks occurred in midafternoon, and photographs were taken of the torpedo boats as they attacked.

Upon first report of the PT boats' apparently hostile intent, four F-8E aircraft were launched from the aircraft carrier *Ticonderoga,* many miles to the South, with instructions to provide air cover but not to fire unless they or *Maddox* were fired upon. As *Maddox* continued in a southerly direction, *Ticonderoga*'s aircraft attacked the two boats that had initiated the action. Both were damaged with Zuni rockets and 20mm gunfire. The third boat, struck by the destroyer's 5-inch, was already dead in the water. After about eight minutes, the aircraft broke off their attacks. In the meantime, *Maddox* had been directed by the 7th Fleet Commander to retire from the area to avoid hostile fire. Following their attacks on the PT's, the aircraft joined *Maddox* and escorted her back toward South Vietnamese waters where she joined a second destroyer, *C. Turner Joy.* The two ships continued to patrol in international waters. Approximately two hours after the action, in early evening, reconnaissance aircraft from

Ticonderoga located the damaged PT's and obtained two photographs. The third boat was last seen burning and presumed sunk.

On 3 August a note of protest was dispatched to the Hanoi Government, reportedly through the International Control Commission for Indo-China. Directed by the President, the note stressed the unprovoked nature of the North Vietnamese attack and closed with the following warning:

> The U.S. Government expects that the authorities of the regime in North Vietnam will be under no misapprehension as to the grave consequences which would inevitably result from any further unprovoked offensive military action against U.S. forces.

On that same day, measures were taken to increase the security of the DE SOTO Patrol, the approved schedule of which still had two days to run. At 1325 hours (Washington time) the JCS approved a CINCPAC request to resume the patrol at a distance of 11 n.m. from the North Vietnamese coast. Later in the day, President Johnson announced that he had approved doubling the patrolling force and authorized active defense measures on the part of both the destroyers and their escorting aircraft. His press statement included the following:

> I have instructed the Navy:
> 1. To continue the patrols in the Gulf of Tonkin off the coast of North Vietnam.
> 2. To double the force by adding an additional destroyer to the one already on patrol.
> 3. To provide a combat air patrol over the destroyers, and
> 4. To issue orders to the commanders of the combat aircraft and the two destroyers; (a) to attack any force which attacks them in international waters, and (b) to attack with the objective not only of driving off the force but of destroying it.

The Second Incident

Late the following evening the destroyers, *Maddox* and *C. Turner Joy,* were involved in a second encounter with hostile patrol boats. Like the first incident, this occurred following a South Vietnamese attack on North Vietnamese coastal targets—this time the Rhon River estuary and the Vinh Sonh radar installation, which were bombarded on the night of 3 August. The more controversial of the two, this incident occurred under cover of darkness and seems to have been both triggered and described largely by radar and sonar images. After the action had been joined, however, both visual sightings and intercepted North Vietnamese communications confirmed that an attack by hostile patrol craft was in progress.

At 1940 hours, 4 August 1964 (Tonkin Gulf time), while "proceeding S.E. at best speed," Task Group 72.1 (*Maddox and Turner Joy*) radioed "RCVD INFO indicating attack by PGM P-4 imminent." Evidently this was based on an intercepted communication, later identified as "an intelligence source," indicating that "North Vietnamese naval forces had been ordered to attack the patrol." At the time, radar contacts evaluated as "probable torpedo boats" were observed about 36 miles to the northeast. Accordingly, the Task Group Commander altered course and increased speed to avoid what he evaluated as a trap. At approximately 2035 hours, while west of Hainan Island, the destroyers reported radar sightings of three unidentified aircraft and two unidentified vessels in the patrol area. On receiving the report, *Ticonderoga* immediately launched F-8s and A-4Ds to provide a combat air patrol over the destroyers. Within minutes, the unidentified aircraft disappeared from the radar screen, while the vessels maintained a distance of about 27 miles. Actually, surface contacts on a parallel course had been shadowing the destroyers with radar for more than three hours. ECM contacts maintained by the *C. Turner Joy* indicated that the radar was that carried aboard DRV patrol boats.

New unidentified surface contacts 13 miles distant were reported at 2134 hours. These vessels were closing at approximately 30 knots on the beam and were evaluated as "hostile." Six minutes later (2140) *Maddox* opened fire, and at 1242, by which time two of the new contacts had closed to a distance of 11 miles, aircraft from *Ticonderoga*'s CAP began their attacks. Just before this, one of the PT boats launched a torpedo, which was later reported as seen passing about 300 feet off the port beam, from aft to forward, of the *C. Turner Joy*. A searchlight beam was observed to swing in an arc toward the *C. Turner Joy* by all of the destroyer's signal bridge personnel. It was extinguished before it illuminated the ship, presumably upon detection of the approaching aircraft. Aboard the *Maddox*, Marine gunners saw what were believed to be cockpit lights of one or more small boats pass up the port side of the ship and down the other. After approximately an hour's action, the destroyers reported two enemy boats sunk and no damage or casualties suffered.

In the meantime, two patrol craft from the initial surface contact had closed to join the action, and the engagement was described for higher headquarters—largely on the basis of the destroyers' radar and sonar indications and on radio intercept information. [Three lines illegible] the count reached 22 torpedoes, a total which caused the Commanding Officer, once the engagement had ended, to question the validity of his report and communicate these doubts to his superiors:

> Review of action makes many recorded contacts and torpedoes fired appear doubtful. Freak weather effects and overeager sonarman may have accounted for many reports.

In addition to sonar readings, however, the Task Group had also reported intercepting communications from North Vietnamese naval craft indicating that they were involved in an attack on U.S. ("enemy") ships and that they had "sacrificed" two vessels in the engagement.

The Response in Washington

Sometime prior to the reported termination of the engagement, at 0030 hours, 5 August (Tonkin Gulf time), "alert orders," to prepare for possible reprisal raids were sent out by naval authorities to *Ticonderoga* and to a second aircraft carrier, *Constellation,* which started heading South from Hong Kong late on 3 August. Such raids were actually ordered and carried out later in the day. "Defense officials disclosed [in public testimony, 9 January 1968] that, when the first word was received of the second attack 'immediate consideration was given to retaliation.' " That apparently began shortly after 0920 hours (Washington time), when the task group message that a North Vietnamese naval attack was imminent was first relayed to Washington. From this time on, amid a sequence of messages describing the attack, Secretary McNamara held "a series of meetings with [his] chief civilian and military advisers" concerning the engagement and possible U.S. retaliatory actions. As he testified before the Fulbright Committee:

> We identified and refined various options for a response to the attack, to be presented to the President. Among these options was the air strike against the attacking boats and their associated bases, which option was eventually selected. As the options were identified preliminary messages were sent to appropriate operational commanders alerting them to the several possibilities so that initial planning steps could be undertaken.

At 1230, the President met with the National Security Council. Having just come from a brief meeting with the JCS, attended also by Secretary Rusk and McGeorge Bundy, Secretary McNamara briefed the NSC on the reported details of the attack and the possibilities for reprisal. Shortly thereafter (presumably during a working lunch with the President, Secretary Rusk and Bundy) and after receiving by telephone the advice of the JCS, McNamara and the others recommended specific reprisal actions. It was at this point that the President approved "a response consisting of an air strike on the PT and SWATOW boat bases and their associated facilities."

Returning from this session shortly after 1500, Secretary McNamara, along with Deputy Secretary Vance, joined with the JCS to review all the evidence relating to the engagement. Included in this review was the communications intelligence information which the Secretary reported, containing North Vietnamese reports that (1) their vessels were engaging the destroyers, and (2) they had lost two craft in the fight. In the meantime, however, messages had been relayed to the Joint Staff indicating considerable confusion over the details of the attack. The DE SOTO Patrol Commander's message, expressing doubts about earlier evidence of a large-scale torpedo attack, arrived sometime after 1330 hours. Considerably later (it was not sent to CINCPACFLT until 1447 EDT), another message arrived to the effect that while details of the action were still confusing, the commander of Task Group 72.1 was certain that the ambush was genuine. He had interviewed the personnel who sighted the boat's cockpit lights passing near the *Maddox,* and he had obtained a report from the *C. Turner Joy* that two torpedoes were observed passing nearby. Accordingly, these reports were discussed by telephone with CINCPAC, and he was instructed by Secretary McNamara to make a careful check of the evidence and ascertain whether there was any doubt concerning the occurrence of an attack. CINCPAC called the JCS at least twice more, at 1723 and again at 1807 hours, to state that he was convinced on the basis of "additional information" that the attacks had taken place. At the time of the earlier call Secretary McNamara and the JCS were discussing possible force deployments to follow any reprisals. On the occasion of the first call, the Secretary was at the White House attending the day's second NSC meeting. Upon being informed of CINC-PAC's call, he reports:

> I spoke to the Director of the Joint Staff and asked him to make certain that the Commander in Chief, Pacific was willing to state that the attack had taken place, and therefore that he was free to release the Executive Order because earlier in the afternoon I had told him that under no circumstances would retaliatory action take place until we were, to use my words, "damned sure that the attacks had taken place."

At the meeting of the National Security Council, proposals to deploy certain increments of OPLAN 37-64 forces to the Western Pacific were discussed, and the order to retaliate against North Vietnamese patrol craft and their associated facilities was confirmed. Following this meeting, at 1845, the President met with 16 Congressional leaders from both parties for a period of 89 minutes. Reportedly, he described the second incident in the Gulf, explained his decisions to order reprisals, and informed the legislators of his intention to request a formal statement of Congressional support for these decisions. On the morning following the meeting, the Washington *Post* carried a report that none of the Congressional leaders present at the meeting had raised objections to the course of action planned. Their only question, the report stated, "had to do with how Congress could show its agreement and concern in the crisis."

In many ways the attacks on U.S. ships in the Tonkin Gulf provided the Administration with an opportunity to do a number of things that had been urged on it. Certainly it offered a politically acceptable way of exerting direct punitive pressure on North Vietnam. In South Vietnam, the U.S. response served to satisfy for a time the growing desire for some action to carry the war to the North. Relative to the election campaign, it provided a means of eliminating any doubts about President Johnson's decisiveness that may have been encouraged by his preferred candidate's image as the restrained man of peace. The obvious convenience and the ways in which it was exploited have been at the root of much of the suspicion with which critics of Administration policy have viewed the incident.

The documents available to this writer are not conclusive on this point, but the evidence indicates that the occurrence of a DRV provocation at this time resulted from events over which the U.S. Government exercised little control. It has been suggested that the incidents were related in some way to pressure coming from the GVN for U.S. action against North Vietnam. However, the patrol was authorized on or prior to 17 July, and General Khanh's oft-cited "Go North" appeal wasn't made until 19 July. The first attack almost certainly was a case of mistaken judgment on the part of the local Vietnamese commander. His probable association of U.S.S. *Maddox* with the South Vietnamese raiding force is indicated by the circumstances preceding the event, the brief duration and character of it, and the long-delayed (not until 5 August) and rather subdued DRV public comment. Moreover, there is little reason to see anything more than coincidence in the close conjunction between the GVN's maritime operations against the North Vietnamese coast and the scheduling of the DE SOTO Patrol. The two operations were scheduled and monitored from different authorities and through separate channels of communication and command. Higher U.S. naval commands were informed of the operations against the two islands by COMUSMACV, but the task group commander had no knowledge of where or when the specific operations had taken place. As Secretary McNamara told Senator Morse, in response to charges that U.S. naval forces were supporting the GVN operation,

> Our ships had absolutely no knowledge of it, were not connected with it; in no sense of the word can be considered to have backstopped the effort.[11]

As retaliatory air raids are being prepared against North Vietnamese PT boat bases, the U.S. Senate debates a resolution introduced by President Johnson. During the debate the following interchange takes place.

MR. BREWSTER [Senator Daniel B. Brewster of Maryland]: . . . I would look with great dismay on a situation involving the landing of large land armies on the continent of Asia. So my question is whether there is anything in the resolution which would authorize or recommend or approve the landing of large American armies in Vietnam or in China.
MR. FULBRIGHT [Senator J. William Fulbright of Arkansas]: There is nothing in the resolution, as I read it, that contemplates it. I agree with the Senator that that is the last thing we would want to do. However, the language of the resolution would not prevent it. It would authorize whatever the Commander in Chief feels is necessary. It does not restrain the Executive from doing it. . . . Speaking for my own committee, everyone I have heard has said that the last thing we want to do is to become involved in a land war in Asia. . . .[12]

Two days later on 7 August, Senator J. William Fulbright sponsors the following Gulf of Tonkin Resolution, which is approved. The vote: House of Representatives—unanimous; Senate—88 to 2.

To Promote the Maintenance of International Peace and Security in Southeast Asia.

Whereas naval units of the Communist regime in Vietnam, in violation of the principles of the Charter of the United Nations and of international law, have deliberately and repeatedly attacked United States naval vessels lawfully present in international waters, and have thereby created a serious threat to international peace; and

Whereas these attacks are part of a deliberate and systematic campaign of aggression that the Communist regime in North Vietnam has been waging against its neighbors and the nations joined with them in the collective defense of their freedom; and

Whereas the United States is assisting the peoples of southeast Asia to protect their freedom and has no territorial, military or political ambitions in that area, but desires only that these peoples should be left in peace to work out their own destinies in their own way: Now, therefore, be it

Resolved by the Senate and House of Representatives of the United States of America in Congress assembled.

That the Congress approves and supports the determination of the President, as Commander in Chief, to take all necessary measures to repel any armed attack against the forces of the United States and to prevent further aggression.

SEC.2. The United States regards as vital to its national interest and to world peace the maintenance of international peace and security in southeast Asia. Consonant with the Constitution of the United States and the Charter of the United Nations and in accordance with its obligations under the Southeast Asia Collective Defense Treaty, the United States is, therefore, prepared, as the President determines, to take all necessary steps, including the use of armed force, to assist any member or protocol state of the Southeast Asia Collective Defense Treaty requesting assistance in defense of its freedom.

SEC.3. This resolution shall expire when the President shall determine that the peace and security of the area is reasonably assured by international conditions created by action of the United Nations or otherwise, except that it may be terminated earlier by concurrent resolution of the Congress.[13]

1964 7 August—U.S. Navy aircraft attack North Vietnamese PT boat bases. U.S. Air Force F-100s and F-105s are deployed to Thailand.

The next day, the United States attempts to make contact with the North Vietnamese government. A State Department note is delivered to the Canadian embassy in Washington. J. Blair Seaborn is the Canadian member of the International Control Commission.

Canadians are urgently asked to have Seaborn during August 10 visit make following points (as having been conveyed to him by U.S. Government since August 6):

A. Re Tonkin Gulf actions, which almost certainly will come up:

1. The DRV has stated that Hon Ngu and Hon Me islands were attacked on July 30. It should be noted that the USS MADDOX was all of that day and into the afternoon of the next day, over 100 miles south of those islands, in international waters near the 17th parallel, and that the DRV attack on the MADDOX took place on August 2nd, more than two days later. Neither the MADDOX or any other destroyer was in any way associated with any attack on the DRV islands.

2. Regarding the August 4 attack by the DRV on the two U.S. destroyers, the Americans were and are at a complete loss to understand the DRV motive. They had decided to absorb the August 2 attack on the grounds that it very well might have been the result of some DRV mistake or miscalculation. The August 4 attack, however—from the determined nature of the attack as indicated by the radar, sonar, and eye witness evidence both from the ships and from their protecting aircraft—was, in the American eyes, obviously deliberate and planned and ordered in advance. In addition, premeditation was shown by the evidence that the DRV craft were waiting in ambush for the destroyers. The attack did not seem to be in response to any action by the South Vietnamese nor did it make sense as a tactic to further any diplomatic objective. Since the attack took place at least 60 miles from nearest land, there could have been no question about territorial waters. About the only reasonable hypothesis was that North Vietnam was intent either upon making it appear that the United States was a "paper tiger" or upon provoking the United States.

3. The American response was directed solely to patrol craft and installations acting in direct support of them. As President Johnson stated: "Our response for the present will be limited and fitting."

4. In view of uncertainty aroused by the deliberate and unprovoked DRV attacks this character, U.S. has necessarily carried out precautionary deployments of additional air power to SVN and Thailand.

B. Re basic American position:

5. Mr. Seaborn should again stress that U.S. policy is simply that North Vietnam should contain itself and its ambitions within the territory allocated to its administration by the 1954 Geneva Agreements. He should stress that U.S. policy in South Vietnam is to preserve the integrity of that state's territory against guerrilla subversion.

6. He should reiterate that the U.S. does not seek military bases in the area and that the U.S. is not seeking to overthrow the Communist regime in Hanoi.

7. He should repeat that the U.S. is fully aware of the degree to which Hanoi controls and directs the guerrilla action in South Vietnam and that the U.S. holds Hanoi directly responsible for that action. He should

similarly indicate U.S. awareness of North Vietnamese control over the Pathet Lao movement in Laos and the degree of North Vietnamese involvement in that country. He should specifically indicate U.S. awareness of North Vietnamese violations of Laotian territory along the infiltration route into South Vietnam.

8. Mr. Seaborn can again refer to the many examples of U.S. policy in tolerance of peaceful coexistence with Communist regimes, such as Yugoslavia, Poland, etc. He can hint at the economic and other benefits which have accrued to those countries because their policy of Communism has confirmed itself to the development of their own national territories and has not sought to expand into other areas.

9. Mr. Seaborn should conclude with the following new points:

a. That the events of the past few days should add credibility to the statement made last time, that "U.S. public and official patience with North Vietnamese aggression is growing extremely thin."

b. That the U.S. Congressional Resolution was passed with near unanimity, strongly re-affirming the unity and determination of the U.S. Government and people not only with respect to any further attacks on U.S. military forces but more broadly to continue to oppose firmly, by all necessary means, DRV efforts to subvert and conquer South Vietnam and Laos.

c. That the U.S. has come to the view that the DRV role in South Vietnam and Laos is critical. If the DRV persists in its present course, it can expect to continue to suffer the consequences.

d. That the DRV knows what it must do if the peace is to be restored.

e. That the U.S. has ways and means of measuring the DRV's participation in, and direction and control of, the war on South Vietnam and in Laos and will be carefully watching the DRV's response to what Mr. Seaborn is telling them.[14]

One week later, the Rules of Engagement (ROE) governing the actions of U.S. forces are changed.

FROM: JCS [Joint Chiefs of Staff] 15 Aug 64
TO: CINCPAC [Commander-in-Chief, Pacific] JCS 7947
SUBJECT: Rules of Engagement (U)

1. This message rescinds JCS 3976.

2. The JCS authorize the destruction of hostile aircraft and seaborne forces by US forces in Southeast Asia under the following rules of engagement:

a. US forces operating in Southeast Asia are authorized to attack and destroy any vessel or aircraft which attacks, or gives positive indication of intent to attack US forces operating in the international waters and air space over international waters of Southeast Asia. This includes hot pursuit into territorial waters or territorial air space as may be necessary and feasible.

b. US forces operating in Southeast Asia are authorized to engage and destroy hostile aircraft over South Vietnam and Thailand. Hot pursuit may be conducted as necessary and feasible over international waters or into North Vietnam, Laos, and Cambodia against hostile aircraft as defined in subpara 2 f (1) (b) below.

c. US forces operating in Laos are authorized to attack and destroy any aircraft which attacks or gives positive indication of intent to attack US forces. Hot pursuit may be conducted as necessary and feasible into North Vietnam, Cambodia, South Vietnam, and Thailand.

d. No pursuit is authorized at this time into the territorial waters or air space of Communist China.

e. US forces entering territorial waters and/or territorial air space as authorized by these rules are not authorized to attack other hostile forces or installations therein unless attacked first by them, and then only to the extent necessary for self defense.

f. Definitions:

(1) Hostile aircraft—A hostile aircraft is defined as one which is:

(a) Visually identified, or designated by the US director of a Joint Operations Center or his authorized US representatives, as a communist bloc aircraft over-flying RVN-Thailand territory without proper clearance from the government concerned;

(b) Observed in one of the following acts:

1. Attacking US or friendly ground forces or installations.

2. Attacking US or friendly aircraft.

3. Laying mines within friendly territorial waters.

4. Attacking US or friendly vessels.

5. Releasing parachutes or gliders over sovereign territory when obviously not in distress; or

6. Acting or behaving in a manner which is within reasonable certainty that air attack on US or forces is intended.

(2) Territorial waters include the territorial sea and waters. The territorial sea is the belt of sea adjacent to three miles in breadth measured from the low water mark [word missing]. Inland waters are waters to landward of the territorial sea.

These rules are not intended, in any manner, to infringe traditional responsibility of a military commander to guard against unprovoked armed attack. In the event of such attack, commander concerned will take immediate, aggressive action [word missing] attacking force with any available means at his command. Declaration of aircraft or vessels as hostile will be made with judgment and discretion. There may be cases where destruction of communist bloc forces would be contrary to US interests, examples of such cases are: due to navigation error, communist civilian aircraft over-fly RVN-Thailand territory; communist aircraft or vessels, manned by defectors attempting to land with the intention of surrendering themselves. All available intelligence should be considered in determining action to be taken in such cases.[15]

1964   16 August—South Vietnam's Military Revolutionary Council elects General Khanh as chief of state.

In a letter of 4 September, the DRV's foreign ministry releases what appears to be its response to the Seaborn initiative.

The DRV Government has more than once stated its eagerness for peace and its constant desire of respecting and correctly implementing the 1954 Geneva Agreements on Viet-nam. . . .

   The DRV Government . . . earnestly requests the cochairmen and the participants of the 1954 Geneva conference on Indochina, in accordance with point 13 of the final declaration of the conference, jointly to study such measures as might prove to be necessary to secure from the U.S. Government an immediate end to all acts of provocation and sabotage against the DRV and to the aggressive war in South Vietnam, as well as the withdrawal of all U.S. troops, military personnel, and arms from South Vietnam, thereby insuring respect for the correct implementation of the 1954 Geneva agreements on Vietnam with a view to maintaining and consolidating peace in Indochina and Southeast Asia.[16]

In September OPLAN 34-A covert operations include the capture of North Vietnamese junks, offshore bombardments, radio broadcasts, and insertion and resupply of psychological and sabotage operations teams. In addition, the U.S. secretary of state "urges" the first air strikes in Laos.

Joint State-Defense Message

6 Oct 64

You are authorized to urge the RLG to begin air attacks against Viet Cong infiltration routes and facilities in the Laos Panhandle by RLAF T-28 aircraft as soon as possible. Such strikes should be spread out over a period of several weeks, and targets should be limited to these deemed suitable for attack by T-28s and listed Para. 8 Vientiane's 581, (excluding Mu Gia pass and any target which Lao will not hit without U.S. air cover or fire support) since decision this matter not yet made.

   You are further authorized to inform Lao that YANKEE TEAM suppressive fire strikes against certain difficult targets in Panhandle, interspersing with further T-28 strikes, are part of the over-all concept and are to be anticipated later but that such US strikes are not repeat not authorized at this time.

   Report soonest proposed schedule of strikes and, upon implementation, all actual commitments of RLG T-28s, including targets attacked, results achieved, and enemy opposition. Also give us any views in addition to those in Vientiane's 581 as to any targets which are deemed too difficult for RLG air strikes and on which US suppressive strikes desired.

FYI: Highest levels have not authorized YANKEE TEAM strikes at this time against Route 7 targets. Since we wish to avoid the impression that we are taking first step in escalation, we inclined defer decision on Route 7 strikes until we have strong evidence Hanoi's preparation for new attack in PDJ, some of which might come from RLAF operations over the Route. END FYI.

You may inform RLG, however, that US will fly additional RECCE over Route 7 to keep current on use being made of the Route by the PL and to identify Route 7 targets and air defenses. The subject of possible decision to conduct strikes on Route 7 being given study in Washington.

FYI: Cross border ground operations not repeat not authorized at this time. End FYI.

END

Rusk[17]

1964   **16 October**—People's Republic of China successfully tests its first atomic bomb. **1 November**—Viet Cong mortar attack on U.S. complex at Bien Hoa airbase kills four Americans and destroys five B-57 bombers. **2 November**—Lyndon Johnson elected president by a landslide. His public position toward Vietnam has been moderate—to "seek no wider war."

In Washington frequent meetings are held and plans are presented to consider what U.S. policy should be in what is agreed upon as a "deteriorating situation" in Vietnam. Ambassador Taylor summarizes the dilemma in a briefing (November 1964):

After a year of changing and ineffective government, the counter-insurgency program country-wide is bogged down and will require heroic treatment to assure revival. Even in the Saigon area, in spite of the planning and the special treatment accorded the Hop Tac plan, this area also is lagging. The northern provinces of South Vietnam which a year ago were considered almost free of Viet Cong are now in deep trouble. In the Quang Ngai-Binh Dinh area, the gains of the Viet Cong have been so serious that once more we are threatened with a partition of the country by a Viet-Cong salient driven to the sea. The pressure on this area has been accompanied by continuous sabotage of the railroad and of Highway 1 which in combination threaten an economic strangulation of the northern provinces.

This deterioration of the pacification program has taken place in spite of the very heavy losses inflicted almost daily on the Viet-Cong and the increase in strength and professional competence of the Armed Forces of South Vietnam. Not only have the Vietcong apparently made good their losses, but of late, have demonstrated three new or newly expanded tactics: The use of stand-off mortar fire against important targets, as in the attack on the Bien Hoa airfield; economic strangulation on limited areas; finally, the stepped-up infiltration of DRV military personnel moving from the north. These new or improved tactics employed against the background of general deterioration offer a serious threat to the pacification program in general and to the safety of important bases and installations in particular.[18]

Reporter Jim Lucas documents what Ambassador Taylor has just called "the very heavy losses inflicted almost daily on the Viet-Cong."

Dec. 14, AP Xa Ben
Suddenly the Viet Cong were everywhere.

They poured out of the burning houses, into the village streets. Some tried to hide beneath thatched eaves and watched in horror as their comrades were shot down in front of them. Others jumped into the river and the canal.

"Get 'em!" yelled Lt. Col. Bill Hammack of Quannah, Tex., as he swung his helicopter to provide better aim for Pfc. Bennie Feltman of Lineville, Ala.

Feltman's machine gun poured it on the swirling ranks below. His tracers arched luridly as they covered the 2000 feet.

Throughout the day we had chased them, knowing where they were holed up in marshy land.

Once, at mid-morning, we had been close enough that they had left clothing and food behind in their holes. The Viet Cong sometimes live in their foxholes. It's hard to dislodge them when they choose to stay and fight. Now, however, they fired and fell back . . . fired and fell back.

"The C-74 Company (an enemy unit) moved to four successive positions in the last four days," Capt. Hayward Riley of Columbia, S.C., had briefed us. "As of 0730 today it was confirmed they were in the vicinity of Objective 41. They've got workshops and a dispensary there."

Riley's boss, Col. Jim Keirsey of Durant, Okla., explained:

"They've broken up into smaller groups to harvest rice and collect taxes. That's why our ambushes have been going so well. We had more small contact last night than we had last month. But it's tougher to catch big units out in the open and make them fight."

By mid-morning, the Rangers had killed two and captured three. They'd brought in three captured weapons.

We had flown over the area in the first hours of Operation Dan Chi 91, crisscrossing it in a propaganda helicopter while a Vietnamese major shouted into the loud speaker:

"Your comrades in the next hamlet have surrendered. Now it is your turn."

Aside from the fact this hadn't happened, it was doubtful that to say so did any good. Winds blew the words before they reached the men on the ground and garbled the message.

WO Ken Hessemer of Portland, Ore., spotted from a light observation plane.

"Lots of trails," he called back. "Now I see people running."

We were pushing them hard, driving them against the river banks. Armored personnel carriers cut weird patterns through the rice paddies. A unit of Rangers was slogging through the mire.

The payoff started when Kessemer radioed: "They're out in the open now. They're going west."

After that it was bedlam—a real turkey shoot.

Armed helicopters came in with their rockets and machine guns. That's what the Commies had been trying to avoid; why they were hiding. Now village after village caught fire, the flames leaping up in mushroom clouds of smoke. The sound was deafening as the rockets tore into the houses.

The Viet Cong were in panic. But there was no place to run, no place to hide. Helicopter after helicopter came in, guns blazing. Many died where they fell. Others dived into the water and died there.

Then it was over. Below, you could hear the sullen roar of flames, and overhead the whirl of the rotors. But all else was quiet. The running men were still. They lay where they had fallen, and the flames enveloped them until the whole of the scene was flames. Later we would try to count them.[19]

Sometimes, however, the "count" of enemy casualties is less than exact. In Bo Hathaway's novel A World of Hurt, *two U.S. Army advisers and their unit of Montagnards ("strikers") are in contact with the Viet Cong. Sergeant Kobus is talking on the radio to an American helicopter gunship.*

"We're pinned down by about a company of 'em," Kobus said. "I think they're dug in along that tree line."

"Is there any firing going on now?"

"No . . . negative. They're layin' low."

"OK, we've only got three minutes on station, but we can hose down the area for you. I want you to consolidate your friendlies and mark your position with smoke. We'll make our run from the southeast."

"Roger." Kobus took a smoke grenade from the radio pack and popped it into the clearing. Yellow smoke plumed upward.

"This is Shark three-two. Confirm yellow smoke at your position."

"Roger."

The first ship came in low and ponderous, like an overweight locust.

With a brapping roar, the six barrels of its mini-gun spewed out fifty rounds each second. The front trees withered like wheat in a hailstorm. The strikers cheered. "That's it," Kobus yelled. "Bring pee on them motherfuckers."

The second ship chugged in and fired two rockets. They shivered the air and erupted into orange and black pumpkins amid the trees. The ship peeled off to the east while its partner came in for a second pass. Involuntarily, Madsen followed them with his eyes like a gunsight. They looked slow and vulnerable. What a thrill to shoot one down.

They made two more passes, alternating between rockets and mini-guns. The lead pilot's voice came back on the radio: "That should keep them off your back for a while. If they get you pinned down again, just give us a call. We'll come back out and even the odds."

"Roger. Thanks a lot." Kobus put down the radio and put on his pack. "OK, Madsen, we're gonna have to go in there and check that area out. It's a rule. When you get an air strike, you gotta check it out and give them a report. Now this time we stick together. None of that shit about you staying up on point. The Americans always gotta stick together. No telling what we're gonna find in there. These fucking slopes will bug out on you in a second. Now, lemme get ahold of that FAC before he leaves." He picked up the radio again and called: "Pirate, Pirate, this is Alpha, Alpha. Over."

"This is Pirate one-five. Over."

"Roger, Pirate. We're going to recon that area now, give you a damage assessment. Can you stay with us in case they're still dug in?"

"All right. I'll fly a little north and see if I can see any movement."

The men were quiet as they entered the woods. Many of the trees were shredded or broken. Some of the rocks were chipped. Where rockets had struck, the vegetation was charred and smoking. They found two dead monkeys and several birds, but no sign of VC.

"Looks like they left," Madsen said.

"Just as long as they went the other way from us, I'm satisfied." They walked in silence for a while. Then Kobus said, "Hell . . . we done our job. Every camp's supposed to keep the VC outa their area. That's our mission here. And that's what we done. Those fuckers won't stop for twenty miles."

They halted while the strikers skinned and cleaned the monkeys and wrapped them in a poncho for the evening meal. One soldier pointed at the skinny carcasses and said, laughing, "VC, VC . . . my bai cac-a-dau VC."

"Cac-a-dau you," Kobus said. "Shit, we're gonna have to give the air force a good damage assessment. The bastards get the ass at us, they won't come out again." He picked up the mike and called, "Pirate, this is Alpha. Over."

"Pirate. Go ahead."

"Roger. Your men did a great job. We got three bunkers and, let's see, five automatic weapons positions destroyed. And . . . they caved in about twenty meters of trench line. Really tore hell out of the place. Over."

"How about body count?"

"Well, they must've dragged them off. We found quite a bit of blood. I'd say they must've had at least six killed. Probably three times that many wounded. Over."

"Anything else?"

"No, no, that's about it. Real fine job. Ah, looks like the rest of them might try to ambush us . . . to get revenge. We gotta push through some pretty rough country to link up with our other unit. Can you stay with us and sorta scout out the area ahead? Over."

"Negative on that. I'm low on fuel. But we can come back out if you get hit again."

"Roger. Negative further here. Out."[20]

1964 31 December		
	TOTAL	NET CHANGE
U.S. military personnel assigned in Vietnam	23,300	+ 7,000
U.S. casualties	YEAR	TO DATE (cumulative)
Killed in action	147	267
Wounded in action	1,039	1,531
(Source: DOD/OASD)		

1965

Assigned to Vietnam in January 1965, Navy Lieutenant Dick Shea records impressions that will later form his book of poems, Vietnam Simply.

> so for some unknown reason
> i volunteered
> and am suddenly 35 thousand feet over vietnam
> in a military iron bird
> it was all ocean a moment ago
> but now a sandy beach
> and a green land
> peacefully there beneath flowing white clouds

welcomes me
sarcastically
the plane bumps in
the runway is filled with holes
and armed guards
which dispel all the tranquility
gathered at 35 thousand
plane door opens
blast of hot air hits me
gangway rolls up
i exit first
cause i was designated courier of some top secret boxes
a stumbling army first lieutenant
and a private first class approach
chaperoned by a major
the first lieutenant impressively orders his detail
of one man
to unload the material
the private calls out the box numbers
the lieutenant shouts out a large busy impressive "check"
and puts a check behind a number
on his impressive clipboard
apparently his only function
the major stands with his hands behind his back
in a state of smiling numbness
the lieutenant importantly signs the received line
then gives me a ride to my first briefing on vietnam
i fill out numerous irritating forms
and hear only one thing at the briefing
    if a suspicious looking vietnamese
    brings a suspicious looking package
    into a place suspiciously full of americans
    and sets it down and leaves
    leave with him

Then Lieutenant Shea observes Saigon.

                american frequented places
                are all cages
                americans are surrounded by chicken wire
                everywhere they go
                    bus windows
                    restaurants
                    bars
                and for good reason
                cause they never are safe

and anyone who's seen a hand grenade go off
is a little bit chicken

i feel safest when
i am alone
the only american

a single american is an awfully small target
to bother with
when there are whole cages of them around[21]

1965   27 January—After five months of short-lived "civilian" governments, the South Vietnamese Armed Forces Council restores General Khanh to power.

---

*That same day Assistant Secretary of Defense J. T. McNaughton drafts his
observations, and Secretary of Defense McNamara comments:*

DRAFT: 27 January 1965 by J. T. McNaughton— Observations Re South Vietnam After Khanh's "Re-Coup"

1) Khanh has given the U.S. a pretext to "dump" South Vietnam. This
option should not be exercised.

2) The new Khanh government could be a "good" one but history is
against it.

3) Max Taylor's effectiveness, with Khanh government, is doubtful.

4) The situation in South Vietnam in general continues to deteriorate.

5) Steady efforts inside South Vietnam can, probably, only slow that
deterioration.

6) U.S. objective in South Vietnam is not to "help friend" but to
contain China.

7) Loss in South Vietnam would merely move the conflict to Malaysia
or Thailand (marginal comment by McNamara—These will go fast). U.S.
won't repeat South Vietnam there! Continue with side effects of accommodation elsewhere in Asia.

8) The three options:
   (a) Strike the DRV;
   (b) "Negotiate"; or
   (c) Keep plugging.

RSM comment: "Drifting."

9) Negotiation, with so few counters, is no way to improve the actual
situation; it might serve to diffuse and confuse to some extent the psychological impact of loss.

McNamara comment: "This is better than drifting."

10) (The Fullbright-Mansfield Church School, for example, has written off South Vietnam; they are seeking solely to cut the damage to our prestige as South Vietnam goes down the drain.)

11) Striking DRV might, but probably won't. RSM comment: Dissent. Help the actual situation. The most serious RSM comment: Dissent. Risk is that the U.S. public will not support a squeeze unless results show soon.

12) Strikes against DRV should be done anyway, first as reprisals. RSM comment to reprisals: "Too narrow. Can use 34A, Desoto, infiltration data, etc. Feel way from there.

13) It is essential that we keep plugging in South Vietnam in any event. Immediate action: (a) Ride along with the new government, make no adverse comments; (b) continue vigorous advisory effort, but add no more U.S. men. RSM comment: "They are in for 6500 more.!"; (c) get dependents out; (d) authorize Westmoreland to use jets. RSM comment: Yes, in emergencies in South Vietnam; (e) React promptly and firmly to next reprisal opportunity; (f) start re-educating U.S. public that Southeast Asia confrontation will last years.

(*Note:* I handed this to RSM 0745, on January 27, 1965, and discussed it for twenty-five minutes. He commented as indicated.)[22]

Four days later Lieutenant Shea comments on the Vietnamese New Year, January 31–February 1.

> tet
> vietnamese new year
> today tomorrow and the day after
> the viet cong sent a message saying
> they were not fighting during tet
> all vietnamese went home
> or disappeared somewhere
> very few guards still on duty
> interesting
> how they call the war off
> and put away their toys for three days
>
> hard for an american military mind to comprehend[23]

1965   **7 February**—While Soviet Premier Kosygin is visiting Hanoi, a Viet Cong attack on the U.S. compound in Pleiku results in nine U.S. advisers killed, 76 wounded.

The same day in Washington, McGeorge Bundy drafts what will one week later become U.S. policy.

A Policy of Sustained Reprisal

7 Feb 1965
We believe that the best available way of increasing our chance of success in Vietnam is the development and execution of a policy of *sustained reprisal* against North Vietnam—a policy in which air and naval action against the North is justified by and related to the whole Viet Cong campaign of violence and terror in the South.

While we believe that the risks of such a policy are acceptable, we emphasize that its costs are real. It implies significant U.S. air losses even if no full air war is joined, and it seems likely that it would eventually require an extensive and costly effort against the whole air defense system of North Vietnam. U.S. casualties would be higher—and more visible to American feelings—than those sustained in the struggle in South Vietnam.

Yet measured against the costs of defeat in Vietnam, this program seems cheap. And even if it fails to turn the tide—as it may—the value of the effort seems to us to exceed its cost.[24]

1965   15 February—People's Republic of China states that it will join the war if North Vietnam is invaded. **18 February**—In Saigon, General Khanh is again ousted in a quick, bloodless military coup.

In late February Swedish poet Goran Sonnevi has been watching the war on television.

On the War in Vietnam

Beyond the TV set, outdoors,
the light changed. The dark slowly became
greyish, and the trees looked black
in the clear pale light
of the new snow. Now it is morning,
everything snowed in. I go out
to clear a path.
On the radio I hear the US
has published a white paper
on the VIETNAM war
accusing North Vietnam
of aggression. On TV
last night.
we saw a film strip taken with

the Viet-Cong; we could hear
the muffled fluttering
of helicopter propellors
from the ground, from the side being
shot. In another film
a few weeks ago
CBS interviewed American
helicopter pilots. One of them
described how glad he was
when he finally got a shot at
a "V.C.": the rockets
threw the VC about nine feet
straight ahead. There's no doubt
we'll have more snow today,
my neighbor says, dressed in black
on the way to work. He embalms
and is nightwatchman
at an insane asylum. The place where I live—Lund
and outskirts—is becoming a whiter
and whiter paper, the sun rises and lights
the open pages, burning and cold.
The dead are numbers, they lie down, whirl about
like snowflakes, in the country wind. Up till now
they figure 2 million have died in Vietnam.
Here hardly anyone dies
except for personal reasons. The Swedish
economic system doesn't kill
many, at least
not here at home. Here
no one goes to war to protect
his interests. We don't
get burned with napalm
to advance a fuedal idea of freedom.
In the 15th and 16th centuries no napalm.
Toward noon here the sun gets rather high.
Soon it will be March 1965.
Every day
more and more dead in America's repulsive war.
There are snowflakes on the photograph
of President Johnson
taken during the last series of bombing raids
on North Vietnam—he is climbing in
or maybe out of a car—more
and more flakes fall on the white pages.
More dead, more self-righteous defenses,
until everything is snowed in again

and the night
finally changes its light outside the windows.

translated from the Swedish
by Robert Bly[25]

The Pentagon Papers *summarizes the events of February and March.*

Imperceptible Transition. By contrast with the earlier Tonkin strikes of
August, 1964 which had been presented as a one-time deomonstration that
North Vietnam could not flagrantly attack US forces with impunity, the
February 1965 raids were explicitly linked with the "larger pattern of aggression" by North Vietnam, and were a reprisal against *North* Vietnam
for an offense committed by the *VC* in *South* Vietnam. When the VC
staged another dramatic attack on Qui Nhon on Feb. 10, the combined
US/GVN response, named FLAMING DART II, was not characterized as
an event-associated reprisal but as a generalized response to "continued
acts of aggression." The new terminology reflected a conscious U.S. decision to broaden the reprisal concept as gradually and imperceptibly as
possible to accommodate a much wider policy of sustained, steadily intensifying air attacks against North Vietnam, at a rate and on a scale to be
determined by the U.S. Although discussed publicly in very muted tones,
the second FLAMING DART operation constituted a sharp break with
past US policy and set the stage for the continuing bombing program that
was now to be launched in earnest. . . .

Initiating ROLLING THUNDER. A firm decision to adopt "a program
of measured and limited air action jointly with the GVN against selected
military targets in the DRV" was made by the President on February
13, and communicated to Ambassador Taylor in Saigon. Details of the
program were deliberately left vague, as the President wished to preserve maximum flexibility. The first strike was set for February 20 and
Taylor was directed to obtain GVN concurrence. A semi-coup in Saigon, however, compelled postponement and cancellation of this and
several subsequent strikes. Political clearance was not given until the
turbulence was calmed with the departure of General Nguyen Khanh
from Vietnam on Feb 25. U.S. reluctance to launch air attacks during
this time was further reinforced by a UK–USSR diplomatic initiative to
reactivate the Cochairmanship of the 1954 Geneva Conference with a
view to involving the members of that conference in a consideration of
the Vietnam crisis. Air strikes executed at that moment, it was feared,
might sabotage that diplomatic gambit, which Washington looked upon
not as a potential negotiating opportunity, but as a convenient vehicle
for public expression of a tough U.S. position. The Co-Chairmen gambit, however, languished—and eventually came to naught. The first
ROLLING THUNDER strike was finally rescheduled for Feb 26. This
time adverse weather forced its cancellation and it was not until March 2

that the first of the new program strikes, dubbed ROLLING THUNDER V, was actually carried out.[26]

An official U.S. Air Force history comments:

The initial series of Rolling Thunder air strikes were both political and psychological in nature. Target selection, forces, munitions used, and even timing of the strikes were decided in Washington. Targets struck were barracks, radar sites, ammunition depots, and military vehicles—all in the southernmost part of North Vietnam. . . .

The first raid was conducted on 2 March when a strike force of 44 F-105s, 40 F-100s, 7 RF-101s, and 20 B-57s, with KC-135 tankers for refueling support, struck an ammunition depot at Xom Bang. Nineteen A-1Hs of the South Vietnamese Air Force struck the Quang Khe Naval Base.

During this attack the strike forces again met what was to remain the greatest threat to air superiority throughout the entire war—antiaircraft artillery fire. The US lost four aircraft during this raid, three while attacking antiaircraft positions. Immediately, flak suppression tactics were re-examined and flak suppression was scheduled only when considered absolutely essential for protection of the primary strike force.[27]

From Hanoi, a Lao Dong Party document dated 5 March considers in part what U.S. strategy might be.

Now, due to the fact that we are not yet strong enough to defeat the enemy but have accumulated real strength, U.S. imperialism sees that it cannot win but has not yet accepted defeat.

U.S. imperialism is discussing the following options:

1. *Widening the war to the North and attacking Southern China.* When thinking about this idea, they see all the more danger, because they will come up against the socialist camp, with China and its 700 million people who now have the atomic bomb. They also know that they don't have enough troops and that they would not be supported by Britain, France, Germany, and Japan. This possibility is therefore very slight but the enemy has thought about it, so we must also be highly vigilant and be prepared for any possible adventurism.

2. *Send U.S. troops to South Vietnam to become the primary force to fight us.* This possibility is also small because they would have to make enormous expenditures in money and material, but would still not be certain of victory, and if they were defeated, they would lose even more face. As for us, if they send U.S. troops, there will be new difficulties and complexities but we will be determined to fight protractedly and, finally, victory will be ours.

3. Besides the above two options, they are discussing a great deal a

third option which is to maintain special war as at present but to increase it one step. In order to carry out this option, U.S. imperialism is striving mightily to create a position of strength militarily and trying to stabilize the political situation in the cities. They try to achieve these two objectives in order to continue to defeat us militarily while at the same time preparing for a political solution on the basis of their position of strength and in accord with their cunning plan.

In the near future, the enemy may carry out bolder military actions in the South and step up provocations against the North.[28]

The next day, what the Lao Dong Party believed to be just a "small possibility" becomes a fact.

On 6 March 1965 the Pentagon issued the following news release:

> TWO U.S. MARINE BATTALIONS TO BE DEPLOYED IN VIET NAM. After consultation between the governments of South Vietnam and the United States, the United States Government has agreed to the request of the Government of Vietnam to station two United States Marine Corps Battalions in the Da Nang area to strengthen the general security of the Da Nang Air Base complex.
>
> The limited mission of the Marines will be to relieve Government of South Vietnam forces now engaged in security duties for action in the pacification program and in offensive roles against Communist guerrilla forces.

On the same day the, Joint Chiefs of Staff ordered CINCPAC to commence the landing of the BLT's [Battalion Landing Teams], and on 7 March Secretary of State Rusk told a national television and radio audience that the Marines would shoot back if shot at, but their mission was to put a tight security ring around Da Nang Air Base, thus freeing South Vietnamese forces for combat.[29]

In Da Nang Lieutenant Shea observes the newly arrived Americans.

> and so
> en masse
> the marines have landed
> bringing with them
> a high state of nervousness
> and inexperience
> and my little city
> is not itself anymore
> whenever american military people
> come into any land
> the people smile and cheer
> the americans are touched by their sincerity

the people's hands go out to the american
and their eyes light up like neon bulbs
spelling out

welcome suckers

and the hands stay out palms up
american military wants are simple
they need the same things in any country they visit
wheels whiskey and whores
(not necessarily in that order)
these three products
are instantly 100% more in cost than before
and the country has an economic boom
here in vn land
all four military services line the streets
they take pictures of anything
buy anything
ride in anything
drink anything
and sleep with anything
little and old kids
line up at the ferry landings
selling straw woven carpets
diarrhea food
themselves

big selling items are marble fish
that can be bought in a shop for a few piastres
but are sold to the uniformed fish on the pier
for ten times as much
cyclo drivers for a large commission
peddle personnel to pig houses of disease
some of the better looking diseases
ride the cyclos
i stand aside
and watch america at work
watch the happy vietnamese faces
watch their bulging pockets
watch them learn to respect the american dollar
watch the american spread his money
watch him drink
watch him proposition
watch him fight with other americans
watch him drink

it certainly makes a person feel proud
to stand back and look at america this way

> to see our ambassadors of the democratic way of life
> build the vietnamese economy
> and raise their aggressive spirit
> so they will be better equipped to fight
> that poor viet cong guerrilla
> that stands on the same pier
> with his palms up to the same americans
> it is hard to tell palms apart
> americans are certainly democratic[30]

The Pentagon Papers *records other American reactions to the arrival of the U.S. Marines.*

Contemporary accounts of the situation in South Vietnam from the non-official viewpoint are unanimous in their recognition of the continuing decay in the political and military capacity of the GVN to resist. The prospect for success if the U.S. did not change its approach to the war was nil. The Viet Cong were clearly winning. To writers like Halberstam and Mecklin, the choice for the U.S. boiled down to two alternatives; either get out or commit land forces to stem the tide. Neither of these writers was likely to view the arrival of the Marines as anything else but indication of a decision to take the second course. Shaplen treated the landing of the Marines as an isolated incident, but he did not accept the rationale that they were in Vietnam for strictly defensive reasons. In commenting on the subsequent arrival of more Marines and the concomitant expansion of their mission to include offensive patrol work, he says: ". . . and sooner or later, it was surmised, they would tangle directly with the Viet Cong; in fact, it was obvious from the outset that in an emergency they would be air-lifted to other areas away from their base."

A glance at some of the commentary of early March 1965 in newspapers and periodicals gives clear indication that the landing of the two Marine BLT's was seen as an event of major significance. Analysis of the import of the event varies, as would be expected, from writer to writer, but almost without exception they read more into the deployment than was made explicit by the brief Defense Department press release. By-lines from Saigon, where reporters had ready access to "reliable sources" in the U.S. Mission, give clear indication that there had been a major shift in attitude as regards the use of U.S. ground forces in Asia. Ted Sell, a Los Angeles Times staff writer, wrote on 10 March 1965: "The landing of the two infantry battalions is in its own way a far more significant act than were earlier attacks by U.S. airplanes, even though those attacks were directed against a country—North Vietnam—ostensibly not taking part in the direct war." Speaking after the Marines were ordered in, one high official said of the no-ground-troops-in-Asia shibboleth, "Sure, it's undesirable. But that doesn't mean we won't do it." It is especially significant that among the writers attempting to gauge the extent of U.S. resolve in the Vietnamese situation, the deployment of ground forces was somehow seen as a much more positive and credible indication of U.S. determination than any of the steps, including the air strikes on the DRV, previously taken.[31]

Two weeks later in Washington, McNaughton again ponders the situation on paper.

Annex—Plan of Action for South Vietnam (3/24/65—first draft)

1. *US aims:*
70%—To avoid a humiliating US defeat (to our reputation as a guarantor).
20%—To keep SVN (and then adjacent) territory from Chinese hands.
10%—To permit the people of SVN to enjoy a better, freer way of life.
ALSO—To emerge from crisis without unacceptable taint from methods used.
NOT—To "help a friend," although it would be hard to stay in if asked out.
2. *The situation:* The situation in general is bad and deteriorating. The VC have the initiative. Defeatism is gaining among the rural population, somewhat in the cities, and even among the soldiers—especially those with relatives in rural areas. The Hop Tac area around Saigon is making little progress; the Delta stays bad; the country has been severed in the north. GVN control is shrinking to enclaves, some burdened with refugees. In Saigon we have a remission: Quat is giving hope on the civilian side, the Buddhists have calmed, and the split generals are in uneasy equilibrium.[32]

On 26 March General Westmoreland (COMUSMACV) delivers to Washington his "Commander's Estimate of the Situation," a report whose "full half inch of foolscap paper" seems to one Pentagon Papers *writer to be "an awesome bulk." Westmoreland's report concludes:*

The most propitious course of action to emerge from the analysis in the Estimate was the second one dealing with the commitment of up to two U.S. divisions, including 17 maneuver battalions, with support. Over and above what was in or authorized to be in Vietnam, Course of Action 2 called for an additional 33,000 men.

In order to illustrate trends in force ratios, Westmoreland postulated that one USMC BLT was the equivalent of three ARVN battalions, and one U.S. Army battalion was the equivalent of two ARVN battalions. Using that rationale, the combat battalions added on through Course of Action 2 would have amounted to 38 ARVN battalion-equivalents. Input on that scale would have had a fair effect on force ratios overall and a very dramatic effect locally in the areas where they were to operate.

Without the benefit of the increased battalion-equivalents provided by

Course of Action 2, the ratio of ARVN (and the two Marine BLT's then in Vietnam) battalions to Viet Cong battalions would have degraded, according to the Estimate, from 1.7 to 1 in March 1965 to 1.6 to 1 in December of that year. This would have been the case despite an accelerated RVNAF build-up and only a modest rate of Viet Cong build-up as in 1964. With the input of Course of Action 2, the equivalent of a 10 month acceleration in the RVNAF build-up could have been accomplished by mid-year and by the end of the build-up period the forces could have been doubled—that is, assuming that the forces in Course of Action 2 were introduced during April, May, and June, a proposal which was barely feasible logistically and which was urged by General Westmoreland.

At the conclusion of his Estimate, General Westmoreland recommended that the U.S. build-up its combat force in Vietnam to 17 battalions by early June at the latest.[33]

1965   29 March—In Saigon, Viet Cong sappers attack the U.S. embassy.

In April U.S. air strikes against targets in North Vietnam intensify. U.S. Air Force historians record the action.

The March 1965 decision to interdict the North Vietnamese rail system south of the 20th parallel led immediately to the April 3rd strike against the Thanh Hoa Railroad and Highway Bridge, known to the Vietnamese as Ham Rong (the Dragon's Jaw). . . .

Shortly after noontime of 3 April 1965, the aircraft of Rolling Thunder Mission 9-Alpha finally climbed into the humid skies of Southeast Asia on their journey to the Thanh Hoa Bridge. This force consisted of 79 aircraft; forty-six F-105s; twenty-one F-100s; two RF-101s; and ten KC-135 tankers. The F-100s came from bases in South Vietnam, while the rest of the aircraft were from squadrons on temporary duty at various Thai bases. The ordnance loads and missions of these planes were as diverse as the fields from which they flew.

Sixteen of the forty-six "Thuds" were loaded with a pair of Bullpup missiles, and each of the remaining thirty carried eight 750-pound general purpose bombs. The aircraft that carried the missiles, and half of the bombers, were scheduled to strike the bridge; the remaining fifteen would provide flak suppression. . . .

The Thanh Hoa Bridge, which spans the Song Ma River, is located three miles north of the town of Thanh Hoa, the capital of Annam Province. It is a replacement for the original French-built bridge which was destroyed by the Viet Minh in 1945—they simply loaded two locomotives with explosives and ran them together in the middle of the bridge.

In 1957, the North Vietnamese, with the assistance of Chinese techni-

cians, undertook the task of again spanning the swift-flowing Song Ma.
Using construction methods that were crude by western standards, the
project moved along ponderously until 1961 when the regime in Hanoi,
needing the bridge to facilitate the movement of supplies to the insurgents in the south, put on the pressure. By working 24-hours a day, the
builders completed the bridge in 1964, and Ho Chi Minh himself presided
at the dedication.

The new bridge at Thanh Hoa was called the Ham Rung (or Dragon's
Jaw) by the Vietnamese. It was 540 feet long, 56 feet wide, and about 50
feet above the river. The Dragon's Jaw had two steel thru-truss spans
which rested in the center on a massive reinforced concrete pier, 16 feet
in diameter, and on concrete abutments at the other ends. Hills on both
sides of the river provided solid bracing for the structure. Between 1965
and 1972, eight concrete piers were added near the approaches to give
additional resistance to bomb damage. A one-meter gauge single railway
track ran down the 12-foot wide center and 22-foot wide concrete highways were cantilevered on each side. This giant would prove to be one of
the single most challenging targets for U.S. air power. . . .

Lt Colonel [Robinson] Risner was designated overall mission coordinator for the attack. His plan called for individual flights of four F-105s
from Korat and Takhli which would be air refueled over the Mekong
River before tracking across Laos to an initial point (IP) three minutes
south of the bridge. . . . After weapon release, the plan called for all
aircraft to continue east until over the Gulf of Tonkin where rejoin would
take place and a Navy destroyer would be avilable to recover anyone who
had to eject due to battle damage or other causes. After rejoin, all
aircraft would return to their launch bases, hopefully to the tune of "The
Ham Rong Bridge is falling down." . . .

The sun glinting through the haze was making the target somewhat
difficult to acquire, but Lt Colonel Risner led the way "down the chute"
and 250-pound missiles were soon exploding on the target. Since these
missiles had to be released and guided one at a time, each pilot shooting
Bullpups had to go around for a second firing pass. This second pass
could slow things down considerably without the precision timing between flights.

The first two flights had already left the target when Captain Bill Meyerholt, number three man in the third flight, rolled his Thunderchief into a
dive and squeezed off a Bullpup. The missile trailed bright orange fire as
it streaked earthward toward the bridge. As smoke from the previous
attacks drifted away from the target, Captain Meyerholt was surprised to
see no visible damage to the bridge as he guided his missile to a hit on the
superstructure and pulled up to go around again. Like its predecessors,
his missile had merely charred the heavy steel and concrete structure.
When a second attack produced the same results, it became all too obvious that firing Bullpups at the Dragon was about as effective as shooting
B-B pellets at a Sherman tank.

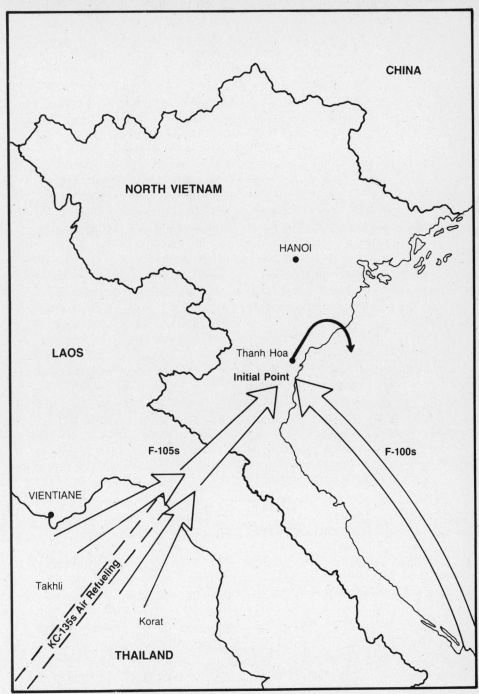

Ingress Routes for the Thanh Hoa Bridge

The remaining missile attacks only served to confirm this observation. When the first of the bomb-carrying Thuds arrived on the scene, the target had barely been scratched. The bombing pilots planned to remedy this situation as they rolled their machines in on the target from 13,000 feet and then tried to keep their aircraft slowed down to the 500-knot release airspeed (the F-105 is notorious for its ability to go downhill rapidly). Hence, the 4,000 foot minimum release altitude came up quickly, with several pilots dropping their string of eight bombs as low as 3,600 feet, only to see them hit on the far bank because of a very strong southwest wind. The last flight of the day, led by Captain Carlyle S. "Smitty" Harris, adjusted their aiming points and scored several good hits on the roadway and superstructure. Heavy smoke and haze, however, precluded any bomb damage assessment by Smitty's flight as they pulled off the target and headed for the Tonkin Gulf, but it was obvious that the bridge still stood. When Smitty looked back at the charred structure, he had no way of knowing that the smoke was really a warning from the Dragon's Jaw.

Aircraft rejoin and recovery went basically as planned, but two aircraft did not make it through the battle. Anti-aircraft fire, considerably more intense than anticipated, had claimed an F-100 flak suppressor and an RF-101. Lt Colonel Risner's Thud also took a hit just as his second missile hit the bridge. Fighting a serious fuel leak and a smoke-filled cockpit in addition to the enemy, he nevertheless nursed his crippled aircraft to Da Nang, in South Vietnam.

On this first attack, ten dozen 750-pound, general purpose bombs and thirty-two missiles had been aimed at the bridge. Numerous hits had charred every part of the structure, yet it gave no evidence of going down. Only the roadway on the south side was damaged enough to prohibit vehicular traffic. The highway on the northern side and the railroad in the center would require only minor repairs. The Thanh Hoa Bridge had suffered far less damage than its attackers had hoped for, and a restrike was ordered for the next day.[34]

The results of the 4 April restrike are telegraphed to Saigon from Korat Royal Thai air force base, Thailand.

THIS IS A ROLLING THUNDER OP-4 SUMMARY REPORT. TAKE OFF REFUELING AND ENTRY INTO TGT AREA WENT AS BRIEFED. TWO MINUTES OUT OF THE TGT STEEL LEAD (AIR COORDINATOR) GAVE THE FLIGHT TO STEEL 3 SINCE STEEL LEAD AND STEEL 2 WERE AIR COORDINATORS. THREE TOOK THE LEAD AND ORINATED [sic] HIMSELF FOR HIS RUN ON A 300 DEGREE HEADING. THREE CALLED IN AND HIS BOMBS IMPACTED ON TGT ON THE EASTERN END OF THE BRIDGE. STEEL 4 CALLED IN ON TGT. STEEL 3 WAS ON FIRE AS SOON AS HE WAS OFF THE TGT. STEEL LEAD CALLED STEEL 3 TWICE AND ASKED HIM IF HE WAS OK. A GARBLED TRANSMISSION WAS HEARD FOLLOWING SECOND CALL BY LEAD. STEEL 3 WAS EMITTING FLAME FOR TWENTY FEET BEHIND AND HEADING ALMOST DUE WEST AT APPROX 2000 FLEET. NEIGHER [sic] PARACHUTE OR AIR-

CRAFT IMPACT WAS OBSERVED ALTHOUGH ALL MEMBERS HAD HIM IN SIGHT UNTIL THE FLAME QUIT.* ALL OF IRON FLIGHTS BOMBS WERE GOOD. COPPER FLIGHTS FIRST THREE A/C HAD EXCELLANT IMPACTS WITH COPPER FOUR'S BOMBS IMPACTING SHORT. MOON'S FLIGHT HAD GOOD BOMBS HOWEVER NUMBER FOUR HAD ALL DUDS. CARBON'S BOMBS WERE FROM GOOD TO EXCELLENT. ZINC FLIGHT WAS BOUNCED BY MIGS AND ZINC 2 CALLED MIGS OUT. HE CALLED ZINC LEAD TO BREAK HARD AS HE HAD A MIG ON HIM: THEN ALMOST IMMEDIATELY ZINC 2 SAID HE WAS HIT AND WAS HEADING 150 DEGREE TRYING TO MAKE THE SHORE LOOSING CONTROL. HE CALLED SEVERAL TIMES AND ASKED IF ANYONE READ HIM. STEEL LEAD SAID HE READ HIM AND TOLD ZINC LEAD TO FIND HIM AND GO RESCUE FREQ. BY THIS TIME SEVERAL A/C HAD SEEN MIGS. STEEL LEAD AND TWO WERE CLEAN AND HEADING EAST IN THE TGT AREA WHEN STEEL 2 CALLED A FLIGHT OF F-105'S OVER THE IP TO TURN HARD LEFT DUE TO TWO MIGS CLOSING ON THEM. I CALLED STEEL LEAD WE HAD MIGS AT 2 O'CLOCK LOW. STEEL LEAD DIDN'T HAVE THEM AND GAVE STEEL TWO THE LEAD. STEEL TWO BROKE INTO THE MIGS AND THEY PASSED 500 FEET BELOW AS ALMOST HEAD ON TO STEEL TWO. THEY WERE MIG 17'S AND HAD N VIETNAM MARKINGS. A REVERSE WAS MADE BUT VISUAL CONTACT LOST WITH MIGS, SINCE THE VIS WAS POOR BECAUSE OF HAZE. ARGON FLIGHT'S BOMBS WERE A LITTLE NORTH OF THE BRIDGE AND SOME HIT ON SHORE. GRAPHITE FLIGHT HAD EXCELLENT IMPACTS ON TGT. ESSO FLIGHT HAD VERY GOOD BOMBS. MOBIL IMPACTS WERE GOOD. SHELL HAD EXTREMELY GOOD IMPACTS ALL ON THE TGT. THE SMOKE WAS [SO] INTENSE THAT PETROL 1 AND 2 WERE INSTRUCTED TO HIT THE SECONDARY TGT. PETROL 1 HIT IN THE 12 O'CLOCK AREA OF THE TGT AREA. PETROL 2 HIT IN THE 6 O'CLOCK AREA OF THE TGT AREA. THE SMOKE WAS VERY INTENSE AND VISUAL BDA [Bomb Damage Assessment] COULD NOT BE AC- COMPLISHED BUT IMPACTS APPEARED TO BE GOOD. PETROL 3 AND 4 DELIVERED LATER WITH NBR 3 TRYING FOR THE SECONDARY AND MISSING BUT NBR 4 HIT ON THE PRIMARY TGT. STEEL 1 AND 2 DEPARTED THE AREA AFTER CADILLAC FLIGHT WENT IN FOR THE BDA THE TGT WAS TORN UP BUT NOT IN THE WATER. RECOVERY WAS MADE WITHOUT INCIDENT.[35]

The U.S. Air Force history summarizes the significance of this mission.

MIGs had been seen on previous missions, but this was the first MIG attack of the war . . . and it was over almost as rapidly as it began. The enemy aircraft had used a diving, high speed pass, coming in behind the bomb-laden Thuds to nail the flight leader and his wingman. There was no chance to get even, as they continued straight ahead and out of the area at maximum speed. Both F-105 pilots were lost. The MIGs had come to protect the prestigious bridge and, in so doing, added a new dimension to what was now a rapidly expanding war. . . .

Although over 300 bombs scored hits on this second strike, the bridge still spanned the Song Ma River. The striking force had inflicted the

*Much later, the pilot of Steel Three, Captain "Smitty" Harris, will be identified as a prisoner of war.

maximum destruction possible considering the weapons available, and the bombs had been accurately dropped through a hail of anti-aircraft fire that, for the first time, included 57mm guns.

The bridge had been severely damaged. Both the northern and southern highways were heavily cratered and large chunks of concrete were missing. Several truss beams had been blown away and bombs had blasted right through the railroad into the river. The eastern span was sagging, but had not gone down. Extensive repairs would be required to make the bridge passable for rail traffic and the highways would never be restored to their former capability. The hard fact was that 750-pound bombs just were not big enough to deliver the *coup de grace* to such a formidable structure.[36]

Later, an interview with two of the North Vietnamese pilots is released from Hanoi.

The commander, rather short, dark-skinned, born in Quang Nam, related the April 4 encounter with a hard suppressed emotion:

"I had never enjoyed such a happy moment as when I received the order to take off and counter the attackers. See, this is the first time our nation has an air force of its own and this is due to the revolution which has also turned us, poor, illiterate and hungry people into fighters of the young Vietnam Air Force.

"All of us spotted the enemy, it seems, at the same time. Sure enough, they were U.S. fighter planes. On seeing them, my blood was up. I immediately gave orders to attack the first F. 105 which I believed was the leader. Hardly had a few seconds elapsed when a flare was seen at its tail. 'Forward! Fire!' I shouted. All of us grappled with the enemy and took pot shots at it simultaneously. Ten seconds after, the U.S. plane belched out a red flame followed with smoke and dived into the fog. Then we turned to the second plane and in no time we discharged all our guns on its belly. The U.S. plane reeled and nosed downward into the fog. It gave out smoke but was not yet deadly hit! We closed with it and fired straight at it. When I zoomed I clearly saw the white cap of the pilot in the cockpit before the plane crashed headlong on the ground.

"As for the morale of the American when he encountered us, our mate will tell you about it," said the commander introducing to us a pilot sitting beside.

He was a very young, strongly-built fellow we had met yesterday night in an emergency meeting of the Party cell.

"We were attacking the second plane," he told us, "when I saw at the rear four others flying in a ladder pattern. One of us and myself reported to our commander and immediately turned about then pounced upon the nearest enemy plane. In the next to no time the head of a U.S. plane as big as a jar mouth flashed through our finders. As was expected the enemy unable to bear such a moral [sic] blow took to flight. We repeated the attack many a time and each time the U.S. pilots could not resist this 'proletarian' move and instead of giving mutual cover they fled helter skelter, abandoning those being attacked to their fate . . ."

The fighter responsible for leading the attack against the planes at the rear was a middle-aged man, formerly a poor fisherman from Viet An, Quang Nam province, in the very place where the Southern Army and people had dealt a death blow at the U.S. aggressors last week. He put on his cap and said to us:

"A pilot must be calm before he gets on board. But yesterday morning, I was still moved when taking my seat in my cockpit. It seemed that Viet An, my native place was calling me, that the Party and Uncle Ho were looking at me! I was thus flying my plane in an excited state and with great confidence. Confidence in my mates and in myself. Above me, on the ground, in the South, in the North, everywhere I have friends and comrades who protect me and follow me with eyes full of affection and confidence . . . No wonder that we have had the better of the enemy!

Vietnam Courier, Hanoi, April 15, 1965[37]

A few days later President Johnson speaks at Johns Hopkins University.

The confused nature of this conflict cannot mask the fact that it is the new face of an old enemy.

Over this war—and all Asia—is another reality: the deepening shadow of Communist China. The rulers in Hanoi are urged on by Peiping. This is a regime which has destroyed freedom in Tibet, which has attacked India, and has been condemned by the United Nations for aggression in Korea. It is a nation which is helping the forces of violence in almost every continent. The contest in Viet-Nam is part of a wider pattern of aggressive purposes.

WHY ARE WE IN SOUTH VIET-NAM?
Why are these realities our concern? Why are we in South Viet-Nam?

We are there because we have a promise to keep. Since 1954 every American President has offered support to the people of South Viet-Nam. We have helped to build, and we have helped to defend. Thus, over many years, we have made a national pledge to help South Viet-Nam defend its independence.

And I intend to keep that promise.

To dishonor that pledge, to abandon this small and brave nation to its enemies, and to the terror that must follow, would be an unforgivable wrong.

We are also there to strengthen world order. Around the globe, from Berlin to Thailand, are people whose well-being rests in part on the belief that they can count on us if they are attacked. To leave Viet-Nam to its fate would shake the confidence of all these people in the value of an

American commitment and in the value of America's word. The result would be increased unrest and instability, and even wider war.

We are also there because there are great stakes in the balance. Let no one think for a moment that retreat from Viet-Nam would bring an end to conflict. The battle would be renewed in one country and then another. The central lesson of our time is that the appetite of aggression is never satisfied. To withdraw from one battlefield means only to prepare for the next. We must say in Southeast Asia—as we did in Europe—in the words of the Bible: "Hitherto shalt thou come, but no further."

There are those who say that all our effort there will be futile—that China's power is such that it is bound to dominate all Southeast Asia. But there is no end to that argument until all of the nations of Asia are swallowed up.

There are those who wonder why we have a responsibility there. Well, we have it there for the same reason that we have a responsibility for the defense of Europe. World War II was fought in both Europe and Asia, and when it ended we found ourselves with continued responsibility for the defense of freedom.

Our objective is the independence of South Viet-Nam and its freedom from attack. We want nothing for ourselves—only that the people of South Viet-Nam be allowed to guide their own country in their own way. We will do everything necessary to reach that objective, and we will do only what is absolutely necessary.

In recent months attacks on South Viet-Nam were stepped up. Thus it became necessary for us to increase our response and to make attacks by air. This is not a change of purpose. It is a change in what we believe that purpose requires.

We do this in order to slow down aggression.

We do this to increase the confidence of the brave people of South Viet-Nam who have bravely borne this brutal battle for so many years with so many casualties.[38]

One American poet, Seth Wade, expresses his reaction to seeing the president on television as follows:

Tonight I Heard the President

Tonight I heard the President
speak through a scratchy cold about freedom,
about people in straw houses who need electricity,
about new sacrifices to old gods
because the people must have freedom and electric lights.
So perhaps they must
and he knows how it must be done.
I, too, have a cold;
perhaps to dead soldiers

one apologizes after all by saying:
I have not chosen a proper subject for thought.
So, writing these words, I think
of the President, who also perhaps cannot sleep
except from weariness of his thought and action.
I think of the President sitting thinking,
in a room only too well lighted,
the cold in the head, the always congested vision.[39]

*A few days later in Hanoi, DRV Premier Pham Van Dong addresses the
National Assembly.*

". . . The unswerving policy of the DRV Government is to respect
strictly the 1954 Geneva agreements on Vietnam and to implement correctly their basic provisions as embodied in the following points:

4 POINTS
1. Recognition of the basic national rights of the Vietnamese people—
peace, independence, sovereignty, unity, and territorial integrity. According to the Geneva agreements, the U.S. Government must withdraw
from South Vietnam U.S. troops, military personnel, and weapons of all
kinds, dismantle all U.S. military bases there, and cancel its military
alliance with South Vietnam. It must end its policy of intervention and
aggression in South Vietnam. According to the Geneva agreements, the
U.S. Government must stop its acts of war against North Vietnam and
completely cease all encroachments on the territory and sovereignty of
the DRV.
2. Pending the peaceful reunification of Vietnam, while Vietnam is still
temporarily divided into two zones the military provisions of the 1954
Geneva agreements on Vietnam must be strictly respected. The two
zones must refrain from entering into any military alliance with foreign
countries and there must be no foreign military bases, troops, or military
personnel in their respective territory.
3. The internal affairs of South Vietnam must be settled by the South
Vietnamese people themselves in accordance with the program of the
NFLSV without any foreign interference.
4. The peaceful reunification of Vietnam is to be settled by the Vietnamese people in both zones, without any foreign interference.
This stand of the DRV Government unquestionably enjoys the approval and support of all peace and justice-loving governments and
people in the world. The government of the DRV is of the view that the
stand expounded here is the basis for the soundest political settlement of
the Vietnam problem.

GENEVA
If this basis is recognized, favorable conditions will be created for the
peaceful settlement of the Vietnam people, and it will be possible to

consider the reconvening of an international conference along the pattern
of the 1954 Geneva conference on Vietnam."[40]

1965 **5 May**—173rd U.S. Army Airborne Brigade lands at Vung Tau,
Republic of Vietnam. **7 May**—U.S. Marine reinforcements land at
Chu Lai.

At home, American poet Clemens Starck ponders:

On a Clear Day

From Telegraph Hill you can see for miles
on a clear day. Today
is May 7,
1965. Overhead
flying in perfect formation,
three F-100's play at war.

The morning papers are already yellow.
Their headlines
threaten me from ten yards away.
And I can't even read.

Is it true the Marines have landed?

I keep walking, what else can I do . . . ?
I think of the sod huts
of homesteaders in the Dakotas.
I am haunted by the ghost of Coolidge,
and the Daughters of the American Revolution.

Imagine!
The American Revolution!
Bunker Hill, the long winter of '77, Washington
crossing the Delaware . . .

It's all over.

Now we are crossing the Red Sea—we,
the Egyptians.[41]

1965 **10 May**—President Johnson decides on another bombing pause.
11 May—Secretary Rusk secretly passes information about pause to
Hanoi via Moscow.

That day, the battle of Song Be begins. One of the forward air controllers (FAC) is interviewed shortly afterward for a classified U.S. Air Force historical study.

I'm Captain John S. Lynch, 54266A, assigned to the 33rd TAC Group as a forward air controller and assigned Phouc Binh Ton Special Zone particular Phouc Long Province. My duty station is Song Be Vietnam. I am a member of Advisory Team 94, very shortly to change over to Special Forces Team B-31.

We were attacked by an estimated regiment on the morning of 11 May 1965 at 1:45 in the morning. It was a coordinated attack against the entire complex here . . . in which we have an airstrip approximately 5,000 feet long, hard surfaced—probably the best strip going north once you leave Saigon in III Corp.

I understand the regiment was Q763 although I cannot confirm this. I heard the figure. I'm not absolutely sure.

However, we are sure of the fact that they hit us with 75mm artillery fire, either pack howitzer or recoilless, 81mm, 60mm, and subsequently a considerable amount of machine guns. At least five 50 caliber machine guns were brought in the immediate vicinity of anti-aircraft protection and innumerable light machine guns—30 caliber and there was one Chinese light machine gun left in the compound. We knew we were in for attack based on intelligence sources. . . .

Because of this, Lt. Col. Alton Park, the advisory team commander, had put us on a 50 per cent alert. We normally maintain 25 per cent otherwise. So all positions were filled, all crew served weapons were manned, all ammunition was distributed and a battle plan had been worked out, if we were attacked what we would do. Because our compound is bordered on the north by the province chief's home and on the south by the 110th A & L Company of the Popular Force Regional force organization. To the west of us is a steep slope and to the east of us is the town, the province headquarters, and across the way is the police compound.

At first indication of an attack . . . (correction about nine o'clock that evening) they had an alert and down on the east side of the mountain they had a slight fire fight, which was reported—supposedly the forward element coming in. Then at 1:45 in the morning, the first rounds came into the compound, simultaneously 75mm fire, 81mm mortar fire. Fortunately one round hit the end room of the compound [, went] into the head on the other side, and did not detonate. Had that one detonated, we would have been in a little trouble with no communications. We did have radios out including the PRC-41 which is the Air Force UHF FAC radio. However, this was taken out of commission by one of the first grenades. Also the VC had infiltrated and the 110 was non-existent and had [fallen] back. So the people were getting grenades simultaneously. They were in the compound in the first 15 minutes. We suffered all our casualties in the first 15 minutes. One man was killed in a mortar position from grenades. They had gotten in and gotten down in the housing area behind the wall and were throwing grenades over this wall. The others were all in the mess hall which was our aid station. They'd come in on the blind side of us. Well, we shot at one man coming across the wire but missed him. They got in the mess hall. There was a fire fight in the mess hall and they threw two satchel charges in. The wounded who were able to get out did, and came back in the hole which I was manning right near the front gate and at that time we exchanged a pretty fair fire fight with the VC in the Mess Hall, a grenade fight and small arms against grenades. . . .

The people in the mess hall did a fine job. One of the doctor's medics, Sgt. Benning, who was killed, did a fine job holding them out. When a satchel charge comes through the door, there isn't much a man and a rifle can do.

So we got our wounded out, kept them coming out the back. Now, the two positions we had in front had been put in at 7 o'clock that night with sandbags. They did not know about these. I think it surprised them by the amount of fire that we gave them. Also the people in the back kept up well disciplined fire power. There was no sporadic shooting or haphazard shooting. It was a concentrated barrage. The 81mm mortar we had in town immediately took over the area to the northwest of us under fire. That's where we could see the recoilless rifle being fired over there or the 75, and we feel that we did some good work there. This went on for a couple of hours, really, the firing. Then it died down considerably.

Then the air started coming in. The helicopters pulled back from the 50's. They made one hell of an attempt to knock them out, but they of course cannot begin to match them. It was about this time that the first B-57 came over, Copperhead 3 who is Captain Tom Craig. He's one of my companions in crime down at Phouc Ton Province at PVT Special Zone headquarters.

At that time we got a radio, got him and we fired on this ridge line here. We got two mortar positions over them, approximately 40 people there and I say approximately—give or take 5 in there.

To the northeast of the ridge line across this Song Be river, we got those with napalm. The 57s took them out. The next target . . . I don't know if we got any in this area to the west of us or not but there was automatic weapons fire coming across there and we didn't receive any more. Then the next target was in town because they had the town and there's a Catholic church right here on the southeast side of town where they were dug in. Some of them were in the church itself firing out and some of them were to the north of the church. There is an open field between the hospital and this church. Later I counted 40 plus positions in there, three 50 caliber positions about 25 meters from one another, all of them were loaded with guns. There was a light .30, [in addition to] 60mm mortar positions with 10 empty cannisters there, and what I think was a .75 position right adjacent to the road. There was a tremendous amount of fire coming out of this area, so we got a radio and two of us went down the road, and down adjacent to the hospital. We could actually see the muzzles of the guns turning. Then we just brought in one B-57 at a time. I was working with an FM radio talking to Copperhead 3, Tom Craig, who in turn would relay to the B-57s and we would bring them in one at a time because of the weather. They could not drop the bombs without being destroyed them- selves so they dropped "safe." As they dropped this pinned the people down and another one would come in and strafe the area.

The first B-57 flight on the scene—I've forgotten the call signs—the lead aircraft was setting there doing pylon turns on these positions. Every time he would get the nose down, he would nose through, come up into the weather a bit, and back down. He received tremendous amount of fire. Then of course as time went on we would do this with all of them, and the fire diminished. And then we got them to come across the town, about like such. There's a heliopad here and open field just south of it and they bombed through here. Then an A1-E flight came in an ex- pended with napalm on the east side of this hill here, and from that point on there was no fire.[42]

On 18 May the DRV government issues a public statement from Hanoi.

". . . According to various sources, the U.S. Government has informed a number of other governments that air raids against the DRV are to be suspended from noon (Washington time) 12 May 1965 till the following week, and that the United States is ready to resume the raids if U.S. and puppet troops are subjected to further attacks in South Vietnam. In mak- ing this perfidious allegation, the U.S. aggressors have no other aim than to cover up their extremely dangerous acts intensifying the war in Viet- nam and Southeast Asia and at the same time to deceive world public opinion on the so-called U.S. peace will . . .

". . . This time, in the face of the mounting movement for an end to the aggressive war in South Vietnam and to the bombing and strafing of the DRV, the U.S. Government has put forward the so-called suspension of air raids against North Vietnam. It has gone so far as to state arro- gantly that the suspension of U.S. air raids on the north must be re- sponded to by a cessation of attacks against the U.S. aggressors and their agents by the people and liberation army in South Vietnam . . .

". . . The DRV Government resolutely exposes the U.S. Govern- ment's trick in the so-called suspension of air raids against North Vietnam as a deceitful maneuver designed to pave the way for new U.S. acts of war. The peace-loving peoples and governments in the world are firmly demanding that the United States end its aggressive war in South Viet- nam, stop for good the savage bombing and strafing raids against the DRV, and scrupulously observe and correctly implement the 1954 Ge- neva agreements on Vietnam. The DRV Government affirms once again that the four-point stand made public on 8 April 1965 is the only sound basis for a political settlement of the Vietnam problem."[43]

1965   June—1st Battalion, Royal Australian Regiment arrives at Vung Tao, Republic of Vietnam. **4 June**—South Vietnamese military leaders create "War Cabinet" headed by Air Marshal Nguyen Cao Ky. **19 June**—Nguyen Van Thieu selected as chief of state; Air Marshal Ky becomes prime minister. **26 June**—COMUSMACV is authorized to commit U.S. forces to battle "in any situation necessary to strengthen the relative position of GVN forces." **27–30 June**—173rd Airborne Brigade offensive in War Zone "D," near Saigon. **1 July**—Viet Cong forces mortar and attack Da Nang airbase, destroying or damaging six American aircraft.

A U.S. Marine Corps historian notes some particular aspects of the Da Nang attack.

The South Vietnamese . . . found a wounded North Vietnamese who turned out to be the intelligence officer of the sapper team. He identified his parent unit as the *3d Battalion, 18th NVA Regiment.*

Although the damage on the airfield was not extensive and there were a few casualties, the spectacular nature of the VC attack caused world-wide publicity and renewed command attention to the vulnerability of the American bases. General Walt, in 1977, remarked:

> During the period of 0200 to 0400 I received phone calls from MACV Hq, CinCPac Hq, FMFPac Hq, Headquarters US Marine Crops, Secretary of the Navy's Office, Secretary of Defense Office and from the White House "Watch Officer" *not* President Johnson. All of the callers wanted to know *all* about the attack and *what* I was doing about it. Fortunately I had given instructions to Colonel Wheeler before the phone started ringing. This points out one of the hazards (for a commander) of having present day instantaneous communications to the battlefield, all over the world.[44]

After hearing the latest news, Undersecretary of State George Ball submits this memo to the president.

Memorandum for the President from George Ball, July 1, 1965

(1) A Losing War: The South Vietnamese are losing the war to the Viet Cong. No one can assure you that we can beat the Viet Cong or even force them to the conference table on our terms, no matter how many hundred thousand *white, foreign* (U.S.) troops we deploy.

No one has demonstrated that a white ground force of whatever size can win a guerrilla war—which is at the same time a civil war between

Asians—in jungle terrain in the midst of a population that refuses cooperation to the white forces (and the South Vietnamese) and thus provides
a great intelligence advantage to the other side. Three recent incidents
vividly illustrate this point: (a) the sneak attack on the Da Nang Air Base
which involved penetration of a defense parameter guarded by 9,000
Marines. This raid was possible only because of the cooperation of the
local inhabitants; (b) the B-52 raid that failed to hit the Viet Cong who
had obviously been tipped off; (c) the search and destroy mission of the
173rd Air Borne Brigade which spent three days looking for the Viet
Cong, suffered 23 casualties, and never made contact with the enemy who
had obviously gotten advance word of their assignment. . . .

The decision you face now, therefore, is crucial. Once large numbers of
U.S. troops are committed to directed combat, they will begin to take
heavy casualties in a war they are ill-equipped to fight in a non-cooperative
if not downright hostile countryside.

Once we suffer large casualties, we will have started a well-nigh irrever-
sible process. Our involvement will be so great that we cannot—without
national humiliation—stop short of achieving our complete objectives. *Of
the two possibilities I think humiliation would be more likely than the
achievement of our objectives—even after we have paid terrible costs.*[45]

1965   28 July—President Johnson announces "immediate" U.S. troop increases in Vietnam, from 75,000 to 125,000.

In August, according to The Pentagon Papers, *a faltering pacification
program is given new emphasis by some old faces who return to Saigon.*

Ambassador Lodge and the "True Believers"

Henry Cabot Lodge returned as Ambassador in August of 1965, and immediately began to talk of pacification as "the heart of the matter." In
telegrams and Mission Council meetings, Lodge told the President, the
GVN, and the Mission that pacification deserved a higher priority. Because he saw himself as an advocate before the President for his beliefs
rather than as the overall manager of the largest overseas civil-military
effort in American history, Lodge did not try, as Ambassador Maxwell
Taylor had done, to devise an integrated and unified strategy that balanced
every part of our effort. Instead, he declared, in his first month back in
Vietnam (September, 1965), that "the U.S. military was doing so well now
that we face a distinct possibility that VC main force units will be neutralized, and VC fortresses destroyed soon," and that therefore we should be
ready to give pacification a new push. While his involvement was irregular
and inconsistent, Lodge did nonetheless play a key role in giving pacification a boost. His rhetoric, even if vague, encouraged other advocates of

pacification to speak up. The man he brought with him, Edward Lansdale, gave by his very presence an implicit boost to pacification. . . .

THE ASSIGNMENT OF LANSDALE:
Handpicked group of about ten* experienced counter-subversion/counter-terrorism workers under direction of Edward G. Lansdale will be going to Saigon to provide Ambassador Lodge with special operating staff in field of political action both at central level and also in connection with rural programs.

COMMENT:
From the beginning, there was misunderstanding over Lansdale's role in Lodge's Embassy. The first cable relects this. The phrase "counter-subversion/counter-terrorism workers," seems to contradict the latter part of the sentence, about "political action." From the start Lodge wanted him to "get pacification going." Thus, less than a month later, Lodge told the President:

> I appointed Edward Lansdale, with his complete approval, to be chairman of the U.S. Mission Liaison Group to the newly created Vietamese govermental body having to do with what we call "pacification," what they call "rural construction," and what means to me *socially conscious practical politics, the by-product of which is effective counter-subversion/terrorism.* I thought it was important for all concerned for him to have a definite allocation where he would have the best chance of bringing his talents to bear. I trust that the hopes of some journalists that he is here in an adversarial relationship with existing US agencies will be nipped in the bud by making him the spokesman for the whole US Mission in this particular regard. (Italics added)

Thus, another action which served to stregthen the pacification priority, although its primary reason probably was to get Lansdale working on something other than Saigon politics.[46]

With the entry of U.S. forces into active rather than reactive combat, both expected and unexpected problems occur. One U.S. Marine Corps historian notes:

The Marines . . . had limited contact with the Vietnamese civilian population and when they had, it had occurred in areas where the people had some basic loyalty to the government cause. This was not the same in the region to the south. It was very difficult to build loyalty to the government of South Vietnam where fathers, brothers, and relatives were part of the VC structure and had been so for a generation. A Buddhist priest who lived in one of the hamlets near Duong Son furnished the Marines with some basic intelligence about the VC strength and organizaton. He revealed that the Viet Cong maintained a roadblock near the railroad

*One member of Lansdale's group, however, is not "handpicked." Assigned by Secretary McNamara, the eleventh man is Daniel Ellsberg.

tracks [in] Duong Son and manned by a four-man squad. A 40-man VC force lived in his village and was busily constructing bunkers, foxholes, punji traps, and setting booby traps. In another hamlet, the VC maintained an observation post to watch the Marines, while an enemy platoon stationed in Duong Son took occasional pot shots at the Marine positions in Duong Son. Enemy political cadres were also active. VC tax agents collected 270 piastres annually from each family living in the area. The priest summed up: "the attitude of the people is generally friendly to the VC and unfriendly to the government forces."

The incident that perhaps best mirrored the perplexities which faced the 9th Marines was the well-publicized search and destroy mission in the Cam Ne village complex on 3 August conducted by Company D, 1/9. It was planned in conjunction with a 3rd Marines operation, BLASTOUT I, carried out by 1/3 and an ARVN battalion approximately four miles south of the Cam Ne complex along both banks of the Yen River. Company D, in addition to supporting this mission, was to clear the Cam Ne complex and relieve the pressure on the two companies of 2/9 in Duong Son.

The company, reinforced by a platoon of LVTs, was to board the tractors at the northern terminal of the Phong Le Bridge, navigate the Cau Do to where it met the Yan River, and land opposite the Cam Ne complex, approximately 1,200 yards downstream. The Marines were to attack to the east and occupy [two other points in] Cam Ne approximately two and a half miles from the line of departure. A battalion command post was established on the northern back of the Song Cau Do in order to coordinate the activities of the infantry unit and its supporting arms. The attack was to begin at 1000 and the Marines were supposed to reach their destination at 1500 that afternoon.

Complications arose at the very beginning. The Marines were unexpectedly reinforced by a CBS television crew at the bridge. Neither the battalion commander, Lieutenant Colonel Ludwig, nor the company commander, Captain H. Brooks West, had been informed that they were to have company.*[47]

What the American public learned on television about Cam Ne from the CBS "reinforcement" is reported the next day, 4 August, by The New York Times.

Burning of Village Described

A correspondent in South Vietnam for C.B.S. television reported yesterday that he had seen United States marines burn 150 dwellings in the hamlet of Camne, despite the pleas of old men and women.

---

*When this manuscript was coordinated with higher headquarters, the reference to the CBS television crew was ordered deleted, with a comment that despite the reviewing officer's dislike of Morley Safer, it should not be marine corps policy to publicize such media activity. The published version does not contain this segment.

The correspondent, Morley Safer, said that the marines had orders, according to an officer in the operation, to burn the hamlet to the ground if fired upon.

"After surrounding the village," Mr. Safer reported, "and receiving one burst of automatic fire from an unidentified direction, the marines poured in 3.5 rocket fire, 79 grenade launchers, and heavy and light machine-gun fire. The marines then moved in, proceeding first with cigarette lighters then with flame throwers, to burn down an estimated 150 dwellings."

Pleas for Delay Ignored

Mr. Safer's report, read on "Evening News With Walter Cronkite," said the marines ignored the pleas of Vietnamese to delay the burnings so that belongings could be removed.

"I subsequently learned," Mr. Safer continued, "that a Marine platoon on the right flank wounded three women and killed one child in a rocket barrage. The day's operations netted about four prisoners—old men. Two marines were wounded, both by their own fire, although this has been denied."

C.B.S. quoted a Defense Department official as having said:

"There is no new policy of toughness towards civilians. Our policy is still to bend over backward even at possible cost of U.S. lives. . . . The U.S. Marine Corps has made a special effort in the Danang area. They have resettled some civilians, set up dispensaries for them and lost a number of marines killed just helping civilians."[48]

Two days later, U.S. Air Force Captain Richard B. Sexton arrives in Vietnam for his second tour as a pilot. A professor of history as well, Sexton will write an extensive analytical and anecdotal diary. Written above his first dated entry is a note that describes how American GIs view their one-year assignment to Vietnam.

80 days have September, April, June, and November. All the rest have 93, except the last month which has 140.

6 August. In many ways this war is like the Civil War. Our Generals don't understand its revolutionary nature and its use of revolutionary means. We have too many McClellands who always overestimate the enemy. The VC are hurting but they still control things because we are afraid to get out of our forts on other than temporary patrols or sweeps. We need to devote fully 50% of our effort to psychological war and civic action. Don't defoliate trees. . . .

Vietnamese are charming. . . . Consider us wonderfully naive because we smile and show emotion openly. Confusion [*sic*] training teaches them to control expression. They are friendly and really like us. Of course there are normal shysters as around any base. But even they respond to a smile. They don't want VC. Have sense of "peoplehood" but not "Nationhood." Nationalism is a Western concept and has affected only the intelligentsia. Most people don't care much about central government. VC use terror effectively to control local areas. Are much worse than government ever was. Collect more taxes, make more demands. However, by the time people realize this it's too late. If people who had experienced both communism and freedom had free choice, they would vote overwhelmingly for freedom.

Catholics realize this is a war of extermination and will fight to the end. Buddhists are fatalists. They will endure whatever is their fate. They don't want VC but are not willing to oppose them. Thus, VC terror works. With bad government, the VC are only a little worse but not enough so to fight. We must give them something to lose. Then they will support Government. Now, gap is small between Government and VC. We must make a wider gap. . . .

Americans cannot comprehend nature of Communist control through terror because there is nothing in our experience to back it. Thus many Americans refuse to believe truth about Communism. Many people are that way until it is too late.

11 August. 173rd US Airborne landing at Holoway and new field in C-123's and C-130's to take part in fight. One plane every 6 minutes. VC are out of contact now.

A lot of reporters here trying to get information. PIO [Public Information Officer] not saying anything. Reporters will make up their own stories.

It is not necessary to kill VC; it is necessary to isolate him from the people.

Army idea of forts—drop of oil—defensive perimeter—is a pile of bunk. Their entire concept of fighting the war with conventional military tactics is wrong. They might win a battle once in a while—like Duc Co— but will lose the war.

Newsmen are told nothing or misleading information so they invent their own stories and they are *wrong*.

26 August. *Time,* August 20, "World" had distorted account of Duc Co, but good account of "Big Joe No. 1." Over radio heard McNamara give interview. He lied. Said 80% of equipment comes from North Vietnam. North equipped with 7.62 mm., all of which is supplied by North. Bullshit! 7.62 is *our* standard and only 20% comes from North. Also, he lied about our role. Said we are not interested in purely internal affairs but only to protect from North and if NVN withdraws, we would too. Bullshit![49]

1965   **16 September**—Colonel Robinson Risner, leader of the first Thanh
          Hoa bridge strike, is shot down over North Vietnam. **8 November**—
          Final elements of Republic of Korea division land in South Vietnam.
          27 November—First large-scale "march for peace" by several thou-
          sand Americans in Washington.

A few days later Secretary McNamara drafts a memo to the president.

Military and Political Actions recommended for SVN
7 December 1965

We believe that, whether or not major new diplomatic initiatives are
made, the US must send a substantial number of additional forces to VN
if we are to avoid being defeated there.

PROGNOSIS ASSUMING THE RECOMMENDED DEPLOYMENTS
Deployments of the kind we have recommended will not guarantee
success. Our intelligence estimate is that the present Communist policy
is to continue to prosecute the war vigorously in the South. They continue to believe that the war will be a long one, that time is their ally,
and that their own staying power is superior to ours. They recognize
that the US reinforcements of 1965 signify a determination to avoid
defeat, and that more US troops can be expected. Even though the
Communists will continue to suffer heavily from GVN and US ground
and air action, we expect them, upon learning of any US intentions to
augment its forces, to boost their own commitment and to test US
capabilities and will to perservere [sic] at higher level of conflict and
casualties (US KIA with the recommended deployments can be expected to reach 1000 a month).

  If the US were willing to commit enough forces—perhaps 600,000 men
or more—we could ultimately prevent the DRV/VC from sustaining the
conflict at a significant level. When this point was reached, however, the
question of Chinese intervention would become critical. (We are generally agreed that the Chinese Communists will intervene with combat
forces to prevent destruction of the Communist regime in the DRV. It is
less clear whether they would intervene to prevent a DRV/VC defeat in
the South.) The intelligence estimate is that the chances are a little better
than even that, at this stage, Hanoi and Peiping would choose to reduce
the effort in the South and try to salvage their resources for another day;
but there is an almost equal chance that they would enlarge the war and
bring in large numbers of Chinese forces (they have made certain prepar-
tions which could point in this direction.

  It follows, therefore, that the odds are about even that, even with the
recommended deployments, we will be faced in early 1967 with a military
standoff at a much higher level, with pacification still stalled, and with

any prospect of military success marred by the chances of an active Chinese intervention.[50]

On 18 December Captain B. C. Wallace, U.S. Air Force, arrives at Ubon Royal Thai air force base, Thailand, to fly F-4C "Phantom" aircraft as a member of the 433rd Tactical Fighter Squadron. He also keeps a daily journal.

Ubon Royal Thai AFB, Thailand
433 TFS
Capt. B. C. Wallace

18 Dec. 1965:
We arrived at Ubon today after an exhausting trip from George AFB, Cal. in a C-130. We broke down in Hawaii and several of us got "polluted" on Mai-Tais. After repairs we proceeded (painfully) to Wake Island, thence Okinawa where a further aircraft problem caused enough delay for a bit of rest. Dave Connett and I went to a hot bath where he proceeded to have two! After an uninspiring tour of a couple of bars we slept until depature time. The short trip to here wasn't too bad after the long haul across the Pacific to Okinawa.

19 Dec. 1965:
Seemingly endless briefings. There are dozens of ground rules to remember and "safe areas" that we must avoid hitting. How do we do that at night, I wonder? Most of our missions are to be in darkness.

20 Dec. 1965:
The squadron flew its first strikes today. I am to fly in the second wave tomorrow. We immediately found out that this is a serious business. Bob Kahn and Joe Moran were hit near Hanoi, losing all but the afterburner on one engine. They suffered a near miss by a SAM missile. Kahn, in the front seat, managed to get them back across most of Laos before it quit. They ejected and were picked up by a "Jolly Green Giant" helicopter. Much whooping it up at the club, but minus Bob and Joe. They were being checked over at the hospital on another base. Korat, I believe.

21 Dec. 1965:
Today it was my turn. We flew the same type of strike as yesterday. It was a daytime, all-out effort of Air Force and Navy directed by the Joint Chiefs of Staff. I was No. 4 in a flight of four flying "MIG cover" for F-105's bombing a bridge on the northeast railroad out of Hanoi into China.

We took on gas from the tanker out over the Gulf of Tonkin and turned northwest flying at a fairly low altitude and "jinking smartly" to avoid any radar tracking or gunfire out of Haiphong, on the coast. The first look I had at North Viet Nam was the coastline between China and

Haiphong. It was surprisingly green. I guess I expected snow or, at least, brown fields. Clouds began to thicken as we went inland. The sky was full of U.S. planes so the MIG's stayed put on Kep Airfield just below. We could see them parked there.

The flight lead was also on his first mission in the area. We had gone too long without an accurate fix on our position and began to get "slightly lost." But since no MIG's were coming up, the F105's were spared that hazard at least. It was apparently enough that the enemy knew where we were even though *we* didn't! According to some of the landmarks, I think we were a bit inside the China border, a brief that I'm keeping strictly to myself. "Big Lyndon" specifically said not to do that!

We departed very low on fuel and sought the emergency tanker under GCI control. There was a great amount of radio chatter. Several Navy aircraft and some F-105's had been hit and were on "Guard" frequency. We had a lot of trouble finding the tanker. When we finally did I was seriously short of fuel because of my No. 4 position in the formation. The FUEL LOW LEVEL light had been on for a minute or two and I was seriously thinking over the ejection procedures. Once on the tanker I was given "first gulp" and did my best, and *quickest,* air refueling ever!

We learned that Bob Jeffrey and George Mims had taken what appeared to be a direct hit just before we entered the target area. Other flight members feel sure that there was no chance of survival for either. Only small pieces of the airplane were seen to emerge from the fireball. George was married one month ago. Bob has a baby son.

My flight lasted four hours. I'm very tired. A rather odd thing happened at the club during the normal post-mission boozing. In contrast to the whooping that went on after Kahn's and Moran's mishap, there was no mention at all of Jeffrey and Mims. Of course, the result was quite different. Still, I found it rather odd that, as far as I could determine, there was no reference at all to their flight. Not like in the movies! But, I'm sure if any of us thought this was a movie he is no longer under that illusion.

After this first mission I feel the same as Bobby Kahn. Today he and Joe returned by helicopter and he "held forth" at the club. He says that if the next 99 are like this one, he may have to change his line of work as well as his underwear!

21 Dec. 1965:
Flew two missions today. Both were in daylight and in North Viet Nam. On the first the weather was overcast so we had to return to Laos and use the bombs to crater a road segment. There was no flak. A welcome change of pace!

On the second strike we hit two bridges. Three of my bombs failed to release and the increased drag precluded landing at Ubon. I landed instead at Udorn Thani in northeastern Thailand. One of the bombs apparently had partially released or had come loose on landing and was barely hanging on the wing. When the ground crew saw it they wisely took off. Not knowing why they looked so startled, but having the average 80 I.Q. of any good fighter pilot, I shut down the engines and, along with my copilot, a younger but slower airman, also left the scene!!

After a lengthy delay we finally departed, sans bombs, for Ubon and arrived at night. It was my third flight of a tedious day and I was as tired as I have ever been in my life. No, more so. It was the record. So in that condition I had to make my first night landing at Ubon. Short runway, no approach lights, no moon. Ladies and gents, I'm ready to chuck this whole thing and deliver mail or milk somewhere. Anywhere.

24 Dec. 1965:
We flew a daytime strike on a storage area in North Viet Nam. I think I missed it but the others said they hit it. Rather a strange way to promote peace on earth on this particular day. A Xmas truce starts tomorrow. I don't know about the enemy, but I can use it.[51]

The Pentagon Papers *history offers a remarkable summary of 1965.*

Meanwhile, Back at The War . . .

The re-emphasis of pacification was, of course, a far more disorderly process than any written review can suggest, and unfortunately must overlook many events and recommendations which were not central to the re-emphasis of pacification. But it is useful and important to review briefly what the Mission was reporting to Washington about the overall effort during 1965, since Saigon's reports should have formed an important part of the background for decision.

This selection should be read not as the "objective" story of what was happening in Vietnam . . . but as a reflection of the beliefs of the Americans in Saigon, and as a reflection of what the Mission wanted Washington to believe.

This selection is entirely direct quotations from MACV's Monthly Evaluation Report. Each month this report began with a summary of the month's events, and the following items represent the running evaluation for 1965: [Emphasis Added]*

> *January, 1965: Review of military events in January tend to induce a decidedly more optimistic view than has been seen in recent months.* Despite adverse influence exerted by national level political disorders and localized Buddhist/student rioting, the military experienced the most successful single month of the counterinsurgency effort. . . . *Pacification made little progress this month.* Although some gains were made in the Hop Tac area, effort in the remainder of RVN was hampered by political activity and religious and student disorders. . . . *If the RVNAF capability can be underwritten by political stability and durability, a significant turning point in the war could be forthcoming.*

*By writer of *The Pentagon Papers.*

February, 1965: . . . GVN forces continued to make progress in III and IV CTZ, maintained a tenuous balance over the VC in I CTZ, and suffered general regression in II CTZ . . . The indicators of RVNAF operational effort . . . all showed a decline. However, losses on both sides remained high due to the violence of encounters and VC tenacity . . . The long term effect of events in February is impossible to foretell. It is obvious that the complexion of the war has changed. The VC appear to be making a concerted effort to isolate the northern portion of RVN by seizing a salient to the sea in the northern part of II CTZ. Here RVNAF has lost the initiative, at least temporarily. However, *US/GVN strikes against DRV and increased use of U.S. jet aircraft in RVN* has had a salutary effect on both military and civilian morale which may result in a greater national effort and, *hopefully, reverse the downward trend.*

March, 1965: Events in March were encouraging. . . . RVNAF ground operations were highlighted by renewed operational effort. . . . VC activity was considerably below the norm of the preceding six months and indications were that the enemy was engaged in the re-supply and re-positioning of units possibly in preparation for a new offensive, probably in the II Corps area. . . . *In summary, March has given rise to some cautious optimism. The current government appears to be taking control of the situation and, if the present state of popular morale can be sustained and strengthened, the GVN, with continued U.S. support, should be able to counter future VC offenses successfully.*

April, 1965: Friendly forces retained the initiative during April and a review of events reinforces the feeling of optimism generated last month. . . . In summary, current trends are highly encouraging and *the GVN may have actually turned the tide at long last.* However, there are some disquieting factors which indicate a need to avoid overconfidence. A test of these trends should be forthcoming in the next few months if the VC *launch their expected counter-offensive* and the period may well be one of the most important of the war.

May, 1965: The encouraging trends of the past few months did not carry through into May and there were some serious setbacks. However, it is hoped that the high morale and improved discipline and leadership which has developed during that period will sustain future GVN efforts. . . .

June, 1965: During June the military situation in the RVN continued to worsen despite a few bright spots occasioned by RVNAF successes. In general, however, the VC . . . retained the initiative having launched several well-coordinated, savage attacks in regimental strength. . . .

July, 1965: An overall analysis of the military situation at the end of July reveals that GVN forces continued to make progress in IV Corps, maintained a limited edge in I Crops with the increased USMC effort and suffered a general regression in the northern portion of III Corps as well as in the central highlands of II Corps. *The VC monsoon offensive, which was so effective in June, faltered during July as VC casualty figures reached a new high.* . . .

August, 1965: An evaluation of the overall military effort in August reveals several encouraging facts. The most pronounced is the steady increase in the number of VC casualties and the number of VC "ralliers" to the GVN. . . . In summary, the general increase in offensive operations by

GVN, U.S. and Third Country forces and a correlative increase in enemy casualties have kept the VC off balance and prevented his interference with the build-up of U.S. forces. The often spoken of VC "monsoon offensive" has not materialized, and it *now appears that the VC have relinquished the initiative in the conduct of the war.*
September, 1965: As the end of the monsoon season approached, the military situation appears considerably brighter than in May when the VC threatened to defeat the RVNAF. Since May the build-up of Free World Military Assistance Forces, coupled with aggressive combat operations, has thwarted VC plans and has laid the foundation for the eventual defeat of the VC. . . .
October, 1965: . . . an increase in magnitude and tempo of engagements as the GVN/FWF maintained the initiative . . . In summary, the military situation during October continued to favor the Allies as the VC experienced heavy casualties from the overwhelming Allied fire power . . . .
November, 1965: The increasing tempo of the war reflected in casualty totals which reached new highs for VC/PAVN and friendly forces. . . . While keeping the enemy generally off balance, GVN/FWMAF were able to maintain and, to some degree, to increase the scope and intensity of friendly-initiated operations.
December, 1965: Military activity in December was highlighted by an increase in the number of VC/PAVN attacks on isolated outposts, hamlets, and districts, towns, and the avoidance of contact with large GVN and Free World Forces. *The effectiveness of this strategy was attested by the highest monthly friendly casualty total of the war,* by friendly weapons losses in excess of weapons captured for the first time since July, and by 30% fewer VC casualties than in November. . . .

This is not the place for a detailed analysis of the reporting of the war, or of the implications of the above-cited evaluations. But several points do seem to emerge:

1. The reports are far too optimistic from January through April, 1965, and a big switch seems to come in June, 1965, when General Westmoreland had already made his 44-battalion request and warned of disaster if they were not forth-coming. May's report begins to show the change in mood, but its ambiguous evaluation is in sharp contrast to the brief backward look offered in September.
2. Pacification is mentioned in the January evaluation, but fades away to virtually nothing in the months of the build-up.
3. The evaluations do not suggest that the main force threat is in any way diminishing by the end of 1965. Indeed, they accurately predict larger battles in 1966. They do not suggest, therefore, that the time had come to start emphasizing pacification *at the expense of exerting more pressure directly on the enemy.* The evaluations do not address this question directly, of course, but they do suggest that if any greater emphasis was to be put on pacification, *it could be done only if there was not a corresponding reduction in the attack effort against the VC.* This, in turn, would imply that if pacification was to receive greater emphasis at the beginning of 1966, it would require either more Allied troops or else might lead to a lessening of pressure on the VC.[52]

Early in 1966 Harrison Salisbury, assistant managing editor of The New
York Times, *accepts the DRV's invitation and travels illegally to Hanoi.
When his articles, which are critical of American conduct, are published,
the Senate Foreign Relations Committee holds hearings on 2 February.
This interchange occurs:*

SENATOR HICKENLOOPER. Did you find installations of significant military
importance in the bombed areas you visited?
MR. SALISBURY. In some areas they exist. In others, they don't, and this is
hard to generalize about.

The principal military objectives which have been bombed in North
Vietnam, and the ones which I described and I described in great detail in
one of my very earliest dispatches, are the highways and the railroads and
the bridges. These are, for the most part, the basic military objectives
that we go after. In addition to this, we attack oil storage capacity, where
it exists, and as I described earlier we knocked that out. There is practically none left.

We attacked certain areas which are transshipment areas where stuff
may be moved, let's say, from Haiphong by barge and then transshipped
by truck or vice versa. We attack such things as motor depots if they
exist, although they are mostly fairly small scale, and then the only other
things of any great consequence that I know of at any rate that we
attacked are antiaircraft installations.

ATTACK ON MIG AIRFIELDS
SENATOR HICKENLOOPER. Did you find that we attacked any major airfields
where the Migs are on the ground, or did we let them alone?
MR. SALISBURY. I didn't see—there is one field as you perhaps know,
where the MIG-21s are based which is outside of Hanoi. I didn't see that
but I think you know it has not been attacked.
SENATOR HICKENLOOPER. Did you find out in your investigation why our
pilots are not allowed to attack that airfield, leaving the Migs sitting there
on the ground to come out and attack us?
MR. SALISBURY. I have read in the Times a good deal about that. I believe
there are specific orders against that.
SENATOR HICKENLOOPER. I understand there are specific orders against
that. My queston was, did you find out why?
MR. SALISBURY. Nobody over there knew why. [Laughter.]
SENATOR HICKENLOOPER. I think they share our wonder here, also.
[Laughter]
MR. SALISBURY. It could be.[53]

1965   24 December—President Johnson announces one week pause in
bombing of North Vietnam.

1965 31 December		
	TOTAL	NET CHANGE
U.S. military personnel assigned in Vietnam	184,300	+161,000
U.S. casualties	YEAR	TO DATE (cumulative)
Killed in action	1,369	1,636
Wounded in action	6,114	7,645
Source: DOD/OASD		

1966

1966   12 March—South Vietnamese Buddhists begin what will be a month-long series of countrywide protests against the SVN military government.

In March Private First Class Carl D. Rogers of the U.S. Army sends a tape-recorded message to the congregation of his New York City church.

Greetings again to all of you at Central Presbyterian. I'm talking tonight against the sounds of a jazz combo next door in the EM Club and I don't know how much of this you're going to pick up and I'm sure you are going to hear a good portion of it and the hollering and screaming that always goes along with it. But we'll do our best to talk above it and let you know a few more thoughts and ideas from our vantage point here in Cam-Ranh Bay. . . .

There are a couple of important things . . . with regard to Oakland. This is the last point where our servicemen touch U.S. soil, because from here they go to the airport and off to Saigon to begin in-country processing. And, consequently, I felt that the men there should have some thoughts to express about what was in store for them in the next year— what their feelings were about leaving their wives and their girlfriends and their home-life here in the States, and going to a foreign country to fight a war. So I asked quite a few. In fact, I asked over a hundred according to my notes . . . and found a couple of surprising things. . . .

Sometimes you'd just be sitting around waiting for formation call and you could get a conversation going with a young guy, and then ask the question, "What do you feel about Vietnam?" And the reaction was the same over and over again: "Well, what do you think I feel? I don't want to go, and **** it—man! I've got a good thing going back in the States. I'm living off base and my wife's with me and we were having a good time and I just bought a new car. . . ." All of these personal concerns are expressed, most of which, I must admit, dealt with their sex life. . . . And, at no point, at no point during the four days that I looked and listened and talked with these fellows did I hear anyone talking about anything relevant to the concerns, the complexities of the whole war situation. . . .

I asked them about how they felt about coming and two of them said, "Well, I really look forward to getting over there so that I can say that I've been and served my time and get the experience for some of the training that we've had," and you could see that he was really, really in his shining hour because of the great publicity the Green Berets were receiving. They kind of walk with a special gait, with their nose in the air because of the feeling that has been generated because of the song and Barry Sadler. So I asked one if he had even read the *Green Berets* and he said, "No, no, I haven't read it," but he certainly heard the record. . . .

After arriving in Vietnam, Private Rogers and his fellow GIs listen to a tape-recorded briefing by their commanding general.

So General Westmoreland tells [us] that the mission is two-fold, and we must fight and beat the Communist aggressor. And then he goes on to say that the second point we must make is to show the Vietnamese people what it is to be a free man. And this got a chuckle from several fellows, because there we sat with our green uniforms on and the hot sun that probably was 110 degrees. For me this had special significance, because I was sitting there in a uniform I detest, in a country that is involved in a war that I don't support, and yet I'm supposed to show these people what it is to be a free man. This is very hard to do. . . .

After getting all of our cards and completing all of the papers for orientation, we were finally packed aboard a C130 aircraft from Tan Son Nhut air base. . . . We headed up here for Cam-Ranh Bay, making six stops along the way at Plei-Ku, Phan-Rang, [Nha] Trang, and a couple of other places. This proved to be one of the most informative six hours that I have ever spent while in this country, because I found an ABC News reporter who was bringing along his TV cameras and a couple of his crew. We were able to get seats together on the plane and spent a great deal of time talking about all of the problems and all of the questions that I wanted to raise. . . .

I was a little surprised to learn that these correspondents are not given additional pay for their efforts here. He said that he would make the same money if he was in Paris covering a fashion show.

And then we talked a little bit about some of the frustrations, because it was quite apparent that he was frustrated with much of what he was facing here. He's been in Vietnam covering the war for five years. He's not an American citizen, and has, at least, that much detachment. But what bothered him most was the inconsistency of Air Marshall Ky at his political conferences and also "The Five O'Clock Follies" as they're known in Saigon, the daily military briefings where much information is given in little pieces.

So, then, of course, I asked about the press and the news media in general, and wanted to find out if he felt that the American reader and viewer of television, listener to the radio, was misinformed or ill informed, as I think *Time* magazine said at one point. And, he said, no, not necessarily, but you must remember that we have a story to write and we have to add originality of a sort, so that our story appears a little bit different from that given by the other networks or the other papers. He said for this reason there is a great deal of leeway, and the truth really is determined so much by the vantage point from which you are writing, as it was in his case. And I think this is so. I found one article that expresses this matter fairly well, by George Carver, Jr. . . . He says that "the current struggle in South Vietnam is an historically rooted phenomenon of infinite complexity, particularly since it involves an externally directed Communist drive for power . . . with a genuine indigenous social revolution. In analyzing such a phenomenon, truth is often a function of one's angle of vision, and myth is not always easy to distinguish from reality." And I can see this. I can see it each day as I read the Army's paper and as I read *Time,* and *Life,* and *Newsweek,* and all of the other publications that we try to get a hold of here. And in talking to fellows I can see how this is so. It is a matter of the angle of your vision.[54]

The "Five O'Clock Follies," as well as the role of the media in general, are described by reporter Elaine Shepard in her book The Doom Pussy.

JUSPAO, Joint United States Public Affairs Office, occupies a heavily reinforced building on the corner of Nguyen Hue and Le Loi, a couple blocks from the Caravelle Hotel. At four-thirty daily, the press attends a Vietnamese briefing. At five o'clock, the Saigon press corps ambles over to JUSPAO, show their press passes to the sergeant on duty, and then navigates the labyrinth of corridors to the briefing auditorium.

Portly and affable Barry Zorthian, whom *Time* calls "the information czar" in Vietnam, is minister-counselor at the US Embassy. Harold Kaplan, former cultural attaché at the US Embassy in Paris, is the witty, knowledgeable spokesman for JUSPAO. He usually leads off the briefing with political information regarding Ambassador Henry Cabot Lodge, Prime Minister Ky, or visiting US Congressmen—who at times descend on the area in near battalion strength. Then officer spokesmen for the military, using brightly lighted and annotated maps, discuss the handouts that have been presented to the newsmen at the door, and elaborate on action in the field. The briefing more often than not disintegrates into a shouting match, especially when the military spokeman refuses to discuss a classified operation. . . .

Shortly before I departed for Vietnam a Washington official told me, "The communists consider this a war for the minds of men. The military is actually secondary. It is a new kind of war for this day and age; different from Korea and World War II—different from anything in our current recollection or thinking. It is ten percent military, ninety percent psychological. We can win or lose through mass communications. This is a war of words as well as bullets.". . .

In March, 1966, there were 360 accredited newsmen in Vietnam, 141 of them US citizens, 67 Vietnamese, 24 British, and 26 Japanese. The rest are Koreans, Filipinos, New Zealanders, and transient correspondents from Canada and other countries. . . .

The granite facts are not easy to come by in Vietnam. The effort to collect them requires plenty of digging. The majority of newsmen, impartial, disciplined, conscientious, careen around the country like highly trained bird dogs uncertain of the scent. The oddballs trying to make a name for themselves in headlines report events out of proportion and perspective. Sometimes the trouble lies back at the foreign desk. One London newspaperman received a cable from his editor requesting an exposé on racial discrimination in the US Armed Forces. Another wrote a solid piece which stated in essence that the United States not only had good cause to be in Vietnam but even had a fair chance of winning. His editors fired back a rocket accusing him of failing to be objective, and informed him that they had altered his copy.

Some newsmen in Saigon complain about the public-information setup. Others consider it the best possible under the circumstances. The bitterest brouhaha to date erupted between Arthur Sylvester, who has the unenviable position of Assistant Secretary of Defense for Public Affairs, and a reporter employed by CBS.

The reporter had produced a TV sequence putting US Marines in a bad light. The reaction was immediate. The reporter then, in print, claimed that Washington officials had warned his network that if they didn't get him out of Vietnam "he's liable to end up with a bullet in his back." The reporter also quoted Sylvester as saying: "Newsmen should be handmaidens of the government."

Sylvester replied in print that perhaps he shouldn't be surprised at "such self-created quotations" coming from a reporter who had so distorted US Marine Corps activity that "he has won the undying contempt of the Marines." And "incidentally," Sylvester added, "that reporter is the only man I ever heard refer to another man, especially a newsman, as a 'handmaiden.' "

In the States I have queried CBS officials. None recalled any Washington threat that reporters might be "shot in the back."

If the story was false it involves the most foolish form of self-advertising. If it is true—even in jest—that a newsman's life was threatened, his colleagues should unite behind him because freedom of the press would be at stake. I would scramble to be the first in line.

If the American public is ill-informed, scores of newsmen are doing their best to correct it and feel their responsibility fully. Though his reports are often at odds with his paper's editorial stand, *The New York Times* columnist Cyrus L. Sulzberger has consistently called for US firmness in Vietnam. He wrote: "It takes two sides to negotiate, and what the other side makes plain is that all it wants is total victory. What the Viet Cong and Hanoi want is peace at no price, and what Peking wants is no peace whatsoever."[55]

In April 1966, while various world governments and organizations, notably the United Nations, attempt to get negotiations started between the warring sides, a North Vietnamese general, Nguyen Van Vinh, addresses a COSVN (Communist Organization of South Vietnam) congress about the Party's position on fighting and negotiating.

Fighting and Negotiating

The resolution of the Party's 11th conference clearly stated that in the process of achieving success a situation where fighting and negotiations are conducted simultaneously may arise. At present, the situation is not yet ripe for negotiations. Fighting while negotiating is aimed at opening another front with a view to making the puppet army more disintegrated, stimulating and developing the enemy's internal contradictions and thereby making him more isolated in order to deprive him of the propaganda weapons, isolate him further, and make a number of people who misunderstand the Americans clearly see their nature.

In a war between a powerful country which waged aggression and a weak country, as long as we have not yet acquired adequate strength, a situation where fighting and negotiations are conducted simultaneously does not exist. Fighting continues until the emergence of a situation where both sides are fighting indecisively. Then a situation where fighting and negotiations are conducted simultaneously may emerge. In fighting while negotiating, the side which fights more strongly will compel the adversary to accept its conditions. Considering the comparative balance of forces, the war proceeds through the following stages:

    —The fighting stage.
    —The stage of fighting while negotiating.
    —Negotiations and signing of agreements.

Whether or not the war will resume after the conclusion of agreements depends upon the comparative balance of forces. If we are capable of dominating the adversary, the war will not break out again. . . .

    —Our policy: to continue fighting until a certain time when we can fight and negotiate at the same time.

This is also a fighting method: repulsing the enemy step by step, and achieving decisive success.

The Party Central Committee entrusts the Politburo with the task of deciding on the time for negotiations.[56]

At the same time, Captain Richard Sexton is assisting in the evaluation of new weapons systems on the AC-47 gunship, first known by the American troops as "Puff, the Magic Dragon," then as "Spooky."

9 April. Today . . . gunnery practice. Will also experiment with tipping one gun down. I bet they forget to reset the gun sight.

Ashau [a Special Forces camp] was a typical indefensible fort in a valley. It worked in the 1800's against Indians but not against modern weapons. US wanted to pull out or reinforce sufficiently to hold. Marines offered to send enough men to seal off valley but at the time President Thieu was in Saigon being fired and no one would make a decision. When Ky mentioned forming constitutional convention he included religious, political, and business groups but no representatives of the peasants, who are the most important. . . .

10 April. Easter Sunday—day off—rested and wrote letters. Early French colonists did a lot of work and gained respect (if not love). Latecomers did nothing, but expected to inherit respect that they never earned. US Armed Forces use war as an excuse for ignorance and mismanagement (so do South Vietnamese). SVN has not started to use available manpower for either civilian or military efforts. I don't mind killing VC; they are a sickness that needs to be cut out. American demonstrators make me sick. They don't need to collect blood for the VC. The VC can get all they need by washing it off their hands.

11 April. Buddhists are more interested in seizing power than in fighting VC. This is the typical parochialism that allowed VC to get started and continue to exist. Buddhists want a theocracy and merchants want corruption as usual. VC cannot win the war now and they know it. They can only hold on and hope the South Vietnamese will tear themselves apart and we either pull out or are forced out.[57]

Three days later a U.S. Air Force major, Theodore J. Shorack, Jr., who is flying A-1s (World War II propeller-driven aircraft), writes the following letter, which was obviously not designed for publication.

14 April 1966
Just got back from Plei-Ku this afternoon. Spent the bulk of two days over there. Flew a mission with them this morning to see how they are conducting their operation in Laos—along the Ho Chi Minh Trail.

Our flying has been cut back quite a bit of late. I'm enclosing a newspaper clipping that is a feeble attempt on the part of D.O.D. to explain it away—note the contradictions. Probably the most basic fact is that McNamara screwed up by his big economy efforts and didn't allow the services to buy enough—soon enough. Just as he screwed up on bringing back the USAF squadrons from overseas and replacing their commitment with units on 4½ month rotation. He is secretly "smuggling" F-100 squadrons back to Japan PCS [Permanent Change of Station] to replace the rotational commitment after making a big hullabaloo to the press about 1½ years ago about saving so much money by bringing these units home to save gold and exchange outflow. Now he's sending squadrons to Southeast Asia, against the war commitment. (The war is fought by PCS units now instead of rotational units.) Then after they are over here quietly transferring them to Japan. There is a F-100 outfit at Missowa that got there via that route. He can't own up to making any sort of mistake.

To his assertion that there is not an ordnance shortage over here: we always have some sort of bombs to hang on the airplanes, so he is right in that sense. However, we frequently do not have the *right kind* of bombs—specifically, sufficient time-delay bombs for the Ho Chi Minh Trail. The shortage is not caused by strikes, riots, and Vietnamese stevedores. It's because Black Bob saved so much money by delaying orders for these goodies. He has made so damn many mistakes for a "whiz kid" that it's pathetic. I hope someday the truth can come out and reveal what a sorry bunch of super-brains we have running our establishment. Starting with LBJ.[58]

That same day Captain Sexton also comments.

14 April.
A scramble at 2235 for XS03476 [map coordinates] but diverted to Saigon. TACC [Tactical Air Control Center] was mad because Corbin used initiative to return to his [original] target. It doesn't matter if we lose the war as long as the paperwork is filled out and some boob still keeps his little empire. . . .

Notes: We fight and kill but try not to hurt anyone needlessly. Of course, innocent people always suffer. Every time we try to do something humane (like tear gas), we are criticized. Some think it is OK to roast VC with napalm or blow him up with a bomb or shoot him between the eyes. The hypocrisy of some moralists is almost beyond belief. Later they will accept it and shrug shoulders. They are not really interested. They just needed a catharsis at the time. VC are like criminals in New York or Al Capone in Chicago or Mafia—but not as well organized.[59]

On 7 May Commander Jeremiah Denton, U.S. Navy, a captured pilot, appears on Hanoi television. He is interviewed by a Japanese correspon-

dent who is a member of the Japanese Communist Party. During the interview, according to Reuters Press, he "would occasionally close his eyes when asked to answer a question." Imprisoned for six years, Commander Denton will be later decorated for having blinked out in code the word "torture" during the interview. On 20 May the following statement is released from Hanoi.

Hanoi in English to American Servicemen in South Vietnam
1300 GMT, 20 May 1966

(Text) Mass organizations and political parties in Vietnam and the world over have extended their warmest greetings to President Ho Chi Minh on the occasion of his 76th birthday. The Vietnamese leader on many occasions has sincerely thanked the American people for their struggle to compel the U.S. Government to end this war of aggression against Vietnam. By so doing, he pointed out, they also help prevent the lives of many young Americans from being uselessly sacrificed in an unjust war against Vietnam thousands of miles away from America.

At President Ho Chi Minh's teaching, the Vietnamese people and army never ill-treated their captured enemy. The humanitarian policy of the Vietnamese leader has been expressed by captured U.S. pilots in the following declarations:

Jeremiah Denton, commander, U.S. Navy, from Aircraft Carrier USS Independence, piloting an A-D-6 plane captured in Thanh Hoa Province on 18 July 1965, declared: The local people treated me most humanely although I was a criminal. I have received adequate food and medical care for injuries and sickness. This good treatment derived from the kindness of heart of the Vietnamese Government and people in spite of my vicious crimes against them.

Robinson Risner, lieutenant colonel, U.S. Air Force, from Air Wing No. 18, stationed in Thailand, piloting an F-105-D, captured in Thanh Hoa Province on 16 September 1965 said: Even though U.S. forces have caused considerable destruction to DRV property creating a natural animosity, this really has not caused the Vietnamese citizens to treat the captured pilots unfairly, but in most cases have been very considerate. Since my confinement here, I have been treated humanely with all my physical needs having been met. And on this occasion I wish to thank the government and the people of the DRV for this consideration.[60]

This official summary of Colonel Risner's debriefing after his release shows what led to the previous public statement.

Col. Robinson Risner (isolation) 31 Oct.—2 Dec. went without food for several days at a time—went without water for 2–3 days sometimes. (at same time no food or/and water?) Most of the time ½ loaf bread and 1 cup water twice a day. Stocks with both legs. They took all but one blanket and 1 suit clothing. Sitting & laying [sic] on a cement slab. General harrassment. "Living in his own filth" much of the time.

Night of 2 Dec. thick pads over eyes bound so that eyeballs were pushed back into sockets. They bound his arms—2 guards per arm, standing on it, pulling on the rope until it squeezed the blood out of the surface of the skin. After the arms were bound up close to the elbow, they went to work on both of them, binding them close to the shoulder, pulling them almost out of the socket. Dislocate right shoulder, left almost. Then marched around for an hour or two, through ditches, up & down stairs, letting him fall. Back to the torture room where same binding treatment was given to legs, then generally "roughed up."

Left bound, arms, legs and eyes with a rope running from his feet to around his neck. At times they had to tie him to a post to "keep me from throwing myself forward on my head." Left this way until willing to talk . . . then treatment was continued the rest of the night because they seemed to want to leave an impression. They were perturbed. When they finally got around to talking to him (around daylight) he made a statement, something to the effect that he was apologizing to the Vietnamese people on the morals and illegal war, and some other items he can't remember. He thinks the statement was played May Day '66. This was taped (recorded) and later they had him write it.[61]

That same month poet Robert Bly edits and writes the introduction for A Poetry Reading Against the Vietnam War.

Giving to Johnson What Is Johnson's

One repulsive novelty of this war is the daily body-count. We count up the small-boned bodies like quail on a gun shoot. The military people would feel better if the bodies were even smaller. If the bodies were smaller, maybe we could get the whole year's kill in front of us on a desk.

I saw a photograph in the *Minneapolis Tribune* recently of a search and kill mission returning to base with the body of the first Viet Cong soldier draped over the jeep hood like a deer. A soldier I know, recently returned, spoke of killing the Viet Cong as though they were big game: he described hitting them in the chest with hollow-nose bullets. He mentioned that the Geneva Convention had outlawed hollow-nose bullets, but his company and regiment used them anyway. It turns out that a hollow-nose bullet is defined as a bullet that has a tiny tunnel running from the tip inward, so that when the bullet hits the body, it suddenly opens up and makes a jagged and massive wound. What the U.S. arms manufacturers do, then, the soldier remarked, is put a small metal or plastic cap on the tip of the bullet so that technically there is no tunnel. As soon as the bullet hits a body, however, the small cap flies off and the

bullet spreads as expected. The soldier defended the practice by remark-
ing that "it was a dirty war." The makers of the Geneva Conventions
had, of course, guessed that wars become dirty; that is why they set up
the convention in the first place. I understand we have also developed an
off-center bullet that turns over as it goes through the air—another way
of getting around the Convention.

These tawdry, pitful tricks are a disgrace to the United States of forty
years ago, let alone the United States of Lincoln. Moreover, *The New
York Times* and *The New York Herald-Tribune* have carried many reports of United States troops torturing Vietnamese prisoners.

During the Algerian war, newspapermen reported torture being carried
out on Algerians by Frenchmen. But the French had watched the Germans torturing French resistance people during the second world war and
their contempt for the German torturers was deep. Most Frenchmen
could not believe the reports of torture were true. Yet they were true.
The reason the French tortured is that they had a bad conscience about
being in Algeria, just as the Germans had a bad conscience about being
in Paris during the War. It was obvious to the French soldiers that they
were fighting the Algerian people as a whole, despite all the official lies
to the contrary.

Americans are in the same situation in Vietnam. They are not libera-
tors. On the contrary, they find the entire people are their enemies. I
have never talked to a soldier back from Vietnam who did not have this
knowledge clearly visible in the back of his frightened eyes. When a
soldier's conscience begins to hurt him, he becomes desperate.

"Two Viet Cong prisoners were interrogated on an airplane flying toward Saigon. The first refused to answer questions and was thrown out of
the airplane at 3,000 feet. The second immediately answered all the questions. But he, too, was thrown out." (Beverly Deepe, *New York Herald-
Tribune,* April 25, 1965)

"So far everything you wrote in your bulletin is true about Vietnam. . . . A week ago our platoon leader brought in three prisoners—I
was part of the group that brought them in. They set up a questioning
station and someone from Intelligence was doing the questioning. This
was the first time I saw anything like this and found we use some dirty
methods too. This guy from intelligence had all three lined up. One was a
woman. He stripped her down to the waist and stripped the two men all
the way. He had a little gadget I thought was a walkie-talkie or something. He stuck one end of this wire to the lady's chest and it was some
kind of electric shock because she got a real bad burn. From what she was
screaming, my buddy and I could figure out she didn't know anything.
Then they took this same wire and tried it on the lady's husband and
brother, but on their lower parts. One of the guys from another platoon
said he saw this happen before a few times and once the guy was killed by
it. . . . Ever since that day I've been sick to my stomach and haven't been
out on patrol or anything. My sergeant tells me I'm suffering from battle

fatigue. . . ." (Letter from American solidier published in Chicago "Women for Peace" Bulletin)

Anyone who knows France knows how much harm the futile sadisms of the Algerian war did to the French in Africa and at home. It increased their self-destruction and self-disgust. A really serious evil of the war, rarely discussed, is the harm it will do the Americans inwardly.[62]

In Bly's book is the following prose poem by Lawrence Ferlinghetti.

Where Is Vietnam?

Meanwhile back at the Ranch the then President also known as Colonel Cornpone got out a blank Army draft and began to fill in the spaces with men and Colonel Cornpone got down to the bottom of the order where there is a space to indicate just where the troops are to be sent and Colonel Cornpone got a faraway look in his eye and reached out and started spinning a globe of the world and his eye wandered over the spinning surface of the world and after a long time he said I See No Relief so they brought him a relief map of the world and he looked at it a long time and said Thank You Gentlemen I see it all very clearly now yes indeed everything stands out very clearly now and I can see the oceans themselves rolling back and Western Civilization still marching Westward around the world and the New Frontier now truly knows no boundaries and those there Vietnamese don't stand a Chinaman's chance in Hell but there's all these Chinamen who think they do and also think they can actually reverse the Westward march of civilization and actually reverse the natural Westward spin of our globe but Gentlemen these are not War Games this is not Space Angels this is the real thing Gentlemen and I know right exactly where this here Vietnam is Gentlemen and I want to make doubly sure that all our own people know right exactly where this here Vietnam is Gentlemen in case any of you should happen to get cornered by some eggheads or someone And just then Ladybird came running and Colonel Cornpone stepped into the cloakroom and whispered to her The world really does rotate Westward don't it? and she being smarter than he as is usually the case whispered back that this here Vietnam was not a place but a state of mind and Colonel Cornpone got that old faraway look again and stepped back onto the front porch and sat there rocking for a long time and then said Gentlemen I am a family man and this is for real and I am hereby ordering the complete and final liberation of Vietmind I mean Vietnam for the roots of the trouble are found wherever the landless and oppressed the poor and despised stand before the gates of opportunity and are not allowed across the Frontier into the Great Society which seems to lie out before me like a land of dreams and so Gentlemen here we go fasten your seatbelts we are powerful and free and united there ain't much we can't do and so Gentlemen let me point out to you exactly where it is we all are going on this here globe because Gentlemen even though I am reputed never to have been out of the United States I do know right where we are going on the brink of Vietmind I mean Vietnam and even though we don't want to stop the world spinning in the right direction even for an instant I do want to slow it down just long enough for me to put my finger for you right on this here sore spot which is Vietmine I mean Vietnam and Colonel Cornpone put out his hand to slow down the world just a bit but this world would not be slowed down a bit this world would not stop spinning at all and Texas and Vietnam spun on together faster and faster slipping away under Colonel Cornpone's hand because the surface of this world had suddenly become very very slippery with a strange kind of red liquid that ran on it across all the obscene boundaries and this world went on spinning faster and faster in the same so predestined direction and kept on spinning and spinning and spinning![63]

Despite all American attempts to destroy it, North Vietnam's Thanh Hoa bridge remains standing. Although repeatedly damaged, it still carries traffic after nightly repairs. As is to happen often during the remainder of the war, the U.S. military attempts something ingenious.

Project "Carolina Moon"—(May 66)

One innovative effort [had taken] shape in September 1965. At that time personnel at the Armament Development Laboratory at Eglin AFB, Florida, came up with the concept of mass-focusing the energy of certain high explosive weapons. The applicability of this concept to new weapon designs was proved in many exhaustive experimental tests in the Eglin complex. Lieutenant General Moore, Commander of the 2nd Air Division in Saigon, was informed of the new mass-focus weapon and its potential against bridges, particularly against the Thanh Hoa Bridge. The new weapon, however, was rather large and would have to be delivered by a cargo type aircraft. General Moore felt that attrition would be high if cargo aircraft were used directly against the Thanh Hoa Bridge. He responded by suggesting that methods of upriver delivery be studied.

As the development of the weapon progressed, it became evident that delivery by C-130 aircraft was feasible and the Tactical Air Warfare Center (TAWC) was directed to form and train an appropriate task force. The weapon, in its final configuration, would weigh 5,000 pounds and resemble a large pancake about 8 feet in diameter and 2½ feet thick. The design was such that the weapon was detonated initially around its periphery with the resultant force of the explosion focused along the axis of the weapon in both directions. The weapon was to be floated down the Song Ma River where it would pass under the Dragon's Jaw, and detonate when sensors in the bomb detected the metal of the bridge structure.

It sounded like a bold plan—and it was. Specialists in many fields were called upon to solve problems associated with extraction techniques, chute deployment, drop accuracy, and river transit of weapon affected by such things as depth and current of the river, position of the tide, and wind draft on its exposed surfaces. This was a formidable task, but acceptable solutions were found and the plan proceeded.

Two C-130 and supporting personnel were sent to Eglin AFB for intensive training and preparation for the upcoming mission. The first crew was led by Major Richard T. Remers; the second by Major Thomas F. Case. Quite simply, the plan was to drop five weapons one to two miles up river from the bridge under the cover of darkness. Entry and exit over the North Vietnamese terrain would be at less than 500 feet to avoid radar detection. The route selected was about 43 miles long, which meant the aircraft would be over enemy territory for at least 17 minutes.

To assist in masking the approach of the C-130, a flight of two F-4 fighter aircraft was scheduled to make a diversionary attack, using flares and bombs, on the highway 10 miles south of Thanh Hoa shortly before the C-130 was to drop its ordnance. In addition, an EB-66 was tasked to carry out jamming in the area during the attack period. The plan was firm, the crews were selected, and training began at an accelerated pace. Training sites in the Eglin area, which had radar returns similar to those anticipated during the 17-minute flight over North Vietnam, were selected.

Their training completed, the two C-130 crews and aircraft deployed to Danang AB on 15 May 1966. Along with the necessary maintenance and munitions specialists, ten mass-focus weapons were provided, allowing for a second mission should the first one fail to accomplish the desired results. The last of the contingent arrived at Danang on 22 May 1966 and began their final preparation for this unique assault on the Dragon's Jaw.

Last minute changes made on the route to the target included intelligence up-dates on automatic weapons and anti-aircraft artillery positions, as well as a review of checklist and rescue procedures. In this regard, an interesting discussion developed between the two crews. Major Remers felt that the aircraft was tough enough to survive moderate anti-aircraft artillery hits, and gain enough altitude should bail-out be necessary. Major Case agreed that the aircraft could take hits, but the low-level flight would preclude a controlled bail-out situation. With these conflicting philosophies, and the fact that either parachutes or flak vests could be worn—but, not both—Major Remers decided that his crew would wear parachutes and stack their flak vests on the floor of the aircraft; Major Case decided that his crew would wear only flak vests and store the parachutes!

The first strike was scheduled for the night of 30 May, but on 27 May, intelligence detected a five-fold increase in AW sites and five new AAA sites. However, a re-evaluation of the plan showed it to be secure and the mission was "on."

Major Remers and his crew took off from Danang at 25 minutes past midnight, turned out over the water at 100 feet altitude and headed north under radio silence. Within an hour, he had guided his bird to the coast-in point in North Vietnam. Maintaining an altitude of 100 feet above the water to avoid enemy radar detection, the big four-engine Hercules crossed the coast of North Vietnam and headed for the bomb release point. Two release points had been selected in the river; one was two miles and the alternate, one mile from the bridge; it was left to Major Remers and his two navigators, Captain Norman G. Clanton and First Lieutenant William "Rocky" Edmondson, to detect the actual drop point.

As they approached the first drop zone, Major Remers climbed the aircraft to 400 feet and slowed to 150 MPH. Having encountered no enemy fire, he elected to press on to the closer drop zone. Shortly after passing the first release point, heavy AW and AAA fire was encountered, but it was too late to turn back. Fortunately, the ground fire, although intense, was inaccurate and missed the C-130 by several hundred feet. The five weapons were dropped successfully in the area closest to the bridge. Immediately after the drop, Major Remers banked his "Herky-bird" sharply to the right, dove back to 100 feet above the ground and made for the safety of the Gulf of Tonkin. The operation has gone flawlessly! The diversionary attack south of Thanh Hoa went as planned and, although it drew an unfriendly reception, both F-4's returned to Thailand unscathed.

Mission effectiveness could not be assessed until the photo reconnais-sance birds made their run at dawn. Needless to say, the crew felt the mission was personally successful—they had survived.

Pent-up emotions of the crew gave way to excited activity by all in-volved in the project as they waited for the recce report. Unfortunately, the pictures revealed no noticeable damage to the Thanh Hoa Bridge nor were any of the bombs seen along the edge of the river. Intelligence could find no trace of the bombs and a second mission was laid on for the next night, 31 May. The plan for Major Case's crew was basically the same with the exception of a minor time change and slight modification to the route of flight.

A change in crew was made at the last minute when Major Case asked "Rocky" Edmondson, the navigator from the previous night's mission, to go along on this one because of his experience from the night before. Ten minutes after its planned 1:00 AM takeoff, the C-130 departed Danang, turned out over water, and headed north. The aircraft and crew were never seen or heard from again.

The flight of F-4s was making its diversionary attack at the designated time when one of the F-4 crews saw anti-aircraft fire and a large ground flash in the vicinity of the Thanh Hoa Bridge approximately two minutes prior to the scheduled C-130 drop time. Photo reconnaissance the next morning revealed no wreckage and an intensive search and rescue mission was flown over the Gulf of Tonkin with no results. Moreover, one of the two F-4 aircraft was shot down that evening and its crew was never recovered.[64]

The prevailing attitudes of many American pilots, as well as the military's public relations tactics, are shown in this popular satire of a news interview.

"What the Captain Means"

CORRESPONDENT: What do you think of the F-4?

CAPTAIN: It's so fuckin' maneuverable you can fly up your own ass with it.

IO [Air Force Information Officer—who is present in order to ensure that only approved statements are released]: What the captain means is that he has found the F4C Phantom highly maneuverable at all altitudes and he considers it an excellent aircraft for all missions assigned.

CORR.: I suppose, captain, that you've flown a certain number of missions over North Vietnam. What did you think of the SAMs used by the North Vietnamese?

CAPT.: Why those bastards couldn't hit a bull in the ass with a bass fiddle. We fake the shit out of them. There's no sweat.

IO: What the captain means is that the Surface-to-Air Missiles around Hanoi pose a serious problem to our air operations and that the pilots have a healthy respect for them.

CORR.: I suppose, captain, that you've flown missions to the South. What kind of ordnance do you use, and what kind of targets do you hit?

CAPT.: Well, I'll tell you, mostly we aim at kicking the shit out of Vietnamese villages, and my favorite ordance is napalm. Man, that stuff just sucks the air out of their friggin' lungs and makes a sonovabitchin' fire.

IO: What the captain means is that air strikes in South Vietnam are often against Vietcong structures and all operations are always under the positive control of Forward Air Controllers, or FACs. The ordnance employed is conventional 500 and 750 pound bombs and 20 millimeter cannon fire.

CORR.: I suppose you spent an R and R in Hong Kong. What were your impressions of the oriental girls?

CAPT.: Yeah, I went to Hong Kong. As for those oriental broads, well, I don't care which way the runway runs, east or west, north or south—a piece of ass is a piece of ass.

IO: What the captain means is that he found the delicately featured oriental girls fascinating, and he was very impressed with their fine manners and thinks their naiveté is most charming.

CORR.: Tell me, captain, have you flown any missions other than over North and South Vietnam?

CAPT.: You bet your sweet ass I've flown other missions. We get scheduled nearly every day on the trail in Laos where those fuckers over there throw everything at you but the friggin' kitchen sink. Even the goddam kids got slingshots.

IO: What the captain means is that he has occasionally been scheduled to fly missions in the extreme Western DMZ, and he has a healthy respect for the flak in that area.

CORR.: I understand that no one in your Fighter Wing has got a MIG yet. What seems to be the problem?

CAPT.: Why you screwhead, if you knew anything about what you're talking about—the problem is MIGs. If we'd get scheduled by those peckerheads at Seventh for those missions in MIG Valley, you can bet your ass we'd get some of those mothers. Those glory hounds at Ubon get all those missions while we settle for fightin' the friggin' war. Those mothers at Ubon are sitting on their fat asses killing MIGs and we get stuck with bombing the goddamned cabbage patches.

IO: What the captain means is that each element in the Seventh Air Force is responsible for doing their assigned job in the air war. Some units are assigned the job of neutralizing enemy air strength by hunting out MIGs, and other elements are assigned bombing missions and interdiction of enemy supply routes.

CORR.: Of all the targets you've hit in Vietnam, which one was the most satisfying?

CAPT.: Well, shit, it was when we were scheduled for that suspected VC vegetable garden. I dropped napalm in the middle of the fuckin' cabbage and my wingman splashed it real good with six of those 750 pound mothers and spread the fire all the way to the friggin' beets and carrots.

IO: What the captain means is that the great variety of tactical targets available throughout Vietnam make the F4C the perfect aircraft to provide flexible response.

CORR.: What do you consider the most difficult target you've struck in North Vietnam?

CAPT.: The friggin' bridges. I must have dropped 40 tons of bombs on those swayin' bamboo mothers, and I ain't hit one of the bastards yet.

IO: What the captain means is that interdicting bridges along enemy supply routes is very important and a quite difficult target. The best way to accomplish this task is to crater the approaches to the bridge.

CORR.: I noticed in touring the base that you have aluminum matting on the taxiways. Would you care to comment on its effectiveness and usefulness in Vietnam?

CAPT.: You're fuckin' right, I'd like to make a comment. Most of us pilots are well hung, but shit, you don't know what hung is until you get hung up on one of the friggin' bumps on that goddam stuff.

IO: What the captain means is that the aluminum matting is quite satisfactory as a temporary expedient, but requires some finesse in taxiing and braking the aircraft.

CORR.: Did you have an opportunity to meet your wife on leave in Honolulu, and did you enjoy the visit with her?

CAPT.: Yeah, I met my wife in Honolulu, but I forgot to check the calendar, so the whole five days were friggin' well combat-proof—a completely dry run.

io: What the captain means is that it was wonderful to get together with his wife and learn first-hand about the family and how things were at home.

CORR.: Thank you for your time, captain.

CAPT.: Screw you—why don't you bastards print the real story, instead of all that crap?

io: What the captain means is that he enjoyed the opportunity to discuss his tour with you.

CORR.: One final question. Could you reduce your impression of the war into a simple phrase or statement, captain?

CAPT.: You bet your ass I can. It's a fucked up war.

io.: What the captain means is . . . it's a FUCKED UP WAR.[65]

1966   23 June—In Saigon, Buddhist uprisings quelled when riot police and troops seize the Buddhist Institute.

On 29 June Ambassador Lodge cables Secretary Rusk with information for the Polish ICC [International Control Commission] representative, about a positive response from Hanoi to U.S. offers for negotiations, via the Italian ambassador to South Vietnam, Giovanni D'Orlandi. This secret approach is code-named "Operation Marigold."

9. THE POLE BEGAN BY SAYING THAT HANOI HAS BEEN DEEPLY DISAPPOINTED BY THE PROPOSALS MADE BY RONNING WHICH, THEY ARE SURE, HAD EMANATED ORIGINALLY FROM THE UNITED STATES AND NOT FROM THE CANADIANS. RONNING HAD PROPOSED THAT THE U.S. STOP THE BOMBING IF NORTH VIET-NAM STOPPED THE INFILTRATION, AND HAD TALKED ABOUT THE EXCHANGE OF PRISONERS' PARCELS AND LETTERS. THIS HAD BITTERLY DISAPPOINTED NORTH VIETNAM. THE FIRST POINT, THEY HAD SAID, WOULD BE UNCONDITIONAL SURRENDER, AND THEY COULD NOT ACCEPT IT, BUT THEY ARE OPEN TO A "POLITICAL COMPROMISE" SETTLING ONCE AND FOR ALL THE ENTIRE VIET-NAM QUESTION.

10. WHEN D'ORLANDI SAID THAT HE WAS SKEPTICAL, THE POLE SAID THAT HANOI WAS PREPARED TO GO "QUITE A LONG WAY." "IT IS USELESS FOR ME TO ADD," SAID THE POLE, "THAT SHOULD THERE NOT BE ANY KIND OF A PRELIMINARY AGREEMENT, HANOI WILL DENY FLATLY EVER HAVING MADE ANY OFFER." ACCORDING TO THE POLE, THE NORTH VIETNAMESE ARE "TIGHTLY CONTROLLED" BY THE CHINESE COMMUNISTS. THE PRELIMINARY TALKS, THEREFORE, SHOULD BE BETWEEN MOSCOW AND WASHINGTON. WHEN AND IF PROPOSALS SHOULD EMERGE WHICH COULD BE CONSIDERED AS A BASIS FOR NEGOTIATIONS, HANOI WOULD AT THAT TIME AND UNDER THOSE CIRCUMSTANCES GET INTO IT. THE POLE SAID THAT HANOI WAS AFRAID OF THE CHINESE COMMUNISTS WHO HAVE AN INTEREST IN DRAGGING ON THE WAR FOR

MANY YEARS. D'ORLANDI ADDED THAT THE POLE WAS EVIDENTLY "PROUD OF HIMSELF" FOR HAVING BROUGHT THESE PROPOSALS ABOUT.

11. THE PROPOSALS ARE AS FOLLOWS:

A. THEY INSIST THAT THE SO-CALLED NATIONAL LIBERATION FRONT "TAKE PART" IN THE NEGOTIATIONS. THE KEY WORD IS "TAKE PART." ACCORDING TO D'ORLANDI, THERE IS "NO QUESTION OF THEIR BEING THE REPRESENTATIVE; THEY ARE NOT TO HAVE ANY MONOPOLY."

B. THERE MUST BE SUSPENSION OF THE BOMBING.

12. THESE ARE THE TWO PROPOSALS.

13. THEN THERE ARE OTHER POINTS, WHICH D'ORLANDI CALLED "NEGATIVE ONES," WHICH ARE THAT (A) HANOI WILL NOT ASK FOR IMMEDIATE REUNIFI-CATION, EITHER BY ELECTIONS OR OTHERWISE, OF NORTH AND SOUTH VIET-NAM; (B) THEY WILL NOT ASK FOR ESTABLISHMENT OF A "SOCIALIST" SYSTEM IN SOUTH VIET-NAM; (C) THEY WILL NOT ASK SOUTH VIET-NAM TO CHANGE THE RELATIONSHIPS WHICH IT HAS IN THE FIELD OF FOREIGN AFFAIRS; AND (D) THEY WILL NOT ASK FOR NEUTRALIZATION. (E) ALTHOUGH THEY WILL ASK FOR U.S. WITHDRAWAL, THEY ARE READY TO DISCUSS A "REASONABLE CALENDAR." (F) ALTHOUGH "WE WOULD LIKE SOMEONE OTHER THAN KY"—TO QUOTE THE WORDS OF HANOI—THEY DO NOT WANT TO INTERFERE WITH THE SOUTH VIET-NAMESE GOVERNMENT. . . .

18. THE POLE SAID THAT HIS GOVERNMENT WOULD BE WILLING TO ARRANGE FOR D'ORLANDI TO MEET WITH APPROPRIATE POLISH SPOKESMEN ANYWHERE— HONG KONG OR SINGAPORE. IN RESPONSE TO A QUESTION BY D'ORLANDI AS TO WHY THEY HAD COME TO HIM, THE POLE SAID THEY WANTED, "AN ABLE DEBATER TO PUT THE CASE TO PRESIDENT JOHNSON, AND WE FEEL THAT THE ITALIAN GOVERNMENT HAS THE SYMPATHY OF THE UNITED STATES GOVERN-MENT." MOREOVER, THE ITALIANS HAVE THE SAME INTEREST WE HAVE IN AGREEMENT BETWEEN WASHINGTON AND MOSCOW, AND IN SHUTTING OUT PEKING.

19. D'ORLANDI'S IMPRESSION IS THAT THE POLES ARE DESPERATELY SEEKING A WAY OUT ON MOSCOW'S INSTRUCTIONS. THIS, HE SAID, MAY NEED FURTHER EXPLORATION. HE HAD THE DEFINITE IMPRESSION THAT NOW HANOI "WAS AMENABLE TO COMMON SENSE" SAYING "THEY DO NOT WANT ANYTHING THAT WOULD NOT STOP THE WHOLE WAR. THEY WANT A POLITICAL SETTLEMENT, AND ARE PREPARED TO GO A LONG WAY."[66]

1966   29–30 June—Ho Chi Minh announces publicly that negotiations are "out of the question" because of U.S. bombing of oil depots very close to Hanoi.

Two weeks later U.S. Air Force Captain B. C. Wallace is finishing his 100-mission tour of duty.

15 July 1966:
No. 2 on a storage area along the beach in the southern "panhandle" of N. Viet Nam. Lead said six or eight machine guns shot at me on my runs but I didn't see it. Several fires were started. Landed at dawn.

17 July 1966:
Flew on Dave Connett's wing on his final mission. It was a spectacular display for his finale. The night was moonless and we were using napalm and CBU's on a storage area.

The above mission turned out to be my final one also. I completed 102 in all but, because of a ruling halfway through the tour, some of the missions into Laos didn't count after 1 February 1966.

Dave (my 6' 4" roommate) and I embarked on a 48 hr. drunk during which we ate a large portion of the Thai rice crop and most of the Jim Beam ration of the Ubon "O" club. Dave had a dental appointment somewhere during the final hours and the expression on the technician's face as he cleaned his teeth and the smell of our flight suits and bad breath will be one of my "most lingering" of the war.

I boarded a C-130 and headed for Bangkok amid the silence of midday as all of the boys slept. There were no goodbyes. I was the last of the "old heads" as the others had long since returned—those who made it. My last few weeks were served as Chief of Safety for the base and the resultant paperwork and supervision of the Safety staff had slowed down my flying. Actually, I gave it "short shrift" I'm afraid, but this war was beginning to formalize and the "staff pukes" were beginning to descend on us with their inspections and other nonsense as I was "promoted" from squadron flying safety officer to Chief of Safety.

At Bangkok we were delayed three full days with aircraft problems but, since it was a charter flight, our expenses (except liquor) were covered by the airline. I took full advantage, with breakfast in bed and lunch by the pool. By the time we finally left I had regained some of my suave. That is, I ate with utensils and only picked my nose in private.

On the return flight I had two or three of our "red bomb" sleeping pills and took them when we left Yokota, Japan after a short stop at Kadena AB, Okinawa. I awoke just prior to landing and greeted the U.S. through glazed eyes. An airline strike was in progress so Ralph Hoyt and a young airman whose wife was in Victorville, Calif., and I chipped in and rented a car and drove to Apple Valley, Calif. Near Mohave, Calif. in the early dawn we were stopped for speeding. Ralph—at the wheel at the time—was properly embarrassed, upset and indignant. I—feeling great, despite the hour—decided that I would invoke the trooper's patriotism and casually remarked that we were returning from the war. As he continued to write out the ticket he complimented us nicely as patriots and defenders of the nation! Ralph insisted on paying the fine since he was driving but I wasn't having any of it. A couple of days later we laughed about it and I paid off. That's the way it *really* ends, folks. Not with the MGM lion, etc., but on a highway at 2 am—hopefully, with a chuckle. Carolyn and two sleepy kids met me at the door and it was finally over.[67]

Unreported by the American press, the "secret war" in Laos has also been escalating. Staff officers at Headquarters 7/13th Air Force, Udorn Royal Thai air force base, use the following briefing notes to inform newly assigned personnel and visiting U.S. senators and congressmen or their committees' representatives who possess Top Secret security clearances. Top Secret data can be revealed only to others who hold this clearance; consequently, no mention is made in public upon a visitor's return home.

"Wars Two and Three"

WE TURN NOW TO LAOS.

HERE WE HAVE A WAR THAT IS CONFUSING BECAUSE SO LITTLE IS GENERALLY KNOWN ABOUT IT. THIS DEARTH OF KNOWLEDGE REFLECTS THE SELF-EFFACING POLICY OF THE UNITED STATES GOVERNMENT WHICH DOES NOT WANT ANY PUBLICITY GIVEN TO OUR VERY CONSIDERABLE ACTIVITIES THERE. . . .

BARREL ROLL IS THE NICKNAME FOR OUR PROGRAM OF CLOSE AIR SUPPORT AND INTERDICTION STRIKES IN NORTHERN LAOS. IN CONSIDERING LAOS ONE MUST REALIZE THAT IT CONSISTS OF TWO DISPARATE GEOGRAPHIC UNITS, NORTHERN LAOS AND THE PANHANDLE OR SOUTHERN LAOS. . . . TO THE LAO GOVERNMENT NORTHERN LAOS IS OF MUCH GREATER CONCERN THAN THE PANHANDLE. COMMUNIST ACTIVITY IN THE NORTHEN LAOS THREATENS THE MEKONG VALLEY, THE TWO CAPITALS AND THE BULK OF THE POPULATION.

HOWEVER, WE MUST ADMIT THAT THE PRIMARY INTEREST OF THE UNITED STATES IN LAOS TODAY IS TO INTERDICT THE HO CHI MINH TRAIL IN THE PANHANDLE.

THE GOVERNMENT OF LAOS IS WILLING TO GIVE US WHAT AMOUNTS TO A FREE HAND IN EXPLOITING AIR POWER TO INTERDICT THE HO CHI MINH TRAIL IN THE PANHANDLE.

HOWEVER, IF THE CAPITALS OF LAOS ARE EVER THREATENED OR IT APPEARS THAT THE COMMUNISTS MAY TAKE THE MEKONG VALLEY, THERE IS LITTLE DOUBT IN THE MINDS OF THOSE WHO HAVE BEEN WORKING WITH THE LAO GOVERNMENT FOR SOME TIME, THAT THE PRESENT GOVERNMENT WILL SEEK AN ACCOMMODATION WITH THE COMMUNISTS. WITH THE COMMUNISTS IN THE GOVERNMENT, WE WOULD NO DOUBT LOSE THE RIGHT TO USE LAOTIAN AIR SPACE IN STRIKING NORTH VIETNAM AND THE HO CHI MINH TRAIL, AND LOSE OUR RIGHT TO STRIKE IN THE PANHANDLE AS WELL. . . . ONE EFFICIENT FRIENDLY FORCE IN LAOS IS THE CAS[CIA]-SUPPORTED FORCE OF NEARLY 20,000 IRREGULARS IN NORTHERN LAOS. IN THE MAIN THESE ARE ETHNIC TRIBAL

PEOPLE—MEO AND YAO TRIBESMEN. THIS SMALL BUT EVER GROWING AND POTENTIALLY SIGNIFICANT FORCE IS YOUNG AND GROWING. THESE GUERRILLAS HAVE SHOWN THE NECESSARY WILL AND DESIRE (ON A RELATIVE BASIS TO OTHER FRIENDLY LAOS FORCES) BUT THEY NEED TIME FOR MATURING AND DEVELOPING THEIR ORGANIZATON. IT IS CONCEIVABLE THAT PRESSURE BROUGHT TO BEAR ON OUR GUERRILLA FORCES MAY BRING THE PROCESS OF DEVELOPMENT TO A GRINDING HALT BY VIRTUE OF THEIR INABILITY TO COUNTERACT OR OVERCOME THE OVERWHELMING PRESSURE OF THE PATHET LAO/VIET MINH. RECENTLY STEPS HAVE BEEN TAKEN BY 7AF TO BOLSTER OUR OPERATION IN BARREL ROLL. STUDIES HAVE BEEN MADE AND ACTIONS ARE UNDERWAY TO WITHSTAND AND COMBAT THE THRUST OF THE PATHET LAO/VIET MINH.

AS A RESULT OF THESE STUDIES, ON ABOUT 18 APRIL, 7AF AGREED TO LAUNCH A MODEST (32 SORTIES PER DAY) AIR OFFENSIVE AIMED PRIMARILY AT ENEMY LOGISTICS BASES. THE OBJECTIVE WAS TO DESTROY THE MUNITIONS, SUPPLIES AND FOOD WHICH THE ENEMY WOULD NEED TO MOUNT AN OFFENSIVE. SECONDARY OBJECTIVES WERE TO DESTROY TROOPS AND VEHICLES AS THE OPPORTUNITY PRESENTED. THE AIR OFFENSIVE IN BARREL ROLL REMAINS DIFFERENT FROM OTHER AIR OPERATONS IN THE THEATER. THE KEY TO THE OPERATION IS THE FAC [Forward Air Controller] FLYING AN O1B AIRCRAFT WHO TAKES INTO THE AIR A DETAILED KNOWLEDGE OF THE LATEST GROUND SOURCE AND PHOTOGRAPHIC INTELLIGENCE IN HIS OPERATING AREA. THE USAF FAC ON OCCASION WILL CARRY WITH HIM THE LEADER OF A GUERRILLA TEAM FROM THE BARREL ROLL AREA WHO WILL POINT OUT HIDING PLACES FOR TROOPS AND SUPPLIES THAT HE HIMSELF FERRETED OUT OF THE GROUND. AS A RESULT OF THIS LIMITED EFFORT FRIENDLY FORCES HAVE REGAINED A LARGE DEGREE OF THEIR COHESION AND CONFIDENCE AND HAVE GONE OVER TO THE OFFENSIVE IN SEPARATE AMBUSHES AND FIRE FIGHTS. . . . WE CAN KEEP THE ENEMY ON THE DEFENSIVE IF THE PRESSURE OF AIR OPERATIONS IN BARREL ROLL IS CONTINUED. THIS WILL REQUIRE MORE STRIKE SORTIES THAN WE HAVE HAD RECENTLY. . . . IN THIS WAY, IF TIME CAN BE BOUGHT, OUR LAOTIAN GUERRILLA FORCES CAN BE DEVELOPED AND INCREASED TO A POINT WHERE THEY CAN BE CONSIDERED BETTER THAN A FAIR MATCH FOR THEIR OPPONENT. THIS, PERHAPS, IS OUR OBJECTIVE IN BARREL ROLL AS WE SEE IT HERE. . . .

THE OTHER HALF OF THE OPERATIONAL PICTURE IN LAOS IS THE STEEL TIGER AREA IN THE PANHANDLE. WE LINK THIS WITH THE INFILTRATION ROUTES IN SOUTHERN NORTH VIETNAM IN WHAT WE CALL ROUTE PACKAGE ONE.

THE PECULIARITIES OF TERRAIN AND GEOGRAPHY IN THE ROUTE PACKAGE ONE—STEEL TIGER NORTH AREAS PROVIDE A LUCRATIVE AREA FOR INTERDICTION. ILLUSTRATED HERE [See frontispiece map] ARE THE LINES OF COMMUNICATION ALONG WHICH ALL VEHICULAR TRAFFIC MUST FLOW IN ORDER TO SUPPORT FORCES IN SOUTH VIETNAM. NOT ILLUSTRATED ARE THE MANY TRAILS, FOOTPATHS AND STREAMS ALSO UTILIZED AS SECONDARY LOC'S [Lines Of Communication].

TURNING NOW TO MU GIA PASS ITSELF—IN SPITE OF THE MANY MISSIONS—
INCLUDING TWO B-52 MISSIONS—THIS PASS REMAINS OPEN. PRIMARY INTELLI-
GENCE SOURCES ESTIMATE THOUSANDS OF COOLIES MAINTAIN THIS ROUTE IN A
CONSTANT STATE OF GOOD REPAIR. . . .

IN ORDER TO ACHIEVE THE DEGREE OF SUCCESS WE DESIRE, IT IS QUITE APPAR-
ENT THAT IMPROVED METHODS OF ACQUISITION OF FLEETING TARGETS SUCH AS
TRUCKS, BULLDOZERS AND OTHER VEHICULAR TRAFFIC MUST BE DEVELOPED.
AT PRESENT, 7AF IS USING THE O-1 AND A-26A FROM NAKHON PHANOM, A1E'S
FROM UDORN, AND AC-47 AIRCRAFT FROM UBON TO PROVIDE 24 HOUR VISUAL
RECONNAISSANCE ALONG THESE LINES OF COMMUNICATION. FORWARD AIR
CONTROLLERS, THROUGH THEIR INTIMATE KNOWLEDGE WHICH THEY ACQUIRE
OF THE AREA THEY PATROL DAILY, ARE ABLE TO PROVIDE TARGETS FOR STRIKE
AIRCRAFT WHICH ARE FRAGGED TO REPORT TO THEM AT CERTAIN SPECIFIED
PERIODS OF THE DAY. ADDITIONALLY, CAS [Controlled American Source—
code name for CIA] HAS INSERTED INDIGENOUS ROAD WATCH TEAMS WHICH,
BY MEANS OF RADIO COMMUNICATION, ARE ABLE TO RELAY FROM GROUND-
TO-AIR AND GROUND-TO-GROUND INFORMATION PERTAINING TO THE MOVE-
MENT OF TRAFFIC ALONG THESE LOC'S. . . .

AS THIS INTERDICTION SITUATION BECOMES MORE AND MORE APPARENT TO THE
ENEMY, IT IS NOT ONLY CONCEIVABLE BUT MOST PROBABLE THAT HE WILL
REACT BY PROVIDING A LESS PERMISSIVE TARGET FOR OUR RECONNAISSANCE
AND STRIKE AIRCRAFT. WE HAVE SEEN SIGNS OF THAT PROCESS DEVELOPING
RECENTLY. OF COURSE, THIS CAN BE CONSIDERED A SIGN OF SUCCESS IN THAT
HIS REACTION WOULD INDICATE WE ARE HURTING HIM, BUT WE MUST CON-
SIDER THE POSSIBILITY OF INCREASED LOSS RATE.[68]

*As overall U.S. casualties increase, a major dilemma becomes apparent,
one that will plague Americans for years to come. U.S. Navy Lieutenant
George Coker explains it in a later interview.*

South Vietnam . . . two helicopters in formation going on a raiding mission. This is a real story. I'm watching the lead helicopter; suddenly
ground fire catches it, the chopper burst into flames, just totally explodes
right there in front of my eyes and crumbles to the ground. Very quickly
we have a rescue group in there. Not a single body can be recovered.
There is nothing but ash. OK; what is the policy? No body, no KIA, so
seven, eight, ten men go down as MIA. That happened. Are these men
alive? Well maybe in this case they go back and say now look Mrs. So
and So, the plane just burned and I'm sure they're MIA not KIA. And
what happens when she gets more and more stories, and she becomes
confused and she meets other MIA's parents and wives and families.
They are confused and they get all these conflicting stories, so now these
guys come back and say that we saw the plane burn up in front of us as
I'm telling you right now. And she doesn't know what to believe. So
maybe she doesn't believe it. She has hope that her husband or son will

come home too. Well, hope is a wonderful thing; I know because it kept me alive and brought me home. But that's because I was alive. I don't think it is going to bring a dead man home. The point here is that we did develop a policy that you had to have a body. So that brings up the next criticism. Why do we have to have a body? Well, it is very simple. You think that's bad, huh? Well, let me tell you a worse situation, and this is real too. We saw the planes go in, we know that there were no chutes, the men are dead, and lo and behold, they show up. This happened on the returning of some of the POW's. It happened in the war, when we were absolutely sure somebody was dead and they showed up prisoners somehow and somehow made it out. A few of the POW's, until the names were released, were listed as KIA. If you think you have problems with MIA's—you have to go and tell somebody now that their KIA is alive, then you really have problems. In short, people realize you can't trust an aviator's judgement all the time and it's not that we don't want to, and it's not that most of the time they're not right, but in this area we can't afford to be wrong once. That's all they need is one KIA suddenly mysteriously showing up alive and all hell breaks loose. Consequently, they come down with a hard, fast policy: no body, no KIA. Even in a situation where you can have numerous witnesses testify to the explosion of an aircraft and absolutely no survivors beyond any shadow of a doubt. Yes, the policy is, in this case a very ridiculous policy perhaps but none the less, a very reasonable policy from another point of view implied here: no body, no KIA. Consequently these seven, ten, helicopter people go MIA instead of KIA. Real Story.

So now we have the beginning of why we have MIA's, why we don't have more KIA's. Then again this happens more than once.[69]

On 15 October 1966 Secretary McNamara sends the president a significant memorandum. In addition to recommending an "electronic barrier" near the DMZ (demilitarized zone separating North from South Vietnam), he suggests "a vigorous pacification program." The Pentagon Papers asserts that much of the emphasis on pacification results from the strongly expressed views of Special Assistant Robert Komer.

The large-unit operations war, which we know best how to fight and where we have had our successes, is largely irrelevant to pacification as long as we do not lose it. By and large, the people in rural areas believe that the GVN when it comes will not stay but that the VC will; that cooperation with the GVN will be punished by the VC; that the GVN is really indifferent to the people's welfare; that the low-level GVN are tools of the local rich; and that the GVN is ridden with corruption.

Success in pacification depends on the interrelated functions of providing physical security, destroying the VC apparatus, motivating the people to cooperate, and establishing responsive local government. An obviously necessary but not sufficient requirement for success of the RD cadre and police is vigorously conducted and adequately prolonged clearing operations by military troops who will "stay" in the area, who behave themselves decently and who show respect for the people.

This elemental requirement of pacification has been missing. In almost no contested area designated for pacification in recent years have ARVN forces actually "cleared and stayed" to a point where cadre teams, if available, could have stayed overnight in hamlets and survived, let alone accomplish their mission. . . .

Now that the threat of a communist main-force military victory has been thwarted by our emergency efforts, we must allocate far more attention and a portion of the regular military forces (at least half of ARVN and perhaps a portion of the U.S. forces) to the task of providing an active and permanent security system behind which the RD teams and police can operate and behind which the political struggle with the VC infrastructure can take place.

The U.S. cannot do this pacification security job for the Vietnamese. All we can do is "massage the heart." For one reason, it is known that we do not intend to stay; if our efforts worked at all, it would merely postpone the eventual confrontation of the VC and GVN infrastructures. The GVN must do the job, and I am convinced that drastic reform is needed if the GVN is going to be able to do it. . . .

One solution would be to consolidate all U.S. activities which are primarily part of the civilian pacification program and all persons engaged in such activities, providing a clear assignment of responsibility and a unified command under a civilian relieved of all other duties. (If this task is assigned to Ambassador Porter, another individual must be sent immediately to Saigon to serve as Ambassador Lodge's deputy.) Under this approach, there would be a carefully delineated division of responsibility between the civilian-in-charge and an element of COMUSMACV under a senior officer, who would give the subject of planning for and providing hamlet security the highest priority in attention and resources. Success will depend on the men selected for the jobs on both sides (they must be among the highest rank and most competent administrators in the U.S. Government), on complete cooperation among the U.S. elements, and on the extent to which the South Vietnamese can be shocked out of their present pattern of behavior. The first work of this reorganized U.S. pacification organization should be to produce within 60 days a realistic and detailed plan for the coming year.

From the political and public-relations viewpoint, this solution is preferable—if it works. But we cannot tolerate continued failure. If it fails after a fair trial, the only alternative in my view is to place the entire pacification program—civilian and military—under General Westmoreland. This alternative would result in the establishment of a Deputy COMUSMACV for Pacification who would be in command of all pacification staffs in Saigon and of all pacification staffs and activities in the field; one person in each corps, province and district would be responsible for the U.S. effort.

(It should be noted that progress in pacification, more than anything else, will persuade the enemy to negotiate or withdraw.)[70]

In addition to pacification planning, U.S. officials in Washington also determine all targets for the bombing of North Vietnam, as reported by authors David Kraslow and Stuart H. Loory.

The device the top officials in the Johnson Administration have worked out for coordinating their efforts is the "Tuesday lunch," named because it convenes usually—but not always—on Tuesday at one o'clock in the family dining room on the second floor of the White House.

To the extent that the President shares important decision-making at all, he does much of it at the Tuesday lunch with the Secretaries of Defense and State, Walt Rostow and Press Secretary George Christian. Occasionally, General Wheeler, the Joint Chiefs chairman, CIA Director Richard Helms and others sit in.

The Tuesday lunch has long since replaced the Cabinet, the National Security Council or the informal, ad hoc "ex comms" (executive committees) of the Kennedy years as the court of last resort on national security matters, foreign affairs and, particularly, Vietnam.

The President and his aides gather around a mahogany Duncan Phyfe oval table in a room papered with scenes depicting the surrender of Cornwallis at Yorktown. They hold their councils of war and peace— covering a wide spectrum of subjects—while black-coated waiters quietly serve them.

The luncheon group is never more specific than when it turns, as it often does, to consideration of individual bombing targets in North Vietnam. The fact is that no road junction, petroleum storage tank, railroad bridge, factory, warehouse, airfield, antiaircraft gun or missile battery, dock or truck depot in the northern part of North Vietnam is struck by American airplanes without the approval of Lyndon Johnson and his Tuesday lunch partners.

The targets submitted for their approval are selected from a master list in the Pentagon known as the "JCS Target List." This is a compilation kept by the Joint Chiefs of Staff of every possible target in North Vietnam, ranging from the least significant to those, like the harbor of Haiphong, that could provoke the Soviet Union and Red China if they were hit. The targets on the list are suggested by field commanders, analysts of reconnaissance photos at Pacific Fleet headquarters in Honolulu and experts working for the Joint Chiefs in the Pentagon.

These targets are "fixed" or strategic installations in the North that have no direct relationship to the ground fighting in South Vietnam. (Those with such a relationship—infiltration routes, for example—can be struck on the order of the American military commander in Saigon without approval from Washington.)

Before the fixed targets ever get to the Tuesday lunch group, they are researched with excruciating care first by officers on the Joint Chiefs' staff and then by civilian officials in the Pentagon. Finally the Defense Secretary sends them to Ben Read, who feeds them into the State Department information grid for study at several levels. State's interest is to see that the political and diplomatic risks of striking any given target are minimized. The State Department analysts study the possibilities, for example, that the property of third nations might be jeopardized in striking a given target or that foreign diplomats visiting in Hanoi might be embarrassed.

The target suggestions are culled, and those ultimately selected presumably must support the three objectives of the bombing McNamara outlined in testimony in 1966 before the House Armed Services Committee:

> (1) To act to improve the morale of the South Vietnamese forces by attacking the North; there is no question but what the bombing will accomplish that; (2) to reduce the flow and/or increase the cost of the infiltration of men and equipment into the South. There is no question but what the capacity of the system has been cut back. . . .
>
> The third objective was to decrease the will of the North Vietnamese to continue the effort in the South at a time when we had proved to them they couldn't win in the South; that is, *affect their will in such a way as to move them to a satisfactory settlement.* (Italics by authors) We haven't reached that point yet. I cannot guarantee to you that the bombing will be a major factor when we do reach it, but I think it may be.

That statement, repeated often by the Pentagon, points up better than anything else on the public record the essentially political nature of the bombing of North Vietnam. If the bombing, then, in any way inhibits the possibility for a satisfactory settlement, it would appear to be undermining the very policy that sanctioned it.

As a result of all the staff work in the Pentagon and at the State Department, the authorization requests for each target were reduced to a single sheet of paper—a kind of report card—on which the suggested strikes were described in summary. Each individual sheet contained a check list for four items:

1. The military advantage of striking the proposed target.
2. The risk to American aircraft and pilots in a raid.
3. The danger that the strike might widen the war by forcing other countries into the fighting.
4. The danger of heavy civilian casualties.

At the Tuesday lunch, President Johnson and his advisers worked over each of the target sheets like schoolteachers grading examination papers. Each of the men graded each of the targets in the four categories.

The decisions were made on the basis of averaged-out grades.

A steel mill near Hanoi, the lunch group might decide, had a marginal

military value, but since both the war-widening danger of striking it and
the risk of civilian casualites were low, it would be authorized. On the
other hand, dropping mines into Haiphong harbor had a great and obvious military value, but it also had a great and obvious war-widening
danger and a high risk to American pilots. So the lunch group refused this
authorization.

In this manner the President and his principal advisers, working over
a lunch table in the White House, showed their intense concern with
individual road junctions, clusters of trucks and structures down to
small buildings in a land thousands of miles away. Their obvious concern lent great weight to the contention that never has more care been
taken in making sure that limited war-making objectives were not being exceeded.[71]

*The American pilots who execute the missions planned at the "Tuesday
lunch" show an uncanny knowledge of the targeting procedures. One of
the popular fighter pilot songs of the day is entitled "Our Leaders," sung to
the melody of "Mañana."*

> At Phillips Range in Kansas
> The jocks all had the knack,
> But now that we're in combat
> We've got colonels on our back,
> And every time we say, "Shit-hot!"
> Or whistle in the bar,
> We have to answer to somebody
> Looking for a star.
>
> CHORUS: Our leaders, our leaders,
> Our leaders, is what they always say,
> But it's bullshit, it's bullshit,
> It's bullshit they feed us every day!
>
> Today we had a hot one
> And the jocks were scared as hell,
> They ran to meet us with a beer
> And tell us we were swell,
> But Recce took the BDA
> And said we missed a hair;
> Now we'll catch all kinds of hell
> From the wheels at Seventh Air.
>
> They send us out in bunches
> To bomb a bridge and die,
> These tactics are for bombers
> That our leaders used to fly,

The bastards don't trust our Colonel
Up in Wing, and so I guess,
We'll have to leave the thinking to
The wheels in JCS!

The JCS are generals,
But they're not always right,
Sometimes they have to think it over
Well into the night;
When they have a question
Or something they can't hack,
They have to leave the judgment to
That money-saving Mac!

Now Mac's job is in danger
For he's on salary, too;
To have the final say-so
Is something he can't do;
Before we fly a mission
And everything's o.k.,
Mac has to get permission from
Flight leader L.B.J.!![72]

*In December U.S. Army Special Forces Lieutenant Jack Lane is in Saigon
for in-country reassignment. Lane is the main character in Alan Clark's
novel* The Lion Heart.

At the MAAG building that morning there was quite a crowd of Special
Forces officers who were being redeployed among the newly arrived
units. A real Madison Avenue colonel was explaining the scheme.

"This guy's legs are so straight he sleeps on the floor," said Dave
Kimche to Lane in a highly audible undertone. "Can't get upstairs."

Lane hadn't seen Kimche for over a year, though they had done the
same refresher course at Bragg. He was crew-cut, but you could see the
sides were quite gray. Lane hoped he didn't look that much older when
he got back to the States.

Kimche went on, lowering his voice somewhat, "A lot of the guys who
are short are opting out of this one. Going back to the Rock for the last
few weeks, and then home."

Lane said, "I've still got six months."

"I got four. But it's going to be a ball from now on. We're gonna really
hit Charlie. I seen the stuff that's coming in."

"I hope so."

He was thinking: All the VC prisoners said—"We beat the French in
four years, if you are five times as strong as the French then we beat you
in five times as many years." All the French said—"We couldn't win and
we know the country—how can you then, coming as strangers?" But that

was probably sour grapes. The French couldn't bear the idea of us succeeding where they had failed. Megand, a natural pessimist, was slightly less discouraging—"*Mon cher garçon,* the Anglo-Saxons *always* win in the end. And anyway, why not *have* a thirty-years' war? It would do the economy no end of good."

"Were you with a good unit, Dave?"

"Frankly, it stunk."

"Me too."

"I never want to see an ARVIN soldier again."

"You'll see them all right—leaning on the civilians in the rear areas while we sort out the VC."

"That's right. 'Pacification.' "

After the lecture, Lane reported to his ASO.

He had been posted, he was told, to the First Battalion of the 78th Division, and was to report to the commanding officer at 1000 hours the following morning, to give "advisory briefing" on the situation in Tay Ninh province, where the division was to be deployed.

"As of now," said the ASO, "you've got about twenty hours' R & R— make the most of it, you're going to have your hands full with those babes."[73]

What Captain Lane could experience in a short R&R is described in Steven Smith's American Boys. *Here, Sergeant Willard Morgan is just four days away from going home.*

He moved up five doors to the Dixie bar. Three soldiers sat around a table with two girls. "Come on and sit down, buddy," one of them said.

"Too much action for me. I'll just have a beer and count the four days I've got left in this place." He sat down and looked out the window, tensing as he thought about home. What would he do? Who would he see? How would he announce his return? The last letter he'd written was to his sister three weeks ago, saying he'd be home before Christmas. Well, he'd be there before that, and he'd probably be drunk a lot. Drunk all the fucking time.

Drunk. What a perfect word. He didn't even have to drink much to get drunk anymore. Maybe that's the way it went: At first you got drunk quickly, then you reached a point where you could hold it for a while, then you'd been drunk so much you could take one beer, think DRUNK, and there you were.

But it wasn't funny anymore, not like in S-1 when he'd down four beers for breakfast. It was funny then, even when he drank a fifth a night, because he never knew where he'd wake up, and someone always told a good story about what he did. It wasn't funny anymore because his guts were a mess and he was weak and fat and smoked fifty cigarettes a day and if he had to run two hundred yards he'd die. Combat was supposed to make you tough. Combat made you shit a lot.

He wondered if Chambers would stay with him in Oakland, wondered if their strained relationship would resolve itself before they left. Orville understood plenty and he accepted too. Morgan wanted him and his sister to get together, even though his sister had a man. She could talk to him about architecture, and they could both take care of him when he was drunk. He knew Chambers was tired of his shit. He disapproved. He understood, he even accepted, but he disapproved. So Chambers didn't respect him anymore. So fuck it.

Maybe it wouldn't be good to have Orville there when he got back. He'd make him feel guilty or constrained. Because Orville didn't find anything funny about people making asses of themselves. Okay, but why be so serious all the time? Lighten up, man. Jesus, if it wasn't grim enough. So you make an ass of yourself. So what? Chambers never made an ass of himself. Gibraltar. Enough, enough, enough. If he made an ass of himself at home, tough shit. The important thing was to make an ass of himself right now. He drank up and left the Dixie.

The sky had clouded over and soon the track that ran in front of the whorehouses would be a river of mud. He walked to the other side of Sin City, stopping about twenty feet in front of the Miami. It had been in the picture from *Time* that his father had sent him shortly after Sin City opened. Old paternal nudge in the ribs about which direction Oriental cunt ran. Sin City. Built to prevent the division from being decimated by the clap. The Army doctors gave shots once a week.

He found Clampitt with a girl in his lap. He and Webster had met Clampitt at finance that morning, and the young gunner had asked to accompany them to Sin City. He was one of Hart's boys who'd made sergeant, but had been breaking away lately and wasn't really that bad. With four days left, who cared anyway?

"You light yet?" Clampitt asked.

"Nope. You?"

"We've just been talking."

"Does she read Spinoza?"

"What?"

"Just to show that there's no hard feelings about you making sergeant, Clampitt, I'm going to buy you a piece of ass. . . . Hey, girl, for how many p. you boom-boom my friend?"

"Boom-boom four hundred p."

"You chop-chop too?"

"No chop-chop. Chop-chop number ten."

"Come on, you chop-chop extra hundred p."

"No chop-chop. Only boom-boom."

He waved five hundred piasters in front of her. "Come on, special chop-chop just for my friend."

"No chop-chop. You number ten thou."

"Six hundred p. chop-chop, boom-boom." He grabbed her shirt and waved the money in her face.

"Let me take my time, Morg," Clampitt said. "You know these Buddhist chicks don't blow. Only the Catholics do."

He started to put the money in his pocket.

"Six hundred p.?" the girl said.

He winked at Clampitt. "That's right, Baby-san. Okay? You take care of my friend. You're not about to reach nirvana anyway." He dangled the bills in front of her again.

"Okay." She took the money, disappeared behind the bar, then quickly reappeared. "Come on, GI," she said to Clampitt.

Ten minutes later Webster bounded through the doorway. "Morg, baby, they got this Pakistani broad at the San Francisco that throws an honest-to-God fuck." He sat down. "You got to try this out. Good, good, gooooooood!"

"Later. You want to go to old town, see what's up?" He felt shitty about Clampitt's whore and wanted to get away.

"Let's relax a little first."

"Okay. Maybe I'll knock off a shot." He went to the bar and made arrangements with a girl who had just come out of the back. He took another beer to the room. She pulled off her pink blouse and black pajama bottoms and flopped on the mat. He removed his shirt and slid his pants and drawers below his knees, leaving his boots on. He looked at the girl, raised the can to his lips, then leaned over and spit a mouthful of beer on her stomach.

"You number ten!" She jumped up.

"Here, wipe it off with my shirt."

She took his T-shirt and wiped her belly. "Be nice, now, GI. Let's have nice boom-boom."

"You play awhile first." He leaned back while she rubbed him.

In five minutes she said, "Come on, GI, you boom-boom now."

He settled into the rhythm and rubbed her thighs with his hands. Her head lolled to one side with her eyes shut and mouth open as if she were asleep. He dropped his face and kissed her salty neck. She smelled like shit. He closed his eyes, put himself back in his room at Berkeley with Emily, the soft-thighed teller from the Wells Fargo Bank, and after a few minutes he came. He got two breaths in before she slid out from under him. He swung his feet over the pallet thinking how much better it was just whacking off. "Jesus Christ," he said when she pulled an Army canteen cup half full of water from under the pallet and splashed her crotch. "You got some real good hygiene here."

"You like boom-boom, GI?"

"Terrific." He restrained himself from pushing her over. He wiped the sweat from his chest and stomach with his T-shirt, put it on, hitched up his pants, and walked out.[74]

Rather than find a girl for himself, however, Captain Lane decides to make a telephone call.

Some time back, nearly three weeks, he'd written to Wanda carefully enclosing an envelope for each of the boys, "to be opened on Christmas Day," and given her checks—one for herself; it was big, a special prize for "poor you, being alone," and another for the boys so that they could all go on a shopping expedition and Tommy and Bang could crash about excitedly in the toy shop before selecting their own choice. So far he'd had no reply. There had been nothing at the post office when he was going through from Na Qwan on Sunday. He supposed it was a good sign. If you're happy you don't write. Knowing this was only half true, his mind quickly compensated: he'd told Wanda that he was being re-posted—she was probably waiting to hear his new address. But she could have sent something, perhaps, just to the APO USAFVN. He had two hours before his appointment at the ASO, and thought he would try the central post office.

In actual fact the post office had been extremely efficient. His credit-card account from American Express was already there, forwarded from the Special Forces box, together with a stockholder's proxy from Sperry-Rand and two issues of the Bache *Listening Post.*

"Can you make a call to the States for me?"

The telephone exchange was very busy. The girl operator he spoke to was wearing too much lipstick and had a dreadful accent. Radio Saigon.

"The delay is up to two hours." She passed the booking form across to him and he wrote out his number.

An hour went by. It would be midnight in Newport. Too bad. Serve her right for not sending a letter. Lane grinned as he thought of Wanda softly curled up in bed to be suddenly waked by the clash of the tele-phone bell. He had his secret knowledge of her body in the middle of the night, when sometimes he would come in very late from fishing trips to tiptoe into the bedroom in the darkness and throw off his clothes and lose himself in that warmth and sweetness.

"Lootenant Lane, please."

"Yes?"

"Your Newport party doesn't answer."

"Please keep it in a bit longer."

"I'm sorry, sir, the circuit has been broken."

"Well, put it in again and keep it ringing this time."

"There will be a delay."

"So?"

"Kindly make out another form."

"Why?" Lane was conscious that there were others in line behind him, impatient with their reservation forms.

"This one has been endorsed 'No Reply.' " She smiled brightly over his shoulder at a pink-faced ensign. "Yes, please?"

Another forty minutes, then it came through.

"Hullo—*Jack!*"

Atmospherics crackled. Their voices came and went on undulating waves.

"Merry Christmas."

"What?"

"I called to say 'Merry Christmas.' "

"This line is terrible."

"I can hear you okay."

"Sure we're okay."

"Tommy?"

"What?"

"HOW'S TOMMY?"

"He's just great."

"And Bang?"

"He's had a cold, but he's better now."

"Completely?"

"Just about."

"Getting over it."

"When?"

"What?"

"When are you coming over?"

"I'm not. At least, I don't think so."

"Merry Christmas, darling."

"Thanks, my sweet. Same to you and the boys. Did you get my letter?"

"He is."

"What?"

"Much better. Bang is."

Hell, this was impossible. What was the matter with Bang, anyway? *Better* didn't mean *well,* it meant *less ill.*

"Darling, this line's hopeless so I'll say good-by for now. Do write. Get the boys to write. Just send it to the APO, Saigon."

"Sure."

"Good-by, my sweet."

"Good-by, darling."

"Fourteen dollars and twenty cents," said the operator as Lane came out of the booth.[75]

1966 31 December		
	TOTAL	NET CHANGE
U.S. military personnel assigned in Vietnam	385,300	+201,000
U.S. casualties	YEAR	TO DATE (cumulative)
Killed in action	5,008	6,644
Wounded in action	30,093	37,738
Source: DOD/OASD		

1967

On 8 February 1967 President Johnson secretly sends this letter to Ho Chi Minh.

His Excellency
Ho Chi Minh
President
Democratic Republic of Vietnam

Dear Mr. President:

I am writing to you in the hope that the conflict in Vietnam can be brought to an end. That conflict has already taken a heavy toll—in lives lost, in wounds inflicted, in property destroyed, and in simple human misery. If we fail to find a just and peaceful solution, history will judge us harshly.

Therefore, I believe that we both have a heavy obligation to seek earnestly the path to peace. It is in response to that obligation that I am writing directly to you.

We have tried over the past several years, in a variety of ways and through a number of channels, to convey to you and your colleagues our desire to achieve a peaceful settlement. For whatever reasons, these efforts have not achieved any results.

It may be that our thoughts and yours, our attitudes and yours, have been distorted or misinterpreted as they passed through these various channels. Certainly that is always a danger in indirect communication.

There is one way to overcome this problem and to move forward in the search for a peaceful settlement. That is for us to arrange for direct talks between trusted representatives in a secure setting and away from the glare of publicity. Such talks should not be used as a propaganda exercise but should be a serious effort to find a workable and mutually acceptable solution.

In the past two weeks, I have noted public statements by representatives of your government suggesting that you would be prepared to enter into direct bilateral talks with representatives of the US Government, provided that we ceased "unconditionally" and permanently our bombing operations against your country and all military actions against it. In the last day, serious and responsible parties have assured us indirectly that this is in fact your proposal.

Let me frankly state that I see two great difficulties with this proposal. In view of your public position, such action on our part would inevitably produce worldwide speculation that discussions were under way and would impair the privacy and secrecy of those discussions. Secondly, there would inevitably be grave concern on our part whether your government would make use of such action by us to improve its military position.

With these problems in mind, I am prepared to move even further towards an ending of hostilities than your Government has proposed in either public statements or through private diplomatic channels. I am prepared to order a cessation of bombing against your country and the stopping of further augmentation of US forces in South Viet-Nam as soon as I am assured that infiltration into South Viet-Nam by land and by sea has stopped. These acts of restraint on both sides would, I believe, make it possible for us to conduct serious and private discussions leading toward an early peace.

I make this proposal to you now with a specific sense of urgency arising from the imminent New Year holidays in Viet-Nam. If you are able to accept this proposal I see no reason why it could not take effect at the end of the New Year, or Tet, holidays. The proposal I have made would be greatly strengthened if your military authorities and those of the Government of South Viet-Nam could promptly negotiate an extension of the Tet truce.

As to the site of the bilateral discussions I propose, there are several possibilities. We could, for example, have our representatives meet in Moscow where contacts have already occurred. They could meet in some other country such as Burma. You may have other arrangements or sites in mind, and I would try to meet your suggestions.

The important thing is to end a conflict that has brought burdens to both our peoples, and above all to the people of South Viet-Nam. If you have any thoughts about the actions I propose, it would be most important that I receive them as soon as possible.

Sincerely,
Lyndon B. Johnson[76]

A few days later Ho Chi Minh replies.

Your Excellency:

On 10 February 1967, I received your message. This is my reply.

Vietnam is thousands of miles away from the United States. The Vietnamese people have never done any harm to the United States. But contrary to the pledges made by its representative at the 1954 Geneva conference, the U.S. Government has ceaselessly intervened in Vietnam; it has unleashed and intensified the war of aggression in South Vietnam with a view to prolonging the partition of Vietnam and turning South Vietnam into a neocolony and a military base of the United States. For over two years now, the U.S. Government has with its air and naval forces carried the war to the Democratic Republic of Vietnam, an independent and sovereign country.

The U.S. Government has committed war crimes, crimes against peace and against mankind. In South Vietnam, half a million U.S. and satellite troops have resorted to the most inhuman weapons and the most barbarous methods of warfare, such as napalm, toxic chemicals and gases, to massacre our compatriots, destroy crops and raze villages to the ground.

In North Vietnam, thousands of U.S. aircraft have dropped hundreds of thousands of tons of bombs, destroying towns, villages, factories, roads, bridges, dikes, dams, and even churches, pagodas, hospitals, schools. In your message, you apparently deplored the sufferings and destructions in Vietnam. May I ask you: Who has perpetrated these monstrous crimes? It is the U.S. and satellite troops. The U.S. Government is entirely responsible for the extremely serious situation in Vietnam.

The U.S. war of aggression against the Vietnamese people constitutes a challenge to the countries of the Socialist camp, a threat to the national independence movement and a serious danger to peace in Asia and the world.

The Vietnamese people deeply love independence, freedom and peace. But in the face of the U.S. aggression, they have risen up, united as one man. Fearless of sacrifices and hardships, they are determined to carry on their resistance until they have won genuine independence and freedom and true peace. Our just cause enjoys strong sympathy and support from the peoples of the whole world, including broad sections of the American people.

The U.S. Government has unleashed the war of aggression in Vietnam. It must cease this aggression. That is the only way to the restoration of peace. The U.S. Government must stop definitively and unconditionally its bombing raids and all other acts of war against the Democratic Republic of Vietnam, withdraw from South Vietnam all U.S. and satellite troops, and let the Vietnamese people settle themselves their own affairs. Such (is the basic) content of the four-point stand of the Government of the D. R. V., which embodies the essential principles and provisions of the 1954 Geneva agreements on Vietnam. It is the basis of a correct political solution to the Vietnam problem.

In your message, you suggested direct talks between the D. R. V. and United States. If the U.S. Government really wants these talks, it must first of all stop unconditionally its bombing raids and all other acts of war against the D. R. V. It is only after the unconditional cessation of the U.S. bombing raids and all other acts of war against the D. R. V. that the D. R. V. and the United States would enter into talks and discuss questions concerning the two sides.

The Vietnamese people will never submit to force, they will never accept talks under the threat of bombs.

Our cause is absolutely just. It is to be hoped that the U.S. Government will act in accordance with reason.

Ho Chi Minh[77]

In March aircraft of the U.S. Navy again attack the Thanh Hoa bridge.

Several strikes were flown against the "Dragon" during the first few weeks of 1967, but with the same disappointing results. In January 1967, however, a US Navy aircraft carrier departed San Diego, California, carrying a new generation of weapons into the Vietnam conflict, the Walleye Glide Bomb, one of the new "smart bombs." The Walleye is a free-fall glide bomb with a 1000-pound warhead which has in the nose a TV camera designed to track and impact on a high contrast aim point. The camera relays what it sees to a scope in the cockpit through which the pilot identifies the target. The pilot sights the target on his scope, positions a set of crosshairs over the pre-selected contrast point, identifies this point to the Walleye, and releases the bomb within its glide and guidance parameters. The key significance of this new weapon is its pinpoint accuracy. It also furnishes a limited stand-off capability, which allows the pilot to release the weapon farther away from the target than is possible with conventional bombs.

In early March 1967, plans were made to attack the Thanh Hoa Bridge as soon as possible with the new Walleye. Missions were flown on 11 March, using the Walleye against military barracks and small bridges to familiarize the pilots with actual weapon employment. Results of these strikes were so successful that the Commander, Carrier Division, Task Force 77, scheduled a Walleye mission against the Dragon's Jaw on 12 March. Attack Squadron 212, designated for this strike, had been provided with a scale model of the Thanh Hoa Bridge to be used in conjunction with a movable light source (simulating the sun) to locate the best points of contrast and the time of day these conditions would occur. Army demolition experts also were on board the carrier to assist in identifying the most vulnerable spots on the bridge structure and the sun's contrasting effect, the pilots and demolition experts agreed that 1412 hours (2:12 pm) on 12 March would provide maximum contrast for the chosen aim point.

The sun shone brightly on 12 March as the pilots rode the escalators from their ready rooms to the flight deck. Although there was a considerable number of AW and AAA sites protecting the Dragon, the strike force for this mission consisted of only three A-4 Skyhawks, with one Walleye each, and two F-8 Crusaders for MIG protection. The mission was planned so that each aircraft would make individual runs on the bridge from south to north in order to give the pilot as much time as possible to locate the aim point, identify it to the weapon, and release it. The flight was launched and joined up over the carrier prior to heading for the target. Enroute, the pilots completed their checks on the weapons systems and declared the mission a "Go."

Over the target, each pilot dove at the bridge at 500 mph and released his weapon as planned. Initially the AW and AAA was very light, but when the third pilot initiated his run, the enemy fire was extremely heavy. As the pilot searched for the aim point, he could see, in his peripheral vision, hundreds of flashes on the ground which he knew all too well to be the enemy guns firing at him. With the aim point sighted, identified to the weapon, and "bombs away," all three pilots headed their Skyhawks toward the Gulf of Tonkin. Photography taken from the strike aircraft showed that all three weapons impacted within five feet of each other on the designated aim point; but, the bridge still stood. . . . Although the bridge had been damaged many times in the past and the North Vietnamese had paid dearly in men and materiel to keep it open, it had become a paramount symbol of North Vietnamese determination.[78]

1967   15 March—Ellsworth Bunker named to replace Lodge as ambassador to South Vietnam. **21 March**—DRV publicly reveals Johnson–Ho Chi Minh correspondence.

Also on 21 March, during a conference in Guam, President Johnson announces that Robert Komer will head up a new organizaton to improve pacification efforts. General Westmoreland remembers.

As my civilian deputy, Komer was to occupy a rung on the command ladder in some ways equivalent to that of General Abrams and was to have the personal rank of ambassador. Yet there was a difference in the two positions: Abrams was my deputy, or second-in-command, in all matters, while Komer was deputy to COMUSMACV for one matter only: pacification.

The Lord knows the President handed me a volatile character in Bob Komer. The nickname "Blowtorch" was all too apt.

To serve as a bridge between Komer and the military, which is a nice way of saying to keep Komer out of my hair, I nominated a smart major general who eleven years earlier had been adviser to Big Minh: George Forsythe. Not yet informed of the assignment, General Forsythe was at his desk in Hawaii when he received a telephone call from the White House. It was Komer, whom he had never met. "Hey, George," Komer blared into the telephone, "pack your bag. I'm going out to be Westy's deputy and run the war for him. You're coming along."

Bob Komer well understood that he had a difficult assignment. He could hardly have missed discerning the irritation some members of my staff felt over a civilian in the command structure. We had, some said, a political commissar. Komer was like a grain of sand in an oyster, and like an oyster, the staff set out to encase the irritant; but Komer was not about to be made into a pearl. He blustered, sometimes blundered, knocked heads together, wrote one caustic memorandum after another to any and all on whatever subject, including strategy. He was determined that everybody know he was there and what he was there to do. When an MP at MACV headquarters stopped his car to allow a vehicle with brigadier general's markings to proceed, Komer demanded a license plate with four stars, although he graciously accepted instead a special identification tag. I had to clamp down when I discovered he was using his old White House ties to send communications direct to the President with draft messages that he wanted the President to send back to the ambassador and me. I also had to convince him to be tactful with the Vietnamese, to speak bluntly only in private lest they lose face with their colleagues.

Yet Bob Komer was the man for the job. He pushed himself and his people hard. He had imaginative ideas, usually sound. Striped pants might work later, but at the start, abrasion was in order and Bob Komer worked overtime at that.

The new organization, which superseded OCO, was known as CORDS, for Civil Operations and Revolutionary Development Support. Because I recognized that pacification was a key to success, I gave CORDS my full support, on occasion surprising some of my military colleagues by overruling them on some matter involving resources, people, or responsibility in favor of Komer. I gave Komer high priority, for example, on the best officers, suggesting such men as Bob Montague, whom I had called on back in 1964 to get HOP TAC going. Because the pacification program had to have adequate military protection, I gave CORDS advisory responsibility for the militia—the Regional and Popular Forces—that had the assignment of local security. I also gave CORDS advisory responsibility for PHOENIX, a project aimed at identifying and excising the VC political infrastructure and run by the South Vietnamese primarily under direction of CIA advisers. Komer put PHOENIX together with assistance of William E. Colby, who was destined to succeed Komer and subsequently to be director of the CIA in Washington. If the guerrilla was to be divested of support from the people, the political control had to be neutralized.

To try to eliminate overoptimistic reporting on pacification, CORDS developed a new method known as the "hamlet evaluation system," or HES. In no way foolproof, the method nevertheless was an improvement in our continuing search for objective evaluation of a nebulous matter.[79]

The CORDS program is a target of satiric attack in Derek Maitland's novel The Only War We've Got. *Here, the new U.S. ambassador to South Vietnam, Goldblatt (Bunker), is driving across Saigon to see Ambassador Risher (Komer), who heads CORDS. Goldblatt has been trying to help settle a feud between South Vietnam's president and vice-president.*

Goldblatt felt optimistic about the outcome of his peacekeeping efforts. Arbitration had reached a stage favourable to agreement, and agreement shone like a beacon at the end of a tunnel. All it needed was for Ambassador Risher to hide three corrupt province chiefs somewhere in his latest pacification scheme. The trouble was, if the latest pacification scheme was anything like its five or six predecessors it would be like trying to hide three pickpockets in a den of thieves. '*Wonder if the Viet Cong have these sort of problems,*' the ambassador mused. Then his heart jumped painfully and a cold spasm crept through his stomach as his limousine pulled into the compound of the Civilian Office of Revolutionary Development and Security (CORDS) and a dark-skinned Vietnamese guard clad in a black Viet Cong uniform and toting an AK-Forty-Seven assault rifle snapped to attention and whipped open the door. The ambassador felt his knees give way under him as he hauled himself nervously from the vehicle; and a second Viet Cong rushed forward and grasped him under the arm. Goldblatt sprang back with a gasp, but the door had been slammed shut behind him, and the first black-clad guard pointed with his rifle at the front steps of the CORDS villa.

'You Go,' he grunted, and the ambassador felt strangely disoriented— as though he had stepped into another void—as he was led shakily across the courtyard by a Viet Cong detachment which had closed in quietly like zombies around him. The hair on his neck and the back of his head sprang up as he entered the villa and yet another grim-faced, black-clad guerilla waved him toward an office at rifle-point. *Don't panic!* his brain ordered his quivering nerves. *Perhaps it is best this way,* a quiet voice whispered somewhere in the far reaches of his consciousness. Inside the office, a faintly familiar figure, clad in a black uniform that strained almost to bursting point over his huge paunch, turned from a map on the wall.

'Why, Mr. Goldblatt. It's good of you to spare me the time!' Ambassador Risher did a quick, dumpy pirouette. 'How do you like it?'

'What the hell's going on here?' Ambassador Goldblatt croaked.

'It's all part of the new pacification programme,' Risher gushed. 'It's called Revolutionary Development.'

'Why the Viet Cong outfits?'

'We're going to beat the Viet Cong at his own game. So we gotta dress like revolutionaries. Great idea, huh?' But Goldblatt groaned with inner agony, and massaged his temples and offered no resistance as Risher placed a chair underneath him and sat him down. 'You look real bad,' Risher said gaily. 'Having problems, huh?'

'No more than usual,' Goldblatt sighed. 'The President and the Vice-President are at each other's throats with tanks and troops and unless you can place three corrupt province chiefs in your programme there'll be a battle on tonight that'll make the real war look silly.'

'No sweat!' Risher twinkled. 'We need all the men we can get for this baby. They'll feel right at home in the Supply Department.'

'Supply Department? Risher, I want to stamp out corruption in this country, not make it worse.'

'But look at it this way, Goldblatt. These slant-eyes have got pride, you know. If we just hand out our supplies, they'll simply give them to the Viet Cong. But if we hand them over to the right people—like those province chiefs—and they sell them to the people, the people will think twice about giving something to the Viet Cong that they've just paid good money for. This way, the province chiefs are kept happy and the people will feel proud because they've earned the stuff by paying money for it and they've not just been given a free handout.' Ambassador Goldblatt sighed again.

'Hey,' said Risher. 'You look like you need a good rest.'

'Let's get on with the briefing,' Goldblatt snapped.

'O.K.,' cried Risher, and he beckoned to a grinning black-clad Vietnamese who stepped into the room. 'Mr. Goldblatt, I'd like you to meet Colonel Nguyen Bé who'll be heading the training side of our new programme. He's a great little guy—hates the Communists and speaks English almost as goddam well as me.'

'Hi, Midder Ambassador,' the colonel grinned, shaking hands with Goldblatt. 'How's your hammer hanging?' Goldblatt recoiled with shock and Risher muttered: 'He's spent a lot of time with the goddam Peace Corps.'

'V.C. number-ten-guddem-cucksuckers!' the colonel chanted.

'I see what you mean,' Ambassador Goldblatt breathed, but Risher was unveiling a stack of charts that hung on the wall.

'Now,' he barked, tapping his pointer against the chart. 'The main reason why the pacification schemes have failed in the past under, er, purely civilian control, is that there was no effective security in areas being pacified, and . . .'

'The pacification schemes did not fail under civilian control,' Goldblatt snapped. 'They were progressing slowly but surely. It's not a job you can do overnight.'

'Well that's just what we aim to do now that we haven't got any goddam civilians screwing up the programme.'

'But *you're* a civilian.'

'There's no such thing as a civilian in war-time,' Risher snapped. He tapped the chart again. 'Lack of security meant that the areas being pacified had little protection against Viet Cong infiltration or attack. Now that the programme is under military control, we can change all that.'

'What are you going to do?' Goldblatt grinned. 'Put troops around every goddam hamlet in the country? There are thirteen thousand of them and you haven't got enough men for that.'

'We are not going to protect the hamlets from the Viet Cong,' Risher barked. 'We are going to take the hamlets right away from the Viet Cong to deny them access to and shelter from the people.'

'How?'

'In broad terms, we're going to uproot all the people—all sixteen million of them—and resettle them in a special heavily-guarded reservation outside Saigon. Then we're gonna defoliate the entire rest of the country

and turn it into a free-fire zone, and anyone caught moving out there—
V.C. or not—is going to get his ass shot off.'

'*You can't do that!!*' Goldblatt barked.

'You got any other ideas?'

'You can't lay the whole country flat!'

'The only way we're gonna win this war,' Risher snapped, 'is to tow this
goddam country out into the middle of the Pacific and bomb the shit out
of it until it sinks.'[80]

*As the American troop buildup accelerates, more GIs arrive than leave.
Larry Heinemann's novel* Close Quarters *has U.S. Army Private First
Class Philip Dosier land in Vietnam sometime during March. He is assigned to an Armored Personnel Carrier (APC) unit. Cross, one of his
sergeants, organizes a welcoming party.*

That night after dark Cross wangled a case of beer out the back door of
the EM Club, which was a tent with a dirt floor and some benches and
picnic tables, and the three of us, Cross and Atevo and I, went down to
the seven-three. It was cooler than the club or the tents. They had both
showered and changed clothes and looked rested, except for their puffy
faces and darkened eyes. Cross opened three cans right away, tapping
them with the pointed tip of the opener to settle the foam, then making
one small cut on one side for air, two full cuts on the other for the
drinking; then he brought out the squat stove and fired it up for a snack,
a can of beef and potatoes from the leftover box. We drank the tepid
chalky beer for a while, watching the beef broth simmer, then Cross said,
"Well, how 'bout some smoke?" and reached under the bench to pull out
an ammo can. There were several packs of cigarettes, Kools and Marl-
boros and Salems, and baggies filled with dope.

"Uh, Cross? What's smoke?" I asked.

"Say?" But then he let out a low chuckle and mumbled something
about fucken new guys. "Why, smoke is M.J. Mike Juliet. Ya know—
grass. Same same smoke. Light up, it won't kill ya. 'Bout the only thing
round here that won't. Guaran-fucken-tee!" He snapped his Zippo and I
sucked the smoke down into my lungs.

"This here is one of the exotic de-lights of the East. Make a short man
see over fences, a tall man see into the clouds, fat dudes crawl under
screen doors. It'll slick up a wet dream, screw up a bad dream, fuck up a
dufus. Cures heartburn, jungle rot, the Gee-fucken-Eyes, all them things.
An' there ain't no muss, no fuss, no puke to clean up after. Smoke is m'
little buddy." I felt a cough, a pain. I blurted out the smoke, coughing
from way down, hacking. Cross laughed and slapped his knee so hard he
dropped his ash.

"Hey, m' man, ain't ya sipped smoke before?" he asked.

"No-o-o," I managed to say between coughs.

"Here, here ya work it too hard. It's a thing ya ain't got to sweat for.

You be good to smoke an' smoke'll be good to you. Ease up, we got boo-coo and we got all fucken night."

After that we sat quiet, smoking and drinking. There was just the hissing of the squat stove and the outgoing H. and I., harassment and interdiction, from the battery of 105 howitzers down the road. I was getting stoned for the first time in my life. Then it occurred to me that the beer was warm.

"Hey, Cross," I said. "You ever get ice?"

"Say? Ice? Yeah." He nodded his head slowly. "Every now an' again. We scrounge it from the icehouse they got at the Tay Ninh Base Camp, sometimes. There's a gook icehouse on the convoy road, the other side of Charlie Papa Alpha. It's a fucken rip-off, but every once in a while a trooper gets a taste in his mouth, or some fucken place, for a cool brew. Yeah, we get ice. That's what the Igloo's for, but you'll get used to warm. You get so you don't mind anything."

He spooned out the beef and potatoes onto a cheap tin dish. I watched the dead ash of his smoke; the beer cans we threw into the dust and moonlight; the cans from the afternoon were still lined up on the deck above my head. Then came the question, from way down, way back. The stupid question, the only question.

"What's it like?" I said. "Outside the wire. In the field. What's it like?"

Atevo sat across from me, wearing this dark canvas slouch hat with the frayed, floppy brim down over his face. He leaned his head back and looked at me with reddened stoic eyes, and said nothing. Cross put aside the tin plate, wiped the mess-kit fork on his trouser leg, and put it aside.

"Heh-heh-heh," he said, "Dosier, m' man, I wondered when you was gonna ask that. An' the answer is: it ain't different a-tall. It don't smell any more fucked up, it don't rain any harder, the gooks ain't any uglier, not by no long shot. 'Bout the only difference is, there ain't no wire. Outside it's just us chickens. And this whole fucken place, from the Red River Delta to the Me-kong, every snatch of sand, every hill and ARVN fort, all the banana groves and rice paddies and hamlets and fucked-up mud hooches, right down to the last squint-eye on this whole fucken farm, you could roll it into one tight-ass ball and none of it is worth the powder to blow it away with. There ain't one, not one square inch of muck within five or six thousand miles of here that I would fight anybody for, except what I'm standing on. And that includes this rubber plantation and fucken Saigon and the goddamn American Embassy. I been here goin' on ten months, m' man. I be goin' home May twenty-first. It ain't soon enough to suit me, but who cares, dig? An' in all that time I never met a squint-eye that I would call anything but gook. 'Come 'ere, papa-san. Lah-dee, motherfucker.' 'Me no VC. No VC.' 'You boo-coo VC, you lyin' slant-eyed, skinny-legged dink. I said come 'ere.' Gooks don't know how ta do shit. Can't get the hang a blackjack, don't even know how to plant somethin' simple-ass, like corn. Fucken-A, m' man, back home all ya got ta do is toss it outa fucken winda and the shit sprouts like weed. I swear, when I leave here you got the run a this fucken ranch. I'm gonna stay in Frisco and stay fucked up. I'm gonna sit me down and just sit, and when I get tired I'll move to a different chair. An' the first dude who fucks with me, I'm gonna crack his hat in two.

"You take Murphy. He'd been here 'bout as long as me an' a better gun you won't find in this fucken platoon, except maybe Atevo here. One night, 'bout a month ago come ta think about it, after weeks and weeks a contac' ever' fucken day, he got some wild hair up his ass and got ta chasing this gook on foot; jumped outa the hatch there and tore off toward the fucken woods, screaming at the top a his lungs. One of the goddamnedest things I seen *anybody* do. An' that chicken-shit gook turned on his fucken heel and shot Murph square in the neck. That's the fucken AK right there. Murph died waitin' on the dust-off. That's why I got the ass at Surtees, 'cause that spook just took his sweet fucken time callin' them in, and Murphy bled ta death. I tell you true, Dosier, I get about half a chance I'm gonna do a number square on his nappy fucken head."

He sat slouched on the bench with his feet out in front of him, flicking ash with his ring finger, leaning his head back against a waterproof and staring up through the crew hatch. His voice trailed off as though it were the end of an early-morning party, with wine bottles and beer bottles lined up along the windowsills and across the floor and everybody out of cigarettes. His words came mumbled and graveled and slow. The pain seemed to draw away from his eyes and settle in his voice and hands. He lit another smoke with a flick of his Zippo, popping seeds, and sucked on his beer. His story wandered through the nights when it rained and the nights when it was clear as water, "where you can't just tell what a thing is, but know just exactly where it's at, ya know?" and the platoon's first pathetic firefights, and down to the firefights they had just come in from.

"Shit, boy. We was at a fire base north a Suoi Tre when a call comes in from the artillery base a couple clicks—that's kilometers, boy—up the way. The dude on the radio said the perimeter was overrun. I know, I was listening. By the way he was talkin' it musta been the gook hordes that's been in the papers all these years. Well, Romeo and a couple tanks from the 34th Armor took off lickity-split through the fucken woods, with Bravo and Charlie Company right behind. And that kid bustin' jungle in the lead tank was busting some bad jungle too. Knocking it back boom-boom-boom. Hell of a lot better than these fucken crackerjack boxes do. We busted through that woodline and Jesus H. fucken Christ, but shit, boy, it looked like every dink in Cochin China was inside that perimeter. The artillery dudes and straight-leg grunts and the gooks was doin' it hand to hand. There was skirmish lines every which way all over the fucken place. That's when Seven-six, Sergeant Bendix, caught a fucken RPG that blew him right outa his hatch. Blew everybody away but Ivy, the driver." And Cross took me down to the seven-six to show me, talking the whole way.

He showed me a ragged hole about the size of my fist in the upraised TC hatch cover, and concentric spirals from the bits of shrapnel coming out from it, like the chamber and grooved rifling you will see if you look down the barrel of a gun.

"It was just about every man for himself," he said as we walked back to the seven-three. "Gooks tried to climb the seven-seven there, and Tweezer and the rest were beatin' them back with a tanker bar and shovels. We got on line with the grunts and dudes from artillery, I pulled into low gear, and drove standin' up one-handed, dingin' gooks with my forty-five and pullin' pins on grenades, counting one thousan', two thousan' three, and dropping them over the side. The tanks was firin' point-blank canister rounds, and seven-one backed one gook upside a tree and ran his ass down, tree and all. An' when some ya-hoo called a cease-fire and the fog cleared there was gook body count and KIA all over everything. Shit, but shit, m' man, the Colonel come down and jus' about creamed his fucken jeans, said there was something like six hundred fuckin' body count. An' it coulda been, I swear. Ain't that right, Atevo? You betcha. We was down about a third of our dudes. An' just about every night after that we had business, mortars and RPGs and probes and sniper fire, and had to drag the seven-six with us every place. Then one night . . . well, who knows, maybe Murphy just got tired. Wore out, ya know? Anyway, one night he goes straight over the top. He jumped outa his hatch like somebody had kicked him and took off with the shotgun after this gook, screaming, '*You cocksucker*.'" Cross pulled out his wallet and the picture of Murphy's wife he had kept, water-ragged and frayed and finger-smudged, a young woman with short combed-back hair in a two-piece bathing suit. He told me about the letter he promised Murphy he would write, but didn't. "It was easy to lie to Murph. Easier than I thought."

"And where does Trobridge come in?" I asked.

"Ol' Four Eyes'd been a gunner on the seven-zero, suckin' on Surtees' hin' tit for his third stripe, so the next morning Surtees put him in the hatch here. An' that fucken Trobridge is a *prime* cunt-head, too. He got a three-inch gash from his me-dulla ob-long-gotto clear around to the bridge of his fucken nose, dead square between his four fucken eyes." Then Cross's speech got crisp and mean. He told about the body count Romeo left in piles and the fucked-up ambushes, and then he told all over again of all the hate he had for Surtees. " 'Bout the nex' firefight we get into, I'm gonna settle his fucken hash, I swear," he said. Then his voice trailed off again into whispers and mumbles.

". . . Ever get so your body just shivers?" he said, loud again. "Like you was pullin' on a bottle of that God-awful junk gook booze. . . . Shivers so bad it's like malaria shakes. Fever and cold sweats and you can't even hold your hand straight, and you feel like you got to puke.

That's all that happens anymore. Jesus, but goddamn I hate warm beer," and he tossed his half-finished can underhanded out into the dust with the rest. It clattered and jangled among the others and I could hear it fizz, the beer spilling out on the ground. He reached above his head then, and yanked his hammock loose and started unbuttoning his cuffs.

"Well, why don' we call it a night, huh?" he said.

"Yes," Atevo said, gathering up his shotgun and flak jacket and slouch hat. "It is getting late."

I got my M-16 and steel pot and the two of us squeezed between the seven-three and seven-one, sidestepping, Atevo saying to Cross, "See you in the morning."

"Roger, roger, roger," Cross said back, his croaking voice trailing off into whispers and mumbles again.

We walked through the motor pool under a vaulted black sky, the stars clear and abundant, with Atevo leading by a step or two. He never used a flashlight, like some did, because the motor pool and the battalion command bunker and the Headquarters Company Orderly Room and the Recon tents, and the paths among them, were in plain view of the woodline, and I got that habit from him. We passed the silhouettes of tracks and deuce-and-a-halfs and the medic and recoilless-rifle jeeps. He stopped at the gateway in the wire where I had been standing earlier—his shotgun over one shoulder and flak jacket over the other, like a short thick cape.

"Let me tell you the first thing you must know," he said. "Do not walk so close. Keep five meters back, and when you go in front I will be five meters behind you."

"Okay," I said, and felt stupid.[81]

1967   **1 April**—U.S. troop strength in Vietnam reaches 430,000 (*Congressional Record*, 9 May). Throughout the United States there are large antiwar demonstrations. **9 May**—U.S. Senate Republican Policy Committee has read into the *Congressional Record* a formal report that deplores the "unilateral American military intervention in Vietnam."

Living in Hanoi during the spring of 1967 is British Consul-General John Colvin. He provides a perspective on the American bombing raids as seen from the ground.

The summer of 1967 began in March, with no real spring, moving from the drizzling chill of winter directly into the temperatures of 100 degrees and corresponding humidity.

A comparable change, from the relative absence of U.S. activity over the northeast quadrant of North Vietnam in the fall and winter to aerial bombardment of some intensity, began in April, although not yet within the 10-mile (prohibited) inner circle of Hanoi. Targets, most of them invisible to us, were struck around the circumference of the city and included airfields, military complexes, industry, storage dumps, and transportation. While the targets were invisible to Hanoi residents, the attackers and—at least in the early stages (for they later left the battle)— the defending MiG fighters could be plainly seen maneuvering at high altitudes. Although there were few combats in the classic sense of dog-fights, the flash of antiaircraft (AA) guns and, very occasionally, the twisting spiral of U.S. planes shot down in flames by surface-to-air mis-siles (SAMs) were seen. Smoke and fires from burning installations rose on the horizon: the crash of the northern antiaircraft batteries alternated with the thunder of high explosives from projectiles striking objectives in the near distance.

For the resident all this was an unwelcome change. Hitherto, we had had to contend only with intermittent visits from reconnaissance aircraft and spasmodic raids from more lethal formations. Even the latter tended to occur in clusters over a period of a week or so and at predictable times, usually at about 2:30 in the afternoon. As I was accustomed to taking a siesta every day after lunch, I had been able to sleep peacefully through most of these raids, waking refreshed to a cup of tea, a later stroll through the streets, conversation at the tennis court in the grounds of the French delegation-general, visits to friends on the Grand Voleur, dinner, and perhaps a movie with the Canadians.

Not much of that was possible after April. Even when attack was manifestly not against the city but against targets in the outskirts or even farther away, the Democratic Republic of Vietnam (D.R.V.) would insist on declaring an air raid on Hanoi itself. The sirens wailed up to 30 times a day: the din and that of the bombs and artillery often precluded sound sleep. No one was permitted out of doors during these incidents on pain of being incarcerated by the militia in one of the city's air-raid shelters, cylindrical concrete holes sunk some four feet deep in the pavements, uncomfortable for those of European height and bulk. . . .

I doubt if even the Soviets felt much devotion to their duties during those days of noise and sweat. Although Mr. Gromyko had told a West-ern interlocutor in the fall of 1966 that U.S. escalation would involve not only Chinese but also direct Soviet intervention with troops, the threat had now been demonstrated as idle. The Russians had—it must have been clear to their embassy—to grin and bear it like everyone else. One of their senior officials, converted from straight vodka to gin and tonic in the course of repeated visits to my house, found the prospect tolerable. (He later died of delirium tremens.) Another, with previous service in London, laid maddening emphasis on his acquaintance with Reggie Maud-ling, pronounced by him "Moddling." A Soviet military attaché, in the time he could spare from complaining about D.R.V. mismanagement of SAMs or from chasing Tonkinese waitresses, recounted interminable dirty stories in an English which few, including Dr. Deb, the Indian medical officer, could grasp.

Some idea of the effects of the bombing outside Hanoi had been given to me earlier by a traveler in North Vietnam; this traveler, although far from pro-American, was careful to distinguish his own de visu observations from the allegations of his North Vietnamese guides. (In this he agreeably differed from the distasteful performance, ultimately disastrous to U.S. policies, of Harrison Salisbury in December 1966. Salisbury's articles appeared in the *New York Times* as his own personal observations made during a visit to North Vietnam; it later became known that they were based almost wholly on North Vietnamese propaganda pamphlets and on statistics provided by D.R.V. officials. His description, for example, of Nam Dinh as a cotton-and-silk town with no military objectives, when the city in fact contained POL [petroleum, oil, and lubricants] storage, a power plant, and a railroad yard, and was surrounded by antiaircraft and surface-to-air missiles, ensured that Salisbury received no Pulitzer Prize. But the articles and their implication, drawn chiefly from North Vietnamese falsehoods, that the United States was deliberately bombing civilian targets carried worldwide conviction. While only the first of many propaganda catastrophes of this kind, Salisbury's *New York Times* articles had a decisive effect throughout America in falsely persuading Americans that their government was engaged on a brutal and inhumane campaign.)

My traveler told me that there had been, as a result of the bombing, only one undamaged bridge between Hanoi and Than Hoa in the southeast of the D.R.V. All the others, including railway bridges, had been damaged or destroyed but subsequently repaired by teams on permanent standby using spare girders and adjustable parts stored in the vicinity. (Pontoon bridges, hidden during the day, had also been observed.) Nevertheless, the journey of 170 kilometers, which took place in the spring of 1967 at night, by lorries in convoy under dimmed lights from the western exit from Than Hoa to 50 kilometers east of Hanoi (when lights were switched on and speed increased), took only 5½ hours. The convoy extinguished all lights under air attack; on that occasion, which was no more than the dropping of a flare, the convoy had been badly bunched and was separated to secure distances by girl wardens apparently stationed in each area for the purpose. (The same journey in early April took seven hours.)

Between Phu Ly, a town along the main route to the south that had been largely evacuated in 1966 and later almost totally destroyed, and Than Hoa, he saw electric light on two occasions only. The first had been in one of the less-ruined streets of Than Hoa and the second in a badly damaged but just functioning power station near the Ham Rong Bridge. He saw no piped water supply in any town or village of the area. The center and the main streets of Than Hoa had been heavily damaged; shops open sold little more than oil, salt, cloth, and occasionally cigarettes. Brick buildings in the countryside, regarded by the North Vietnamese as automatic targets, were said to have been evacuated, with hospitals, schools, etc., now being housed in bamboo houses. Education continued, and medical care under primitive conditions (mud floors, no piped water or light, insufficient doctors) was fairly devoted and as efficient as the circumstances permitted. Casualties, particularly those caused by bomb casings, were said to be widespread among the peasantry and not easy to cure. Doctors were mainly "pharmacists," although there were a few good surgeons, frequently operating by flashlights. In and around all towns or villages attacked, the traveler observed Vietnamese antiaircraft guns of various calibers.

Bombing, other than along the railway line, where it appeared to be concentrated near halts, small stations, and their attendant hamlets, had sometimes seemed in this area to lack the precision shown against targets such as bridges and oil tanks elsewhere in the country. Villages, ostensibly no more than agricultural cooperatives, had been "wiped out" by 500-pound bombs, of which the craters were clearly visible; civilian casualties and damage to civilian housing in villages and towns seemed very high, again largely due to North Vietnamese AA defenses sited in built-up areas on their perimeters. . . .

On the morning of May 19, 1967, I visited my vice-consul, Geoffrey Livesey, in his quarters behind the consulate. Below the apartment lay a green courtyard planted with small trees and scrub vegetation; his servant's rooms with their louvered doors were below the balcony running around two sides of the square.

Geoffrey gave me a drink. The overhead fan in the living room turned briskly, rendering a little more tolerable the damp, heavy midday heat. The thought of another four months of that cruel summer was depressing. But Livesey was not only young and adventurous, he was also uncomplaining, and I had no wish to intrude less stoical concerns on his self-sufficiency. The air-raid sirens sounded, and we walked out onto the balcony.

As we stood there, seven or eight United States F-105 Thunderchief fighter-bombers, flying at scarcely more than roof-top height and no more, it seemed, than 100 yards away, shot across our vision at what appeared—so tight was the space in which the whole incident was framed between houses and sky—enormous speed. They had come on us suddenly out of nowhere, the hard, gray, sleek aircraft, in superb formation at approximately 600 mph, disappearing for an instant behind the trees and buildings that lay between us and the power station (thermal power plant) less than one mile to the south, and then quickly climbing clear and away. As they had hurtled past us, so close it seemed we could almost touch them or call to the pilots, we had seen the rockets fired from the pods under their wings. Almost simultaneously, such lights as were on in the apartment went out, the fan stopped turning, and a column of dust, smoke, and flame rose from the direction of the power station. (As the planes had penetrated the city's defenses by coming in under the radar screen, the first antiaircraft batteries opened up only when the raiders had not only departed but were probably 20 miles away.) As we were shortly to observe, the performance of this squadron disposed of every Communist or other illusion about the laxity of American bombing or the imprecision of U.S. bombing techniques.

The all-clear wailed; stillness descended. The apartment, without the touch of air from the revolving fan, was already crushingly hot.

Because we had no wish to be falsely accused of acting as spotters or observers for the U.S. Air Force, we did not usually go out of our way deliberately to inspect the results of air raids. But on this occasion, personal considerations demanded that we at least look at the target on the ground.

Antiaircraft guns, surrounded by their agitated crews, were sited among the rain trees in the park. There was an air of tense activity, almost hysteria; orders were bellowed in glottal tones. The men ran around their positions as if further attack were imminent. Fists were shaken at the sky; little groups of civilians whispered apprehensively together. The war was at last in the middle of Hanoi; the city, simmering in the heat, responded. The harsh determination on the faces of the gunners, the discipline and urgency gave an impression of devotion to country that was frightening in its implacability. It was also, because the air defenses had no chance at all against similar raids, pathetic and oddly moving. Perhaps neutral diplomats in London during the blitz also caught the mood of the defenders and, if only subconsciously and during the height of the battle, identified with guts and courage against the enemy. It was a strange, multiform, and disturbing moment.

The power station, an oblong gray brick or concrete building, was about 100-feet high with a ground plan of some 600 by 300 feet; it was topped by tall black chimneys and surrounded by terraced houses. The flames had died down by the time we approached it, but the dust still rose from fallen masonry. The building had been repeatedly struck by high explosives: the chimneys had collapsed, and the whole structure, gaping with holes caused by the rockets, seemed also to be listing drunkenly to one side. (We also viewed it from the other side, on our return home by the dyke road.) There was, in our opinion, no hope at all for it. The acccuracy of the attack had also been such that out of the complex of the 50 or so small private houses around the power plant, only three had been at all damaged, and those from blast rather than direct hits.

[The next day,] . . . the lights went on, the fans started to turn, and the rattle of the box air conditioner began. Across the street, the repair factory was once more brightly lit.

There was no more means then, than there is even today, of determining what had happened. The power station could have been less gravely damaged than we had supposed; mobile generators could have been brought into the area (for electric current was not restored to the entire city, only to our quarter and to a few governmental and other buildings); or another but more distant power station could have taken the load. The lesson, however, was of the astonishing preparedness and resourcefulness of the D.R.V.; only continual air attack of a kind that Rolling Thunder had not yet initiated would surmount those qualities.

But Rolling Thunder did, thereafter, or so it appeared to us, begin to do precisely that, although without again striking the power plants or other targets in central Hanoi. The objectives, attacked without respite for the next two weeks, remained on the periphery of the city. The noise of bombing and gunfire was almost continual, and the damage to Vietnamese equipment and weapons considerable; but by the time I left for London on consultations in early June, morale, health, and the flow of war materiel to Hanoi had not decisively diminished.[82]

1967 **17 June**—Secretary McNamara forms a *Pentagon Papers* task force to write a classified history of the Vietnam War. One member of this group is Daniel Ellsberg. **30 June**—As campaigning for the September South Vietnamese presidential elections becomes intense, Air Marshal Ky withdraws to become the vice-presidential candidate with Chief of State Thieu.

One of the new arrivals in July is a U.S. Marine Corps lieutenant, David Kramer, the protagonist of Robert Roth's novel Sand in the Wind.

Da Nang, July 1967
The two groups of men studied each other—one group in a fenced-off area, the other passing by it. Each face searched the faces of those in the other group, seeking clues to what they themselves had looked like thirteen months past or what they would look like thirteen months hence—one group uneasy and alert, just off a plane from Okinawa; the other group laughing, joking, confident, ready to board it after waiting since before dawn for four or five of the longest, happiest hours they had ever experienced, now seeing the plane that would take them home and at last sure of something so long in doubt—their own survival.

The newly debarked group, some of them still glancing backwards, was led to the rear of the nearest building. They milled around nervously while waiting for their seabags. Beyond the barbwire fence less than twenty yards away, they could see a vast, shimmering plain of rice paddies stretching to the dark mountains miles in the distance. Dikes of gray-brown mud cut the plain into thousands of perfect squares, each a different shade of green. Scattered and almost lost against this plain of rice paddies were the small dark forms of the peasants who worked them.

An asphalt walkway ran along the near side of the fence, and every few minutes a young Vietnamese girl or two would pass by. The soldiers' eyes would follow these delicately beautiful girls. Their loose fitting black or white slacks ruffled beneath the long, brightly colored silk dresses slit to the waist on both sides. Occasionally the girls would be carrying white parasols which accented the shiny black hair that fell gracefully down the hollows of their backs. Among the soldiers walked other, older, Vietnamese women in black slacks and dingy white blouses. Straw, cone-shaped hats blocked the sun from their lined faces. Many of them had crudely shaped cigars gripped between their yellow-stained teeth. These older women moved about with their heads down and their eyes scanning the ground for cigarette butts and pieces of paper to be swept into the dustpans they carried.

Occasionally a soldier would walk by holding a rifle balanced upside down on his shoulder, his hand on the front end of the barrel and a tag dangling from the stock. These weren't the M-14's or M-16's they had carried in the bush, but SKS's, formerly carried by Viet Cong or NVA soldiers. The newly arrived men stared at these rifles with envy, sometimes saying to themselves or to a friend, "When I leave Nam, I'll have one of them too."

A truck pulled up and the seabags in it were quickly tossed to the pavement. The men milled among them until, finding their own, they'd heave it on their shoulders and carry it towards the building. They would hesitate at the entrance until their eyes adjusted to the dim interior, then split up and join the appropriate lines to receive their orders. Rows of huge timbers supported the flat, corrugated roof and dwarfed the men standing near them. At one end of the building, a harsh artificial light glared down upon a few battered desks. A high counter separated this small area from the rest of the interior. Long lines of men stretched from the counter to the opposite end of the building. Other men sat or lay upon hard wooden benches. The atmosphere was similar to the gloom of a large, run-down train terminal.

In one of the shorter lines reserved for officers, there were only seven men. A major was talking to three of the others, all second lieutenants. This would be his second tour and he was enjoying the role of the old salt letting the boots know what they were in for. Behind these four, two more second lieutenants talked about a drunk they'd had in Okinawa. The last man in line, also a second lieutenant, faced away from the counter. His dark hair, though short, was cut somewhat longer than the "skin jobs" of the officers in front of him. He had the patient yet annoyed expression of someone accustomed, but never adjusted, to standing in line. A half-smoked cigarette hung insolently from the corner of his mouth. He removed it and turned towards the counter. The line slowly shortened as he studied the spit-shined boots of those ahead of him.

When he reached the counter, the clerk looked up with relief seeing that he was the last man to be processed. The lieutenant handed the clerk his orders.

"Lieutenant Kramer?"

"Yes."

"You'll be going to the Fifth Marine Regiment in An Hoa. Know anything about the Fifth?"

"No."

"The Arizona?"

Kramer shook his head.

"I wouldn't be in too much of a hurry to learn, sir. There'll be a truck by in about twenty minutes to take you to Ninth Motors. You'll be able to get a chopper from there. Wait right out front, somebody'll call your name."

Kramer nodded, lifted his seabag, and carried it to the entrance. Shading his eyes with his free hand, he looked for a place to set it down. The area was covered with prone bodies. Stepping over and between them, he made his way to an empty spot and jerked the seabag off his shoulder. He glanced at his watch, then stretched out on the ground using the bag as a pillow. After lying there a few minutes, he changed his mind and sat up, not wanting 'some lifer' to bother him about being unofficerlike. He glanced around with aloof curiosity, surprised at how calm and relieved he felt—glad to have all the training over with and not too concerned about what was to follow. What was there to be concerned about? Since his arrival everything he'd seen, every step he'd taken, had been expected, as if he'd done it a hundred times before. It was all a cliché. How simply he'd entered it, been caught within its slow momentum. Nothing remained but to follow it through—passively.[83]

In Laos, also in July, an event takes place that is typical of some of the situations faced by American advisers there. This letter is from Headquarters 7/13 Air Force, Udorn, Thailand, to Headquarters, U.S. Air Force, Washington.

27 July 67

Subject: Spirits

Among the normal T-28 logistics difficulties, a T-28 was recently declared NORS-G [Not Operationally Ready for Service—Grounded] by the Royal Lao Air Force for bad spirits. Lao pilots refused to fly the aircraft on combat missions. Clearance was obtained for a one-time flight to Udorn. Here, Buddhist monks were able to exorcise the bad spirits. The cost was $7.62 covering the cost of candles and herbs for the ceremony and Salem cigarettes, tooth paste, and soap for the monks. This was considered a small price to pay for continued utilization of a $181,000 aircraft.[84]

After four months in Vietnam, the main character in the novel Close Quarters, *APC driver Dosier, has become an experienced combat veteran. Here, he and his company go on patrol.*

We mount up out of Carolyne and take the battery of 105s with us. The Cow Catcher, Seven-three Delta, me; I pull the whole battery out of the mud. Five tubes and deuce-and-a-halfs and jeeps and lunch baskets and everything. Then Romeo drives the road. Morning here. Afternoon there. Night laager by the Suoi Dau cutoff. The next morning and afternoon and that night, same same. I don't touch ground for three days. Quinn and me stay fucked up.

I bust jungle out to Ap Six, another Chieu Hoi ville. When we break through the woodline the ten Deltas bring the tracks on line and we race the last five hundred meters over dry rice paddy. Some dinks take off for the woods to the left. Seven-seven and seven-eight peel off after them, firing over their heads, then lower. They drop four head of cattle and blow two papa-sans ass over teakettle with the fifties. We drive through truck gardens and in under the shade trees, among the cart trails and footpaths between hooches. I stop at the first hooch I come to with Quinn and the seven-four on my right flank. The others move on. There is an old mama-san sitting in the shade around the side, watching the peanut harvest dry. There's raw peanuts spread all over the back yard. I can see them through the doorways. Trobridge, whom Quinn has now nicknamed Dipstick, and the new gunners, Dewey and Walthers, jump down to check everything out. I shove the Cow Catcher into park, leaving it idle, and stand on the driver's seat with my shotgun Jesse James fashion—one foot on the chicken-wire grill, one hand on the trigger, a round in the chamber, the barrel resting over the other forearm—watching the flanks.

Dewey and Walthers came on the same plane from Cu Chi with Quinn. Dewey did not know, couldn't figure, had no idea what the shaving brushes were for. Stepik said that Dewey was what is known in the trade as a mark, but after a while he caught on. Walthers, a fuzzy-haired guy like Steichen, sat in awe of us for the first week, and it was too simple, too easy to kid him, because he believed every lie we could think up.

Dewey grabs the old woman by the back of her blouse.

"No VC!" she shouts, and shakes her gray-haired, wrinkled old head. "No VC. VC numba fucken ten. VC numba fucken ten *thou!*"

Trobridge looks down his ugly lumpy nose at her and says, "Shut yer yap, mama-san." Dewey holds her back while Dipstick and Walthers go through the hooch. Dipstick thrashes around, throwing dishes and saucepans and crockery out into the front yard, while Walthers and Dewey stand and watch. Trobridge and Walthers go out back. Dewey tells the woman to squat, which she does, and goes around the side to cover them. I can hear the muffled crunching of peanuts and more crockery, and then: "Aha!" Dipstick comes chugging around the side of the hooch, holding a crossbow-looking contraption over his head. There is a C-ration can nailed to the business end of it and a stiff wire bolt rigged with a trip wire. It's got to be a homemade mousetrap or something like that.

"Booby trap," says Trobridge. "It's a fucken booby trap! You *lie*, mama-san," he says, leaning down into her face. "You boo-coo VC." The woman squats beside him under the upheld mousetrap, trying to think of a way to explain it. Her lips and gums and teeth are stained red with betel nut.

Quinn and Steichen stand head and shoulders above the weeds and brush on the seven-four not twenty meters away. They stand on the deck, laughing and shaking their heads. "Go gettum, Dipstick!" they yell.

"She's gook!" says Trobridge. "She's gook! Dozer, call the El-tee an' tell 'im we got us a gen-you-wine VC gook!" He is so excited that he cannot restrain himself from jumping up and down, pointing at her broadly with the mousetrap.

"Romeo Six," I say into my CVC microphone, "Seven-three Delta here. Eagle-eye Seven-three says he gotta Victor Charlie, cross his heart and hope to die. Whadaya wanna do with 'er?"

"This is Six. Roger, what is your location?"

"Near as I can make it out, we are directly to your rear. Hang a one-eighty and ya can't miss," I say.

"Roger. Be there in zero five. Tell Seven-three to stand fast. Copy?"

"Roger dodger," I say. Then I turn to Trobridge. "El-tee says ta take a break in place," but it is too late. Dipstick has already torched the hooch and is dragging a flaming rag to the haystack. The woman screams and tries to run after him, but Dewey has her by the scruff of her blouse and keeps pulling her down to her heels. Six-niner, the El-tee's track, comes wide around the smoking hooch just as the thatch catches and a couple small-arms rounds cook off with a muffled pop. Everybody, including me, hunches and flinches for that instant, then looks over at Trobridge as much to say, "Well I'll be goddamned."

The El-tee announces over the radio that Seven-three has a VC hooch. Quinn swings the seven-four around to my rear, facing the rice paddies, and shuts down. Then he and Steichen and Whiskey j. and Dewey go around back. Quinn and Whiskey j. quickly frag the well; find a bomb-shelter entrance, frag it a couple times, and pull off a couple rounds into the opening. Then they move off into the bushes out of my line of sight. Trobridge stands at the side of the six-niner, showing the El-tee the mousetrap. The woman squats on her heels in the middle of the yard, watching after Quinn and the rest. "Fucken GI," she says, and slaps the ground disgustedly.

"Hey, mama-san," I shout.

She looks at me from under the brim of her cone hat. Everybody looks at me.

"You think that's fucked up?" With my gun I point to her hooch, smoking thickly and crackling. A pig squeals. A dog barks. Trobridge shouts nonsense at someone. There is a bull buffalo just to my left with his nose-ring thong tied to a palm tree with a simple slipknot. He has been following the Cow Catcher and Trobridge and the old woman out of the corners of his eyes. He looks over at the burning hooch, looks at the Cow Catcher, looks at the old woman and the six-niner behind her, and tugs at the slipknot, stretching his neck and flaring his nostrils.

"Mama-san, you *really* think that's fucked up?" I shout, and point to Dipstick and the hooch and haystack again. "Well, clap your slanted eyes on this." And I switch the shotgun off safe and take aim on the buff's head from the hip. I work the pump and squeeze off the rounds. Blam. Blam. Blam. Blam. Blam. Blam. I lean forward against each recoil, the slide of the shotgun slippery and sweaty and oily in my hand. The recoil nudges softly against my hip. The buff keeps rolling his eyes, stamping his hooves, and stretching and yanking against the nose-ring thong with flared nostrils and dug-in heels. It takes me six rounds of double-aught buckshot to bring him down. The first round catches him between the flat of his curved-back horns. He flinches and shakes his head and pins back his ears, and pulls back on the nose-ring thong. The second round hits the side of his chest. He flinches again, baring his teeth, and paws the ground, snapping up dirt in small hard chips. The third round hits him square in the snout. He staggers on his forelegs, stumbling, and slacks the thong. He shakes his head again, flinging dribbles of blood in an arc on the damp, packed earth. The woman screams and collapses on the ground, whining and thrashing her arms and pounding on the hard ground with the flat of her palms. I catch the buff again as his head is turned—right on the back of the neck. His flanks twitch. His eyes wide, showing the whites. His jaw slacks and he slobbers gobs of red and creamy foam. The next round catches him under the chin. It blows away the nose ring and thong and a hand-sized chunk of slack flesh and blackened teeth. He falls to his knees, bellows, and shakes his head more violently, which scatters more blood and scummy foam from his lips and the hole in his chin. The last round broadsides him across the face, blowing off the corners of his black bristled lips. He falls to his side, bleeding gushes from his neck and head and snout in front of the hooch, which is now flaming and falling into itself with glowing bits of thatch trailing off with the smoke.

There are other shots off in the distance: the short kakak kakak kakakak of an AK; the quick sharp report of a frag; the crisp, methodical three-round bursts of a semiautomatic M-16—Quinn. There are deep-throated baritone shouts and engine noises muffled in the woods and calls on the radio of more gooks. There is more shooting, fifties and pigs, and frags.

I stand in the driver's hatch amid the thickening hooch and hay smoke which fills the yard. The buff lies on his side heaving his chest and working his legs in fits. It snorts blood, flashing its tail wanly, breathing in hoarse, sucking gasps and sharply exhaled sighs. The woman still screams in the steep-slanted rays of smoky sunlight; crying hysterically, keening.

Terrified. Frightened to death we will kill her. The gunpowder smoke rises from the muzzle and open chamber in slow steady wisps. The woman lies on her back with her hands over her eyes, weeping and rocking, knees up. Troopers from the six-niner and other tracks take pictures of the hooch and buff and her, and rummage around the hooch going through her stuff to find something to take with them when we go—cheap hand scythes, bowls and cups, and pots and pans. I reload the tube and the chamber with rounds from the sack hanging on the infrared scope inside. Beside me the engine rumbles at idle.

And it all came on a whim. She was gook. The hooch was gook. The buff was a gook buff. But it always came with that hard-faced, uncaring, eye-aching whim; like hands squeezing down on hands, a sort of rock-scissors-paper trick. Slowly, slowly, so slow it is only glimpsed in time-lapse, those two or three scraps of good and real and soft things left of you are sucked down into a small hard pea. And the rest? Everything else brazes over and thickens and blackens—even the nap dreams. I hear them crunch when I punch them, like walking on a scallop-shell path.

I stand in the sunlit smoky shade with bits of straw ash floating down around me, the woman hysterical and whimpering and the buffalo dead still. And I smell the fear, as clearly as I can make out Quinn's booming, mumbled baritone voice, and it smells the same as rotted burning flesh.

We wind up the afternoon with three live ones, not counting mama-san. We torch all the hooches and hay mounds, frag the bomb shelters, kill and run off the livestock, capture, kill, fuck up everybody else we can find. Seven-seven and seven-eight stroll back from the woodline with two shot-up body count dragging on the ground behind them, tied at the ankles. We take the prisoners to Fire Base Georgianne and that night the ARVN MPs come out with the resupply to get them.[85]

1967   3 September—The Thieu/Ky slate wins 35 percent of the popular vote in South Vietnam and is declared elected.

Shortly after the elections, CIA agent Knox, the protagonist of James Trowbridge's novel Easy Victories, *arrives in Vietnam. He is met at the airport by a CIA employee known only as "B.D.," who drives Knox through Saigon.*

"What do you mean?" [Knox's] stomach went suddenly queasy as B.D. nudged up to an old Vietnamese on a bicycle and blew the horn. The Vietnamese veered away without looking back. A moment later he was riding only inches away from the car as they passed, his eyes fixed on something only he could see.

B.D. nudged the rear of a pedicab and blew the horn again, then swerved to the right and passed with a burst of speed slowing abruptly to avoid an ox cart filled with rough sawn lumber. . . . "In short, I mean they're bastards." He was still either picking his teeth or biting his fingernails.

"I thought we were out here to win the hearts and minds of these people."

"You can screw that. The only way to get through to the Viets is to get them by the balls. Then their hearts and minds got to follow."

Knox braced against the floorboard as an old Renault bumped out of a side alley and turned into the line of traffic. B.D. veered around it. A three-wheeled motorcycle with a metal basket in front and two Vietnamese girls in it passed them in a steady stream of blue exhaust. Knox's eyes smarted. "What kind of motorcycle is that?"

"It's a cyclo. Most people call them motorized junks. Only vehicle in the world uses the passenger as the bumper."

"They look dangerous."

"Everything's dangerous over here."

"You don't think we should be out here."

"I didn't say that. All I said was, 'Get them by the balls and their hearts gotta follow.' Hell's bells, man, you think these people are ready for democracy? Ask one of them. They can't even spell it. Things like democracy, liberty, all that pretty stuff in the speeches is so much crap to them. They can't think any further than the next bowl of rice."

"Why do you stay out here if that's the case?"

"The Agency pays me pretty well. Besides that, I've got a responsibility to myself to see this war through." B.D. laughed, and it was high, almost a giggle, not what you would expect from a man his size. "The fighter pilots and Special Forces types say this is our only war and we've got to nurse it along; maybe I stay just to see pricks like them get their noses out of joint."

They were past all the checkpoints now. They rattled over a connecting road in the process of being paved, though great potholes stood out in the gravel, and they had to slow down for one especially large hole puddled with rainwater. They were through an intersection then, by a large hospital painted white with symmetrical crosses in red on the roof. They traveled along a fairly broad street lined on both sides with villas behind high walls and new hotels and the skeletons of other buildings standing in rickety scaffolding. "This is Cach Mang," B.D. said. "It becomes something else up ahead. At a bridge. That's where Saigon really begins."

"Do you think we're winning the war? No one back in the States seems to know. Some team comes out here and makes a report that everything is rosy. McNamara says the war will be won in another year. Then you catch the evening news."

"We're bombing the hell out of the North."

"Then you think we'll get the North Vietnamese to the conference table?"

"Shit no. All we'll do with the bombing is get us to the conference table. If that happens we'll probably lose the war no matter what anybody in Washington says. And we won't be defeated by Ho chi Minh or Nguyen vo Giap; we'll be beaten by CBS and the *New York Times*."

"You sound like the war's getting you down."

"Sometimes it gets to you when you see a lot of people getting rich off the black market. If I had a mind to I could make a couple of thousand in the black market every month, real easy."

The station wagon rattled over a rough stretch where the street had been dug up to lay a new water pipe. "I thought that sort of thing went on only between the Asiatics, you know, stealing stuff from the ports."

"That goes on all the time. It's small potatoes. Every now and then Ky gets some pressure put on him when a big congressional junket comes through in a day. Ky sends around some trucks to load up all the stuff they can find on the streets. 'Course, everybody's had plenty of time to move things and they're back on the street two days later. All the congressmen who've come out have been pricks. You know, get their pictures in the paper wearing jungle fatigues and inspecting some pig farm or new well. Stay in the Caravelle every night, then leave. Anyway, the big money is in currency manipulation. You can get as high as one hundred fifty to one, sometimes even one hundred seventy to one hundred dred MPC for US green. Then you convert the MPC back to green and start all over again."

"What's MPC?"

"Christ, man, didn't you change your money to scrip at the airport?"

"Was I supposed to? And what's scrip?"

"MPC. Scrip. Same difference. Everybody over here gets paid in military pay certificates. MPC. You have to change your US dollars into MPC when you arrive, and you can't deal with the Vietnamese in anything but piastres." B.D. struck a match to a cigarette and sucked in the smoke. "No sweat, you can change your green at the office. Wait till you get a look at it. The ten-buck MPC has a woman on the back that looks exactly like Jackie Kennedy. Christ help me."

He laughed, a high, almost obscene laugh, showing gross uneven teeth stained brown from cigarette smoke. Smoking too much, perspiring too easily, dressing badly, always tearing something, drinking only beer and swilling that; but very sensitive, dedicated, though trying not to show it, and extremely competent. He would be assigned to help Knox learn the trade, though neither knew it just then, and had either of them known he would not have been particularly pleased. For B.D. was certain in his assumption that man would be destroyed by the gods, or lack of them— whatever—it really made no difference to him, but he still retained his dignity as a man, a human entity, and that was the one, the sole and only material mortal treasure not hostage to fortune.

Later, Knox receives his first briefing by his superior, Mr. Balfour.

"Just remember there're no James Bonds in this kind of business. No pretty spies trying to get into your pants. No roll-over cameras, no one-time pads, no miniature radio transmitters, no fast cars. Just plain old-fashioned vetting and writing it up by the book, lots of IIRs to write, God yes, lots of those—"

"What's an IIR?"

Mister Balfour put down his Coke glass and looked reflectively at Knox. "You don't know what an IIR is? Just what *did* they teach you at school about report writing?"

"Well, they showed us how to make an EEI but no one said anything about an IIR."

Mister Balfour sighed. "Trust the school to be two years behind the times. An IIR is the same thing an EEI used to be."

"Back at the school they're still calling them EEIs."

"Khristonacrutch, man, get it through your skull that you can't go by anything that fuckin' school taught. This is the real thing out here, no old fairies prancing around telling you how they did it when Donovan had all those wild-ass schemes to liberate the French and arm them with sling-shots made from old condoms. The real world's out there and it's got you by the scroats unless you bugger it first."

"Yessir."

Mister Balfour finished the Coke in the glass and poured more from the can, being careful this time to stop before it foamed over. "Anyway, there'll be lots of IIRs to write and everybody from the Ambassador on down wants a good job. That's his policy, and it goes without saying that because it's his policy it's also my policy. You've got to always keep in mind that these reports go to MACV as well as our own internal distribution, the Ambassador's staff, that new DIA thing McNamara started and of course State. So they've got to look professional. You'd be surprised how many times some general at MACV or an area specialist in Foggy Bottom distrusts a report because it isn't neat enough, professional-looking enough."

"Aren't the other intelligence services getting distribution, too?"

"Yes, oh hell yes. And they're sending us data, some of it's good stuff. I'm not knocking them, but we're the ones with the reputation to keep up. And naturally we don't want the other shops to swing onto some intelligence which they can use to upstage us. So if you get some really good information let us know about it here and don't put it out to the Army or Air Force types until we've had a chance to pass on it."

The air conditioner was slipping cool air almost unnoticed into the room. Knox felt suddenly cold, then hot again. He sneezed.

"Bless you," Mister Balfour said. "You'd better get cleaned up. Take a couple of aspirin as well. A lot of our people coming over get colds their first week here. Keep them for a long time, too. Something about the change of climate and doing it so quickly. Just don't get too hot or too cold too quickly. I like my people to stay healthy." Mister Balfour got up from behind his cluttered desk and for the first time offered his hand. Knox stood and took it. The clasp was limp and somewhat sweaty despite the cool air. He could see that Mister Balfour was not wearing an undershirt.

"I'd like to know some more about this Operation Phoenix thing."

"Later, later. One of the section chiefs runs it as his personal baby, more or less. I don't know a great deal about it myself. Remember, we're just seeing if it's going to fly. My job is to stay on top of the overall big picture. B.D. will take you around to the right people."[86]

In mid-September, enlisted marine Chester McMullen writes a letter from his new assignment.

Sept. 15, 1967
PhuBai, RVN

Whatever later developments may provide, let it be said at the outset here, I really like it. No fooling, this is it, maybe, for which I have been looking.

I am here in Phu Bai, having flown this morning by C-119 from DaNang. This is where I will mostly be. Phu Bai, you will notice on your map, is some distance north of DaNang, approximately 13 miles south of the city of Hue and about 40 miles south of the DMZ. Arriving here, I was offered several types of jobs, including an almost identical clerical position as the one in Beaufort. The most appealing seemed a chance to work in the Group Legal section. I was interviewed by the legal NCOIC and Legal Officer, and later was told I was hired. Good. I look forward to that, as it should be more interesting than the usual admin. stuff I'm used to. I have been briefed very little on what I'll be doing, so will report on that in a while when I'm better versed myself. They work a 10–12 hour day, seven days a week here. There is not much else to do but work.

Combat responsibilities, such as patrols and perimeter defense, are normally on a rotating duty basis. The abnormality enters if we are hit here. This hasn't happened since Sept. 1 and that was mainly pre-election harassment, but they are pretty edgy yet. There were 4 killed and 54 wounded in that attack, mostly mortars in the living area.

The living area: We are in the process of converting from tents to makeshift plywood huts, known as hutches. Lumber and plywood are scrounged, as is aluminum and our nails, etc. I live in a nearly completed hutch. Since the last attack, everyone has been busy digging bunkers. This is not easy, owing to the rain—which will get worse. The bunker committee of my hutch (pronounced hootch) showed me the grand design for our bunker. We will be very safe inside, when completed, if waist-deep in mud.

Most interesting about my job: here is also the legal branch for Dong

Ha. Dong Ha, as you can see on your map, is about 6 mi. south of the DMZ. Con Thien is the only thing we've got further north. Things at Dong Ha are pretty bad. They get hit daily and live mostly underground there now. Our legal office sends someone there a few days a week. As the office consists of only the Legal Officer, the NCOIC (a sergeant) and myself and another PFC, I should get to go to Dong Ha quite a bit. And that should be interesting. Some of the older hutches are rather elaborate inside. They have gotten hold of enough materials to make them thoroughly waterproof, partition off the areas around the cots, giving some privacy, added shelves and planked off the rafters to make a storage attic. We plan to improve our hutch as soon as the bunker is completed. The' hutch next door has had to abandon their bunker. They have an 8 foot deep lake. We will hurry to finish ours ere the rains really come.

Among the items in my 80lb. issue of combat gear yesterday is an M-14 rifle with 100 rds. of ammunition. Despite all my efforts to sell myself on the M-16, I feel much more comfortable with this M-14. There are all kinds of noises here. Especially during dark. Explosions, artillery, mortars, rifle fire on the perimeter. They say there is nothing to worry about as long as you can hear it. I go around with one eye on the nearest dive-pit and one ear waiting for the alert siren—meaning "incoming." Incoming rockets, mortar or artillery rounds.

Although we have an almost dry place to sleep, and cold water and gravity operated showers and good chow and the place is comfortable and cozy, there are lots of nice things that just aren't here. People have already been advising me of things to send home for to make my little stay more pleasant. People also say—ho, ho—he says he likes it here— ho, ho, ho. You wait, they say, and they are probably right. When the rains come, they say, you will not be dry or sleep dry or wear dry clothes or see anything dry for 6 months. Every place is already ankle deep in mud at least. It must really be something when the rains come.

There are some niceties which can be bought from the gooks. This morning, I bought a small, sturdy wooden chest-foot locker, which I hope will help in the fight to keep things dry. Very clever. It is made from a discarded 105 recoilless rifle shell box. Also I bought a small bowl for shaving and a mirror to nail to the wall, also for shaving. These cost, respectively, 450 piasters and 80 piasters—about $4.80 all together. $5 = 590 piasters. We exchanged our currency for Military Pay Certificates (Govt. script bearing pictures of pretty girls and monetary denomination) and piasters. MPC are for use on base—piasters for dealing with the Vietnamese. No American money is allowed.[87]

At the same time, CIA agent Knox also finds a place to live. He has met a Vietnamese girl, Rosette.

Rosette found him a house on Tran cao Van Street, not very far from the site on Thong Nhut where the new American Embassy was being built. It was a small villa which had once been servants' quarters behind the larger house of the owner. It was similar to B.D.'s except that it was not enclosed within the main courtyard but was outside, and was reached by going down a narrow alley between high walls which opened into its own small courtyard. It was also reached by a gate cut in the wall if Knox did not use the alley. Sometimes the owner parked his old black Renault in the alleyway, and unless it was parked very close against one wall Knox had to go through the main courtyard and the gate. But he did not mind, for the car effectively blocked the alley and made a good grenade screen.

He paid a good price for it, even signing a lease for a lower price than he was really paying, the owner looking at him slyly as he signed the faint blue graph paper. He did not even ask Rosette how she had found it, for already he knew that she had her ways. He paid twenty-five thousand piastres a month instead of the fourteen thousand the lease specified, and the landlord said he would install an air conditioner. And when it was installed the USAID shield with the brown and white hands clasping had been painted over, though Knox could still see the outline of the shield dimly through the hastily applied paint.

There was an aquarium in the living room, something stored there by the owner. A two-hundred-liter glass-sided tank with the caulked seams dry but still serviceable. Rosette brought him some fish. They were small and delicate, with long, lacy fans for tails and sleek torpedo shapes, graceful in every movement. He was to spoil all that when he unknowingly put in a Siamese fighting fish he brought home in a glass fruit jar from the fish market. That was all to come later, after he had discovered the tropical fish market and the bull-necked fighting fish with the iridescent colors and ethereal fins and the little boys who sold fish from plastic bags held hooplike on concentric rings of wire growing like a Christmas tree from the fender of a bicycle's rear wheel. But he did not discover the savage viciousness of the fighting fish until afterward, and then of course it was too late. All he had left was the one fighting fish until Rosette brought him some more fish and changed the water; and, when he was not looking, threw the fighting fish into the yard to let it die.

Knox had three rooms, a large living room with the usual cheap plastic sofa and a table with chairs already warp-legged past all hope of ever sitting evenly, a screen that hid the rusty refrigerator and the alcove which served as a kitchen with the two-burner gas stove he would hardly ever use and one small iron skillet. Two more rooms, one for a bedroom with a sparse wooden frame for the bed and foam rubber for a mattress; the other he would never use except for the people he would meet who would stay there because it had a bed and a toilet, too, even though the chain on the water closet had rusted through and been repaired with a length of plastic piping.

Knox was the prince and possessor of this empire, to include the portable Sanyo radio and the aquarium, for as long as he paid the rent of twenty-five thousand piastres a month, or, in terms he could more easily grasp, $213 at the official rate.

He lived there and liked it after a fashion, because he had to share it with no one, except Rosette, unless he wanted to; and no one from the office ever came to know where he actually lived, even though he conscientiously entered the address in the duty agent log. He did not have a telephone. Telephones were luxuries you learned to live without, and that was just as well considering the phone system. He did have the uncomfortable feeling that B.D. knew where he lived and what he was doing.

The office was close enough to walk to, but he tried to be mysterious. Knox left and returned at odd hours, and went by various routes. Sometimes he would go around by the Basilica or the back streets by the Botanical Gardens. There he would see urchins on rooftops flying small kites made from newspaper with long fierce tails, held captive against the incessant lure of the wind by incredibly long thin threads wound around San Miguel beer bottles.

And Rosette would be there. Only infrequently at first, then more often, and discreetly, for he had a cleaning woman who came every morning except Sundays for one thousand piastres a month and did a reasonably good job of keeping the villa clean. To avoid the talk he thought would follow disclosure he kept Rosette hidden, apart in her own separate cubicle of the life he was neatly ordering. Making for himself a secure little island in the midst of time.[88]

Despite the growing numbers of American troops, one of the major American programs is the training of the Republic of South Vietnam's Armed Forces (RVNAF). Attempts are constantly being made in Saigon and Washington to quantify the results. The Pentagon Papers *notes:*

At the Pentagon, Systems Analysis sought measures of RVNAF effectiveness in a comparison between the performances of Vietnamese and American units in selected categories: VC/NVA KIA ratios, battalion days of operations, days of enemy contact, number of operations, weapons loss of ratios, etc. Summarizing the results of some of these statistical studies, Systems Analysis stated in September 1967:

> Per man, Vietnamese forces were about half as effective as U.S. forces in killing VC/NVA during the eleven months (Aug 66 through Jun 67) for which detailed data are available. Effectiveness differs widely among Vietnamese units of the same type and between units in differing parts of the country. Poor leadership is the key reason for inefficiency in most cases.

The MACV staff rebutted many of the premises on which the statistical comparisons had been based and again revealed the difficulty in developing meaningful statistical measures with respect to anything Vietnamese. Their most telling criticism of the Systems Analysis comparison of U.S. and Vietnamese units was the following:

(a) It is generally accepted that US maneuver battalions have a combat effectiveness ratio of about 3:1 to RVNAF maneuver battalions due to their greater unit firepower and depth of combat support/combat service support forces; RVNAF also lacks the mobility assets available to US units.

(b) Approximately one-third of the RVNAF maneuver battalions are committed to direct support of Revolutionary Development, a mission which constrains the overall potential to find, fix, and fight the enemy forces. In this analysis an RVNAF unit that is 45 percent as effective as US units which have three times the RVNAF combat effectiveness would appear to be doing very well. In fact, anything over 33 percent would reflect superior performance.

But here again one can be misled. One reason that ARVN was given the RD [Revolutionary Development] support mission in the first place was its demonstrated inability to engage effectively and destroy the enemy main force. RD was regarded as a residual and semi-passive role more suited to ARVN capabilities. And so the statistical arguments raged, partisans marshalling whatever statistics they could to defend what in most cases were their own preconceived notions.

All of this is not to imply that qualitative estimates, diagnoses, pre-scriptions, and prognosis were lacking in 1967. At the Guam Conference with the President, General Abrams' appointment as the new Deputy COMUSMACV had been announced along with the others already mentioned and his responsibility for overseeing the U.S. advisory effort with RVNAF reemphasized. Upon return to Saigon prior to his own departure Lodge [had] sent a message to the President stressing the importance of RVNAF:

> MACV's success (which means the success of the United States and of all of us) will . . . willy-nilly, be judged not so much on the brilliant perfor-mance of the U.S. troops as on its success in getting ARVN, RF and PF quickly to function as a first-class counter terror, counter-guerrilla force.

Lodge concluded with a glowing endorsement of Abrams as the man to see that RVNAF did become an effective force. There is ample evidence that Abrams did work with great energy to do just that.[89]

Another analysis of U.S. effectiveness in North Vietnam is quite different, as expressed by British Consul-General Colvin.

Rolling Thunder was not pursued during the early part of my 10-day absence but began again toward the end of my stay in England. Rumors in Saigon, when I passed through on my way back north, spoke of a projected American strategy to bomb the North Vietnamese dykes on a massive scale. Certainly, millions of deaths had been caused under the French regime and untold agricultural and other damage by a natural flooding of the Red River; to breach the dykes artificially would bring the same result, putting even Hanoi under water to a depth of at least 11 feet. I do not believe that this option was ever seriously considered at the highest levels in Washington. Anyway, the policy was never executed, and the rumors may have been no more than deception, as a further means of pressure on the D.R.V. authorities. This did not deter the D.R.V. from announcing almost every day on Hanoi radio (VNA) or in *Nanh Dan*, the party daily, that the USAF was carrying out such attacks; although these statements were quite untrue, many of the missions bought collapsible boats against the perceived likelihood of major flooding. I was discouraged by my government from either buying a boat or commissioning the construction of an air-raid shelter under the consulate. Both actions, it was thought, might have been seen by the North Vietnamese as an act of collusion by America's supposed ally at Hanoi with presumed aggressive planning by the United States against the D.R.V. The argument, it is worth recalling today, seemed sensible at the time.

In the fall of 1966 or the winter of 1966–1967, a delegation from the Czechoslovak government had arrived in Hanoi to advise the North Vietnamese on the modalities of carrying the propaganda war to the continental United States. The flow to Hanoi of grisly "Western" journalists, television "personalities," disaffected minority groups, "tribunals," "parliamentary" commissions, "concerned" writers, "independent" or "international" jurists, doctors, trade unionists, and other riff-raff, most of whose expenses were paid by the D.R.V. government, began and hardly ever stopped. The tide of hatred for America, pulled by falsehoods of Marxist, neo-Marxist, or Trotskyist professional manufacture, started thereafter to infiltrate the American media and eventually the "intellectual" establishment. By the summer of 1967 it was clear, even to an isolated diplomatic mission in Hanoi, that the American effort to prevent a totalitarian regime from obliterating a free country was being resisted by the totalitarians as much—and with the connivance of their supposed opponents—in America as in Vietnam. (One publication, incidentally, described me as "the lanky British ambassador [*sic*], a veteran of 22 [*sic*] years in Indochina, who stalked the Hotel Metropole in white colonialist linen suit.") The picture presented, of undersized and "freedom-loving" northern democrats bravely struggling against a brutal aggressor, was not one recognizable in either Saigon or Hanoi; in the south, aggression, atrocity, and repression seemed, rather, the D.R.V.'s characteristics, and in the north, regimentaion and the absence of political liberty. But neither the extermination by the People's Army of Vietnam of entire southern communities nor the massacres in the north during land reform distracted American intellectuals from the prospect of humiliating, if not butchering, their own country. . . .

By September . . . [in Hanoi] evidence of malnutrition was now clear, and among adults as well as children. Food, other than that little provided by collectivized agriculture and private plots in the D.R.V., was not coming in from China, North Vietnam's main source of supply. American bombing of the entry points into Vietnam from that country, as well as Sino-Soviet differences, had had their substantive effects. In the streets, offices, and factories, the population could barely get about their duties; even the residence staff, better fed than the rest of their compatriots, dragged themselves 'round the house. The hospitals were filled with cases of hunger edema as well as of wounds. (Bombing of the power lines of Hanoi at that time brought another danger, fortunately of short duration, that of failure of the electric water pumps; for three days there was no water supply throughout the district. Mass epidemic, in the already unsanitary conditions of the capital, could not have been far away.) The symptoms of disease noted in late July had begun to spread. The economy was at last breaking down. The country and its people were close to a collapse which, for the first time, no amount of excited exhortation could correct.

And every morning since I reached Hanoi, the streets of the quarter had been lined with war materiel brought in overnight from China across the Paul Daumer Bridge, amphibious vehicles, artillery, armored fighting vehicles, Sergeant surface-to-air missiles on flatbeds, saucily parked even outside the British and Canadian missions. By the time that I returned from London in June, their numbers had somewhat decreased. By August and September there were none at all. . . . the trains were coming no longer.

So that in the last few months I had come to believe that the country's endurance had reached its limits. If the appearance of the leaders at the recent National Day celebrations had been any indication, it might have been thought that they too might be coming to recognize this, in spite of the loss of political investment that negotiations might represent. But the tone and substance of some remarks by Pham Van Dong on September 3, on the other hand, were harder and less flexible than ever. And I had, until recently, to repeat my consistent impression that there was still almost nothing that the people could not be asked to do and almost no lengths to which they could not be persuaded to go, even if on their hands and knees; it was as difficult, I knew, to convey this mental climate as it was depressing to live in it. I had believed, until August, that the D.R.V. regime would pursue the conflict even if they had, like Samson, to pull the pillars down on themselves and on all of us. . . .

The D.R.V. in late September, when I left that unhappy country for England, was no longer capable of maintaining itself as an economic unit nor of mounting aggressive war against its neighbor. . . .

The strength of the American bombing campaign of summer 1967 had rested not only on its weight but on its consistency, hour after hour, day after day. The strategy, as well as damaging or destroying—in ports, on railway lines, and on storage areas—the capacity of the D.R.V. to feed itself and to maintain invasion, had also, for the first time, allowed the North Vietnamese no time to repair war-making facilities. No sooner

were they repaired than they were struck again; Tonkinese ingenuity had
been defeated and, by the remorseless persistence of the campaign, their
will eroded to near-extinction.

But although some spasmodic bombing in the northeast quadrant took
place after September, it was on a greatly reduced scale and frequently
interrupted by long periods of inactivity during "peace initiatives," all
illusory if not contrived, and anyway occasions when the campaign should
have maintained, even increased, momentum. Above all, that factor—the
persistence of the campaign—which had sapped North Vietnamese endurance was discarded. . . . Victory—by September 1967 in American hands—
was not so much thrown away as shunned with prim, averted eyes.[90]

As seen in John Cassidy's novel A Station in the Delta, *CIA agent Toby
Busch arrives at his new duty station in the southern part of the country.
The man who meets him asks how Toby got his CORDS job as pacifica-
tion (P) officer.*

"All the section heads at the station there were lined up to interview me,
and they all said how good a job they knew I could do in their sections,
but I had a good look at that station, and I said to myself, My God, this is
just like a headquarters in the field, and I can do without headquarters
duty. So, when they said My Tho needed a P officer, I said: 'I accept!
Where's My Tho and what's a P officer!' "

Ben laughed delightedly.

"And here I am," Toby concluded, with an expansive sweep of his
hand.

"My new boss."

Toby looked at him quickly, but saw that Ben had made the remark
with a matter-of-fact good humor. Toby began to relax in the presence of
his new associate.

He looked around at the countryside as they bounced down the road. It
was flat delta land, with rice paddies, an occasional clump of trees, small
thatched dwellings. A little child was sitting on a water buffalo off to their
left, and brought him a flashback of a picture he had seen in his sixth-
grade geography book. Cochin China.

"So, how are things in Can Tho?" Ben asked.

"Well, I guess they're all right, but I don't know what standard to use.
I've never been there before. In fact, I've never been on this side of the
Pacific before."

"You're a clean slate."

"Right."

"That can be an advantage."

"I suppose so."

"How do the people in Can Tho think we're doing out here in the
provinces?"

"You mean in the pacification program and things like that?"

"Yeah."

"They seem to be fairly optimistic. Not too good, but not too bad."

Ben nodded thoughtfully. "And what do they think in Saigon?"

"The Saigon people seem to think we've got the VC on the run out in the provinces."

"That figures. Saigon says we're winning, Regional Offices in Can Tho say we're doing fairly well. The picture seems to be colored by the distance."

"And what does the Provincial Pacification Officer from My Tho say?" asked Toby.

"I say we're gettin' our butt waxed."

"The hell you say."

"They're just kickin' the shit out of us here. And not only here, but all over the delta. I can't speak with any authority about the other regions, but the delta, Region Four, is in trouble. Ski is the only guy in the region that isn't as uneasy as hell, and that's because he's got almost no VC up there. Hell, Kien Tuong Province doesn't have much of *anything!*"

"Have all of you been reporting these things to Saigon and Can Tho?"

"They've got the same facts we have. They just interpret them differently."

"It doesn't seem possible that people would put such different interpretations on the same set of facts."

"They look at the statistics. They're at a distance. Statistics is a poor way to estimate your position in unconventional warfare. The closer you get to the action, the less the statistics mean to you."

"Well, they get action in Saigon too, don't they?"

"Oh, sure. They get grenades and bombs and things like that. But there's no doubt about who controls Saigon. And Can Tho, too. Can Tho gets mortared now and then, but they've got the Ninth ARVN close by. But we're out here trying to reclaim towns and hamlets from the VC. The statistics say we're doing it, but a ride around the countryside says like *hell* we are!"

"I've got my work cut out for me, then. We've got to get good intelligence in to Can Tho and Saigon."

"Right."

The countryside certainly didn't look like a battlefield. He saw a man and a woman squatting at work in a large vegetable garden. It was a big enough plot to be a supplier for a town market. The conical straw hats hid the laborers' faces, and gave them the appearance of motionless symbols of the peace that seemed to pervade the land. From the air he had seen the lines of craters made by the B-52 bombs, but from ground level among the rice paddies and vegetable gardens he saw none of the ravages of war. Saigon had seemed to be laced together with barbed wire, and Can Tho looked nearly as besieged as Saigon, but here, where the action was, there seemed to be no trace of it, no fear of it, and no preparations for it.[91]

On 8 October PFC McMullen writes another letter home.

Oct. 8, 1967
Phu Bai
This is too much! Rich has kept from my eyes the October issue of
Playboy. There are none at all in Phu Bai. Some copies, the first copies
of the September *Playboy,* arrived only a short time ago. I had bought
this in early August in Los Satanos. Everyone here waits for the October
Playboy like the desert waits for rain, like bean sprouts wait for spring,
like kids wait for Christmas. Like the Second Coming, New Year's Eve
and the end of the war all falling on the same day, we await the October
Playboy. We would rather see the 3rd MarDiv PX (the only store in this
neck of the woods) stock the October *Playboy* than we would see them
get in some soap and toothpaste. We would give blood and bones for a
glimpse at the advertisement on the back cover of the October *Playboy.*
We would walk unarmed and with a target strapped to our back from
here to Hanoi to talk to someone who has met someone who has seen
someone who was near a copy of the October *Playboy.* And Rich has
prevented the October *Playboy itself* from coming to us! Prevented, in his
bland assumption that Phu Bai has everything that everywhere else has,
an honest to God, real life copy of the October *PLAYBOY ITSELF* from
coming here. I feel no mercy towards him. My men were angry, very
angry. They wanted to go at once and bring him here to stand before a
tribunal of Phu Bai marines and explain himself before they dismembered
him. But I was kind and said they could only shoot him. And so now they
wing their way to Gainesville, Rich's doom secure in the bulge of their
shoulder holsters. He never should have done it.[92]

1967   21 October—In Washington, 50,000 protestors march on the
             Pentagon.

---

*In Vietnam, Private First Class Henry Winsted, a character in William
Pelfrey's novel* The Big V, *prepares for his first combat mission.*

It was still dark at the reveille formation. Beating helicopters used the
strobe lights under their noses to come down behind us. The first sergeant
had to raise his voice. After the formation I went to chow alone; Kell
went back to the barracks to sleep.

I woke him at seven-thirty and we went to the arms room together. I
drew my M-16 and three bandoliers; he had a grenade launcher and nylon
vest with pockets for the rounds. He had taped his name to the fiberglass
stock, "Sergeant T. E. Kell." Spelled the word *sergeant.*

I also drew two frag grenades and two yellow smoke grenades. Kell helped me strap them to the pistol belt properly so the pins couldn't get snagged on a bush and detonate—he said that had happened to a guy in Delta company last month, brought the max on his young ass. He also helped me adjust the straps of the ruck frame so it would ride as high as possible on my back. If I didn't do that, the radio would kick my ass bigger than shit. It probably would anyway, humping off Jude, but you try to make it as easy as you can. I put three magazines in each pouch on the pistol belt. I tied the other two bandoliers across my chest Pancho Villa-style. Wore the steel pot low on my skull, weighted pistol belt tight and low on my hips. Combat ready. Tiger.

I really *did* feel combat ready. Real frags, live rounds all over your body, rifle. Tiger, Airborne all the way. Fuck me. I don't know.

Kell had drawn big sergeant stripes on the camouflage cover of his helmet, in red ink. Stock of the M-79 tucked into his armpit like a hunter with a shotgun, short barrel broken open. He grabbed his faded ruck sack and we were off. The leather fronts of his jungle boots were scuffed white. I felt embarrassed, walking behind him, new cruit written all over me.

A deuce-and-a-half was waiting beside the orderly room. C-rations and crates of red hand-flares were stacked level with the railings, just enough room between the tailgate for us to stretch out on the floor facing each other. At least I could roll over the tailgate quickly if we were hit.

Welch came out of the orderly room with the slate, to check us off. "All set, Winsted?"

I nodded. The barrel of my rifle rested against my shoulder.

"Be more comfortable if you take that damned ruck sack off and sit on the fucker."

I looked at him.

"What's it like to be a goddamned commando, Welch?" Kell asked.

"Sucks ass, Sergeant Kell."

Sergeant Kell. Welch had E-5 stripes himself. I looked at Kell, noting that he was sitting on the ruck. But I would wait until Welch left to take mine off.

The driver came out wearing a flak jacket; another guy with flak jacket and a sixteen got in the cab with him.

"Take it easy, sarge," Welch yelled.

There was an oriental arch over the road as you left the battalion area, "Good luck, Regulars."

The truck jerked going through the gears; I slipped the ruck off and pushed it under me without getting up. The division LRRPs—long-range recon patrol, pronounced "lerps," the elite—were strutting towards the PX in tailored camouflage fatigues and cowboy jungle hats as we rolled toward the gates. Bright infantry-blue hat bands.

The MPs were frisking the gooks, feeling their bodies just like a police-man in a movie, before letting them in. They were mostly young girls and old men, used as KPs, waitresses, and PX cashiers. All had yellow plastic-covered ID cards pinned to their shirts and blouses. They wore the wide straw hats you see in postcards and movies; I remember being struck that they really did.

A PFC MP with a slate came to our truck and glanced over the tailgate. "No flak jackets?"

"Didn't give us any," said Kell.

"Fuck it." He checked his slate and yelled at the driver to go.

We were out of Camp Enari. Alone. Thick brush and trees on both sides of the frayed ribbon asphalt.

"I thought we were gonna convoy," I yelled to Kell.

"We're just on our way to the convoy point. Don't worry, it'll be a convoy. Probably five miles long. Nobody goes on Highway Fourteen without a convoy."

Fuck me. Highway Fourteen. I had heard of it on television and at Fort Polk.

We reached the dirt field in five minutes and stayed there for two hours before all the vehicles were assembled and the gunship escort arrived. There was a hill with an artillery battery across from the field. First time they fired I quivered. The buck sergeant laughed.

"That was eight-inch. They bring the max, shoot twenty-three miles. I think Fi Bait called in eight-inch at Dak To."

Before our truck had come to a full stop the gooks were all over us. Mostly old men and kids.

"You buy watch . . ."

"You buy girlie pictah . . ."

"Shoe shine, numah fuckin one . . ."

Pastel silk blouses on the girls, bare feet in rubber shower thongs. Giggling and nodding their heads as they spoke. Shining black hair falling down their backs.

A kid climbed the tailgate with a shoe shine box and Kell knocked him off with the barrel of his M-79.

"Hoa, numah fuckin ten!" the kid yelled. "Cheap Charlie."

He gave Kell the finger and spat in the yellow dirt. Kell pulled an HE round from his vest and threw it at him.

"Hit the road, little fucker."

It hit him on the heel, the kid screamed but looked down and quickly picked up the M-79 round. He held it up to Kell and smiled at him before putting it in the shoe shine box, then took off running and disappeared in the crowd.

"Don't let 'em sell you nothing, Henry. If you do they'll be two hundred of 'em all over the truck 'fore you know it."

Another shoe shine climbed in on my side and started shining my boot.

"Me numah one shine, Joe. Numah fuckin one."

"No want shine," I said.

He kept working. A girl saw him and ran up to the tailgate. Not over twelve or thirteen years old, the black hair shimmering to her waist. "You want buy pictah, Joe?" Smiling, white teeth and soft child's voice.

She pulled an album from the top of her blouse and opened it, leaning over the tailgate for balance.

"See."

The first picture was a GI getting a blow job from a gook girl.

"No, me no want pictah."

Kell laughed.

An old man appeared on top of the C-rations with an arm of watches, another kid climbed up with a knife.

"Me no want. Me no want," I kept saying.

Kell just shook his head. "I told you."

I started screaming, "Me no want!"

But they kept hovering, the old man with a Hollywood Ho Chi Minh beard and stub black teeth. "Numah one watch, Missah Joe," smiling big and nodding his head.

Several GIs from the other trucks had gotten down and were walking around. Two stopped below us, watching the gooks. Two more kids had climbed on; the girl was flipping through her album and pointing to each picture.

"New *fuckin* cruit," one guy yelled.

He had a joint in one hand, Remington shotgun tucked into the other arm. The steel pot was tipped back on his head, peace sign and FTA on the camouflage cover.

"Twenty-three *days*, motherfucker. I got twenty-three motherfuckin days."

The other guy laughed and pulled the shotgun trying to move him on. My gook girl kept flipping through the album. The shoe shine was doing the second boot.

"Twenty-three days and I'm home, motherfucker. How many days *you* got? How many ya say?" leaning his ear forward. "Fuck you."

He threw the other guy's arm off the shotgun. The gooks stopped yapping and eyeballed him.

"You dumb fucker. You *dumb* motherfucker. You got twenty-three *lifetimes.*"

He put the joint in his mouth and let it hang on the lower lip, like a movie star would a cigarette. He walked on with the shotgun over his shoulder like a stateside troop walking guard with an M-14.

Kell kicked the shoe shine in the ass and drew the M-79 back as if to hit the old man. They scrambled down, all yelling "Numah fuckin ten." The little girl with the pictures spat and gave us the finger.

"Don't pay that guy no mind, Henry. Fucker's so high he don't know where he is. Sorry fucker. Time'll pass for you. Don't worry."

I wasn't thinking about time. Gooks. Remington shotgun, joint.

"How long have you got?" I asked.

"One-two-five. Next month I'll be a motherfuckin two-digit midget."

I hadn't thought about whores being there, though at Fort Polk you heard all the stories. Convoys were where you always got it.

They had been working all along the trucks, making sure there were no MPs around before approaching anybody. They all came to me right off, instinctively knowing the cruit. Maybe he cherry boy, maybe he pay ten dollah MPC.

"Come on, we make boom boom, Joe."

Tight American-style pants instead of the loose black pajamas the others had. That's the way you can always tell a gook whore, pants or a mini-skirt. The only one worth looking at had a pair of red Bermuda shorts.

"No want," I said.

"Hey, Mile-wide, *I* boom boom."

Kell pointed to the ugliest one in the bunch. The others put their hands over their mouths, even Mile-wide raised her eyebrows and giggled. I don't know how he could have wanted her, circular face with pudgy jowls, and flopping tits. He dropped the steel pot and vest and jumped down, keeping the M-79 and one HE round.

"Won't you get the clap?"

"Who the fuck cares, Henry boy? If I get the clap I can go back to the rear for shots."

"Come on, Joe," the others kept saying. "Me numah one girl Numah one boom boom."

Another guy came out of the woods and his girl ran laughing to join the group.

I remember being struck that they were all so simple, even innocent about the whole thing. Soft glimmering black eyes, giggling like children.

The slender one in shorts had pallid but soft cheeks. She began moving her hands around the waist and hips. Moaning and winking.

"Oh, Joe. Me boo-coo horny. Come on Joe." Wiggling the hips as she worked the thin fingers up under the blouse, "Me numah one, Joe. Come on."

Long shining black hair. Lips parted moaning, working the hands up to the breasts, actually squeezing the right nipple under the blouse. "Boom boom, boom boom. Me love you Joe."

The others kept giggling hysterically.

"Come on, Joe. Only five dollah MPC," whole body rolling in a belly dance, "me so horny."

She finally got pissed off with my gazing and silence, dropped the blouse and frowned, stomping the ground. She spat on the tailgate and spun around, soft shining black hair swishing across her back.

"Numah fuckin ten. Cheap Charlie."

The others screamed, slapping each other's shoulders as they moved on to better prospects.

When Kell came striding back he was still buttoning his pants.

"Worth it?" I asked.

"Shit no."

Only two more old man peddlers came by before we left; I think word got around that we weren't buying. Kell cursed and drew the M-79 back like a club before they could climb the tailgate.

The helicopters streaked up from behind the artillery hill, dropped, then buzzed us, turbines grinding, streaking, diving straight in at us. Two of them, not more then twenty feet off the ground with the fierce-looking rocket pods and mini-guns poised on each side. I ducked on that first pass. Door gunners with the big sixties.

"Hogs," Kell yelled. "They ain't nothin. Wait till you see the Cobras work out. They bring the *max*."

The MPs sent an armored vehicle ahead of each truck. APCs, tanks, and gun trucks. Each gun truck had three quad fifties—a quad fifty is four synchronized fifty-caliber machine guns working almost like a giant mini-gun—and high steel plate all around the bed. One had "Highlander Hellions" painted on the plating, another "Aces High."

The gunships kept performing as we rolled, diving, circling, roaring. Vehicles stretched fifty feet apart, a ten-minute lapse between passes.

In places the bush had been cleared a hundred meters back from the road with stumps and black skeleton trees, like a forest fire. On some low hills you could see a tank or armored personnel carrier with cyclone fence around it to detonate in-coming RPG—rocket-propelled grenades—before they could pierce the armor. We accelerated crossing a bridge. I remember fearing it meant mines or ambush—which I suppose it could have been, but if it hadn't been my first convoy I would have thought nothing of it. There were two sandbag bunkers at each end, a sixty in each bunker and the gunners flashing the peace sign as we passed. Gook kids dove into the river on both sides. They would clutch the barbed wire, lean forward, and let go squealing. At the other end a bunch of naked kids clapped and waved at us. Some held their fingers in a V, the hand sign for "Gimme cigarette, Joe."

It was over two hours to Clarissa. Landscape monotonously serene, occasional fields of elephant grass, endless horizon hills and peaks. The rolling hills reminded me of Kentucky, I shook my head thinking about it. Of course it was actually the triple canopy—trees sometimes a hundred feet high, hiding the bamboo groves, below that thorns and vines covering ravines and swamps and streams. Sometimes after an arc light—a B-52 strike—the bamboo is twisted and tangled so thick you can't get through. It's like hacking at steel pipe and wire, and you may have to go three or four hours to get around it.

There was a Montagnard village just outside Clarissa, with straw houses on stilts. A water buffalo stood in a mud pit in front of one house. All the kids flashed the cigarette sign; the old men stood by the entrance ladders giggling and waving. We slowed going through.

I knew we must be getting there but I hadn't pictured it as right next to a village. The wire and bunker line started immediately at the end of the village, rusting concertina stacked three coils high and tangle-foot stretched over the yellow dirt behind it, then more concertina and twenty feet of open ground before the bunkers. Every third bunker was a tower made of heavy timber, like Fort Apache except for the corrugated aluminum roof and machine gun. The MPs at the gates waved us through and we turned off from the rest of the convoy to a road parallel to Highway Fourteen.

When we reached the Regulars' area—"Regulars by God" spelled out in front of the tents in infantry-blue .105 cannisters—a guy ran out of the S-1 tent and flagged us.

"Winsted and Kell?" he yelled.

We nodded. He had spit-shined boots and no shit, suntanned.

"You're going forward right now. Charlie company's gonna CA, gotta get you out before it starts."

Each of the lined tents had a guidon-shaped sign, infantry blue with the crossed rifles and the name of the company.

CA. Combat assault. Charlie company was milling at the pad and watched us jump from the truck. My steel pot fell off, like a first-grader dropping the chalk at the blackboard. The men standing or pacing, some with thumbs tucked into the pistol belt. One machine gunner was kneeling to tie a towel around his sixty, so he could balance it on his shoulder. Just like in a damned movie.[93]

At about the same time, PFC McMullen writes home again after visiting Dong Ha, another American base.

Nov. 7, 1967
Phu Bai
Dong Ha is alright. It is prettier than Phu Bai, has grass and trees, is up on top of a hill so you can see around, see the DMZ across the river. Their messhall is cleaner than Phu Bai's and, best of all, there are no rats in the hooches. I never slept so freely—no rats. Running to the bunkers could drive one nuts there, though. When you must run to your bunker it is very frightening, but when you must do it several times a day, it is nerve-wracking as well. As I was sleeping so freely, as was said, two water buffalo wandered into a nearby minefield and blew themselves away in two successive hooch-rattling explosions which were easily mistaken for incoming artillery. Everyone "flew" to the bunkers again. When you must go to the bunkers from a sound sleep that is the most frightening of all. You are not sure where they are hitting; and know that you are awfully slow and confused (though in fact you have probably never moved faster) and that in a second you will be blown to pieces. After the water buffalo incident, I returned to rat-free sleep.

North Vietnamese artillery from across the DMZ (and from the

South side of the DMZ, as well), is the main problem at Dong Ha; that and rockets, whereas mortars are our main concern at Phu Bai. Woe if we should get rockets here. What a fear that would be. Anyway, Dong Ha is OK, if a little of a shock after our "peaceful lull" here in Phu Bai.[94]

Meanwhile, a few kilometers northwest of Phu Bai, the U.S. Marine outpost of Khe Sanh is seeing increased enemy activity. Michael Herr's Dispatches *describes the scene.*

Somewhere Out There, within artillery range of the Khe Sanh Combat Base, within a twenty-mile radius, a day's march, assuming the "attack posture," concealed and silent and ominous, lay five full divisions of North Vietnamese Regulars. This was the situation during the closing weeks of 1967:

Somewhere to the southwest was the 304th NVA Division. Due east (somewhere) was the 320th. The 325C was deployed in an unknown fashion to the northwest, and the 324B (a cause for real alarm among enemy-division buffs) was somewhere to the northeast. There was also an unidentified division just the other side of the Laotian border, where their big artillery had been dug so deeply into the mountainsides that not even our B-52's could harm them. All of that terrain, all of that cover, ridge after ridge, murderous slides and gorges, all cloaked by triple canopy and thick monsoon mists. And whole divisions were out there in that.

Marine Intelligence (While I see many hoof-marks going in, I see none coming out), backed by the findings of increasing Air Force reconnaissance missions, had been watching and evaluating the build-up with alarm since spring. Khe Sanh had always been in the vicinity of major infiltration routes, "sat astride" them, as the Mission put it. That slight but definite plateau, rising abruptly from the foothills bridging Laos and Vietnam, had been of value for as long as the Vietnamese had been at war. The routes now used by the NVA had been used twenty years earlier by the Viet Minh. Khe Sanh's original value to the Americans might be gauged by the fact that in spite of the known infiltration all around it, we held it for years with nothing more than a Special Forces A Team; less than a dozen Americans and around 400 indigenous troops, Vietnamese and Montagnard. When the Special Forces first moved in there in 1962, they built their teamhouse, outbuildings, club and defenses over bunkers that had been left by the French. Infiltrating columns simply diverted their routes a kilometer or so away from the central Khe Sanh position. The Green Berets ran out regular, extremely cautious patrols. Since they were almost always surrounded by the infiltrators, Khe Sanh was not the most comfortable duty in Vietnam, but there was seldom anything more than the random ambush or the occasional mortaring that was standard for A Teams anywhere in-country. If the NVA had considered Khe Sanh tactically crucial or even important, they could have taken it at any time. And if we had thought of it as anything more than a token outpost—you can't have infiltrators running around without putting someone in there for a look—we could have created it as a major base. No one builds bases like Americans.

In the course of routine patrols during the early spring of 1966, Special Forces reported what appeared to be a significant increase in the number of enemy troops in the immediate Khe Sanh area, and a battalion of Marines was sent to reinforce the patrols. A year later, in April and May of 1967, during large but routine Search-and-Destroy operations, the Marines found and engaged battalion-strength units of North Vietnamese holding the tops of Hills 881 North and South, and a lot of people were killed on both sides. The battles grew into the bloodiest of the spring. The hills were taken and, weeks later, abandoned. The Marines that might have maintained the hills (Where better to observe infiltration than from a vantage of 881 meters?) were sent instead to Khe Sanh, where the 1st and 3rd Battalions of the 26th Marine Regiment rotated, increasing their harassment of the NVA, hoping, if not to drive them out of the sector, to at least force their movements into predictable patterns. The 26th, a hybrid regiment, was formed out of the TAOR of the 5th Marine Division, a numerical designation which remained on paper even after the actual command of the regiment became the responsibility of the 3rd Marine Division, headquartered at Dong Ha, nearby in the DMZ.

By summer, it became obvious that the battles for 881 North and South had engaged a relatively small number of the enemy thought to be in the area. Patrols were stepped up (they were now thought to be among the most dangerous in I Corps), and additional elements of the 26th Marines were airlifted into what was now being called the Khe Sanh Combat Base. The Seabees laid down a 600-meter tarmac airstrip. A beer hall and an air-conditioned officers' club were built, and the regimental command set up its Tactical Operations Center in the largest of the deserted French bunkers. Yet Khe Sanh continued to be only a moderate, private concern of the Marine Corps. A few old hands in the press corps knew vaguely about the base and about the small ville of about a thousand Montagnards which lay four kilometers to the south. It was not until November, when the regiment had grown to full and then reinforced strength (6,000 Marines, not including units added from the 9th Marine Regiment), with 600 Vietnamese Rangers, two detachments of Seabees, a helicopter squadron and a small Special Forces Compound, that the Marines began "leaking" the rather remarkable claim that by building up the base we had lured an unbelievable number of enemy to the area.[95]

On 21 November General Westmoreland, COMUSMACV, returns to the United States at the order of the president to deliver the following TV address to the nation.

With 1968, a new phase is now starting. We have reached an important point when the end begins to come into view. What is this third phase we are about to enter?

In Phase III, in 1968, we intend to do the following:

Help the Vietnamese Armed Forces to continue improving their effectiveness.

Decrease our advisers in training centers and other places where the professional competence of Vietnamese officers makes this possible.

Increase our advisory effort with the younger brothers of the Vietnamese Army: the Regional Forces and Popular Forces.

Use U.S. and free-world forces to destroy North Vietnamese forays while we assist the Vietnamese to reorganize for territorial security.

Provide the new military equipment to revitalize the Vietnamese Army and prepare it to take on an ever-increasing share of the war.

Continue pressure on North to prevent rebuilding and to make infiltration more costly.

Turn a major share of frontline DMZ defense over to the Vietnamese Army.

Increase U.S. support in the rich and populated delta.

Help the Government of Viet-Nam single out and destroy the Communist shadow government.

Continue to isolate the guerrilla from the people.

Help the new Vietnamese government to respond to popular aspirations and to reduce and eliminate corruption.

Help the Vietnamese strengthen their policy forces to enhance law and order.

Open more roads and canals.

Continue to improve the Vietnamese economy and standard of living.

THE FINAL PHASE

Now for phase IV—the final phase. That period will see the conclusion of our plan to weaken the enemy and strengthen our friends until we become progressively superfluous. The object will be to show the world that guerrilla warfare and invasion do not pay as a new means of Communist aggression.

I see phase IV happening as follows:

Infiltration will slow.

The Communist infrastructure will be cut up and near collapse.

The Vietnamese Government will prove its stability, and the Vietnamese Army will show that it can handle Viet Cong.

The Regional Forces and Popular Forces will reach a higher level of professional performance.

U.S. units can begin to phase down as the Vietnamese Army is modernized and develops its capacity to the fullest.

The military physical assets, bases and ports, will be progressively turned over to the Vietnamese.

The Vietnamese will take charge of the final mopping up of the Viet
Cong (which will probably last several years). The U.S., at the same
time, will continue the developmental help envisaged by the President for
the community of Southeast Asia.

You may ask how long phase III will take, before we reach the final
phase. We have already entered part of phase III. Looking back on
phases I and II, we can conclude that we have come a long way.
   I see progress as I travel all over Viet-Nam.
   I see it in the attitudes of the Vietnamese.
   I see it in the open roads and canals.
   I see it in the new crops and the new purchasing power of the farmer.
   I see it in the increasing willingness of the Vietnamese Army to fight
North Vietnamese units and in the victories they are winning.

Parenthetically, I might say that the U.S. press tends to report U.S.
actions; so you may not be as aware as I am of the victories won by South
Vietnamese forces.
   The enemy has many problems:

He is losing control of the scattered population under his influence.
   He is losing credibility with the population he still controls.
   He is alienating the people by his increased demands and taxes, where
he can impose them.
   He sees the strength of his forces steadily declining.
   He can no longer recruit in the South to any meaningful extent; he
must plug the gap with North Vietnamese.
   His monsoon offensives have been failures.
   He was dealt a mortal blow by the installation of a freely elected
representative government.
   And he failed in his desperate effort to take the world's headlines from
the inauguration by a military victory.[96]

William Eastlake's novel The Bamboo Bed *views General Westmoreland's
optimism from a different perspective.*

Hill 904 was a big son of a bitch. It was called 904 because it was 904
meters high. Hill 904 was a tough son of a bitch. Almost every American
unit in the highlands had tried to take it. Some had succeeded, some had
failed, some had taken it many times at great cost. Other times the
Unfriendlies had given it to the Americans. They'd killed all the Americans they cared to kill that day and pulled out. But one fine day the
Unfriendlies decided to hold Hill 904. It was the same day the Americans
decided to take it. So uphill the Americans went. The Unfriendlies, being
in a magnificent position on top of Hill 904, killed all the Americans in
sight. You would have thought, Captain Knightbridge thought, that the
Americans would have learned from the British at Bunker Hill. The
British lost the flower of their army trying to take Bunker Hill from the
Americans. The Americans just sat there on the hill and killed every

British flower in sight. On Hill 904 it was the Americans that were the cut flowers. On Hill 904 it was the Americans who had all the latest, most modern equipment against some farmers, dug in on a hill. Up the Hill 904 the Americans went. Down the Hill 904 the Americans came. It all happened so quickly they did not have a chance to bring back their dead buddies with them. I wonder where the bodies went? The Americans did this again and again and again and again. Why? Because it was a habit now. The Americans were hooked on Hill 904. They climbed the mountain because the mountain was there. Hill 904 became the enemy. They called it the hairy ball, it was that tangled and twisted with jungle and the shit of war, the bodies and the shell holes, heads, arms, legs, coconuts, breadfruit, coffee cans, cocks, balls, C rations, rice, Winston cigarettes, letters from home, telegrams from the Hasbrouck Heights New Jersey Boosters Club congratulating them on their victory, beer cans, gin bottles, marijuana wrappers, Bibles, hymn-books, a Guide to Better Living, autographs of Hubert Horatio Humphrey and the movie stars who visited the Hill on a calm day, millions of gallons of red blood as though it had been sprayed there by defoliation mission, all of a year's output of something from a chemical company for which the stockholders received a supplemental year's-end dividend and caused the stock to jump up three and five eighths, socks, condoms, letters from home, despair and pity and heartbreak and death and pity and heartbreak, that's what Hill 904 was made of.

So up the hill the Americans went, the same day the Unfriendlies decided to hold it, and the battle went on and on and on until the Americans had almost no dead to give. So General William Westmoreland, who had graduated from West Point fifteen years before Knightbridge and who was in charge of the whole show, decided that this was the time to make the statement that we were winning the war. That did not help. So General Westmoreland decided that this was the time to quit the field. For General Westmoreland to quit the field. So General Westmoreland got on an airplane with Ambassador Ellsworth Bunker and both of them went back to the United States of America and announced that they were winning the war. That did not help. Hill 904 was still held by the Unfriendlies. Then one fine day Clancy took it. It cost Clancy ninety-four men, but he took it when all had failed. General Westmoreland and Ambassador Bunker came back to Vietnam. Ambassador Bunker went back to doing whatever ambassadors do who walk a crooked mile to run a crowded country. General Westmoreland gave Clancy a medal.[97]

1967   November—Secretary of Defense McNamara persuades President Johnson to accept his resignation, but agrees to stay on until 29 February.

Having assumed the cover identity of an American newsman, CIA agent Knox, in Trowbridge's novel Easy Victories, *accompanies South Vietnamese Colonel Hiep on an Operation Phoenix mission.*

Colonel Hiep had set up his command post in the square. At one time the market had been covered and shops and market stalls had surrounded it. But now it was burned out. Hiep pointed to a triangular block of concrete ringed with skeins of concertina wire. The block was surmounted by a piece of helicopter rotor blade. The monument was some twelve feet high and was situated in the exact geometrical center of the square.

"VC monument. You take pictures please." Knox obediently snapped several pictures. He even moved around and took some from different angles.

"What does this damn thing commemorate?"

"The shooting down of a helicopter," Fumarole said. "Some Charlie gunner got a bicycle and a month's pass in the deal. His local unit most likely threw up this piece of junk to celebrate the achievement."

Two Special Police were attaching demolition strips of gelignite to the base and halfway up the sides of the monument. Another was running thin electrical wires back to a small hand-held detonator. The two Special Police finished strapping the charges in place and scurried away. They had been pretty efficient. And the wires were not attached to the detonator until they were clear. Pretty good. For Vietnamese. The other Special Police handed the detonator to Colonel Hiep. A staff officer blew a whistle and everybody took cover. Colonel Hiep spun the handle of the detonator and the monument disintegrated under the implosion of the charges. A thick pall of acrid smoke and dust hung in the still air. Some of it settled on Knox and stuck to his skin and clothes in a fine paste.

A priest in white vestments came out of the church across the square. Hiep walked over with pistol drawn. The priest stood waiting calmly with hands folded in front of him. Knox could see that the church was freshly painted. The cross which surmounted the small cupola had been struck by a piece of shrapnel from the demolition of the VC mounument and was leaning askew.

Hiep was talking to the priest in rapid Vietnamese. The priest heard him out and answered calmly. Knox edged around the two men and glanced inside the church. An irregular double row of bullet holes in the sheet-tin roof marked an earlier visit by a helicopter gunship or an A-1E. The shrapnel had also knocked out several windowpanes. But it was still very much a church. Orderly and clean. Freshly swept and the few missals arranged in neat, even piles on a bench in the rear.

Outside in the square the priest was being hustled away. A PRU was placing a black hood over the man's head. The priest's hands were already tied and someone had tagged him with a neatly printed detainee card run through a fold of his cassock with thin copper wire with the ends twisted. His white vestments had been shucked off and thrown in a rumpled heap in the shadow of the church. Several other detainees were already squatting in a small circle under a chinaberry tree. Some of them had hoods. Some did not. A guard made the priest sit down in the group.

Knox took a picture of that, too. They looked for all the world like a pathetic klavern of Ku Klux Klansmen. But he did not feel like laughing.

The high-pitched twitter of rotors and a shadow fleeing briefly across the square marked the arrival of a helicopter. It set down like a huge dragonfly in the middle of the square where the monument acclaiming the destruction of another of its kind had stood until recently. The blades threw up a cloud of dust and everybody turned their backs to the blast. Knox covered his nose with the collar of his fatigue blouse. But it did no good. He still got a lot of grit in his nose and mouth. The major who had been at the briefing the night before got out of the helicopter. He seemed pleased with himself. He joined Colonel Hiep and Sweeney and spread open a map with plastic overlay marked by red grease pencil.

"We zapped five Charlies trying to get through the cordon."

"We haven't done much here," Sweeney said. "They must have got word we were coming. All the troops are gone. There's been no return fire. Only men left in the hamlet are old men and the priest."

The major frowned. "Sounds like something got screwed up somewhere. Maybe that briefing of yours last night. There was a whole shitpot full of people moving around outside."

Sweeney glared at him. They conferred another minute or two and then the major departed. Again in dust and last year's dried leaves.

Some of the PRUs were eating food they had taken from houses. One had disposed of all his psywar leaflets and was using the heavy plastic bag to hold vegetables and a live chicken. It made an awkward bundle. Particularly since the chicken was thrashing and kicking spasmodically. The operation was taking on a festive air.

A Special Police came up from the direction of the river to report he had found the marks of a lot of sampans along the bank. Sweeney received the news dourly. "That explains why no draft-age men are around. The able bodies were warned and took off."

Fumarole was eating a crab apple. He passed one to Knox and Knox took a bite, then spat it out. "They just had to have their big briefing last night," Fumarole said. "Hell, if I had known Sweeney was going to let Hiep pretend to run this show I wouldn't have come. And fuck what the Station said. Put that in your report to Balfour."

Knox said nothing.

Sweeney and Smith were questioning a woman just added to the group of prisoners. The Special Police interpreter was not very expert. The woman looked at them sullenly.

"How much do the VC collect from you in taxes?"

"No know no VC," she said in broken English.

"Where did you learn your English?"

"In Da Nang. I work there many year."

"How much does the whole village pay, and don't lie to me."

"No know VC. Me Buddhist. Buddhist no know VC."

"How many times do the VC song teams come here?"

"No many."

"What do they say?"

"They say Americans get tired soon. Go home."

Sweeney shrugged and turned away. Knox was very thirsty. He had been looking for water for some time now but had seen none. Other than the canteens carried by the Vietnamese. He told Fumarole and Fumarole located a large pottery crock in one of the houses. Knox had to splash out the film of dust and mosquito larvae on top and drink from cupped hands. The water was lukewarm and tasted of things he did not like to think about.

Four Special Police were interrogating a man in the back of the house. One of them touched the man's feet from time to time with the bud of a lighted cigarette. They were all firing questions at the man without giving him time to answer. The man also had a thin woven cord of nylon holding his mouth open. One of the Special Police grabbed the man's hair and smashed his face against a table. Blood dripped from a split lip. An eye puffed almost shut.

Knox walked out of the house feeling as thirsty as he had before Fumarole showed him the crock. All the villagers the PRUs and Special Police had been able to locate were huddled in the square. A psywar lieutenant was standing on a basket and lecturing the old men and despondent women about the benevolence of the government in Saigon. Other Special Police were tacking up big posters of Ky and Thieu. Sweeney was standing with the two informers. They had hoods of their own made from rough burlap with slits cut for eyeholes. They pointed to people in the crowd and they were tied and led away to the growing band of detainees. The last man taken was so old he could not walk fast. His guard raised the man's bound arms behind him until the old man's torso was parallel to the ground. When that did not hurry the old man along and he stumbled the guard dragged him the rest of the way by his bound arms. He dumped the old man into the group of prisoners. The old man somehow managed to get his feet under him and squatted. His shaven head bobbed slightly from side to side with the effort of breathing. His eyes were closed.

"That's taking it pretty rough on the old man," Knox said.

"You never know," Smith said. "He could be the head Cong for the area."

Knox heard a shot from the house where he had found the water pot. He went back inside the house and saw the body of the Vietnamese who had been interrogated by the Special Police. The man's body twitched and a Special Police shot him again with the muzzle of the carbine pressed against the man's ear. The twitching stopped. The Special Police filed out past Knox and the last man struck a match to a pile of thatch in the corner by the water crock. The house burned readily.

Back in the square, the Census-Grievance people were returning identification cards to the people who had had them. The knot of prisoners had grown considerably. A swirl of hot wind blew out from the burning house and Knox smelled the faint cinnamon odor of burned flesh. The priest was talking quietly to the old man through his hood. The old man's head was still bobbing steadily with a peculiar rhythm all its own.

"May as well get the hell out of here and see if Interrogations can get more from these people than we can," Sweeney said. Then to Smith: "What's the score?"

"Five KIAs shot running away, the major reported. Then one prisoner killed while trying to escape. That makes six in all. No friendly casualties."

Sweeney nodded. "Maybe we salvaged something after all."

"What do you think of Operation Phoenix?" Fumarole said.

"Like trying to root the Democrats out of Chicago," Knox said.[98]

1967 December—President Johnson announces a Christmas pause in the bombing of North Vietnam, asking for a positive reaction from the DRV.

Under Robert Komer's CORDS program, the senior American adviser in each province is required to submit monthly reports to the MACCORDS director in Saigon. The December report from Quang Tri province is written by Robert Brewer. Many of the province advisers' reports for December indicate sharply increased Viet Cong preparations, as noted in 2. (c) below.

QUANG TRI Province

Period Ending 28 December 1967

1. STATUS OF THE RD PLAN:

   a. December was marked by moderate activity in the field and intensive work in the in-province training classrooms. The cold, wet weather in the first two weeks slowed the flow of commodities to the field and made construction work in the RD hamlets difficult. This slowdown was offset by many courses conducted for hamlet and village officials, and for RD and Static Census Grievance Cadre. By mid-month the weather improved and work in the field accelerated. Despite the holidays and weather, the revised RD program for 1967 appeared to be on schedule. There also was considerable energy expended in drafting the Province Pacification Plan for 1968.

b. The continuing emphasis on eliminating the VC infrastructure produced modest gains. The tempo of combined operations at sector and subsector level incrased, and ICEX target lists were in great demand. The Province Chief finally released one platoon of the 105th NPFF Company for duty in the primary RD area. Hamlet self-defense forces known as Revolutionary Development Peoples Groups (RDPG), also began receiving arms from the Province Chief. Hamlet and village leaders continued to ask for the arming of RDFG. Previously there was some reluctance on the part of the people to defend themselves.

c. The "town meeting" concept continued to develop with GVN officials assuming the responsibility of calling the meetings and achieving meaningful results. . . .

2. . . .

b. *Enemy Situation*: The number of reported enemy locations and movements increased significantly in December, as well as the number of enemy-initiated incidents. There were 2 enemy rocket attacks, 3 ambushes, 3 assassinations, 2 instances of harassing fire, 2 mining incidents, 5 mortar attacks and 1 attempted sabotage of the Ga Bridge. The reported planned attack on Quang Tri City and Allied installations between 18 and 20 December was limited to a mortar attack on Ai Tu airfield. Reports from returnees and POW's indicate the enemy is suffering from lack of food and replacements; and general hardships.

c. *Infrastructure*: The Viet Cong infrastructure increased their efforts to gain more control in RD fringe areas. There were reports of several important political meetings in VC-controlled areas, espousing the doctrine of removing the "puppet" government. The VC were very active in collecting bamboo stretchers, mats, and rice, *a strong indication of a planned large-scale attack*. [emphasis added] They were also successful in obtaining civilian laborers for one or two days. Most of this activity was centered in VC-controlled areas. However the VC showed their strength in Cam Lo by assassinating the Cam Lo Census Grievance director in his house near Cam Lo District Headquarters.

In a recent Chieu Hoi Report it was noted that the Quang Tri Province Committee ceased publication of its newspaper "Cuu Nuoc" (National Salvation) and put all their efforts behind the Tri-Thien military region publication "Thong Nhat" (Unification). The VC seemed to be running short on effective, high-level party members and they must further centralize their political efforts. Targeting of the VC infrastructure by the ICEX Committee continued.[99]

In Washington, year-end statistics are tabulated and circulated. These figures seem to indicate a definite improvement in the pacification effort.

POPULATION DATA
TOTAL SCORE—COUNTRYWIDE MARCH THROUGH DECEMBER, 1967[100]

Population in Thousands	MARCH	JUNE	SEPTEMBER	DECEMBER	NET CHANGE MARCH–DECEMBER
Population Weighted Index	2.33	2.42	2.50	2.54	
Secure/Good					
A Hamlets	300.9	489.4	646.8	694.9	394.
B Hamlets	2,861.9	3,128.7	3,489.7	3,481.3	619.
C Hamlets	4,221.8	4,360.5	4,044.2	4,279.1	57.
Non-Hamlet	3,210.1	3,277.3	3,135.1	3,059.4	−150.
Total	10,594.7 (63.3%)	11,255.9 (65.6%)	11,315.8 (66.5%)	11,514.7 (67.0%)	920.
Contested/Poor					
D Hamlets	2,235.7	1,976.2	2,087.2	2,157.6	−78.
E Hamlets	480.0	402.3	337.2	318.6	−161.
Other Hamlets	.0	152.3	91.7	68.3	68.
Non-Hamlet	274.0	290.8	237.4	243.6	−10.
Total	2,989.7 (17.9%)	2,821.6 (16.4%)	2,753.5 (16.2%)	2,808.1 (16.3%)	−181.
VC Controlled					
VC Hamlets	2,955.8	2,923.2	2,809.5	2,748.4	−207.
Non-Hamlet	196.4	164.2	134.1	112.5	−83.
Total	3,152.2 (18.8%)	3,087.4 (18.0%)	2,943.6 (17.3%)	2,860.9 (16.7%)	−791.
Total Population	16,736.6	17,164.9	17,012.0	17,183.7	447.

HAMLET DATA
TOTAL SCORE—COUNTRYWIDE MARCH THROUGH DECEMBER, 1967

Number of Hamlets	MARCH	JUNE	SEPTEMBER	DECEMBER	NET CHANGE MARCH–DECEMBER
Secure/Good					
A Hamlets	99	168	213	231	132
B Hamlets	1,639	1,776	1,902	1,809	170
C Hamlets	3,138	3,245	3,137	3,300	162
Total	4,876	5,189	5,252	5,340	466
Contested/Poor					
D Hamlets	2,348	2,156	2,206	2,230	−118
E Hamlets	599	528	483	445	−154
Other Hamlets	0	686	713	825	875
Total	2,947	3,370	3,402	3,500	533
VC Hamlets	4,262	3,978	3,987	3,882	−380
Total Hamlets	12,085	12,537	12,641	12,722	637

In Saigon, after conferring with his station chief, CIA agent Knox discusses the intelligence situation with his associate, B.D.

B.D. smoked a cigarette between the time they were outside Mister Balfour's office door and the time it took to walk to B.D.'s office. He slumped in his chair and drank ice water straight from the pitcher until the sweat showed dark through his shirt. He lit another cigarette and looked at Knox through the smoke. "Go and sin no more."

Knox ignored him and picked up an IIR. "This is the tenth IIR I've seen this month saying the VC are going to launch an attack on Binh Thuy Air Base during the next full moon. Don't you think this is all a bit much?"

"Don't worrry about it. Just get it looking good and send it out. At least we've got our ass covered. If you predict it long enough when it really happens you've got something in file to drag out and say to all and sundry, 'Haw, motherfucker, I told you so.' "

"It's a waste."

"Like I say, every rule is its own reward. Never mind the facts, give them the straight trivia."[101]

Although the traditional Western New Year's truce has been agreed to by both sides, a major truce violation incident is described in Larry Heinemann's novel Close Quarters. *On New Year's Eve, Philip Dosier and his fellow APC drivers are standing alert in their vehicles.*

So while Teddy lounged in the hatch above us, Quinn and Dewey and I lounged on the benches, sitting knee to knee, talking in low voices. Well after dark, we could barely see each other's faces in the starlight. Dewey was telling us about the last New Year's Eve party he'd been to.

"I got so fucken ripped. Wound up passed out under the buffet. Next morning I woke up on the porch mat without a stitch on, and this fat pig of a broad was lying on the floor next to me. *I* don't know what happened, but *she* had a big shit-eating grin and kept hugging me."

"Don't ya know if ya got laid?" asked Quinn.

"Fucken-A, Quinn. I don't even remember taking my clothes off."

"M' man, ya better get yer shit to-gether." And just then a claymore blew. Quinn and I shot our heads up through the crew hatch. To the left a grayish cloud of smoke rose straight into the air, and two troops lay belly down behind their bunker, looking around themselves. The Alpha Company second platoon leader came over the air.

"What was that? What's going on?"

"Two-six, this is Two-eight," came another, younger voice. "Disregard. Just some short-timer getting one off for the back-in-the-world New Year."

"Send that man to my location," said Two-six, sounding peeved. "And everybody turn down the radios. I can hear all of you."

Quinn turned down the volume until it was just audible. And we sat back again, but barely a moment later the second platoon's LP, three dudes sitting shoulder to shoulder in a foxhole twenty meters into the woods, came over the air. The dude spoke in halting and careful whispers, giving each word its own breath. "Lima. Pa-pa. Two. Got. Move. Ment." I looked at Quinn, then Dewey, and began to rise. The tracks on line got very quiet; quiet enough to hear light sneaking footfalls in the perimeter behind us.

"Lima. Pa-pa. Two," the dude softly whispered again. I knew that he sat scrunched down over his lap, put the mouthpiece ever so close to his lips, and covered his secret message with his hand. "Count six—eight bodies—coming your location."

"Roger," said Alpha Two-six. "Eh, Romeo seven-three? Gimme some recon-by-fire."

I gave him a roger and climbed into the hatch, pushing Teddy up and out. I put on the CVC, cocked the fifty, and swung it around square to the front. Beginning ten meters in front of the woodline, I squeezed off a long burst, walking the rounds up to chest high. I moved the gun to the left and fired, then the right. I swept and fired. A long burst. A short burst. Another long burst. The hundred rounds were gone, scattering hot fifty brass and links around the gun mount and inside around my feet. I reloaded quickly and listened. The LP came back over the air again, whispering quickly, this time giving it in one breath.

"More-bodies-twenty-thirty-boo-coo-can-we-pull *back?*"

"This is Two-six. Negative," the dude said flatly. In other words, good-bye. And all that night I listened for the LP's dying words, a booming shout through the jungle as the gooks stood over them, zipping them up with bursts of AK. "Hey, Alpha Two-six! Fu-uck you! See you in goddam fucking hell, Two-six!" (But the next morning the three of them, all black dudes, would stumble out of the woods without waiting for relief, dragging the radio and their rifles and such, soaked to the skin and ass-whipped. Their eyes *that* big around as though they'd seen something that would last them to the grave. The dudes would walk past the Cow Catcher, shaking their heads at one another and mumbling, "Nev-ver fucken a-gin, man. Nev-ver fucken a-gin, you hear me?")

Quinn and Teddy moved in behind their guns, bringing boxes of frags and ammo with them and standing on the benches. Dewey took my shotgun and stood in the crew hatch just behind my armor shield, not sure what to do. Teddy, with those lean arms of his, watched Quinn in his black T-shirt and flak jacket all night long, doing what he did.

Then it began—fifties and sixties and frags and AKs and RPGs—down toward the road where the seven-four had parked—frags and claymores and sixteens on auto and more AKs, lots of AKs—on the south side of the laager by Bravo Company and to the east by the grunts. And a moment later Quinn and Teddy and Dewey and I started in, because there they came. First the muzzles and sight blades, then the khaki

trousers and handmade, homemade rubber sandals, the black-cloth web
gear and straight black hair. A squad of dinks, maybe more. And we all
began at once—machine guns and AKs and grenades and RPG rounds
coming in hitting somewhere, spraying ice-blue and red and whitish
shrapnel. I picked a silhouette or shadow or shirt and pulled off rounds
with both thumbs on the butterfly trigger. Long bursts and short bursts.
And Quinn and Teddy took turns lobbing grenades, pulling the pins with
their thumbs, tossing the pin rings back over their shoulders, counting
one thousand one, one thousand two, then heaving the grenades up and
over the canopy. Sometimes they got an air burst. A burst of automatic
AK fire would tangtangtangtang against the fifty gun shield where I
stood, crouching behind the gun. All that noise like cackling and throaty
rattling, a junk box poured out on the ground, all clatter and jangle and
screaming. The three batteries opened up, firing at will, sailing HE
rounds into the jungle, and the shrapnel came back into the laager,
whizzing hotly, and sometimes banging against the gun shields with a
clang. Then word came down that air strikes were coming in, watch your
head, so we slacked off a minute and waited. The Phantoms came in low
over the treetops, one after another, dropping canisters of napalm with
each pass. Then somebody said that they were calling in the eight-inch
and 175 guns from Katum and Suoi Dau. Someone else said there was a
break in the line over by the grunts and they were doing it hand-to-
fucking-hand, Romeo get ready to pull off the line and move over. And I
said, yeah, I could dig it, and Quinn slapped the sixty gun shield with the
heel of his hand as much to say, yeah, come on, let's go. But we never
did. The Phantoms kept coming, shrieking and screaming low over the
clearing, setting napalm fires with each pass. The fifties and pigs and
gunships and mini-guns and small arms kept putting out rounds. The
dinks kept coming up to the woodline, out into the clearing. We could
hear the booming volley after volley of eight-inch and 175s whistling in,
getting air bursts, because they could set the fuses for time and had the
time down right. The 155s and 105s behind us squeezed off canister
rounds point-blank above the screaming and yelling, and Quinn and
Teddy lobbed grenades and worked the pigs and I banged out ten- and
twenty-round bursts, walking the rounds in and out, in and out of the
woodline just as Quinn had done a couple days before. I could hear the
Alpha Company CO screaming bloody fucking murder over the radio,
screaming so loud we heard him well enough without. And I never moved
so fast in my life, tearing open ammo boxes, cocking and firing and
cursing, sweated up and squinting with the rest. Alpha Company fire
teams moved back and forth behind us trying to find clear fields of fire.
There were more incoming mortars and rockets and Chicom grenades,
and somebody said a 105 crew got blown away, tube and all, and then
gunships came around again with mini-guns and fifties and belt-fed grenades. God, my God, I could hear the wounded screaming, behind us
and in the woods and down front. The medics came up to the track on

our right and dragged off two dudes, one dude screaming nonsense at the top of his lungs, fuck you fuck you fuck you. There was a rattle of straight-pipe mufflers backing off from high RPMs, and everybody was trying to talk on the radio at once. We kept putting out rounds and more Phantoms came around again, more and more yet—every Phantom in War Zone C, every Phantom in Cochin China—and there was a constant clatter of the mini-guns, spraying red-orange tracers like a cow pissing on a flat rock. The green tracers of the AKs arcing upward, and heavy incoming hit the LZ and battalion operations. And, Jesus, somebody said over the air, Jesus shit, they said, there they are, get'm, get'm, kill'm. Get down and get some.

And the rattle started all over again. A call came for medics and litters and extra hands to report to the LZ on the cart trail, but we just put out rounds and watched the silver and black light from the 105 illumination rounds swinging the shadows back and forth. Another bunch of dinks broke through the woodline off to the right, the dude in front with a pistol and the guy behind with an RPG launcher, locked and loaded. Then blap-slap-slide, there was a whomp! and a blast of gray curling smoke, and when the smoke cleared they were gone and the woodline right behind was in shreds. That's when I remembered our claymores—we still had a dozen claymores out. The gunships—with blinking running lights and landing lights—circled, one behind the other, firing long bursts, brrrrrrap, and the eight-inch and 175s and 155s and 105s came in volleys, ka-rack, and thack-thackthack as the shrapnel caromed through the woods. The medics came back for three dudes in the bunker on our far left and the air strikes settled in on the Bravo Company side of the perimeter. I saw three mo-gas fires and another blew while I looked straight at it—black and gray and scarlet, a brilliant black and fiery orange mushroom, one guy flying off the back in flames. The El-tee came over the air ("Seven-three? Seven-two? Seven-four? Seven-one?" You could hear the worry in his voice as though he was lost himself and hadn't talked to another human for days. Hello? Anybody?), and asked if we were all right. I piped up on the CVC, "Fucken-A bet yer sweet tooties, El-tee." Seven-one and Seven-two answered right after that, but we couldn't raise Seven-four and Dewey wanted to go down and see, but I reached around and grabbed him by the shirt and screamed at him to stay put.

I went through box after box of hundred-round belts, grabbing the fifty with both hands, shoulders hunched and tense, and rolled out twenty-round bursts with both thumbs on the butterfly trigger. The rounds chopped up the corpses that lay in front of us and chewed up the wood-line to chest high. The sound, the feel, the thick smell of gunpowder and gritty sweat and smoking thirty-weight oil mixed with a sniff of fear—that sweet sticky ooze—and the sheer physical joy at the noise the fifty made as it tore into the bodies and the woods. The recoil worked its way up my arms until it blurred my vision; until it was an aggravating overpowering ache in the small of my back that dragged me closer—nose to nose—to the sputtering gun flashes and a senseless, rhymeless, fluid madness. But it was not panic. No, it was never panic. Panic does not explain that crackle in the air. It almost amounted to a spark arcing between the thumbs. My body was all used up; all screams and gasps and migraine ache. The barrel smoked and stank white hot, so I poured some thirty-weight on the barrel and feed tray, and it steamed and smoked and smelled of grease. The firefight slacked and thickened, slacked and thickened all night long.

We ran out of grenades and claymores and one of the pigs hanged fire, so Quinn wound up with the shotgun and I used my forty-five, squeezing off well-aimed shots, just like the range.

Suddenly the sun rose over the trees. I stood behind the fifty, leaning back against the damp armor shield; my mouth so dry and thick I couldn't work up anything to spit. The air strikes were gone. The Huey and Cobra gunships were gone. The artillery had ceased fire. I stared at shot-up trees and beaten-down woodline grass, blinking my aching eyes, and only when I saw a movement of an arm and flak jacket—some dude stepping gingerly among the corpses to the right—did I understand that the firefight was over. Then I saw the bodies, dozens it seemed like, and a litter of ammo boxes and packing cardboard and the cartridge brass, the dud Chicom grenades and frayed ends of claymore wires—firefight junk—jungle junk.

Quinn still stood in the crew hatch, the shotgun over his forearm, his chin on the stock, his hand and fingers at the trigger.

"You okay?" he asked slowly.

"Yeah," I replied. "You?" . . .

Later that morning a Chinook came in with a load of newsmen, looking so bad-ass spiffy in their Saigon-cowboy suits—starched tiger fatigues, spit-shined boots, and silly fucking bush hats.

Yessiree! The Great Truce Day Body Count! All you got to do to get on the dinnertime news is blow away more people than live in Hadley-burg; sit up all night nipping gooks, and then lounge around the grave site cleaning your nails and picking your teeth, waiting your turn to be interviewed by some housecat with a dick job and a shorthand notebook—but don't forget to sweep up a little so the folks think you're neat, and comb your hair a little like the old days so Ma knows it's you. There was a free-lance camera clown, Korean or Japanese, and a network newsman with slicked-back gray hair, slinging a tape recorder over his shoulder with the mike to his mouth, looking for all the world like a playground director. He and the dude with the 16 mm walked fast, making it around the seven-six just in back of us, not even taking the time to look down and figure out what it used to be, like it was garbage in the gutter, and went straight for the grave.

The dude with the 16 mm waltzed up and asked if he could stand on the deck so he could get a better shot.

"Shore," I said, getting up from the bench. "Why, just *any*-fucken-thing for the workin' press!"

"But first ya got to take ma fucken picture," said Quinn, flicking his ash and pointing to himself with his smoke. "Take *all* our pictures. An' I'll take *yer* fucken picture. Jus' let us get our guns an' shit, an' take our picture an' you kin stan' any-fucken-place you wan'. Stan' on yer fucken head, f'rall I fucken care." So the guy stood there with that camera resting on his shoulder, while we dragged out clean shirts and our bush hats and some ammo belts and bandoliers and pineapple frags, machine guns and rifles and forty-fives, worn low on the hips, and my shotgun. We stood in a loose semicircle and John Wayned it for the guy, standing there spraddled-legged and reared back, grinning real bad-like and laughing, having ourselves a good old-fashioned hawhawhaw. He panned back and forth a couple times and then said that was it, so I helped him up to the deck with an oopsie-whoopsie-daisy and he stood behind Teddy's sixty and took his movies. By then the reporter had the Bravo Company CO by the shirt and the two of them stood in front of the grave while Bravo Company helped the bodies into the ditch with a flip of a boot—the dude with the 16 mm clicking and grinding away to a fare-thee-well.

"And Bravo Comp-nay did this an' we did that, ya see. Now, the straight-leg grunts o'er there was dukin' it with the gooks hand ta hand, but that ain't nuthin', 'cause Bra-vo Comp-nay, why, we is jus' 'bout the most evil bunch a motherfuckers in this whole val-ley. Yessireebob, if it hadn't been for Bra-vo Comp-nay—the name is Rock, Captain Richard Rock, Are-oh-cee-kay, sir—if it hadn't been for the Bra-vo Comp-nay these gooks'd be coming ashore at San De-ay-go. No shit!"

I leaned against the armor smoking my smoke, watching Mr. Network slick back his hair, taking down every lie with a straight face. I wanted to shout: Hey, dipstick! Come on over here! See this garbage here? A gun-glove freak burned right down to his socks at this very place. All this silver junk and that black junk used to be just like the Cow Catcher here. See that there, that's fingers and that's most of an arm, and under that box is an ankle and foot. I'm sorry about the rest, but if ya want ta catch it, go on down to the six-niner and the El-tee will be tickled pink to show you the sack, or maybe you can catch it before they throw it aboard the KIA dust-off. But he just kept standing there, jacking his jaw while Bravo Six, that skinny fucking lifer, rapped him a crock of bullshit.

Then some dude with a red Santa Claus beard and a 35-mm camera slid up to us as we sat around the back, smoking.

"My name is Fuziozoopopolis," he said, or something fucked up and dufus-sounding like that. "I'm from UPI," or was it the AP?

"Yeah?" I said, looking up. "No shit."

"Yes," he said, putting a leg up on the ramp, chummy fashion. "Say, what do you men think about all this?"

I glanced over at Quinn. "Say? Think?" I said, "Am I s'posed ta think something?"

"My name is Quinn," said Quinn. "Cue-you-eye-en-en."

"You were here last night, right? I mean, what's on your mind right now?" the guy said, bending forward, note pad poised.

"His name is Dosier, Dee-oh-es-eye-ee-are," said Quinn.

"See that garbage back there? Found a dude in that this morning. See them dinks in the ditch? Fuck 'em. But say, m' man, lemme ask you a question. Why the fuck you come out here?"

"Don't you know? I'm a journalist. You're news this morning."[102]

1967 31 December		
	TOTAL	NET CHANGE
U.S. military personnel assigned in Vietnam	485,600	+100,300
U.S. casualties	YEAR	TO DATE (cumulative)
Killed in action	9,377	16,021
Wounded in action	62,024	99,762

Source: DOD/OASD

1968

1968   1 January—DRV announces that it will hold talks with the United States if all bombing and "other acts of war" against North Vietnam are halted.

During the first three weeks of 1968 the marines in the Khe Sanh area, as described in a U.S. Marine Corps history, see increased activity.

On 20 January, a Marine company made contact with a North Vietnam-ese battalion entrenched between Hill 881 South and Hill 881 North, two miles northwest of Khe Sanh itself. The 3d Battalion, 26th Marines (Alderman), attacked, killing 103 of the enemy. The second battle of Khe Sanh had begun. Next day, 21 January, the enemy overran the village of Khe Sanh. Refugees came crowding into the perimeter. The outpost on

Hill 861 and the base itself came under attack. The largest ammunition dump at Khe Sanh blew up under the mortar and artillery barrage.

Colonel Lownds asked for another battalion. General Tompkins told General Cushman that, unless otherwise directed, he intended to send his Division reserve, the 1st Battalion, 1st Marines, from Quang Tri to Khe Sanh. But this was one of the battalions scheduled to revert to Task Force X-Ray, so General Cushman directed Tompkins to send the 1st Battalion, 9th Marines (Lieutenant Colonel John F. Mitchell), a 3d Marine Division battalion, which was at Camp Evans. Mitchell's battalion arrived at Khe Sanh that same day, 21 January. Over one thousand civilian refugees were moved out by air.

On 26 January, General Lam agreed to send a Ranger Battalion to Khe Sanh and promised to send another one later if needed. The 37th Rangers, their on-board strength down to 318, came in on the 27th from Phu Loc. That same day, two more batteries of Marine 105mm. howitzers joined the garrison.

There were now five infantry battalions at Khe Sanh, supported by three batteries of 105mm. howitzers, a battery of 4.2-inch mortars, and a battery of 155mm. howitzers. Three batteries of 105s fell short of the rule-of-thumb ratio of one battery to each infantry battalion. More guns could have been moved into the perimeter, but this would have increased the congestion within the base. Further, it was foreseen that the controlling factor in direct support artillery would not be the number of tubes, but rather the number of artillery rounds that could be supplied by air.

Offsetting this slight deficiency in direct-support artillery were 18 long-range U.S. Army 175mm. guns within supporting range: 14 of them at Camp Carroll, and 4 at the Rockpile (Thon Son Lam).

Also at the Khe Sanh Combat Base (KSCB), there were six 90mm. gun tanks, ten ONTOS with their 106mm. recoilless rifles, two Army M-42s mounting dual 40mm. "dusters," and two Army M-55s with quad caliber .50s.[103]

In late January General Westmoreland issues his instructions to American forces for what has now become the annual Tet (Vietnamese New Year) truce period.

SECRET 02698
SUBJECT: OPERATION HOBBY HORSE (U)

1. (S) GVN HAS ANNOUNCED THAT A 36 HOUR TET CEASEFIRE WILL BE OBSERVED DURING THE PERIOD 291800H TO 310600H JAN. THE US POSITION FOR TET HAS NOT BEEN FORMALLY DECLARED AT THIS TIME, ALTHOUGH IT IS EXPECTED TO CONFORM WITH THE GVN POSITION EXCEPT 14 SPEKUF N AREAS. THE RULES GOVERNING MILITARY ACTIONS DURING THE CEASEFIRE ARE EXPECTED TO PARALLEL THOSE ESTABLISHED FOR THE NEW YEARS CEASEFIRE. THIS INFORMATION WILL BE PROMULGATED AS RECEIVED.

2. (S) OPERATION HOBBY HORSE, OUTLINED HEREIN, WILL BE IMPLEMENTED ON RECEIPT OF THIS MESSAGE IN ORDER TO MAXIMIZE OUR TACTICAL POTENTIAL FOLLOWING THE TET CEASEFIRE AT A TIME CAREFULLY SELECTED TO COINCIDE WITH THE ENEMY'S GREATEST VULNERABILITY. HOBBY HORSE WILL BE EXECUTED IN TWO PHASES:

A. PHASE ONE. EFFECTIVE IMMEDIATELY, COMMANDERS WILL INITIATE A COMPREHENSIVE AND INTENSIVE INTELLIGENCE COLLECTION EFFORT TO IDENTIFY AND PINPOINT ENEMY TROOP LOCATIONS, BASES AND FACILITIES, AND LOC LOCATIONS. THE INTELLIGENCE COLLECTION PROGRAM WILL BE STRESSED IN PARTICULAR DURING THE TET CEASEFIRE PERIOD. THIS HQ WILL PROVIDE, BY SEPARATE MESSAGES, SPECIFIC INTELLIGENCE TASKING INSTRUCTIONS COVERING AIR AND GROUND RECONNAISSANCE, AND REPORTING PROCEDURES FOR THE PERIOD. CONCURRENT WITH THE DEVELOPMENT OF INTELLIGENCE INFORMATION, ALL COMMANDERS (INCL RVNAF AND FW) WILL PREPARE DETAILED ATTACK PLANS AND FIRE PLAN FOR ALL WEAPONS SYSTEMS INCLUDING ARTY, NGF, TACAIR, AND ARCC LIGHT, WHICH WILL BE EXECUTED DURING PHASE TWO, HOBBY HORSE.

B. PHASE TWO: A TRADITIONAL HOLIDAY. TET IS OF EQUAL SIGNIFICANCE TO BOTH NVN AND RVN FORCES. IN THE EVENT THE ENEMY HONORS TO ANY EXTENT THE SPIRIT OF A TET CEASEFIRE, A DEGREE OF LAXITY AND VULNERABILITY AMONG ENEMY FORCES MAY BE EXPECTED DURING AND IN THE SHORT TERM FOLLOWING TET. HOWEVER, WITHIN THIS PERIOD IT MAY BE ANTICIPATED THAT ENEMY ALERTNESS MAY REACH A PEAK AT THE IMMEDIATE TERMINATION OF THE CEASEFIRE PERIOD, WITH A FURTHER RELAXATION FOLLOWING THEREAFTER IF NOT ATTACKED BY FIRE OR MANEUVER. COMMANDERS WILL THEREFORE CONTINUE THEIR INTENSIVE SURVEILLANCE TO DETERMINE THE MOST ADVANTAGEOUS TIME SUBSEQUENT TO THE CEASEFIRE PERIOD TO STRIKE THE ENEMY WHEN HE IS MOST VULNERABLE AND LEAST EXPECTING AN ATTACK. IT IS ASSUMED THAT OPTIMUM TIMING OPPORTUNITIES FOR INITIATING THESE SUDDEN AND CONCENTRATED OFFENSIVE STRIKES WILL VARY BY AREA, AND TARGET. THE DISCRETION AND JUDGEMENT OF THE RESPONSIBLE COMMANDER WILL PREVAIL IN ALL INSTANCES.

3. (S) IN THE PAST, FREE WORLD FORCES HAVE DERIVED NO DISCERNIBLE MILITARY ADVANTAGES FROM HOLIDAY CEASEFIRES. IT IS ESSENTIAL, THEREFORE, THAT OUR INTELLIGENCE CAPABILITIES BE EMPLOYED TO THE LIMIT OF THE IMPOSED CEASEFIRE CONSTRAINTS DURING THE TRUCE PERIOD; AND THAT THE FULL WEIGHT OF OUR FIREPOWER AND MANEUVER MOBILITY BE APPLIED WITH PRECISION, MASS AND PREEMPTIVE SUDDENNESS AND THE POINT TO THE GREATEST ENEMY VULNERABILITY FOLLOWING THE CEASEFIRE.

4. (S) TO BE FULLY EFFECTIVE, HOBBY HORSE PLANNING MUST BE CLOSELY COORDINATED WITH RVNAF/FW COUNTERPARTS. . . .

6. (U) ACTION ADDRESS ACKNOWLEDGE RECEIPT BY MSG OR TELEPHONE MACV 2927 OR EAC 381.[104]

In the novel A Station in the Delta, *CIA regional officer Bill Voight and CIA operations officer Chet Wolleson are celebrating the TET holiday at Can Tho. They discuss recent intelligence information that has been provided by pacification officer Toby Busch.*

It was midnight, and the Tet party in Can Tho was at its peak. Bill Voigt stood by the bar of the little lounge in the compound and looked foggily at the crowd of merry-makers. Dino was dancing with one of the nurses. Jerry was shaking a set of liar's dice with Russ, the commo man. A couple of people from an Ohio State University Research Team that was quartered at the far end of the compound were sitting with several of the USAID public relations people, who also had offices in the area. All of Bill's regional staff were there, as well as the Phong Dinh Province staff, and Wilbur Hamilton.

Even Chet had unwound more than Bill had ever known him to do; had, in fact, gotten somewhat bagged on CC and water.

The Christmas truce had been peaceful, and things had been quiet ever since, except for that astonishing ambush Toby Busch's people had run into. No question about it, they had uncovered an important hideout, probably of the Yenan Battalion. He would make sure Toby got full credit for that. Although, on the other hand, Little Jack surely ought to have handled that search operation better than that. *Christ, eighteen men killed.*

He looked at Chet, who was leaning on the bar beaming at nothing.

"Looks like our uneasiness about Viet Cong action during Tet was off the mark, Chet," he said. "Everything's calm and peaceful."

"Yeah," Chet replied. "Except for Busch, I guess. He's got his own private Tet offensive going."

"His Tet offensive? What's he doing, planning another search operation right away?"

"No, it's what he says the VC are planning. He's hollering that the VC are going to attack us tomorrow."

"Oh?" responded Bill idly, toying with the glass on the bar before him. "What's he got, some kind of a crystal ball?"

"No," muttered Chet, with something that sounded like a cross between a snort and a giggle, "I don't think either one of his balls is made of crystal, but I think his head is made of Jell-O."

"Well, you gotta admit he found a VC hideout the other day."

"Yeah, and got eighteen more men killed."

Bill did not respond. There was no point in arguing with Chet, especially about something he had such unreasoning responses to, and most especially when he was drunk.

"Him and his goddamned penetration," said Chet, taking a drink from the nearly empty glass.

"Penetration?"

"Yeah. Wunnerful great big goddamned penetration he says he's got. Brings me all kinds of crap from it."

"What's he been bringing you?" Bill asked, suddenly sober. "I've never seen any of it."

" 'Course not! Why should you be bothered with it? It's a whole piss-pot full of stuff, but he never was able to get enough information on his agent so we could clear him, and then he said the agent was under surveillance, and he was out of touch, and then he was back in touch with a dead drop, and he comes down here with a great big goddamned battle plan of the Viet Cong and expects me to put that out in an intel—at the same time the Saigon penetration operation is getting constant take, straight from the horse's mouth, that it's all a deception, and—"

"Chet, listen to me," said Bill sternly. "Did Busch bring reports in about a Tet attack—specific information?"

"Yeah."

"When?"

"Yesterday morning. I looked it over. Bunch of bullshit!"

"Where did he get the information?"

"I just told you. From some guy that says he's a local force battalion commander."

"Come on," said Bill. "I'm going with you to your office. I want you to get that stuff out and show me."

Chet shrugged and walked behind Bill across the driveway into the ROIC offices.

Ten minutes later Bill was leafing through the papers Toby had left, his eyes wide with astonishment, sweat starting from every pore.

"Chet," he said, looking intently at the other man, who was sitting drowsy-eyed across the desk, "at the very best, what you've done here is the stupidest thing I've ever seen, and at worst it's downright criminal!"

"Come on," said Chet indignantly. "That stuff—"

"This stuff may be true, or highly exaggerated, or even false, but it is intelligence that should have been disseminated with IMMEDIATE precedence the minute you got it. You've got all the elements necessary here for the customer to study the information and judge for himself. And yet *you* interposed your own judgment that it is false, and stopped it cold."

"It *is* false," said Chet.

"You'd better be saying prayers for the rest of the night that it is," said Bill, "and even if it is false, this action of yours of sitting on a report is going to go into your record. You've let a personal feeling about another officer distort your judgment and get in the way of your professional obligations."

"Now, just hold on a goddammed minute!" Chet exclaimed. "How in hell can they do anything to me for—"

"And," Bill continued, "if the information turns out to be true, you're going to spend the rest of your career running errands in headquarters, unless they decide to fire you. So, as I say, you better hope it isn't true.

"Now I want you to get every one of the officers in here, and Laura too. We're going to have a staff meeting, and I'm going to do as much as possible to get us ready and warn the rest of the country."

Chet rose and made as if to protest.

"Move!" Bill said coldly. "Move your ass like you've never moved it before!"

The staff assembled with the boisterous good humor of the party they had left, but Bill's steely purposefulness brought them around quickly. Each man was ordered to check the locations of the persons under his supervision, and do whatever he could to alert them, all over the delta. They must not give out any specific information over the single sideband, but the matter was urgent enough, and far enough along, that they would allow the Viet Cong monitors to conclude that something urgent was causing a great deal of traffic.

Having energized and dispatched his staff to alert the entire region, Bill dictated a paragraph that was to accompany the cabled intelligence report the reports officer was even now preparing.

"Make this FLASH precedence," he said to Laura.

Chet protested. "Christ, if you alert the whole world that way, and then it turns out—"

"Come here, Chet," Bill said, leading his deputy outside, where nobody could hear them. When they were alone, he grabbed Chet's arm.

"Next time you butt in on this," he rasped, "I'll say whatever I've got to say in front of anybody that's around. But this is one more time I'm going to answer you in private. If it hadn't been for your stupidity, I wouldn't be having to lay my own reputation on the line by putting out a FLASH message. This information could have gone with nothing but a priority, or maybe an immediate precedence if it had been handled the minute you got it. As it is, FLASH precedence may save something, maybe not much.

"Now, if you can be of any help around here, pitch in. If not, get the hell back to the bar, or to bed."

Bill marched back into his office and dictated the cable.

His reports officer was just coming in with the finished intelligence report when he was signing off on the operational information to go with it.

"Thank God Busch is a pro," said the reports officer. "That report was a beauty just as he turned it in. All I had to do was look up some references, and fix up the dissemination line."

"It looks serious, doesn't it?"

"I gotta say that report is damned convincing. Chet must have been out of his mind—"

"Here is the ops information to go with your intel," Bill said, handing the page to the reports officer just as the commo man came in to pick up the material for transmission.

THE FOLLOWING INFORMATION WAS OBTAINED FROM A SOURCE AT THE MIDDLE LEVEL OF THE VIET CONG MILITARY COMMAND. HE IS A NEW SOURCE, AND

UNTESTED. THE RELIABILITY OF HIS INFORMATION CANNOT BE JUDGED, AND WE REALIZE THAT IT CONTRADICTS THE VOLUMINOUS REPORTING SAIGON STATION HAS BEEN RECEIVING FROM A HIGH-LEVEL VIET CONG SOURCE IN THE PAST (SEE REFERENCES), BUT FIELD ASSESSMENT BOTH OF THIS AGENT AND OF HIS INFORMATION LEADS ROIC TO BELIEVE THAT THIS REPORT IS ACCURATE. THE WEALTH OF DETAILS WITHIN THE AREA OF AGENT'S KNOWLEDGE, THE TENOR OF HIS JUDGMENTS AND SPECULATIONS IN AREAS BEYOND HIS COMPETENCE, AND THE COINCIDENCE BETWEEN HIS INFORMATION AND THE RESULTS OF A RECENT SEARCH OPERATION IN DINH TUONG PROVINCE, WHICH THE AGENT COULD NOT HAVE KNOWN AT THE TIME OF HIS REPORT, ARE ELEMENTS THAT INVITE CAREFUL CONSIDERATION. THIS REPORT IS MORE, AND IT IS BETTER, THAN WOULD HAVE BEEN LOGICAL OR REQUIRED BY A DECEPTION OPERATION. ROIC BELIEVES IT TO BE TRUE, AND THIS REGION IS BEING PREPARED FOR ACTION AS WELL AS POSSIBLE AT THIS LATE HOUR.

FOR REASONS THAT WILL BE CLARIFIED ELSEWHERE THIS REPORT IS LATE GETTING INTO CHANNELS. IT IS FOR THIS REASON THAT IT IS BEING TRANSMITTED WITH FLASH PRECEDENCE.

"OK," said Bill, signing off on the documents and handing them to Russ. "Let's get this on the air, while the rest of us get some weapons issued and get set for whatever is coming."[105]

The same evening in Saigon, Red Cross International Volunteer Service employee Jane Stirling is in her hotel room, sleeping. One of the major characters in Hugh Atkinson's novel The Most Savage Animal, *Jane is due to depart the next day for a meeting in Geneva.*

She started up when the telephone rang, her heart beating painfully, in a confusion of dreams, striving to identify the room, to identify herself, to leave that place into which all the past weeks had tumbled in grotesque dislocation.

'It's Clark Clyde, Jane. I just wanted to say goodbye. I've got an early meeting in the moring.'

She came to herself gratefully, reached for the light switch. 'I'm sorry. What was that? I was sleeping.'

'It's Clark Clyde. I just wanted to wish you goodbye.'

'Where are you going?'

'I'm not going anywhere. I mean I'm going to Quong Lo. I'm not going back with you to Geneva.'

She brushed at her hair, frowning.

'I don't understand, Clark.'

'Are you in bed?'

'On the bed. What's the time?'

'Nine o'clock. If you're not in bed can I buy you a drink?'

She had thought it was the middle of the night. 'You can buy me a dinner.'

Seated together in the Hotel Caravelle, Clark Clyde stared dismally at the menu. He had barely finished a big meal before telephoning Jane. . . . 'There are rumours about an attack. Did you know the VC mortared Ton Son Nhut this afternoon?'

'The General told me. The General doesn't like war. . . . Let's share a châteaubriand.'

'A châteaubriand?" Clark Clyde was miserable. 'Are they very big?'

'Not too big for a big man like you. I'll have shrimp cocktail for a start.'

'I don't believe I'll have a starter.'

'A lady can't eat alone. It isn't manners.'

Clark Clyde shut his eyes. 'Very well. Shrimp cocktail for two.'

The Caravelle was a new hotel, a gay place in the evenings. They were at the end of the meal when they heard the heavy concussions, a muffled whump, whump, whump that seemed to vibrate the air. The chatter quietened. The guests waited, the men's faces suddenly sharpened.

'Artillery?' somebody asked.

Again the concussions whumped the room.

'No. More like heavy bombing.'

A correspondent scraped back his chair, wiping his mouth with a napkin.

'I'm going up on the roof.' He took his wine from the bucket. 'Come on, bring the glasses.'

They watched other hurried departures.

'Do you want to go?' Clark Clyde asked. 'Up on the roof, I mean. There might be something to see.' He emptied his glass and Jane's, and stuffed them in his pockets.

The parapet was lined with figures, bottle and glasses before them, exchanging calls and conjecture. A jet screamed near by, its tailpipe flaring.

'Sock it to them, man,' someone shouted.

There were more whumps, other distant explosions.

'What do you think? Is it Ton Son Nhut?'

'More the other way, near Cholon.'

On the dark horizon the sky lit with blazing streaks of colour, like fierce shooting stars.

'Helicopter gunships. They're putting the rockets in.'

Blazing parachute flares burned holes of luminosity in the dark. Tracer shells rose hotly, bent and expired.

'It's Cholon side. Somewhere back of Cholon.'

Again the fierce shooting stars struck at the ground from low on the horizon. The air whumped again.

The shouts and laughter on the roof grew louder.

'Sock it to them. Sock it to the little bastards.'

Jane thought of . . . small men in bare feet and sandals, hurrying to wrap weapons in mats, tying rice belts around their waists.

'It looks like cracker night,' Clark Clyde said. 'That's all—just like cracker night.'

Another jet screamed over the city. A woman in an evening dress tried to find it. 'Hurry up. You'll be late for the party.'[106]

Immediately, General Westmoreland issues the following order.

SECRET 30 JANUARY 68

1. (C) THE GVN HAS CANCELLED THE 36 HOUR CEASEFIRE FOR TET. ACCORD-INGLY, THE TET CEASEFIRE FOR U.S. FORCES (REF) IS HEREBY CANCELLED.

2. (C) EFFECTIVE IMMEDIATELY ALL FORCES WILL RESUME INTENSIFIED OPERA-TIONS, AND TROOPS WILL BE PLACED ON MAXIMUM ALERT WITH PARTICULAR ATTENTION TO THE DEFENSE OF HEADQUARTERS COMPLEXES, LOGISTICAL IN-STALLATIONS, AIRFIELDS, POPULATION CENTERS, AND BILLETS. ALL UNITS WILL BE PARTICULARLY ALERT TO DECEPTION MEASURES BY THE ENEMY AND BE POISED TO AGGRESSIVELY PURSUE AND DESTROY ANY ENEMY FORCE WHICH ATTACKS.

3. ACKNOWLEDGE RECEIPT . . . BY TELEPHONE MACV 2927, OR EAC 381.[107]

ACT III

January 1968–May 1970

In Vietnam,
The wind Doesn't Blow,
    It Sucks

                    BOMB HAIPHONG.

Better yet, get bombed.

            Only Lifers Get Bombed

Then Bomb Haiphong
        with LIFERS

—GI latrine graffiti, Saigon

An official South Vietnamese government study describes major actions of the enemy Tet Offensive.

Che sara sara with the Viet Cong nation-wide offensive on and gaining momentum. In the first hours of the campaign it was feared that Hanoi was about to realize its final objective of conquering South Vietnam. During the holiday period a total of 28 provincial capitals were attacked along with the sprawling metropolis of Saigon-Cholon. The following summarizes the situation.

In the nation's northernmost provinces, militarily known as I Corps, the Communists attacked Hue at 0200 hours on 31 January, then followed up with similar assaults on Quang Tri, Quang Tin, and Quang Ngai only two hours after the Hue push. In II Corps—the Highlands and the coastal provinces—Phan Thiet was hit at about the same time while the highland resort of Dalat was attacked during the early hours of 2 February.

In the provinces surrounding Saigon, militarily known as III Corps, the Communists also launched a series of well-coordinated attacks against vital military and political installations during the early hours of 31 January. The headquarters of the 25th Infantry Division in Hau Nghia province was assaulted the following morning. In the early hours of 1 February, installations in Binh Duong and Bien Hoa provinces were assailed. Long-Khanh was to be added to the list the following night.

In the Mekong Delta (IV Corps) Communist pressure was acutely felt in Phong Dinh, Vinh Long (1 Feb.), in Kien Hoa, Dinh Tuong, Kien Giang, and Vinh Binh (2 Feb.), in Kien Tuong (4 Feb.), and finally at the headquarters of the 44th Special Zone at Cao Lanh in the early hours of 5 February. Go Cong was the target for another V.C. assault the following night and Bac Lieu was struck five days later.

Chronologically, the V.C. *Tet* offensive included the following actions:

Tet's Eve: Qui Nhon, Kontum, Pleiku, Darlac, and Nha Trang; all these cities are located either in the highland or central coast.

31 January: Saigon-Cholon, Gia Dinh, Can Tho and Vinh Long (III and IV Corps); Phan Thiet (II Corps); and Hue, Quang Tri, Quang Tin and Quang Ngai (I Corps).

1 February: Kien Hoa, Dinh Tuong, Go Cong, Kien Giang, Vinh Binh (IV Corps); Binh Duong and Bien Hoa (III Corps); On this day the enemy pressure lost some of its momentum throughout the country although in such places as Saigon, Hue, Ban Me Thuot, Kontum, My Tho and Vinh Long, the situation still could be described as dangerous. After sunrise, Kien Tuong town and a few garrisons in Long Khanh province were attacked but the assailants were quickly repulsed.

2 February: Dalat (II Corps).

3 February: Enemy activities definitely decreased throughout the nation. Only in Hue did the Communists continue their occupation of the Citadel. In other cities the insurgents sought security by hiding among the people but they were rooted out. On that and the following day they also attempted to attack the provincial town of Go-Cong and the headquarters of the 44th Special Military District. They failed.

6 February: The situation in Hue, Saigon, and Can Tho continued to be a source of worry for military commanders. Particularly in Phong Dinh province, in the Mekong delta, V.C. pressure slowed down for a while, then became more intense in mid-February. In other parts of the country, especially in I and IV Corps, the Communists continued pounding populated areas with mortars and rockets.

7 February: For the first time in the war the Communists used tanks to attack an Allied position. A Communist armored column crossed the border from Laos and swept through the small village of Lang Vei near Khe Sanh. This brought about the collapse of the defensive system at Lang Vei. Only 72 of the defenders could get to Khe Sanh with the remaining 316 men considered either killed or missing. In the meantime U.S. marines joined the Battle of Hue and dislodged the Communists from the residential areas of the former imperial capital.

10 February: V.C. troops entered Bac-Lieu City and set afire an estimated 1,000 houses. Except for Saigon and Hue, all other South Vietnamese cities had been cleared of Communist troops by now. In Saigon, the fighting was located in the suburbs and in Hue it was in the areas of Cua Huu and the Bach Ho Bridge.

28 of the 48 cities and provincial towns of South Vietnam were attacked by the enemy.[1]

Tet in Saigon: as described in the novel Officers' Wives. *Having returned to visit her husband, who is ending his second tour of Vietnam duty, Amy Rosser is asleep in her hotel room.*

She was awakened by a tremendous explosion that sent bits of plaster raining into her face. She stumbled to the window, which now had a big crack in it. Below in the street, some kind of Army vehicle was burning. Men in black pajamas were running past it. One stopped, hoisted a bazooka to his shoulder, and the man beside him shoved a rocket into it. The rocket whizzed down the street and another explosion made the old hotel shudder. On the outskirts of the city a Fourth of July display of red tracers and white flares filled the sky. What in God's name was happening? Another coup? The government of Vietnam had been fairly stable for the past two years.

Amy called the desk. "What's going on?" she said.

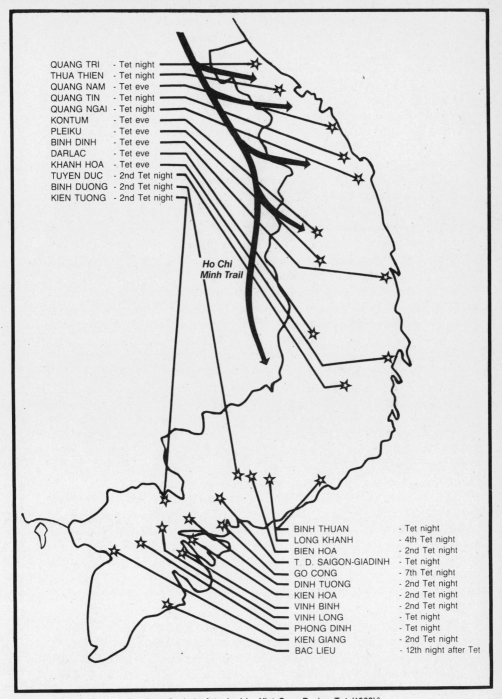

QUANG TRI - Tet night
THUA THIEN - Tet night
QUANG NAM - Tet eve
QUANG TIN - Tet night
QUANG NGAI - Tet night
KONTUM - Tet eve
PLEIKU - Tet eve
BINH DINH - Tet eve
DARLAC - Tet eve
KHANH HOA - Tet eve
TUYEN DUC - 2nd Tet night
BINH DUONG - 2nd Tet night
KIEN TUONG - 2nd Tet night

Ho Chi Minh Trail

BINH THUAN - Tet night
LONG KHANH - 4th Tet night
BIEN HOA - 2nd Tet night
T. D. SAIGON-GIADINH - Tet night
GO CONG - 7th Tet night
DINH TUONG - 2nd Tet night
KIEN HOA - 2nd Tet night
VINH BINH - 2nd Tet night
VINH LONG - Tet night
PHONG DINH - Tet night
KIEN GIANG - 2nd Tet night
BAC LIEU - 12th night after Tet

Province Capitals Attacked by Viet Cong During Tet (1968)[2]

"Beaucoup VC," gasped the operator. "Stay in room."

VC in Saigon? Amy stayed in her room. There was nothing else to do. Outside, a full-fledged battle was raging. Tanks and armored personnel carriers rumbled past, blasting the now unseen enemy. The tinkling sound of ambulance bells drifted through the dawn. Across the Saigon River in the Bui Phat slum a half dozen fires were raging.

About 7 A.M. Adam called. "Are you all right?" he asked.

"Yes. What's happening?"

"An all-out VC offensive. They're attacking every provincial capital from Quang Tri to Ca Mau."

"Where are you?"

"At Phoenix City BOQ. They just blew out all the windows."

"Is there fighting at Ban Me Thuot?"

"Heavy. It's heavy almost everywhere."

"I thought we were winning this war."

"It's a desperation gesture. We've been praying for them to come out and fight. I still can't believe they're doing anything so crazy. They must be factoring in the political value of it."

Amy tried to get some news on the radio in her room. All she heard at first was a confusing mixture of Viennese waltzes and Vietnamese popular songs. She learned later that the VC had captured the radio station in downtown Saigon but the South Vietnamese had cut off the transmitters and switched the station to an alternate unit outside Saigon, where the operators had nothing but tired music tapes to play. Eventually, as the day progressed, news began to come in from Armed Forces Radio. The Viet Cong had penetrated an amazing number of cities. At Qui Nhon they were ranting revolutionary appeals over the captured radio station. At Ban Me Thuot, the headquarters of George's brigade, the town was a chaos of gunfire and explosions. Outside, Saigon continued to reverberate with small-arms and cannon fire. A squad of sappers had attacked the U.S. Embassy but all had been killed by midmorning.

Adam called every hour or two. He was trying to get back to Phu Bai, but nothing was flying out of Tan Son Nhut. The airport was under attack by several battalions of Viet Cong. Not until the following day did he get a flight back to General Ingalls' headquarters. Amy meanwhile abandoned the hotel and wandered around Saigon, watching (along with crowds of Vietnamese) furious fire fights across the river in Bui Phat and other sections of the city, as government troops attacked isolated pockets of Viet Cong.

At one of these street scenes, she heard a gravel voice calling her name. "Mrs. Rosser? Amy?" She turned to blink up at the toothy face of Brooks Turner, her reporter friend and neighbor from Alexandre Dumas Street. "What the hell are you doing here?"

"I flew in to spend Tet with my husband. He's up at Ban Me Thuot. Probably fighting for his life."

"I think it's the other way around. The Great General Offensive and

People's Uprising, as they call it in Hanoi, seems to have failed miserably. There was no uprising. In most places the people just hid in their cellars. The ARVN is fighting like they've never fought before."

"How nice."

"You worried about George? I've got a guy in Ban Me Thuot. Let's go back to the villa. We may have some copy from him."

Brooks hustled her into his Renault and drove rapidly across Saigon to Alexandre Dumas Street. It was as peacefully suburban as it had been in 1963. Brooks said that her old villa was occupied by one of the twenty-seven generals now in Saigon. "A pompous asshole named Eberle. You know him?"

"Slightly," Amy said.

In the house, three exotic Eurasian secretaries, any one of whom could have posed for a *Playboy* centerfold, greeted Brooks with giddy smiles and simultaneously managed to frown at Amy. They thought she was competition. They relaxed somewhat when Brooks introduced her as the wife of his old friend Lieutenant Colonel Rosser. Brooks began shuffling through pages of copy that the secretaries had typed from correspondents elsewhere in Vietnam. "Holy shit," he said. "Listen to this."

He began to read from the middle of his stringer's story.

"The situation at Ban Me Thuot was critical. The Communists were roaming at will throughout the city, shooting South Vietnamese officials and Americans. Attempts by ARVN units to fight their way into the city were stalled by heavy resistance. I was at the airport, a fiercely contested site. The VC had heavy machine guns on two sides of it. Suddenly over the nearby jungle ridges, like the cavalry of old to the rescue, came the helicopters of the 1/3 Maneuver Battalion of the 1st Brigade of the 5th Airmobile Division, commanded by Lieutenant Colonel George Rosser. Down onto the bullet-swept airstrip they came, their armored helicopters pounding the dug-in VC with rockets and machine guns. One helicopter was hit by a shell from a recoilless rifle. It spun into a crumpled mass of smoldering metal; injured men could be seen crawling out of it. Colonel Rosser, whose command of the 1/3 was supposed to end today, instantly organized a rescue operation. Leaping into an ARVN armored personnel carrier, he ordered his radioman and a dozen troopers aboard it and roared across the airfield into a death-storm of VC automatic-weapons fire. While his gunships worked on the enemy from above, Rosser and his squad leaped from the personnel carrier and dragged wounded men back to the vehicle. Five of his men were hit, none of them seriously. As they went back for the last man in the downed chopper, another recoilless rifle round struck home and the gas tank exploded. Lieutenant Colonel Rosser plunged into the flaming interior to drag the unconscious pilot to safety. Rosser was badly burned on the face, hands and chest but he refused evacuation and organized his battalion for an immediate attack on VC positions around the airport. In two hours, the airport was cleared and the 1/3 was moving through Ban Me Thuot. As I write this, they are heavily engaged. Lieutenant Colonel Rosser is still in command."

George? Amy thought. *George?*

She had to sit down. Brooks Turner thought it was normal feminine fragility. He had no idea that Mrs. Rosser was weak-kneed because she had just discovered that all these years she had been living with a real soldier but had never given him a chance to prove it.

George. One of the brave. *George.*

"It was his last day in command?" Brooks Turner was asking her. "That's one hell of a story."[3]

Tet in Ban Me Thuot: as reported in the official South Vietnamese history:

The entire enemy assault force, regular and irregular, was estimated at about 3,500 men. It foreboded great danger for the city garrison, which had never faced such an overwhelming enemy force before. With such a large manpower commitment the enemy seemed intent on taking over the city and turning it into either a rear base or a political capital for the Communist-led National Liberation Front.

After a week of fighting, the enemy failed to occupy any Vietnamese military installations or compounds. His force spread into the populated areas and engaged in seesaw battles against the city defenders who were supported by armor, artillery and air strikes which extensively damaged the property and life of the local civilian population.

The 1/8 Tank Squadron and the 3/8 APC Squadron played the key part in the defense of the city and in defeating the enemy. The use of tank cannons, however, caused civilian casualties and property damage. Though these casualties and property damage were very regrettable accidents of war they were almost unavoidable.

The organic garrison soldiers of the 23rd Tactical Zone Command headquarters made up the only infantry unit defending the city. There were not many of them however. The enemy outnumbered and outgunned them.

Although the enemy was able to exploit the factor of surprise the failure of their attacks served to demoralize their fighting men. They elected to fight a defensive war from populated areas to include civilian houses and a few public buildings. Apparently they were ordered to stick to their positions and fight as long as possible and at all costs. Therefore their lost [sic] was heavier than the lost [sic] they suffered in jungle battles.

Commencing with the second day of their offensive the enemy units failed to stage any more assaults on any Vietnamese military compounds. They dug in and fought defensively. Many enemy positions were almost sitting ducks for Vietnamese armor and artillery. This style of fighting cost the enemy the highest combat casualties known in the city area since the beginning of the war.

Friendly forces suffered 148 killed, 315 wounded and 22 missing. The

23rd Infantry Division alone suffered 112 killed, 268 wounded and three missing in action. Equipment losses included 41 weapons, three tanks and two armored carriers burned, four other armor vehicles damaged and a number of radio transceivers and vehicles.

The enemy paid dearly. They had 924 of their men killed and 143 captured, they lost 243 weapons including 46 which were crew served.

The civilian population also suffered severely 176 were killed, 403 wounded and forced to live in eleven temporary refugee centers. Material damage included 3,319 houses destroyed completely and 479 houses at least 50% damaged 18,823 persons were made homeless and military dependents suffered a sizeable portion of the casualties and property damage. There were 66 killed, 48 wounded and 1095 houses destroyed with 323 housing units 50% damaged.[4]

Tet in Phu Bai: On each of the next two days, Private McMullen writes a letter home.

Feb, 6, 1968
Phu Bai
Leave me alone.

Feb, 7, 1968
Phu Bai
Perhaps I should elaborate somewhat.
While you (and others) have gadded about your cheerful landscape in search of happiness, a great deal has been decided (in secret places) (behind closed doors)
The part that will interest you the most is that—
There will be no more good old days—ever again.
In short—we have lost.
The changes will be slow at first—you will not be able to face it for a while longer yet.
BIG THINGS
HAVE FAILED.
   —and I am going
   far away.
   Please. I do not
   wish to hear
   anything
   anymore
   and I
   have
   nothing
   to say
   to anyone.[5]

Tet in Hue: Meanwhile, this battle is becoming the bloodiest engagement of the war. American journalist Michael Herr observes:

The courtyard of the American compound in Hue was filled with puddles from the rain, and the canvas tops of the jeeps and trucks sagged with the weight of the water. It was the fifth day of the fighting, and everyone was still amazed that the NVA or the Cong had not hit the compound on the first night. An enormous white goose had come into the compound that night, and now his wings were heavy with the oil that had formed on the surface of the puddles. Every time a vehicle entered the yard he would beat his wings in a fury and scream, but he never left the compound and, as far as I knew, no one ever ate him.

Nearly two hundred of us were sleeping in the two small rooms that had been the compound's dining quarters. The Army was not happy about having to billet all of the Marines that were coming through, and they were absolutely furious about all of the correspondents who were hanging around, waiting until the fighting moved north across the river, into the Citadel. You were lucky to find space enough on the floor to lie down on, luckier if you found an empty stretcher to sleep on, and luckiest of all if the stretcher was new. All night long the few unbroken windows would rattle from the airstrikes across the river, and a mortar pit just outside fired incessantly. At two or three in the morning, Marines would come in from their patrols. They'd cross the room, not much caring whether they stepped on anyone or not. They'd turn their radios on and shout across the room to one another. "Really, can't you fellows show a bit more consideration?" a British correspondent said, and their laughter woke anyone who was not already up.

One morning there was a fire in the prison camp across the road from the compound. We saw the black smoke rising over the barbed wire that topped the camp wall and heard automatic weapons' fire. The prison was full of captured NVA and Vietcong or Vietcong suspects; the guards said that the fire had been started to cover an escape. The ARVN and a few Americans were shooting blindly into the flames, and the bodies were burning where they fell. Civilian dead lay out on the sidewalks only a block from the compound, and the park that ran along the Perfume River was littered with dead. It was cold during those days, the sun never came out once, but the rain did things to the corpses that were worse in their way than anything the sun could have done. It was on one of those days that I realized that the only corpse I could not bear to look at would be the one I would never have to see.[6]

Tet in Hue: The South Vietnamese historians report atrocities.

The enemy virtually controlled the entire city on the evening of Tet Day or January 30. During the next two days enemy troops and agents moved about in the city freely. They were controlling the people as if they were operating in VC territory.

The VC called people out of their homes to "political study meetings," classified them into categories—civil servants, soldiers, police and just plain citizens. Except for the last category all the people summoned were detained overnight at the Government Delegate's office building on the right bank of the Perfume River. They were allowed to go home the next morning.

People speculated that the enemy was starting a three-stage mass arrest and murder scheme. The case mentioned above was a lighter one while the serious case involved those civilians detained in the Gia Hoi area which was under even firmer enemy control. In this area the enemy succeeded in carrying out all of the three stages of his sinister scheme.

First he sealed off the occupied area, herding the people together and classifying them into categories. The just plain citizen category was told to form civic organizations. This process was designed to help the enemy have tight control on the populace. Each of the organizations had a representative to take orders from the enemy. These plain citizens were told to continue to work normally and to keep public order. Then enemy troops and agents came to each house confiscating all private radios in an apparent effort to cut the people off from the outside world. At the same time they spread the rumor that the entire Thua Thien province and the whole country had come under their control.

In the next step they called on all national government employees, such as public servants, soldiers and police, to surrender their individual weapons and to report to their military place of duty in order to benefit from clemency measures. Failing to comply they would have to face severe punishment. Large numbers of such people turned themselves and their weapons in to the Communists and were allowed to freely return and stay home for two days. None were forced to do anything for the enemy. The move was apparently designed to deceive the public.

The third stage was the actual mass arrest and terror drive against these former employees of the local government.

After these two days of having been freed people were asked to attend "political meetings" by the enemy cadremen who came to each of their homes. A number of people never came back or were ever heard of again. The number of "missing" increased with each passing day. These people had been murdered somewhere in the city after reporting to the "political meetings." They had never suspected they would meet tragic death; nor had they been aware of the time they were to die. Survivors and enemy agents, captured in the later stages of the Hue battle, recounted that the victims had been told to dig air raid trenches during the daytime. Then they were actually led to these so-called trenches in the night to be massacred by the submachine-gun fire or simply buried alive. Apparently the victims had never suspected they were digging their own mass graves. In many cases the victims were murdered and shoved into the graves soon after they had finished digging.

An estimated 1,000 people were murdered and massacred in this way by the Viet Cong in the suburbs of Hue. They had been public servants,

soldiers and those who had experienced personal feuds with pro-
Communist elements during the political disturbances in preceding years.
Major mass graves were later found at the Gia Hoi high school, the Tang
Quang Tu pagoda, the Bai Dau area (some 30 mass graves here alone)
and Emperor Tu Duc's tomb (another 20 mass graves here). The bodies
recovered from these and other mass graves showed evidence of atrocious, painful deaths. A number of bodies were headless or limbless—or
both. Others had their hands tied behind their backs. Still others were
tied together in groups of tens or fifteens, indicating that the victims had
been shoved into the mass graves and buried alive.[7]

Tet in Hue: In the city, a corporal named Joker in Gustav Hasford's novel
The Short Timers *looks across the Perfume River at a North Vietnamese*
soldier who resembles an ant.

The ant fires.
   Machine-gun bullets knock the ant over.
   The gunship swings around to verify that it is a confirmed kill.
   As machine-gun bullets snap into the wet sand, the ant stands up, aims
its tiny AK-47 assault rifle, and fires a thirty-round magazine on full
automatic.
   The Huey gunship explodes, splits open like a bloated green egg. The
gutted carcass of aluminum and plexiglass bounces along, suspended in
the air, burning, trailing black smoke. And then it falls.
   The flaming chopper hits the river and the flowing water sucks it down.
   The ant does not move. The ant fires another magazine on full automatic. The ant is shooting at the sky. . . .
   The remaining two gunships attack.
   The ant walks off the beach.
   The gunships hit the beach and sand dunes with every weapon they've
got. They circle and circle and circle like predatory birds. Then, out of
ammunition and out of fuel, they buzz straight into the horizon and
vanish.
   Delta Company applauds and cheers and whistles. "Get some! Number
one! Out-fucking-standing! Payback is a motherfucker!"
   Alice says, "That guy was a grunt."
   While we wait for the gunboats to come and take us back across the
River of Perfumes we talk about how the NVA grunt was one hell of a hard
individual and about how it would be okay if he came to America and
married all our sisters and about how we all hope that he will live to be a
hundred years old because the world will be diminished when he's gone.
   The next morning, Rafter Man and I get the map coordinates of a mass
grave from some green ghouls and we hump over to the site to get
Captain January his atrocity photographs.
   The mass grave smells really bad—the odor of blood, the stink of
worms, decayed human beings. The Arvin snuffies doing the digging in a

school yard have all tied T-shirts around their faces, but casualties due to uncontrollable puking are heavy.

We see corpses of Vietnamese civilians who have been buried alive, faces frozen in mid-scream, hands like claws, the fingernails bloody and caked with damp earth. All of the dead people are grinning that hideous, joyless grin of those who have heard the joke, of those who have seen the terrible secrets of the earth. There's even the corpse of a dog which Victor Charlie could not separate from its master.

There are no corpses with their hands tied behind their backs. However, the green ghouls assure use that they have seen such corpses elsewhere. So I borrow some demolition wire from the Arvin snuffies and, crushing the stiff bodies with my knee until dry bones crack, I bind up a family, assembled at random from the multitude—a man, his wife, a little boy, a little girl, and, of course, their dog. As a final touch I wire the dog's feet together.[8]

On 12 February, with the fighting diminishing everywhere except Hue, PFC McMullen responds to a letter he has just received.

Feb. 12, 1968
Phu Bai
You surprise me. I had no idea you had an idea where Hue and Phu Bai are even located. Why are you so concerned? Everything is just fine. Why indeed is everyone so concerned? If they are really concerned about what is happening in Vietnam, why are they paying their taxes? Why indeed are they not lying down in the streets by the scrillions?

Did I tell you? Just a few short months ago I read in the paper that many citizens all over our great nation drove around during the daytime, one weekend, with their automobile lights on! To show their support for the boys in Vietnam. Let me tell you how truly moved I was by this sacrifice on their part. Many of us wept openly and unashamedly when the news arrived. The sight of our dear flag, glimmering in the Vietnamese twilight, above the Vietnamese soil, that night, stirred us all more deeply than we were usually stirred, Ah yes. "By the rockets red glare, the bombs bursting in air" . . . ah yes.[9]

In Washington that same day, the Joints Chiefs of Staff recognize a number of problems resulting from the Tet Offensive and make some recommendations to the secretary of defense.

3. *Assessment of the Situation in Vietnam.*

a. The VC/NVA forces have launched large-scale offensive operations throughout South Vietnam.

b. As of 11 February 1968, Headquarters, MACV, reports that attacks have taken place on 34 provincial towns, 64 district towns, and all of the autonomous cities.

c. The enemy has expressed his intention to continue offensive operations and to destroy the Government of Vietnam and its Armed Forces.

d. The first phase of his offensive has failed in that he does not have adequate control over any population center to install his Revolutionary Committees which he hoped to form into a coalition with the NLF.

e. He has lost between 30 and 40 thousand killed and captured, and we have seized over seven thousand weapons.

f. Reports indicate that he has committed the bulk of his VC main force elements down to platoon level throughout the country, with the exception of six to eight battalions in the general area of Saigon.

g. Thus far, he has committed only 20 to 25 percent of his North Vietnamese forces. These were employed as gap fillers where VC strength was apparently not adequate to carry out his initial thrust on the cities and towns. Since November, he has increased his NVA battalions by about 25. The bulk of these and the bulk of the uncommitted NVA forces are in the I Corps area.

h. It is not clear whether the enemy will be able to recycle his attacks on a second phase. He has indicated his intention to do so during the period from 10 to 15 February.

i. South Vietnamese forces have suffered nearly two thousand killed, over seven thousand wounded, and an unknown number of absences. MACV suspects the desertion rate may be high. The average present for duty strength of RVN infantry battalions is 50 percent and Ranger Battalions, 43 percent. Five of nine airborne battalions are judged by MACV to be combat ineffective at this time.

4. *MACV, RVNAF posture*—COMUSMACV has expressed three major concerns:

a. The ability of the weakened RVNAF to cope with additional sustained enemy offensive operations.

b. Logistic support north of Danang, because of weather and sea conditions in the Northern I Corps area, enemy interdiction of Route 1, and the probability of intensified combat in that area.

c. The forces available to him are not adequate at the moment to permit him to pursue his own campaign plans and to resume offensive operations against a weakened enemy, considering the competing requirements of reacting to enemy initiatives, assisting defending Government centers, and reinforcing weakened RVNAF units when necessary.

5. It is not clear at this time whether the enemy will be able to mount and sustain a second series of major attacks throughout the country. It is equally unclear as to how well the Vietnamese Armed Forces would be able to stand up against such a series of attacks if they were to occur. . . .

8. In addition to examining the criticality of deployments to South Vietnam, we must look to our capacity to meet the possibility of widespread civil disorder in the United States in the months ahead. It appears that, whether or not deployments under any of these plans are directed,

sufficient forces are still available for civil disorder control. These include National Guard forces deployed under State or Federal control, composite units brought together in each CONUS Army area, and some of the troops from 1st and 2nd Armored Divisions and 5th Infantry Division (Mech). . . .

11. Based on the foregoing assessment of the situation and problems facing COMUSMACV and the analysis of courses of action contained in the Annexes, the Joint Chiefs of Staff conclude and recommend that:

a. A decision to deploy reinforcements to Vietnam be deferred at this time.

b. Measures be taken now to prepare the 82nd Airborne Division and 6/9 Marine division/wing team for possible deployment to Vietnam.

c. As a matter of prudence, call certain additional Reserve units to active duty now. Deployment of emergency reinforcements to Vietnam should not be made without concomitant callup of Reserves sufficient at least to replace those deployed and provide for the increased sustaining base requirements of all Services. In addition, bring selected Reserve force units to full strength and an increased state of combat readiness.

d. Legislation be sought now to (1) provide authority to call individual Reservists to active duty; (2) extend past 30 June 1968 the existing authority to call Reserve units to active duty; and (3) extend terms of service for active duty personnel.[10]

Three days later, with the fighting in Hue still continuing, PFC McMullen writes again.

Feb. 15, 1968
Phu Bai
In truth, I am sickofitall. Only about one hundred days to go now. Somehow I must totter through those days to the great rest and solitude at the end of them.

I will scream and shout and rant and grow violent if anyone bothers me, says anything to me. Beware . . . Boy of Hostility.

Speaking of champions, soon I go into training for the heavyweight title. I will be great. The greatest. And when they activate the reserves, I will go to jail.

Quite seriously, I assume that sometime during the next four years that I will be subject to recall, there will be some blunderful crisis that will necessitate calling up the reserves. When they read the big roster, McMullen will be among the missing. Life is long. There is no need to do anything I don't want to. I will go to jail for a while. No big thing.

I am really trying to be nice and civil this letter, but my heart is not in it. I would love to punch people. Perhaps that in itself would be worth a few months in jail. Just to start punching people. Wham. Pow. I hate. Klobber. Pow. Wham.[11]

In Washington, on 20 February the Senate Foreign Relations Committee holds hearings on the subject of the Gulf of Tonkin incident. Shortly before he leaves office, Defense Secretary McNamara is questioned by members of the committee.

EXTENT OF U.S. PARTICIPATION IN SVN OPERATIONS AGAINST NORTH IN 1964
THE CHAIRMAN: Mr. Secretary, would you describe the organization, the extent of U.S. participation in South Vietnamese operations against the north during 1964?
SECRETARY MCNAMARA: I can't describe the exact organization although I will be happy to try to obtain the information for you.

The operations of the South Vietnamese against the North were carried out by South Vietnamese personnel, utilizing to some degree U.S. equipment. The boats, as I think I stated before this committee in August 1964, were, I believe, wholly supplied by the United States. I was going to say, in part; I think they were wholly supplied by the United States.

The United States was informed of the operations to insure that they did not interfere with patrols of the kind that we are describing now.

I believe, also, some U.S. personnel may have trained, or participated in the training, of some of the South Vietnamese personnel participating in the operations.

The operations, however, were under the command of the South Vietnamese and were carried out by the South Vietnamese. There were no U.S. personnel participating in it, to the best of my knowledge.

AMOUNT OF U.S. TRAINING AND SUPPLIES
THE CHAIRMAN: Do you recall, what did America do beyond training and supplying the equipment, do you know? You should know.
SECRETARY MCNAMARA: No. In the first place, I don't believe we carried on all the training, although I think there were some U.S. personnel participating in it.

In the second place, we did provide some of the equipment, but I don't believe we provided all of it.

Thirdly, we were informed of the nature of the operations but we did not participate in them and we did not command them. . . .
SENATOR GORE: Well, let us see if we differ on this matter. Today in your statement you say this, and this is page 2:

> As I stated then and repeat now our vessels played absolutely no part in and were not associated with this activity. There was then and there is now no question but that the United States Government knew, and that I knew personally, the general nature of some countermeasures being taken by the South Vietnamese in response to North Vietnamese aggression. As I informed Congress the boats utilized by the South Vietnamese were financed by the United States. What I said then, and I repeat today, that the *Maddox* and the *Turner Joy* did not participate in the South Vietnamese activities and they had no knowledge of the details of these opera-

tions, and that in no sense of the word could they be considered to have backstopped the effort.

Now, here is what you said to the committee on the 6th:

I would like to cover three points. First—

THE CHAIRMAN: Of August 1964.
SENATOR GORE: Of August 1964.

First, our Navy played absolutely no part in, was not associated with, was not aware of any South Vietnamese actions, if there were any. I want to make that very clear.

NEW STATEMENT ALTERS TESTIMONY OF AUGUST 1964
This was stricken from the record that was published. You state further, and I read again what was stricken from the record—

It was not informed of, was not aware, had no evidence of and, so far as I know today, has no knowledge any, any possible South Vietnamese actions in connection with the two islands that Senator Morse referred to.

Now, in your statement today you modified that. You said they had no knowledge of the details of these operations. That was not the question at all. So there is a considerable difference in what you said to the public today on this point and what you said to the committee on August 6, 1964. I read further, and all I am reading here, Mr. Secretary, was stricken from the record.
SECRETARY McNAMARA: Could I interrupt you one moment, Senator Gore?
SENATOR GORE: Yes, sir.
SECRETARY McNAMARA: Possibly through oversight you omitted a very important sentence in that August 6, 1964, statement because you read a sentence that started with the word 'It" when the word "It" in relation to what you said previously might have reflected back on the Navy to mean the Navy, whereas it meant the *Maddox,* and the sentence you omitted was, "The *Maddox,* operating in international waters, carrying out the routine patrol we carry out of the type we carry out at all times, it was not informed of it," meaning the *Maddox* was not informed of it.
SENATOR GORE: That is correct. The Department or you struck that from the record.
SECRETARY McNAMARA: I said the *Maddox*—
SENATOR GORE: It differs from what you said to the public today.
SECRETARY McNAMARA: I beg your pardon?
SENATOR GORE: Let me read two sentences.
SECRETARY McNAMARA: Let me make clear what this says and what the committee understood at the time, that the *Maddox* was not informed of, was not aware of, had no evidence of, no knowledge of any possible South Vietnamese actions in connection with the two islands that Senator Morse referred to. That was my belief then, it is my belief today, and I

personally had the commander of the patrol called within the last 72 hours to check and make sure that my understanding was still correct, and he says he did not have knowledge then of the possible South Vietnamese actions in connection with the two islands Senator Morse referred to.

SENATOR GORE: Well, your first statement there is that our Navy played absolutely no part in—

SECRETARY MCNAMARA: I think the word, when I say our Navy played no part in, I think that is true; was not associated with, that is true. I said it was not aware of, I think that is ambiguous. I was using the word "Navy" referring to the task force. But I think that it is ambiguous.

Later in the paragraph I think it is clear I was referring in the whole paragraph to the task force. But I certainly agree with you that the word "Navy" in the first sentence is ambiguous.

UNITED STATES KNEW OF 34A OPERATIONS

SENATOR GORE: Well, of course, we know now from the cables that the *Maddox* was, in fact, informed of the 34 Ops.

SECRETARY MCNAMARA: You do not know now that they had knowledge of—

SENATOR GORE: The details.

SECRETARY MCNAMARA (continuing): Possible—not the details. You do not know now they had knowledge of what I said they did not have knowledge of, which is possible Vietnamese actions. You know very well that the Navy meant *Maddox* in this context in that first sentence because I myself reported that the Navy had furnished the boats to the South Vietnamese, and you, meaning the Congress, so reported in the congressional debate, so there could have been no misinterpretation then, and I do not think there is now of that paragraph.

SENATOR GORE: Well, I won't review the cables. They are already in the record.

There is another sentence which you spoke to the committee about on page 24 of the executive hearings, that was deleted. I will read the whole sentence lest—and then I will identify what is stricken:

> I testified the other day that the American vessels were or the American vessel was, it was the MADDOX at that time, was operating on a southerly course in routine patrol in international waters in this area.

The following part of the sentence is stricken, "and that vessel had absolutely no knowledge of any actions of any kind by the South Vietnamese in South Vietnam or outside of South Vietnam."

The cables certainly contradict that.

SECRETARY MCNAMARA: I do not believe so, Senator Gore.

SENATOR GORE: Will you give me those cables?

SECRETARY MCNAMARA: Yes, sir; I have them here, and I will be happy to see that they are inserted in the record right here. The cables instruct the commander of the *Maddox* to stay outside certain restricted areas. They do not tell him who is operating in the areas or against what targets or at what times. They simply say, "Stay north and east of a line between two points 17 degrees, 17 plus degrees, in such and such easterly longitude."

Later that instruction is modified to say, "Stay north of 19 degrees 10 minutes north."

SENATOR GORE: Well, Mr. Secretary, you said earlier that the commander of the *Maddox* knew what 34 operations stood for.

SECRETARY MCNAMARA: I did not say. I think you will find in the record that I did not say that.

SENATOR GORE: Didn't he say that, Mr. Chairman?

KNOWLEDGE OF SHIP COMMANDERS LIMITED

SECRETARY MACNAMARA: You will have to check the record and see that. I said he did not know the time schedule of operations or of the targets or of the details of the operations. He did know that he was to stay out of certain restricted areas. He knew the term "34-A" because it was included in a message that was sent to him.

SENATOR GORE: But did not know what it stood for?

SECRETARY MCNAMARA: I do not believe he knew what it stood for, and he certainly did not know anything about these particular targets or dates or the nature of operations.

One good evidence of that is that he misidentified 34-A vessels as Russian vessels.

THE CHAIRMAN: Didn't he later say in one of his cables that the North Vietnamese were very agitated about their presence there and regarded them as part of the 34-A operations, in one of the later cables? I think he said that is why he was apprehensive and suggested that they call off the further operation.

The cable—let me see, I think—let me see, this is very puzzling to me. Is this the one at the top? The cable from the *Maddox*, "The above patrol will"—this is to the *Maddox*—"clearly demonstrate our determination to continue these operations. Possibly draw North Vietnamese Navy patrol boats to northward away from the area of 34-A operations and eliminate DeSoto patrol interference with 34 operations."

Then, on the 4th of August, some 15 hours before the second incident, the operational commander of the *Maddox* and the *Turner Joy,* who was aboard the *Maddox,* sent the following to the commander of the 7th Fleet:

> Evaluation of info from various sources indicates that DRV considers patrol directly involved with 34-A Ops.
>
> The DRV considers United States presence as enemies because of these ops and have already indicated readiness to treat us in that category.
>
> B. DRV are very sensitive about Hon Me. Believe this is PT operating base and the cove there presently contains numerous patrol and PT craft which have been repositioned from northerly bases.

I cannot imagine a commander who sent that saying that they considered him a part of the 34 operations without knowing anything about what 34 operations was.

SECRETARY MCNAMARA: Well, I can only tell you what he tells us, which is that he did not know the nature of the 34-A operations, the targets, the times, the boats, the courses, or anything at that time.

THE CHAIRMAN: The details.

SENATOR GORE: That was not what you told the committee though, Mr. Secretary.

SECRETARY MCNAMARA: It is what I believe I told the committee, Senator Gore.

PUBLIC STATEMENTS BY THE ADMINISTRATION DECEPTIVE

SENATOR GORE: You told the American people today they did not know about the details of the operation. What you said to the committee, back in 1964—let me find it:

> Our Navy played absolutely no part in, was not associated with, was not aware of, any South Vietnamese actions if there were any. . . .

SENATOR GORE: Let me state quite candidly my feeling of doubt and question. I hope that further inquiry will resolve these doubts and questions. I feel the Congress and the country were misled about the closeness of operation of DeSoto patrol and the South Vietnamese raids by vessels that we had furnished, by men we had trained, operating with the advice of our military advisers in South Vietnam. That is No. 1.

I know I have been misled. It may be partly my fault. I am not excusing myself.

Secondly, I feel that I was misled that this was an entirely unprovoked attack, that our ships were entirely on routine patrol. The fact stands from today that they were intelligence ships; that they were under instructions to agitate North Vietnam radar, that they were plying close to the shore within 4 miles of the islands under orders in the daytime, retiring at night; that they were covered with immediate air cover which, in itself—that they were covered with military aircraft which you said on television the other day which would be provocative off of North Korea. Why it would not be provocative off of North Vietnam I do not know.[12]

1968 23 February—Viet Cong and North Vietnamese forces withdraw from Hue.

Shortly afterward U.S. Marine Sergeant William Ehrhart leaves Vietnam and writes this poem.

Coming Home

San Francisco airport—

no more corpsmen stuffing ruptured chests
with cotton balls and not enough heat tabs
to eat a decent meal.

I asked some girl to sit
and have a Coke with me.
She thought I was crazy;
I thought she was going to call a cop.

I bought a ticket for Philadelphia.
At the loading gate, they told me:
"Thank you for flying TWA;
we hope you will enjoy your flight."

No brass bands;
no flags,
no girls,
no cameramen.

Only a small boy who asked me
what the ribbons on my jacket meant.[13]

At the month's end PFC McMullen writes home again.

Feb. 27, 1968
Phu Bai
We will not be going to Khe Sanh after all. The witness whom we were
going there to see has been wounded and medevaced to the States. We
will not be too sad at not going to Khe Sanh soon. They have many bad
things there.

Of the glorious war, I have decided it is time for the U.S. to admit we
cannot win and leave—before we lose. Further, if the Kommunists want
to take over the world, I would rather wait and fight them in my backyard
than in this hole. Further still, the predominant sentiment here is—

I'd rather save my ass
Than Johnson's face.

Anyway, you must get me one of those Support Our Boys—Bring
Them Home-type license plates, bumperstickers or whatever. I will put it
in my area at the hootch.

So far away we are here from girls. Someone came back from R&R
and said how soft girls were.[14]

*Michael Herr experiences what PFC McMullen has referred to as the "bad
things" at Khe Sanh.*

Sometimes you'd step from the bunker, all sense of time passing having left you, and find it dark out. The far side of the hills around the bowl of the base was glimmering, but you could never see the source of the light, and it had the look of a city at night approached from a great distance. Flares were dropping everywhere around the fringes of the perimeter, laying a dead white light on the high ground rising from the piedmont. There would be dozens of them at once sometimes, trailing an intense smoke, dropping white-hot sparks, and it seemed as though anything caught in their range would be made still, like figures in a game of living statues. There would be the muted rush of illumination rounds, fired from 60-mm. mortars inside the wire, dropping magnesium-brilliant above the NVA trenches for a few seconds, outlining the gaunt, flat spread of the mahogany trees, giving the landscape a ghastly clarity and dying out. You could watch mortar bursts, orange and gray-smoking, over the tops of trees three and four kilometers away, and the heavier shelling from support bases farther east along the DMZ, from Camp Carrol and the Rockpile, directed against suspected troop movements or NVA rocket and mortar positions. Once in a while—I guess I saw it happen three or four times in all—there would be a second-ary explosion, a direct hit on a supply of NVA ammunition. And at night it was beautiful. Even the incoming was beautiful at night, beautiful and deeply dreadful.

I remembered the way a Phantom pilot had talked about how beautiful the surface-to-air missiles looked as they drifted up toward his plane to kill him, and remembered myself how lovely .50-caliber tracers could be, com-ing at you as you flew at night in a helicopter, how slow and graceful, arching up easily, a dream, so remote from anything that could harm you. It could make you feel a total serenity, an elevation that put you above death, but that never lasted very long. One hit anywhere in the chopper would bring you back, bitten lips, white knuckles and all, and then you knew where you were. It was different with the incoming at Khe Sanh. You didn't get to watch the shells very often. You knew if you heard one, the first one, that you were safe, or at least saved. If you were still standing up and looking after that, you deserved anything that happened to you.

Nights were when the air and artillery strikes were heaviest, because that was when we knew that the NVA was above ground and moving. At night you could lie out on some sandbags and watch the C-47's mounted with Vulcans doing their work. The C-47 was a standard prop flareship, but many of them carried .20- and .762-mm. guns on their doors, Mike-Mikes that could fire out 300 rounds per second, Gatling style, "a round in every square inch of a football field in less than a minute," as the handouts said. They used to call it Puff the Magic Dragon, but the Ma-rines knew better: they named it Spooky. Every fifth round fired was a tracer, and when Spooky was working, everything stopped while that solid stream of violent red poured down out of the black sky. If you watched from a great distance, the stream would seem to dry up between bursts, vanishing slowly from air to ground like a comet tail, the sound of the guns disappearing too, a few seconds later. If you watched at a close range, you couldn't believe that anyone would have the courage to deal with that night after night, week after week, and you cultivated a respect for the Viet Cong and NVA who had crouched under it every night now for months. It was awesome, worse than anything the Lord had ever put down on Egypt, and at night, you'd hear the Marines talking, watching it, yelling, "Get some!" until they grew quiet and someone would say, "Spooky understands." The nights were very beautiful. Night was when you really had the least to fear and feared the most. You could go through some very bad numbers at night. . . .

And at night, all of it seemed more possible. At night in Khe Sanh, waiting there, thinking about all of them (40,000, some said), thinking that they might really try it, could keep you up. If they did, when they did, it might not matter that you were in the best bunker in the DMZ, wouldn't matter that you were young and had plans, that you were loved, that you were a noncombatant, an observer. Because if it came, it would be in a bloodswarm of killing, and credentials would not be examined. (The only Vietnamese many of us knew was the words "Bao Chi! Bao Chi!"—Journalist! Journalist! or even "Bao Chi Fap!"—French journalist!, which was the same as crying, Don't shoot! Don't shoot!) You came to love your life, to love and respect the mere fact of it, but often you became heedless of it in the way that somnambulists are heedless. Being "good" meant staying alive, and sometimes that was only a matter of caring enough at any given moment. No wonder everyone became a luck freak, no wonder you could wake at four in the morning some mornings and *know* that tomorrow it would finally happen, you could stop worrying about it now and just lie there, sweating in the dampest chill you ever felt.[15]

At about the same time, in Cassidy's novel A Station in the Delta, *CIA Regional Officer Bill Voigt, who had sent the last-minute warning of the Tet attacks, is in his office.*

Russ came in with a message, and Bill could tell by his face what the message contained.

"I am very sorry, Bill," Russ said, and quickly left.

REGRET TO INFORM YOU THAT YOUR SON, WILLIAM VOIGT, JR., WAS KILLED IN ACTION ON FEBRUARY 26. ALL CONCERNED DEEPLY DISTRESSED THAT REFERENCE MESSAGE REACHED YOU BEFORE OFFICIAL NOTIFICATION, WHICH WAS INEXPLICABLY DELAYED.

The phone rang, and Bill picked it up with a trembling hand. It was the adjutant at the Regional Adviser's office. "Bill," he said, "I've just received a message from Two Corps . . ."

"Yes, Hank," said Bill. "I know what's in it. I've just had the news from my own people."

"I don't know why this was delayed."

"It's all right. Those things can happen."

"I'll send this one right over."

"I'll appreciate it. How did it happen, do you know?"

"Yes. Apparently he did a brave thing, and it's not just the blah-blah that usually comes in these messages."

"What did he do?"

"He was trying to rally a remnant of Rangers after a bad ambush, and he went into one of those mud forts to bring some of them out."

"He went into a mud fort?"

"Yeah. A B-Forty hit it. He was killed instantly."

Bill sat as if frozen, the phone still in his hand.

"You still there, Bill?"

"Yeah. Sorry. Yeah, I'm still here."

"You OK?"

"Sure."

"There's nothing a fellow can say, Bill. Awfully sorry to give you such news."

"That's OK. Listen, do you think arrangements could be made for me to take him home personally?"

"I'm sure it could be arranged, if that's what you want to do."

"Will you work on it, then? I'll have to get my own people's permission for leave of absence, but I don't think that will be any problem."

"Leave it to me, old friend. I'll see that this doesn't get delayed. I'll be in touch with you."

Bill hung up the phone and sat motionless. He was feeling nothing yet. It was too soon. Such a calamity takes time to begin shaking a man's soul. He had had experiences in the past. The worst time was yet to come. He would weep for Will later today and tomorrow, but the real trial would come when he went home to his wife, bringing her only son back to her in a coffin.

He called Laura in and dictated a cable asking headquarters' permission to accompany Will's body to Massachusetts for burial. He also cabled headquarters to ask that his closest friend through all the years, a man whom he and his wife had known and loved since the old Burma days, be the one to go to her now with the news.

Then he went to the dining room. It was back to normal now, and the Vietnamese employees were serving breakfast to a capacity crowd. . . . Two navy public relations officers, whom he knew by sight, came to the table with another man and asked if they might sit there. Bill motioned them into the chairs. The other man was a reporter. . . . Bill regarded him blankly, not really paying attention.

"And so, I went out on that carrier, you know, and what do I have to put up with but an escort. It was a young jg that wouldn't let me out of his sight."

"Well," said one of the public relations men, "that's standard operating procedure, you know."

"Yeah, I know. I also know that what they wanted was to keep me from moving around the ship and talking to the people I wanted to talk to, and getting the story I was after. But I got away from the stupid son of a bitch anyway, and found just the guys I was looking for, and got the story I wanted."

"What was the story you wanted?"

"I wanted to find out what the morale really was like on that ship. Whether the guys were smoking a lot of marijuana, whether there were many of them that had deserted or wanted to desert."

Bill could not resist interjecting a comment. "I'd think you could find a better story where the fighting is still going on. There's plenty of it."

"You're wrong, my friend," said the reporter. "The news isn't here in Vietnam. The news is back home. People are sick and tired of this stupid war, and what the people are interested in hearing is that their army and navy feel the same way. These kids want out. Now. Canada and Sweden are full of 'em, you know. At least there are *some* young guys in our country that have got enough brains and guts to figure out what's right and do it."

Bill stood up as if to leave, but instead of turning to go, he brought his fist around in a crunching haymaker that caught the reporter full in the mouth. The reporter's head snapped back and he flew backward against a nearby table, knocking it over and scattering the startled occupants in all directions. Bill moved over to where the man sat, groggy from the force of the blow. Blood from a cut lip was dripping on his fatigues.

"You slimy bastard," Bill snarled. "You've got a war that's tearing millions of lives apart on land and what do you do? You go on board a ship to look for drugs and deserters. That's all this war means to a chicken shit like you—a chance to beat the competition with a story of how worthless and demoralized our soldiers are, and how great and noble the Viet Cong are. Money and fame, that's what you're after, and you don't care how you get them!"

Everybody in the dining room was sitting in silence, staring at the scene. The reporter made as if to rise.

"If you get up now," Bill said, "I'll finish the job on you. You better sit there and listen because it looks like the only way the press is ever going to get the truth is get their hard heads beaten in.

"You're sitting in the middle of a battle that's been won, won flat and hands down by us and our allies, but do you print that? No, you sure as hell don't, because that message, even though it's the God's truth, that everybody in this room knows, doesn't happen to agree with the gospel according to Saint Walter.

"Now, buster, if you want to tell your editors who punched you in the mouth, and who would be glad to kill you if you were worth killing, tell them it was the CIA Regional Officer in Charge, and that if they want to ask me why, I'll be glad to tell them.

"And what I'll tell them, you miserable chicken shit, is that our soldiers have won this battle, and this war, but you and your smart-ass friends, and your wiser-than-anybody editors, have lost it. And so every single death and every drop of blood through all these years, that you've had so much fun showing on the screens with your snide remarks, it's all been for nothing.

"And that is *your* fault!

"I hope you and your friends can live with that, because there is no forgiving it, and twenty years from now you're never going to be able to explain it!"

He stalked out.

The rest of the people in the dining room, who had been frozen into immobility by this sudden violent drama, began to straighten up the furniture and get back to normal. The public relations men helped the reporter to his feet and took him into the bar, where Sheila brought a basin with some water and some first-aid supplies, and began to treat his cut lip.

"Jesus Christ," said the reporter through his swelling lips, "what kind of Neanderthal is that guy?"

"He's a very sweet man," said Sheila. "You just caught him at a bad time."[16]

The North Vietnamese, however, have a different perspective on the Tet Offensive.

The Liberation Armed Forces and the compatriots of South Viet-Nam, on 30 January 1968, simultaneously rose up in 64 cities and provincial capitals and in many rural areas adjoining the cities. Revolutionary political power was established in Hue and in many newly liberated rural areas. The *Lien Minh Cac Luc Luong Dan Toc, Dan Chu Va Hoa Binh* (the Alliance of National, Democratic, and Peace Forces) in Saigon and Hue was born. The United National Front against the United States and for national salvation in South Viet-Nam was expanded.

The General Offensive and Uprisings in the early spring of 1968 dealt a lightning blow to the Americans and puppets, not only destroying a significant part of the enemy troop strength and destroying a colossal amount of the enemy's war materiel but also overturning the strategic position of the enemy and forcing the enemy to suddenly abandon its "search and destroy and pacify" plan and to pursue the defensive and passive strategy of "clear and hold". With more than 1 million U.S. and puppet troops, the White House and Pentagon leaders continued to complain about a shortage of troops. The countryside was left undefended and the "pacification" plan was bankrupted. The enemy had to pull back in order to defend in the cities and to defend the inner and outer perimeters, but, nevertheless, continued to fear surprise attacks by the Liberation Army.

Conversely, the war situation of the South Vietnamese [Communist] Army and people had never been as favorable and their strategic posture had never been as strong as it has been since the general offensive and uprisings of early spring 1968. The South Vietnamese revolution not only had a firm battle posture in the jungle and mountain area and in the countryside but also acquired a new front in the urban areas. The South Vietnamese Army and people brought the revolutionary war right to the hideouts of the Americans and puppets. The key agencies and vital installations of the enemy were dealt painful blows and were paralyzed and disrupted.

The General Offensive and Uprising is a process. Waves of attacks and uprisings continuously occur. Series of attacks are combined with regular attacks. Our people have become increasingly stronger the more they have fought and increasingly energized. Throughout 1968, the South Vietnamese Army and people knocked out of action 630,000 of the enemy, including 230,000 U.S. and satellite troops.[17]

1968   29 February—Defense Secretary McNamara's resignation becomes effective. He is replaced by Clark Clifford.

To the American advisers, the impact of the Tet Offensive is shown by this report, typical of those from the majority of provinces, from Quang Ngai Province Senior Adviser James A. May.

3 March 1968

TO: Deputy for CORDS
        III MAF
        Da Nang, Vietnam
Quang Ngai 05 Province   Period Ending: 29 February 1968

1. (C) STATUS OF THE REVOLUTIONARY DEVELOPMENT [RD] PLAN:
    a. The 1968 RD Program received a massive set back during the month of February due to heavy and partially successful VC attacks resulting in almost total collapse of security throughout the province (except Duc Pho). It will require at least another month to regain control of the terrain and population taken over by the VC. A longer period must ensue before the psychological damage has been repaired and full confidence in the GVN restored to its January 1968 level. Many Vietnamese officials, including the Province Chief, are confused, frightened, indecisive and even defeatists.
    b. On the positive side, the VC attacks have swept the twin veils of complacency and self-delusion from many eyes, US as well as GVN.

Many Vietnamese officials have begun to work as they never have before, in order to survive. Both American and Vietnamese officials are reexamining their RD theory and practice in order to devise a strengthened action program that cannot be emasculated by VC harassment and offensives. Such a program is being hammered out amid much healthy controversy. The "we must have an order from Saigon" syndrome is still one of the VC's most powerful allies in blocking local GVN action. CORDS officers have had to use both intensive and extensive leverage sometimes to the point of counter productivity, in order to force at least some essential action by their counterparts. The months ahead will require even more advisory pressure to overcome their inertia and seize the initiative from the VC. . . .

A. GENERAL:

(1) The security situation in the Province remained basically unchanged during the month, with the exception of the eastern area of Tu Ngia District, where, with the return of some RD teams and RF/PF units to their operational areas, there was some improvement over the low state of security existing at the first of the month. However, hopes for a rapid return to the security posture existing prior to the enemy's TET offensive have been thwarted by the enemy's continued harassment of friendly units and terrorist activities directed against the local populace.

(2) In Nghia Hanh District, the security situation is even more critical. There has been no improvement at all during the month. Enemy main force, local force, and guerrilla units continue to have complete freedom of movement and the opportunity to harass at will. The enemy's success in gaining control of the uncommitted population in the district was greater than in any other area of the Province, and, as a result extensive friendly operations throughout the district will be necessary before a return to the pre-TET security is achieved.

(3) In Binh Son, Mo Duc, and Duc Pho Districts the situation has been returned to the approximate status quo prior to the TET offensive. Extensive sweep operations by the Americal Division in Binh Son have assisted in removing temporary VC areas of influence, as they have to a certain extent in Son Tinh. The SIA for the Duc Pho DIOCC indicates that the VC continue to use the eastern areas of Duc Pho District, to include the areas in and around Duc Pho District Headquarters, for resupply. Because Duc Pho District did not come under heavy attack during the TET offensive there was no basic change in the security threat, with the important exception of the almost total annihilation of C/219 Sapper Co., due to the Americal Division operations.

(4) Route #1 remains open from the northern to southern end of the Province, though harassing incidents have increased during the month.

(5) Total incidents initiated by the enemy during the month were 94, as compared to 76 in January and 65 in December 1967.

B. ENEMY SITUATION:

(1) After the relocation of elements from virtually every local force (LF) unit in Quang Ngai Province to the area of Quang Ngai City for the attack of 31 January, all the units involved have slowly drifted back to their former areas of operation. Though no unit escaped heavy casualties during the offensive, indications are that the VC, partially because of a successful propaganda campaign and partially because of an extension of their area of influence, have been able to recruit replacements with greater ease than they have known for the past year.[18]

The impact of the Tet Offensive on the American people, however, results primarily from one episode shown on TV: Saigon Police Chief General Loan executing a captured enemy soldier.[19]

Later, poet Gerald Lange writes about his reaction to watching the Tet Offensive on television.

Poem for Brig. Gen. Nguyen Ngoc Loan:
Chance News Item

These days I watch the news cautiously
You can't be too careful
I keep my hand on the knob
just in case

you see
I was not prepared
you raised the pistol to his head
and shot him too quickly

I don't think you truly understood
the needs of the American viewing audience
you see
it never happened that way
on television before

christ I could barely whisper
I could barely remember how to scream

you have to work up to these things slowly
murder is such a difficult thing to get right

fatigue sleeves rolled to the elbow
tendons hard to the task
you were playing a part
that I could understand

but you shot him too quickly
I was not prepared

the violent contortion of the facial muscles
the slow stiffness of the dying limbs
the blood squirting to equilibrium
christ

and then to be cut off
and sit through station identification
and a three minute commercial
how do you think we must have felt

now months later
I see where you got yours
carried out of a Saigon alley
on the back of an American Marine

you seemed smaller than I remembered[20]

*On 3 March Defense Secretary Clark Clifford's Vietnam Working Group
makes recommendations to President Johnson.*

1. Meeting General Westmoreland's request by deploying as close to
May 1 as practical 20,000 additional troops (approximately 1/2 of which
would be combat).
2. Approval of a Reserve call-up and an increased end strength adequate to meet the balance of the request and to restore a strategic reserve
in the United States, adequate for possible contingencies.

3. Reservation of the decision to deploy the balance of General West-moreland's new request. While we would be in a position to make these additional deployments, the future decision to do so would be contingent upon:

a. Continuous reexamination of the desirability of further deployments on a week-by-week basis as the situation develops;

b. Improved political performance by the GVN and increased contribution in effective military action by the ARVN;

c. The results of a study in depth, to be initiated immediately, of a possible new strategic guidance for the conduct of US military operations in South Vietnam.[21]

Still unacknowledged by the U.S. government and unknown to most of the American people, the war in Laos has also intensified. Arthur J. Dommen records the fall of a vital outpost.

Communist thrusts menaced government positions near Paksane, Sara-vane, and Attopeu. The Communists drove government troops out of Lao Ngam in the northern foothills of the Bolovens Plateau, thereby gaining a commanding hold on a region crisscrossed with trails and rich in produce. The valley of the Done River as far as Pakse came within the sphere of Pathet Lao requisitioning and recruiting activity. Lao Ngam became the terminus of new camouflaged roads that generally followed the line of Route Nationale 23 south from Muong Phine, then broke off and crossed the Done River at a series of fords downstream from Sara-vane. The capture of Thateng allowed the Communists to link up Lao Ngam with a new embarkation point near Ban Phone thirty miles south of the old mountain trail terminus of Ban Bac on the Kong River. Following the Tet Offensive, launched in South Vietnam on January 31, 1968, North Vietnamese traffic in Laos reached a record peak in March when 17,000 trucks were believed by American sources to be operating along the Trail as Hanoi bent all efforts to sustain the "generalized offensive" strategy in the South. . . .

THE CAPTURE OF PHOU PHA THI
In Sam Neua Province, the North Vietnamese had made several unsuccessful attempts to drive the Americans off Phou Pha Thi, from which bombers were directed onto targets in the Red River delta. The position appeared so inaccessible that the North Vietnamese outfitted some of their antiquated Russian Antonov biplanes to carry mortar shells with which to bomb the radio and radar antennas on the summit. The lumbering craft made easy targets, and their raids were little better than suicide missions; the exuberant Americans at Phou Pha Thi gave visitors pieces of the wreckage of two of the biplanes as souvenirs.

By February, 1968, however, the North Vietnamese high command meant business and launched three battalions of the 766th Regiment against Phou Pha Thi. They took the airstrip and fought their way up the last slopes in hand-to-hand combat. The place was defended by Meo and Thai irregulars. Heavy bombing had not been able to prevent the North Vietnamese from building a road through the jungle to the foot of the peak. As the ring tightened around them, twelve U.S. Air Force technicians abandoned their van and, using ropes, lowered themselves down the almost sheer cliff face to their rear and sought shelter in caves. One by one they were killed by grenades dropped over the edge of the cliff by the North Vietnamese above. A thirteenth American, a ground air controller, slipped through the North Vietnamese lines and was later rescued by helicopter. On March 11, the handful of Americans and their loyal Meo guards, on whom the men in the air had depended for so long, were no more.[22]

1968   12 March—Peace candidate Eugene McCarthy makes an extremely strong showing in the New Hampshire Democratic Party presidential primary. **16 March**—Robert Kennedy, brother of the former president, announces his candidacy for the Democratic Party nomination for president.

In South Vietnam that same day, according to three Associated Press reporters, what is designed to be a routine mission starts for Company C of the 1st Battalion, 20th Infantry, 23rd (Americal) Division of the U.S. Army.

So now, on March 16, Charlie Company was winging southeast on its 15 minute flight to My Lai. Below was the neat quilt-patch pattern of the farmlands and rice paddies, broken up by necklaces of trees, the rivers and the straight, sharp line of Highway 521. It was morning, but already the spring heat of Vietnam made the air sultry and moist. The sun was over the South China Sea, a silvery, shimmering expanse in the distance.

The helicopters traveling southward passed over the western edge of the village, dipped farther south and came north again—making a counter-clockwise sweep in their landing pattern. Artillery still was exploding on the outer perimeter of the village. Helicopter gunships were still sending down their rockets but, incredibly, in the huts some My Lai inhabitants were eating breakfast. Only very few people could be seen as the helicopters dropped down.

My Lai 4 from the air was amoeba-shaped, mostly green, with the brown bamboo roofs of the hooches poking through. Thick jungle growth shielded neighbor from neighbor. There was a trail running east-west along the south edge and it was crossed by another one, slashing straight southward between farms to Highway 521—My Lai's road to the markets

of Quang Ngai City. That trail crossing was a landmark of the hamlet's
life and so was it to be of its death.

Trees marked the limits of the village at the east and then there was a
clearing of a few hundred meters. Beyond that was another line of green
vegetation and a shallow drainage ditch that was 4–5 feet wide in spots as
it meandered south and west. The water was scummy and brown from the
mud stirred by the basking water buffalo. Later that day it would run red.

Rusty Calley rode to battle like a leader, taking the first helicopter
ferrying Charlie Company to My Lai 4. Because of the artillery fire, the
copters circled before making their final approach.

"We came in on our final and the guns opened up," Calley said [later].
"The door gunner on our chopper didn't open up because the gunships
were almost right off the side of him. But the only really significant thing
I remember there, that on final, the AC [aircraft commander] turned
around and told me we had a hot one, we were coming in hot and I
believe he said, 'When I get low, un-ass.'

"And we definitely did. I think my first man went out the chopper
when we were still at 15 feet. I went off, it was about five feet off the
ground."

Lt. William L. Calley Jr. had arrived at My Lai 4.

"Well, after we got on the ground and got set up and in our position,
there was a few minutes' delay before we actually started our assault. The
gunships were still working on the village and we kind of just sat back and
waited for an order. The order came down to start our assault. We came
up with an initial heavy burst of fire, but, within three or four steps, most
of the men were knocking back down to semi-automatic fire and assaulted straight through the village. It was pretty rough going. It was hard
to keep a line formation there because of the hedgerows and the buildings
and the trees and everything would channelize men into files and they
would have to break back out and it was pretty raggedy-andy going
through there as a line formation.

"I have no idea as to the time concept of how long it took us to move
completely through the village. When I got to the eastern edge, my
formation had broken down. I immediately had to get my squad leaders
to get my men reformed up to move out."

If the VC 48th was going to fight that day, it hadn't chosen to make its
stand at My Lai 4. Medina came on the radio. What was holding Calley
up?

"I told him I had some bunkers yet to check out and that I wanted to
check, and I still had that small portion of the hamlet to the southeast.
And also there was a lot of enemy personnel I still had with me . . .
ahead of me."

Calley said Medina told him to hurry and get his men moving again—
"and get rid of the people I had there that were detaining me. When I
broke out of the village on the southern trail, I at that time ran into Paul
Meadlo that was there with a large, well, a group of people."

Paul Meadlo, 20 then, was a dark-haired, broad-chested youth and a PFC rifleman in Calley's platoon. Calley said he asked Meadlo if he knew what he was supposed to do with "those people."

"He said he did," Calley went on. "I told him to get moving, get on the other side of the ditch. I am talking about the main ditch that was right there in front of us."

Calley said he was having other problems. He spied one of his men, Dennis Conti, molesting a Vietnamese woman, he said later. "I told him to get his pants back up and get over to where he was supposed to be."

Then he turned to a sergeant, L. G. Bacon, and told him where to set in his guns. "He rogered and the next conversation I had was with section again, Capt. Medina. He asked me why I was disobeying his orders. Well, I explained to him why, what was slowing me down, and at that time he told me to waste the Vietnamese and get my people out on line, out in the position they were supposed to be."

Calley said he yelled to Bacon and told him to get his men searching the bunkers. Then he started over to S. Sgt. David Mitchell's position and noticed Meadlo still standing there with a group of Vietnamese. Calley yelled to the PFC.

"I told him if he couldn't move all those people, to get rid of them. He gave me a reply. I don't know what it was."

Then, Calley said, he heard a considerable volume of firing. . . .

There was an official report of that day at My Lai 4. This was Lt. Col. Barker's confidential combat action report, dated March 28th. It was in marked contrast with what came to be known about this small place in a small war. Barker wrote of "the many hedgerows [that] offered the enemy considerable cover and concealment from the attacking friendly forces."

He wrote of the artillery barrage preceding the arrival of Charlie Company and said it "resulted in 68 VC KIAs (killed in action) in the enemy's combat zone. Company C then immediately attacked to the east, receiving enemy small arms fire as they pressed forward."

He wrote that "all casualties requiring evacuation were removed from the area by helicopters, including wounded VC and some of their civilian supporters."

And he wrote: "This operation was well planned, well executed and successful. Friendly casualties were light and the enemy suffered heavily. On this operation the civilian population supporting the VC in the area numbered approximately 200. This created a problem in population control and medical care of those civilians caught in the fires of opposing forces. However, the infantry unit on the ground and helicopters were able to assist civilians in leaving the area and in caring for and/or evacuating the wounded."

And he concluded with a recommendation that medical and police teams and such henceforth be brought into such an operation to "facili-

tate population control and medical care and . . . free infantry personnel
for combat operations."

Then he affixed his name.[23]

Poet W. D. Ehrhart expresses a prevailing GI attitude at this time.

Guerrilla War

It's practically impossible
to tell civilians
from the Vietcong.

Nobody wears uniforms.
They all talk
the same language
(and you couldn't understand them
even if they didn't).

They tape grenades
inside their clothes,
and carry satchel charges
in their market baskets.

Even their women fight;
and young boys,
and girls.

It's practically impossible
to tell civilians
from the Vietcong;

after awhile,
you quit trying.[24]

1968   **18 March**—President Johnson meets with friends and advisers, including George Ball, Dean Acheson, and Maxwell Taylor, all of
whom are no longer part of the present U.S. government.
22 March—President Johnson announces that General Westmoreland is to be recalled to become chief of staff of the U.S. Army.

---

*On 30 March the acting U.S. secretary of state sends a "Literally Eyes
Only" message to the U.S. ambassadors in Southeast Asia. In part, the
message states that the next day the president will deliver a speech that will
contain the following emphasis:*

[2] a. Major stress on importance of GVN and ARVN increased effectiveness, with our equipment and other support as first priority in our
own actions.

b. 13,500 support forces to be called up at once in order to round out the 10,500 combat units sent in February.

c. Replenishment of strategic reserve by calling up 48,500 additional reserves, stating that these would be designed to strategic reserve.

d. Related tax increases and budget cuts already largely needed for non-Vietnamese reasons.

3. In addition, after similar consultation and concurrence, President proposes to announce that bombing will be restricted to targets most directly engaged in the battlefield area and that this meant that there would be no bombing north of 20th parallel. Announcement would leave open how Hanoi might respond, and would be open-ended as to time. However, it would indicate that Hanoi's response could be helpful in determining whether we were justified in assumption that Hanoi would not take advantage if we stopping (sic) bombing altogether. Thus, it would to this extent foreshadow possibility of full bombing stoppage at a later point.

The ambassadors are given some instructions.

a. You should call attention to force increases that would be announced at the same time and would make clear our continued resolve. Also our top priority to re-equipping ARVN forces.

b. You should make clear that Hanoi is likely to denounce the project and thus free our hand after a short period. Nonetheless, we might wish to continue the limitation even after a formal denunciation, in order to reinforce its sincerity and put the monkey firmly on Hanoi's back for whatever follows. Of course, any major military change could compel full-scale resumption at any time.

c. With or without denunciation, Hanoi might well feel limited in conducting any major offensives at least in the northern areas. If they did so, this could ease the pressure where it is most potentially serious. If they did not, then this would give us a clear field for whatever actions were then required.

d. In view of weather limitations, bombing north of the 20th parallel will in any event be limited at least for the next four weeks or so—which we tentatively envisage as a maximum testing period in any event. Hence, we are not giving up anything really serious in this time frame. Moreover, air power now used north of 20th can probably be used in Laos (where no policy change planned) and in SVN.

e. Insofar as our announcement foreshadows any possibility of a complete bombing stoppage, in the event Hanoi really exercises reciprocal restraints, we regard this as unlikely. But in any case, the period of demonstrated restraint would probably have to continue for a period of several weeks. . . .[25]

The next day, 31 March, President Johnson speaks to the nation. His rewritten ending surprises even his closest advisers.

Tonight I renew the offer I made last August—to stop the bombardment of North Viet-Nam. We ask that talks begin promptly, that they be serious talks on the substance of peace. We assume that during those talks Hanoi will not take advantage of our restraint.

We are prepared to move immediately toward peace through negotiations.

So tonight, in the hope that this action will lead to early talks, I am taking the first step to deescalate the conflict. We are reducing—substantially reducing—the present level of hostilities. And we are doing so unilaterally and at once.

Tonight I have ordered our aircraft and our naval vessels to make no attacks on North Viet-Nam, except in the area north of the demilitarized zone where the continuing enemy buildup directly threatens Allied forward positions and where the movements of their troops and supplies are clearly related to that threat.

The area in which we are stopping our attacks includes almost 90 percent of North Viet-Nam's population and most of its territory. Thus there will be no attacks around the principal populated areas or in the food-producing areas of North Viet-Nam.

Even this very limited bombing of the North could come to an early end if our restraint is matched by restraint in Hanoi. But I cannot in good conscience stop all bombing so long as to do so would immediately and directly endanger the lives of our men and our allies. Whether a complete bombing halt becomes possible in the future will be determined by events.

Our purpose in this action is to bring about a reduction in the level of violence that now exists. . . .

I call upon President Ho Chi Minh to respond positively and favorably to this new step toward peace.

But if peace does not come now through negotiations, it will come when Hanoi understands that our common resolve is unshakable and our common strength is invincible. . . .

Finally, my fellow Americans, let me say this:

Of those to whom much is given, much is asked. I cannot say, and no man could say, that no more will be asked of us.

Yet, I believe that now, no less than when the decade began, this generation of Americans is willing to "pay any price, bear any burden, meet any hardship, support any friend, oppose any foe to assure the survival and the success of liberty." Since those words were spoken by John F. Kennedy, the people of America have kept that compact with mankind's noblest cause. . . .

And in these times as in times before, it is true that a house divided against itself by the spirit of faction, of party, of region, of religion, of race, is a house that cannot stand.

There is division in the American house now. There is divisiveness among us all tonight. And holding the trust that is mine, as President of all the people, I cannot disregard the peril to the progress of the American people and the hope and the prospect of peace for all peoples. . . .

What we won when all our people united just must not now be lost in suspicion, distrust, selfishness, and politics among any of our people.

Believing this as I do, I have concluded that I should not permit the Presidency to become involved in the partisan divisions that are developing in this political year.

With America's sons in the fields far away, with America's future under challenge right here at home, with our hopes and the world's hopes for peace in the balance every day, I do not believe that I should devote an hour or a day of my time to any personal partisan causes or to any duties other than the awesome duties of this Office—the Presidency of your country.

Accordingly, I shall not seek, and I will not accept, the nomination of my party for another term as your President.

But let men everywhere know, however, that a strong, a confident, and a vigilant America stands ready tonight to seek an honorable peace—and stands ready tonight to defend an honored cause—whatever the price, whatever the burden, whatever the sacrifices that duty may require.

Thank you for listening.

Good night and God bless all of you.[26]

In Vietnam the next day, according to the Seventh Air Force HQ (Saigon) Weekly Intelligence Summary, some significant new developments occur.

I CORPS.

11. (C) The enemy may have deployed SAM's into South Vietnam. On 1 April at 0548 hours a Marine F-8 pilot observed what he described as a SAM launched at his aircraft from a point 15 kilometers northwest of Khe Sanh (XD 728476). There was no electronic warning, but the aircraft successfully avoided the missile which exploded at approximately 15,000 feet. There was another SAM site reported just south of the DMZ above Camp Carroll last month. However, this is the first occasion where a missile has actually been launched. Several interrogation reports have described various missiles located north of the DMZ apparently headed for South Vietnam. While the missiles were often described as surface-to-surface, it is possible that the informants mistook SAM's for another type of missile.

12. (C) An agent who has previously provided valid information, including early warning of the TET offensive, alleges that Quang Ngai and Quang Tin Provinces will come under strong ground attacks during April. He further alleges that, as a result of these attacks, the NVA/VC will offer to negotiate with the following demands:

a. Quang Tri and Thua Thien Provinces must go to North Vietnam.

b. From the southern border of Thua Thien Province to Nha Trang City must be ruled by a coalition government which includes the VC.

c. The rest of South Vietnam would remain under GVN control. There was no evaluation of this information provided. . . .

III CORPS.

2. (C) A series of recently captured documents provides the most comprehensive information to date of the Communist's plan for the TET offensive and reveal in some detail plans for future VC/NVA action against III Corps. Together, these documents emphasize the seriousness with which the enemy views the TET offensive failure, reveal continuing efforts to overcome deficiencies, and reflect the enemy's plans for eventual renewal of offensive activity in the Saigon area. These references to a second offensive against Saigon are now considered to be long range plans. A 21 Feb COSVN document states that it is not advisable to conduct large-scale attacks on towns and cities in the immediate future because the 'enemy' defenses have been strengthened. The documents stress the fact that the main reason for the failure to attain all of the goals of the TET offensive was primarily a lack of coordination.[27]

1968   3 April—The DRV replies to President Johnson: its representatives will meet with those of the United States. For months, the parties will argue over the selection of a site and the shape of the table.
4 April—In Memphis, Tennessee, civil rights leader Dr. Martin Luther King, Jr., is assassinated.

During this period the Khe Sanh base has held despite enemy shelling and probes. A U.S. Marine Corps history describes how the siege is lifted.

Operation Pegasus was launched on 1 April. The ARVN portion of the operation was called Lam Son 207; the ARVN had long since given up trying to give each operation a gutsy, evocative nickname. 1st Air Cavalry Division, with an ARVN airborne battalion moving with them, was to leap-frog into successive positions east and then south of Khe Sanh. Less dramatically, the 1st Marine Regiment (Hughes) and three ARVN battalions were to move overland westward from Ca Lu to open up Route 9 itself.

On the first day out, 1st Marines, moving against very little resistance, got to their objective west of Ca Lu; and 3d Brigade, 1st Air Cavalry (Campbell) established a fire support base five miles east of Khe Sanh.

On 4 April, 26th Marines attacked southeast from Khe Sanh itself. First link-up between the Marines and cavalrymen came on 6 April when 1st Battalion, 9th Marines (Mitchell) met the approaching 1st Air Cav troopers. Later that same day, 1st Air Cav and ARVN airborne elements reached Khe Sanh. On 9 April, for the first time in 45 days, no shells fell on the base; and U.S. forces went back into Lang Vei Special Forces camp, meeting virtually no resistance. By 12 April, Route 9 was open to truck traffic.

Two days later, on 14 April, 3d Battalion, 26th Marines (Lieutenant Colonel John C. Studt) took Hill 881 North. Operation Pegasus was now declared over.

The battle for Khe Sanh had been fought according to plan: the Marines had buttoned up their defenses; the enemy had been engaged with massive firepower, air and artillery; the defenders had been adequately re-supplied by air; land communications were restored with the return of good weather.

Writes General Westmoreland: "The key to our success at Khe Sanh was firepower, principally aerial firepower. For 77 days, Air Force, Navy, and Marine aircraft provided round-the-clock, close-in support to the defending garrison and were controlled by airborne Forward Air Controllers or ground-based radar. Between 22 January and 31 March, tactical aircraft flew an average of 300 sorties daily, close to one every five minutes, and expended 35,000 tons of bombs and rockets."

During the same period, Strategic Air Command's B-52s had flown 2,602 sorties and dropped over 75,000 tons of bombs. Marine howitzers at Khe Sanh and Army 175s supporting from Camp Carroll and the Rockpile had fired over 100,000 rounds, nearly 1,500 shells a day.

Between 21 January and 8 April, 14,000 or more tons of supplies were delivered by Marine and Air Force air to Khe Sanh. Sixty-five percent of the deliveries were by parachute drop from C-130s and C-123s. In all, there were some 679 drops. During the same period, 455 aircraft landed at Khe Sanh. Television may have given the American public the impression that anything attempting to land at Khe Sanh was shot down. Actually only four fixed-wing aircraft—a C-130, a C-123, an A-4, and an F-4— appear to have been destroyed by enemy action.

Perhaps a tougher problem in aerial logistics than the air drops on KSCB (the main drop zone was between the perimeter and the rock quarry) was the re-supply of the two Marine battalions occupying the hills to the north. This was done by Marine helicopters flying in "gaggles" averaging seven aircraft and coming straight from Dong Ha to each of the hill positions. Coming down on these minuscule landing zones was like placing the chopper on the center of a bull's eye and was only feasible because of the covering close air support provided by Marine fixed-wing aircraft using smoke, napalm, and bombs. Exact helicopter losses are elusive but it appears that at least 17 choppers were destroyed or received "strike damage" and that perhaps twice this number received some degree of battle damage.

In any case, there was never a serious supply shortage. General Westmoreland rightly called the logistic air effort the "premier air logistical feat of the war."

In no way was Khe Sanh another Dien Bien Phu. The Marines had never thought that it would be.[28]

*On 15 April, his tour of duty nearing its end, PFC McMullen replies to a
letter from a friend.*

April 15, 1968
Phu Bai
Gee, things went boom in the night (in Gainesville). I'm awfully sorry to
hear that. Hey, Guys, I said. Things're really rough back in the world:
Listen to this. Things go boom in the night there.

We all laughed and laughed. Hohoho.

Really. One sniper bullet. You wake me up in the middle of the night
to tell me one sniper bullet was (maybe) fired from a dorm near you.
Henny Penny and Ducky Lucky maybe you should have told, Ha Ha.

So far as I could read from the paper you sent, everyone got all riled up
and the national guard came and some people got arrested and maybe a
few people threw rocks and set some fires. What is so big about that?
This is only April. And it is only 1968. You just wait, honkie, you just
wait. Worse things are coming. Wait a few summers yet maybe. Hicksville will really burn.

I myself would like to preside over the Conflagration of Los Angeles.
While LeRoi Jones lights the torch to New Jersey.

You speak of white backlash as if it were a thing of the future. It's here,
been here a while, growing with all the other sickness of your sick country.
You are white backlash, you and all the others who say, yes, I'm for them
having their rights, but this violence and rioting are just too much. Only
wait, sickies. Your country is, if you have not noticed, the most racist in the
world. Only slightly worse than South Africa, but still worse. It is a racism
that runs right to the sick core. (Meanwhile your mighty Republic is gutting
a nation and people in Asia). But I won't go into that here. Only now I will
tell you that you have seen nothing yet. You have not seen civil disorders,
but the first sparks of the revolution. You wait.[29]

*At this time in Saigon, correspondent Michael Herr goes to a party with a
new friend.*

His name was Davies, and he was a gunner with a helicopter group based
at Tan Son Nhut airport. On paper, by the regulations, he was billeted in
one of the big "hotel" BEQs in Cholon, but he only kept his things there.
He actually lived in a small two-story Vietnamese house deeper inside of
Cholon, as far from the papers and the regulations as he could get. Every
morning he took an Army bus with wire-grill windows out to the base and
flew missions, mostly around War Zone C, along the Cambodian border,
and most nights he returned to the house in Cholon where he lived with
his "wife" (he'd found her in one of the bars) and some other Vietnamese
who were said to be the girl's family. Her mamma-san and her brother
were always there, living on the first floor, and there were others who

came and went. He seldom saw the brother, but every few days he would find a pile of labels and brand names torn from cardboard cartons, American products that the brother wanted from the PX.

The first time I saw him he was sitting alone at a table on the Continental terrace, drinking a beer. He had a full, drooping moustache and sharp, sad eyes, and he was wearing a denim workshirt and wheat jeans. He also carried a Leica and a copy of *Ramparts Magazine,* and I just assumed at first he was a correspondent. I didn't know then that you could buy *Ramparts* at the PX, and after I'd borrowed and returned it, we began to talk. It was the issue that featured left-wing Catholics like Jesus Christ and Fulton Sheen on the cover. *"Catholique?"* one of the bar girls said later that night. "Moi aussi," and she kept the magazine. That was when we were walking around Cholon in the rain trying to find Hoa, his wife. Mamma-san had told us that she'd gone to the movies with some girl friends, but Davies knew what she was doing.

"I hate that shit," he said. "It's so uncool."

"Well, don't put up with it."

"Yeah."

Davies' house was down a long narrow alley that became nothing more than a warren at the end, smelling of camphor-smoke and fish, crowded but clean. He would not speak to Mamma-san, and we walked straight up to the second floor. It was one long room that had a sleeping area screened off in an arrangement of filmy curtains. At the top of the stairs there was a large poster of Lenny Bruce, and beneath it, in a shrine effect, was a low table with a Buddha and lighted incense on it.

"Lenny," Davies said.

Most of one wall was covered with a collage that Davies had done with the help of some friends. It included photos of burning monks, stacked Vietcong dead, wounded Marines screaming and weeping, Cardinal Spellman waving from a chopper, Ronald Reagan, his face halved and separated by a stalk of cannabis; pictures of John Lennon peering through wire-rimmed glasses, Mick Jagger, Jimi Hendrix, Dylan, Eldridge Cleaver, Rap Brown; coffins draped with American flags whose stars were replaced by swastikas and dollar signs; odd parts clipped from *Playboy* pictures, newspaper headlines (Farmers Butcher Hogs to Protest Pork Price Dip) photo captions (President Jokes with Newsmen), beautiful girls holding flowers, showers of peace symbols; Ky standing at attention and saluting, a small mushroom cloud forming where his genitalia should have been; a map of the Western United States with the shape of Vietnam reversed and fitted over California; and one large, long figure that began at the bottom with shiny leather boots and rouged knees and ascended in a microskirt, bare breasts, graceful shoulders, and a long neck, topped by the burned, blackened face of a dead Vietnamese woman.

By the time Davies' friends showed up, we were already stoned. We could hear them below, laughing and rapping with Mamma, and then they came up the stairs, three blacks and two white guys.

"It sure do smell *peculiar* up here," one of them said.

"Hi, you freaky li'l fuckers."

"This grass is Number Ten," Davies said. "Every time I smoke this grass over here it gives me a bad trip."

"Ain' nuthin' th' matter with that grass," someone said. "It ain' the grass."

"Where's Hoa?"

"Yeah, Davies, where's your ole lady at?"

"She's out hustling Saigon tea, and I'm fucking sick of it." He tried to look really angry, but he only looked unhappy.

One of them handed off a joint and stretched out. "Hairy day today," he said.

"Where'd you fly?"

"Bu Dop."

"Bu Dop!" one of the spades said, and he started to move toward the joint, jiving and working his shoulders, bobbing his head. "Bu Dop, budop, bu dop dop *dop!*"

"Funky funky Bu Dop."

"Hey, man, can you O.D. on grass?"

"I dunno, baby. Maybe we could get jobs at the Aberdeen Proving Grounds smokin' dope for Uncle Sugar."

"Wow, I'm stoned. Hey, Davies, you stoned?"

"Yeah," Davies said.

It started to rain again, so hard that you couldn't hear drops, only the full force of the water pouring down on the metal roof. We smoked a little more, and then the others started to leave. Davies looked like he was sleeping with his eyes open.

"That goddam pig," he said. "Fuckin' whore. Man, I'm paying out all this bread for the house, and those people downstairs. I don't even know who they are, for Christ's sake. I'm really . . . I'm getting sick of it."

"You're pretty short now," someone said. "Why don't you cut out?"

"You mean just split?"

"Why not?"

Davies was quiet for a long time.

"Yeah," he finally said. "This is bad. This is really bad. I think I'm going to get out of here."[30]

1968   **3 May**—In Washington, President Johnson announces that the United States and the DRV have agreed to Paris as a site for peace talks, to start on 10 May. **May**—In South Vietnam, Communists begin "second phase" of their spring offensive. Forewarned, U.S. and ARVN forces suppress all attacks. **6 June**—Los Angeles. Presidential candidate Robert F. Kennedy, Jr., is assassinated.

At this time, the last group of marines, as described in William Huggett's Body Count, *enter the American base at Khe Sanh. One marine's flak jacket is inscribed as follows:*

YEA THOUGH I WALK THROUGH THE VALLEY OF THE SHADOW OF DEATH I WILL FEAR NO EVIL FOR I AM THE MEANEST MOTHERFUCKER IN THE VALLEY.

At dusk they filed into the great base; and every man felt the awesome hush. So many had died here. The bunkers seemed to stretch on and on into the gloom, a zigzagging trench between each bunker. In silence they passed rows of rusted coils of sagging concertina wire stacked five and seven rolls high. Beyond that were the cross-woven patterns of straight barbed wire, knee and waist high. Between these was the thatch row of German barbed tape, tangled fields of metal strips edged with razorlike flanges instead of barbs. Beyond that, scattered through the wires, were the Claymore mines, a load of buckshot plastered onto the front of a curved block of TNT, with electric detonating cords running back into the bunkers. There was one last row of concertina wire and finally the misty valley stretched out to the hills where the NVA made the final circle.

"Christ, it's big!"

"Gives me the creeps."

It had been three weeks since the contact at Banks' Hill, and the company was assigned to perimeter guard duty at Khe Sanh even though the base was largely evacuated.

They moved on toward the COC, Command of Camp, bunker and waited. The COC and the medical bunkers were deep in the ground, only the top making a little bulge on the surface. It looked like a big boil, crudely bandaged with tarps and canvas. Here and there was a little wooden appendage for air.

Along the runway great hulks of twisted metal bore witness to the inferno it had once been. Grotesque trucks with jagged, deformed bodies lay everywhere. Burned-out airplane frames reared into the sky like weird sculpture. Open trash pits stank. Everything lay discarded and rusting as if it were a city abandoned before a plague. Now it was only quiet and still. A ghost town—deserted and old. Rats manned the dilapidated bunkers.

A sergeant came to show them to their positions. The perimeter seemed endless as they filed past bunker after bunker.

"You've got that sector. It's the sector One-Nine used to have."

"One-Nine *Battalion*," Hawkins exclaimed; "we're only a company!" He began to count the bunkers and realized that there would only be two men to a bunker with several empty bunkers in between, fifty percent watch all night.

Their platoon section was so long it would take Hawkins an hour to check the lines—even in the daytime. He stumbled along the trench and stopped at the yawning hole of the bunker he and Joseley would man.

"Let's see what we got." He struck a match and timorously poked his head through the hole. Immediately there was a scurrying of little bodies; but it was the odor that hit him—of old urine, rotten C-rations, and moldy dankness. Something like putrid Camembert cheese.

"Whew! People slept in there." He lit another match and stepped in again. It was a hole about five and a half feet high; three feet dug into the ground, and two feet above the ground level piled up with sandbags to complete the structure. Odd strips of metal and crooked wooden poles formed the frame for the roof. Hawkins' eyes lighted as he saw a bed, a hospital stretcher. The poles were stuck into the dirt wall at one end and propped on sandbags at the other. He put his hand down, testing. The canvas was slick wet. His hand jerked away.

"Let's sleep outside, Lieutenant."[31]

1968   27 June—All U.S. troops withdraw from the Khe Sanh base, leaving it to be reoccupied by the enemy.

As the fighting diminishes all over Vietnam, American soldiers, much like Private Robert Chatain in his story "On the Perimeter," experience the routine of night guard duty.

Discourse

They liked to divide the members of the security platoon evenly along the length of the perimeter, no two "veterans" in any one bunker, and fill out the remaining positions with ordinary clerks on detail from the various units of Long Binh. Occasionally the roster put me with people from my old company, but usually I spent the night with strangers. In the intimacy of the bunker they could not keep their mouths shut. I had to listen, smoldering, to hours of rumor, complaint, prejudice, and platitude. By the time dawn carried them back to their safe barracks I would know whether they had been drafted or had volunteered for the draft or enlisted or been tricked into enlisting or railroaded by their local boards, their families, or the courts; I would have found out where they had received training, how they had come to Vietnam, what they thought they had discovered about themselves, God, and their country, and when they would get out; I would have heard some of their most interesting Army experiences; I would have been told their opinions on the manners and morals of the peoples of Europe, Asia, and the other places their uniforms had taken them, and I would have learned their attitude toward the

war, toward international communism, toward the peace movement, and
finally toward the chance that they might be killed during the night, a
possibility that I sometimes came to anticipate with pleasure long before
they had finished talking.[32]

*During the summer of 1968, many other young Americans such as Tim
O'Brien are also discussing "manners and morals," as shown by this passage from* If I Die in a Combat Zone.

I'd never been a demonstrator, except in the loose sense. True, I'd taken
a stand in the school newspaper on the war, trying to show why it seemed
wrong. But, mostly, I'd just listened.

"No war is worth losing your life for," a college acquaintance used to
argue. "The issue isn't a moral one. It's a matter of efficiency: What's the
most efficient way to stay alive when your nation is at war? That's the
issue."

But others argued that no war is worth losing your country for, and
when asked about the case when a country fights a wrong war, those
people just shrugged.

Most of my college friends found easy paths away from the problem, all
to their credit. Deferments for this and that. Letters from doctors or
chaplains. It was hard to find people who had to think much about the
problem. Counsel came from two main quarters, pacifists and veterans of
foreign wars, but neither camp had much to offer. It wasn't a matter of
peace, as the pacifists argued, but rather a matter of when and when not
to join others in making war. And it wasn't a matter of listening to an
ex-lieutenant colonel talk about serving in a right war, when the question
was whether to serve in what seemed a wrong one.

On August 13, I went to the bus depot. A Worthington *Daily Globe*
photographer took my picture standing by a rail fence with four other
draftees.

Then the bus took us through corn fields, to little towns along the
way—Rushmore and Adrian—where other recruits came aboard. With
the tough guys drinking beer and howling in the back seats, brandishing
their empty cans and calling one another "scum" and "trainee" and "GI
Joe," with all this noise and hearty farewelling, we went to Sioux Falls.
We spent the night in a YMCA. I went out alone for a beer, drank it in a
corner booth, then I bought a book and read it in my room.

At noon the next day our hands were in the air, even the tough guys.
We recited the oath—some of us loudly and daringly, others in bewilder-
ment. It was a brightly lighted room, wood paneled. A flag gave the place
the right colors. There was smoke in the air. We said the words, and we
were soldiers.

I'd never been much of a fighter. I was afraid of bullies: frustrated
anger. Still, I deferred to no one. Positively lorded myself over inferiors.
And on top of that was the matter of conscience and conviction, uncer-

tain and surface-deep but pure nonetheless. I was a confirmed liberal. Not a pacifist, but I would have cast my ballot to end the Vietnam war, I would have voted for Eugene McCarthy, hoping he would make peace. I was not soldier material, that was certain.

But I submitted. All the soul searchings and midnight conversations and books and beliefs were voided by abstention, extinguished by forfeiture, for lack of oxygen, by a sort of sleepwalking default. It was no decision, no chain of ideas or reasons, that steered me into the war.

It was an intellectual and physical stand-off, and I did not have the energy to see it to an end. It did not want to be a soldier, not even an observer to war. But neither did I want to upset a peculiar balance between the order I knew, the people I knew, and my own private world. It was not just that I valued that order. I also feared its opposite—inevitable chaos, censure, embarrassment, the end of everything that had happened in my life, the end of it all.[33]

In August Private Robert Chatain is standing night guard duty on the perimeter.

Miami

The passing of the broom from one bunker to the next was a time-honored ritual that had survived the earlier attacks on the ammunition depot, the physical deterioration of the bunkers during the months since their construction, even the coming of the monsoon and subsequent reduction in the amount of dust to be swept from the bunks and floorboards. No one remembered when the last inspection of the bunker line had been made, but still the broom passed every night. It was a good chance to catch up on the news.

"You hear about Fine?"

"No."

"Got orders for the Congo. Diplomatic mission. Far out."

"Hm."

"You haven't heard about the new offensive in September?"

"No."

"Supposed to be a big offensive in September, big as Tet."

"Hm."

"You hear about all the fucking money they dug up near Qui Nhon?"

"No."

"A hundred and fifty grand, all in fifty-dollar bills. The Treasury Department says there isn't supposed to be any fifty-dollar bills over here. We're paying for both fucking sides of this war."

"Hm."

"You hear about the Republicans?"

"No."

"Nominated Richard Nixon."
"Hm."[34]

1968   20 August—U.S.S.R. invades Czechoslovakia.

Again on night guard duty, Private Chatain and his buddies talk.

Czechoslovakia

The well-informed were discussing current events over the field phone. I listened, but stayed out of it.

"If they've taken Dubček to Moscow he's probably dead by now."

"I just didn't believe they'd actually go through with it."

"The radio stations knew about it in advance and set up secret spots to broadcast from. They kept everybody cool."

"You've got to hand it to kids who throw stones at tanks."

"Well, there are good guys and bad guys in the Kremlin just as there are good guys and bad guys in Washington. The bad guys won."

A new voice cut in. "We should bomb the shit out of them."

"One war at a time, huh?"[35]

During the next few days, Private Chatain learns of events taking place at the Democratic National Convention.

Chicago

First I heard that large demonstrations were planned, which was to be expected, and that the Mayor had announced he would keep order, which was also to be expected. Then I heard that twenty thousand troops would be on hand and that sixty black GI's had staged a sit-down strike at Fort Hood when ordered to go. From an amateur political analyst I understood that Gene had no chance, George had no chance, and if Hubert didn't take it on the first ballot, Teddy would get the nod. I was reminded that labor troubles in the city had affected transportation and communications. I discovered that the FBI had unearthed plans to dump LSD into the city's water supply. I read that the Unit Rule had been abolished, a "peace plank" had been proposed by a minority of the Platform Committee, and Georgia's Lester Maddox group had not been seated pending the outcome of a challenge by a rival delegation. A sergeant told me about a lot of violence in Lincoln Park. I found out that the peace plank had been respectably defeated. I was informed that city police had apparently gone crazy, injuring hundreds of people. A crowd had been pushed through the plate-glass window of the Hilton Hotel's Haymarket Lounge, someone reported. I saw a remarkable *Stars and Stripes* headline which read,

"Police Storm Hotel, Beat McCarthy Aides." There was speculation that newsmen were being deliberately assaulted. I learned that Hubert Humphrey had received the Democratic nomination. I was told of a silent candlelight parade by delegates from the Amphitheater to the Loop.[36]

In Chicago, from 28 to 29 August, Vietnam veteran Carl Rogers is one of the demonstrators.

Chicago

As the grey smoke filled the air around us, our eyes burned and watered. We couldn't breathe, even through the water-soaked cloths that "old-timers" in the peace movement had given us earlier . . . I cursed at the Guards whom I had been defending up to that moment, as I too had been in uniform not long before. Now I was full of rage. And I was full of fear as I watched them insert clips of ammunition into weapons like that I had carried in Vietnam . . .

Rows of guards followed jeeps with barbed wire strung across the front of them. It didn't talke the kids long to give them a name: Daley's Dozers. Slowly they pushed through the street and the crowd scattered back into the park where once again clubs began to crack skulls. For the second night McCarthy headquarters in the Hilton Hotel was turned into an emergency hospital . . . The sound of "Happy Days Are Here Again" was blaring from the color television. And there was Hubert Horatio Humphrey saying: "At this convention we have recognized the end of an era and the beginning of a new day."

He didn't know the half of it.[37]

1968   31 October—President Johnson announces complete halt to "all air, naval, and artillery bombardment of North Vietnam." **5 November**—Richard M. Nixon elected president of the United States.

1968   31 December

	TOTAL	NET CHANGE
U.S. military personnel assigned in Vietnam	536,100	+50,500

U.S. casualties	YEAR	TO DATE (cumulative)
Killed in action	14,589	30,610
Wounded in action	92,818	192,580

Source: DOD/OASD

1969

On 8 January 1969 President-elect Nixon sends his national security adviser-to-be, Henry Kissinger, a note:

In making your study of Vietnam I want a precise report on what the enemy has in Cambodia and what, if anything, we are doing to destroy the buildup there. I think a very definite change of policy toward Cambodia probably should be one of the first orders of business when we get in.[38]

1969 **16 January**—After months of bickering, the United States and the DRV announce agreement on a round conference table for the Paris peace talks.

After circulating twenty-eight questions to involved agencies, Dr. Kissinger receives 548 pages of replies, subsequently summarized as NSSM-1 (National Security Study No. 1) on 21 January, 1969, the day after President Nixon's inauguration.

Summary of Responses to NSSM 1
The Situation in Vietnam

The responses to the questions posed regarding Vietnam show agreement on some matters as well as very substantial differences of opinion within the U.S. Government on many aspects of the Vietnam situation. While there are some divergencies on the facts, the sharpest differences arise in the interpretation of those facts, the relative weight to be given them, and the implications to be drawn. In addition, there remain certain areas where our information remains inadequate.

There is general agreement, assuming we follow our current strategy, on the following—

(1) The GVN and allied position in Vietnam has been strengthened recently in many respects.

(2) The GVN has improved its political position, but it is not certain that GVN and other non-communist groups will be able to survive a peaceful competition with the NLF for political power in South Vietnam.

(3) The RVNAF alone cannot now, or in the foreseeable future, stand up to the current North Vietnamese-Viet Cong forces.

(4) The enemy have suffered some reverses but they have not changed

their essential objectives and they have sufficient strength to pursue these objectives. We are not attriting his forces faster than he can recruit or infiltrate.

(5) The enemy is not in Paris primarily out of weakness. . . .

1. NEGOTIATING ENVIRONMENT (QUESTIONS 1–4)

There is general U.S. government agreement that Hanoi is in Paris for a variety of motives but not primarily out of weakness; that Hanoi is charting a course independent of Moscow, which favors negotiations, and of Peking, which opposes them; and that our knowledge of possible political factions among North Vietnamese leaders is extremely imprecise. There continues wide disagreement about the impact on Southeast Asia of various outcomes in Vietnam. . . .

2. THE ENEMY (QUESTIONS 5–10)

Analyses of various enemy tactics and capabilities reveal both significant agreements and sharp controversies within the Government. Among the major points of consensus:

A combination of military pressures and political tacts [sic] explains recent enemy withdrawals and lower levels of activity.

Under current rules of engagement, the enemy's manpower pool and infiltration capabilities can outlast allied attrition efforts indefinitely.

The enemy basically controls both sides' casualty rates.

The enemy can still launch major offensives, although not at Tet levels, or, probably, with equally dramatic effect.

Major controversies include:

CIA and State assign much higher figures to the VC Order of Battle than MACV, and they include additional categories of VC/NLF organization.

MACV/JCS and Saigon consider Cambodia (and specifically Sihanoukville) an important enemy supply channel while CIA disagrees strongly.

3. THE SOUTH VIETNAMESE ARMED FORCES (QUESTIONS 10A–13)

The emphatic differences between U.S. agencies on the RVNAF outweigh the points of agreement. There is consensus that the RVNAF is getting larger, better equipped and somewhat more effective. And all agree that it could not now, or in the foreseeable future, handle both the VC and sizeable NVA forces without U.S. combat support. On other major points there is vivid controversy. The military community gives much greater weight to RVNAF statistical improvements while OSD and CIA highlight remaining obstacles, with OSD being the most pessimistic. Paradoxically, MACV/CINCPAC/JCS see RVNAF as being less capable against the VC alone than does CIA.

4. PACIFICATION (QUESTIONS 14–20)

Two well-defined and divergent views emerged from the agencies on the pacification situation in South Vietnam. One view is held by MACV and Embassy Saigon and endorsed by CINCPAC and JCS. The other view is that of OSD, CIA and State. The two views are profoundly different in terms of factual interpretation and policy implications. Both views agree on the nature of the problem, that is, the obstacles to improvement and complete success. What distinguishes one view from the other is each's assessment of the magnitude of the problem, and the likelihood that obstacles will be overcome. . . .

6. U.S. MILITARY OPERATIONS (QUESTIONS 24–28)

The only major points of agreement with[in] the U.S. Government on these subjects are:

The description of recent US deployment and tactics;

The difficulties of assessing the results of B-52 strikes, but their known effectiveness against known troop concentrations and in close support operations;

The fact that the Soviets and Chinese supply almost all war material to Hanoi and have enabled the North Vietnamese to carry on despite all our operations.

Otherwise there are fundamental disagreements running throughout this section, including the following:

OSD believes, the MACV/JCS deny, that there is a certain amount of "fat" in our current force levels that could be cut back without significant reduction in combat capability.

MACV/JCS and, somewhat more cautiously CIA ascribe much higher casualty estimates to our B-52 strikes.[39]

Four days later a U.S. Marine operation called "Dewey Canyon" is launched. Typical of the company-sized "search and destroy" actions conducted in previous months, the highlights of the first week of this operation are later summarized for the commanding general, III MAF. Here is the report for 28 January from which the numbers will be fed into a computer and provide the data base for statistical reports on the progress of the war.

280910HJ Company I (YD 158146) was fired upon by 4 NVA using S/A in shelter. Returned S/A fire and killed 2 NVA. While sweeping through a fortified position, encountered a platoon size NVA force in bunkers and hootches. Fired S/A and arty, then regrouped and was reinforced by the CP group and one platoon. Held up attack and hit enemy with air strikes. Results, 1 friendly KIA and 9 WIAs and 3 NVA KIAs. Further search of air strike area uncovered 3 shelters $8' \times 12' \times 20'$, 3 bunkers, 2 SKS rifles, 2 AK-47 rifles, 1 RPD LMG with 3 drums of ammo plus assorted 782 gear. Also picked up, were assorted medical supplies and documents. 281000HJ Company M (YD 192158) found 10 bunkers $9' \times 5' \times 5'$, 3 bunkers $6' \times 5' \times 8'$ and 7 burning shelters. There was a large assortment of cooking and household items, 18 machetes, 2 rice grinders, 10 dead pigs, and 12 live ones; 15 chickens, 50 lbs of meat, corn, vegetables, and rice mixed. Killed livestock and destroyed structures. 281015HJ Company L (YD 187124) found sleeping area large enough for 25–30 people. Also, found 1 individual crawling through bushes and apprehinded [sic] same. He claims to be civilian but is wearing a military uniform. Person is crippled and about 30 years of age. 281130HJ Company I (YD 158157) under heavy S/A fire from estimated 2 NVA squads. Returning S/A fire, reinforced by CO CP and one platoon; mortar and arty missions in progress. 281500HJ Company N (YD 193155), while searching a bunkered area, observed 2 NVA running and killed both. In their possession were 25 lbs rice, 1 rain suit, 3 ponchos, assorted tobacco and cigars. Both soldiers were well groomed in Khaki shirts and shorts. 281630HJ Company (YD 190124) found 3 bunkers and 2 shelters, 3 SKS rifles with bayonets, assorted clothing, cooking utensils, 30 lbs rice and some medical gear.[40]

On 12 February the following episode takes place at a mission briefing in Thailand.

The place was the big briefing room of the famed 8th TFW [Tactical Fighter Wing] at Ubon Air Base, Thailand. We F-4 types had filed in before sun-up for a very important first light Mu Gia Pass mission. The Wing Commander was there, as was the Vice, the DO, and our Squadron Commanders. Serious business. In his regular briefing place, Lt. Gary Gernhardt our intel officer got up with Lt. Al Saunders and read the following: 7th AF message 121920Z. In the early morning of 11 February at 0220 local, seismic sensors indicated a large movement in strings nine through thirteen. At 0348 local, the Bangkok seismographic center reported a reading of .83 on the Richter scale, the highest ever recorded, in the northern panhandle area of Laos near the Vietnam border. The land formation in this high karst region is composed of limestone and calcium carbonate which erodes easily and hence bares the karst. This composition is also easily reduced by water and dynamic oscillation, such as brought on by B-52 bombing, to a porus [sic] and, hence, unstable condition thereby weakening the rock substructure. At 0620 local a Nail FAC observed what appeared to be a large rift in Mu Gia Pass that extended far to the south through Ban Phanop Valley. Due to bad weather, he was unable to follow the phenomena [sic]. At 0940 local, a Wolf FAC in the Ban Karai region descended through a break in the overcast and reported a large portion of the Dog's Head had shifted into the river at Ban Laboy ford area. Weather immediately closed in preventing further reconnaissance. At this moment, ground team reports are being collated. 7th AF Blue Chip in conjunction with Air Force System Command personnel concur that should this phenomena [sic] continue at its present rate it will cause a situation affecting future USAF tactics. Current prognostication indicates a 96 percent chance that in the next 48 to 60 hours, 50 percent of southern North Vietnam and related communist held portions of Laos will detach itself from the Indochina Peninsula land mass and float into the Tonkin Gulf thereby coming under US Navy jurisdiction hence releasing the USAF from further participation.[41]

In a much more serious vein, three days later the commander of the Pacific Air Forces sends this instruction for all U.S. Air force commanders in Thailand to brief their men.

SECRET LIMDIS
SUBJ: UPI ARTICLE—SOUVANNA PHOUMA

UPI STORY FROM VIENTIANE, DATED 12 FEB, ALLEGES THAT PRIME MINISTER PRINCE SOUVANNA PHOUMA ADMITTED THAT US PLANES ARE BOMBING NORTH VIETNAMESE TROOP CONCENTRATIONS AND INFILTRATION ROUTES IN LAOS. EMBASSY VIENTIANE REPORTS SOUVANNA SAID OUR—MEANING ROYAL LAO GOVERNMENT—PLANES NOT US PLANES.

PRESENT DEFENSE DEPT POLICY FOR RESPONSE ON US OPERATIONS IN LAOS STILL APPLIES AND IS QUOTED AS FOLLOWS: QUOTE. THE PREFERABLE RESPONSE TO QUESTIONS ABOUT AIR OPERATIONS IN LAOS IS NO COMMENT. IF PRESSED, YOU ARE AUTHORIZED TO STATE, AT THE REQUEST OF THE ROYAL LAOTIAN GOVERNMENT, THE UNITED STATES HAS SINCE 1964 BEEN CONDUCTING RECONNAISSANCE FLIGHTS OVER LAOS ESCORTED BY ARMED AIRCRAFT. BY AGREEMENT WITH THE LAOS GOVERNMENT, THE ESCORT FIGHTER AIRCRAFT MAY RETURN FIRE IF FIRED UPON. UNQUOTE.[42]

At almost the same time, in James Webb's novel Fields of Fire, *Marine Lieutenant R. E. Lee Hodges arrives to begin his tour of duty.*

Hodges began processing in Da Nang. At Division headquarters, he and several other new Lieutenants were granted a quick audience with the Assistant Division Commander, then briefed by a string of Colonels regarding the Division's area of operations. One of the Colonels produced a detailed map, on which he had carefully placed a mass of dots, one for each enemy contact in a certain place. The map was loaded with dots. In some places they were speckles, like polka dots, and in others they gathered to make large red smears.

The red dots reminded Hodges of blood, and their collective presence was like a slap that awakened him to the reality of the bush. They were only dots, but each one, according to the Colonel, represented someone killed or wounded. The Twenty-fifth Marines area of operations, where Hodges was headed, was a large red smear.

The first night he lay on a mildewed cot inside a tent at the Motor Transport battalion's compound, which housed Division transients. On a far ridge, all night long, a .50-caliber machine gun expended ammunition in deep burps. Shadows from distant flares lit one side of the wall, on and off, and Hodges felt vulnerable, naked in his ignorance. He didn't have the slightest idea why the .50-cal kept firing while the compound where he slept was not even on alert. It irritated him. He was finally in Vietnam, but he wasn't a part of it.

The following morning he and two others took a convoy from Da Nang to the combat base at An Hoa. It was a journey into darkness and primitivity, as little by little the comparatively lush surroundings of Da Nang fell by the wayside. Strings of American bases and well-kept villages gave way to wide, ruptured fields, saturated with little ponds, permanent bomb craters from the years of war. The multitude of gravestones and pagodas beginning just outside Da Nang bore chips and divots from a hundred thousand bullets. Hodges could make out old fighting holes along many of the ridges, where units had dug into their night perimeters months and years before. He felt young, even more naive, a stranger to an ongoing game that did not demand or even need his presence.

At Liberty Bridge, the Vu Gia and Thu Bon rivers joined, isolating the An Hoa Basin from the rest of civilized Vietnam. The convoy crossed the river on a pull barge, one truck at a time. There was no bridge at Liberty Bridge. The old bridge had been blown by the VC years before, and the new bridge was not yet completed. On the far side of the rivers, after they passed a combat base that sat on a large J-shaped hill, was land as chewed and devastated as the pictures Hodges had seen of Verdun. Whole treelines were torn out by bombs. All along the road were tatters of villages that had been ripped apart by the years of fighting. Fields were porous with bomb and mortar craters. The scattered hootches that served as homes for the villagers were no more than straw thatch, often patched with C-ration cardboard, appended to large earthen mounds where the families that remained hid from the battles.

The convoy road ended at An Hoa. There was nothing beyond the combat base but the mountains, across the river, which stretched all the way to Laos. The enemy owned the mountains. Hodges quickly comprehended the isolation, studying the wasted terrain on all sides of the narrow country road. It was as if the convoy had passed through a distance-warp when it barged across the river, and had ended up a million miles from Da Nang.

An Hoa, for all its red dust and oven heat, seemed an oasis. He watched the base as the convoy approached, attempting to distinguish its structure. None was apparent. An outpost appeared, surrounded by reams of concertina and barbed wire, then another. The tents of the larger base were packed onto one red hill, then fell into a draw and continued on another bald ridge. Hodges remembered that it was a futile effort to attempt to find order, that An Hoa was merely another legacy passed on from French times, turned into an American base because there had already been an airstrip capable of use.

There's barbed wire, he finally decided, surveying a wounded countryside swollen with anger. That'll do for starters.

More processing in An Hoa. Regiment to battalion to company. He dragged his Valpac from place to place, receiving instructions about how to be a Good Lieutenant. His stateside utilities became completely soaked from his sweat. Finally the company supply clerk brought him to the supply tent, where he stored his Valpac and was issued jungle utilities and boots, a flak jacket, a helmet, and the full ration of combat gear. His new boots were embarrassingly unscuffed. His flak jacket was too bright a shade of green, undulled by the dust of the Basin, which penetrated every type of weave known to man. But, finally, he could begin to blend in.

That night the base was mortared and he shared a small bunker with four other men and a few fleeting rats. He heard the mortars fall in random bursts across the base and could not fight back a feeling about how neat it was. By God, he pondered, leaning like an unconcerned old-timer against the bunker wall, it's finally happening to *me*.

The next day, as he was walking to an indoctrination class with another new Lieutenant, the base was rocketed. He sprinted to a dry ditch and dove in, feeling like a true combat veteran. One rocket landed perhaps fifty meters away, directly on top of a tent, and he began composing in his own mind how he would put that into a letter to someone. But then he climbed out of the ditch and almost stepped on the severed hand of a man who had been inside the tent. It lay on the road, in perfect condition, having been blown more than a hundred feet by the rocket's explosion. The man's wedding ring was in perfect place. Someone from near the tent shouted that the First Sergeant was dead.

And it wasn't fun anymore.

On his second night in An Hoa he was awakened by a company clerk who told him that the company was in contact, and asked him if he wanted to watch. It was past midnight. He couldn't quite understand the man's meaning. Do I want to *watch*, he pondered over and over, gathering his flak jacket and helmet and weapon. Do I want to watch. Why? Is it on TV?

But he dutifully followed the man and joined several clerks from the company office on top of a large sandbag bunker. They pointed north, across the river, and he followed their fingers as his eyes searched into the hell that was known as the Arizona Valley.

And he sat, feeling slightly obscene, as if he were a peeping tom to someone's private doings, and watched his company dying across the river. Red and green tracers interlaced and careened into the black night air. Mortars and B-40 rocket-propelled grenades flashed and impacted, spewing dirt with whumps that he could hear from the three-mile distance he was watching. Illumination flares dangled like tiny streetlights in the distance.

He was washed with a mix of helplessness and fear that overrode any emotion he had ever experienced, and continued to stare, an armchair spectator to the sport of dying. And tomorrow, he said over and over as he watched, tomorrow that will be my very own Vietnam.[43]

1969   1 March—Two battalions of the North Vietnamese 174th Regiment and three battalions of the 148th Regiment launch an offensive in northern Laos.

On 2 March the problems of U.S. Army Captain Maurey Schwartz finally come to an end. This anonymous narrative receives wide distribution in Vietnam.

SUBJECT: Recommendation for Medal of Honor

5 Sep 68
FROM: CO, 1st Airplane Co.
TO: Bn S-1
1. Recommend Capt. Maurey Schwartz be considered for award of the Congressional Medal of Honor for his heroic actions in the DMZ on 4 Sep 68.
2. Capt. Schwartz was flying his 01 Birddog reconnaissance airplane on a routine reconnaissance mission when he was called by a platoon of Marines in heavy contact with NVA forces in the DMZ. The Marines were surrounded by enemy forces and receiving heavy casualties when Capt. Schwartz dived his airplane in over the enemy positions, firing his marking rockets on the NVA heavy weapons gunners. After making several passes and expending all his rockets, taking several hits from enemy ground fire in the process, Capt. Schwartz took his AR15 rifle and, placing it on automatic, made several more passes, spraying the enemy with a heavy concentration of fire. On his last pass, Capt. Schwartz's airplane was hit by an NVA 50-caliber round. The plane went out of control and hit a tree, as Capt. Schwartz was flying very low in order to place his fire more effectively. Capt. Schwartz was fortunately only slightly injured and was dusted off several hours later. His actions saved the Marine platoon from almost certain destruction and finally resulted in their victory over the enemy forces. Capt. Schwartz personally accounted for 397 NVA soldiers killed by aerial action and 43 automatic and crew-served enemy weapons destroyed.

1st Ind
5 Oct 68
FROM: S-1
TO: S-2
1. What was the enemy situation that day?

2d Ind
26 Oct 68
FROM: S-2
TO: S-1
1. Bad!
2. If it hadn't been for Capt. Schwartz and the platoon of Marines blocking the enemy, they could have started a new offensive that day, catching us flat-footed.

3d Ind
10 Nov 68
FROM: S-1
TO: AG
1. Forwarded for your recommendations and consideration.
2. Recommend approval.

4th Ind
29 Nov 68
FROM: AG
TO: Safety Officer
1. Forwarded for your comments.
2. Don't we have a regulation against aviators flying below 500 feet except during takeoff and landing?

5th Ind
15 Dec 68
FROM: ASO
TO: AG
1. That's affirm. You signed it yourself.

6th Ind
5 Jan 69
FROM: AG
TO: Chief of Staff
1. Forwarded for your advice.

7th Ind
15 Jan 69
FROM: CofS
TO: AG
1. After consultation with Embassy staff officers in Saigon, I feel we should reconsider this recommendation due to the touchy political situation. Since the President has halted the bombing of North Vietnam and cut down activities in the DMZ, it may upset the Paris peace talks if the enemy is reminded that Marines and our aviators were operating in the DMZ.

8th Ind
26 Jan 69
FROM: AG
TO: S-1
1. Your attention is invited to previous indorsements.
2. I am especially concerned about that regulation stating our aviators will not fly below 500 feet. Recommend you counsel your pilots on flying safety.

9th Ind
15 Feb 69

FROM: S-1
TO: CO, 1st Airplane Co.
1. Your attention is invited to previous indorsements.
2. Henceforth, aviators of this command are forbidden to fly in or near the DMZ.
3. You will take appropriate action to insure that, in the future, your aviators adhere strictly to regulations forbidding low-level flying.
4. It has also been noted that you are still carrying Capt. Schwartz's wrecked airplane on your property book. You are reminded that regulations require elimination of unsalvageable property with minimum delay.

10th Ind
23 Feb 69
FROM: CO, 1st Apln Co.
TO: S-4
1. Your attention is invited to preceding indorsement.
2. You will take immediate action to drop Capt. Schwartz's aircraft, number 52-837763, from this unit's property books.

11th Ind
2 March 69
FROM: S-4
TO: Capt. Maurey C. Schwartz
THRU: S-1
1. You are hereby notified that a report of survey is being initiated against you in the amount of $18,944.29, the cost of one aircraft, 0-1E, tail number 52-837763, lost by you through carelessness and flagrant disregard of flying safety regulations in or near the DMZ on or about 4 Sep 68.
2. You are further advised that you will appear before a general court martial to be convened at Brigade Headquarters tomorrow to answer charges of willful disobedience of a standing regulation, to wit: low-level flying in violation of current safety regulations. You are further being charged with destruction of Government property, to wit: One 0-1E airplane, of a value of more than $50, through neglect and reckless behavior.
3. You are further advised that the State Department, through the U.S. Embassy in Saigon, has requested your immediate transfer from duty in Vietnam to avoid possible political repercussions of your flagrant disregard of the Demilitarized Zone when you attacked Vietnamese citizens on the ground within the DMZ.
4. Further, you are being relieved from flight status pending investigation of your misconduct. Your transfer to duty as U.S. Military Attache to Antarctica will be effective upon completion of your court martial.[44]

Two days later Major Mark Berent, an American pilot stationed in Thailand on his second combat tour, makes the following comments in a letter to a good friend.

4 March '69

We've lost so damn many here it no longer seems real. (And even now it is only about 70% of what it was like over North Vietnam.)

I fly in a night attack squadron and if our birds aren't smacking into the 2–3000 foot karst ridges suddenly rising from nowhere, they are stitched end to end by 23mm, 37mm, or 57mm. Just dive bombing at night sans moon, with much haze (up to 10,000′) (from burning rice paddies for the next crop's fertilization), viz [visibility] 2–3 miles, isn't conclusive to longevity.

Naturally I'm forbidden by all sorts of silly directives to mention exactly where I fly, but the astute reader of *Time, Newsweek,* or the *NY Times,* or any one of scores of publications can obviously pronounce the four letter word.

It's such a ridiculously piddly effort at such high cost it borders on criminal negligence. Our effort up North, though slow starting for the same political reasons that shut it off, at least was producing better results for the cost. Namely a high pitched squeal from the NVN and NFL leaders.

We gave the contributions of hundreds of pilots away when Johnson attempted his last gesture toward immortality.

Now the pilots who are dead have no foreseeable tangible trade-in security for SVN. Only the living, the half a thousand or so pilots in the Hanoi Hilton have a value—for the North Vietnamese—as pawns, hostages to gain further concessions at the so-called negotiation table.

"Negotiation" my ass; "Giveaway" or "Sellout" is more appropriate. . . .

The "sellout" I refer to is the great god "world opinion." Whoever created that demon far surpassed any ancient horror tale. Since when is world opinion based on the mewlings of a variety of flap-wristed psuedo-intellectuals who hide, un-read, behind slogans.

I'm aware, Mike, a lot of what I'm writing is at least herein unsupported. Also perhaps emotional and as such incoherent or perhaps without too much continuity. By careful study, quotes, editing, etc., I could probably cough up a reasonably supported thesis. I'm just too damn tired. . . .

After all, I do agree with why we are here. I just happen to totally disagree with how we are going about it. And I feel a hell of a frustration. At least when I flew in the South there were positive results. An SF camp saved, circled US or ARVN troops helped out, etc. (to name a few dramatic but nonetheless valuable incidents.)

So I suppose one could quote "job dissatisfaction" as one of the obtuse motivations behind what I say.

Damn war anyhow. Curse you Red Baron. Or just fuck it![45]

In Washington, Dr. Henry Kissinger is at a meeting that is characterized by arguments over the still unapproved plan to attack Communist sanctuaries in Cambodia.

Having previously submitted my thoughts in a memorandum, I did not speak. Rogers finally agreed to a B-52 strike on the base area containing the presumed Communist headquarters. These deliberations are instructive: A month of an unprovoked North Vietnamese offensive, over a thousand American dead, elicited after weeks of anguished discussion exactly *one* American retaliatory raid within three miles of the Cambodian border in an area occupied by the North Vietnamese for over four years. And this would enter the folklore as an example of wanton "illegality."

After the meeting, the Joint Chiefs sought to include additional attacks on North Vietnamese troop concentrations violating the Demilitarized Zone. Laird and I agree that it was more important to keep Rogers with us and the proposal was not approved.

The B-52 attack took place on March 18 against North Vietnamese Base Area 353, within three miles of the Cambodian border (see the map on page 248). For this strike the Pentagon dug into its bottomless bag of code names and came up with "Breakfast"—as meaningless as it was tasteless. When an air attack hits an ammunition or fuel depot there are always secondary explosions that provide nearly conclusive evidence of a successful raid. The initial assessment by the crew of the March 18 Breakfast strike reported "a total of 73 secondary explosions in the target area ranging up to five times the normal intensity of a typical secondary."[46]

One week later, as the Laotian monsoon season nears, with its heavy regular rains, the commander of the Seventh Air Force sends this message to all his subordinates in Thailand and Vietnam.

CONFIDENTIAL/DO

FOR COMMANDERS FROM GENERAL JONES.

ALL AIR UNITS OPERATING IN LAOS HAVE THE OPPORTUNITY TO PARTICIPATE IN SETTING A RECORD ON NUMBER OF TRUCKS DESTROYED DURING A ONE MONTH PERIOD IF WE REDOUBLE OUR EFFORTS FOR THE LAST FEW DAYS OF MARCH. REQUEST THAT ALL COMMANDERS TAKE SPECIAL ACTION TO MEET SORTIE REQUIREMENTS AND DESTROY AS MANY TRUCKS AS POSSIBLE. SORTIES FRAGGED TO HARD TARGETS WILL STILL REQUIRE AUTHORITY FROM APPROPRIATE CONTROL AGENCIES PRIOR TO DIVERTING TO ATTACK TRUCKS. GOOD HUNTING.[47]

1969 29 March—Vietnam veteran Ron Ridenhour sends twenty-nine copies of a letter to senators, congressmen, and President Nixon. The letter's subject: the 1968 massacre of civilians at My Lai. **30 April**—U.S. military personnel in Vietnam reach peak strength of 543,400.

In early May Tim O'Brien is part of an operation in a small Vietnamese village that will shortly become well known around the world.

My Lai in May

The villages of My Lai are scattered like wild seed in and around Pinkville, a flat stretch of sandy red clay along the northern coast of South Vietnam. "Pinkville" is a silly, county-fairish misnomer for such a sullen piece of the world. From the infantryman's perspective, zigzagging through one of the most heavily mined areas in the war zone, there is little pink or rosy about Pinkville: mud huts more often deserted than not, bombed-out pagodas, the patently hostile faces of Pinkville's inhabitants, acre after acre of slush, paddy after paddy, a dirty maze of elaborate tunnels and bomb shelters and graves.

The place gets its name from the fact that military maps color it a shimmering shade of elephant pink, signifying what the map legends call a "built-up area." Perhaps it once was. Perhaps Pinkville once upon a time was a thriving part of Quang Ngai province. It is no longer.

Pinkville and the villages called My Lai were well known to Alpha Company. . . . In January, a month or so before I arrived in Vietnam, . . . Alpha Company took part in massive Operation Russell Beach, joining forces with other army elements, boatloads of marines, the navy and air force. Subject of the intricately planned and much-touted campaign was Pinkville and the Batangan Peninsula. Both had long served as Charlie's answer to the American R & R center—friendly natives, home-cooked rice, and nearly total sanctuary from American foot soldiers. Despite publicity and War College strategy, the operation did not produce the anticipated results, and this unit learned some hard lessons about Pinkville. There was no reliable criterion by which to distinguish a pretty Vietnamese girl from a deadly enemy; often they were one and the same person. The unit triggered one mine after another during Operation Russell Beach. Frustration and anger built with each explosion and betrayal, one Oriental face began to look like any other, hostile and black, and Alpha Company was boiling with hate when it was pulled out of Pinkville.

In May we were ordered back. Inserted by chopper in the villages of My Khe, a few thousand meters south of the My Lai's, we hit immediate contact. The Viet Cong were there, waiting in ambush across the paddy. The people of My Khe 3 were silent; they let us walk into the ambush, not a word of warning.

The day was quiet and hot, and I was thinking about Coke and rest. Then the bushes just erupted. I was carrying the radio for the company commander, and I remember getting separated from him, thinking I had to get up there. But I couldn't. I lay there. I screamed, buried my head.

A hand grenade came out of the bushes, skidded across my helmet, a red sardine can with explosives inside. I remember my glimpse of the thing, fizzling there beside me. I remembered rolling to my left; remember waiting for the loudest noise of my life. It was just a pop, but I remember thinking that must be how it sounds to a dead man. Nothing hurt much. Clauson, a big fellow, took the force of the grenade. I lay there and watched him trot a few steps, screaming; then he lay on his back and screamed. I couldn't move. I kept hollering, begging for an end to it. The battalion commander was on the radio, asking where my captain was, wanting to talk to him, wanting me to pop smoke to mark our position, wanting me to call the other platoons. Bullets were coming from the bushes. Clauson was gone, I don't know where or how, and when I put my head up to look for him, I couldn't see anyone. Everything was noise, and it lasted on and on. It was over, I knew, when Mad Mark came out of the bushes, carrying a tall, skinny guy named Arnold over his shoulder. He swiveled Arnold into a helicopter, and we went north, into the My Lai's.

Along the way we encountered the citizens of Pinkville; they were the nonparticipants in war. Children under ten years, women, old folks who planted their eyes into the dirt and were silent. "Where are the VC?" Captain Johansen would ask, nicely enough. "Where are all the men? Where is Poppa-san?" No answers, not from the villagers. Not until we ducked poppa's bullet or stepped on his land mine.

Alpha Company was fatigued and angry leaving My Lai 5. Another futile search of a nearly deserted village, another fat zero turned up through interrogation. Moving north to cross the Diem Diem River, the company took continuous sniper fire, and it intensified into a sharp thunder when we reached the river and a bridge, seventy-five meters long and perfectly exposed, the only way across. One man at a time, churning as fast as the rucksacks and radios and machine guns allowed, the unit crossed the Song Diem Diem, the rest of the troops spraying out protective fire, waiting their own turn, and we were scared. It was a race. A lieutenant was the starter, crouched at the clay runway leading into the paddy, hollering "Go" for each of us, then letting loose a burst of fire to cover the guy. The captain, first man to win his race, was at the finish line. He gave the V sign to each man across. It may have signaled victory or valor. It did not mean peace. The men were angry. No enemy soldiers to shoot back at, only hedgerows and bushes and clumps of dead trees.

We were mortared that night. We crawled about in gullies and along paddy dikes, trying to evade. We saw the red quick flashes of their mortar tubes, but no one dared fire back, for it would do nothing but give away more precisely our position. The captain had me call headquarters to get gunships, and in the middle of the communication the mortar rounds fell even closer, and Johansen muttered that they were bracketing us, walking their rounds in from two directions, and on our hands and knees, my antenna dragging along in the paddy, the night purely black, we crawled forward and backward and finally into a village of My Lai, where we spent that night. Platoons lay out in the water of the paddies. They were afraid to move.

In the next days it took little provocation for us to flick the flint of our Zippo lighters. Thatched roofs take the flame quickly, and on bad days the hamlets of Pinkville burned, taking our revenge in fire. It was good to walk from Pinkville and to see fire behind Alpha Company. It was good, just as pure hate is good.

We walked to other villages, and the phantom Forty-eighth Viet Cong Battalion walked with us. When a booby-trapped artillery round blew two popular soldiers into a hedgerow, men put their fists into the faces of the nearest Vietnamese, two frightened women living in the guilty hamlet, and when the troops were through with them, they hacked off chunks of thick black hair. The men were crying, doing this. An officer used his pistol, hammering it against a prisoner's skull.

Scraps of our friends were dropped in plastic body bags. Jet fighters were called in. The hamlet was leveled, and napalm was used. I heard screams in the burning black rubble. I heard the enemy's AK-47 rifles crack out like impotent popguns against the jets. There were Viet Cong in that hamlet. And there were babies and children and people who just didn't give a damn in there, too. But Chip and Tom were on the way to Graves Registration in Chu Lai, and they were dead, and it was hard to be filled with pity.[48]

At the same time in the United States, Congressman Morris Udall, among many other Americans, becomes involved in the media-reported problem of civilian casualties. He receives this letter from the Department of Defense.

8 May 1969

Honorable Morris K. Udall
House of Representatives
Washington, D.C. 20515

Dear Mr. Udall:

The following information is provided in response to your April 11 referral of a letter from Dr. Andre Bruwer of Tucson.

Your constituent requested information concerning the use of various types of ordnance and the number of civilian casualties in South Vietnam. As you know, information regarding consumption of specific types of bombs in Southeast Asia is classified and therefore not available to the general public.

With regard to your constituent's second question, there are no accurate and meaningful figures available on civilian casualties in Vietnam. However, estimates indicate that the total civilian casualties each year are probably about one quarter of the number cited by your constituent. The consensus of responsible and knowledgeable people in Vietnam is that civilian casualties resulting from US and allied military operations are minimal.

Although human errors of judgment and mechanical failures have on occasion resulted in civilian casualties during US operations, the Commander, Military Assistance Command, Vietnam has taken every precaution to insure that our forces employ firepower in a disciplined and discriminatory manner. This has been effective in limiting civilian casualties.

The problem of civilian casualties is difficult to solve in all wars; it is compounded in South Vietnam by the presence of Viet Cong strongholds in villages. These villages are taken under attack only when intelligence has verified that they are actually occupied by the Viet Cong. To the maximum extent possible, civilians are informed of an impending attack and given sufficient time to move to safe locations. In areas where air strikes are required, leaflets and loudspeaker broadcasts are used to alert the local populace. The problem is equally difficult when our ground forces attempt to recapture a village that has been seized by the Viet Cong, but all possible measures are taken to insure the safety of noncombatants.

The United States will continue to make every effort to avoid taking the lives of innocent civilians. I want to assure you that our military commanders in Vietnam are deeply aware of the need to avoid any useless sacrifice of lives.

I hope this information will be helpful in replying to Dr. Bruwer.

> Sincerely,
> Jack L. Stempler
> Assistant to the Secretary
> (Legislative Affairs)[49]

On 14 May President Nixon delivers his first televised speech on Vietnam.

This brings us, then, to the matter of negotiations.

We must recognize that peace in Vietnam cannot be achieved overnight. A war which has raged for so many years will require detailed negotiations and cannot be settled at a single stroke.

What kind of a settlement will permit the South Vietnamese people to determine freely their own political future? Such a settlement will require the withdrawal of all non-South Vietnamese forces from South Vietnam and procedures for political choice that give each significant group in South Vietnam a real opportunity to participate in the political life of the nation.

To implement these principles, I reaffirm now our willingness to withdraw our forces on a specified timetable. We ask only that North Vietnam withdraw its forces from South Vietnam, Cambodia and Laos into North Vietnam, also in accordance with a timetable.

We include Cambodia and Laos to ensure that these countries would not be used as bases for a renewed war. The Cambodian border is only 35 miles from Saigon: the Laotian border is only 25 miles from Hue.

Our offer provides for a simultaneous start on withdrawal by both sides: agreement on a mutually acceptable timetable; and for the withdrawal to be accomplished quickly.

If North Vietnam wants to insist that it has no forces in South Vietnam, we will no longer debate the point—provided that its forces cease to be there, and that we have reliable assurances that they will not return. . . .

To make very concrete what I have said, I propose the following measures, which seem to me consistent with the principles of all parties. These proposals are made on the basis of full consultation with President Thieu.

—As soon as agreement can be reached, all non-South Vietnamese forces would begin withdrawals from South Vietnam.

—Over a period of 12 months, by agreed-upon stages, the major portions of all U.S., Allied and other non-South Vietnamese forces would be withdrawn. At the end of this 12-month period, the remaining U.S., Allied and other non-South Vietnamese forces would move into designated base areas and would not engage in combat operations.

—The remaining U.S. and Allied forces would move to complete their withdrawals as the remaining North Vietnam forces were withdrawn and returned to North Vietnam.

—An international supervisory body, acceptable to both sides, would be created for the purpose of verifying withdrawals, and for any other purposes agreed upon between the two sides.

—This international body would begin operating in accordance with an agreed timetable, and would participate in arranging supervised ceasefires.

—As soon as possible after the international body was functioning, elections would be held under agreed procedures and under the supervision of the international body.

—Arrangements would be made for the earliest possible release of prisoners of war on both sides.

—All parties would agree to observe the Geneva Accords of 1954 regarding Vietnam and Cambodia, and the Laos Accords of 1962.

I believe this proposal for peace is realistic, and takes account of the legitimate interests of all concerned. It is consistent with President Thieu's six points. It can accommodate the various programs put forth by the other side. We and the Government of South Vietnam are prepared to discuss its details with the other side. Secretary Rogers is now in Saigon and will be discussing with President Thieu how, together, we may put forward these proposed measures most usefully in Paris. He will, as well, be consulting with our other Asian allies on these measures while on his Asian trip. However, I would stress that these proposals are not offered on a take-it-or-leave-it basis. We are quite willing to consider other approaches consistent with our principles.

We are willing to talk about anybody's program—Hanoi's four points, the NLF's 10 points—provided it can be made consistent with the few basic principles I have set forth here.[50]

The next morning, three days of riots break out in Berkeley, California, as police, backed by California National Guard troops, attempt to dislodge the squatters of People's Park, a vacant lot appropriated by various groups for gardens and recreation. Antiwar activist and writer Merritt Clifton is there.

The Hueys shrieked in low, so low I might have downed one with a well-aimed rock. But there were no rocks. Entering Sproul Plaza at the end of Telegraph Avenue, each spewed a yellow-green cloud, rising slightly to clear Sather Gate. I thought of fish, dumping milt. A sea of high school classmates surged, parted like the tide.

And in the brief lull between Hueys came their screams. Blue-jacketed, helmeted, gas-masked billyclubs split heads and booted crotches, advancing in a robot-like phalanx. Khaki fixed bayonets cut off escape. Kids vomited; broke out in blisters; cried for water. But Ludwig's Fountain offered only dry gum-wrappers. Some clutched one another, keeping heads low. Others raised each other out of their own puke. An older handful hurled half-empty gas cannisters back at the clubs. And then more Hueys came. I could see no longer through the yellow-green curtains.

Prevailing winds protected us, the press, outside the cordon. "Jesus Christ!", a KRON cameraman muttered, squinting down. He tried to get himself a cigarette, one-handed. Dropped the pack. Stopped the camera, set it down, picked the pack up, then cast it aside.

I held my rail, staring. These were my friends and classmates, the gentlest, brightest kids I knew. Kids from my art class, who'd volunteered to build a park, People's Park, on an unused, sunbaked lot. Leni, named for Lenin, an avowed Communist who didn't yet understand communism meant Gulags, as surely as fascism meant Auschwitz; Danny Gold, a high school Disraeli, who saw in the park a miniature Israel, and could not realize that Palestinians had land rights too; others whose names I'd forgotten, poets and painters and musicians who'd often mastered beauty, yet at 15, 16, and 17 had not discovered violence. Hill kids, mostly, who'd remained in segregated, tracked college prep classes, while black and white met in shop and detention hall; who'd sung 'We Shall Overcome' in Glee Club, while I'd fought with knives and razor-blades in the lower corridors; who'd collected allowances and spent them on Beatle records, while I'd worked weekends and vacations, painting Oakland ghetto apartment houses. I'd tried to warn them, tried to speak of pits in yards where three-year-olds were made to fight like dogs, parents betting on the outcome; of covering blood on walls with two coats of white latex; of the world I knew, where 'rights' meant that fists could earn, 'peace' was something carved on tombstones, and 'love' was but a tender form of rape. They'd never understood. When union goons had brought them sod, stolen from a strikebound mass transit construction site, they'd taken it for 'free', and laid it, unaware company goons would claim it back through the law. When older, college-aged leaders told them to hold the park, they'd slept there, not noticing that those leaders slept at home. When the 'Blue Meanies' broke their heads, storming the park at dawn, they'd begun to learn.

Huey after Huey after Huey. Vietnam in Berkeley. In the TV's echo, counting Nixon's returns, I heard those radical leaders exhorting their victims to "Storm your Bastille! Seize your Harper's Ferry!" They'd appealed through bullhorns to ideals and glory, new Napoleons. Almost alone, I'd remained in class. I'd only heard the rifle-fire on Bloody Thursday, yesterday; only greeted the first limping survivors as they straggled back, not been among them. Club-swinging cops drove the rest like cattle. Then I'd joined the thick of it. I'd had no choice. . . . I peered over the top while police dragged 300 of my classmates to waiting Black Marias. They were hauled to Santa Rita Prison; thrown into outdoor barbed-wire pens until parents bailed them out. Two girls I knew were gang-raped by Alameda County sheriff's deputies, men who might have been their fathers. One guy I knew caught the edge of a birdshot blast in the back. But I didn't see that. I only saw the Hueys, formation after formation. "You're bombing your fucking children!", a woman reporter screamed up at them from beside me. She wept, shaking her fist; buried her head in my shoulder, expecting me to hold and comfort her, though she must have been twice my age. I couldn't move. Wild boars sometimes ate their young, I reflected, reciting an old Yorkshire proverb: "Dogs is inferiors and horses is inferiors, but pigs is equals."

At ten, five years before People's Park, I'd stood with my skateboard on those same steps. Baffled, I'd heard poets John Thompson and Doug Palmer read 'obscene' poetry, later watching police carry away those who 'sat in' after the two were arrested. That had happened in an almost carnival atmosphere, frat-rats holding a sympathetic bawdy songfest. Now I blundered away from the woman, away from another staggered file of Hueys appearing over the rooftops—[51]

In June a new political entity comes into being in Vietnam. An official DRV history comments on the progress to date.

During the first 6 months of 1969, the [Communist] South Vietnamese Army and people wiped out or captured 330,000 of the enemy including 145,000 U.S.* and satellite troops. In January 1969, the U.S. imperialists were forced to hold official talks with the delegation of the NFLSVN at

*Official Department of Defense figures, 1 Jan 69 to 30 Jun 69: U.S. killed in action: 3,074; 3rd nation killed in action: 396; U.S. wounded in action: 25,785; 3rd nation wounded in action: 1,025 (DOD/OASD 27 Mar 75).

the four-sided Paris Conference. With that, the South Vietnamese people opened a new front, the diplomatic front. The South Vietnamese people are continuously attacking the enemy and scoring great victories on all three fronts (the military, the political, and the diplomatic). The liberated area has been expanded and many of the liberated zones adjoin the urban areas. A people's revolutionary administration was established not only at township and district levels but even at province level and in the large cities.

On 6 June 1969, the patriotic forces held the South Vietnamese National Congress of Delegates and unanimously elected the *Chinh Phu Cach Mang Lam Thoi Cong Hoa Mien Nam Viet Nam* (the Provisional Revolutionary Government of the Republic of South Viet-Nam) and the *Hoi Dong Co Van Ben Canh Chinh Phu* (the Advisory Council Alongside the Government). The Provisional Revolutionary Government was a decisive victory in the process of perfecting the system of revolutionary political power in South Viet-Nam, a genuinely national and democratic political power. The birth of the revolutionary administration shook the puppet regime and the U.S. henchmen at the roots.[52]

1969 8 June—President Nixon makes announcement that the United States will unilaterally withdraw 25,000 troops. **11 June**—Cambodian Prince Sihanouk announces diplomatic relations at chargé d'affaires level with the United States. He says that "our Vietnamese Socialist friends are . . . overtly Vietnamizing our territory" and that Cambodia will "fight . . . to maintain territorial integrity."

In June the U.S. Congress passes the following resolution.

S. RES. 85, 91ST CONGRESS, NATIONAL COMMITMENTS RESOLUTION, JUNE 25, 1969
Whereas accurate definition of the term "national commitment" in recent years has become obscured: Now, therefore, be it
Resolved, That (1) a national commitment for the purpose of this resolution means the use of the Armed Forces of the United States on foreign territory, or a promise to assist a foreign country, government, or people by the use of the Armed Forces or financial resources of the United States, either immediately or upon the happening of certain events, and (2) it is the sense of the Senate that a national commitment by the United States results only from affirmative action taken by the executive and legislative branches of the United States Government by means of a treaty, statute, or concurrent resolution of both Houses of Congress specifically providing for such commitment.[53]

In mid-July President Nixon writes to DRV President Ho Chi Minh.

July 15, 1969

His Excellency Ho CHI MINH,
President, Democratic Republic of Vietnam, Hanoi.

DEAR MR. PRESIDENT:

I realize that it is difficult to communicate meaningfully across the gulf of four years of war. But precisely because of this gulf, I wanted to take this opportunity to reaffirm in all solemnity my desire to work for a just peace. I deeply believe that the war in Vietnam has gone on too long and delay in bringing it to an end can benefit no one—least of all the people of Vietnam.

My speech on May 14 laid out a proposal which I believe is fair to all parties. Other proposals have been made which attempt to give the people of South Vietnam an opportunity to choose their own future. These proposals take into account the reasonable conditions of all sides. But we stand ready to discuss other programs as well, specifically the 10 point program of the N.L.F.

As I have said repeatedly, there is nothing to be gained by waiting. Delay can only increase the dangers and multiply the suffering.

The time has come to move forward at the conference table toward an early resolution of this tragic war. You will find us forthcoming and open-minded in a common effort to bring the blessings of peace to the brave people of Vietnam. Let history record that at this critical juncture, both sides turned their face toward peace rather than toward conflict and war.

Sincerely,
Richard Nixon[54]

Also in July COSVN ([Communist] Central Office) holds its 9th Conference and produces the following resolution.

Part II. Future Enemy Schemes and Our Immediate Tasks

The Americans' subjective intention is to carry out the *precept* of deescalating [the war] step by step; to strive to seize the initiative in a passive position; to win a strong position on the battlefield as they de-escalate; *to de-escalate in order to "de-Americanize" the war but not to immediately end* the war; to reinforce the puppet army as American troops are withdrawn; to have necessary time for having appropriate de-escalation steps; and at *every de-escalation step, to strive to launch partial counter-offensives in fierce competition with our forces.*

At present, there is very little possibility that the enemy will carry out a massive troop build-up and expand the limited war to the whole country;

however, we still need to keep our alertness. There are *two possible developments* to the war as follows:

> *One:* In the process of de-escalating the war, the Americans may suffer increasing losses and encounter greater difficulties; therefore they may be *forced to seek an early end to the war* through a political solution which they cannot refuse. Even in this case, there will be a period of time from the signing of the agreement ending the war until all American troops are withdrawn from South Viet-Nam. During this period of time, our struggle against the enemy will go on with extreme complexity and we will have to be extremely alert.
>
> *Two:* If our attacks in all aspects are not sufficiently strong and if the Americans are able to temporarily overcome part of their difficulties, they will strive to prolong the war in South Viet-Nam for a certain period of time during which they will try to de-escalate from a strong position of one sort or another, and carry out the de-Americanization in a prolonged war contest before they must admit defeat and accept a political solution.

In both these eventualities, especially in the case of a prolonged de-escalation, the Americans may, in certain circumstances, put pressure on us by threatening to broaden the war through the resumption of bombing in North Viet-Nam within a definite scope and time limit, or the expansion of the war into Laos and Cambodia.

Whether the war will develop according to the first or second eventuality *depends principally on the strength of our attacks in the military, political and diplomatic fields,* especially our military and political attacks, and on the extent of military, political, economic and financial difficulties which the war causes to the Americans in Viet-Nam, in the U.S.A. itself, and over the world.[55]

From the same conference, as quoted by Dr. Henry Kissinger, come these specific COSVN intentions.

a. *Fiercely attack American troops,* inflict very heavy losses on them, cause them increasing difficulties in all fields. . . .

b. *Strongly strike the puppet army, annihilate the most obdurate elements of the puppet army and administration, paralyze and disintegrate the remaining elements.* . . .

c. *Strive to build up our military and political forces and deploy them on an increasingly strong strategic offensive position.* . . .

d. Continue to destroy and weaken the puppet administration at various levels; *especially, defeat the enemy's pacification plan; wipe out the major part of the puppet administration . . . and promote the role of the Provisional Revolutionary Government.*

e. On this basis, *smash the Americans' will of aggression; force them to give up their intention of ending the war in a strong position, and to end the war quickly and withdraw troops* while the puppet army and administration are still too weak to take over the responsibility of the Americans, *force the Americans to accept a political solution,* and recognize an independent, democratic peaceful and neutral South Viet-Nam with a national, democratic coalition government working toward reunifying Viet-Nam. [Italics in original.][56]

At the same time American policy is also undergoing change, as Dr. Kissinger records.

The Beginning of Troop Withdrawals

After the May 14 speech outlining our compromise terms for negotiation, we turned to the unilateral withdrawal of American troops. We had inherited, in one of the less felicitous phrases of foreign policy in this century, a general commitment to "de-Americanize" the war. The Johnson Administration had begun the effort to strengthen the South Vietnamese army, but there were no plans for American withdrawals. . . . Nixon favored withdrawal. . . . In a news conference of March 14, he had laid down three criteria for our withdrawals: the ability of the South Vietnamese to defend themselves without American troops; negotiating progress in the Paris talks; and the level of enemy activity. Nixon's strategy in the early months, in fact, was to try to weaken the enemy to the maximum possible extent, speed up the modernization of Saigon's forces, and then begin withdrawals. He thought that would be a public relations coup. . . .

These issues were to be discussed at a meeting of the President and his senior advisers on the Presidential yacht *Sequoia* on July 7. Rogers, Laird, Wheeler, Attorney General Mitchell, General Robert Cushman (Deputy CIA Director), and I were present. In the event, the principal topic of discussion was the meaning of an apparent lull in the fighting. Did it result from Hanoi's exhaustion, from a new negotiating strategy, or from an attempt by Hanoi to achieve de-escalation by tacit understandings? It was symptomatic of the intellectual confusion of the period that in the relief felt when a military lull eased both casualties and domestic pressures, no one asked the question whether the lull might not reflect the fact that our strategy was succeeding and should therefore be continued. Instead, there was unanimity that we should respond by a reciprocal slowdown. It was decided to make a basic change in the battlefield orders for General Abrams. The existing "mission statement" for US forces in Southeast Asia, inherited from the Johnson Administration, declared the ambitious intention to "defeat" the enemy and "force" its withdrawal to North Vietnam. The new mission statement (which went into effect on August 15) focused on providing "maximum assistance" to the South Vietnamese to strengthen their forces, supporting pacification efforts, and reducing the flow of supplies to the enemy. As it turned out, the President at the last moment changed his mind and countermanded the new instructions. But Laird had already issued them, and they stood. I do not know whether the changed orders—which were quickly leaked—made any practical difference. Given our commitment to withdrawal, they reflected our capabilities, whatever our intentions.[57]

1969   25 July—Laotian Prime Minister Souvanna Phouma charges in Paris that 60,000 Vietnamese are waging war in Laos. Souvanna admits that he has authorized U.S. bombing raids on the Ho Chi Minh Trail.

Despite the beginning of U.S. troop withdrawals, replacements for those who complete their one-year tours continue to arrive. Now an "old guy," Lieutenant R. E. Lee Hodges, in Webb's Fields of Fire, *meets a friend.*

Hodges met a classmate from his Basic School platoon in the mess hall when he went to eat his last hot meal before departing on the operation. It was lunch: B-ration freeze-dried hamburgers topped with brown gravy made from powder, a dirt-filled lettuce salad, and Kool-Aid. The classmate had only recently arrived in Vietnam, after finishing combat engineer's school. They had not been close in Basic School, yet Hodges greeted him as a long-lost friend, the man's enthusiastic awe a reminder of how it had begun for him five months before. Grasping the man's hand and staring into rested, curious eyes, Hodges sensed an innocence that was as far away as his own childhood. He thought of the advice of Major Otto, who had spoken so honestly to him the day he departed for the bush, and again lamented the fact that the Major was in Da Nang on the Division staff. His friend's face convinced him that he and Otto now shared a jealous ethos, gained in fear and dirt and blood and hassle, that would have made it possible to talk, really talk, for the first time. This was me, mused Hodges, listening to his friend's questions. But it isn't anymore.

The classmate had kept up with the doings of all the other Lieutenants who had graduated with them. He knew who had washed out of flight school. He knew who was up for medals. He knew who had died.

Hodges downed his meal without enthusiasm, listening absently while thinking of the operation he would embark on in only a few hours. There was a tickle in the back of his head that mildly resented this new arrival's knowledge. From the man's perch in engineer's school, in the calm of a Fort Belvoir building, he had kept score, as if it were a basketball game, while Hodges and the other grunts had slugged it out in isolation from each other.

But it was irrelevant, anyway, at least right then. Basic School, with all its earnestness and idealism, was an unreachable part of his life, blocked off from him by combat's warp of terror. Flight school was for other people. Medals were for heroes. Relevance was Snake and Cat Man and Cannonball. Importance was keeping them alive through another week.

Twenty dead, his friend was saying, giving the numbers with the careless abandon of one who had never experienced the quick death of a friend, then commenting in the same breath on the unbearable heat and dust of An Hoa. Seventy grunt lieutenants in our Basic Class, and twenty dead in five months.

The deaths reached Hodges, brought him from his moody contemplation of the coming operation. The twenty dead would not pass through his mind like the other chatter from his classmate. He chewed a piece of gritty lettuce, considering it a luxury, and remembered Basic School, only a half-year removed, yet like a dream from innocent childhood. The platoon runs, the feisty chants, the nights they would return to O'Bannon Hall after field problems and climb three flights of steps to the floor that held their rooms, leaving thick mud trails from their boots and camouflage smears along the handrails. Singing in loud unison:

> "Fuck, fuck fuck this TBS shit,
> Three more weeks and we'll be home.
> Then it's off to Vietnam, lose a leg or lose an arm,
> And be pensioned by the Corps forever more!"

But not believing it.

Twenty dead. His friend continued, giving all the details of how each man had died, seemingly more amazed that so many were capable of dying in such a dirty little war than with the fact that they had actually died. He knew all the details, and was able to transfer each death neatly into a lesson, a comment on the character of the man who had died. The family man died on the day his son was born. The super-hero assaulted a North Vietnamese bunker and caught a grenade in the stomach (it had never happened to John Wayne). The best athlete willed his own death after losing both legs to a mine. The salty ex-enlisted wiseass refused to listen to the advice of a Kit Carson Scout and walked his platoon into an ambush. The class jokester's helicopter had caught vicious fire going into a hot landing zone, and had crashed, then blew up, the ammunition inside the helicopter detonating and killing every man (a most ironic way to go, the jokester would have agreed).

On and on, as if they were textbook deaths. The lessons irritated Hodges. His friend had no right to package them so neatly, to make them sensible.

And how would he characterize mine, Hodges wondered again and again as the man issued his examples. He knows I came from Okinawa by my own free will. Oh, God. I'd be the gungy one. Hodges shrugged. Ah. What the hell does he know, anyway. And who the fuck cares.

Hodges drained his last bit of Kool-Aid. It was time to round up his platoon. He stood and shook his classmate's hand, feeling he had little in common with the man anymore. "Remember how we all were afraid it would end before we got a chance to get a piece of it?"

The man clasped Hodges' hand. It was the eyes, Hodges finally decided. Too—enthusiastic. "We can still win it, I think. Don't you?"

Hodges heard himself issue a surprised chuckle. "I don't know anything about it anymore."[58]

On 30 August President Ho Chi Minh's reply to President Nixon's 14 May letter is received in Paris.

Hanoi, Aug. 25, 1969

His Excellency RICHARD MILHOUS NIXON,
President of the United States, Washington.

MR. PRESIDENT:
I have the honor to acknowledge receipt of your letter.

The war of agression of the United States against our people, violating our fundamental national rights, still continues in South Vietnam. The United States continues to intensify military operations, the B-52 bombings and the use of toxic chemical products multiply the crimes against the Vietnamese people. The longer the war goes on, the more it accumulates the mourning and burdens of the American people. I am extremely indignant at the losses and destructions caused by the American troops to our people and our country. I am also deeply touched at the rising toll of death of young Americans who have fallen in Vietnam by reason of the policy of American governing circles.

Our Vietnamese people are deeply devoted to peace, a real peace with independence and real freedom. They are determined to fight to the end, without fearing the sacrifices and difficulties in order to defend their country and their sacred national rights. The over-all solution in 10 points of the National Liberation Front of South Vietnam and of the provisional revolutionary government of the Republic of South Vietnam is a logical and reasonable basis for the settlement of the Vietnamese problem. It has earned the sympathy and support of the peoples of the world.

In your letter you have expressed the desire to act for a just peace. For this the United States must cease the war of aggression and withdraw their troops. . . .[59]

1969   3 September—Ho Chi Minh dies.

On 5 September the public information officer at Fort Benning, Georgia, issues the following press release:

"1/Lt. William L. Calley, Jr. is being retained on active duty beyond his normal release date because of an investigation being conducted under Article 32 of the Uniform Code of Military Justice. Lt. Calley, who was to have been separated from the Army on 6 Sep 69 is charged with violation of Article 118, murder, for offenses allegedly committed against civilians while serving in Vietnam in March, 1968."[60]

In Cambodia, the SVNLA (South Vietnamese [Communist] Liberation Army) is also having some personnel problems, but for a different reason. Captured later, this document is translated by U.S. intelligence.

Document No 1

Notebook entries, August to
September 1969 by a cadre of
J-12 Section (possibly Border
Area Office, Political Staff
Department, Headquarters
SVNLA)

1. Importance of border areas: The border between Cambodia and Vietnam is 930 kilometers long. The areas along it constitute a rear area which directly influences the resistance war in South Vietnam. Supplies and weapons are brought through this area.

2. *Characteristics:* Through these areas we could establish contact with the world and the great rear area. For this reason, the U.S. and puppets are striving to cut us completely from Cambodia.

I. SCHEMES

1. The U.S. and Puppets are trying to isolate the South Vietnam Revolution. The U.S. has poured in money to bribe the Cambodian Government in order to control the border areas and drive us out.

To achieve their purpose, they have sent out spies from SVN and Cambodia to the border areas. These spies, (from South Vietnam) composed of Special Forces, commandos, and reconnaissance agents are disguised as cadre and Liberation troops, wearing same uniforms, and carrying the same equipments as the Liberation troops.

The spies who came from Cambodia mingled with the people under the pretense of visiting their relatives or doing business [or enlisting in our ranks]. They inquired about our bases and storage facilities and then sent either Special Forces or B-52 bombers to attack us.

In short, what the Cambodians knew, they reported to the U.S. and Puppet troops who then used air and artillery to attack us in the border areas. (The U.S. troops launched the following attacks in the border areas.)

Attacked our base areas in March 69.

Attacked Areas 50 and 71 in May 69.

Attacked Area 91 in August 69.

Recently, they attacked Sau Ro's area, eight kilometers inside the Cambodian territory.

2. They kidnapped our personnel, seized the documents then either killed or released the victims. They claimed that the victims were arrested by the Cambodian authorities, in reality, they seized the documents which they sold to the Americans who then used the information to launch heliborne troops to attack our border area.

The ultra-rightists constantly criticized the Cambodian [Government]. They said that the B-52's attacked Cambodian territory because Cambodia harbored the "Viet Cong."

The enemy is trying to win Cambodia's sympathy in order to control the border areas.

He is attempting to destroy our rear area, our support area and create dissensions between the Vietnamese and Cambodian peoples.

He criticized the Cambodian people and Government and those who support us.

In conclusion, the border area is a very important area which we are striving to secure in order to protect our agencies and forces which are located there to support the battlefield.

II. THE CAMBODIAN GOVERNMENT CONSISTS OF THREE TYPES OF MEMBERS

1. *The rightist faction:* This faction consists of people with narrow-minded nationalism. They always seek to create dissension between the Vietnamese and Cambodian peoples and push the Cambodian Government to cut all relations with us, to cease supporting us and stop all trade activities with us.

2. *Ultra-Rightists:*
This faction consists of totally pro-American individuals.

3. *Neutral Faction:*
This faction consists of those who have a progressive political tendency. They want to support us and maintain Cambodia's independence and neutrality.

Due to the confusing political situation in Cambodia and the diversity of factions within the Cambodian government, we have met many difficulties in our diplomatic relations with Cambodia from the Central down to the local levels. . . .

After we win victory, Cambodia will live side by side with our country, a peaceful country with a correct policy. For this reason, Cambodia cannot fail to support us. . . .

Our position:
1. Our position is strong and our political stand is sound. This is clearly realized by the Cambodian Government.

2. We gained the sympathy of the Cambodian labor class. Therefore, we are required to observe the following points:

When encountering difficulties caused by the Khmer people, we should not be confused, but remain calm and believe in the Front. If we are captured [by the troops], we should display a firm political attitude, affirm our position and abstain from making irresponsible statements.

Conversely, if we meet favorable conditions, we should not lose our vigilance.

Our shortcomings:
1. We did not respect the [Cambodian] territorial integrity.
2. The messing, billeting, and movement regulations of our troops were not strictly observed. We fired carelessly and killed people and cattle. This adversely affects our influence upon the Khmer people.
3. Our soldiers were not courteous and did not display equality toward the Cambodian people in dealing with them.

They failed to live up to the code of the People's Army. In some areas, they either lowered the prestige of the revolutionary forces or revealed military secrets. They failed to understand the Cambodian people. They did not discriminate between friend and foe. . . .

Our mission:
Our chief mission is to continue to win Cambodia to our side for the benefit of our frontlines, our messing, and our billeting at the border. . . .

Review of our past attitude:
We did not respect the territorial integrity of Cambodia and looked down on the Cambodian people. For instance, our messing, billeting, and movement have had adverse effects on the Cambodian people's standard of living.

Our personnel were afraid of only Cambodian officers who rode motorcycles, but [five words illegible].

They paid little regards to the Cambodian people.

They were inclined to impress the Cambodian people with their weapons and thought they could bribe them with money.

They have not made positive efforts to assist our [Cambodian] friends and promote solidarity [between our two people]. . . .

The best measure is to heighten our vigilance under all circumstances.

Border [unit]
Presently, each unit has one set [of kitchen utensils]. It is requested that the utensils be increased by 50% so that they can entertain guests. The rear service needs the following items:

One cauldron for each units [*sic*]
Seven cauldrons for the inter-unit.
Each cauldron should be large enough to cook rice for 12 people.
One machete for each unit.
One saw for each inter-unit.
Clothing for [Unit] 89. Since the beginning of this year, we have only received eight suits and 95 meters of nylon.

Allowance for administrative office and for reception of guests (August 69).

Allowance for repair of bicycles not issued (Sept. 69).[61]

In mid-September Dr. Kissinger sends a memorandum to the president.

Memorandum for the President (September 10, 1969)

FROM: Henry A. Kissinger
SUBJECT: Our Present Course in Vietnam

I have become deeply concerned about our present course on Vietnam. This memorandum is to inform you of the reasons for my concern. It does not discuss alternative courses of action, but is provided for your background consideration. You know my recommendations.

While time acts against both us and our enemy, it runs more quickly against our strategy than against theirs. This pessimistic view is based on my view of Hanoi's strategy and the probable success of the various elements of our own.

I. U.S. STRATEGY

In effect, we are attempting to solve the problem of Vietnam on three highly interrelated fronts: (1) within the U.S., (2) in Vietnam, and (3) through diplomacy. To achieve our basic goals through diplomacy, we must be reasonably successful on *both* of the other two fronts.

a. *U.S.*

The pressure of public opinion on you to resolve the war quickly will increase—and I believe increase greatly—during the coming months. While polls may show that large numbers of Americans now are satisfied with the Administration's handling of the war, the elements of an evaporation of this support are clearly present. The plans for student demonstrations in October are well known, and while many Americans will oppose the students' activities, they will also be reminded of their own opposition to the continuation of the war. As mentioned below, I do not believe that "Vietnamization" can significantly reduce the pressures for an end to the war, and may, in fact, increase them after a certain point. Particularly significant is the clear opposition of many "moderate" leaders of opinion, particularly in the press and in the East (e.g., *Life* Magazine). The result of the recrudescence of intense public concern must be to polarize public opinion. You will then be somewhat in the same position as was President Johnson, although the substance of your position will be different. You will be caught between the Hawks and the Doves.

The effect of these public pressures on the U.S. Government will be to accentuate the internal divisiveness that has already become apparent to the public and Hanoi. Statements by government officials which attempt to assuage the Hawks or Doves will serve to confuse Hanoi but also to confirm it in its course of waiting us out. . . .

This view of their strategy is supported by our estimates of enemy infiltration. They *could* infiltrate more men, according to intelligence estimates, despite growing domestic difficulties. The only logical reason for their not having done so is that more men were not needed in the pipeline—at least for a few months—to support a lower-cost strategy of protracted warfare. It seems most unlikely that they are attempting to "signal" to us a desire for a *de facto* mutual withdrawal, although this cannot be discounted. There is no diplomatic sign of this—except in Xuan Thuy's linkage of points two and three of the PRG program—and I do not believe they trust us enough to "withdraw" a larger percentage of their men than we have of ours, as they would be doing.

Hanoi's adoption of a strategy designed to wait us out fits both with its doctrine of how to fight a revolutionary war and with its expectations about increasingly significant problems for the U.S.

III. CONCLUSION

In brief, I do not believe we can make enough evident progress in Vietnam to hold the line within the U.S. (and the U.S. Government), and Hanoi has adopted a strategy which it should be able to maintain for some time—barring some break like Sino-Soviet hostilities. Hence my growing concern.[62]

The next day Dr. Kissinger sends another memo, which includes the following statement.

Given the history of over-optimistic reports on Vietnam the past few years, it would be practically impossible to convince the American people that the other side is hurting and therefore with patience, *time could be on our side.* First of all we are not sure about our relative position—we have misread indicators many times before. Secondly, even if we conclude that the allied military position is sound, we don't know how to translate this into political terms—and the political prospects in South Vietnam are much shakier. Thirdly, the Administration faces an extremely skeptical and cynical American audience—the President is rightly reluctant to appear optimistic and assume his own credibility gap. Finally, to a large and vocal portion of the dissenters in this country, the strength of the allied position is irrelevant—they want an end to the war at any price.[63]

1969   16 September—President Nixon announces a further withdrawal of 35,000 U.S. troops.

Also in Washington, planning for what Dr. Kissinger refers to as the "student demonstrations in October" is underway. Writer Paul Hoffman is there.

By mid-September, discontent with the Nixon Administration's Vietnam policy had become an ominous rumbling beneath the surface of the American body politic.

In part, Nixon seemed to be suffering from the same old credibility gap that had plagued Lyndon Johnson. Cartoonists delighted in transforming Nixon's ski nose and jowly jaws into Johnson's craggy Texas features, an implication that there was no difference between the policies of the two Administrations.

On Vietnam, as on so many other issues, the new President tried to steer a middle course between the hawks and doves. He wound up, as on so many other issues, fully satisfying neither side.

He could pledge to end the war. Yet there were no signs the war was anywhere near a conclusion. And he could stand before the troops in Vietnam and call their fight—in a sadly inappropriate quotation from Winston Churchill—America's "finest hour."

He could promise to de-Americanize the war while it still continued, withdrawing 25,000 American troops in the spring and another 35,000 in the fall. Yet the pace of the pull-out was such that, if it continued at the same rate (as New York City's Mayor John V. Lindsay pointed out), it would take nine years to finish the job.

In Paris, the peace talks dragged on inconclusively—this time under a new chief American negotiator, former U.N. Ambassador Henry Cabot Lodge—and the U.S. sometimes seemed to face more opposition from its South Vietnamese ally than from its North Vietnamese opponents.

And in Vietnam, the fighting continued—albeit, at a reduced rate. Some Administration spokesmen boasted of a week in which only sixty-four died. By mid-October, 38,887 Americans had been killed in action in Vietnam. And there was no end in sight. . . .

By mid-September, the students had returned to class. Brown and the Moratorium leaders found no trouble in re-assembling the "Kiddie Corps." On campus after campus, demonstrations, marches and anti-war rallies were planned for M-Day. . . .

By October, the Moratorium committee included thirty-one full-time, paid staff workers and an outside army of 7,500 adult organizers.

"We're seeing one of the benefits of the McCarthy campaign," said staffer David Mixner. "You call four people in Iowa and you don't have to tell them what to do. They know how to organize, get up literature, deal with the press, rent halls. They know how to handle it."

Still, the whole operation was small-bore, a protest largely confined to the fringes of political action—college students, professional pacifists, and Democratic doves out to harvest a little political capital from the protest.

Then suddenly, spontaneously, Moratorium backing blossomed. All across the country, in sources the organizers had hardly thought to tap, came gestures of support. The seeds of discontent, planted months before, had sprouted—flowering in full bloom. As *Time* Magazine put it:

"Small-town housewives and Wall Street lawyers, college presidents and politicians, veteran demonstrators and people who have never made the 'V' sign of the peace movement—thousands of Americans who have never thought to grow a beard, don a hippie headband or burn a draft card—planned to turn out on M-day to register their dismay and frustration over Viet Nam."

The Harris Poll in June showed the American public supported the President's Vietnam policies by a narrow margin, forty-seven to forty-five per cent. Three months later, clear majority opposed the tack Nixon was taking, fifty-seven per cent to thirty-five.

The opposition arose in the most varied places. The Harvard University faculty voted 225 to 81 to condemn the war. It was the faculty's first statement on a political matter in nearly two hundred years—the last being opposition to King George III's tea tax in 1773. In Westport, Connecticut, perhaps the nation's must affluent suburb, the town council voted 17 to 15 to adopt a resolution calling for immediate pull-out. The presidents of seventy-nine colleges and universities signed a statement advocating pull-out. And Asian experts at the RAND Corporation, long considered the brains behind (or the pawns of) the military establishment, wrote a letter to *The New York Times* protesting the nation's war policies.

On Capitol Hill, seventeen Senators and forty-seven Representatives of both parties announced their support for the Moratorium. One group of Congressmen announced their plan to keep the House in all-night session debating the war as their contribution to M-Day.

Boston's Richard Cardinal Cushing came out for M-Day. So did the Rev. Eugene Carson Blake, general secretary of the Protestant World Council of Churches, and Rabbi Jacob Rudin, president of the Synagogue Council of America. So did scores of lesser churchmen of all denominations.

Among the few organizations taking an official stand against the Moratorium, as Brown had predicted, was organized labor. Meeting in Atlantic City, New Jersey, delegates to the AFL-CIO Convention voted 999 to 1 to back the President. But the 2,500,000-member alliance of the Teamsters Union and the United Auto Workers supported M-Day.

And Whitney Young, executive secretary of the Urban League, and one of the nation's few Negro leaders who still supported the war, finally came around. The Urban League depends on the support and cooperation of big business. Young's conversion could be taken as a sign that opposition to the war was no longer unfashionable in the top ranks of American industry.

In short, opposition to the war had become respectable.[64]

On 14 October DRV Premier Pham Van Dong publishes an open letter to American antiwar protesters. It is read into the Congressional Record *by Congressman Rogers C. B. Morton, Republican National Chairman.*

Dear American Friends: Up until now the U.S. progressive people had struggled against the war of aggression against Vietnam. This fall large sectors of the U.S. people, encouraged and supported by many peace- and justice-loving American personages, are also launching a broad and powerful offensive throughout the United States to demand that the Nixon Administration put an end to the Vietnam aggressive war and immediately bring all American troops home.

Your struggle eloquently reflects the U.S. people's legitimate and urgent demand, which is to save U.S. honor and to prevent their sons and brothers from dying uselessly in Vietnam. This is also a very appropriate and timely answer to the attitude of the U.S. authorities who are still obdurately intensifying and prolonging the Vietnam aggressive war in defiance of protests by U.S. and world public opinion.

The Vietnamese and world people fully approve of and enthusiastically acclaim your just struggle.

The Vietnamese people demand that the U.S. government withdraw completely and unconditionally U.S. troops and those of other foreign countries in the American camp from Vietnam, thus allowing the Vietnamese people to decide their own destiny by themselves.

The Vietnamese people deeply cherish peace, but it must be peace in independence and freedom. As long as the U.S. government does not end its aggression against Vietnam, the Vietnamese people will persevere in their struggle to defend their fundamental national rights. Our people's patriotic struggle is precisely the struggle for peace and justice that you are carrying out.

We are firmly confident that with the solidarity and bravery of the peoples of our two countries and with the approval and support of peace-loving people in the world, the struggle of the Vietnamese people and U.S. progressive people against U.S. aggression will certainly be crowned with total victory.

May your fall offensive succeed splendidly.

> Affectionately yours,
> Pham Van Dong,
> Premier of the DRV Government.[65]

1969 15 October—Antiwar protests and demonstrations are staged all over the country. Planning begins for other, larger rallies to be held on 15 November. **28 October**—After holding secret hearings, Senator J. William Fulbright states in an interview that U.S. involvement in Laos is a "major operation" run by the CIA and approved by the past three administrations. **12 November**—Reporter Seymour Hersh publishes a story and interview in thirty U.S. newspapers. The subject: "Massacre at My Lai 4."

Three days later, "M-Day," Moratorium Day, arrives, as noted by Paul Hoffman.

Saturday, November 15
The day dawned bright and clear—but cold for an outdoor rally, with temperatures bouncing down to the freezing mark.

At the first of the march contingents formed on the Mall, Mobe staffer Susan Miller, the last of the March Against Death, deposited the last name placard in the wooden coffins. But before they could be moved to the mall for a memorial service came the first of a series of incidents with counter-demonstrators. This group, wearing the distinctive red-white-and-blue armbands, insisted on adding the names of the 3,000 Vietnamese killed in Hue during the 1968 Tet offensive. The Mobe leaders agreed. Before the coffins were carried off, the super-patriots seized a Viet Cong flag and set it afire. . . .

At 10:25 a.m.—twenty-five minutes after the appointed hour—the mass march began. Three drummers, their instruments muffled in black crepe, set the pace. Behind them came an honor guard of next-of-kin to those who died in Vietnam carrying the ten coffins. Behind them, a man dragging a 300-pound wooden cross. And then the front row of marchers, seventeen abreast, bearing the banner

SILENT MAJORITY FOR PEACE.

Then another row of the honorary grand marshals—Mrs. Coretta King, Dr. Spock, Rev. Coffin, Senators McGovern and Goodell, and others. And behind them, row upon row, unto the hundreds of thousands.

The procession was a huge panoply of banners and flags. From Pennsylvania Avenue and 15th Street I could see American flags, some right-side-up, some upside-down; red-white-and-blue flags with the dove of peace; the red flag of revolution; the black flag of anarchy; banners of all colors with the omnipresent peace symbol

and dozens and dozens of the red-white-and-yellow flag of the Viet Cong, some—apparently inadvertently—upside-down. Cong flags far outnumbered American. For perhaps the first time in the annals of recent protests, the sight of the Cong flag did not provoke the wrath of the moderates—or the police. Outside the Washington Hotel, two men grabbed a

Cong flag from two youths at curbside. "We want our flag back," the pair protested, as sympathizers gathered behind them. One of the patriots pulled a knife to defend the captured banner. The scene had the makings of an ugly confrontation. Then a Washington cop stepped in, took the flag and returned it to its owners, took the knife, broke the blade and returned it, also.

The signs—some hand-lettered, some mass-produced—were even more varied than the banners.

> NIXON, THIS IS OUR LAST MARCH—
> THE FIRE NEXT TIME

proclaimed one placard. Not a dozen yards behind it was a huge portrait of Martin Luther King and the inscription

> NON-VIOLENCE . . . OUR MOST
> POTENT WEAPON

There were the usual slogans

> STOP THE WAR
> END IT NOW
> PEACE NOW

One hand-painted sign said simply in lower-case letters

> all too long i have dwelt with those who hate peace

There were the identification banners: of the colleges—NYU, Grinnell, Chapel Hill; the unions—Local 1199, Drug and Hospital Workers, District 65, Distributive Workers, the orange-and-black eagle-placards of Cesar Chavez' Farm Workers; the militant organizations—SDS, Youth Against War and Fascism, and way up front

> GIs AGAINST THE WAR

These numbered about one hundred soldiers and sailors all on active duty. One Mobe staff member estimated that perhaps a third of them had gone AWOL to join the march, having been denied passes by local commanders.

There were poster portraits of the heroes of the New Left—King, Castro, Robert Kennedy, Malcolm X and Ho Chi Minh. And everywhere one looked there were the hand-lettered signs glorying in the gibe of Spiro Agnew

> EFFETE SNOB

or

> EFFETE SNOB FOR PEACE

For four hours, Pennsylvania Avenue was a solid mass of humanity—mainly young, mainly white. The peace movement had yet to sink its roots into the heart of the black community. Those who neared or passed the untrustworthy age of thirty sometimes tried to sing, "We Shall Overcome," but mostly the students counted cadence with the slogans of the New Left:

> Ho, Ho, Ho Chi Minh
> NLF is going to win

or

> One, two, three, four
> Richard Nixon (or Tricky-Dicky) stop the war

usually followed by

> Two, four, six, eight
> Organize to smash the state

As I stood at curbside, a man beside me started commanding the parade. He was fiftyish and spoke with an Ozark accent. His face was weathered, his hair close-cropped. He was obviously an obscure bureaucrat in some government department. "It's quite remarkable," he said. "American students used to be the most apathetic in the world. It used to be quite the thing to eat goldfish or steal panties. Who'd ever think they'd feel so strongly about anything to do something like this?"

Curbside along the Avenue was a human chain of 3,000 Mobe marshals—at some points, a double chain—linked arm-in-arm channeling the steady flow of humanity. The Mobe had promised that the march would be peaceful and they intended to keep it that way. Not once did the police have occasion to break through the line of marshals. And only occasionally were the marshals mobilized. One incident came at 14th Street when about fifty helmeted radicals carrying Cong flags and a banner of something called the "Buffalo Nine," tried to break through the chain, presumably to march on the off-limits White House. They chanted.

> War, war, one more war. Revolution now!

But the revolution failed to pierce the phalanx of unarmed marshals. Although some marshals were toppled to the ground, the line held.

Later, a group of a half dozen radicals locked arms and raced through the parade formation near the Washington Monument. "You dumb 'peace please' people," one shouted, "we want revolution." Again, marshals quieted the outburst. There was another incident at the rally itself, while Senator McGovern was speaking, as a rebel band tried to storm the stage, "Fascists!" they shouted at the marshals. "You're as bad as the pigs." "Stop the picnic! Start the revolution!" There was some shoving, a few punches were thrown, but in the end, the line held.

At 15th Street, where the March had to swing south off the Avenue, a female marshal—her eyes closed, her head shaking ecstatically, her long blonde hair tossing from side to side—kept calling, "Keep coming, you beautiful people!"

Coming they kept. Early in the day, Police Chief Wilson put the number of marchers at 250,000, though he conceded his estimate might be a bit low. By all accounts, another 50,000 to 100,000—too late or too tired to march—joined up at the Washington Monument for the rally. The Mobe put the final figure at 800,000—obviously a gross exaggeration. My own guess, no more or less valid than anyone else's, would be slightly upward of 300,000 in the march, another 100,000 or more at the Monument.

By any estimate, it was the largest single political demonstration in American history—far exceeding the 250,000 at the 1963 civil rights rally at the Lincoln Memorial. And that had been held on a hot summer day! . . .

The Yippies had received a permit to parade at the Justice Department after the rally. By the time those who remained at the Mall were singing "give peace a chance," those who had given up on peace were attempting to storm the offices of Attorney General Mitchell.

Thousands had drifted away from the rally, down Constitution Avenue to watch the action. By best accounts, only about 800 to 1,000 of the 10,000 or so at Justice were activists interested in violent confrontation. At first, the parade was peaceful—if noisy. Carrying a host of Viet Cong flags and a huge papier-mache caricature of Mitchell, the militants— Yippies, SDS and others—as well as sympathizers and crowds of curious swarmed around the building chanting, "Stop the trial!" and "Free Bobby!"

Then, by a sort of underground grapevine, the activists started massing around the Constitution Avenue entrance. Someone pulled down the American flag from the department pole. It was tossed into the crowd and was quickly ripped apart. "Tear it up! Kill it! It's dead! The flag is dead!" a girl screamed. Another American flag was burned and the Viet Cong standard was hoisted up the pole. A paint bomb splattered a splotch of crimson against the limestone wall. About eight windows were broken by rocks. One group of militants started rattling the huge iron gates, demanding admittance.

Mitchell and Kleindienst watched the melee from their fifth-floor of-fice. According to Mrs. Mitchell, the Attorney General thought "it looked like the Russian Revolution going on."

Police Chief Wilson, who said his forces had acted too precipitously in the use of gas at DuPont Circle, now took the lead and tossed the first tear-gas cannister. It was followed by dozens of others and again the "pepper-foggers" were brought into use.

Time and again, Mobe marshals with bullhorns braved the gas from one side and the rocks from the other to urge the demonstrators to desist and disperse. "This is what Nixon wants," one screamed, "You're just playing into their hands."

"These peace marshals are unbelievable," said Yippie Rubin, his wig held down by a hippie headband, wearing a sweatshirt emblazoned with a bomb and the words, "The Conspiracy." "I told them I was the head marshal and they were all fired."

. . . The police hurled gas and formed slowly advancing cordons; the demonstrators fell back, scattering and again and again attempting to re-form. As some of the militants were sent scurrying into the downtown shopping area, there was an outburst of window-breaking.

As on Friday night, there was no sign of club-swinging by the police, but thousands of innocent bystanders got gassed—some who had come to watch the Yippies do their thing, some peacefully passing by on their way home from the march and rally only to be trapped in the ebb and flow of action, some local residents who had simply gone shopping in downtown Washington, only to emerge from the stores into a tear-gas barrage. Because of the sharp wind off the Potomac, the police were forced to toss the gas grenades far behind the ranks of the militants, into the throng of bystanders or trapped passers-by. Several persons were injured when they were struck by the cannisters.

The combat continued for more than an hour. Eventually, one hundred thirty-five were arrested, almost all charged with disorderly conduct. Yippie Rubin defended the confrontation. "We anti-war people may occasionally throw rocks, but the government drops six-ton bombs on Vietnam."

While the eyes of all were turned to Justice, there was an ironic footnote back at the Mall. I am indebted to Alfred G. Aronowitz for his account:

"In the end, America's children were sent home with the knowledge that they weren't welcome in Mr. Nixon's America. With ten minutes still left before the rally permit expired, a shoulder-to-shoulder line of cops charged over the hill from the Washington Monument, firing tear-gas cartridges at the several hundred who were still warming themselves around bonfires or waiting for buses.

"The cops charged through the snow fences around the stage, arresting everyone in their path, including William Hanley, the Boston sound specialist who had rushed out of his trailer-truck to defend his delicate electronic equipment.

"After a weekend of outstanding restraint, the cops had finally succumbed to the last temptation, a little hint that Washington was ready only to tolerate those people and didn't really welcome them. Not only did they arrest Hanley, but they also arrested members of his crew, who had worked around the clock for two days to assemble the stage and the sound towers and who were now busy disassembling them. Then the cops charged through the press tent, knocking over tables, telephones and typewriters and arresting everyone who had taken refuge there from the tear gas. . . .

"Hanley and his crew were immediately ordered released by Mayor Walter Washington, but the incident is now one of those fishbones of contention that history has had to swallow."[66]

Three days later the U.S. Senate Foreign Relations Committee holds two days of hearings on Vietnam with administration officials. Here, the secretary of defense is being questioned.

PRESIDENT NIXON'S CHANGE OF ORDERS TO GENERAL ABRAMS

SENATOR MANSFIELD: Well now, to your knowledge, Mr. Secretary, did the President of the United States, when he was in Vietnam last July, issue to General Abrams any change in the orders then in existence?

SECRETARY LAIRD: That is correct. He did.

SENATOR MANSFIELD: And what was that order which he gave to General Abrams which signified a decided change?

SECRETARY LAIRD: The order which he gave to General Abrams verbally at that time was to minimize U.S. casualties to the greatest extent possible, protect the security of the U.S. forces, and move forward as rapidly as possible with a program to Vietnamize the war.

SENATOR MANSFIELD: Was that a protective reaction policy?

SECRETARY LAIRD: The President did not use that term. I used that term in March, Senator Mansfield.

SENATOR MANSFIELD: I am trying to get it at a given point. Would you describe that as——

SECRETARY LAIRD: I would describe that as a protective reaction policy. These orders of the President were then formalized in regular military standing orders.

SENATOR MANSFIELD: Orders by the President to General Abrams and through him to his subordinates.

SECRETARY LAIRD: Military orders are issued by the Joint Chiefs of Staff, but they follow the directions of the Commander in Chief, the President of the United States.

SENATOR MANSFIELD: What I understand the President did was to put into effect what you advocated the previous March.

SECRETARY LAIRD: That is correct.

FIRST USE OF TERM "PROTECTIVE REACTION" POLICY

SENATOR MANSFIELD: I was under the impression that the order itself was initially issued by the President last July, that a month or so ago at a press conference which you held at the Pentagon you brought out the use of the term "protective reaction" for the first time that I ever heard it. I think you had a General Barnes on a standby basis to make some explanations about the Vietnamization or pacification of the area which he held. And then the following Sunday, when I was in Salt Lake City, I saw Secretary Rogers on television. He emphasized the tactic of protective reaction which to me seems to be a decided shift away from any kind of maximum pressure on search and destroy, which means in effect that what we can have [are] sweeps to anticipate and protect anything which might be coming up. I know that you will not agree with this, but it seems to me that that is a pretty decided step, if not a long step, toward a cease-fire and standfast.

SECRETARY LAIRD: It would be depending upon what the enemy does.

Later, the secretary of defense replies to a series of questions written by the committee.

CASUALTIES

QUESTION: If the Vietnamization program proceeds as you hope, how many casualties do you estimate the United States will suffer and how much will the war cost next year? In 1971?

ANSWER: I would hope to reduce U.S. casualties to zero as quickly as possible. However, U.S. casualties are primarily dependent upon three factors: the level of enemy activity, the number and type of U.S. combat forces, and the method of U.S. operations. We do not control enemy activity which in turn affects the level of U.S. forces and how they operate. Thus, it is impossible to predict with any accuracy the number of U.S. casualties which we will suffer in 1970 or 1971. [Deleted.]

COST

The current estimate for the cost of the war in FY 1970, including allocated costs of research, equipment procurement and continental U.S. training and logistics support, is $23.2 billion. The incremental cost of the war, that is the yet additional defense cost due to the war, is considerably less and approximates $15 billion. With respect to what the war will cost by the end of another year, such estimates are not possible at this time due to the fact that precise numbers and schedule withdrawals cannot be determined. As President Nixon stated, this will largely depend on the capability of the South Vietnamese to assume greater responsibility for the war and the actions of the North Vietnamese.

QUESTION: How many of the South Vietnamese generals fought with the French? With the Viet Minh?

ANSWER: Of the 54 RVNAF general officers on active duty 50 served with the French, two served with the French and Viet Minh and the remaining two did not serve with either group.

QUESTION: Do you anticipate any morale problem with U.S. troops as a result of a military victory being ruled out but fighting continuing with no end in sight?

ANSWER: No, I do not anticipate any significant morale problems.[67]

1969   21 November—For the next two weeks the story of Lieutenant Calley and the My Lai massacre becomes widely publicized in the American media.

The "major U.S. operation in Laos," revealed just five weeks earlier by Senator Fulbright, is documented by U.S. Air Force Major Albert E. Preyss in one of the many tape recordings he sends home to his family. Major Preyss is flying A-1 aircraft at Nakhon Phanom air base, Thailand.

approximately 175 rounds of 37mm. all intended for us and it was just unbelievable because Jim and I had to keep talking and advising each other where we were in relation to the fires that we had started on the ground, so that we wouldn't run into each other. We were in and out of the clouds and flying instruments as much as anything else, because at one time I was making a 4-G turn in a 60-degree bank in the clouds and all I could see was the one napalm fire on the ground that I was using for a reference. That was really something. We kept expending ordnance and Black Lion kept calling us to drop more, drop more, drop more, expend everything and we told him that we were and were doing our best and we told him how tough our situation was and he just kept pleading and I really mean—pleading! We stayed there for one hour delivering ordnance against those 82mm mortars and the two 37mm. guns. I don't know how successful we were, but I know one thing—for at least an hour those 37mms instead of shooting at Black Lion, were shooting at us, so we at least caught their attention—not that I wanted it.

O.K. so . . . it finally get so tight there between the ground, the clouds, the guns, that we used up all our ammunition, except for our 20mm. and we made 1 or 2 gun passes and then we just called it quits and we climbed up above the cloud layer, we had to actually climb through it this time— couldn't find any more holes and of course we've already lost more than one airplane running into a hill but at least I'm very, very familiar with the terrain area and we knew what heading to climb out on while we were going through the clouds.

Well, we got on top and Black Lion was still pleading with us for help. So what we did then was to drop some flares down through the clouds and ask Black Lion if he could see the flares and then tell us where the guns were in relation to those flares . . . and we could see the glow of the flare through the clouds. So he gave us directions and we rolled in from about 10,000 feet, pointed straight at the ground and fired our 20mm. and actually pulled off going through the clouds. It was really a sight to be firing all those four guns while we were going through the clouds . . . it just lit up the inside of the cloud like a Christmas tree and the flashes were so bright that I just had to put my head down in the cockpit and fly instruments on the pull up.

Well, that was some mission and we got back here about 8:30–9 o'clock in the evening, landed about then, briefed and all and of course it was the war story of the day and everybody's heard about it now and I guess we're gonna write this one up for a medal now. I tell you I think it was worth it. In fact Ron went up there this morning to help them out and he went down through the clouds all by himself and his wingman couldn't hack it and he tried to help out Black Lion, who was still calling for help this morning. Ron says he never believed that he would do that kind of nonsense, but he just felt more or less compelled by the situation. That's the way it goes—a situation just seems to dictate your actions and you really don't have much control over it.

So we got over to the club about 10 or 10:30 for dinner. Somehow I think I missed lunch yesterday. So I was a bit hungry and there wasn't much on the menu. I ordered burgundy beef and I don't know what kind of a concoction it was. It was just beef and some sort of sauce and rice . . . and I don't know what the chef had put in it, it tasted like curry flavoring, but God, it was terrible, but I was hungry so I just stuffed myself with it anyway.

Then Jim and I thought we ought to go over to the bar there and have a drink to celebrate our safe arrival home and we got together with a group of the guys and were listening to a band that had come in—some Thai musicians—and a couple of go-go girls—and one drink led to another and left there about 1:30 or 2 o'clock and I guess I had, oh, I don't know how many drinks, too many, and I walked back to the hootch area here. I was feeling good when I left the club but by the time I got back to the hootch I was feeling pretty lousy, so I thought I'd walk around the block a couple of times. I really got sick and I just heaved all over the grass all around the area here—a little bit here—a little bit there. I just couldn't shake it—I know the drinking didn't help, but I think that dinner really got to me and then the excitement of the evening finally all caught up at once. I was really very, very glad to be alive.[68]

A few days later senators Cooper and Church sponsor a successful amendment to a bill that funds the U.S. military.

Cooper-Church Amendment to the Defense Appropriations Act, FY 1970, December 15, 1969

"SEC. 643. In line with the expressed intention of the President of the United States, none of the funds appropriated by this Act shall be used to finance the introduction of American ground combat troops into Laos or Thailand."[69]

1969   15 December—President Nixon announces a further withdrawal of 50,000 U.S. troops, to be completed by April 1970.

1969   31 December

	TOTAL	NET CHANGE
U.S. military personnel assigned in Vietnam	475,200	−68,200
		(from April peak)

	YEAR	TO DATE (cumulative)
U.S. casualties		
Killed in Action	9,414	40,024
Wounded in action	70,216	262,796

Source: DOD/OASD

1970

On 2 January 1970 a captured Viet Cong soldier completes writing a lengthy transcript that reveals details of COSVN Conference 10 (10 to 15 October 1969). In addition to stating that there are now "4,000,000 . . . youths from North Vietnam" fighting against the "U.S. and puppet" forces, he reports that the following information was briefed at the conference.

1/ Enemy's and Our International Situations

President Nixon has a younger brother who is a Major and a pilot bombing the North; he was shot down by the soldiers and citizens of the North; he parachuted down and was captured alive (name unknown). His wife has recently made the following proposition to the Government of the North:

'If the Government of North Vietnam releases my husband, I will pay a compensation of 50 million dollars'; The Government of North Vietnam did not accept, but allowed her to visit her husband; when she went to Hanoi she was permitted to stay 7 days with her husband to treat him properly. The Government of North Vietnam then made a counter-proposal:

'When you return to America, agitate in the House of Representatives, the Senate, the Congress and among the American people to rise up and demand that their husbands, sons and sweethearts return home and stop the war in Vietnam. If you are able to do that, then your name will carry great honor and you will have helped the people of Vietnam rapidly achieve freedom. If you carry out the above conditions, the Government of North Vietnam promises to you the following:

'Guarantee the life of your husband; release your husband and return him safely; waive all compensation for war expenses.' Nixon's sister-in-law accepted the conditions of the Government of Vietnam.

In August 1969, this woman returned to her country to begin mobilizing the largest demonstration ever held in America. There were demonstrations which lasted for 48 hours, with each person carrying a placard with a name (of those Americans, living and dead, in Vietnam) through the streets of major American cities; then they deposited the placards into a large coffin at the US Senate.

Because of the facts presented above, at present in America there are many successive and violent demonstrations on the same subject:

That America must stop the war in Vietnam (a leading slogan); the second slogan or call is the demand for the release of their husbands, sons and sweethearts; only then will the South enjoy peace; America must withdraw its troops today and not make promises for tomorrow.

Faced with this situation, Nixon frustratingly coped with it, and was forced to accept the opinions of the American people.[70]

On 15 January another intelligence report is presented in a Saigon briefing at the headquarters of the U.S. 7th Air Force.

LAOTIAN AIR DEFENSES
THIS PORTION OF THE BRIEFING DEALS WITH ENEMY AIR DEFENSES IN LAOS. . . .

SINCE THE NOV 68 BOMBING HALT OVER NVN, THE LAOTIAN AAA DEFENSES HAVE BEEN CONTINUALLY STRENGTHENED BY NVN AID. TO PROVIDE GREATER SECURITY FOR THEIR MAJOR LOC'S AND THEIR TRUCKS AND SUPPLIES TRANSMITTING THEM, THE NORTH VIETNAMESE HAVE MORE THAN TRIPLED THE LAOTIAN AAA ORDER OF BATTLE SINCE NOV 1968. AT THAT TIME, THERE WERE ABOUT 200 GUNS LOCATED IN LAOS; HOWEVER BY THE END OF THE DRY SEASON IN 1969, THE COUNT HAD PEAKED AT ALMOST 600 GUNS. SINCE THEN, THE COUNT HAS STEADILY RISEN AND AS OF THE END OF NOV OF THIS PAST YEAR, HAS ALREADY SURPASSED THE 650 MARK.[71]

Five weeks later Dr. Kissinger acts on the DRV's agreement to "private" negotiations in addition to the public Paris talks.

The house in Choisy-le-Roi where we met with the North Vietnamese might have belonged to a foreman in one of the factories in the district. On the ground floor there was a small living room connected to an even smaller dining room, which opened into a garden. In the living room two rows of easy chairs, heavily upholstered in red, faced each other. The American group—I, Richard Smyser (my Vietnam expert), Tony Lake, and General Walters—would sit alongside the wall to the left of the door; the North Vietnamese delegation, numbering six, sat along the other wall. There were four or five feet of floor space and eons of perception separating us.

At the first meeting on February 21, 1970, Xuan Thuy greeted me and led me into the living room to meet the man whose conceit it was to use the title of Special Adviser to Xuan Thuy, although as a member of the governing Politburo he outranked him by several levels. . . .

In the afternoon it as Le Duc Tho's turn. He began by challenging my assessment that events had moved in our favor since August. "Only when we have a correct assessment of the balance of forces," said Le Duc Tho in his role as Leninist schoolmaster, "can we have a correct solution." He revealed the importance Hanoi attached to our public opinion by giving it pride of place in his presentation. He denied that Nixon's public standing had improved, citing a Gallup Poll which showed that the number of Americans favoring immediate withdrawal had risen from 21 to 35 percent. This, however, was "only" public opinion. "In addition, I have seen many statements by the Senate Foreign Relations Committee, by the

Democratic Party, by Mr. Clifford, which have demanded the total withdrawal of American forces, the change of Thieu-Ky-Khiem,* and the appointment of a successor to Ambassador Lodge." I replied sharply that I would listen to no further propositions from Hanoi regarding American public opinion; Le Duc Tho was there to negotiate the Vietnamese position. Painful as I found our domestic dissent, I did not think it compatible with our dignity to debate it with an adversary. It took several meetings to get that point across and I never succeeded totally.

Le Duc Tho next attacked our military assessment. He cut to the heart of the dilemma of Vietnamization. All too acutely, he pointed out that our strategy was to withdraw enough forces to make the war bearable for the American people while simultaneously strengthening the Saigon forces so that they could stand on their own. He then asked the question that was also tormenting me: "Before, there were over a million U.S. and puppet troops, and you failed. How can you succeed when you let the puppet troops do the fighting? Now, with only U.S. support, how can you win?"

From this analysis, Le Duc Tho's conclusions followed inexorably. He insisted that military and political problems be dealt with simultaneously—a position from which he never deviated until October 1972. According to Le Duc Tho, the only military subject for discussion was the unconditional liquidation of our involvement. The six-month deadline for withdrawal proposed by the NLF was fixed and would run regardless of other agreements. However, even if we withdrew, Hanoi would stop fighting only if there were a political settlement. This, in Le Duc Tho's view, presupposed the removal of the "warlike" President Thieu, Vice President Ky, and Prime Minister Khiem and the creation of a coalition government composed of three groups: those members of the "Saigon Administration" (without Thieu, Ky, and Khiem) who genuinely stood for "peace, independence and neutrality"; neutral forces who met the same criteria; and the Communist NLF. The NLF would determine who stood for "peace, independence and neutrality." This coalition government, loaded as it was in Hanoi's favor, was not, however, the final word. With one-third of it composed of Communists, with the remainder approved by the Communists, with all anti-Communist leaders barred, it was then to negotiate with the fully armed NLF for a definitive solution. Tho comforted me that this generous scheme would open hopeful prospects: "If you show goodwill and serious intent, a settlement will come quickly."[72]

Although both private and public negotiations emphasize the situation in Vietnam, it is in Laos where most of the air and ground combat occurs in early 1970. U.S. Air Force Colonel Edward Kenny describes the events of February.

*Tran Thien Khiem, who had replaced Tran Van Huong as Prime Minister of South Vietnam. [footnote in original]

1. (S) INTRODUCTION:

a. Following the loss of the key defensive position of Phou Nok Kok in January (See DOCO End of Tour Report—January 1970) enemy pressure continually increased. During February friendly units were progressively dislodged from their forward positions. The enemy gained access to the PDJ, and following several sharp engagements at L-22 the entire PDJ fell into enemy hands and General Vang Pao ordered the evacuation of Xieng Khoangville. Three days later LS-108 at Moung Soui also fell to the enemy. Thus, by the end of February all the gains realized by Operation About Face had again reverted to enemy control.

2. (S) LOSS OF THE PLAINE DES JARRES:

a. During the early part of February the enemy pushed the friendly forces further back along Route 7 from Ban Ban to Noug Pet. There were reports of intensive efforts by the enemy to reopen this section of Route 7 as a prelude to an offensive against the PDJ. Finally, on 12 February the long expected offensive started. . . . Eight sites in Military Region II (MR II) came under heavy attack on the night of 11–12 Feb. Coincident with these heavy attacks the vital Xieng Khouang Airfield (L-22) was attacked by two "DACON" companies of NVA with a third in reserve. Dacon companies are special composite elite units referred to by the Lao as suicide companies. . . . The friendly forces held firm and inflicted at least 74KIA casualties on the enemy forces. Evidently, however, this first attack on L-22 was a diversion. The main attack that night was against Phou Houay, a high point dominating the Route 7/71 Junction (Ref 2). This attack was successful and Phou Houay fell to the enemy. The attack was launched under near zero-zero weather conditions precluding the effective use of air support. There was continuing pressure on the remaining friendlies in the Route 7/71 Junction area during the 12th. Enemy tanks and elements were reported west of Ban Ban moving toward the 7/71 Junction (Ref 3). The 7/71 Junction is at the northeastern end of the PDJ and once past this junction the enemy can fan out over the entire PDJ. That night, 12–13 Feb, a large enemy convoy of eight tanks, eight armored cars and sixty trucks was reported east of Khang Khay heading toward Khang Khay and L-22.

b. During the 13th of February all friendly forces fighting to the east of the PDJ were ordered to withdraw to forward positions around the PDJ. Also, the forces that had been attempting to hold the Route 7/71 Junction were withdrawn to avoid encirclement. Thus the gateway to the PDJ was now in enemy hands; troops and supplies could pour into the PDJ unimpeded by any friendly ground forces. Xieng Khouang Airfield (L-22) continued to receive nightly attacks during 12–19 Feb. During this time the remaining government outposts in and around the PDJ were rapidly overrun. On the night of 14 Feb six outposts fell, and on 15 Feb 23 positions west of the 7/71 Junction were abandoned due to enemy pressure. On the night of 17 Feb Long Tieng (LS-20A) was hit by a small group (7) of NVA while Xieng Khouang Airfield came under heavy attack by troops supported by approximately four tanks (Ref 6). Finally, in the early morning hours of 21 Feb, the Xieng Khouang Airfield was lost (Ref 7). With the loss of this position General Vang Pao decided to evacuate his troops from Xieng Khouangville. Thus the entire PDJ was now in enemy hands.

3. (S) LOSS OF MOUNG SOUI (LS-108):

a. With the loss of Xieng Khouang Airfield friendly forces became scattered and disorganized for a short period. Also, it became readily apparent that Moung Soui was in imminent danger of attack. This Lima Site is important because RLAF T-28 aircraft use it for strikes in the PDJ and surrounding areas. The only other nearby base from which T-28's can be launched is at Long Tieng (LS-20A). However, due to conditions at LS-20A the T-28's cannot carry a full ordnance load when staging from there. At the time L-22 fell there were only 200ADC troops defending Moung Soui. This figure was increased somewhat when some of the troops who left L-22 arrived in the Moung Soui area however. The enemy had one of three obvious choices. He could push on to Moung Soui, then down Route 4/7 to its junction with Route 13. This would isolate the Royal Capital of Luang Prabang from Vientiane, as well as denying LS-108 to the RLAF. Another choice was to continue his offensive in the direction of Long Tieng (LS-20A). If the enemy could sustain his momentum this move might very well cause the collapse of all organized opposition. The third choice available was to slow his advance and consolidate his gains.

. b. The enemy chose the first alternative. Rather than stopping his advance and consolidating his gains he continued his drive against Moung Soui. By maintaining pressure against the confused and demoralized RLG forces he considerably enhanced the probability of great gains with minimal losses. On 24 Feb Moung Soui came under attack and fell late the same afternoon.[73]

On 6 March President Nixon delivers another address concerning the war.

I turn now to the precise nature of our aid to Laos.

In response to press conference questions on September 26, December 8 and January 30, I have indicated:

—That the United States has no ground combat forces in Laos.

—That there were 50,000 North Vietnamese troops in Laos and that "more perhaps are coming."

—That, at the request of the Royal Laotian Government which was set up by the Geneva Accords of 1962, we have provided logistical and other assistance to that government for the purpose of helping it to prevent the Communist conquest of Laos.

—That we have used air power for the purpose of interdicting the flow of North Vietnamese troops and supplies on that part of the Ho Chi Minh Trail which runs through Laos.

—That, at the request of the Royal Laotian Government, we have flown reconnaissance missions in Northern Laos in support of the Laotian Government's efforts to defend itself against North Vietnamese aggression and that we were engaged in "some other activities."

It would, of course, have posed no political problem for me to have disclosed in greater detail those military support activities which had been initiated by two previous administrations and which have been continued by this administration.

I have not considered it in the national interest to do so because of our concern that putting emphasis on American activities in Laos might hinder the efforts of Prime Minister Souvanna Phouma to bring about adherence to the Geneva Agreements by the Communist signatories.

In recent days, however, there has been intense public speculation to the effect that the United States involvement in Laos has substantially increased in violation of the Geneva Accords, that American ground forces are engaged in combat in Laos and that our air activity has had the effect of escalating the conflict.

Because these reports are grossly inaccurate, I have concluded that our national interest will be served by putting the subject into perspective through a precise description of our current activities in Laos.

These are the facts:

—There are no American ground combat troops in Laos.

—We have no plans for introducing ground combat forces into Laos.

—The total number of Americans directly employed by the U.S. Government in Laos is 616. In addition, there are 424 Americans employed on contract to the government or to government contractors. Of these 1040 Americans, the total number, military and civilian, engaged in a military advisory or military training capacity numbers 320. Logistics personnel number 323.

—No American stationed in Laos has ever been killed in ground combat operations.

—U.S. personnel in Laos during the past year has not increased while during the past few months, North Vietnam has sent over 13,000 additional combat ground troops into Laos.

—When requested by the Royal Laotian Government, we have continued to provide military assistance to regular and irregular Laotian forces in the form of equipment, training and logistics. The levels of our assistance have risen in response to the growth of North Vietnamese combat activities.

—We have continued to conduct air operations. Our first priority for such operations is to interdict the continued flow of troops and supplies across Laotian territory on the Ho Chi Minh Trail. As Commander-in-Chief of our armed Forces, I consider it my responsibility to use our air power to interdict this flow of supplies and men into South Vietnam and thereby avoid a heavy toll of American and allied lives.

—In addition to these air operations on the Ho Chi Minh Trail, we have continued to carry out reconnaissance flights in Northern Laos and to fly combat support missions for Laotian forces when requested to do so by the Royal Laotian Government.

—In every instance our combat air operations have taken place only over those parts of Laos occupied and contested by North Vietnamese and other Communist forces. They have been flown only when requested by the Laotian Government. The level of our air operations has been increased only as the number of North Vietnamese in Laos and the level of their aggression has increased.

Our goal in Laos has been and continues to be to reduce American involvement and not to increase it, to bring peace in accordance with the 1962 Accords and not to prolong the war.[74]

1970   13 March—With Cambodian Chief of State Sihanouk out of the country, anti-Viet Cong/North Vietnamese demonstrations become riots in Phnom Penh. The Cambodian government demands that all Viet Cong and North Vietnamese troops withdraw from Cambodia by 15 March. **18 March**—As Cambodian troops attack Viet Cong and North Vietnamese sanctuaries, Lieutenant General Lon Nol's coup overthrows Prince Sihanouk. The Cambodian national assembly concurs unanimously.

In Washington, according to Dr. Kissinger, the U.S. government is completely surprised.

For Lon Nol and Sirik Matak, the crucial step was their act of bravado to take up the popular battle against the hated—and far superior—forces of the North Vietnamese and Viet Cong. For Sihanouk, the crucial step was his week of hesitation, because what Lon Nol and Sirik Matak feared, and Podgorny advised, the United States also believed and preferred: that Sihanouk's bold reentry into Phnom Penh to face down his opponents would have turned the tide of events and was in everybody's best interest. Once returned to power, Sihanouk could have resumed his balancing role from his traditional position, which I described to Nixon . . . as one of "placing himself deliberately on the extreme left wing of the right wing." We would almost certainly have cooperated with this effort. By March 20 events were racing out of control.

The role of the United States through these events was hardly as purposeful as some imagine, or as effectual as others pretend. Preoccupied with Laos for the first three months of the year, and with no intelligence personnel in Phnom Penh, we found our perceptions lagging far behind events. We neither encouraged Sihanouk's overthrow nor knew about it in advance. We did not even grasp its significance for many weeks. My own ignorance of what was going on is reflected in two memoranda to Nixon. Though he received daily summaries of key events, I did not send forward a longer analysis of the first (March 11) demonstrations against Sihanouk until March 17, a week's delay that indicates that Cambodia was scarcely a high priority concern. Even more striking is my suggestion in that analysis that it all could have been an elaborate trick by Sihanouk:

> Given the sharp competition between Sirik Matak and Sihanouk, it is possible that Sirik wanted to present Sihanouk with a fait accompli, or to challenge him to a test on gounds where Sirik Matak's position would be popular. On the other hand, nobody has challenged Sihanouk so directly in years, and it is quite possible that this is an elaborate maneuver, to permit Sihanouk to call for Soviet and Chinese cooperation in urging the VC/NVA to leave, on the grounds that he will fall and be replaced by a "rightist" leader if the VC/NVA stay in Cambodia.
>
> The recent behavior of Sihanouk and the RKG [Royal Khmer Government] would fit either thesis—i.e., that this is a collusive gambit; or that Sihanouk in fact faces a challenge from Sirik Matak and Lon Nol.

The motivations of the principal actors in Phnom Penh were quite obscure to me, not least because Lon Nol had been among those profiting from the smuggling trade with the very Communist forces that his government now challenged. On March 19 in another memorandum to the President, I still thought Sihanouk might attempt to return to Phnom Penh and put some of the pieces back together:

> Lon Nol has heretofore been content to be Number Two, but this appears to be a straight power challenge. In popular anger against Vietnamese Communist incursions, he has found a good issue to challenge Sihanouk (and the Army fanned up that anger), but Lon Nol's dealings with the Communists do not suggest that he is a fervent anti-Communist or anti-Vietnamese patriot.
>
> *Future Choices.* This situation will probably move in one of three ways:
>
> —A Lon Nol/Sirik Matak-dominated new Government supported by the Army, with little popular support and forced to buy popularity with anti-Vietnamese slogans and economic progress.
>
> —A shaky compromise akin to the barons' truce with King John in 1215, permitting Sihanouk to come back as Chief of State but with much limited powers. This would be an unstable situation, as Sihanouk maneuvered, probably successfully, to outflank and eliminate his challengers.
>
> —A Sihanouk victory, by turning the Army against Lon Nol.
>
> *The Implications for Foreign Policy and for Us.* Khmer nationalism has [been] aroused against the Vietnamese Communist occupation. Any future government will probably have to be more circumspect and covert about its cooperation with the Vietnamese. Lon Nol has chosen this issue, and he will need to be able to demonstrate publicly that he is taking action against the Vietnamese occupation. Similarly, Sihanouk will not for some time open himself to the charge of being "soft on the Vietnamese."
>
> This will create serious problems for the VC/NVA, which will have considerable reason to take a more hostile line toward Cambodia.

None of my reports to the President discussed any US intelligence involvement or expressed any particular pleasure at the coup. Nor was CIA reporting more prescient, doubtless in part because the Agency had been banned from Phnom Penh. It was not until March 18—the day of Sihanouk's ouster—that a CIA report was circulated in Washington. Its burden: that the Lon Nol–encouraged riots were a precursor to a coup against Sihanouk if Sihanouk refused to go along with an anti-Hanoi policy. The information had been acquired the week before from an Asian businessman not otherwise identified. The delay in distributing this report and the CIA's failure to predict the overthrow of Sihanouk were later the subject of an investigation by the President's Foreign Intelligence Advisory Board. I do not recall any document predicting the coup that came to my attention before the event, and I have not unearthed one in my papers. Of charges of intelligence failure, it should be remembered that the leader against whom it was directed had a far greater incentive to know the truth in his country, and he failed to anticipate the plot.[75]

1970 **23 March**—With DRV, PRG, and Pathet Lao concurrence, Prince Sihanouk declares from Peking that he will form a "national union" government and army. **27–28 March**—South Vietnamese troops, with U.S. air and helicopter support, make first publicly announced ground attacks against Communist base areas in Cambodia. **30 March**—With U.S. air (including B-52) support, the North Vietnamese/Pathet Lao advance in northern Laos is checked.

The next day in Vientiane, Laos, as seen in the novel The Laotian Fragments, *the U.S. air attaché sends copies of two messages to the chief forward air controller, Major Blake. Only the second one is transmitted to Washington.*

Draft copy of DIA [Defense Intelligence Agency] Summary. OUSAIRA [office of U.S. air attaché] Vientiane, to DIA, Washington, 31 March. Attached is a memo, which follows as the next item.

1. All evidence points to the fact that Long Tieng has been held, but for reasons which are not, repeat, not entirely clear. Even though Sam Thong was reoccupied today without opposition and the enemy there has apparently abandoned his positions on the north ridge, even though Vang Pao's troops now occupy all territory around Long Tieng, there is an air of deepening mystery infusing the entire operation.

2. Some of the questions are: How many NVA were actually out there? How many friendly troops did *we* have? What were the enemy's real intentions? Why didn't they take Long Tieng any of the three days prior to the rains, when they apparently outnumbered a demoralized, tired

handful of men? After the rains, what happened to them? Might there have been, in fact, only a few sapper companies, whose instructions were to harass us? Did they extend their supply lines too far and get caught by the rains? Does VP [Vang Pao] really believe there were "thousands" of NVA out there? Did they actually bring in all that heavy equipment and did it get stuck in the mud? Was our interdiction campaign successful, so that the enemy really did not have all that big stuff in after all? Did our airstrikes chew them up so much that they could not continue? Were they afraid of determined resistance by the combined Meo-Lao forces? Did we win a battle, or did the rains save our ass? Or just what the hell went on up there, anyway? I'll be swacked if I know. All I know is that everyone I've had the pleasure of serving with here deserves the highest praise his country can give him.

Memo from OUSAIRA, Vientiane, to Major Blake, dated 31 March.

Bill:

Attached is a draft of the DIA Summary I wish I had the guts to send. But I don't. Furthermore, I doubt if it would do any good anyway. I think you can understand by now, however, why I have decided to submit my retirement papers immediately, even before the results of the promotion board are announced. I don't think I can take another Long Tieng, even if I'm not here to see it. And, quite frankly, I don't see why I should be expected to. If I had any answers to give you, I'd pass them on—but I don't.

So I'm going to leave the whole fucking thing in someone else's lap, my friend, and it's not my baby anymore. Incidentally, I suspect the feeling is somewhat mutual in Washington. I may have been fired. I've just been informed that my replacement is due in next week, three months earlier than I had expected him.

Call me at your convenience when you're down, and I'll buy you that drink I've been promising. From now on, color me FIGMO [slang acronym for "Fuck It, Got My Orders"].

JB

PS. Here's a copy of the DIA message I *did* send. Note the qualifiers.

DIA Summary (Xerox copy), OUSAIRA, Vientiane, to DIA, Washington, 31 March.

1. According to General Vang Pao, Commander of Military Region II, the siege of Long Tieng has been lifted. He has called upon all his people to return to their homes, and has announced that the enemy has suffered a disastrous defeat. Plans are already underway to assist refugees in returning to the valley.

2. In the face of what was reported to be a vastly superior enemy force, defenders consisting of allied soldiers from many contiguous regions suc-

cessfully withstood an 11-day assault which included 122mm rockets, mortar and artillery fire, and direct attacks. Despite extremely poor weather and miserably dangerous flying conditions, U.S. air support assured the success of this major engagement. General Vang Pao himself has said, "If it were not for your (the U.S.) help, an NVA general would now be living in my house."

3. When the weather was below visual minimums, radar bombing continuously pounded the enemy, destroying unknown numbers of supplies and no doubt inflicting numerous casualties. Our small force of Raven FACs repeatedly distinguished themselves, even while living under conditions of privation and hardship when ordered to evacuate. Nearly constant air attacks disrupted the enemy's timetable, and when the weather finally cleared, massive airstrikes harassed a withdrawing, no doubt demoralized North Vietnamese division.

4. All praises should go where they are most deserved: to the valiant soldiers of General Vang Pao; to the intelligence community, who kept so well abreast of developments; to the USAF officers and men, both FAC and strike pilots, who relentlessly and efficiently did their jobs; and finally, to the combined determination of all joint forces involved, whose courage and devotion to duty ensured that Long Tieng, this year, would not fall.

Holograph note in Col. Barnes' hand: "You see, Bill? Both versions are true—that's why it's all so tragic."[76]

As shown by this 3 April priority, "Info Perishable" message, the American intelligence community is quite concerned about the consequences of the widening of the war to include Cambodia.

3 APRIL 70
FROM: [Washington]
TO: [Multiple Addresses]

PEKING'S POLICY TOWARDS CAMBODIA:

(C-NFD) THE DENIAL OF SPECIAL PRIVILEGES TO THE COMMUNISTS BY THE NEW GOVERNMENT OF CAMBODIA HAS FAR REACHING CONSEQUENCES ON CHICOM'S [Chinese Communists'] OUTLOOK TOWARD SOUTHEAST ASIA. THE CLOSURE OF SIHANOUKVILLE TO PEKING'S LOGISTICAL SUPPORT OF THE VIET CONG AND THE DENIAL OF SANCTUARY TO COMMUNIST TROOPS IN CAMBODIA WOULD SERIOUSLY JEOPARDIZE PEKING'S PRIME GOAL OF PROTRACTED PRESSURE ON U.S. AND ALLIED FORCES IN SOUTHEAST ASIA. THE COMMUNIST FORCES IN THE STRATEGIC DELTA AREA OF VIETNAM DEPEND HEAVILY ON LOGISTICAL SUPPORT THROUGH CAMBODIA, AND DISRUPTION OF THIS AVENUE WOULD MAKE THEM VULNERABLE TO ALLIED PROSECUTION.

RADIO PEKING HAS WIDELY PUBLICIZED THE MESSAGE OF OFFICIAL BACKING RECEIVED BY SIHANOUK FROM SOUTHEAST ASIAN COMMUNIST LEADERS. A DI-

RECT ATTACK UPON THE LON NOL REGIME WAS ISSUED BY PEKING ON 1 APRIL.
THIS IS PROBABLY AN EFFORT BY PEKING TO EXERT MAXIMUM PRESSURE ON THE
NEW 'SALVATION' GOVERNMENT TO ACCEDE TO A COMPROMISE AGREEMENT
CONCERNING THE USE OF CAMBODIA BY COMMUNIST FORCES. IF SUCH A COMPRO-
MISE IS NOT FORTHCOMING, IT IS PROBABLE THAT PEKING WILL LOGISTICALLY
SUPPORT COORDINATED INSURGENCY ATTACKS ON CAMBODIA BY THE PATHET
LAO, VIET CONG, AND NORTH VIETNAMESE. THE PRIMARY AIM WOULD BE TO
REINSTALL A SYMPATHETIC GOVERNMENT IN PHNOM PENH. AN UNCONFIRMED 2
APRIL ASSOCIATED PRESS REPORT FROM PHNOM PENH STATES THAT SIHANOUK IS
NOW IN HANOI.[77]

*At this time Donald Kirk is one of the many American correspondents
whose attention suddenly shifts to Cambodia. He flies to Phnom Penh.*

The Cambodian leader is Sirik Matak, who easily impressed Americans by
seizing upon the concept of "la guerre populaire" and urging continued
offensives against the enemy, particularly while Lon Nol was recuperating
in Hawaii. Primary responsibility for conduct of the war, however, rested
not with Sirik Matak but with a council of perhaps half a dozen generals in
charge of a general headquarters within the ministry of defense.

The question, of course, is whether Cambodia's generals are at all
better qualified militarily than Sirik Matak, by profession a diplomat who
served as ambassador to China, Japan and the Philippines before Sihanouk temporarily "retired" him in 1968. Most senior Cambodian officers
were trained by French officers in conventional infantry tactics that bear
little relationship to the peculiar brand of hit-and-run warfare waged by
Communist troops along major roads leading toward Phnom Penh. Lon
Nol himself, after having attended Saigon's fashionable Lycée Chasse-
loup-Laubat (ten years ahead of Sihanouk), began his career as a civilian
magistrate under French colonial authorities in 1936. He did not enter
military service until 1952, when he was appointed commander of Bat-
tambang province, and had no formal training until 1955, when he
studied for several months at the French-advised Royal Khmer Military
Academy.

Unlike Lon Nol, many of Cambodia's officers spent several years in
France—or else, before 1963, studied in the United States under the old
military assistance and advisory program. General Fernandez, for instance, has been to France three times: first in 1951 at infantry school,
again in 1953 at staff school, and, finally, from 1959 to 1961 at the
Advanced School of Warfare, the equivalent of the various war colleges
in the United States for potential top officers. Often, however, the experience of training in France was more valued socially than professionally.
Sihanouk himself was raised speaking French—and far preferred to discuss political and military problems in French than in Cambodian. (General Fernandez, like other one-time Sihanouk lieutenants, reflects his
French background and close associations with the prince. "Poof," he

said, pursing his lips and turning up his palms in a typically French gesture of frustration, when asked if he knew whether or not any officers
were still selling arms to the Communists.) . . .

The weakness of government forces in the spring of 1970 was understandable, but army officers could present no such excuses for the failure
of a vaunted "counter-offensive" up Route Six, a critical highway north
of Phnom Penh, the following September. For the first time in the war,
according to Lieutenant Colonel Am Rong, the Cambodian army spokesman in Phnom Penh, Cambodian forces were "seizing the initiative" and
beginning to drive the North Vietnamese from strongholds they had held
since the previous spring and summer. Along with oher reporters and
photographers, I clambered into a Mercedes-Benz, the standard convey-
ance for reaching any of the fronts in this elusive, multifronted war, and
hurried to the scene of the latest fighting, some sixty miles to the north.

The aim of the offensive was to open up Route Six as far as the town of
Kompong Thom, a major government enclave some eighty miles north of
the capital, but it was questionable if the special "task force" spearhead-
ing the drive could even get into the village of Taing Kauk, into which
Communist troops had dug a complex network of trenches and bunkers.
The weakness of the task force was all the more humiliating in view of the
American role in the operation. Cambodia and the United States, after
all, had solidified an unwritten agreement under which Washington was
providing full air support (described as "interdiction of North Vietnamese
supply routes" by Defense Secretary Melvin Laird) as well as new weapons, ammunition and even training for Cambodian troops in South Vietnam. Indeed, at least 1,000 of the 5,000 men poured into the offensive
had just completed a three-week refresher course in South Vietnam after
American transport planes had evacuated them from untenable positions
in the sparsely populated, jungly northeastern provinces.

Two American planes, a slow-moving C-119 "gunship" laden with machine guns and a phantom jet on a photo-reconnaissance mission, were
wheeling and diving overhead when I reached the tail of the task force near
a blown-out bridge outside of Taing Kauk. Cambodian soldiers were
lolling in hammocks slung between mud-spattered buses and French armored cars on which they had driven from Phnom Penh, and a work crew
was attempting to rebuild the bridge with a new orange-colored steel
girder, supplied by the Americans. I walked across the girder, past soldiers
fishing and swimming in a canal by a rice paddy, to the "front," several
hundred yards up the road. Bullets cracked and twanged, occasionally
kicking up geysers of water in the rice paddies. French-trained junior
officers shouted "Avancez!" Their charges, bunched together in defiance
of commonsense rules of safety under fire, fought from trenches cut into
the road by North Vietnamese saboteurs. A squad of Cambodians moved
slowly toward the cement framework of an old schoolhouse. They poked
through ashes and gaping holes in the walls, already bombarded by American planes. Automatic-rifle fire crackled from the shadows.

Major Hang Yieu, battalion commander, barked orders in Cambodian from one of the trenches. More soldiers inched forward along a wall beside the schoolhouse. In a moment the rifle fire died down, and the American planes faded in the distance. Standing beside the major, I saw the bodies of three Cambodian soldiers lying next to an entrance to the schoolgrounds. "It is normal for an offensive," Hang Yieu remarked, somewhat laconically, neither sadly nor callously, as some of his soldiers stared at the bodies. Fifty feet ahead lay the bodies of two North Vietnamese, their hands still clutching a long pole on which had hung a sack of rice. Across from them was the body of one more Cambodian soldier, his white sneakers shining in the midday sun.

"It will be a long time before we reach Kompong Thom," said Hang Yieu as some of his troops fired a few final perfunctory shots into the school building, now apparently deserted by the last enemy snipers. As if to prove the major's point, most of his men slouched under some trees in the shade of abandoned village homes. Others foraged for pigs and chickens or drank water from a well. "We are waiting for our support," the major explained. A mile behind him, some of the "support" slowly lumbered forward—a few buses, armored cars, and hospital trucks identifiable by their red crosses. "We think maybe 2,000 or 3,000 Communist troops are ahead of us," Hang Yieu said, but his estimate seemed grossly exaggerated. Twenty or thirty snipers could easily have held up the entire column. The fighting on the fringes of Taing Kauk, in fact, dramatized the pattern of the operation, if not of the entire war. The enemy's main purpose was to harass, delay and pin down Cambodian forces while opening new supply and infiltration routes through eastern and central Cambodia to South Vietnam.

"Cambodian troops are advancing slowly but steadily," announced Colonel Am Rong (whose name, it has often been noted, seemed peculiarly appropriate) the morning after I returned to Phnom Penh. In fact, however, the North Vietnamese, sneaking around Cambodian positions, soon cut the road in several places behind them and threatened to surround them. It was all the Cambodians, supported by American air strikes, could do to fight their way into Taing Kauk, set up a more or less permanent base in the shelled, strafed, and bombed-out town, and hold the North Vietnamese at arm's length with occasional sporadic patrols into the tree lines.[78]

1970 **8 April**—Attacking Cambodian troops are driven back by North Vietnamese/Viet Cong forces near the South Vietnamese border. **20 April**—President Nixon announces that 150,000 more U.S. troops will be withdrawn from Vietnam by spring 1971.

By April, despite operations by ARVN units in Cambodia, North Viet-
namese/Viet Cong forces are advancing on Phnom Penh, and the Lon Nol
government has detained or killed thousands of Vietnamese residents of
eastern Cambodia. On 22 April the acting chairman of the Joint Chiefs of
Staff sends the following message to his Asian commanders.

Subj: Situation-in Cambodia

1. As you are certainly aware, there is highest level concern here with respect to the situation in Cambodia. This concern has been heightened by the following:

a. It appears that the success of NVA and VC troops to date have encouraged them to expand what may have been limited objectives initially to a current drive to isolate Phnom Penh.

b. Most lines of communication leading into Phnom Penh from the north, east, and south have been interdicted by enemy forces and the security of Phnom Penh and the Cambodian Government appears to be seriously threatened.

2. Considerations are continuing as to how best to respond to this situation in a timely manner. As you know, limited US materiel support to the Cambodian Government has begun; however, we are of the view that this will have only minor impact on the current momentum of the VC/NVA. Further, we believe that a more direct approach through attack of enemy support areas along the South Vietnam/Cambodian border would probably have much greater effect on the enemy in the near term. With the enemy over-extended, he presents us with opportunities that we should not let slip by. Further, the threat to Phnom Penh and the present concern of higher authority may be conducive to relaxation of some of the current constraints under which we are operating. If this happens we should be prepared to take advantage of the opportunity.

3. Actions which we might consider and on which I would like your views follow:

a. More US involvement in detailed ARVN planning for cross-border operations.

b. Preparations to provide US fire support and logistic support for ARVN units operating cross-border.

c. Preparation for selective use of US troops in most productive base areas, if US policy permits.

d. Plans for employment of Khmer CIDG [Civilian Irregular Defense Groups] troops.

e. Diversion of some of the small arms and ammunition now en route to the PSDF [People's Self-Defense Forces].

With respect to employment of the Khmer CIDG we could:

a. Fly them to Phnom Penh to support the FARK. [Forces Armées Royale Khmer].

b. Use them for cross-border operations supported from SVN.

It would appear that the later [*sic*] would be more productive. In this case we could relieve the Khmer of their present CIDG border post duties and concentrate them in one or more areas where they could devote full attention to cross-border operations. In this way we could continue to support them from bases in SVN. Under proper circumstances they might be accompanied by Vietnamese Special Forces (LLDB) [*Luc Luong Dac Diet,* "Special Forces" in Vietnamese] or US Special Forces. We would like your appraisal of their probable effectiveness if:

(1) Vietnamese Special Forces remain with them; or

(2) They operated without either Vietnamese or US Special Forces accompanying them.

With respect to small arms delivery, it would appear that we might consider delivering arms by sea to Vung Tau and then by air to Phnom Penh. We would want delivery to be covert if possible; however, this may not be feasible over a long period or if large quantities are involved.

We would appreciate your views on the above suggestions and any others that you believe would be effective in relieving pressure on Phnom Penh and the Cambodian Government. Whatever plans we embark on should be designed for early implementation and be effective over the next few weeks to take advantage of the remaining dry season. Highest authority is particularly interested in steps that we can take now to reflect our support for Lon Nol and to cause the North Vietnamese to reappraise their actions. We believe that the first step should be ARVN operations against critical base areas in the following target priorities:

a. Headquarters and Communication Centers.

b. Caches and Depots.

c. Troop concentrations.

The US would support this initial step up to the border, working with the South Vietnamese, and should be prepared to take further actions into Cambodia if the political situation permits.

(U) Since we must provide recommendations to higher authority, would appreciate your views by 0800 Washington time on 22 April.[79]

On 30 April President Nixon addresses the nation.

Good evening, my fellow Americans. Ten days ago, in my report to the Nation on Viet-Nam, I announced a decision to withdraw an additional 150,000 Americans from Viet-Nam over the next year. I said then that I was making that decision despite our concern over increased enemy activity in Laos, in Cambodia, and in South Viet-Nam.

At that time, I warned that if I concluded that increased enemy activity in any of these areas endangered the lives of Americans remaining in Viet-Nam I would not hesitate to take strong and effective measures to deal with that situation.

Despite that warning, North Viet-Nam has increased its military aggression in all these areas, and particularly in Cambodia. . . . In contrast to our policy, the enemy in the past 2 weeks has stepped up his guerrilla actions, and he is concentrating his main forces in these sanctuaries that you see on this map, where they are building up to launch massive attacks on our forces and those of South Viet-Nam.

North Viet-Nam in the last 2 weeks has stripped away all pretense of respecting the sovereignty or the neutrality of Cambodia. Thousands of their soldiers are invading the country from the sanctuaries; they are encircling the Capital of Phnom Penh. Coming from these sanctuaries, as you see here, they have moved into Cambodia and are encircling the Capital.

Cambodia, as a result of this, has sent out a call to the United States, to a number of other nations, for assistance. Because if this enemy effort succeeds, Cambodia would become a vast enemy staging area and a springboard for attacks on South Viet-Nam along 600 miles of frontier, a refuge where enemy troops could return from combat without fear of retaliation.

North Vietnamese men and supplies could then be poured into that country, jeopardizing not only the lives of our own men but the people of South Viet-Nam as well.

Now, confronted with this situation, we have three options.

First, we can do nothing. Well, the ultimate result of that course of action is clear. Unless we indulge in wishful thinking, the lives of Americans remaining in Viet-nam after our next withdrawal of 150,000 would be gravely threatened.

Let us go to the map again. Here is South Viet-Nam. Here is North Viet-Nam. North Viet-Nam already occupies this part of Laos. If North Viet-Nam also occupied this whole band in Cambodia, or the entire country, it would mean that South Viet-Nam was completely outflanked and the forces of Americans in this area, as well as the South Vietnamese, would be in an untenable military position.

Our second choice is to provide massive military assistance to Cambodia itself. Now, unfortunately, while we deeply sympathize with the plight of 7 million Cambodians, whose country is being invaded, massive amounts of military assistance could not be rapidly and effectively utilized by the small Cambodian Army against the immediate threat.

With other nations, we shall do our best to provide the small arms and other equipment which the Cambodian Army of 40,000 needs and can use for its defense. But the aid we will provide will be limited to the purpose of enabling Cambodia to defend its neutrality and not for the purpose of making it an active belligerent on one side or the other.

Our third choice is to go to the heart of the trouble. That means cleaning out major North Vietnamese and Viet Cong occupied territories—these sanctuaries which serve as bases for attacks on both Cambodia and American and South Vietnamese forces in South Viet-Nam. Some of these, incidentally, are as close to Saigon as Baltimore is to

Washington. This one, for example [*indicating*], is called the Parrot's
Beak. It is only 33 miles from Saigon.

Now, faced with these three options, this is the decision I have made.

In cooperation with the armed forces of South Viet-Nam, attacks are
being launched this week to clean out major enemy sanctuaries on the
Cambodian-Viet-Nam border.

A major responsibility for the ground operations is being assumed by
South Vietnamese forces. For example, the attacks in several areas, including the Parrot's Beak that I referred to a moment ago, are exclusively
South Vietnamese ground operations under South Vietnamese command,
with the United States providing air and logistical support.

There is one area, however, immediately above Parrot's Beak, where I
have concluded that a combined American and South Vietnamese operation is necessary.

Tonight American and South Vietnamese units will attack the head-
quarters for the entire Communist military operation in South Viet-Nam.
This key control center has been occupied by the North Vietnamese and
Viet Cong for 5 years in blatant violation of Cambodia's neutrality.

This is not an invasion of Cambodia. The areas in which these attacks
will be launched are completely occupied and controlled by North Vietnamese forces. Our purpose is not to occupy the areas. Once enemy forces
are driven out of these sanctuaries and once their military supplies are
destroyed, we will withdraw.

These actions are in no way directed at the security interests of any
nation. Any government that chooses to use these actions as a pretext for
harming relations with the United States will be doing so on its own
responsibility and on its own initiative, and we will draw the appropriate
conclusions. . . .

Tonight I again warn the North Vietnamese that if they continue to
escalate the fighting when the United States is withdrawing its forces, I
shall meet my responsibility as Commander in Chief of our Armed Forces
to take the action I consider necessary to defend the security of our
American men.

The action that I have announced tonight puts the leaders of North
Viet-Nam on notice that we will be patient in working for peace, we will
be conciliatory at the conference table, but we will not be humiliated. We
will not be defeated. We will not allow American men by the thousands
to be killed by an enemy from privileged sanctuaries.

The time came long ago to end this war through peaceful negotiations.
We stand ready for those negotiations. We have made major efforts,
many of which must remain secret. I say tonight that all the offers and
approaches made previously remain on the conference table whenever
Hanoi is ready to negotiate seriously.

But if the enemy response to our most conciliatory offers for peaceful
negotiation continues to be to increase its attacks and humiliate and
defeat us, we shall react accordingly.[80]

Dr. Kissinger offers his perspective on the president's speech.

All the critical themes of the later explosion were present before the President's speech: We were escalating the war. No military action could possibly succeed; hence, claims to the contrary by the government were false. We were alleged to be so little in control of our decisions that the smallest step was seen as leading to an open-ended commitment of hundreds of thousands of American troops. A credibility gap had been created over any effort to achieve an honorable exit from the war. Thus, the press greeted the arguments in Nixon's speech on April 30 with a simple counterassertion: They did not believe him. It was "Military Hallucination—Again" according to the *New York Times:* "Time and bitter experience have exhausted the credulity of the American people and Congress." To the *Washington Post* it was a "self-renewing war" supported by "suspect evidence, specious argument and excessive rhetoric." To the *Miami Herald* "the script in Cambodia shockingly is the same as the story in Vietnam in the days of Kennedy and Johnson. We have heard it all before—endless times." Debate was engulfed in mass passion.

Just as it was burgeoning before April 30, the new increase in tempo had begun with calls for strikes and marches by the student leaders, who had proved their skill in producing confrontation in previous seasons of protest. The President's statements, oscillating between the maudlin and the strident, did not help in a volatile situation where everything was capable of misinterpretation. His May 1 off-the-cuff reference to "bums . . . blowing up campuses," a gibe overheard by reporters during a visit to the Pentagon, was a needless challenge.[81]

Three days later General Abrams (COMUSMACV) reports to Washington and to General Weyand at the Paris peace talks about the initial results of the Cambodian incursion.

FM COMUSMACV
TO [addressee deleted]

SUBJECT: CAMBODIAN OPERATIONS (OPERATION ROCK CRUSHER AND OPERATION TOAN THANG 43), PERIOD 0222000H TO 031200H MAY 70 (U).

1. (C) GENERAL:

A. OPN ROCK CRUSHER. ELEMENTS PARTICIPATING IN OPERATION ROCK CRUSHER CONTINUED MOVEMENT TO THE SOUTH TO ESTABLISH BLOCKING POSITIONS FOR COORDINATED EFFORT WITH IV CORPS. ELEMENTS OF TF 318 CONTINUED TO SECURE ROAD TO SVAY RIENG. TASK FORCES A, B, AND C MOVED FROM THEIR NDP'S TO PRE-PLANNED OBJECTIVES TO CONDUCT SCREEN AND SEARCH OPN IN AREAS. . . . CONTACT HAS BEEN LIGHT AND SCATTERED.

B. OPN TOAN THANG 43. ALL INDICATIONS FROM THE FIELD ARE THAT OPERA-TION TOAN THANG-43 ACHIEVED COMPLETE SURPRISE AND CAUGHT THE ENEMY

FLAT-FOOTED. IN ADDITION TO THE OUTSTANDING OPERATIONAL RESULTS,
LARGE AMOUNTS OF MATERIEL HAS BEEN DESTROYED OR CAPTURED TO INCLUDE
TRUCKS, MEDICAL SUPPLIES, FOODSTUFFS AND MUNITIONS. DURING THE PERIOD
CONTACT REMAINED LIGHT AS ELEMENTS EFFECTED LINK-UP OPERATIONS AND
CONTINUED SEARCHING. A SIGNIFICANT CACHE OF 65 TONS OF RICE WAS
UNCOVERED.[82]

*The next day, 4 May, in Berkeley, California, a man and a woman are
cooking dinner. The following is excerpted from Michael Rossman's story
entitled "The Day We Named Our Child We Had Fish for Dinner."*

"What shall I do with the filet?" asked Karen from the kitchen. "There
are bones in it."

"Cook it," I said.

"I don't like it with bones."

"They come out easier after it's cooked. That's the way fish are."

"Oh, never mind." Clatter of pans, water running. Indistinctly: "Screw
you, anyway."

"What was that?"

"I said, never mind."

"And what else? What after that?"

Clatter of pans, running water. I pulled myself up again, weary, and
went into the kitchen. She was standing over the stove, stirring instant
mashed potatoes. I couldn't read her back. I held her. "I think we're
tearing ourselves apart because the world is coming apart."

"I think you're right," she said.

"Water the plants," I told her, as I went back into the front room,
grimly ignoring the radio, the phone. "That's the thing to remember now,
remember to water the plants."

It was the fourth night of Cambodia. I was watching the ferns when our
brother Lonnie from San Diego came in. "Carol called to find out when
you're coming back," I reported. "She says they're working for a school-
wide strike on Thursday. The English Department already voted to go
out. Farber brought them round, and the paper's agreed to support it."

"All up and down Telegraph they're talking about Kent State," he
said, his face still flushed from walking, intense through his spectacles.
"There's little knots of freaks just talking, all along the street. It's true,
four were killed, the National Guard shot them down in the parking lots.
I can't believe it." . . . Later Tom calls, from over in the next house, to
tell me that Reagan has just ordered all the state colleges and universities
closed through Sunday at least. Another first for California, the Golden
State.

Three years before Cambodia I visited Kent, Ohio. Spring 1967. The
media were just discovering the Haight and the Hippy. I was on my first
round of visiting campuses, just starting to sort things out, to adjust my

perspective from Berkeley-provincial to a national scope, and learn what
work I could do in our ghetto. For the moment, I was writing a story on
what the war was doing to what we then called the Student Movement,
and I wanted some unknown dreary large public campus to play off
against Antioch and Oberlin. So I chose Kent State, found a contact, and
spent a couple of days there.

I mostly remember the flat apathy of the faces I met while on campus,
these students of lower-class blood slack-weary from the mineral-drained
hills of upland Ohio, many of them serving time for the upward mobility
of the teaching credential. The buxom girls chattering in the morning
Pancake House, as I sat over fourth coffee, road-grimed, hugging my
sleeping bag.

Flat, that campus, flat. Some months earlier a first hiccup of antiwar
protest had turned out a hundred for a lonely march. Now I found all told
maybe a dozen committed to keeping active, trying to find a way to move
it on. Isolated, embattled, embittered, taking refuge in an overtight group
whose talk was laced with hurtful humor and flashes of longing.

They took me home for the night, the house was old and they had made
their warm mark on its surfaces; they lived in what would become a com-
mune, and then a family. Over late coffee we talked about organizing,
about guerrilla theater, about holding together for warmth. Hang on,
brothers and sisters, I said to them, some Spring is coming. And I left them
the large *Yellow Submarine* poster I designed for Mario's birthday—an
anarchist program for a disruptive festival of joy, "a generally loving retaliation against absurd attack." The poster commemorated the 1966 Second
Strike at Berkeley—for us in the West, the first event in which freaks and
politicos joined in public ritual, in song and an elaborate masque. We
discussed community programs, wild with the energy of coming together,
and broke into spontaneous joy, singing chorus after chorus of "Yellow
Submarine"—imagining all our friends on board, the blue sky, the life-
green sea.

Then next October, before I left to begin my second round of traveling
campus work, we put on our feathers at dawn and marched 7,000 strong
down into Oakland to block the doors of the Induction Center. After we
got the shit clubbed out of 200 people, we tied up the downtown for the
rest of the week, dodging the heat and chanting, "We are the people!" in
the intersections.

So long ago. *Saturday in Kent they trashed the town in protest, breaking 56
windows.* I was in Rock Island, Illinois, with my brother Russell from our
theater troupe, talking about the death of a culture and teaching college
kids how to begin to play again, to live in their bodies. *Sunday in Kent
they burned down the Army ROTC building.* I was home in Berkeley, in
the house we call Dragon's Eye. Sixteen of our family were learning to
play a holy gambling game together, device for pooling psychic force,
handed down from the Indians through Stewart Brand of the Pranksters.

Today in Kent on the fourth of Cambodia 2,000 turned out, and they shot 4 dead in the parking lots. O let us laugh and canter. O I will play the Fool, grant me my mad anger, I still believe that art will see us through. . . .

(Rewriting now on the sixth of Cambodia, the plastic "underground" radio turns real as it tells me how the girl's leg broke as they beat her and threw her off the wall, an hour ago up on campus, and how 2,000 National Guardsmen have been ordered into Urbana, Illinois. I've spent ten separate weeks in Urbana, we have family there. Vic centers it, he works in wood and is making a cradle for the baby. Last month I saw him. He was organizing a craft-food-garage cooperative. The week before he had charged the pigs for the first time to help rescue a brother, was still shaken.) . . .

Here now in Berkeley it is the fourth night of Cambodia. Kent State is catching up fast. We shall have to go some to keep ahead.

Cold wind coming. Sky turning black, the missiles sulk in their cages, the green net of the ocean grows dangerous thin, the terrorism of bombs begins, the Minutemen multiply bunkers, the economy chokes ánd staggers, the blacks grow yet more desperate, the War is coming home. I figure I'm likely to die in this decade, perhaps in this city I love, down the street beyond the neighborhood garden, in some warm summer twilight when people sit on their porches and the joy of live music drifts out from their windows. That's a cold political judgment, without much to do with what's also true: that since I woke at fifteen I've never been able to imagine past about thirty-five, it's been only a blank in my mind, always the same through the years, down to now, when I'm thirty. Do you mind if I finger my intimate fragments in front of you, awkwardly? I can't fit them together. But what else is a man to do in this mad time, pretend that everything's only at its usual standard of incoherence? . . . If we are let live through this decade and the next, we will be strong, strong, our women will be powerful and our men beautiful.[83]

ACT IV
May 1970–January 1973

Give Nixon Time with his withdrawal PROGRAM

Withdrawal is something Nixon's
father should have done
58 years ago

You SHITHOUSE Philosophers
have all the answers

BETTER THAN YOU NON-THINKING
LIFERS.

—GI latrine graffiti, Saigon

In Washington, Dr. Kissinger observes the aftermath of Kent State.

The Administration responded with a statement of extraordinary insensitivity. Ron Ziegler was told to say that the killings "should remind us all once again that when dissent turns to violence it invites tragedy."

The momentum of student strikes and protests accelerated immediately. Campus unrest and violence overtook the Cambodian operation itself as the major issue before the public. Washington took on the character of a besieged city. A pinnacle of mass public protest was reached by May 9 when a crowd estimated at between 75,000 and 100,000 demonstrated on a hot Saturday afternoon on the Ellipse, the park to the south of the White House. Police surrounded the White House; a ring of sixty buses was used to shield the grounds of the President's home.

After May 9 thousands more students, often led by their faculty, descended on the capital to denounce "escalation" and the "folly" of their government. A thousand lawyers lobbied Congress to end the war, followed by thirty-three heads of universities, architects, doctors, health officers, nurses, and one hundred corporate executives from New York. The press fed the mood. Editorials expressed doubts about the claims of success in Cambodia emanating from the Pentagon. Beyond these peaceful demonstrations antiwar students proved adept at imaginative tactics of disruption merging with outright violence. Some two thousand Columbia University students sat down in the road in the rush hour. Fires were set on several college campuses as bonfires for peace. At Syracuse University fire destroyed a new building as twenty-five hundred students demonstrated nearby. Students demonstrated in the financial district of New York City on May 7 and 8. In retaliation, construction workers building the World Trade Center descended on Wall Street and beat the protesters with clubs and other makeshift weapons. The incident shocked some into the realization that a breakdown of civil order could backfire dangerously against the demonstrators. But it did not slow down the pace of protest; it only encouraged Nixon in the belief that the masses of the American public were on his side.[1]

In James Webb's novel Fields of Fire, *Will Goodrich, a former marine corporal, has returned to Harvard University.*

Cambodia. He had seen the President's address on television, and remembered all the silly, irritating restrictions of Vietnam combat, and

actually felt pleased about the announcement, in a detached sort of way.
It was all irrelevant anymore, none of it mattered, but if it had to continue, at least it should be rational. And Cambodia seemed rational.

He was asleep when the door buzzer rang. It blasted flatly through his
slumber, again and again. He found his trousers and crutches and made
his way through the apartment to the door. He opened it and faced two
men he had never seen before. One was short and stocky, with dull blond
hair and a wide, placid face. He wore a Pendleton shirt and frayed Levis.
The other was frail and hook-nosed, with lit, angry eyes and an impatient
posture. He wore a jeans jacket, with a clenched fist and a Viet Cong flag
on the back. Both had shoulder-length hair.

The short man spoke. His voice was deep and modulated, almost sad.
"Are you Will Goodrich?" He nodded toward the empty trouser leg. "I
assume you are."

Goodrich leaned forward on his crutches, wiping his face in an attempt
to shake the drowsiness. "Yeah. What do you need?"

"Can we speak with you for a moment?"

Goodrich checked his watch. It was past midnight. The short man
caught his gesture. "I'm sorry about the time. We've been working
steadily for a couple hours now, and we have to be ready to go tomorrow
first thing. So it had to be now. We'll be up all night."

"Doing what?" Goodrich gestured for them to come inside, and made
his way to the couch. They followed, the short man still talking.

"Getting ready. It's going to be big tomorrow. It will be the biggest one
we've had. I'm sorry. You probably don't know us."

The frail, impatient companion finally spoke. "But you saw Tricky
Dick's speech tonight, didn't you? The fucking fascist. The bastard's sick,
man."

The short man continued. obviously tolerating his companion's outbursts with some discomfort. "I'm Paul Kerrigan. This is Sid Braverman.
We're part of the Student Coalition To End The War. You probably
aren't aware of what's going on at the campus. People are pretty upset
about this Cambodia thing."

Goodrich was mildly surprised. "Really?"

Braverman nodded quickly, inspecting Goodrich's stereo. "That's
right. They're tearing that place apart, man."

Kerrigan corrected him. "Well, not really. Not *yet,* anyway. But it's
pretty active. And tomorrow we're having a full-fledged rally. We're
setting up a platform, down where they used to hold the football rallies.
You know the place."

Goodrich smiled vaguely through a lingering drowsiness. "Oh, yeah. I
used to be in the band. We were all at the rallies."

Kerrigan and Braverman exchanged tentative glances. Kerrigan spoke.
"Well, we're lining up speakers for tomorrow. And as near as I can
determine, you're the only person who's really been *in* it, you know what
I mean?"Goodrich nodded. Kerrigan continued, encouraged by the nod.

"We think you could really give the rally some credibility if you would speak at it."

Braverman joined in. "Yeah, man. You could really lay it on everybody about how bad the Nam stinks. You know, like what did you see that was worth giving a leg for—" Kerrigan cut him off and he shrugged as if preoccupied.

They both seemed slightly embarrassed, as if they had unwittingly tipped their hands. Goodrich absently rubbed his stump and managed to smile to them. "Look. You don't have to try and buffalo me. I know why you want me to speak, and it doesn't have a hell of a lot to do with what my opinion might be." Goodrich mimicked the announcer at the rally, gesturing like a circus master of ceremonies. "Here, folks, on our very stage, is graphic evidence of experiment gone afoul. Specimen reports unfavorable reactions to terror and misery. Examine left trouser leg, which is now empty. Specimen is entirely credible to make observations on experiment. Now specimen will say, in his very own words, that it was shitty. Take it awayyyyy, Goodrich."

Goodrich lit a cigarette. "Does that embarrass you? It shouldn't. But let's start with honest premises, all right? Now. If I did this—and to be honest, I'm not terribly worked up about it—what would you expect me to say?"

Kerrigan folded his arms, studying Goodrich. "Well, within reason, you could say whatever you wish. I mean, we don't expect you to come out and ask for more troops to the war zone, or anything like that."

"No. That's not what I had in mind."

"And what we *really* need is somebody who is able to talk about how shitty it was in the Nam. How senseless the killings were. How it felt to see your buddies get wasted. The whole immorality bit. You know, the desecrations, the tortures, the atrocities. I'll bet in the Marines you saw a lot of that."

"That's all a bunch of shit."

"What?" Both stared incredulously at Goodrich.

"It's all a bunch of shit. I have more standing to say that than any person in this school. And I say it's a bunch of shit."

Braverman peered at Goodrich with unmuted hostility. "With My Lai in the paper every day you tell me it's a bunch of shit?"

"I didn't say things don't happen. And I don't know anything about My Lai. But it's a bunch of shit to say it's regular or even condoned. Look, man. I fought with myself about this for *months*. I even turned a guy in for murder. I thought it was my duty. But I just *don't know anymore*. What you guys are missing is the confrontation. It loses its simplicity when you have to deal with it."

Braverman and Kerrigan appeared confused and hostile. Goodrich continued. "Look at the people. Are they murderers? You don't know. You haven't dealt with them, and you haven't been through what they've been through. It's easy to sit here and say that. But you haven't had it eat away at you. It gets you. It gets everybody, man. It took five months, but it got me, even, and good Christ if it got me it gets everybody. You drop someone in hell and give him a gun and tell him to kill for some god-damned amorphous reason he can't even articulate. Then suddenly he feels an emotion that makes utter sense and he has a gun in his hand and he's seen dead people for months and the reasons are irrelevant anyway, so *pow*. And it's utterly logical, because the emotion was right. That isn't murder. It isn't even atrocious. It's just a sad fact of life."

He pondered the two. "You know why I'm all fucked up?" He waved his stump, forcing them to look at it. "Because of a little girl. That's right. A little babysan sucked me right out into the open so the NVA could start an ambush." They did not seem particularly surprised: The People's War Against Imperialism. Right in the books, Will. He continued. "I was a team leader. I had a kid who was going to shoot her. I knocked his rifle down. Just in time to see him shot in the face." Still no reaction from them. Also in the books: The Goo That Was Your Best Friend's Face. Already been done once. Sorry, Will. Be original, will you?

"Do you know how it feels to know you caused that? I'll see his face staring down at that babysan for the rest of my life. And I'll tell you what. If I hadn't had the shit blown out of me, it would have given me great pleasure to hunt that little girl down and blow her away."

He eyed them with a shrewd grin. "And I'll bet a month's pay that you two would have been the first to join me in the hunt. It's like role-playing. Activists will always be activists, and you'd be the first to get uptight."

Braverman seethed with anger. "I've had enough. Take your artificial leg and shove it." He rose from his chair and began to walk to the door.

Kerrigan still pondered Goodrich. "I'm sorry you feel that way." He folded his arms again. "You said something about your own statement. Do you have a statement you'd like to make?"

"I don't know. Like I said, the idea doesn't exactly move me. But they—you—should know what you're doing to a lot of people. It's isn't this simple, man. You're hurting a lot of people."

"Do you want it to end?"

"The war? Sure I want it to end."

"Can you start your speech with that? That you want it to end? As long as you make that clear, you'll serve our purposes." Kerrigan shrugged. "You said you appreciated honesty. We need your statement. After that, I'll give you a couple minutes." He smiled, then turned to leave. "But I'd appreciate it if you'd hold back on your theories."

He drove to the wide, flat field, scene of so many innocent events in years gone by, pep rallies and rock concerts. There was a good crowd on it, scattered here, close together there, some sitting on its outskirts in little groups as if it were indeed a picnic. There was an air of merriment among the gathered students. They were camouflaged in jeans and khaki, masked with unkemptness, almost as if they were secretly ashamed of the largeness of their own futures, or felt constrained to deny the certainties of their own lives.

Kerrigan and Braverman had arranged for him to park near the speaker's platform, along the road. He stopped the car and undid his artificial leg, as they had asked, leaving it in the car. Then he made his way up the platform, on his crutches.

The crowd had begun to chant. "HO. HO. HO CHI MINH. THE N.L.F. IS GONNA WIN."

He stood uneasily on the platform, agonizingly self-conscious of his legless state. Just below him a girl in cut-off jeans sat comfortably on someone's shoulders. Her arms were outstretched, fists clenched, moving up and down in rhythm to the chants. Her face smiled excitedly. Her shirt was tied in a knot above the belly button, and unbuttoned except for the bottom two buttons. Her breasts were huge. They also bounced with the rhythm. Goodrich watched the breasts bounce merrily and tried to remember if he had ever experienced such lovelies. He hadn't.

Across the field the flag came down. A new one rose. It was red and blue, with a bright gold star in its center. Goodrich's insides churned mightily. He told himself that he was able to intellectualize such frivolity, that although it would have enraged those like Snake and Bagger, he himself understood it. But soon he stopped pretending: He was shaking with a deep rage. If he had been stronger, he would have crossed the field and lowered the flag himself. Or so he consoled himself as he peered at waiting eyes, isolated on the stage.

"HO! HO! HO CHI MINH!"

And a thousand corpses rotted in [the] Arizona.

"THE N.L.F. IS GONNA WIN!"

And a hundred ghosts increased his haunted agony.

Snake, Baby Cakes, and Hodges, all the others peered down from uneasy, wasted rest and called upon the Senator to Set The Bastards Straight. And those others, Bagger, Cannonball, and Cat Man, now wronged by a culture gap that overrode any hint of generational divide. Goodrich took the microphone and cleared his throat. Well, here goes. He thought of them again, wishing some of them were in the crowd.

"IT'S TIME THE KILLING ENDED." He was surprised at the echoes of his voice that careened across the field. The crowd cheered. It shocked and emboldened him at the same time. Kerrigan and Braverman were watching him closely. He nodded to them and they nodded back. Braverman was squinting. "I'D LIKE TO SEE THE WAR END. SOON." More cheers. He gave the two men a small smile. There. I said it. Dues are paid.

He eyed the crowd. His blood was rushing. His head pounded from the rapid pulsing of the blood through his temples. "ISN'T THAT WHY YOU CAME HERE? TO TRY AND END IT?" More cheers.

Yeah. Groovy. End the war. "THEN WHY ARE YOU PLAYING THESE GODDAMN *GAMES*? LOOK AT YOURSELVES. AND THE FLAG. JESUS CHRIST, HO CHI MINH IS GONNA WIN. HOW MANY OF YOU ARE GOING TO GET HURT IN VIET- NAM? I DIDN'T SEE ANY OF YOU IN VIETNAM. I SAW DUDES, MAN. DUDES. AND TRUCK DRIVERS AND COAL MINERS AND FARMERS. I DIDN'T SEE YOU. WHERE WERE YOU? FLUNKING YOUR DRAFT PHYSICALS? WHAT DO YOU CARE IF IT ENDS? YOU WON'T GET HURT."

He stood dumbly, staring at querulous, irritated faces, trying to think of something else to say. Something patriotic, he mused feebly, trying to remember the things he had contemplated while driving to the rally. Or maybe piss them off some more. Another putdown, like some day they'll pay. Pay what? It doesn't cost them. Never will cost them. Like some goddamn party.

He gripped the mike, staring at them. "LOOK. WHAT DO ANY OF YOU EVEN KNOW ABOUT IT, FOR CHRIST SAKE? HO CHI FUCKING MINH. AND WHAT THE HELL HAS IT COST—"

Kerrigan stripped the mike from his nerve-damaged hand without ef- fort, then peered calmly through the center of his face, not even bothering to look him in the eye. "You fucking asshole. Get out of here."

Goodrich worked his way down the platform, engulfed by confused and hostile stares. Many in the crowd were hissing at him. He chuckled to himself. Snake would have loved it, would have grooved on the whole thing. Senator, he would have said, you finally grew some balls.

He noticed the car then. There were swastikas painted in bright red on both doors. On the hood, someone had written "FASCIST PIG." Across the narrow street a group of perhaps twenty people watched him, all grinning conspiratorially. Braverman stood at their head, holding a can of spray paint.

The paint was still wet. Goodrich smeared it around with his hand, then took his shirt off and rubbed it. The markings would not come off. Finally he stopped his futile effort and stared at the leering Braverman. He thought of flying into a rage, of jumping into his car and running over all of them, but he found that he was incapable of great emotion. It would never make any sense, and there was no use in fighting that. He swung his head from side to side, surprising everyone, including himself, by making a series of sounds that resembled a deep guffaw. Finally he raised his head.

"Fascist, huh? Hey, Braverman." He pointed a crutch. "Pow." Then he drove away.[2]

Retired U.S. Air Force Major Walter McDonald shows one aspect of the combat veteran's feelings in this poem.

Veteran

I get as far as the park
this time.
Spectators queer as animals
circle me like a campfire.
They hope I'll fall.

Leaves lie in the park
like tiny bombs
ready to explode. Someday
someone raking
will strike a fuse.
We'll all be killed.

My stumps itch
inside their legs,
lightweight aluminum
clump clump. One of my arms
goes out of control, shifts smoothly
like a transmission, salutes.

They think I'm
shooting a bone
at them. I'm trying
to turn back. They're closing in,
this is Da Nang, their eyes
rake me like AK-47's.[3]

Another veteran, Michael Berkowitz, remembers the fighting in a Saigon suburb during the 1968 Tet Offensive and writes this poem about his motivation to protest. Ben Tre suffered such extensive damage that a U.S. Army officer was widely quoted in the press as saying, "We had to destroy the town in order to save it."

Ben Tre Suburb

You ask us why we're out here, carrying signs
Out in this god-forsaken asphalt shopping center
You who sent us to level the verdant jungles of Vietnam.

A man takes a leaflet
and rips it up without reading it.
A woman faces us so bristling with hate
that her glasses shake to the end of her nose.

> "You communists," she finally
> manages to squeeze
> out her contorted mouth.

> Communists like those
> we were sent over to fight?

Go home, you shout.
But we have none.
You sent us abroad.
And now the world is our home.

Now wherever you send us
We meet our brothers,
Not our enemy.

Why are we here
In front of the supermarket, the auditorium,
the theater, your favorite restaurant.
We're here because it's the only way to reach you—
Before the next war.[4]

On 8 May, President Nixon holds a news conference.

QUESTION: *One of the consequences of the Cambodian action was the fact that the other side boycotted this week's peace talks in Paris. There is some question as to whether our side will attend next week. Have you made a decision on that?*

THE PRESIDENT: Our side will attend next week. We expect the talks to go forward. And at the same time we are cleaning out the enemy sanctuaries in Cambodia, we will pursue the path of peace at the negotiating table there and in a number of other forums that we are presently working on.

QUESTION: *Mr. President, Secretary of Defense Laird said last week that if the North Vietnamese troops should move across the DMZ [demilitarized zone] in force, he would recommend resumption of the bombing. What would be your reaction to such a recommendation in those circumstances?*

THE PRESIDENT: I am not going to speculate as to what the North Vietnamese may do. I will only say that if the North Vietnamese did what some have suggested they might do—move a massive force of 250,000 to 300,000 across the DMZ against our Marine Corps people who are there—I would certainly not allow those men to be massacred without using more force, and more effective force, against North Viet-Nam.

I think we have warned the leaders of North Viet-Nam on this point several times, and because we have warned them I do not believe they will move across the DMZ.[5]

1970   12 May—In Saigon a joint U.S./RVN communiqué announces the capture in Cambodia of enough weapons and ammunition to sustain a five-month enemy offensive. **27 May**—Defense Secretary Laird announces that there will be "no U.S. advisers in Cambodia after June first."

In Laos, North Vietnamese/Pathet Lao troops open two uncharacteristic offensives: one in the north, the other in the southeast, near the previously untouched town of Saravane. The 11 June Rules of Engagement (ROE) revision is published the day after North Vietnamese troops occupy Saravane.

SUBJECT: AIR OPERATIONS IN STEEL TIGER

REF MSG IS STEEL TIGER TEMPORARY OPERATIONS RULE NUMBER ONE AND SHOULD BE CORRECTED TO READ AS FOLLOWS: (PARA FOUR) QUOTE: U.S. AIR OPERATIONS BY "SLOW MOVER" AIRCRAFT, GUNSHIPS AND FLARE SHIPS ARE AUTHORIZED WITHIN THE SARAVAN 5KM RESTRICTED AREA IN DIRECT SUPPORT OF GROUND FORCES AND AGAINST CLEARLY DEFINED MILITARY TARGETS OF OPPORTUNITY. NO "FAST MOVER" AIRCRAFT WILL ENTER THE 5KM RE-STRICTED AREA. ALL TARGETS MUST BE VALIDATED BY EITHER AIRA SVKT, A FAC WITH X-RAY OR A FAG PRIOR TO STRIKE. ALL STRIKES WILL BE UNDER CONTROL OF A FAC/FAG. FAC AIRCRAFT MUST HAVE X-RAY OR BE [IN VISUAL] CONTACT WITH THE GROUND. STRIKES WILL NOT BE CONDUCTED WITHIN 500 METERS OF VILLAGES UNLESS RECEIVING AAA (14.5 ZPU OR LARGER) FIRE FROM THE VILLAGE. GROUND FIRE BEING RECEIVED FROM THE AIRSTRIP AT SARAVAN MAY BE RETURNED. HOWEVER, CAUTION WILL BE PRACTICED NOT TO DESTROY THE STRIP. THE TOWN OF SARAVAN ITSELF WILL NOT BE STRUCK UNDER ANY CIRCUMSTANCE. NAPALM IS APPROVED FOR TROOPS IN CONTACT AND MAY BE AUTHORIZED BY EITHER AAIRA SAVANAKHET OR AAIRA PAKSE. ALL AIRCRAFT NOT IN DIRECT SUPPORT OF GROUND OPERATIONS WITHIN THE 5KM CIRCLE WILL CONTINUE TO AVOID SARAVAN BY 5KM AND 5,000 FEET AGL.[6]

That same week Professor Roy G. Francis gives the commencement address at Hartford High School, Hartford, Wisconsin.

My World—and Welcome to It

3 June 1970
Well, you've made it. It's over. All the pleading, cajoling, threatening and seeming endless parade of class hours somehow filled, are over. Twelve long years of being obliged to look to the future have ended. And here you are, on the brink of something, not wanting to look behind you lest you recognize triviality when you see it, and not able to look very far into the future. . . .

For the first time in a quarter of a century, the heart confronts the mind on the campus. The period from 1945 to 1965 was disconcerting and somewhat deadening. The strained objectivity of the scholar, the stance of "ethical neutrality," the pretence that the real world was not of immediate importance, all suggested to the student body that the college really did not care about man at all. Active students dare to care.

Unfortunately, many of you parents here tonight have concluded on the basis of inadequate evidence that either a few devilish kooks are leading otherwise good kids astray or you have sired a whole generation of ingrates who seek only to destroy all that you have built. I suggest to you that neither of these is correct. What is happening on our campuses represents the concerns and the will of the majority of students. The silent student largely assents to the dissenting voice of the moderate activist. As usual, Mr. Agnew is wrong in suggesting otherwise. . . . Now, I will be the first to admit that Mr. Nixon has the same right as all of his predecessors in having a court jester. However, I am surprised at our being unable to laugh at what is obviously a political satire. Taking Nixon's vice president seriously is a sign of how uptight we have become.

You see, either Agnew is privy to Nixon's policy decisions or he is not. If he is, then his assertions that campus dissent will lead to things like the massacre at Kent State sound more like a threat than a prediction. Further, if he does have access to state secrets, then he in fact cannot speak with the casual freedom of the average citizen. If he has knowledge we do not, then he has a responsibility to speak with less virulence than others. Not all of us are vice presidents, no matter how dumb we may appear to be. But Mr. Nixon may not trust him: He may not have this special knowledge. If, therefore, he is just like the other 200 million people who are confused about our policies, there is no reason to accord him a status other than that given to all previous vice presidents. One must joke about his pretence to wisdom, that's what vice presidents are for. . . .

All of you here who feel that the National Guard were within their rights at Kent State would symbolically pull the trigger of a rifle aimed at the young men and women you see graduating tonight. The anguished outcry heard on our campuses after the President ordered troops into Cambodia directly involved more than half of the students in our colleges and universities. These were not the actions of a mere one or two percent. It is true, of course, that hard-core radicals, and even "trashers," did their best to manipulate honest outrage for their own ends. But they failed—and you must sense that the outrage was genuine and widespread.

I can say without any chance of contradiction that our continued participation in the Vietnam War—or must we now admit its escalation and say the war of Indochina?—is totally rejected by the current generation. During World War II, men were impatient with the slowness of the draft and enlisted by the millions. Today, there would be no combat force without the draft. Those college students who do defend our presence in Vietnam are (a) protected by student deferment and (b) not enlisting themselves. In other words, it takes an act of Congress, unevenly and occasionally illegally administered, to get an adequate number of bullet stoppers on the Asian mainland.

Historic reasons for having once begun the Vietnam slaughter no longer obtain. The present situation has become frighteningly clear. The price for mere continuation of the fighting, let alone further escalation of the war, is the total destruction of Democracy here at home.[7]*

On 30 June, President Nixon reports to the nation on the Cambodian "incursion."

THE MILITARY OPERATIONS

Ten major operations were launched against a dozen of the most significant base areas with 32,000 American troops and 48,000 South Vietnamese participating at various times. As of today, all Americans, including logistics personnel and advisers, have withdrawn, as have a majority of the South Vietnamese forces.

Our military response to the enemy's escalation was measured in every respect. It was a limited operation for a limited period of time with limited objectives.

We have scrupulously observed the 21-mile limit on penetration of our ground combat forces into Cambodian territory. These self-imposed time and geographic restrictions may have cost us some military advantages, but we knew that we could achieve our primary objectives within these restraints. And these restraints underscored the limited nature of our purpose to the American people.

My June 3 interim report pointed up the success of these operations and the massive amounts of supplies we were seizing and destroying. We have since added substantially to these totals. A full inventory is attached as an appendix to the report. Here are some highlights.

According to latest estimates from the field, we have captured:

—22,892 individual weapons—enough to equip about 74 full-strength North Vietnamese infantry battalions and 2,509 big crew-served weapons—enough to equip about 25 full-strength North Vietnamese infantry battalions;

—More than 15 million rounds of ammunition or about what the enemy has fired in South Vietnam during the past year;

—14 million pounds of rice, enough to feed all the enemy combat battalions estimated to be in South Vietnam for about four months;

—143,000 rockets, mortars, and recoilless rifle rounds, used against cities and bases. Based on recent experience, the number of mortars, large rockets, and recoilless rifle rounds is equivalent to what the enemy shoots in about 14 months in South Vietnam;

—Over 199,552 anti-aircraft rounds, 5,482 mines, 62,022 grenades, and 83,000 pounds of explosives, including 1,002 satchel charges;

---

*According to Professor Francis, "The results were amazing. While the graduating class gave me a standing ovation, their parents did not. Indeed, only some of them applauded—and they were in the minority. The School Board passed a resolution that night condemning the speech if not me. There was great turmoil in that little town. But I did get one letter signed by about a dozen people (including the vice-president of a small business and his wife) thanking me for dragging the town closer to the then present time."

—Over 435 vehicles and destroyed over 11,688 bunkers and other military structures.

And while our objective has been supplies rather than personnel, the enemy has also taken a heavy manpower loss—11,349 men killed and about 2,328 captured and detainees.

These are impressive statistics. But what is the deeper meaning of the piles of enemy supplies and the rubble of enemy installations?

We have eliminated an immediate threat to our forces and to the security of South Vietnam—and produced the prospect of fewer American casualties in the future.

We have inflicted extensive casualties and very heavy losses in material on the enemy—losses which can now be replaced only from the North during a monsoon season and in the face of counteraction by South Vietnamese ground and U.S. air forces.

We have ended the concept of Cambodian sanctuaries, immune from attack, upon which the enemy military had relied for five years.

We have dislocated supply lines and disrupted Hanoi's strategy in the Saigon area and the Mekong Delta. The enemy capacity to mount a major offensive in this vital populated region of the South has been greatly diminished.

We have effectively cut off the enemy from resupply by the sea. In 1969, well over half of the munitions being delivered to the North Vietnamese and Viet Cong in Cambodia came by sea.

We have, for the time being, separated the Communist main force units—regular troops organized in formal units similar to conventional armies—from the guerrillas in the southern part of Vietnam. This should provide a boost to pacification efforts.

We have guaranteed the continuance of our troop withdrawal program. On June 3, I reaffirmed that 150,000 more Americans would return home within a year and announced that 50,000 would leave Vietnam by October 15.

We have bought time for the South Vietnamese to strengthen themselves against the enemy. . . .

THE FUTURE

Now that our ground forces and our logistic and advisory personnel have all been withdrawn, what will be our future policy for Cambodia?

The following will be the guidelines of our policy in Cambodia:

1. There will be no U.S. ground personnel in Cambodia except for the regular staff of our Embassy in Phnom Penh.

2. There will be no U.S. advisers with Cambodian units.

3. We will conduct—with the approval of the Cambodian Government—air interdiction missions against the enemy efforts to move supplies and personnel through Cambodia toward South Vietnam and to re-establish base areas relevant to the war in Vietnam. We do this to protect our forces in South Vietnam.

4. We will turn over material captured in the base areas in Cambodia to the Cambodian Government to help it defend its neutrality and independence.

5. We will provide military assistance to the Cambodian Government in the form of small arms and relatively unsophisticated equipment in types and quantities suitable for their army. To date we have supplied about $5 million of these items principally in the form of small arms, mortars, trucks, aircraft parts, communications equipment and medical supplies.

6. We will encourage other countries of the region to give diplomatic support to the independence and neutrality of Cambodia. We welcome the efforts of the Djakarta group of countries to mobilize world opinion and encourage Asian cooperation to this end.

7. We will encourage and support the efforts of third countries who wish to furnish Cambodia with troops or material. We applaud the efforts of Asian nations to help Cambodia preserve its neutrality and independence.[8]

At this time, the narrator of Jay Boyer's unpublished novel As Far Away as China *is a U.S. Air Force lieutenant assigned to a base in Vietnam. He describes what he sees shortly after his arrival.*

During our indoctrination, the Base Commander said he should tell those officers new to Southeast Asia that the people here think we're gods. But that is not quite the case. Not gods. More like creatures from another planet who have inexplicable powers.

Once you get outside the village, for instance, women carrying lame children may approach and beg you to make them right.

They are in some ways beautiful people. Even the aged, squat in doorways and beneath their conical hats. It is as if they have been beatified. Still, there are so many contradictions. The same fisherman who will offer to rent you his teenage daughter will walk barefoot for miles to take his nephew to the free clinic.

Though there is a small city nearby, the village outside the base is really a hamlet. Most bases draw merchants, hookers, bars and all the rest. That's been discouraged here. We're too small, I suppose, maybe too near the action. Maybe that's not it at all.

Anyway, it is really a hamlet. The houses are built facing the water, all in a line. There is about fifty feet between them. And as the river bends around, the makeshift shops begin moving away from the river, forming a horse shoe.

All of this is surrounded by barbed wire.

In the middle of the horse shoe, there are rice paddies. On the outside, away from the river, there is a field and paved road. And on the far side of the road, there is the base, the landing strips.

I spend hours trying to describe these things, trying to explain what it's like in my letters. How to talk about the people. The way the village smells. The naked children along the roadside.

I don't know how many F-4s there are here, but there are plenty. At one end of the runway, several sit fully armed and cocked at all times. The area is brightly lit by ground light and, from the sky, looks like a Christmas tree.

All of the F-4s are camouflaged. They are painted in splotches of fatigue-green, khaki and black. All except for the latest one which was flown in from Okinawa before the camouflaging was accomplished. It is causing quite a stir.

The villagers have grown used to the high thin screech of the fighters as they take off for missions or land. It is a piercing sound which, when the planes near the ground, seems to vibrate in your skin.

Though I cannot hear the difference, Mamasan says the new fighter, the silver one, makes a different sound. Without an interpreter she cannot make me understand what the difference is.

But I suspect it is the way it looks more than the way it sounds. I tell her this as best I can. In the sunlight, I say, using hands and noises, when it takes off, it gleams against the sun and seems to split the clouds apart.

Just when I think I have made my point, she tells me it is not an airplane at all. She says it is a blade and, if we do not stop it, it will slice open the sky's belly.

Keith is our Administration Officer. He doesn't fly anymore, he just administers. He sits at his desk sorting through miles of paper.

I'm a FAC, a Forward Air Controller. Because the F-4s fly too high and too fast to see what they are firing at, it's my job to mark the target. I fly an O-1, a single engine Cessna 172 converted only slightly for combat. Except for the phosphorous rockets, it is much the same little plane that men climb out of every Sunday in Des Moines or St. Paul wearing Bermuda shorts and sunglasses.

Under each wing there are phosphorous rockets. I mark the targets with them. Only I can fly low enough, slow enough. I fire the rockets at the targets and they smoke white, then the F-4 Phantoms fire at the smoke.

After an air strike, after I've marked the targets and the F-4s have come in, it is my job to calculate the damage. I keep my clipboard at my side. There are lots of mimeographed work sheets. BOMBS ON TARGET. PERCENTAGE OF TARGET DESTROYED. MILITARY STRUCTURES DESTROYED.

Some have three columns, some have more.[9]

In August William Stubbs is reassigned to the American embassy in Phnom Penh, Cambodia. A letter to Sven Kraemer of the National Security Council describes his initial impressions.

The thoughts expressed below are, of course, my personal ones. They undoubtedly reflect certain prejudices, acquired primarily while serving in Phnom Penh during another era (1963–64) and in Vietnam from 1964 to 1967. During the latter period, I served on the staff of Deputy Ambassador Porter (who was charged with coordinating the pacification program) as well as on the staff of the ill-fated OCO and its successor CORDS. I should state at the outset that many of my views were shaped by experiences and revelations of those assignments.

In August 1970, I was very pleased to return to Cambodia for a second assignment. Cambodia was, admittedly, suffering some military setbacks at that time, but there were several reasons for optimism:

—the war was obviously one of foreign aggression, with Khmer dissidents estimated at 10,000 or less,

—the Government of Cambodia, as well as its military and civilian personnel, enjoyed a great deal of popular support,

—the Government of the United States was providing military and economic assistance, but was pledged to avoid the pitfalls of a large mission, combat troops and advisers.

It seemed to me, in short, that we had an excellent opportunity to apply some of the lessons we learned (or should have learned) in Vietnam,

To facilitate the policy of Vietnamization, and perhaps for other reasons, it was decided that it was in our national interest to support Cambodia. Our support would take the form not of personnel but of equipment and funds, which would assist a country to resist aggression. An important part of this resistance would depend on popular support for the government, an element which had been crucially lacking in Vietnam. The government of Cambodia not only appeared to have popular support, it appeared to be anxious to prove to the population that the government could offer a better life than the enemy, that the government troops could protect the people while remaining well-behaved, and that civil servants were just that . . . servants of the civil population rather than their exploiters. In essence, the government of Cambodia, after less than a year at war and left to its own resources and traditions, seemed to be well on the way to appreciating, and perhaps even applying, the most important of the lessons of South Vietnam: *prove to the people that you can protect them and provide them a good life, and the people will support you against invaders and dissidents.*

United States Government support to Cambodia was to consist of economic aid, which would assist in stabilizing a wartime economy, and military equipment. The military equipment would strengthen the FANK*

*Forces Armées Nationales Khmers

shield, behind which Vietnamization could proceed, and with the help of which the government of Cambodia could carry out activities aimed at increasing popular support and stimulating resistance to the enemy. I was not, of course, privy to grand strategy, but it seemed at the time that the long term hope was that Cambodia—with our aid but without a large infusion of Americans—could become strong enough to survive, at least until peace came to Vietnam through negotiations or other means.

That was my general appraisal of the situation upon my arrival in August 1970. I believe our policies were well-conceived, and that the Ambassador and other persons sent here to carry them out were exceptionally capable. It was a small, hard-working Embassy in the last months of 1970, and political duties, as well as the task of providing equipment to FANK, were executed with amazing effectiveness.[10]

1970   7 September—With U.S. air support, FANK (Forces Armées Nationales Khmers) forces start offensive in Cambodia. **14 September**— FANK offensive halted by fierce opposition of North Vietnamese and Khmer Rouge troops.

In September North Vietnamese General Vo Nguyen Giap, the architect of the Viet Minh's defeat of the French in 1954, addresses a Communist military conference in Hanoi.

Comrades, we are meeting here today to discuss the organization of the implementation of the Central Military Party Committee's resolution on the tasks related to military science. On behalf of the Central Military Party Committee, I warmly welcome you, Comrades, who have come from various Armed Services and Branches, from various agencies of the High Command, from the Military Institutes and Schools, from the Military Zones, from the Provinces, and from various battlefields to attend this conference. . . .

The war has now spread throughout Indo-China. This requires an increasingly close combat coordination among the armed forces and people of Viet-Nam, Cambodia, and Laos. . . .

We have the duty to prepare ourselves so that, in case the enemy adventurously unleashes a war of aggression against the North, our armed forces and people can readily defeat and resolutely annihilate him. Before our eyes are the U.S. imperialists, the extremely insidious and cruel archimperialists. Despite their repeated defeats, they still are very stubborn and crafty. They are concocting, day and night, new schemes and tricks to oppose our people's resistance. They have spent billions of dollars, have set up hundreds of companies and agencies specializing in studying the Vietnam war, have arduously developed their economic and

military strength, and have devoted modern science and technology and
all psychological warfare tricks to massacring and deceiving our people in
the hope of retrieving themselves from the danger of complete defeat.
Therefore, it is more necessary than ever before to firmly grasp the rules
governing the war, to firmly grasp the enemy's schemes and maneuvers
and the rules governing his activities, and to firmly grasp the procedures
for and the methods of preparing for and waging our war in order to
serve national salvation and national defense.

Vietnamese military science is obviously an invincible military science,
because it has undergone many challenges in the realities of our people's
protracted and fierce struggle against the big and powerful imperialists for
decades now. *Our military science has defeated the military science of the
U.S.* imperialists—the craftiest and cruelest enemy of mankind. Our military science has completely bankrupted the outmoded ideas of the imperialists concerning the decisive role of their armed forces' strength, their
modern equipment and weaponry, their modern air force, and so forth in
the war and has inflicted shameful defeats on their modern armed forces
on the battlefields.[11]

1970 20 November—After a U.S. Air Force reconnaissance aircraft is
shot down over North Vietnam, heavy bombing is resumed against
antiaircraft emplacements. This bombing is also cover for the helicopter assault on the SonTay Prisoner of War Camp near Hanoi.
U.S. forces enter and exit successfully, but no American POWs are
found.

---

*On 14 December U.S. senators Cooper and Church again sponsor a suc-
cessful amendment to a bill that funds U.S. policies in Southeast Asia.*

**Cooper-Church Amendment
to the Special Foreign Assistance Act of 1971
as Amended, H.R. 19911, P.L. 91–652**

Sec. 7. (a) In line with the expressed intention of the President of the
United States, none of the funds authorized or appropriated pursuant to
this or any other Act may be used to finance the introduction of United
States ground combat troops into Cambodia, or to provide United States
advisers to or for military, paramilitary, police, or other security or intelligence forces in Cambodia.

(b) Military and economic assistance provided by the United States to
Cambodia and authorized or appropriated pursuant to this or any other
Act shall not be construed as a commitment by the United States to
Cambodia for its defense.[12]

In December Private Thomas Kingsley arrives in Vietnam and writes the following three letters.

Dear Mom and Dad,

This country is so beautiful, I don't believe it! It reminds me of Canada. It's so calm, picturesque, and serene. Presently I'm at Cam Ranh Bay. It's like a small resort town.

Love,
Tom

Dear Mom and Dad,

It's hard to experience Christmas when it's 110 degrees out. However, in between beers I managed to dream what it was like on the morning of Christmas. We didn't have to work today—they gave us a special dinner and free beer—so if this letter sounds incoherent it's because I had more beer than dinner. Merry Christmas!

I bought myself a camera, so I should have a lot of good shots when I get back. As I said before, this place is really beautiful, and I was not surprised to find that many lifers bring their wives and families out here to live.

I spent Christmas with some close friends (you'd be surprised how fast you meet "friends"), listened to Bob Hope on the radio—he was about 30 miles away—and went to a show they had on our firebase. I still haven't reached my final destination, so don't try to write yet. It will be another week before I find out what I'll be doing and where.

So far everything has been real quiet and everything is going fine. There are always rumors flying around though. The lifers say the war is over and everyone is pulling out. We were told we would be pulling out the 15th of January—that doesn't mean me, specifically—it means my division, the 1st Cavalry; no telling when they'll get to my company.

By the way, I enjoyed Christmas a day earlier than you did.

Merry Christmas and Love,
Tom

Dear Mom and Dad,

You'll have to excuse the handwriting again; I'm using a single cracked board as a backboard, and my hands are terribly dirty.

I have finally reached my end destination (I don't mean that facetiously!), a place called Mace Firebase. During the welcoming orientation it was stated only two men have been killed in the last six months from this battalion, which numbers about 600 men. So I guess I am in a fairly safe location.

The name Air Cavalry refers to air mobility. Wherever we go we are transported by helicopter. You know how I am afraid of height; well, these people are scaring the hell out of me! I guess these helicopters are safe, though, but it seems to me they are held together with string and chewing gum; they rattle, shake, and lurch something terrible. All kidding aside, though, these helicopters are really efficient. They carry rockets, machine guns, small bombs, and other assorted weapons. They fly both daytime and nighttime missions, by means of a large searchlight on the latter. Transport helicopters carry about ten men each and are flanked and protected by gunships (helicopters loaded with armament).

Before we go on a mission, artillery will clear out an area with heavy bombing. They will then shift their target to the perimeter of the area we are to land in, in case the enemy wishes to attack us. When we are dropped off, the gunships will hover in the area until our position is positively fortified; then it will make runs in the surrounding area up to a mile out looking for the enemy. Sounds pretty safe, doesn't it. I hope so!

Right now I am on guard duty. I sit in a bunker with three other guys and listen to what is happening on the other side of the barbed wire. The other side of the wire is off limits to everyone after six o'clock and you're supposed to shoot on sight. However, we never do—too many drunken GI's around. Just a while ago there were two kids playing about 100 yards from the wire. Naturally we didn't shoot them, even though they could have been VC, but instead called headquarters, who in turn sent a party out to question them. All was legitimate and the kids were sent on their way.

By the way, have a good time on New Year's Eve, even though this letter is late.

Well, it's getting dark now so I have to concentrate on my work.

Love,
Tom[13]

1970 **30 December**–U.S. Navy turns over combat role to SVN Navy. Some 17,000 U.S. Navy advisers remain with the 40,000-man SVN Navy.

1970   31 December

	TOTAL	NET CHANGE
U.S. military personnel assigned in Vietnam	334,600	−140,600

U.S. casualties	YEAR	TO DATE (cumulative)
Killed in action	4,221	44,245
Wounded in action	30,643	293,439

Source: DOD/OASD

1971

Early in 1971 COSVN convenes another conference on the progress of the war. This summary, probably written in January to February 1971, shows the Viet Cong/North Vietnamese/Khmer Rouge intentions for the year.

The 18 March 1970 coup d'etat and the subsequent expansion of the war of aggression by the U.S. imperialists to Cambodia, which was intended to support the Vietnamization program in South Viet-Nam, failed to enable them to attain their proposed goals of destroying our agencies, storage facilities, and base areas, destroying and depleting our main forces, halting the revolutionary movement in Cambodia, and saving the Lon Nol clique from a dangerous situation.

On the contrary, this created conditions for the Cambodian revolutionary movement to leap forward and strengthened the unity of the peoples of Laos, Cambodia, and Viet-Nam in their struggles. A unified front was established through which the Indochinese peoples are fighting their common enemy, the U.S. imperialists and their henchmen. A large strategic theater of operations was developed, binding the three countries together, linking the big frontline with the big rear area, and turning Indo-China into a unified battlefield. In this theater, Cambodia is the most vulnerable point of the U.S. and puppets, South Viet-Nam is the main war theater with a decisive bearing on the common victory, and Laos is a significant area of operations.

In 1970, the U.S. imperialists ventured to expand the war in Cambodia, but failed to save themselves from the dangerous situation. On the contrary, they suffered heavier military, political, and diplomatic failures and became further bogged down and strategically deadlocked. The U.S. withdrew its troops while puppet troops had to replace U.S. troops and concurrently play the key role in supporting the puppet Cambodian troops. Since enemy troops were forced to disperse thinly, the enemy experienced increasing difficulties in his pacification and Vietnamization plans and will certainly meet defeat.

Because the enemy exerted great efforts to implement the Nixon doctrine in South Viet-Nam and Indo-China, we had to surmount great difficulties and trials in the resistance against the U.S. for national salvation.

The [revolutionary] movement in the rural area was subjected to unprecedented disturbances by barbarous enemy attacks through his pacification and encroachment programs. However, we were still able to maintain the operational positions of our infrastructure and armed forces.

We managed to maintain and in some areas even expand, our control over villages and hamlets in spite of the presence of enemy outposts. In many areas, we even undermined or reduced the effectiveness of the enemy defensive and oppressive control system.

The [struggle] movement in urban areas against the burden born from the Vietnamization plan developed on a large scale with support from all social classes. They openly demanded U.S. troop withdrawals, an overthrow of the Thieu-Ky-Khiem clique, and the establishment of a Government which would restore peace. The movement was supported by uncommitted factions and many personalities of various [political] parties, including those in the puppet National Assembly and the puppet government. Such a movement has caused continual failures for the U.S.-Thieu-Ky-Khiem clique in its efforts to rally a political force to support its oppression of revolutionary forces and opposition parties.

In this extremely fierce and complicated war, our main force units effectively fulfilled their role by attracting, containing and destroying many enemy mobile forces to successfully support political and armed [struggle] movements in South Viet-Nam and Cambodia. Through their successful maintenance and expansion of our strategic bases and corridors, they have proven to be increasingly significant in the new war position of the Indochinese people.

The great victories achieved on the battlefield by the people of the three Indochinese countries, in conjunction with positive diplomatic activities, won increasingly broad support and cooperation from all democratic and peace-loving people throughout the world and isolated the Nixon clique and its lackey governments. . . .

Noteworthy is the fact that although they would continue to withdraw their troops, they would retain an important element of U.S. and satellite forces to operate with puppet forces which are large in number but low in morale. These troops are reinforced with equipment and given additional training and support from U.S. troops, especially the U.S. Air Force, therefore they have considerable firepower and great mobility. They have a new defensive and oppressive control system designed to safeguard both rural and urban areas, therefore they have the hope to maintain and improve their position.

Nevertheless, they also have very fundamental difficulties that cannot be surmounted even with the large military and economic potentials of the ringleader imperialists. They have to deescalate the war, continue to withdraw their troops, and rely on the puppet government and Army which are increasingly demoralized and politically weakened. They have to cope with three Indochinese countries which have power and sound leadership in addition to their tradition of fighting the aggressors. They also have to face the peace movements in the U.S. and throughout the world demanding the end of the war of aggression in Viet-Nam and Indo-China.

The basic enemy weaknesses and our objective advantages are as follows:

The more the U.S. speeds up the Vietnamization program, the more the puppet government is compelled to expedite its dictatorial and fascist policies on conscription, troop upgrading, taxation and inflation, and to send puppet troops to the battlefields to die in the place of U.S. soldiers. By so doing, the puppet government would aggravate the contradictions between itself and the people of various classes, including the uncommitted class and a large number of puppet government personnel. It would make the demands for social welfare, economic improvement, freedom, democracy, culture, the end of war, and restoration of peace become more pressing. It would ripen the political awareness demanding U.S. troop withdrawals and the replacement of the Thieu-Ky-Khiem government by a new one which would restore peace; aggravate the political, economic, and financial crises; and deepen the internal dissensions in the puppet government. These are the objective conditions necessary for us to expand the struggle movement against the Americans for national salvation and rally the new forces including the uncommitted class, puppet soldiers and personnel, and a number of personalities in the puppet government to promote a new movement against the U.S. and the Thieu-Ky-Khiem clique.[14]

In late January Private Thomas Kingsley writes two letters with differing perspectives on the same subject.

Dear Mom and Dad,

We've been at the LZ now for two days. The only duty we have to do for the five days is guard duty nightly—which lasts for one hour per person. When we first arrived back from the jungle, there sitting in front of our little caves was a truck-load of beer and Coke. During the daytime we play football, softball, volleyball, and other games. The greatest joy is that we're served three hot meals a day.

I sent home three cartridges of film to be processed. Half of them probably won't come out—some were taken from helicopters, trees, mud holes, and all kinds of other hazards.

It's a shame I couldn't caption the pictures because you probably won't understand what they're about. But at least you'll see what we wear, our surroundings, and other insights. I couldn't get any good shots of how we sleep because it's always too dark; we always travel in triple canopy jungle (three levels of growth). Which is why the jungle is so safe—we have literally cut our way through and therefore have only one passageway to protect. We set up trip flares across the path (a wire across the path attached to a flare) and land mines. If the enemy attempts to come any other way we will hear them.

Our first mission was completely uneventful, which doesn't displease me in the least. Our leader explained that for TET we are going out into the jungle and hiding for 15 days. By the way, I've found the jungle is the safest place to be. No one knows where you're at, you can hear people coming a mile away, and it's very easy to protect yourself and hide. No one expects a large TET offensive this year. But enough of tactics.

Our LZ, which we have nicknamed Peggy, is about 25 miles northeast of Bien Hoa. We never travel more than 10 miles in any direction from Peggy.

If I'm not writing on the lines, take into consideration I'm writing this by candlelight. I also lost my pen in the darkness—that's why the change of color.

I expect to hear from you shortly.

Love,
Tom

Dear Bob,

The first month has passed unceremoniously and uneventfully, which doesn't displease me in the least. There have been times, though, when I have been scared to death—a couple of times I thought it was all over. I look back now and laugh because it wasn't even close.

The first night on guard I almost shot up a firefly, which I thought was a gook with a flashlight. The second night I heard someone yelling at me. So I woke up the guys around me and they said it was a frog! Sounded just like a person.

There is not supposed to be much of a TET offensive—encompassing only mortaring of large cities. Our leader says we are just going into the jungle and hide—staying in one position. Needless to say, he has a good head on him. We never do the things we're supposed to.

Sooner or later, though, the fan has got to hit the shit. Companies all around us are running into contact, and I firmly believe I will not leave here without being shot or injured first. I hate to say it, but that's how it is; the odds of finding trouble are too great, something's got to happen sometime. And anyone who tells you the war is over is full of shit.

I'm so embittered I don't believe it—but there is nothing you can do. I'm not nervous at all, but you just realize something's got to happen. Right now we're laying in ambush for gooks coming our way that attacked the company next to us, killing two.

And it seems no one gives a damn besides us grunts in the bush. You people in the world don't know what's happening because the Army won't let you know and the goddamn lifers in the Army could care less— as long as the death count is reasonable—say under 40 a week.

It's really hell, man. I saw a medivac operation after a company had been hit by our own artillery. Four dead—everyone was injured, most just slightly. But it was sickening. They carry the dead by a rope hanging from a helicopter (the dead man is inside a plastic bag) and just lower him to the ground—then throw them on a truck!

The fourth one was still alive when he came in—he was in the copter—

and died a while later. He had no right leg at all; and seeing it just turned me to jelly, man—and guys just sitting around crying—it really shakes you up. And for no goddamn reason at all!

The kids spit at you—there's a bitter hatred between us and the South Viet Nam troops because they carry new weapons and we don't; and we do all the goddamn fighting while they sit on their asses all the time. Man, it makes you burn.

And I haven't seen any action yet—none of my friends have been hurt and no one in my company has been injured. But it will only be a matter of time. And how do you react—how do you blow off steam? A lot of guys grow a hatred for all gooks—that's why we have My Lai. Others take it out on the Army; in Nam they average two frags a week (fragging is where a man simply pulls the pin on a hand grenade and tosses it at a lifer).

It's bigger than that, though—it's the whole goddamn country—to allow such an atrocity to happen. I suppose because nobody really realizes what's happening here or can't imagine or picture it. I know I couldn't.

But I'll tell you, man, if I ever get back there and hear someone say Viet Nam was worthwhile or it was our obligation—I'll hit him right in the face. Because this is nothing but a shame—such a big mistake at such a huge cost. You can't believe it till you see it.

Oh well, enough rambling. I'm writing this in the morning and last night I had a good cry—because I was thinking too much—that's why all the emotion. Don't tell Mom or Dad or Mary about this letter because they think everything is okay.

Usually I get lost in books or cards and don't do much thinking. It's hard writing letters to them, too, because you have to slant everything into a good light. You know, Mom hasn't been feeling well, so needless to say, my letters to her have been very light toned, showing enthusiasm, etc. It would really affect her if she knew the whole situation. So don't let on that her son is experiencing traumatic happenings.

I sent her home a lot of pictures to be developed, so if you want to see the kid wearing a lot of smiles, go visit Mom and Dad. They would appreciate your company.

I expect to get a lot of letters about trivia from you now 'cause, man, I sure need it. Need something to take my mind off this place.

Sorry about the tone of this letter, but as the old saying goes—"You can bullshit some of the people some of the time . . . " I'll be hearing from you.

Tarzan[15]

1971   **8 February**—With U.S. air and helicopter support, large numbers of South Vietnamese forces invade Laos to destroy supplies and cut the infiltration routes.

In James Webb's novel Fields of Fire, *Private Dan is a member of the South Vietnamese army. His unit participates in the Laos invasion.*

Laos, 1971

OPERATION LAM SON 719 There was an urgent, unstoppable rumble and the ground trembled, vibrating angrily. The dust rose in a hazy blanket that covered the hill and coated lungs and stung eyes. Across the narrow valley was a stream of steady flashes and a black cloud that grew quickly behind the flashes, puffing up like exhaust fumes from a poorly tuned truck. Dan pressed his sweating face into the dust and clutched his rifle and wondered at the ground beneath him as it quivered. It was the arc light again. Perhaps that will stop them, he thought, knowing that nothing would stop them.

The arc light finished and a black cloud hung low over the thick green canopy of the ridges across the valley. There was a moment of hesitating silence. They will come now, he decided. The B-52s are gone and there is nothing to stop them. As if on cue the artillery crunched into the hill, saturating it and the valley in front of Dan with angry clouds, devastating crunches. 152s. They will kill us all, Dan decided. So strange to die in this country I do not know. But, he sighed, hugging the barren ground, that is the nature of things. I warned them. I told them but they would not listen. A Private is not listened to. And it was so logical. A Private knows intrinsically what a General must learn through experience. That is because a Private thinks with caution since he will be killed. A General can be daring when only the Private will die for his mistakes. But it is useless to think about it. Thoughts will not change it.

The night before the operation began they had sat in the abandoned ruins of Khe Sanh and watched the jets as they saturated the Laos road with bombs and napalm. There had been much talk about Khe Sanh among the soldiers. This is where the Marines killed so many North Vietnamese, they had agreed in awe. A great battle for the Marines. Now it was abandoned and the airstrip was tatters of curled plating that used to be runway and the bunkers had dissolved into the earth. And the Marines were gone. But it was a great battle. Thousands of ghosts haunted the dark perimeter.

There had been a pep talk by the company commander. He had clasped his hands in front of his chest, intent. "Tomorrow will begin the greatest test for our Army," he had said. "Tomorrow we attack Laos."

Dan could not fully comprehend Laos. Nor did he understand why it was a test. To him it was absurd. So many problems right here, he thought. So many North Vietnamese soldiers in my valley. And no Government soldiers there, since the Marines left. And yet we are attacking this Laos.

Finally his reticence was overwhelmed by his common sense. "And what is this 'Laos' that it is so important," he had asked. "Why do we attack this 'Laos'?"

The *Dai Wei* had looked at him with contempt. "It is a country," he answered. "We attack it because enemy soldiers and supplies are there. Many soldiers. Much supplies. It will be a great victory."

Dan shrugged, meeting the company commander's eyes. "Enemy soldiers and supplies are everywhere. There are easier places. We do not know this 'Laos.' "

The officer had become angered. He walked over to Dan, standing over him. "Are you a General, then? Three years you spend doing nothing with the American Marines. Before that you are the enemy. And now you are a General. We attack Laos for the good of the country."

Dan was not afraid of the *Dai Wei*. The man could only beat him. "We do so many things for the good of the country," he answered. "We kill so many. We destroy so much. And what is a country? Is it a group of people who think alike and work together and want all other people to leave them alone? Then my valley is a country. Is it a piece of land that can be separated from other land? Then my valley is a country. Two rivers come together and a cliff joins them at their wide part. I do not do this for the people of my valley. And I do not know your country."

The officer slapped Dan hard on the face. "Your valley is VC. You are VC. I should kill you." The officer slapped him again. "You want me to put you in prison so you will not have to attack Laos with us. Peasant coward. *Que lam.*"

Dan stared tiredly at the officer. "I am not afraid," he said slowly. "I do not have to be afraid to think it is wrong."

The officer stomped off and Dan sat down and lit a cigarette. Across the border another air strike was dropping bombs along the road. The air strikes are like a magnet, Dan mused. They know what we are going to do. They will wait for the right time and mass on the road and destroy us. It is so stupid.

A group of soldiers crowded eagerly around Dan when the officer left. His willingness to stand his ground in the face of certain pain and ridicule gave him a strong charisma. There were many in Dan's squad who felt the way he had spoken. They did not resent his past. He had been with them for six months, and had always been reliable.

And there were the stories. Dan's melodious baritone sang out the pain of his past in a hard, unemotional ballad that they loved to listen to. They were eager to learn of the VC and were mildly assuaged when Dan spoke of them with digust. The VC had taken his family and his land and thus his life, for the sake of discipline. He would never forgive them. It was the only passion he felt and it was a personal one. The other soldiers interpreted his passion as one against the VC movement. He did not attempt to distinguish the hate for them. It would not change anything for him.

And they were eager to learn of his years with the Marines. Dan spoke of the Marines with mild warmth. They were good years for him and the warm ember of their remembrance was the only pleasure he was able to speak of. So many great battles. So much respect. "I would have stayed with them until I died," Dan would tell his eager listeners. "It was the best life for me. But they left and there was no place to go. I could not return to my village because of the VC. I have not seen my valley since I was conscripted." Dan never questioned why the Marines left. It was the nature of things that they would leave. Always the foreigner leaves. This was not their home.

They spent an eerie, restless night amid the ghosts at Khe Sanh, and in the morning began following Route 9 into Laos. The fog was dense and heavy in the lungs and its isolating thickness created an air of unreality about the column's movements. Dan was surprised when Laos appeared no different than Vietnam. He had been sure that different countries would look different. But they are all the same, he had mused in awe. What is this that it is Laos and not Vietnam?

For two weeks they twisted along narrow trails, under thick canopy and bamboo trellises where canopy ended. There was almost no resistance. The *Dai Wei* ridiculed Dan occasionally. "So we do not know this 'Laos,' eh, General? So it is wrong?" Dan did not answer. The North Vietnamese will speak for me, he thought.

He was right. When the column was far enough into the trap that supply lines could be cut, the NVA massed with thousands of troops and hundreds of pieces of heavy equipment. Whole battalions were overrun and destroyed. Dan's battalion had been attacked the day before, and had moved onto a scarred, barren hill in order to defend.

The heavy artillery had shelled the hill for a full day. Dan's battalion now shared an unspoken but permeating conviction that they would be defeated soon. The men stayed in hastily dug fighting holes only because they were more afraid of running than of fighting. There was an undercurrent of panic in every unit.

A medevac helicopter made it through enemy guns and landed on the hill, and was immediately swamped with frightened men. Soldiers hung on to the outsides of the helicopter when the insides were too full. American crewmen cursed the panicking soldiers and kicked at them, knocking them off the helicopter railings so they could depart.

Dan crouched inside his fighting hole, not understanding the depth of the other soldiers' panic. Why would a man risk his life on a helicopter railing, wondered Dan. It is so stupid. When the helicopter lands he will only be taken by the officers and sent somewhere new to die.

The artillery fire became more intense. The hill was under a cloud of dust. Then there was a creaking rumble to the front, where the arc light had been, and the narrow valley filled with a dozen Russian tanks. The artillery shifted to behind the hill and the tanks charged out of the trees to the front of it, spitting huge explosions and churning curtains of dust behind them. The soldiers watched a Cobra gunship scream above the tanks, pumping rockets. The gunship disintegrated in the air. Someone on the ridge behind the tanks had blown it up with a Russian SAM missile. A second gunship screamed in and also exploded.

When the second gunship blew up there was a high, collective scream of terror and the battalion snapped. Masses of troops and officers fled the hill, running through the artillery barrage behind it. The tanks climbed the hill, taking it easily, and consolidated on the other side of it. Behind the tanks a battalion of NVA advanced in skirmishes, moving quickly up the hill. The Political Officer of the NVA battalion spoke melodiously into a loudspeaker. "*Hoan ho Bac va Dang!* Surrender to us and you will not be harmed. We are fellow countrymen! Throw down your arms and join us in our struggle! Surrender and you will not be harmed!"

Dan had watched the tanks in amazement. There are so many, he had marveled. And they are so good. He knew it would be no use to run. They would kill the ones who ran. He lay curled inside his hole as the tanks passed over him. Then he heard the loudspeaker. He sensed with his natural, uncanny shrewdness that the message was a true one. They truly believe these things, he remarked inwardly. Countrymen. Struggle. They were the words he himself had urged upon villagers years before, when the VC took him into the villages at night.

Dan stood in the haze of dust and put both hands into the air, leaving his rifle in his hole. He joined a group of surrendering men, the men crawling out of similar hiding places, arms in the air. His face was the definition of endurance, cracked with a small, ironic smile. He was not afraid. If they killed him it did not matter. But they would not kill him. He was sure of that. He knew the words they desired to hear and his strong, melodious voice would carry the words into their senses and they would nod and accept his words as urgent truth.

The group of beaten, surrendering men was swallowed by the North Vietnamese. The NVA soldiers were flushed with their victory and eager to interrogate their prisoners.

Dan sighed. They seemed so naive. And it was such a game.[16]

In late February Private Thomas Kingsley writes to his friend Bob again.

Hi, old buddy,

I'm a little calmer today for no apparent reason. I guess I'm getting used to this crap. After I finished that last letter, we made contact three more times that day—I didn't sleep very well that night. Then we made contact once on each of the next two days. So I'm getting used to it. (That takes me right up to today.) A couple of guys got hurt and three gooks were killed, I think (no one knows for sure)—we found one. Although I was very teed off when I wrote the last letter, I still feel exactly the way I did then. When we get back to the LZ I'm sure one of the boys will do the commanding officer in. The two guys who got hurt were the fault of the

CO again—the guy is completely ignorant. Enough of the war stories, though.

Yes, I can receive packages, but just remember everything I receive I have to carry on my back—don't have a locker to store it in—so don't be sending me 18 hardbacks.

I found an article in Playboy, an advertisement put out by a group that opposes the war (Viet Nam Veterans Against the War). My friend Bob and myself got the whole squad together and joined in each sending a contribution. We also all signed a petition stating our feelings and gave it to the CO.

You asked about the jungle. Well, I was really scared at first—you run into spiders (huge ones), an occasional snake, and other animals, but they never bother you. You can be sleeping and they'll run right over you, but unless you sit on one, they don't bite. The biggest spider out here couldn't kill a person—but it could sure lay you up for a while—but then I could use a couple of weeks out of the bush. I sleep in a hammock that's killing my back—you know what they are, tie each end of a giant rag to a tree!

I just had a great idea—what I could really use which would remind me of civilization, would be a bottle of rum. They send out a couple of Cokes on log day, so I'd have a mix. I could mix it in my canteen cup. (March 6th is my birthday)—hint.

Well, I have to get a letter off to Mary.

Take it easy,
Tom[17]

At about the same time Private First Class "Hawk" Hawkins loses a friend and receives an unexpected opportunity, as seen in Charles Durden's novel No Bugles, No Drums.

Nobody seemed to notice that Garcia was dead. First coupla days there were some jokes. But nobody gave a fat rat's ass Garcia was dead. Tough shit. Might be me tomorrow. Count your days 'n' keep your ass covered. "Yet by your courage in tribulation, by your cheerfulness before the dirty devices of this world, you have won the love of those who have watched you. All we remember is your living face, and that we loved you for being of our clay and spirit." Chicano slum kids don't come from middle-America's clay, or spirit. I mean, what fuckin' Iowa pig farmer, Mississippi sharecropper, Westchester County Jew, California grape grower, Harlem spade, or Spokane shop owner is gonna admit bein' of the same clay and spirit as some dumb wetback who got his ass ripped in Nam? Those who have watched *us* have done it through the bottom of a beer glass in sleazy bars, or lookin' over a forkful of potatoes. We were lucky to get three minutes between an Anacin commercial and the stock market report. We were a pain in the ass, and just so many numbers on some dude's board in Saigon, the Pentagon, and the international desks of the networks. Once a week the voice, for thirty seconds, became somber and the announcements seeped into the ether: Forty-five Americans were reported killed in Vietnam this week. The Dow Jones Industrial average was off today, down three points to 983. No one loved us for bein' of their clay 'n' spirit. They were grateful to those of us who went away quietly, without makin' too big a fuss 'r screamin' Hell no, we won't go!

Four days after Garcia got it, First Sergeant Minnow called Poe, Dago 'n' me to his office. "Garcia's parents have asked for a body escort, someone from his outfit. You three have been chosen."

"Why me?" Dago asked.

"We ain't got any other Mexicans."

"I'm Italian."

"Same thing. You're leavin' tomorrow mornin' for Danang, where you'll pick up the body for flight to Oakland, then San Diego. You'll be briefed. Get your class-A's ready."

"That's it?" Dago asked. "We don't know shit about escortin' bodies, First Sergeant. What's the scoop?"

"You'll be briefed, Cocuzza."

Dago looked a mite pissed when we left. I was stoned out on the idea of gettin' outa Nam, even if it was only for a few days. Poe was quiet. "Man, how come you're so fuckin' down on it?" I asked Dago.

"It's a setup. I know it."

"How?"

"I don't know, but I feel it. That fucker's settin' me up, y' know?"

I couldn't see how, but I wasn't into Dago's doin's enough to know anything except he was apparently makin' a shit-load of money. When he'd gone off to make arrangements for his absence, Poe said to me, "I can't go."

"Wha' th' fuck's with you two?"

"I can't go."

"Why?"

"I can't trust Whipple alone for four or five days with my pigs."

"I got your fuckin' pig hangin'." I grabbed my crotch. "Here's your goddamn pig."

"You aren't supposed to talk to the Corporal of the Pigs like that, pfc Hawkins."

"Stuff it. Do you realize we're gonna see the land of the Big PXs?

Round-eyed girls. Clothes that ain't olive goddamn green? Food . . . think of it, man. Real food."

"It's supposed to be a funeral, Hawk. For a fallen comrade."

"That can't last more'n half a day, right? We got time."

"I hope you don't seem that delighted that Garcia got it while you're standing by his grave. His parents might not understand."

"You think that's why he tried to tie it on with that water-boo? So we'd get a chance to get outa here?"

"I think you're flaky." He stopped at the openin' to his bunker. "You're changing, Hawk."

"Ain't we all?"

"May be. Just may be."

Next mornin', about an hour before we were s'posed to leave, Dago went out. He wasn't gone more'n fifteen minutes, and I didn't think anything of it till he came back, dropped a duffel bag on the floor 'n' said, "Put your clothes in here." The bag was almost full. I picked it up. I *tried* to pick it up. I made maybe two feet before it thumped back to the floor. "Put my clothes where?"

"In there."

"You shittin' me, man? That fucker weighs about a hundred pounds now, and the room that's left ain't enough to change your mind in."

"It weighs eighty pounds. Y' got room enough for all y' need."

"Wha'th'fuck's in there?"

"Grade-goddamn-A Thai grass. One thousand dollars a pound, wholesale."

My mind went through some rapid-ass tote-boardin'.

"Eighty thousand dollars!"

"For that one. There's two more. One f' you, one f' Poe. You both get a cut."

"A quarter of a million dollars?" My voice squeaked. "Two hundred 'n' fifty *thousand* US dollars?"

"I may not get more'n two hundred thou' since I'll hafta dump it quick. But that's minimum."

"Dago . . . we'll be shot. They won't bust us. We'll be shot down on the streets like gooks in a free-fire zone. You're crazy. You know that? *Crazy.* How in God's name do you think you can smuggle—how much is it?—anyway, don't matter. You can't get away with that shit!"

"No sweat." He snapped his fingers like he was in the Top of the Mark and wanted the check.

" 'No sweat,' he says. How much is there?"

"A hundred keys."

"Two hundred 'n' twenty pounds?"

"Actually, it's two-forty. But twenty pounds is f' my friends."

"Two hundred 'n' forty fuckin' pounds of grass . . . no sweat? Am I s'posed to believe *that*?"

"Have I steered y' wrong yet?"

"No, man."

"Well?"

"I mean, no! I'm not goin' to do it. You're stone flaky. Cracked at the seams. No way."

"Not even f' twenty-five percent of what ya bag brings?"

"Not even for—twenty-five percent?" Whirrrr . . . "Twenty thousand?"

"Give that man a big cigar! Twenty thousand it is."

"Even if *I* do, Poe'll never go for it."

"He's already agreed."

"He doesn't need twenty thousand any more'n I need another year in Nam."

"He's agreed, Hawk. Would I lie?"

"What's in it for him?"

"Votes."

"Votes? Votes for what?"

"Votes f' the senatorial seat in the next election of a Virginia senator."

"You're from *Jersey*. How you gonna vote in Virginia?"

"Not me, y' dumb fuck. Teamsters. My uncle's a teamster, tied in with their political wing. I tell 'im this dude did me a favor an' he needs votes. All the fuckin' truck drivers in Virginia are gonna line up to vote f' Poe."

"His *old man*'s already senator."

"Poe's gonna run against 'im."

"Fuck me. Anyway, he can't be that old."

"He'll be thirty, two days before the election—three years from now. Anyway, we gonna get us a mess of round-eyes 'n' party till the cows come home . . . ain't that how you fuckin' rednecks say it?"

"What we say is hang it in your ass. I'll do it, but I still don't see how."

"Just do what I tell y' to do, no questions. An' keep ya goddamn mouth shut. Dig?"

"I dig."

"My, my, you aren't as dumb as I thought."

"And you may fuckin' well not be as smart as you think."

"Y' better hope the hell I am."[18]

Another way to make money from the war can be seen by the first two pages of Burton Tauber's "Preliminary Prospectus" on pages 476–477.

On 6 March Private First Class Thomas Kingsley writes a birthday letter.

(My Birthday)

Good morning,

It's about 10:00 and I'm just sitting around in my hammock—I don't know how much longer it's going to hold me. We're in the mountains, and it's absolutely beautiful! We're right at the very top and the sights are something else—I can see the Red China Sea from my hammock!

Another good thing, there are no gooks here because there is no water. So, the next 10 days or so will be like a vacation. Rumor has it this will be our last jungle mission—after this we'll be pulling guard duty at Bien Hoa, which would please me greatly—I've been out here for three months now without a break. I guess the Army is trying to make the deadline of May 1, to extract all jungle forces out of combat positions. We would then be used as a back-up force (while pulling guard) so for me it's very important that Vietnamization works—otherwise it won't be much of a break if we have to keep bailing the ARVN's out. The 10,000 GI's in Laos are back-up forces, but little good that title is doing them! The first Air Cavalry Division will definitely not be sent to Cambodia or Laos because our obligations in this region are too demanding; plus we're located too far away. It will be interesting to see what effect this Laos thing will have on the whole war.

I imagine there will be a long lull after the Laos battles. On the last mission we were running into contact 2 or 3 times a week, but I would say ¾ of the gooks were unarmed. During that mission I felt there was actually no real danger—that if contact was made it was by our initiative—not that we go out looking for trouble, far from it. But I think they have orders not to engage our forces unless absolutely necessary. We run into gooks, though, while traveling down paths or something like that. Many orders of our gung ho, John Wayne-type commander are ignored or carried out with less than high enthusiasm if there's a chance of getting hurt. Like I said before, we just try to hide in the jungle.

I'll be sending a tape home soon.

Love,
Tom[19]

On 22 March President Nixon answers questions in an interview with ABC Television's Howard K. Smith. The subject is the recent invasion of Laos.

MR. SMITH: Well, now, sir, they give the impression of retreating from Laos now, and there is still a whole month of dry season before the rains come. If they retreat now, won't the Communists have plenty of time to repair their trails and repair their pipelines before the rains come?
THE PRESIDENT: They can never gain back the time, Mr. Smith. Six weeks

$1.00

PROSPECTUS

225,000,000 SHARES

THE WAR IN VIETNAM

Common Stock
(No Par Value)

THIS OFFERING INVOLVES A HIGH DEGREE OF RISK

At the present time there is no established trading market for the Common Stock of the Company. The Company does not have a record of earnings or success, and the price of the shares being offered hereby was determined by the Company and may be deemed arbitrary.

THIS MATTER HAS NOT BEEN APPROVED OR DISAPPROVED BY THE SECURITIES EXCHANGE COMMISSION, THE CONGRESS OF THE UNITED STATES, THE AMERICAN PEOPLE, OR ANY OTHER GOVERNMENTAL AGENCY, EXCEPT THE PENTAGON, NOR HAS ANY AGENCY PASSED UPON THE ACCURACY OR ADEQUACY OF INFORMATION DISCLOSED WITH REGARD TO THIS MATTER. ANY REPRESENTATION TO THE CONTRARY IS A CRIMINAL OFFENSE.

	Price to Public(1)	Underwriting Discounts and Commissions	Proceeds To Company
Per Share			
Total	$120 Billion		

(1) Does not include additional costs and effects, including, but not limited to, inflation, destruction of youth and properties, divisiveness of the populace, destruction of the concepts underlying the republic and other related costs.

This offering involves:

(a) Special Risks concerning the Company. See "Introductory Statement."

(b) Annual call for additional funds and assessment on shareholders.

THE ADMINISTRATION   THE JOINT CHIEFS OF STAFF

This prospectus was written by Burton R. Tauber. It is being offered to the public by Workman Publishing Company, Inc., Monocle Periodicals, Inc., Pentacle Press, Inc.

Workman Publishing Company, Inc., 231 East 51st Street, New York, New York 10022

Until   (90 days after the date of this Prospectus), all dealers effecting transactions in the shares offered hereby whether or not participating in this distribution, may be required to deliver a Prospectus. This is in addition to the obligation of dealers to deliver a Prospectus when acting as underwriters.

No dealer, salesman, member of the Administration or any other person is authorized by the Company to give any information with regard to the Company to the Congress of the United States, including the Senate Foreign Relations Committee, or to make any representation other than as contained in this Prospectus in connection with the offering described herein. This Prospectus does not constitute an offering to sell or a solicitation of an offer to buy from any person in any State in which it is unlawful to make such offer or solicitation. The delivery of this Prospectus or statements by officers of the Company at any time do not imply that the information herein is correct as of any time subsequent to the date hereof.

TABLE OF CONTENTS

IN CONNECTION WITH THIS OFFERING, THE COMPANY MAY OVER-ALLOT OR EFFECT TRANSACTIONS WHICH STABILIZE OR MAINTAIN THE MARKET PRICE OF THE COMMON STOCK OF THE COMPANY AT A LEVEL ABOVE THAT WHICH MIGHT OTHERWISE PREVAIL IN THE OPEN MARKET. SUCH STABILIZ-ING, IF COMMENCED, MAY BE DISCONTINUED AT ANY TIME.

is a period in which the Communists not only have found, as we pointed out earlier, that the supplies to the South have been drastically cut.

During that 6-week period they have had chewed up great amounts of ammunition, great amounts of materiel that otherwise would have gone south and would have been used, incidentally, against many Americans fighting in South Viet-Nam, and also in that 6-week period the South Vietnamese have developed a considerable capability on their own and considerable confidence on their own. They are better units to handle the situation as we withdraw.

Now, insofar as what they are going to be able to do for the balance of this dry season is concerned, I can only suggest that I cannot predict what will happen today, tomorrow, or the next day. There is going to be some more severe fighting as the South Vietnamese continue to withdraw from Laos. That we expected. . . .

Now, what does this mean for the future? Well, I think when we judge whether this operation is going to be labeled a success or a failure, we cannot judge it before it is concluded, and we cannot judge it even after it is concluded. We can only see it in perspective because its goals were long range—long range being, first, to insure the continuation of the American withdrawal; second, to reduce the risk to the remaining Americans as we withdraw; and third, to insure the ability of the South Vietnamese to defend themselves after we have left. Those were the three goals of this operation.

How do we know whether or not those goals will be achieved? Well, I will say this. My interim assessment based on General Abrams' advice and the advice that I get from all people in the field is this: As far as our withdrawal is concerned, it is assured. The next withdrawal announcement will be made in April. It will be at least at the number that I have been withdrawing over the past few months; and second, as far as the danger to the American forces remaining, particularly in the northern part of South Viet-Nam, there are 100,000 there, as you know, that danger has been substantially reduced. That operation has already accomplished that much.

Third, as far as the ARVN is concerned—and here I come back to an expert—General Abrams, who tells it like it is and says it like it is, says that some of their units did not do so well but 18 out of 22 battalions conducted themselves with high morale, with great confidence, and they are able to defend themselves man for man against the North Vietnamese.

And so that I would say insofar as achieving our goals of assuring American withdrawal, reducing the threat to the remainder of our forces, and, finally, our goal of seeing to it that the ARVN develops the capability to defend itself, that the operation in Laos at this interim period has made considerable progress in achieving those goals.[20]

That same day Private First Class Thomas Kingsley's parents receive this last letter.

Mr. and Mrs. Frederick E. Kingsley:

The Secretary of the Army has asked me to express his deep regret that
your son, Private First Class Thomas E. Kingsley, died in Vietnam on 20
March 1971. He was on a military mission when an automatic explosive
device placed by a friendly force detonated. Please accept my deepest
sympathy. This confirms personal notification made by a representative
of the Secretary of the Army.

> Kenneth G. Wickham
> Major General USA
> The Adjutant General
> Department of the Army
> Washington, D.C.[21]

Although death notices are shattering, more prolonged agony is experienced by families of men classified MIA (Missing In Action). Jean Ebbert expresses a navy wife's view in this poem.

MIA?

I've always liked daffodils,
So impudent, so militant,
A brilliant row unbowed to spring rains.

But I've never cared to plant bulbs.
Too impatient to trust in a promise,
I always chose seedlings already in bloom.

Last fall, however, I risked the bulbs.
This is the time, I thought, I'll try!

> Three weeks earlier the ship had
> sailed down the channel, carrying
> men, planes, ammunition, supplies,
> and the hearts of two thousand women.
>
> The ship would cruise until spring
> in dangerous waters, its planes
> would fly through hazardous spaces.

I made the preparations carefully.
Each bulb was committed to earth.
Now there was nothing to do but wait.

Waiting calls for patience, maturity.
I don't do it very well.
But you don't have to do it very well, you just have to do it.

> Letters from the ship said the men
> were waiting, too. The war was said

to be "winding down." The missions
flown were described as "routine."
There were routine briefs, routine
launches, and, of course, routine
losses. The rate of attrition was
said to be close to a peacetime
level. A spokesman for the Department
of Defense called the losses
"acceptable."

Winter ended.
The daffodils were coming up.
"All things come to him who waits."

Not quite all. Seventeen came up.
The eighteenth was missing in . . . in . . . in what?
What had gone wrong, down in the dark earth?

A gardener told me that seventeen out of eighteen was "acceptable."
He meant well. How could I be rude?
How could I say I hardly saw the seventeen that made it,
                    I saw only the eighteenth that was . . . missing?

I'm told I must not lose heart, that someday I'll try again.
Maybe. Maybe next year, or the year after that.

But not daffodils.[22]

1971   25 March—South Vietnamese troops complete their retreat from
Laos. **7 April**—President Nixon announces the withdrawal of
100,000 more U.S. troops. **19–24 April**—One thousand members
of VVAW (Vietnam Veterans Against the War) demonstrate in Washington. **24 April**—A week of protests culminates with an antiwar
rally in Washington—size estimated at 200,000 to 500,000 people.

---

*In Laos, the situation for the Royal Lao government is not favorable.
General Oudone Sananikone records a further, unpublicized expansion of
the war.*

In late April or early May 1971, I accompanied Souvanna Phouma to
Bangkok. . . . Along with us was the chief of the Thai liaison mission to
Vientiane who briefed his prime minister of the situation in Laos.
    The discussions with Prime Minister Thanom were brief and conclusive
because careful preparations had been made before hand by both delegations, the Thais and the Lao. The Thai volunteer units—two battalions—

were ready to go and all we had to settle was where they would be deployed.

We agreed that two considerations would govern the area of deployment; first, the units should be used far from Vientiane to minimize the amount of information about the operation that would be available to the diplomatic missions and foreign press in the capital; second, the Thais should be employed in an area of serious threat. Southern Laos was the logical choice. Not only was it remote from Vientiane, but a new NVA offensive had . . . overrun Paksong on the Bolovens Plateau and was threatening Pakse.

The two battalions were deployed immediately following the conference and placed at Ban Houei Sai, north of Paksong. The battalions barely had time to organize the terrain when, the first night on the position, the NVA struck in force. Making skillful use of their mortars and fighting all night, the Thais held the position. When morning came, the bodies of two hundred North Vietnamese soldiers were counted on the final protective wire and some as far in as the battalion command post. This initial success greatly buoyed the confidence of the Thai officers and the commander of the Thai expeditionary force, an outstanding officer who had been a classmate of mine at Fort Leavenworth.

Following the sound military maxim—reinforce success—Souvanna Phouma approved the Army staff's recommendation to deploy the next Thai contingent to Military Region II on the Plaine des Jarres. Vang Pao, commanding the irregular Lao forces on the Plaine, was being hard pressed by the best troops the NVA had to offer. The NVA was making a maximum effort to destroy Vang Pao's force because it had been so successful in disrupting NVA operations in the border areas. Here was a chance to repeat the successful engagement at Ban Houei Sai in which the Thai volunteers had proved so effective and perhaps restore the lost momentum to Vang Pao's irregulars.

Accordingly, two Thai volunteer infantry regiments, with supporting regular artillery, were lifted to the Plaine Des Jarres. Confident of success, the force dispatched its security elements and began advancing across the open, rolling grasslands toward the enemy. The NVA, however, would not be twice burned. It was ready with its heavy artillery registered and its infantry poised for the attack.

The battle began with a very heavy artillery concentration, including 130-mm and 122-mm guns, pouring down on the Thai battalions. While the Thais were pinned down by the fire, the NVA infantry assaulted and virtually destroyed the volunteer battalions. Thai casualties were heavy and hundreds of Thais became prisoners of war.

But this disastrous experience on the Plaine Des Jarres did not diminish the Thai enthusiasm for sending volunteers to Laos. The Thai commitment continued . . . and the volunteers engaged in a number of heavy actions in Military Region II in which the NVA employed its largest artillery and the Thais had to call on U.S. B-52's to avoid destruction.[23]

1971   3 May—Undersecretary of State John Irwin confirms publicly for the first time that B-52s have been flying regularly in Laos.

On 18 May the following message indicates not only the decreasing U.S. commitment to the war but also the managerial methodology of U.S. resource allocation.

TO: COMUSMACV

FM: PACAF/DO

S E C R E T/DO

SUBJECT: FORECAST OF OPERATIONS (U)

1. DURING THE WEEK 23 THRU 29 MAY 71, 370 TACAIR, 30 GUNSHIP, 40 B-52 SORTIES WILL BE AVAILABLE DAILY FOR STRIKES IN SOUTHEAST ASIA. TACAIR IS DOWN 43 SORTIES FROM THE PREVIOUS FORECAST LARGELY DUE TO A DECREASE IN NAVY SORTIES AVAILABLE. FOR PLANNING, THE SORTIE AVERAGES WILL BE: STEEL TIGER 60.0 PER CENT; BARREL ROLL 12.7 PER CENT; CAMBODIA 11.9 PER CENT; RVN 15.4 PER CENT. PLANNED SORTIE RATES, BASED ON POSSESSED AIRCRAFT, ARE: F-4's 1.0; F-100's 1.0; A-1's 0.7; B-57's 0.8; AND A-37's 1.5.

2. STEEL TIGER WILL BE ALLOCATED APPROXIMATELY 222 TACAIR AND 15 GUNSHIP SORTIES PER DAY. GUNSHIPS ARE DOWN ONE AC-130 FROM LAST WEEK DUE TO BATTLE DAMAGE AND AIRCRAFT UNDER MODIFICATION. INTERDICTION WILL CONCENTRATE ON THRUPUT ROUTES, WITH ROUND-THE-CLOCK STRIKES TO STOP THRUPUT UNTIL THE MONSOON RAINS MAKE THE ROADS IMPASSABLE. TACAIR WILL BE SCHEDULED TO ABCCC DAY AND NIGHT TO PROVIDE STRIKES AGAINST TRUCKS AND LUCRATIVE TARGETS. THE NIGHT INTERDICTION EFFORT WILL CENTER AROUND AC-130 GUNSHIPS, WITH F-4's PROVIDING COVER AND FLAK SUPPRESSION. B-57's WILL STRIKE AT NIGHT ALONG THE WESTERN ROUTE STRUCTURE, AND NAVY A-6's WILL STRIKE UNDER COMMANDO BOLT ON INPUT ROUTES. NIGHT OWLS WILL OPERATE ON INPUT ROUTES.

3. APPROXIMATELY 47 TACAIR AND 5 GUNSHIPS WILL BE ALLOCATED TO BARREL ROLL DAILY. TACAIR WILL PROVIDE INTERDICTION AND GROUND SUPPORT FOR FRIENDLY FORCES. GUNSHIPS WILL PROVIDE AIR COVER AT NIGHT IN THE PRIMARY BATTLEFIELD AREA. QUICK REACTION F-4's WILL PROVIDE SUPPORT IF REQUIRED.

4. APPROXIMATELY 57 TACAIR AND 2 GUNSHIP SORTIES WILL BE ALLOCATED TO RVN DAILY. 35 PREPLANNED AND 20 IMMEDIATE TACAIR SORTIES WILL BE AVAILABLE FOR AIR SUPPORT IN RESPONSE TO GROUND COMMANDERS REQUESTS. TWO NIGHT OWL TRAINING SORTIES WILL ALSO STRIKE IN RVN. ALLOCATION OF ATTACK SORTIES TO THE FIELD FORCES AND MILITARY REGIONS WILL BE AS DIRECTED BY COMUSMACV.

5. APPROXIMATELY 44 TACAIR AND 8 GUNSHIP SORTIES WILL BE ALLOCATED TO OPERATIONS IN CAMBODIA DAILY. TACAIR WILL BE PROVIDED BY A-37'S, SUPPLEMENTED BY ADDITIONAL TACAIR AS REQUIRED BY TACTICAL EMERGENCIES.

6. COMMANDO VAULT MISSIONS WILL BE FLOWN AS REQUIRED EMPLOYING C-130/BLU 82 WEAPONS. APPROXIMATELY 210 SORTIES FOR THE WEEK WILL BE FLOWN IN SUPPORT OF PSYCHOLOGICAL WARFARE OPERATIONS.[24]

1971   13 June—Daniel Ellsberg releases *The Pentagon Papers* to *The New York Times*. **28 June**—Ellsberg indicted for stealing classified information.

In July correspondent Donald Kirk returns to Vietnam.

Saigon: July, 1971
Turn left off one of the main streets leading to the gates of sprawling Tan Son Nhut air base and you find where it's at in Saigon. It happens on "Soul Alley," where the brothers get together, get close, real tight and rap, let it all out, and none of the rabbits or lifers, as career military men are inevitably known, dares bother them. Check it out, dig it, around five or six o'clock of an evening when they start getting back from their jobs as clerks and communications specialists, security guards and drivers, or whatever else the army makes a man do in this country. The brothers, almost all of them enlisted men in olive drab fatigues, stroll down the alley while soul music blares from the little bars and clubs, and some of them settle down for a game of cards in the few hours before night falls. Then, around midnight, Soul Alley empties as they retreat to their rooms in the cement block apartment houses and homes with tin roofs that crowd the neighborhood.

"Technically, we're not even supposed to be here," says one of the brothers, talking to an intruder in the shadows of a small shop purveying cold canned soft drinks, stolen or purchased for illegal resale from the military base exchange on Tan Son Nhut. "We're supposed to be living on the base. It's the only way we can get away from the harassment, the 'man,' the 'lifers.' Here we can live the way we want to and do what we want. It's home to us." Soul Alley, in fact, is home to only a small percentage of black GIs in Vietnam–200 or 300 at most, including deserters and AWOLs, some of whom have been living along the maze of surrounding walkways for months and even years. Soul Alley attracts hundreds more blacks for a few hours, an evening, or a weekend before they return to their quarters and duties at posts surrounding Saigon. Even if the majority of the approximately 20,000 blacks in Vietnam have never visited Soul Alley, almost all of them have heard of it and view it as a symbol of their desires and needs in what many of them describe as a white man's army fighting a useless war.

"You get to live with the Vietnamese. You stay in the same houses with them," says a GI, explaining the symbolism, the sense of identification, inherent in a place like Soul Alley. "You find out the problems the Vietnamese go through to live from day to day. They're striving, the same as our people. They want to progress, same as we do. Here's President Thieu staying in his palace making money and these people are hustling for bread. Check it out. Same as President Nixon in the White House, and the blacks gettin' nothin'. There it is."

The GI, who goes by the soul name of Brother Rap, articulates better than most of his friends the underlying attitude of thousands of blacks now serving in Vietnam. It was only a few years ago, in September, 1965, that this correspondent, asked to write an article on racial problems among GIs in Vietnam, interviewed black soldiers from all services, in all regions of the country, and discovered their attitude was almost universally enthusiastic and highly motivated. They had gripes, as do most GIs regardless of racial, ethnic, or social background, but basically they liked the army, were grateful for the opportunities it provided, approved of the war and thought we were beating "Charlie," as the Viet Cong were then known. (Now GIs refer to the VC as "gooks," "dinks," and "slopes." The term "Charlie" for Viet Cong is regarded as somewhat old-fashioned.) Indeed, I often found black GIs more vocal in defense of the war than white soldiers. "The army's tough, but it's good for us," a lanky Philadelphian told me in 1965 while on patrol in jungles north of Saigon. "We can get rank here where we can't even get jobs on the outside."

"The army treats us like dirt," Brother Rap goes on, after I tell him about my first experience, nearly six years ago, in interviewing black soldiers. "If you're white and you're in the army and you don't dig black, you can be real mean. You can put false charges against us. You can give us little details." Another GI, previously silent during my conversation with Brother Rap, interrupts. "The army's the most prejudiced place I've ever been in," he says, and then unhesitatingly gives his name: Specialist Fourth Class William Gary, a twenty-three-year-old from Chicago. "I don't mind saying who I am," Gary explains. "Anybody wants to know who I am and how I feel, they're welcome to it." Gary, like most of the blacks to whom I spoke, bitterly criticizes the army for small, seemingly petty daily offenses rather than having sent him here in the first place.

"You can go on sick call and you're black and they give you some detail," says Gary, toying with a chain of beads with a black cross around his neck. "You go see the IG [Inspector General] or chaplain, and they won't do a damn thing for you. You sit around down here minding your own business and the MPs come on lookin' for you, sayin' you're AWOL."

Whether or not such complaints are entirely justified, they are representative of the changing, angry mood among black GIs. Not all of those whom I met, in interviews from the mountainous, jungle-covered northern provinces to the flatlands around Saigon, complain about racial discrimination as such, but not one of them believes, really, in either the army or the war. They are clearly attuned to both racial and student problems in the States and aver, almost to a man, that they'd rather join their brothers in "the real war back in the world" than go on fighting in Vietnam. The attitudes of black GIs to some extent parallel those of white soldiers, who are extremely embittered by their military experience, but resentment among blacks penetrates much deeper. Whites talk of returning to more or less conventional lives—homes, families, jobs and school. Blacks tend to discuss "revolution" and "liberation" from the "system" and react swiftly, sometimes violently, to racial slights and slurs. Blacks and whites, more so than at any time since the end of formal segregation in the armed forces more than twenty years ago, tend to cluster in their own cliques and rarely talk or socialize with each other. Blacks assert their identity and independence in hair styles, dress, language, music—just as they "hang together" on Soul Alley, their own segregated neighborhood, whenever they get a chance.

"If you pulled all the blacks out of Vietnam, you'd have the biggest revolution you've ever seen in the United States," says another brother whom I meet in one of the bars off Soul Alley. "You better believe," he goes on, "when Nixon pulls us out there won't be no more United States. The blacks know demolition. The blacks know how to shoot. We're gonna use all that stuff 'back in the world' " (the term GIs inevitably use to mean "back in the States"). These words may appear exaggerated, but blacks in Vietnam have begun to organize just as their brothers have done at home. During our conversation one of them pulls out a plastic card printed on one side in red, black, and green stripes. "That's the flag of the Black Liberation Front of the armed forces," he explains, noting his own name above that of the president, Bobby Wilson, on the back.

"Bobby Wilson never talks to people," says the brother, in response to my suggestion that he arrange an interview. "He's here, though. We know him." The GIs rated the Black Liberation Front and the Black Panthers as the two most influential organizations among black GIs in Vietnam.[25]

Also in July U.S. Air Force Lieutenant Richard Doyle arrives in Vietnam as an intelligence officer. He keeps an introspective diary.

A Vietnam Diary

9 July 71
I've been what they call "in country" a week today. I'm close to Saigon, at Bien Hoa. I'm living in a hootch with the flyboys—my contemporaries, my "peers". But I'm at odds with them and what they stand for just as I face a personal, inner dilemma. What am I *really* all about and, more specifically, just how much of that vitriolic anti-war, anti-military, anti-establishment stuff will stay with me here, where I'm a part of it and where

I need the air force to survive? At least I think I do. Like other people, I must have things to do, a feeling of worth and esteem. In Idaho I filled my life after I left the base each day and entered the other culture we had there—friends, music, discussion, a feeling of brotherhood in a cause, a cause of peace. And that was how the days were accomplished in Idaho. Not so here. They're much more serious about everything here and, of course, this is the war. But I can't leave it at the gate. These courageous young officers with pictures of wives and families-just-begun on the walls spend their days looking for things and people to destroy. And I sleep in the same building with them. And worry about rocket attacks. You'd think that would motivate me to press the attack on Charlie, to maximise my own security perhaps. Somehow it doesn't. Of course I'm scared but my reaction isn't one of revenge. I simply don't feel part of this struggle. Indicative of the difficulty experienced by the foreign policy makers in making the domino theory more visceral. The tack I am taking involves examining my feelings on self-defense and the protection of loved ones if threatened with violence and the extension of such feelings to something like this war. That would seem to be the only possible justification for killing people. Because balanced against any other criterion must be considered the fact that every man shares one experience—the human experience. To deny someone else that experience is my concept of sin. It (killing) is such an irreparable act. This irreparability dictates to me the necessity of determining beyond the vaguest doubt the requirement for killing. If you lack such conviction, killing is a sin. And it would also appear that one man's determination that another should be denied the human experience is fantastically arbitrary and arrogant. . . .

17 Jul 71
I keep thinking about that admonition by Einstein (from Russell's autobiography) to the effect that one must do nothing which offends one's conscience, even if ordered to do so by the state. The Americans spoke of a "higher duty" at Nuremberg. Then we commit a Vietnam and will have nothing to do with draft evaders and CO's who, in some cases, are playing such roles out of a sense of obligation to mankind or to the better instincts of this country or to their own conscience, as the term implies. They are, in my opinion, heroes. I don't know why I care. I wish I had not had to make the choice. Now that I'm here my worst doubts about the war are confirmed. And I am part of the killing and wish I was not. I feel dirty.

Surviving here is requiring a schizophrenic effort which pales the one I've lived with in the last two years. Because the war has come home.[26]

With increasing public scrutiny of all aspects of Cambodian operations, there is also the problem within the U.S. military on the precise interpretation of the ROE (Rules of Engagement). This query on 4 August from one of the U.S. Air Force fighter wings is an example.

FM 8TFW/UBON AFLD THAI
TO 7AF/TAN SON NHUT AB RVN
S E C R E T
SUBJ: ROE CLARIFICATION (U).

1. CONSIDERING THE SENSITIVITY SURROUNDING U.S. AIR OPERATIONS IN CAM-
BODIA, IT IS NECESSARY FOR THE 8TFW TO RECEIVE CLARIFICATION OF THE
FOLLOWING CAMBODIAN ROE PROBLEM AREAS.

A. REF A, PARA 2C, LINES 1 AND 2 STATES THAT "STOENG TRENG WILL BE
CONSIDERED AN URBAN AREA AND, AS SUCH, WILL NOT BE STRUCK." REFER
PARA 3C STATES THAT "URBAN AREAS ARE DEFINED AS THOSE DEPICTED AS
BUILT-UP AREAS ON AN ARMY MAP SERVICE 1:50,000 SCALE MAP." HOWEVER,
THE APPROPRIATE ARMY MAP SERVICE (AMS) 1:50,000 SCALE (6136 II, SERIES
L7016) MAP DOES NOT DEPICT STOENG TRENG AS A BUILT-UP AREA. THE LEG-
END ON THIS, AND OTHER 1:50,000 SCALE MAPS, INDICATES A BUILT-UP AREA
AS A DISTINCTIVELY TINTED AREA WITH WELL DEFINED BOUNDARIES. THE
ACTUAL NO-BOMB AREA SURROUNDING THE CITY OF STOENG TRENG, THERE-
FORE, IS ILL-DEFINED. TO PREVENT POSSIBLE ROE VIOLATION, RECOMMEND 7AF
ESTABLISH A REASONABLE, BUT WELL DEFINED, NBR "BOX" AROUND THE CITY
OF STOENG TRENG.

B. BASED ON CURRENT ROE (REF A, PARA 1D(1) AND PARA 3D; REF B, PARA 2C)
IS OUR INTERPRETATION CORRECT THAT FIXED-WING GUNSHIPS CAN EXPEND
AGAINST TARGETS IN VILLAGES OR HAMLETS LOCATED WITHIN 1000 METERS
EITHER SIDE OF ALL CATEGORY "A" LOCS? [Lines Of Communication, i.e.,
roads.]

C. REF B, PARA 2D, H (NOTE) STATES THAT "AN INHABITED VILLAGE OR
TOWN IS DEFINED AS A GROUPING OF 15 OR MORE STRUCTURES THAT THE
FANK [Forces Armées Nationales Khmers] HAS NOT IDENTIFIED AS UNIN-
HABITED." VARIOUS ANS 1:50,000 SCALE MAPS SHOW THE EXISTENCE OF
STRUCTURES ALONG MANY CATEGORY "B" LOCS. IF THESE STRUCTURES ARE
LOCATED IN A VERY CLOSE GROUP, IT IS RELATIVELY EASY TO DISTINGUISH IT
AS A VILLAGE OR HAMLET. HOWEVER, A PROBLEM ARISES WHEN THESE STRUC-
TURES ARE NOT CONTAINED WITHIN A CLOSE-KNIT GROUP. IN MANY AREAS, A
SERIES OF 15 STRUCTURES OR MORE MAY BE SPACED INTERMITTENTLY ON
BOTH SIDES OF A CATEGORY "B" LOC FOR A DISTANCE OF SEVERAL KILOME-
TERS. THE QUESTION ARISES AS TO WHETHER OR NOT IT IS PERMISSIBLE TO
EXPEND AGAINST A MOTORIZED VEHICLE OR WATERCRAFT ON A CATEGORY
"B" LOC IF THAT VEHICLE OR WATERCRAFT IS TRAVELLING ALONG, OR
STOPPED IN, AN AREA WITH INTERMITTENTLY SPACED STRUCTURES LOCATED
ALONG THE LOC? IN ADDITION, REQUEST A CLEARER DEFINITION OF A
VILLAGE IN THE CAMBODIAN AREA OF OPERATIONS.

2. ANY GUIDANCE CONCERNING THE PREROGATIVES OF THE FIXED-WING GUN-
SHIPS TO ATTACK SUSPECTED TARGETS ALONG CATEGORY A AND B LOC'S
SUCH AS THOSE DESCRIBED ABOVE SHOULD CONSIDER BOTH THE SITUATION

WHEN THE AC-130 IS ASSISTED BY A FAC AND THE SITUATION WHEN IT IS
SELF-FACABLE.

3. CLARIFICATION OF THE ABOVE PROBLEM AREAS WILL SIGNIFICANTLY RE-
SOLVE THE POSSIBILITY OF ROE VIOLATIONS AND AID IN THE OVERALL INTERDIC-
TION EFFORT IN CAMBODIA.[27]

*From the perspective of the Communist Khmer Rouge, however, instruc-
tions on how to counter U.S. airpower in Cambodia are not so complicated.
This captured directive is translated by Lieutenant Colonel Sok Sambaur,
Khmer Air Force, on 15 August 71.*

Aircraft Shooting Lesson

1. *How to shoot OV-10*—We must lead it by three times the length of
its fuselage. We must shoot by ripple (bursts). We shoot only when he
dives. If he is in level flight or turning, don't shoot. Do not shoot at any
time when he is pulling up from a dive. We must wait until he dives to
shoot at him. If he strafes or drops bombs, the attack lasts only 30
minutes to an hour.

2. *How to shoot MIGS*—(MIG is interpreted as any jet fighter). The
MIG is the fastest. We must lead it by four times the length of its fuselage. The manner of shooting is the same as above, by ripple. There are
two situations when we shoot him. Sometimes we are walking along,
and he sees us and dives. We must get down and watch whether he
bombs right on us or far from us. If his pass is away from us, we can
shoot. If he dives straight at us, we must flatten out as soon as possible
since we have no trenches. We must lie on our back-sack, ready to
shoot at his second pass. If there is a big tree nearby, we must move
toward it for shelter and shoot again. His attack never lasts over one
hour to an hour and a half.

3. *How to shoot chopper*—He has speed of 150 km/hr. We must lead
him by two lengths of his fuselage. With our CKC (individual weapon—
bolt action rifle), we must all shoot together at the same time. We must
watch how he swings and sways. We always must swing with him. This
means that our eyes must be on him all the time.

4. *How to shoot A-1 (or T-28)*—This aircraft has a speed of 600 km/hr,
and it carries only four bombs and a few rounds of ammo. We must lead
him by three times the length of his fuselage, because he almost has the
speed of an OV-10. We must all shoot together at the karman (juncture
of wings and fuselage), pointing our guns at the same place when he is
diving.[28]

*With national elections in South Vietnam scheduled for 3 October, cam-
paigning begins. Comments on local politics and the progress of Vietnamization are contained in this province report for August.*

Province Report
(RCS: MACCORDS 31.01 R2)

DATE: 1 September 1971
Period Ending: 31 August 1971

Phu Yen Province

1. (C). OVERALL STATUS OF THE COMMUNITY DEFENSE AND LOCAL
DEVELOPMENT EFFORT.
a. A number of months ago, even before the first lower house candidate
announced his intention to seek elective office, Judge Nguyen Dinh Hoe
outlined to this reporter the methods which would be used in an attempt
to "rig" the elections. According to the judge, the GVN would resort to
"hanging the VC hat on the heads" of those candidates who held a
chance for victory but did not fit into the government's game plan. Additionally, the judge recounted that scores of government troops and cadre
would be mobilized and through means both fair and foul, the approved
candidates would be elected. As a result, it came as no surprise when the
local GVN employed exactly such tactics during this month's election
campaign. The GVN's efforts to determine the election outcome was
handled with the typical arrogance and incompetence that has been witnessed in many other government undertakings. Perhaps the most damn-
ing indictment against the local administration is that its most feared and
hated rival, An Quang Nguyen Cong Hoan, won a smashing victory
despite orders to GVN cadre at all levels to thwart his election. Hoan,
like the less fortunate Congressmen Cao Van Chieu and Huynh Dieu,
had the "Viet Cong Hat" placed squarely atop his head in various GVN
directives and the campaigns of all three were described by the local
GVN as a Communist plot. On a brighter note, from the GVN point of
view, Truong Van Nguyen—the darling of the GVN and grandson of the
local founder of the Dai Viet party—squeaked out a victory for Phu
Yen's remaining seat. Literally thousands of GVN personnel, including
most of the RD cadre, were mobilized to insure a victory for Nguyen.
  b. The Province Chief, LTC Nguyen Van To, has consulted a Nha
Trang fortune teller who had predicted that Phu Yen will have a new
leader before the end of the year. LTC To has given every indication that
he believes the prediction. Individuals in the local business community
are once again complaining loudly about corruption and its current rate of
escalation. Similar reports in the past have generally proved to be accurate and have indicated that the official under suspicion was making "one
last haul" before his relief. Nguyen Van Ngac, brother of the Province
Chief and member of the local police force, appears to be devoting his
efforts full time to dubious commercial activities. Perhaps, indeed, the
end is in sight for the To administration.
  c. Regional and Popular Forces were not particularly active but the
Koreans—for the second straight month—took up the slack. The 26th

ROK regiment completed an operation in Base Area 236 which claimed over 300 enemy killed. Based on past experience, however, abductions should rise dramatically in the Tuy Hoa valley in the near future as the Viet Cong impress new recruits to replace many low level, rear support and production cadre lost to the ROKs.

    d. The Hieu Xuong District Chief, LTC Le Van Trong, whose name was mentioned prominently in connection with the plunder of the Phu Hiep air base, reportedly will be sacked sometime in the near future. If Trong's removal is, in fact, tied to the Phu Hiep caper, he will become the 18th victim of that scandal. It is interesting to note, however, that while transfers and administrative jail terms have been handed out freely, not a single "ill-gotten" piaster has been recovered. The workings of the GVN are, indeed, strange.[29]

1971   **3–4 September**—Men later identified as "the White House Plumbers" break into the office of Daniel Ellsberg's psychiatrist, Dr. Fielding, in search of evidence to support the U.S. government *Pentagon Papers* case.

Most U.S. pilots, however, are not concerned with political scandals, either at home or in Vietnam. The narrator of As Far Away as China *provides a perspective from the air on a problem that plagues all U.S. military men.*

This afternoon, waiting for the F-4, I begin to fly long lazy S patterns above the hootches, the white building, the jagged rocks. I've been trained to do this. One more way of cutting down on the possibility of being hit by sniper fire. As I bank into another leg of the S, though, I forget why I'm doing it, I just do it.

When the Phantom is overhead, I go down to take a closer look. They sit on the edge of the plateau, rising into a small mountain. There are two clusters of hootches built near the rocks. The hootches are in groups of three, a white wooden building sitting between.

As the F-4 begins to roll and climb, I can see a muzzle, probably a Soviet-made S11, extend through the side of the one farthest back.

While the F-4, camouflaged in a mottle of greens and blacks and browns, circles overhead, I move toward the target and point the nose straight down. I have no sense of diving. Like always, it is as if everything is coming up at me.

I contact the fighter pilot and ask for one run of strafing fire from his 50 caliber machine guns, then one run of napalm.

I reach over my head and flick the safety, then the first switch which sends my right outboard rocket down to the left of the huts.

There will not be much room to work in. The sharp angle of the rocks, the steep ascent of the mountain on three sides of the hootches, means that the F-4 will have to maneuver deftly. It is only the two hootches further back that the ground troops want destroyed. It is there that the gun emplacement sits.

The F-4, appearing to be coming too low and too fast to be accurate, looking as if it will snap from the force of the dive or snag on the upper ledges, prep fires with its 50 caliber machine guns, the row of dirt and sand rising and disappearing like numbers on a calculator.

He repeats the steep arc of his first run, diving toward the target, then, as the plane begins its ascent, drops one can of napalm, and, a bit later, a second.

The first canister falls end over end then strikes the ground and detonates, exploding, sending debris in every direction and setting the last hootch on fire.

I can see that the second canister, though, has missed the target. As my mind telescopes, I can see that it is falling to the rear of the white building and now is bouncing along the ground, seeming to suspend itself in midair each time as if it were a film in slow motion, and only now, only now when I'm sure it was a dud does it explode. . . .

I bank into still another leg of the S pattern. Though I've seen the explosion, the flames billowing and changing color before they give off that familiar black smoke, the front of the building remains intact.

But it is not until I get closer that I begin to see what has happened. As I fly overhead, holding the clipboard with my knees, I see that men and women are coming out of bunkers in the rocks. The mouths of the bunkers were so well disguised that I could not see them before. I would not be able to see them now if there weren't people coming out of them.

Dropping down to under 100 feet, watching the F-4 disappear into the horizon, I see that the men and women are taking makeshift wheelbarrows from beneath a camouflage of bamboo, wheeling them as fast as they can toward the burning hootches. I watch them disappear behind the white building which, I can see now, has been gutted and its white front stands like some Hollywood prop.

They are carrying things in their wheelbarrows, methodically as if they are carrying brick. One load after another. Making neat piles off to the side.

It is only now that I am flying lower that I can see how badly damaged the building is. Though the front is miraculously untouched, the rest of it is no more than a charring skeleton.

It is not until I get closer still, though, that I begin to realize what is going on. The older women are wheeling the bodies of children. Surely they are children because now the ones that are still alive are being brought out by the younger women, held across their outstretched arms like linen.

Flying in tight little patterns, I can see there aren't enough wheelbarrows to go around. The old men, their hands empty, are following behind their wives and daughters.

The old men too hold their hands at their sides, necks forward, their legs slightly bent, as though in some aged mime they are pushing away their own invisible dead.

There are thatched roofs and trees all around us. Here, beneath the trees, a boy with a switch rides a buffalo. And behind the trees, beneath flat reed hats, figures stoop to shoots in the water.

It is not what you see from the air. The sun is going down and the water glistens. You would not know there were dikes. Or shoots, or water. Because of the way the sun glistens, it is all flat and green and there is no horizon to speak of.

Not just here near the stand, but in all directions.

If you were to cross the paddies, you could do it on the run, your feet barely skimming. That is the sense you have. But sooner or later you would surely fall off.

I hold the clipboard on my lap, a ballpoint pen between my fingers. I have seen civilians killed before, of course. The VC and NVA use them as cover. It's just the way they work. These things happen, I tell myself.

I go through a little speech to myself, the ordinary speech, a few lines I carry with me just in case. It's a little speech about the nature of this war, but today it doesn't do much good. I listen to the words as though they are coming from someone else, from some understanding neighbor.

It's strange how you learn to survive here. You learn about time as you never have before. You learn what the past is to the present. You reduce as much as you can to a calculus of sights and sounds, of patterns and strategies, as if that can find you the proper order. You try to separate yourself from what is going on here. You try not to figure out what it is doing to these people, to your friends, to yourself. That's the best you can do. You try to do more than just react to the catalog of facts you establish in your head and you'll go haywire.

That is why I'll just fill out the reports and go. I will not look back at the little old men beneath their conical hats. The faces of the women sitting with their hands clasped about their knees, past terror, rocking back and forth. I will not see the women carrying screaming children, I have never seen them before, their eyes wide and fixed on me flying high above them.

Like always I will just estimate the wounded, the dead, the extent and nature of the damage.

When I flip through the forms today, though, one row of discrete blocks after another, I find I have no idea where to begin.

I flip through the forms, one row of discrete blocks after another.

Flying away from it all, the stick back a little, the nose slightly above the horizon, I look into the clouds which, today, up here, are a delicate combination of blues and whites and pinks. Even without my altimeter, I know I am rising.

I thought I'd learned better than this. I tell myself you have to learn to leave things behind here. This is a world of the dead, the maimed, the destroyed. You have to deal with them as if you are some adjuster for a very large insurance company. When all of it begins to get you, you just straighten out your files.

That's what I tell myself.

When I get back, after I have had my Coke, I open the folder and spread the forms on the bed. I decide to do them in pencil.[30]

1971   19 September—In Saigon President Thieu uses riot police to quell anti-government demonstrations. 3 October—President Thieu re-elected with 90 percent of the vote.

In Cambodia, on 7 October, U.S. embassy employee William Stubbs comments about the situation there.

The government troops who were so well-behaved and well-loved by the people a year ago have greatly increased in number. Such a rapid increase has naturally brought problems of leadership and discipline, as there was no large corps of experienced officers and NCO's to deal with the raw recruits. The troops, often unpaid, seem to be more and more frequently engaging in theft and looting, both in urban and rural areas. Such behavior does not endear them, or the government they represent, to the population.

One solution to the problem of troop misbehavior would be to prevent armed forces from entering populated areas, including villages. But at present there are many areas of Cambodia where military personnel are the only representatives of the government, and if the troops are removed there is no one to fill the resulting vacuum and provide the government presence necessary for obtaining popular support in resisting the enemy.

There are many Cambodians who believe that popular support is waning. They point to their own estimates of Khmer dissidents, and state that a year ago there were 10,000 and today the total has increased to 15,000—up 50%. Regardless of whether these figures are entirely accurate, it would not seem to me a politically healthy situation if the government is losing people at a rapid rate while it gains ground slowly. I therefore cite again what I consider to be the essential lesson of Vietnam: the government, to obtain the support of the population, must prove to the people that it can protect them, and simultaneously provide a better life. . . .

A year has passed, and one is able to see a genuine difference in FANK's performance. The equipment we have provided and the training we have helped to arrange in Vietnam have obviously increased the capabilities of the fighting force. Government troops are liberating areas that have been held by the enemy for a year or more, and several significant battles have been won. This is all very encouraging. But there are accompanying discouraging factors.

All . . . programs have promising aspects, but none of the three is comprehensive in providing simultaneously the necessary protection and development. Equally unfortunate is the fact that all three programs suffer from an acute lack of funds and material resources. Finally, and perhaps most discouraging from my own point of view, few persons within our Embassy view this situation as a crucial one. Our major effort, certainly when judged by the greatly increased number of persons engaged in it, is the provision of military equipment. We seem to be slipping slowly into the same bog which trapped us in Vietnam: a belief that the war can be won with a well-equipped conventional army; a belief accompanied by a neglect for political programs aimed at retaining popular support for the government.

I should state immediately that I would not seek to transplant the CORDS program, the Hamlet Evaluation System or any of a number of political action programs for Vietnam to Cambodia. But I do believe we must turn our attention and divert some of our funds to the problems which these programs have dealt with, and that this can be done with no increase in personnel.

We can, for instance, use all the political influence and leverage we possess to attempt to persuade the GKR to put its pacification and development programs under one roof. This would not be easy, for the man who becomes responsible for such a unified effort would wield a great deal of power and perhaps gain a large popular following. We can urge the GKR to continue with its plans for a national cadre training center, plans which included assistance and advice from Col. Nguyen Van Be of Vung Tau. The project was stopped, according to Hang Thun Hak, because of objections from ranking FANK officers. We can suggest, perhaps insist, that certain items of military equipment which we provide be turned over to local self-defense forces, and propose proper training programs for these forces. Finally, we can provide funds, through a separate appropriation if necessary, for a GKR agency which would deal with the overall problem. The government we support, of course, need not necessarily be the present configuration of personalities.

The provision of funds need not and should not be accompanied by an increase in Embassy personnel. The GKR, with some wise counsel from ranking members of our Embassy and additional advice from competent Vietnamese, should have the ability to organize and implement programs which gain the support of the population. But they need financial assistance to do it, and they must be urged to focus their attention on the problem. If they are not able to do it with their own personnel, I doubt seriously whether any corps of American advisers can do it for them.

It is, of course, possible that they will make a valiant effort, with our support, and fail. But I am becoming more and more convinced that if they do not make the effort, or if we do not support it, the army may continue to gain ground but the government will eventually lose the population and the country will fall. If it has been decided that the fall of Cambodia would be contrary to our national interest, we should seek out all reasonable means to prevent that fall. Washington appears to see an increase in military and A.I.D. personnel and programs as sufficient steps. But similar steps were taken in Vietnam with results now evident. I would hope that it should not be necessary for us to rediscover the wheel in Cambodia, but at present it appears to me that we are applying few of the lessons we should have learned.[31]

Also in October writer C.D.B. Bryan interviews a wounded U.S. Army lieutenant colonel. In any accident much like the one that happened to Private Thomas Kingsley, an enlisted man under the colonel's command has been killed by a short round fired by American artillery.

The colonel paused for a moment, then said, "Look, to digress for a moment, the whole reason why I volunteered for Vietnam the second time was because I honestly felt I could be a better battalion commander, could accomplish the mission with less loss of life, than a lot of the people who were going over there. I felt this because of the tremendous experience I had had fighting with the Vietnamese Airborne in 1965 and 1966. After my first tour I came home with probably the greatest feeling of satisfaction I've ever had in anything I've ever done. I slept in the mud, ate rice and Vietnamese food with chopsticks for one solid year. Everywhere the Vietnamese went, I went. I was one of them. And I felt, I really felt, that I was honestly helping people. I met some fantastic people in that outfit, Vietnamese for whom I have the greatest respect in the world. These people were desperate. Many of them were from North Vietnam and had fled the Communists in 1954. They were true patriots fighting for their country, for their lives! I came home from that year feeling I had been fighting for freedom and democracy. Now, wait," he said, holding up his hand in anticipation of an interruption. "When I volunteered for Vietnam in 1965, it was for 'God, Country, and Mom's Homemade Apple Pie.' I got to Vietnam, and we were surrounded at Dak To. Well, when you get surrounded and the sun goes down with you sitting there thinking you may not see it come up again the next morning, it takes a helluva lot more than God, Country and Mom's Apple Pie— those words emblazoned across the sky—to keep you going."

Lieutenant Colonel Schwarzkopf pushed himself up from his chair and stood facing me. "I think we went to Vietnam in the first place for the principle of democracy. I'm not saying that that's what it all turned out to be, and I'm not saying that that was the end result. I'm saying only that this is the principle we went to Vietnam for. Well, what kept me going while we were surrounded was by that time I had honestly met enough truly fine, dedicated South Vietnamese officers in the Vietnamese Airborne Division who sincerely and honestly believed that we were fighting for their country, for their freedom and that I—as an American taught from the time I was knee-high to a grasshopper that one stands up and fights for democracy—that I was over there to help. . . .

"The public seems to have lost faith in the military because of the war in Vietnam," Schwarzkopf continued. "After all, we're only an arm of policy of the United States government. We're public servants. If the public no longer has confidence in us, then what good are we? I think right now in the officer corps there are an awful lot of people who feel confused about the public's attitude. I came into the Army because I wanted to serve my country. I took an oath saying that I'd protect this country from all enemies foreign and domestic—I didn't say *I'd* determine who the enemies were! I said I'd merely protect the country after somebody else made that determination. So this war comes around in Vietnam; the duly elected government officials send us, the Army, to fight the war. We go to Vietnam and fight the best way we know how— not needlessly wasting lives for the most part. We did the best we could, and it dragged on and on and on. Many of us were sent back a second time. A lot of young officers have been sent back a third time. I'm talking about the kid who went over first as a platoon leader, returned as a captain and commanded an infantry company and then, a third time, went over as a major. Three times he's gone off not knowing whether he was going to come back alive. He's got ten years in the service and in that ten years has been separated from his wife and family for three of them. He didn't go off to Vietnam because he wanted to. He was sent by his country. Now, suddenly, public opinion is violently antimilitary as though it had all been this kid's idea! So here he is, a young Army major with ten years' service and he's going to sit down and think, 'All of a sudden I'm being blamed for all this,' and he hurts. He's hurt! He doesn't understand why he's bearing the brunt of this animosity when the guys who sent him to Vietnam seven years ago are now back on college campuses writing articles about how terrible it is that he's there in Vietnam!" . . .

"But I think this is an important point: the government sends you off to fight its war—again, it's not *your* war; it's the government's war. You go off and fight not only once, but twice, okay? And suddenly a decision is made, 'Well, look, you guys were all wrong. You're a bunch of dirty bastards. You never should have been there!' Now this is going to make me think long and hard before I go off to war again. This is me, Norm Schwarzkopf, personally. I don't think there will ever be another major confrontation where huge armies line up on both sides. If that happens, it's inevitably going to be nuclear weapons and the whole thing. So I think all wars of the future are going to be—and again, God forbid, I hope we don't have any. War is a profanity. It really is. It's terrifying. Nobody is more antiwar than an intelligent person who's been to war. Probably the most antiwar people I know are Army officers—but if we do have a war, I think it's going to be similar in nature to Vietnam and Korea. Limited in scope. And when they get ready to send me again, I'm going to have to stop and ask myself, 'Is it worth it?' That's a very dangerous place for the nation to be when your own army is going to stop and question."

We carried our coffee back to the table. He sat cradling the mug between his palms. "I *hate* what Vietnam has done to our country! I *hate* what Vietnam has done to our Army!"[32]

1971   **20 October**—Cambodian leader Lon Nol declares a state of emergency and rule by decree. **12 November**—President Nixon announces the withdrawal of 45,000 more troops and states that the "U.S. ground offensive has ended."

Lieutenant Richard Doyle comments in his diary:

22 Nov 71
The second rainy day in a row here, pretty dismal. Nixon has apparently scored well with the public by bringing the army out, especially just before Xmas. It's always been difficult for the air force to ellict (sp) sympathy for their expensive, electronic troops anyway, so here we sit. The saddest aspect of all is not our remaining here. It is rather the ease with which the American public has been bought off. When the number of "GI's" or "American soldiers" being killed is practically nil, the antiwar fervor dwindles. But this sub-continent remains the scene of battles and deaths and sadness. Most people simply cannot be concerned with the deaths of Indo-Chinese. And Nixon's attitudes on the draft evaders is really a sin. The potential for good is there if he could only embrace it.[33]

1971 December—North Vietnamese and allied indigenous forces open
new offensives in Laos and Cambodia.

---

*This parody of a military bulletin board notice indicates the feelings of
many U.S. servicemen in Vietnam at the end of 1971.*

Yearly GI'S Bulletin

NUMBER 69   CHRISTMAS EVE

EFFECTIVE UNTIL ETS [ESTIMATED TIME OF SEPARATION] UNLESS SOONER SENT
HOME DUE TO TERMINATION

1. *DETAILS FOR THE WEEK*: NONE
2. THE FOLLOWING CHRISTMAS SONG IS QUOTED FOR INFORMATION AND COMPLI-
ANCE

CHRISTMAS IN VIETNAM

(TO JINGLE BELLS)

DASHING THROUGH THE MUD, IN A JEEP THAT SHOULD BE JUNK,
OVER THE ROADS WE GO, HALF OF US ARE DRUNK.
WHEELS ON DIRT ROADS BOUNCE, MAKING ASSES SORE,
LORD I'D SOONER GO TO HELL THAN FINISH OUT THIS WAR.
CHORUS: JINGLE BELLS, MORTAR SHELLS, VC IN THE GRASS,
               WE'LL GET NO MERRY CHRISTMAS CHEER UNTIL THIS YEAR HAS
                  PASSED.
               JINGLE BELLS, MORTAR SHELLS, VC IN THE GRASS,
               TAKE YOUR MERRY CHRISTMAS CHEER AND SHOVE IT UP YOUR ASS.

CHRISTMAS TIME IS HERE, AS EVERYBODY DUCKS,
PEOPLE THINK IT'S DEAR, GI'S THINK IT SUCKS.
ALL AT HOME ARE GAY, CHILDREN ARE AT PLAY,
WHILE WE ARE STUCK OUT HERE SO GOD-DAMNED FAR AWAY.

CHORUS: JINGLE BELLS, MORTAR SHELLS, VC IN THE GRASS,
               WE'LL GET NO MERRY CHRISTMAS CHEER UNTIL THIS YEAR HAS
                  PASSED.
               JINGLE BELLS, MORTAR SHELLS, VC IN THE GRASS,
               TAKE YOUR MERRY CHRISTMAS CHEER AND SHOVE IT UP YOUR ASS.

THE MORAL OF OUR SONG, IT'S PLAIN AS IT CAN BE,
PLEASE NO MORE MIDNIGHT CAROLS SING AND SCREW YOUR CHRISTMAS TREE.
THERE'S ONE MORE THING LEFT TO SAY, BEFORE WE HAVE TO LEAVE,
VIETNAM IS NOT THE PLACE TO BE ON CHRISTMAS EVE.

CHORUS: JINGLE BELLS, MORTAR SHELLS, VC IN THE GRASS,
               WE'LL GET NO MERRY CHRISTMAS CHEER UNTIL THIS YEAR HAS
                  PASSED.
               JINGLE BELLS, MORTAR SHELLS, VC IN THE GRASS,
               TAKE YOUR MERRY CHRISTMAS CHEER AND SHOVE IT UP YOUR ASS.[34]

1971 31 December		
	TOTAL	NET CHANGE
U.S. military personnel assigned in Vietnam	156,800	−177,800
U.S. casualties	YEAR	TO DATE (cumulative)
Killed in action	1,381	45,626
Wounded in action	8,936	302,375

Source: DOD/OASD

1972

As 1972 begins, the peace talks still seem stalled.

Latest U.S./South Vietnamese Peace Plan Detailed

Background: Late in 1969, President Nixon initiated a series of high-level private negotiations with North Vietnam to explore the possibility of new approaches to a peace settlement. On January 25, 1972, he laid the record of these secret negotiations before the American people along with the full details of our latest peace plan.

U.S./SOUTH VIETNAMESE PROPOSALS
WITHDRAWAL OF FORCES·

—All U.S./Allied forces would withdraw from South Vietnam within six months of an agreement in principle on an overall settlement.

—Our withdrawals (together with prisoner releases) would start as soon as such an agreement is reached and would continue while a final agreement covering such political issues as elections is worked out. Our withdrawals would be completed when a final agreement is signed. .

—We do not insist on withdrawal of enemy forces at the same time as U.S./Allied forces withdraw. We ask only that Hanoi accept the principle that all armed forces of the countries of Indochina must remain within their national frontiers. Without abandoning the principle of mutuality, we are flexible on timing and willing to withdraw our forces before North Vietnam withdraws its forces.

—Alternatively, we are willing to fix a date for the unilateral withdrawal of U.S./Allied forces provided all prisoners are released and there is agreement on a cease-fire.

RELEASE OF PRISONERS

—Prisoners of war (PWs) would be released concurrently with U.S. troop withdrawals, beginning as soon as an overall agreement in principle has been reached.

—Alternatively, PWs would be released as part of an agreement only on military issues, including a fixed date for U.S. withdrawal and a cease-fire.

—Or, as we proposed in October 1970, we are ready to negotiate separately the immediate, unconditional release of all prisoners as a simple act of humanity.

CEASE-FIRE

—There should be a cease-fire throughout Indochina, to begin when an overall agreement is signed and to include a prohibition on further infiltration of North Vietnamese forces into other countries of Indochina.

—Alternatively, we would negotiate a cease-fire as part of an agreement on PW releases and U.S./Allied withdrawal, rather than as part of an overall agreement.

POLITICAL SETTLEMENT

—A free, democratic presidential election would be held in South Vietnam within six months of the signing of a final agreement.

—An independent body would be set up as soon as final agreement is reached to organize and run the election.

—All political forces, including the National Liberation Front (NLF), could participate in the election and be represented in the independent electoral body.

—There would be international supervision of the election.

—The President and Vice President of South Vietnam would resign one month before the election. The Chairman of the South Vietnamese Senate, as caretaker head of the Government, would assume administrative responsibilities except for those involving the election.

—All U.S./Allied forces would be withdrawn before the election.

OTHER MAJOR ELEMENTS

—Both sides would respect the 1954 and 1962 Geneva accords.

—South Vietnam, along with the other countries of Indochina, would adopt a foreign policy consistent with the military provisions of the 1954 Geneva accords.

—There would be international supervision of the military elements of an agreement.

—The U.S. would accept limitations on its military and economic assistance to South Vietnam, if North Vietnam accepts limitations on aid from its allies.

—The U.S. would be prepared to undertake a massive post-war reconstruction program in Indochina of several billion dollars, in which North Vietnam could share.

NORTH VIETNAM/NLF POSITION

The other side does not accept our eight-point peace plan and continues to insist that their position as set forth in the July 1971 "seven-point proposal" and February 1972 "elaboration" be accepted as a basis for agreement. Their two fundamental demands—total, unconditional U.S./Allied withdrawal by a fixed date and the replacement of Saigon's current leadership by a coalition regime—have not changed.

Their current proposals, in brief, include the following principal elements:

—Unconditional U.S./Allied withdrawal including cessation of air activity directed against Vietnam;

—The Vietnamese themselves will settle the problem of "Vietnamese forces in South Vietnam";

—Prisoners will be released on the terminal date of U.S./Allied withdrawal provided an overall agreement is reached;

—The immediate resignation of President Thieu, an end to the present Saigon Government's "warlike policy" and the dismantling of its "oppressive machinery";

—Elections after these steps are taken and a new coalition regime has been set up.[35]

1972   26 January—Radio Hanoi broadcasts DRV's rejection of President Nixon's proposals. **21–28 February**—President Nixon visits the People's Republic of China.

Five weeks later, as seen in this chapter from Walter McDonald's unpublished novel Waiting for the End, *some American officers are taking their daily exercise.*

The Track

By noon Bien Dien sweltered in heat, the humid air heavy like deep depression. The clouds had not built far enough to block out the sun, which beat down almost too bright to see. For the first time since the rocket blast last night, the base was quiet, as if totally shut down. I could not hear a jet or bombs or gunfire anywhere. The whole war seemed to have been called off.

I felt my back baking already as Lebowitz guided me, jogging the three blocks to the track, a dirt oval bulldozed around a field laid out for football but covered now in dead yellow grass, a collapsing rusting goalpost at each end. Lebowitz said that in the old days, with a half million Americans in Vietnam, the base was famous as Bien Dien-by-the-Sea, its beaches a favorite R and R center. But after most of the troops were withdrawn, there weren't enough left for proper patrols, and the VC began mining the beaches. Now they were off limits, and jogging was the best hot way to relax.

A road paralleled the track and cut north to the flight line a few blocks away, hidden by hangars and quonset huts. Along the other side of the field were wooden bleachers built between the forty yard lines, a platform at the fifty like a parade reviewing stand. Behind the bleachers a sagging cyclone fence ran the length of the field and on beyond were rows and rows of tin and wooden shacks where Vietnamese airmen lived with their families. And at the far end of the field, beyond a great wall smothered with vines, there was a huge French mansion with a red roof and trees everywhere around it, like parts of the jungle.

There were a dozen or more men in trunks already on the track, some of them jogging fast, some shuffling along with their heads down, their arms hanging. Lebowitz drew the towel from his neck and wiped his face and threw the towel on the field. His thin face was drawn, almost emaciated, and his eyes were deep set in dark hollow sockets, his stiff hair pepper white.

"Six times around for a mile," he said, not breaking stride.

"How many miles do you go?" I asked, my bones already heavy in the heat.

"Four, five, I'll let you know."

He ran light on his feet, a thin man with long muscles. He kept his fists straight out in front of him, knuckles up. He was taller than me by several inches, his long stride hitting three for my four. His high voice chattered like a separate thing that could not be winded.

"See that guy rounding the endzone? That's Fleming. He runs every day. The only guy here who can outlast me."

"Yeah," I said, still trying to fall in with his pace. "I see him."

Fresh from the States, I was used to handball and an indoor track, and running here in this humidity was like treading deep water with boots on.

I watched Fleming round the turn and enter the straightaway, running fast with determined desperate lunges past a group of slower joggers and along the row of Vietnamese shacks. Two or three children broke from the bushes and ran toward the track, whirling and darting away out of sight as Fleming ran past. When the children broke toward the group following him, one of the men lunged at them and the children scattered.

We approached the turn and the old wall of the French estate towered before us, lush with vines, shaded by the great limbs of trees beyond the walls.

"The Frenchman's place," Lebowitz said, tossing his thumb at the wall. "It's their private club, now."

I had read about Bien Dien before leaving Saigon. I knew it was one of the American bases built in the sixties, bulldozed not merely out of jungle but out of an old French colonial plantation on the bay by the name of Bien Dien. At the peak of United States involvement, eighteen thousand

Americans crowded the base, along with a handful of French still running their plantation and a few hundred Vietnamese. Now, only four hundred Americans remained, and thousands of Vietnamese, and still the handful of French, who lived apart and never troubled themselves with Americans except invitations to the base commander and his staff at Christmas and the fourth of July and Bastille Day.

I heard a board thudding just beyond the wall and then a splash cut trimly into water.

"Swimming pool," Lebowitz said, his face parallel to the wall, his fists pumping. "Those cats still think they're in the Promised Land."

We turned down the backstretch and came even with the shacks. There was an awful smell, like rotten cabbages and wine.

"You numbah ten!" a child's voice screamed, the worst insult possible. "You 'mericans numbah ten!"

Lebowitz never turned his head toward that supreme insult, just kept jogging the same steady pace. And when the child screamed at us again, Lebowitz called back friendly, "You numbah one! You numbah one, boychild!"

He answered my silence as we jogged on. "Want to trade places with them?"

"No way," I said.

"You're right," he said. "No way. If we can't be friends with the kids, there's no way."

Shackler and Malatesta arrived from the officers' hootches, and we fell in behind them as they entered the track, jogging heavily. Shackler lunged along, leaning forward like a heavyweight, but Malatesta brought his knees high and trotted with his shoulders thrust back as if he were marching.

"They hit the village again?" Lebowitz called.

"Naw," Shackler replied, not looking back. "Must be getting ready to hit the base."

Rumors. At breakfast someone had said three NVA divisions had crossed the demilitarized zone and were last detected twenty kilometers north of the base. Estimates of casualties from last night's mortar attack ran as high as dozens of Americans and hundreds of Vietnamese killed and god knows how many wounded. Someone said the VC had overrun half of Plei Nhon and massacred scores of villagers during the night.

I waited for someone else to speak, but all ran quietly, all alone. Now and then we would fall into step and there would be the thump thump thump of our running. Then the steps would syncopate and break rhythm and in the heavy depressing heat ˙ would find myself having to concentrate to maintain stride.

Fleming caught us in the second lap and passed without looking, his breath heaving, the tendons in his neck stretched tight. He was a good-looking kid with blond hair and flushed cheeks and he looked too young to be out of high school. He raced on, as if trying to outdistance fear.

Each time we passed the great wall I would listen and once I thought I heard sensual laughter, and another time I heard music, slow and light and peaceful, like Paris in springtime.

A muscular, middle-aged man ran past us, deeply tanned, an old sergeant or a colonel, his stiff white hair glistening with sweat. Around his waist was a wide leather back support, gleaming black, a .38 holstered on one side and a knife scabbard stitched to the other.

"Watch him," Lebowitz said. "He won't go near the shacks."

Sure enough, the man ran swiftly along the inside of the track, next to the football field.

"Hates kids?" I asked.

"Naw," he said, grinning. "Just afraid someone's gonna nail him before it's over. He's not the only one."

After three laps Shackler and Malatesta dropped out, panting heavily, but Lebowitz jogged on, staring ahead. I glanced at them walking slowly back towards the quarters, their arms limp. I felt more like that than running, but something in my legs kept going and after a few paces I caught up with Lebowitz again.

"It all counts towards DEROS," he said grimly. Date of Earliest Return from Overseas: months, impossible months from now.

We must have jogged around that track for an hour. One by one the others dropped out and returned to the quarters for showers and back to duty. After awhile there were only Lebowitz and I and, lapping us every two or three rounds, Fleming, haunting the day with his fear.

Lebowitz paced me like a record spinning around and around, lap after lap. I caught my mind wandering off the track, dozing, drugged with fatigue and the heat. I no longer heard the children jeering at us, only now and then a woman's high strange scolding from inside the shacks or a crying baby. I listened for the swimming pool to splash again or for music, but there were not even birds singing in the Frenchman's jungle beyond the wall. After awhile even Lebowitz hushed and there was only the thump of our toes jogging on dirt.

My lungs numbed in the heat and my legs came to feel like things apart, able to go on and on. My eyes burned with sweat, and I squinted so tight I could hardly see anymore, and because they stung it was impossible to think. I was adjusting, though, lost in rhythm, like a mechanical animal caught on the rim of existence, going round and round, getting closer to DEROS. It felt good and I was slipping deep in dreams when I heard a noise with my name on it.

"Moose. It's time, Moose," Lebowitz called.

I jolted to a halt off the track and dropped my arms. My hands were numb. I heard jets roaring from the flight line. Drenched in sweat, tasting salt and iodine, I shuddered. It was overcast, the sky boiling with clouds, and in the distance there was thunder, or bombs, and I had the feeling there was still a long, long way to go.[36]

An official U.S. Air Force history describes what the joggers hear as "thunder, or bombs."

The hammer fell on Easter Weekend, 1972. Soon after midnight, in the early-morning darkness of Good Friday, 30 March, thousands of Communist mortar, rocket, and artillery rounds began battering South Vietnamese positions along the northern border of the Republic. By mid-day, multitudes of North Vietnamese regulars had moved across the so-called Demilitarized Zone (DMZ), assaulting fire bases and linking with other Communist units already to the south. Bewildered by the mass and ferocity of the attacks and the pressures on their communications, the defenders quickly fell back from the advanced posts.

For the next several days, thick overcasts, low ceilings, and rain helped shield the Communists in the DMZ region from air attack. The invasion was open and direct—largely absent were those tactics of camouflage and dispersion typical of Communist methods in the past. Three North Vietnamese divisions—some 40,000 troops in all—delivered the main blows, driving against Quang Tri city and later, Hue. Further weight came from certain weapons seldom or never seen previously in South Vietnam. Among these were the Soviet T-54, T-34, and older PT-76 tanks, the Soviet-made SA-2 and SA-7 anti-aircraft missiles, the Russian 130-mm. gun, and the AT-3 wire-guided anti-tank missile. The 130-mm. gun, with a firing range of 17 miles, was especially effective in sustaining the invasion. Defending the region were largely untested South Vietnamese infantry, reinforced by two brigades of Vietnamese Marines and the local Regional and Popular Forces. Fewer than 9,000 men spread over the northernmost 300 square miles—a force clearly inferior to the attackers.

A second major Communist invasion took form simultaneously, gaining momentum in the forested and rugged highlands north and west of Pleiku. Moderate-scale attacks on the region's fire support bases began on 30 March. Within a few days, pressures intensified on more than a dozen posts, including the ridge positions west of Kontum and Dak To. Communist units threatened the important roadway between Pleiku and Kontum, and on 3 April occupied high ground near the Dak To airfield, bringing it under artillery fire and closing down air operations. By mid-April, the invading force in Military Region II included about 20,000 troops, most of whom had entered Vietnam since the first of the month. Communist objectives included the several bases and towns in the highlands, apparently with the idea of establishing full political control of the region. Other attacks on district towns in coastal regions, and efforts against supply lines connecting Pleiku to the coast, threatened, in effect, to divide Vietnam in half.

Although the South Vietnamese had anticipated the appearance of some tanks in the highlands, the mass and variety of heavy equipment used by the Communists was a surprise. As in Military Region I, the Communists deployed several variations of the T-54 and PT-76, and the track mounted

twin 57-mm. anti-aircraft gun with target acquisition radar. The North
Vietnamese secretly moved this weaponry into position prior to the assaults over new roads built beneath the thick jungle canopy.

A third major drive unfolded in the border provinces immediately
north and northwest of Saigon. The Allies had been aware since early
March of concentrated Viet Cong propaganda efforts in the regions between Cambodia and Saigon. The first attacks came in the rubber plantation region of northern Tay Ninh province—600 rounds of recoilless rifle
and rocket rounds pounded the fire support base at Lac Long at dawn 2
April. Two days later Communist tanks carried the position. The pressures in Tay Ninh, however, were but diversions for the main blows
launched by three Communist divisions on 5 April in Binh Long Province. The main objectives in Binh Long were the towns and airfields in
Loc Ninh, An Loc, and Quan Loi, along with positions astride highway
13, the main roadway connecting the region with Saigon. Again, Communist purposes appeared both political and military—first to establish a
regional government, and second, to prepare for possible further operations against more vital objectives such as Saigon itself. As elsewhere, the
Binh Long drive featured the employment of substantial numbers of
tanks and weaponry more advanced than that used in the past.

Both sides recognized the pivotal significance of the moment. President
Thieu called upon his nation to rally, describing the invasions as "the
final battle to decide the survival of the people." Hanoi, captured documents later indicated, believed that anti-war factions in America would
limit any strong reaction to the invasion; the Communists expected the
battlefield victories would inflict losses on American forces, defeat the
Vietnamization program, and undermine Nixon's stature at home.[37]

The official air force history documents some specific episodes.

An American Air Force Captain guided his OV-10 Bronco through the
layers of overcast, concentrating on his flight instruments but alert for
those glimpses of terrain that would permit transition to visual reference.
The pilot's mission was to locate survivors of an EB-66 electronic warfare
ship, downed a few hours earlier near the Demilitarized Zone (DMZ)
dividing the two Vietnams. Since the start of the Communist attacks on
the fire support bases above Quang Tri three days earlier, Allied airmen
had strenuously tried to work the region to combat the yet unclear enemy
thrust. Constant low ceilings and poor visibility, however, had masked
the full strength and movements of the North Vietnamese invaders.

Almost directly over the Ben Hai River, at the center of the DMZ, the
OV-10 broke into the clear. Staying under the low clouds, the pilot
"jinked" hurriedly back and forth to avoid small-arms fire from below.
The young officer radioed excitedly to another OV-10 still overhead: "My
God, you should see the people down here—all over the place—People,
Tanks, Trucks, the whole nine yards—and everybody is shooting." Cap-

tain Richard M. Atchison, listening in the second OV-10 overhead, remembered, "that's when we knew that big things were coming." . . .

In preparing for the invasion, the North Vietnamese vastly expanded their anti-aircraft capabilities in the region. Allied pilots reported that the intensity of fire near the DMZ was equal to that encountered during earlier raids in the Hanoi area. Besides the 23-mm., 37-mm., and 57-mm. weapons used in the past, the Communists introduced 85-mm. and 100-mm. guns into and south of the DMZ. In the weeks before the invasion, Allied pilots realized that the Communists were also bringing in significant numbers of surface-to-air missiles. Lt Colonel Gabriel A. Kardong, commander of the USAF FAC unit at DaNang, elaborated on the missile build-up:

> The SA–2 missile was considered a threat only in North Vietnam and parts of Laos until the latter part of January 72. Preparatory to the April invasion the DMZ area was jammed with hundreds of AAA pieces, artillery, and SAM–2 missiles. On the 17th of February I narrowly evaded a SAM–2 while flying at 1,200 feet in the DMZ. That day, 81 SA–2's were fired in the DMZ area and downed three F–4 aircraft. . . .

Here is one account of a SAM encounter by an OV-10 crew-member:

> They started to hammer us hard. We got a SAM warning, I looked up and saw three of them high, and just about the time Rocky started to break, I saw two more coming low. The two low ones passed behind us, the three high started to come down on us. Suddenly I saw a big puff, beepers are going off and just as we were coming up to the beach, I heard a call coming from Covey 282. They were hit about two miles off our left wing— he just flat went down. We were doing our own act—Rocky broke to the right, but a SAM was coming from the tail; whether it had gone up and made a turn, I'll never know, but Rocky took the aircraft and put it straight down and the SAM went off in full view of the canopy at about 300 feet. Shook us up badly, we had to go over the beach and take a water bottle break. . . .

On the afternoon of 2 April, two EB-66's (Bat-21 and 22) out of Thailand were flying eastward just south of the DMZ. The two electronic warfare craft were escorting a cell of B-52's, bombing near the DMZ. Bat-21 carried a six-man crew which included a pilot, navigator, and four electronic warfare officers (EWO). Three SAM's were launched at Bat-21. One of the EWO's called a SAM missile warning on the right side of the aircraft. That meant that the SAM had been fired from inside South Vietnam. The missile hit the plane directly in the ECM compartment area, and the bird went down. One "beeper" came on the air [when an aviator bails out of his aircraft, his survival radio is activated and starts sending out an audible "beeping" signal on emergency frequencies], that from the navigator's survival radio. Apparently he was the only one who bailed out.

Captain Jimmie D. Kempton, piloting an OV-10 out of DaNang AB, talked to Bat-21's navigator, Lt Colonel Iceal E. Hambleton, as he descended in his chute. The area was completely blanketed by clouds so getting an exact position on the survivor was difficult. Capt Kempton descended under the clouds and located Hambleton visually, his chute still visible from the air.

Concidentally, an airborne search and rescue task force [a typical air rescue task force included one or two HH-53 "Super Jolly Green" rescue helicopters and 4–8 A–1E propeller driven attack aircraft] was operating nearby. It had been launched from DaNang to evacuate some U.S. Army advisors from Quang Tri but that mission had been cancelled. Two A-1's from the rescue force, Sandy 07 and 08, heard the emergency calls and headed north toward Hambleton's position. Amid intense ground fire, the Skyraider pilots spent the next couple of hours talking with Hambleton on the radio and trying to keep the North Vietnamese from capturing him. The A-1's were flying under low clouds hanging over the river valley, which made the job ever tougher.

Working with Hambleton was an experience that none of the Sandy pilots would ever forget. He called off positions of fire, watched the ordnance impact, and gave the crews corrections based on his observations. Hambleton could see and hear troops within 100 meters of his position. During these crucial hours, "he saved his own life by maintaining his cool."

Meanwhile, Kempton had flown southward, making calls to find someone to go in and pick up Hambleton. Soon he was returning with four U.S. Army helicopters in tow—two UH-1B "Cobra" gunships and two UH-1H passenger-carrying "slicks." Approaching Hambleton's position, two of the four choppers were shot down. One UH-1H was completely destroyed with no survivors. The Cobra, Blue Ghost 28, was able to reach the beach, and its two crewmen were soon picked up. But darkness was approaching fast. There would be no pickup for Colonel Hambleton that night.

At 2100 hours, Nail 59 relieved the DaNang FAC's. Nail 59 was flying a new version of the OV-10 aircraft with the Pave Nail system on board [Pave Nail OV–10's were equipped with precision Loran c/o navigation equipment, a light intensification viewer, a laser designator, and a computer system; two crewmen were used—pilot and weapon systems operator]. The Pave Nail precision Loran equipment had proved itself on rescue operations by providing accurate survivor position information at night and in bad weather. Nail 59 made contact with Hambleton on the ground. By using a series of radio bearings off the survival radio and their Loran equipment, Nail established his exact position in a few minutes. Hambleton was about a thousand meters north of the town of Cam Lo on the north bank of the Mien Giang River.

MIXING RESCUE AND WAR

Throughout the night, FAC's from DaNang and Nakhon Phanom (NKP), Thailand, maintained continuous patrol over Hambleton [FAC's from

DaNang AB, South Vietnam had call signs Covey and Bilk while the
FAC's from NKP in Thailand used the call sign Nail]. Shortly before
dawn on April 3, two Pave Nail OV-10's from NKP—one crewed by
Captain Rocky O. Smith and Captain Richard M. Atchison—underwent
briefings and pre-flight preparations, leaving NKP so as to arrive over
Bat-21 at first light.

Hambleton had meanwhile taken refuge in a big clump of bushes surrounded by a very large field, and reported that there were North Vietnamese troops still all around. The first task for the overhead FAC's, then,
was to put down a ring of area-denial ordnance, surrounding Hambleton's
position. Because of the foul weather, visual airstrikes were not possible.
Smith and Atchison relayed the Loran coordinates of Hambleton's position back to the Task Force Alpha targeting center at NKP for analysis.
There, personnel checked recent photography of the area, corrected the
target coordinates for mapping errors, and put together the information
necessary for Loran airstrikes [this procedure had been developed in a
joint FAC–Task Force Alpha program and used extensively in previous
rescue operations in 1971–1972]. The strike data was then passed back to
the FAC's on the scene. Within hours, Smith and Atchison were clearing
in flights of fighters. The fighters used their Loran bombing equipment to
place the ordnance down around Hambleton's position.

Smith and Atchison landed at DaNang instead of their home station in
Thailand. They met with the Covey FAC's and Army advisors there and
explained their capability, exchanged target information, and established
a zone of operation north of the Cam Lo River. In this safety zone
around the survivor, the U.S. Air Force would control all airstrikes and
artillery fire.

On the second day of the operation, an SA-2 claimed Nail 38, with Bill
Henderson and Mark Clark on board. . . . Atchison gave this account:

> Just as they started to turn, they caught it right in the tail booms. Blew
> that OV–10 to pieces. Just a tumbling ball of fire, sailing down to the
> river. Two chutes came out of the fireball—beautiful. Mark landed south
> of the river, south and east of Hambleton. Henderson landed north in a
> big field—within 500 meters of Bat–21. Henderson told me after his re-
> lease that ten or fifteen people came out of the woods and chased him. He
> found a clump of bamboo and jumped in—they couldn't find him. That
> night a group came out and started cutting down the bamboo. They used
> it for camouflage. They worked right over Bill's shelter. He doubled up
> with machetes going over his head. They cut all of his bamboo down—he
> was then taken north. Mark found a barbed wire enclosed area—figured it
> was a good place to hide. He crawled under the wire. We worked the
> whole area over with Loran weapon deliveries—then the clouds broke and
> we worked the fighters visually.

For the rest of that day and the next two days, the FAC's and fighters
worked the area over. There were plenty of targets, since the Army
advisors had selected about 600 in addition to the North Vietnamese

artillery fire bases. Reports of tanks moving down from the DMZ promised further good hunting.

One episode illustrated the meaning of battlefield interdiction. A
"Covey" FAC out of DaNang spotted a column of tanks moving down
Highway One (The Street Without Joy) toward Dong Ha City. He called
a Pave Nail FAC to come over and take a look—get a good position on
them.

> It was one of our preplanned targets. In fact the column was moving
> between two preplanned targets, so we went on secure voice and started
> it back through Task Force Alpha to 7th Air Force. In about 30 minutes
> 6 "Bufs" [B–52's] came in and rippled that road. They got 35 tanks, and
> we found out later the command bunker of the NVA division in that
> area.

For the rest of that day and the next two days Seventh Air Force worked
the whole area over heavily. Objectives were twofold—first, to stop the
invasion forces, disrupt their movement and cut their supply lines, and
second, to beat down the defenses around Hambleton and Clark so that a
pickup could be made. After several days of continuous air attack, the
area looked relatively quiet. A FAC said later,

> We had bombed it, we had destroyed all the troop camps, all the bridges,
> and the headquarters buildings, all the fire bases inside that area. There
> was no movement.

On 6 April, the first attempt was made to pick up the two survivors. Jolly
62, the rescue helicopter, was escorted by a flight of A-1E Sandys, entering from the southeast. The plan was to run in over Clark's position on a
northwesterly heading, cross the river and the road, pick up Hambleton,
make a left turn, pick up Clark about one kilometer away, and exit out to
the South.

Jolly 62 got across the river safely, but as they started to go for Bat-21,
they came under fire from a village. Jolly 62 was really getting hosed
down—they started to turn right, heading right for the village, when
somebody in the helicopter pressed down on the radio transmit button. . . . The FAC and the Sandys were screaming "turn left, don't turn
right, turn left." But Jolly 62 couldn't hear because that mike button was
down. The right turn put them into more heavy machine gun fire, sieving
the helicopter. The Sandy pilots watched as Jolly 62 limped back across
the river, but "a flame shot out below the main rotor . . . the helicopter
nosed up, rolled left 90°, and pieces started falling from the aircraft . . . it
hit the ground on its left side . . . fire continued to burn . . . finally
consuming the entire aircraft." Clark had also been watching from his
location south of the river, and had seen a North Vietnamese signalman
on the river bank with a big red scarf. Whenever aircraft came in at low
level, he would wave his scarf, and all hell would break loose. That scarf
activated every gun in the area.[38]

1972   6 April—Authorized by President Nixon, Operation "Rolling Thunder," the bombing of North Vietnam, resumes.

An official secret air force monograph written shortly afterward details a significant battle occurring at another provincial capital, An Loc.

On 12 April, President Thieu visited Binh Long Province to survey the battlefield situation and to emphasize his role as commander in chief. He made a public statement that district capitals might be abandoned, but that provincial capitals were to be defended at all costs. Colonel Miller stated that for Thieu, An Loc was "a Bastogne, a place where a stand or die defense would decide the fate of the enemy offensive closest to the national capital." When the actual battle for An Loc began on the following day, U.S. Ambassador Bunker pointed out that the battle had to be considered of "major psychological importance" because of Thieu's public statements.

By the night of 12/13 April, "ringed by enemy regiments, battered by enemy artillery, roofed with anti-aircraft fire with defenders driven into the perimeter of the town itself," the VC/NVA considered An Loc ready for capture. Artillery was heavy all day on the twelfth and throughout most of the evening until it reached a "crescendo" after 0300. At 0530, the indirect fire touched off the ammunition dump and POL storage areas. At 0730, out of the northeast, two dozen tanks including PT-76s led a major ground attack against An Loc.

At 0800, as the noise of indirect fire diminished, the rumble of T-54 tanks was heard in the streets of An Loc. The tanks rode in "cockily" with turrets open and commanders in view. Led to believe that the VC already occupied the city, the crews were exercising great care so that they would not shoot troops in the streets. They thought their mission was a ceremonial one—to go to the Provincial Chief's residence and run up the North Vietnamese flag. The ARVN troops in the streets quickly disposed of this myth by immobilizing the lead tanks with M-72 Light Anti-Tank Weapons (LAWs). Cobra helicopter gunships also took a heavy toll of the tanks with FFAR rockets. Thus the first attack was blunted through a combination of enemy ignorance and aggressive action by allied forces.

A second ground attack from the northwest began at 1015. ARVN airborne troops moving from the south to relieve An Loc met battalion sized resistance about the same time, thereby stopping the relief column. By 1330 the invading forces, including tanks, controlled the airstrip on the northeast in addition to the northern half of An Loc itself. At this time, General Hollingsworth received an inquiry from the Senior U.S. Adviser to the ARVN 5th Division concerning withdrawal of all American advisers as had been past policy in such situations. Hollingsworth decided to keep key American advisers at An Loc and Army advisers later said that they thought this decision was a big one in the allied success in holding the capital.[39]

Meanwhile, as noted in the air force history, the attempt to rescue the two downed American pilots continues.

The rescue had become an important struggle within the larger battle, as Allied airmen continued to sow the "circle of hate" around their men, and punish the gun positions and troops that fired on the Jollys and Sandys. The two survivors continued to hide and evade while remaining in contact with their small survival radios. Hambleton said later that "The radio was the most wonderful thing I had. I made it last 12 days on one battery. . . . the radio was my biggest help."

The area around Hambleton and Clark was still pretty hot. Some of the airmen wanted to try another pickup, others said no—too risky. There was talk about putting in a U.S. Army light observation helicopter at night. As the FAC's talked to the Army advisors at DaNang about the possibilities,

> In walked a U.S. Marine Colonel, built like a fire hydrant. He said, "I understand you have people you want taken out." Yes sir, we do. "Well, I have a full carrier of guys that would love to do that." We showed him where they were—he took a Marine ground team amd some ARVN rangers and they went up the river.

After receiving word of the new plan Clark and Hambleton started working their way down river to meet the Marines. Clark was closest to the river. He swam and floated down river and met the team first. Hambleton had to come through a mile of mine field—it took four hours to reach the river. After resting, he crossed the river, found a log and began floating downstream. After dawn, he hid in the foliage along the bank.

For three nights, Hambleton made his way slowly down river, his progress constantly followed by the FAC's. On the fourth day he sighted a sampan; using a pre-arranged signal he called out his rank and favorite color. The Marines on the sampan acknowledged—they took Hambleton aboard and covered him with leaves. The ordeal was nearly over. After 12 days, Bat-21 was on the way home.[40]

At An Loc, even though the first two North Vietnamese attacks have been repulsed, the city is under siege.

Surrounded by artillery, anti-aircraft weapons, and ground troops, general conditions in the city steadily deteriorated. In addition to the government military forces in An Loc, there were approximately 10,000 civilians, mostly refugees, who added to the already serious water, sewerage, food, and shelter problems. The VC/NVA fully realized that these civilians greatly complicated the problems of the defenders of An Loc, and they made every effort to guide additional refugees into the city and to keep all the civilians confined to the besieged area. Major Raymond Haney, a U.S. adviser to the ARVN 5th Infantry Division at An Loc, related that a French/Vietnamese priest and, later, Buddhist monks, attempted to evacuate civilian refugees to the south. On both occasions the VC/NVA shelled the refugees, driving them back into the city. Haney saw the aftermath of the shelling—fallen refugees "laying in the ditches like cordwood."

Under such conditions, morale of the defenders had to be strengthened if the enemy siege was to fail. This was to prove an enormous task. Shortages of food and water would have been a sufficient detriment to morale in themselves. Perhaps even more eroding on morale, however, were medical and sanitation problems. At first all the seriously wounded were kept in the hospital—military and civilians alike. On the night of 13 April, the hospital and its 300 patients became the target for hostile 105mm and 155mm shells, resulting in the total destruction of the hospital and most of the patients as well. With no hospital facility available and medicines in short supply, wounds sustained during shelling and battle did not receive adequate medical care at An Loc. Unable to be medevaced out because of the intense AAA, the ARVN troops watched their wounds redden, fester in the heat, and turn gangrenous. Commanders and buddies could only try to keep flies away from the wounds and hope that no more of them would get hurt. To sustain a serious head, chest, or stomach wound was almost always a death sentence. Innumerable cases of disease, including cholera, spread quickly among the defenders imprisoned in the bunkered shelters for hours at a time during intense shelling. Under such conditions, even the barest minimums of sanitation could not be achieved and accumulated filth hastened the spread of disease and misery. The untreated wounds, diseases, and indirect fire led to so many dead that it became necessary to resort to mass burials in shallow graves using lime dropped from aircraft.

Intensifying the problems, the shortages and the inconveniences, the pain and the apprehension, was the shelling, day after day, minute after minute. The accurate enemy guns destroyed almost everything of material value to the defending forces. Even when the ARVN gun crews attempted to confuse the hostile gunners by constantly shifting positions of government guns, the new positions were quickly spotted and shelled. Most enemy observation points were from positions outside the defense perimeter. While they poured sniper fire into the defense positions, hostile troops on rooftops in the northern part of An Loc relayed information to VC/NVA. Within the defense perimeter six young women were discovered with radio transmitters concealed in their brassieres. Accused of relaying information to enemy gun crews, the women were tied up and left "in an impact area where NVA artillery subsequently killed them."

The point of discussing the conditions on the ground in the besieged city is to show why the ground commanders so desperately sought aerial support for resupply and medical evacuation. Unless these two things could be achieved, An Loc was lost. Intelligence reports indicated that the VC/NVA were counting on the rapidly accumulating morale problems to force surrender of the city and to encourage ARVN desertion. At this time, Colonel Miller asserted that the enemy "enjoyed" the fact of no resupply and no helicopters landing. He asserted that "come hell or high water, both should be accomplished."

From the first days of the battle, allied commanders realized the importance of aerial resupply, but the problem was considered to be more of a logistical management one rather than one in which supplies would have to be "fought through" to the defenders. The first days' experience did little to change this apparent view. From 7–19 April, the Vietnamese and American CH-47s and VNAF C-123s and HU-1B helicopters flew 93 sorties delivering 301 tons of supplies. Unless one of these supply missions aborted prior to drop, all consigned goods were received by the government centrally constituted supply authorities. Outside the defense perimeter the VC/NVA needed supplies for survival also. Thus furious fire fights occurred over stray bundles falling down between the opposing forces.

Frustration was everywhere—in the air and on the ground—over the seemingly hopeless task of supplying the city. As the days went by, direct fire grew heavier and was increasingly more accurate. This heavy fire contributed greatly to the poor drop and recovery results, and ground commanders were concerned that drops were becoming more harmful than helpful to their cause. The classic example was that of a VC officer captured on the east side of town by ARVN defenders. While being interrogated, the officer requested a can of fruit cocktail because he said he had become accustomed to eating it since some American drops had been recovered by his unit. A U.S. officer who witnessed the scene, and who was subsisting on brackish water, canned fish, and rice, found the request extremely depressing.[41]

On 20 April the PRG (Communist Provisional Revolutionary Government) delegate to the Paris peace talks writes a letter to the U.S. Congress.

Letter from Mme. Nguyen Thi Binh to U.S. Congress
April 20, 1972

The honourable members of the U.S. Congress.

In the capacity of one of the leaders of the National Front for Liberation and the Provisional Revolutionary Government of the Republic of South Vietnam, I wish to write to you, on the present, extremely serious situation in Vietnam, a situation that concerns both our peoples and our countries.

For more than 3 years now, President Nixon has been making repeated promises to the American people about "U.S. disengagement" in Vietnam, but he has actually prolonged and expanded the war throughout Indochina and is dangerously intensifying the hostilities.

After pouring over 6 million tons of bombs and shells on our land since he took office, President Nixon is sending B–52 bombers, tactical aircraft and warships to release everyday thousands of tons of bombs and shells on North and South Vietnam, indiscriminately killing Vietnamese women and children. Going even farther than Mr. Johnson, President Nixon has ordered B–52's to bomb Hanoi, Haiphong and other populous areas of North Vietnam. Mr. Nixon said that such actions were necessary to "protect the lives of the American troops" and "to defend the self-determination" of the South Vietnamese people. In fact, he has thrown in the material strength and the honour of the United States in an attempt to maintain Nguyen Van Thieu, a hated U.S. agent whose immediate resignation is firmly demanded by the South Vietnamese people, and to preserve a regime which is symbolized by "tiger-cage" jail-cells built with the American people's money. This is what Mr. Nixon calls his policy of "Vietnamization" of the war.

For many years the American people have been deceived by the successive administrations in Washington about what was happening in Vietnam. The resolution on the so-called "Tonkin Gulf incident" allowed the Johnson administration to introduce over half a million U.S. troops to South Vietnam and to bomb North Vietnam. What did all this lead to? At present, by repeating about the so-called "invasion by North Vietnam," Mr. Nixon wants the United States to live again the same old tragedy, to embark on the path of new military adventures, to cause savage destructions and killings to a country whose people have done no harm whatsoever to the United States and its people. . . .

According to the U.S. Constitution, the Congress has the power to decide on the question of war and peace. Therefore, I urge you to stop President Nixon in taking an adventurous path fraught with unpredictable consequences. . . .

There is no other solution to the South Vietnam problem than that the Nixon administration should stop its intensification of the war in South Vietnam, end its escalation of the air war against North Vietnam, and resume the work of the Paris conference with a real desire to negotiate.

I am firmly confident that justice will overcome cruelty, and truth will overcome fallacy. Please accept, ladies and gentlemen, the assurances of my highest consideration.

[signed] Nguyen Thi Binh, member of Central Committee of the NFL, foreign minister of the PRG of the Republic of South Vietnam.[42]

The next day two members of the U.S. Congress visit Madame Binh in Paris.

Mme. Binh Receives Bella Abzug, Patsy Mink on 21 April

Liberation Radio [Clandestine] in Vietnamese to South Vietnam 1400 GMT 24 Apr 72 B

[Text] Minister Nguyen Thi Binh, head of the PRGRSV delegation to the Paris conference, on 21 April 1972, received Mrs. Bella Abzug, representative, Democrat, of New York, and Mrs. Patsy Mink, representative, Democrat of Hawaii.

The two representatives expressed indignation at the new bombings by the U.S. Government of both zones of Vietnam, particularly of Hanoi and Haiphong, and promised that they would step up their activities in the U.S. Congress to demand that the Nixon administration bring all U.S. troops home, end the bombing of North and South Vietnam, and resume the Paris conference on Vietnam.

Minister Nguyen Thi Binh clearly expounded the PRGRSV's stand at the Paris conference on Vietnam and stressed the South Vietnamese people's determination to defeat the U.S. Vietnamization of the war policy and make available the Vietnamese people's basic rights. Minister Nguyen Thi Binh cordially invited the two American women to dinner. The meeting took place in a friendly and understanding atmosphere.[43]

The next week a familiar target is attacked in North Vietnam.

Operation Freedom Dawn

With the authorization to reinitiate the bombing of North Vietnam, several air operations plans were drawn up to satisfy the interdiction requirements directed by the upper echelon planners. One of these plans, Freedom Dawn, included, among other targets, the Thanh Hoa Bridge. The plan called for a small tactical strike force to destroy the Dragon's Jaw with the new family of guided bombs. . . . These weapons consisted of Electro-Optical Guided Bombs (EOGBs) and Laser Guided Bombs (LGBs) in the 2,000-pound and 3,000-pound class. The EOGB was a contrast weapon, similar in concept to the Walleye first used in 1967 by the US Navy. The EOGB, however, was a 2,000-pound bomb with a small TV camera attached to the nose which transmitted a picture of what it was viewing to a scope in the attack aircraft. The pilot would point the aircraft and weapon at the target area thereby allowing the Weapon Systems Operator (WSO) in the rear cockpit of the F-4 to find the target on the scope, refine the contrast aiming point and designate the target to the weapon. Once this was accomplished, the pilot would release the bomb and quickly depart the target area, leaving the EOGB to guide itself toward the designated aim point. Target weather and cloud cover was a factor when delivering EOGB's, but if the weapon could see the target when it was released from the aircraft it would usually impact the aim point.

The LGB was somewhat different. A laser sensor was mated to the nose of a 2,000 or a 3,000-pound bomb which enabled it to guide itself toward a target illuminated with low power laser energy. The problem of illuminating the target with this laser energy was solved by attaching a pod beneath the fighter aircraft. This pod contained an optical viewing system and laser emitting capability, both operated by the WSO in the backseat of the fighter. With this system, the pilot could point his aircraft toward the target while his WSO optically located the precise target aim point and illuminated it with his laser equipment. The pilot would then release his bombs and depart the target area leaving the LGB to guide itself to the target. An advantage of this system was that more than one aircraft at a time could drop LGBs on the same target, with all weapons using the same illumination point to guide on. Both the EOGB and the LGB resulted in less aircrew exposure and greater accuracy than conventional weapons. A disadvantage was that the target had to be continuously illuminated by the laser for the LGB to be effective. If clouds obstructed the view of the illuminating pod the LGB would become an unguided bomb and probably miss the target. . . .

The operation was to be carried out by 12 F-4 Phantoms from the 8th TFW, eight of them loaded with 2,000-pound guided weapons. A flight of 4 Phantoms was to lay a chaff corridor from the initial point to the target so that the eight bomb-laden F-4s could operate in a relatively sterilized radar environment. Bad weather in the target area had been the cause of several last minute postponements of the mission, but on 27 April 1972, reports indicated the weather had cleared sufficiently over Thanh Hoa to permit the strike. . . .

With several thousand pounds of fuel obtained from the tankers, the fighters headed for the bridge. The chaff delivery aircraft had gone out in front to form the protective corridor in advance of the strike aircraft. However, as the strike aircraft approached the IP, a glance in the direction of the target revealed heavy cloud cover which could hamper the use of the guided bombs. The heavy cloud cover and poor visibility precluded the use of LGB illuminators to designate the target continuously. It was a day for the EOGB weapons. The aircraft carrying the EOGBs then positioned themselves for the strike, and let loose with five EOGBs. The extremely heavy anti-aircraft fire filled the skies with hundreds of white, gray and black puffs of smoke from exploding AAA shells. A number of SA-2 SAMs were fired at the aircraft, but SAM effectiveness was reduced by the chaff—so much so that the Phantoms escaped without a scratch. Post-mission photo reconnaissance showed the damage to the bridge to be extensive enough to render it unusable to vehicle traffic. The EOGBs had severely shaken the structure, but stubborn to the end, the Dragon's Jaw would need one more punch.[44]

1972   1 May—South Vietnam's province capital of Quang Tri falls to North Vietnamese troops. **8 May**—President Nixon orders the mining of Hanoi and Haiphong harbors, as well as increased bombing of North Vietnamese lines of communication. The Senate Foreign Relations Committee publishes "Thailand, Laos, and Cambodia:

January, 1972—A Staff Report," which provides the first official details of U.S. and Thai air and ground support to Laotian and Cambodian forces.

The An Loc battle continues.

At 0030 on 11 May heavy artillery fire directed against An Loc removed all doubt about VC/NVA intentions. Major Ingram said that the barrage was so heavy that to leave your bunker was "certain death." Captain Moffett said that the noise

> kept going up to a crescendo . . . it sounded like somebody was popping popcorn—shaking it just all over the city . . . and about 4 or 4:30 it stopped—bam—just like somebody dropped down a baton. Everything stopped at once.

The contrast between rounds every five seconds climaxing an over 7000 round barrage and the relative quiet that followed brought great apprehension. But, inexplicably, the enemy paused before attacking while VNAF and USAF TACAIR streaked toward the city. At 0500 a combined tank and infantry attack struck with fury at defense perimeters and quickly established a salient in the ARVN defenses in both the northeast and western sections of town. Colonel Ulmer, who replaced Colonel Miller as Senior Adviser to the ARVN 5th Division, wrote that the VC/ NVA strategy was to continue to drive into these two salients. With this tactic, the enemy hoped to link up and thus split the ARVN defenders into two enclaves. The ARVN commander's response to this tactic was to rapidly shift his 5th Airborne Battalion between the two salients, preventing their link and holding them in place until air power could help eliminate the salients. In addition to these two major thrusts, tanks and heavy troop contacts were reported all over the perimeter.

The forceful attack by the VC/NVA was met by a spirited and effective defense. ARVN troops who learned the effectiveness of M-72 LAWs against tanks in the April attacks not only stood their ground but sought out tanks to engage. By noon these ground troops had destroyed seven tanks, principally with their LAWs. Cobra gunships equipped with 2.75 inch FEAR rockets engaged other tanks, destroying or immobilizing four more. When the first waves of hostile forces moved forward, FACs directed whatever ordnance was available to them to slow the attacks. For example, when a reported battalion of enemy troops or approximately 500 men threatened to overrun the 36th Ranger Battalion, the FAC ordered "Daisy Cutters" dropped 200 meters in front of the ranger positions. The resulting blasts halted the attack and turned back the hostile troops. The TACAIR pilots responding showed great bravery and professionalism as well. In the midst of the battle, TACAIR received a distress call from General Hung's command bunker, under point blank range fire from a NVA tank. Lt Colonel Gordo Weed answered the call with his

A-37 equipped with two 250 lb. bombs. On the first pass the first bomb scored a direct hit on the tank, but—the bomb was a dud! The tank stopped firing at the bunker, but it was not immobilized. Again braving a hail of 37 mm and .51 caliber ground fire that had already downed one A-37, he released his second bomb as well. The resulting explosions destroyed the tank and routed its supporting infantry troops.

The very successful day for TACAIR on 11 May was also a very costly one. As part of their general attack plans, the VC/NVA had added additional AAA batteries to an already impressive array. One U.S. Army captain on the ground said he had "never heard so much 37mm and 23mm firing" in his life as he heard that morning. The enemy had clustered the weapons for self protection as well as to shoot down allied aircraft. At one location were four or five 37mm and the same number of 23mm weapons all surrounded by .51 caliber weapons. One A-37, one Cobra, and two FAC operated O-2s fell to the murderous fire by late afternoon. . . .

While the ARVN seemed to be holding successfully on the ground the second day of the renewed attack, things took an ominous turn in the air. During the day, several possible sightings were made of Soviet-made SA-7 STRELA missiles being fired at F-4s and FACs. At 1837, an AC-130 Spectre reported five such missiles fired at him. The first four exploded 1000 feet below the aircraft. The fifth was on a light path to miss the aircraft, but jinked into the AC-130. Although there was extensive damage, the aircraft was able to return to base. Because of the already serious AAA hazard, Cobras were operating with difficulty and FACs had already had their minimums raised to avoid the AAA. In addition, the A-37 low level napalm strikes had also been stopped. Now the SA-7 threatened other low level aircraft and techniques as well.[45]

Carrying out orders for increased bombing in North Vietnam, U.S. Air Force pilots once more return to Thanh Hoa.

[Starting on] the 10th of May, Operation Linebacker I . . . air strikes were flown against targets in the Hanoi-Haiphong area and reduced to rubble many key objectives previously "off limits."

After three days of Linebacker activity, the Thanh Hoa Bridge once again was highlighted on the daily mission orders. The mission was to be similar to that flown on April 27th except the weather was forecast to be better and two additional aircraft were scheduled, making a total of 14 strike aircraft. Guided bombs were on the agenda again; however, this time, nine 3,000-pound LGBs would be used in conjunction with fifteen 2,000-pound LGBs and forty-eight 500-pound conventional bombs.

On the morning of 13 May, the attacking force members annotated their maps with updated SAM plots and received final briefings on enemy AAA defenses, air-refueling tracks, positions of supporting ECM forces and the SAR procedures. The target weather was briefed as good. The strike took off on schedule and rendezvoused with the KC-135 tankers for the pre-strike refueling.

The pilots then set an easterly course across southern North Vietnam to the Gulf of Tonkin, and from there north to the target area. Approaching the target, everyone could see that the weather forecaster had been correct. No trouble—some clouds were evident and the flights positioned for attack.

With the target in sight, the lead aircraft rolled in for the kill, unleashing his LGBs at the bridge. Plane after plane followed, with each pilot hoping that the anti-aircraft flashes on the ground did not signal a shot destined for his aircraft. As they dropped more bombs on the target, the last few pilots saw large clouds of dust spewing and belches of fire as the bombs exploded on the bridge. After the final aircraft had pulled away from the target, the strike pilots knew the bridge was down. The pilots headed for home—mission accomplished.

No aircraft had been damaged, even though the AAA and SAM fire had been intense. Post-strike photography by RF-4Cs confirmed the strike pilots' assessment. The western span of the bridge had been knocked completely off its 40 foot thick concrete abutment and the bridge superstructure was so critically disfigured and twisted that rail traffic would come to a standstill for at least several months.[46]

1972   9 June—Chief Province Adviser John Paul Vann—considered by all sides to be the most controversial, dedicated, respected American in Vietnam—is killed in an aircraft crash.

As the North Vietnamese spring offensive begins to falter, another committee of the U.S. Congress holds hearings in Washington. The U.S. press has reported that instead of being retired normally, the commander of Seventh Air Force, Saigon, has actually been fired for exceeding his authority.

Hearing Before the Armed Services Investigating Subcommittee of the Committee on Armed Services, House of Representatives Ninety-second Congress, Second Session, Under the Authority of H. Res. 201

HEARING HELD JUNE 12, 1972

STATEMENT OF GEN. JOHN D. LAVELLE (USAF, RETIRED)

GENERAL LAVELLE: Mr. Chairman, it is a pleasure to appear before your subcommittee today, and to explain the circumstances surrounding my recent retirement. I was assigned, as General Ryan said, as commander of the 7th Air Force on August 1, 1971, just shortly before the start of the buildup of the North Vietnamese forces and their massive infiltration into Laos and South Vietnam which eventually resulted in the heavy fighting and eventual overrun of the Plain of Jars in Laos and the more recent invasion of South Vietnam. When I first took over, it was in the middle of the rainy season; however, starting in late September, as the rains subsided and the roads started to dry out, there was increased activity as the North Vietnamese infiltrations began. From this time, the infiltration, accompanied with the increased aggressiveness of the North Vietnamese, was constantly on the build. . . .

As you know, the air war in South Vietnam is tightly controlled and operated under quite specific rules of engagement. These rules of engagement had not changed substantively since we ceased bombing North Vietnam in 1968. However, the environment over there had changed considerably. I don't think there were any missile sites or radar controlled heavy antiaircraft artillery in the southern part of North Vietnam in 1968. In February of this year, in addition to the sophisticated air defense control system, there were many occupied surface-to-air missile sites, along with many radar controlled heavy antiaircraft artillery. The North Vietnamese also used a new tactic which greatly reduced warning to our crews of missile launches.

The rules of engagement, although being fairly specific, also require some interpretation or judgment factor added. With this air defense buildup, increased aggressiveness of the North Vietnamese and the large number of North Vietnam regular army units that had infiltrated south or moved into position to move across the DMZ, I chose to make a very liberal interpretation of these rules of engagement. In certain instances against high priority military targets I made interpretations that were probably beyond the literal intention of the rules. I did this since the crews were operating in an environment of optimum enemy defense. It was these isolated instances reported as protective reaction strikes that resulted in General Ryan recalling me and questioning me on what we were doing.

Mr. Chairman, in view of the publicity of the last 2 days I would like to digress from the script, and point out that these protective reaction strikes that I am talking about were in the neighborhood of 20, probably less; they were four- or eight-airplane strikes, they were not massive raids. They were against missile sites, missiles on transporters, airfields, the 122- and 130-millimeter guns and radars. They were not "extensive raids."

From General Ryan's viewpoint in Washington, I had exceeded my authority. I can sit here now and understand his position, but at that time as the commander on the spot concerned with the safety of the crews and, at the same time trying to stop the buildup that was going on, I felt that these were justifiable actions. . . .

MR. PIKE: Were you concerned that the bomb damage report showed damage to trucks or a SAM transporter or to POL, rather than to something that you were allowed to hit?

GENERAL LAVELLE: No, sir.

MR. PIKE: Tell us why. You said they were missile-related equipment. Is that it?

GENERAL LAVELLE: Yes, sir.

MR. PIKE: Did you feel that under the rules of engagement, as you interpreted them, your right to attack missiles would include a missile on a transporter?

GENERAL LAVELLE: Yes, sir.

MR. PIKE: When you say these trucks were missile-related equipment, how were they missile-related equipment?

GENERAL LAVELLE: We had picked up, or identified by reconnaissance, missiles on transporters parked alongside the road, waiting for the bad weather, to come through the pass, to come into Laos. They were never alone. The missiles had associated equipment, generator, vans, fuel, or just equipment for the personnel. But we never found a missile on a transporter by itself. We found missiles and trucks with them.

MR. PIKE: General Lavelle, as to these three incidents on the 25th of February, how did you establish that this took place 7 miles on the wrong side of the border instead of 7 miles on the right side of the border?

GENERAL LAVELLE: Photographs, sir.

MR PIKE: The photographs showed the trucks still there; is that it?

GENERAL LAVELLE: No, sir. When the photographs were brought to my attention, they showed the missiles and trucks there waiting to come into Laos. I directed that we go hit those missiles and trucks.

MR. PIKE: All right.

GENERAL LAVELLE: Mr. Pike, I would like to add, if I may, a few more points here.

In December and January, before we made these strikes, there were four missile firings from Laos, two of them at gunships and two of them at fighters. We expended a tremendous amount of effort attempting to find and destroy those missile sites in Laos.

First of all, they never fired at our aircraft unless it was through the weather or at night. I think I am correct in saying they were all fired through the weather, so we couldn't locate them after they fired.

Secondly, when the weather broke in one instance, I flooded the area with reconnaissance aircraft, trying to find the missiles. We took a picture at 12:10 p.m. of a road intersection, by one reconnaissance aircraft, perfectly clear. A second reconnaissance aircraft came by at 12:30 and photographed a missile on a launcher, 20 minutes later.

Now, when they got in the jungle we just couldn't find them. And when these missiles and associated equipment were lined up waiting for bad weather to come into Laos, this is when we hit them.

MR. PIKE: Would it have been permissible for you to have hit those targets between the 26th and the 31st of December?

GENERAL LAVELLE: 26th and 31st; yes, sir.

MR. PIKE: Would it have been permissible for you to have hit those targets on the 17th and 18th of February?

GENERAL LAVELLE: No, sir—because of their location, Mr. Pike.

MR. PIKE: Because they were too far north?

GENERAL LAVELLE: Yes, sir.

MR. DANIEL: General Lavelle, in continuation of Mr. Lennon's interrogation with respect to the New York Times article, are you now in a position to set the record straight as far as that article is concerned? And, if so, do you intend to do so?

GENERAL LAVELLE: Sir, I have not talked to the press at any time.

MR. DANIEL: I am not suggesting you do. I wondered what your feeling was about it.

GENERAL LAVELLE: I planned not to do anything about it until after this hearing, and I told Mr. Hébert I would not.

MR. DANIEL: Who was the prime selector of targets during the time that has been discussed here today? Who selected the targets that you could hit?

GENERAL RYAN: The Secretary of Defense.

MR. DANIEL: Mr. Chairman, like Mr. Dickinson, I want to commend both the witnesses. I think they have served their positions well. I can certainly understand why each of them acted the way he did. I can also understand why so much frustration has come out of this war.[47]

By this time it is apparent that the North Vietnamese spring offensive has been checked. What happens at An Loc is typical.

A POW report indicated that the NVA Division received 360 replacements in May, but none during the first eighteen days in June. The troops received rice only once each day and "Morale was low due to fear of B-52 strikes, sickness, and poor leadership."

In spite of these problems encountered by the interdicting forces, the relief column still moved too slowly to suit American advisers. General Hollingsworth felt that ARVN was just not trying hard enough. He considered the C-130 heavy drops to the ARVN 15th Infantry Regiment "to be a misuse of assets" because it was "inefficient" and it degraded "the incentive for the 21st Division to open Highway 13." Thus he requested the drops be halted, but COMUSMACV did not concur, and the drops continued.

For the city of An Loc, enemy stubbornness in the capital and on the highway, plus bad weather inhibiting TACAIR, prolonged the formal siege. Lt. General Nguyen Van Minh, Commanding General of MR III, had no doubt about the eventual outcome, however. With over 3100 ARVN and 1500 territorial forces troops combat effective at An Loc, his principal concern was getting the more than 1000 wounded medevaced out of the city. On 12 June, the last of the VC/NVA were driven from the town itself and on 14 June, reinforcement of An Loc with 1650 fresh troops by U.S. helicopter was completed. With things seemingly under control, General Minh declared the siege "over" on 18 June.[48]

1972   29 June—President Nixon announces the resumption of the Paris
peace talks. **30 June**—Since 1 January, despite the North Vietnamese spring offensive, the United States has withdrawn 109,800 military personnel. Remaining in Vietnam: 47,000 U.S. soldiers. Casualties from January through June have been 178 Americans killed,
809 wounded. The South Vietnamese, however, have suffered
19,595 killed, 50,325 wounded—their highest six-month losses of
the war so far (DOD/OASD 27 Mar 75). **12 August**—At Da Nang,
the last U.S. ground troops leave Vietnam. Remaining are 43,500
American service personnel in administrative and supply jobs, plus
helicopter and air crews. **22 August**—Republican National Convention renominates President Nixon by a vote of 1,347 to 1.

At the convention is Vietnam veteran Ron Kovic, who is paralyzed.

It was the night of Nixon's acceptance speech and now I was on my own
deep in his territory, all alone in my wheelchair in a sweat-soaked marine
utility jacket covered with medals from the war. A TV producer I knew
from the Coast had gotten me past the guards at the entrance with his
press pass. My eyes were still smarting from teargas. Outside the chain
metal fence around the Convention Center my friends were being
clubbed and arrested, herded into wagons. The crowds were thick all
around me, people dressed as if they were going to a banquet, men in
expensive summer suits and women in light elegant dresses. Every once
in a while someone would look at me as if I didn't belong there. But I had
come almost three thousand miles for this meeting with the president and
nothing was going to prevent it from taking place.

I worked my way slowly and carefully into the huge hall, moving down
one of the side aisles. "Excuse me, excuse me," I said to delegates as I
pushed past them farther and farther to the front of the hall toward the
speakers' podium.

I had gotten only halfway toward where I wanted to be when I was
stopped by one of the convention security marshals. "Where are you
going?" he said. He grabbed hold of the back of my chair, I made believe
I hadn't heard him and kept turning my wheels, but his grip on the chair
was too tight and now two other security men had joined him.

"What's the matter?" I said. "Can't a disabled veteran who fought for
his country sit up front?"

The three men looked at each other for a moment and one of them
said, "I'm afraid not. You're not allowed up front with the delegates." I
had gotten as far as I had on sheer bluff alone and now they were telling
me I could go no farther. "You'll have to go to the back of the convention hall, son. Let's go," said the guard who was holding my chair.

In a move of desperation I swung around facing all three of them, shouting as loud as I could so Walter Cronkite and the CBS camera crew that was just above me could hear me and maybe even focus their cameras in for the six o'clock news. "I'm a Vietnam veteran and I fought in the war! Did you fight in the war?"

One of the guards looked away.

"Yeah, that's what I thought," I said. "I bet none of you fought in the war and you guys are trying to throw me out of the convention. I've got just as much right to be up front here as any of these delegates. I fought for that right and I was born on the Fourth of July."

I was really shouting now and another officer came over. I think he might have been in charge of the hall. He told me I could stay where I was if I was quiet and didn't move up any farther. I agreed with the compromise. I locked my brakes and looked for other veterans in the tremendous crowd. As far as I could tell, I was the only one who had made it in.

People had begun to sit down all around me. They all had Four More Years buttons and I was surprised to see how many of them were young. I began speaking to them, telling them about the Last Patrol and why veterans from all over the United States had taken the time and effort to travel thousands of miles to the Republican National Convention. "I'm a disabled veteran!" I shouted. "I served two tours of duty in Vietnam and while on my second tour of duty up in the DMZ I was wounded and paralyzed from the chest down." I told them I would be that way for the rest of my life. Then I began to talk about the hospitals and how they treated the returning veterans like animals, how I, many nights in the Bronx, had lain in my own shit for hours waiting for an aide. "And they never come," I said. "They never come because that man that's going to accept the nomination tonight has been lying to all of us and spending the money on war that should be spent on healing and helping the wounded. That's the biggest lie and hypocrisy of all—that we had to go over there and fight and get crippled and come home to a government and leaders who could care less about the same boys they sent over."

I kept shouting and speaking, looking for some kind of reaction from the crowd. No one seemed to want to even look at me.

"Is it too real for you to look at? Is this wheelchair too much for you to take? The man who will accept the nomination tonight is a liar!" I shouted again and again, until finally one of the security men came back and told me to be quiet or they would have to take me to the back of the hall.

I told him that if they tried to move me or touch my chair there would be a fight and hell to pay right there in front of Walter Cronkite and the national television networks. I told him if he wanted to wrestle me and beat me to the floor of the convention hall in front of all those cameras he could.

By then a couple of newsmen, including Roger Mudd from CBS, had worked their way through the security barricades and begun to ask me questions.

"Why are you here tonight?" Roger Mudd asked me. "But don't start talking until I get the camera here," he shouted.

It was too good to be true. In a few seconds Roger Mudd and I would be going on live all over the country. I would be doing what I had come here for, showing the whole nation what the war was all about. The camera began to roll, and I began to explain why I and the others had come, that the war was wrong and it had to stop immediately. "I'm a Vietnam veteran," I said. "I gave America my all and the leaders of this government threw me and the others away to rot in their V.A. hospitals. What's happening in Vietnam is a crime against humanity, and I just want the American people to know that we have come all the way across this country, sleeping on the ground and in the rain, to let the American people see for themselves the men who fought their war and have come to oppose it. If you can't believe the veteran who fought the war and was wounded in the war, who can you believe?"

"Thank you," said Roger Mudd, visibly moved by what I had said. "This is Roger Mudd," he said, "down on the convention floor with Ron Kovic, a disabled veteran protesting President Nixon's policy in Vietnam.". . .

Suddenly a roar went up in the convention hall, louder than anything I had ever heard in my life. It started off as a rumble, then gained in intensity until it sounded like a tremendous thunderbolt. "Four more years, four more years," the crowd roared over and over again. The fat woman next to me was jumping up and down and dancing in the aisle. It was the greatest ovation the president of the United States had ever received and he loved it. I held the sides of my wheelchair to keep my hands from shaking. After what seemed forever, the roar finally began to die down.

This was the moment I had come three thousand miles for, this was it, all the pain and the rage, all the trials and the death of the war and what had been done to me and a generation of Americans by all the men who had lied to us and tricked us, by the man who stood before us in the convention hall that night, while men who had fought for their country were being gassed and beaten in the street outside the hall. I thought of Bobby who sat next to me and the months we had spent in the hospital in the Bronx. It was all hitting me at once, all those years, all that destruction, all that sorrow.

President Nixon began to speak and all three of us took a deep breath and shouted at the top of our lungs, "Stop the bombing, stop the war, stop the bombing, stop the war," as loud and as hard as we could, looking directly at Nixon. The security agents immediately threw up their arms, trying to hide us from the cameras and the president. "Stop the bombing, stop the bombing," I screamed. For an instant Cronkite looked down, then turned his head away. They're not going to show it, I thought. They're going to try and hide us like they did in the hospitals. Hundreds of people around us began to clap and shout "Four more

years," trying to drown out our protest. They all seemed very angry and
shouted at us to stop. We continued shouting, interrupting Nixon again
and again until Secret Service agents grabbed our chairs from behind and
began pulling us backward as fast as they could out of the convention
hall. "Take it easy," Bobby said to me. "Don't fight back."

I wanted to take a swing and fight right there in the middle of the
convention hall in front of the president and the whole country. "So this
is how they treat their wounded veterans!" I screamed.

A short guy with a big Four More Years button ran up to me and spat
in my face. "Traitor!" he screamed, as he was yanked back by police.
Pandemonium was breaking out all around us and the Secret Service men
kept pulling us out backward.

"I served two tours of duty in Vietnam!" I screamed to one newsman. "I gave three-quarters of my body for America. And what do I
get? Spit in the face!" I kept screaming until we hit the side entrance
where the agents pushed us outside and shut the doors, locking them
with chains and padlocks so reporters wouldn't be able to follow us out
for interviews.

All three of us sat holding on to each other shaking. We had done it. It
had been the biggest moment of our lives, we had shouted down the
president of the United States and disrupted his acceptance speech. What
more was there left to do but go home?

I sat in my chair still shaking and began to cry.[49]

1972   **28 August**—President Nixon announces that the U.S. draft will end
by July 1973. **15 September**—South Vietnamese forces recapture
the province capital of Quang Tri. **14 October**—As U.S. bombing
of the Ho Chi Minh Trail continues, an announcement from Hanoi
acknowledges that a Pathet Lao delegation is being sent to Vientiane for discussions on ending the war in Laos.

---

*At the height of the U.S. political campaign, Secretary of State William
Rogers cables elements of recent radio and TV commentaries to embassy
personnel in Southeast Asia.*

SUBJ: RADIO/TV COMMENTARY ON CAMBODIAN POLITICAL DEVELOPMENTS

1. FOLLOWING IS ESSENTIAL WORDING COMMENTARY BROADCAST BY ERIC SEVA-
REID ON CBS TV EVENING NEWS OCTOBER 20.

". . . TODAY, A NEW SE ASIAN COMRADE-IN-ARMS, PRIME MINISTER LON NOL,
ABOLISHED THE CAMBODIAN CONSTITUTION AND ANNOUNCED THAT HE WOULD
NO LONGER PLAY THE SO-CALLED GAME OF DEMOCRACY AND FREEDOM BECAUSE
IT INTERFERES WITH MILITARY VICTORY OVER THE COMMUNISTS . . . THE CAM-
BODIAN LEADER MAY WELL HAVE DAMAGED HIMSELF WHERE IT HURTS. IN THE

POCKETBOOK. HIS TIMING COULD NOT HAVE BEEN WORSE. POWERFUL FORCES IN CONGRESS ARE JUST NOW TRYING TO PUT A CEILING ON THE AMOUNT OF TAXPAYERS' DOLLARS THAT THE NIXON ADMINISTRATION CAN SPEND IN CAMBODIA. THE ADMINISTRATION WANTS A MONEY COMMITMENT WITH AN OPEN TOP, WHILE DENYING THAT OUR INVOLVEMENT IN CAMBODIA IS OPEN-ENDED. AT LEAST, CONGRESSMEN DON'T THINK THE ADMINISTRATION CAN HAVE IT BOTH WAYS. ADMINISTRATION STATEMENT WRITERS HAD A DREADFUL TIME COMPOSING A HANDOUT OR PUTTING THE BEST POSSIBLE FACE ON THE COLLAPSE OF THE ELECTION PROCESS IN VN, AND NO DOUBT THEY WILL FIND PHRASES TO COVER THE CONSTITUTIONAL COLLAPSE IN CAMBODIA . . ."

2. ESSENTIAL WORDING MARVIN KALB RADIO COMMENTARY OCTOBER 21: "THE SENATE BEGINS DEBATING FOREIGN AID BILL TODAY AND A HOUSE-SENATE COMMITTEE CONTINUES DEBATING A MILITARY PROCUREMENT BILL. BOTH MEASURES CARRY ANTI-WAR AMENDMENTS BEHIND HIM [*sic*] LIKE HORSES PULLING A CARRIAGE THAT MAY BECOME TOO HEAVY. THE FOREIGN AID BILL, A NEW COOPER-CHURCH AMENDMENT THAT WOULD RESTRICT FUNDS FOR INDOCHINA ONLY TO THE WITHDRAWAL OF AMERICAN FORCES; NOTHING MORE NOTHING LESS. MILITARY PROCUREMENT BILL CARRIES SO-CALLED MANSFIELD AMENDMENT THAT WOULD DECLARE US POLICY TO BE THE WITHDRAWAL OF AMERICAN TROOPS FROM INDOCHINA BY NEXT SPRING CONTINGENT ONLY ON THE RELEASE OF AMERICAN POW'S BY NORTH VIETNAM. EACH AMENDMENT REPRESENTS ANOTHER SLICE INTO ADMINISTRATION PEROGATIVES [*sic*] IN INDOCHINA, ANOTHER EFFORT BY ANTI-WAR SENATORS AND CONGRESSMEN TO FORCE THE WHITE HOUSE TO GIVE UP THE DEFENSE OF INDOCHINA AS ESSENTIALLY A BAD INVESTMENT FOR THE US. IT IS TOO SIMPLISTIC TO DESCRIBE THESE LEGISLATORS AS DOVES. MANY ARE REALLY DISILLUSIONED HAWKS, OTHERS BASICALLY UNINTERESTED IN A NEVER ENDING WAR IN ASIA, COMMITTED TO A NEVER ENDING WAR AGAINST POVERTY AND INJUSTICE AT HOME. THE LABEL REALLY IS NOT IMPORTANT. THE MOOD IS AND THE MOOD IS ONE OF FRUSTRATION AND DISGUST. THE LATEST REASON HAS SURFACED IN CAMBODIA. PREMIER LON NOL WHO REPLACED PRINCE SIHANOUK IN THE SPRING OF LAST YEAR DISBANDED THE CAMBODIAN PARLIAMENT SEVERAL DAYS AGO, LARGE CROWDS OF BUDDHIST MONKS THEN DEMONSTRATED AGAINST LON NOL. THEY CARRIED BANNERS SAYING "WE WANT TO LIVE IN DEMOCRACY." LON NOL GOT ON NATION-WIDE RADIO THEN AND ASKED SHOULD WE VAINLY PLAY THE GAME OF DEMOCRACY AND FREEDOM WHICH WILL LEAD US TO COMPLETE DEFEAT OR SHOULD WE CURTAIL ANARCHICAL FREEDOM IN ORDER TO ACHIEVE VICTORY. LON NOL THEN ANSWERED HIS OWN QUESTION: "THE GOVERNMENT HAS MADE ITS DECISION. WE HAVE SELECTED THE WAY THAT WILL BRING US TO VICTORY." VICTORY IS ONE OF THOSE MILITARY WORDS. UP UNTIL SIHANOUK WAS OUSTED FROM POWER SUCH WORDS WERE NOT PART OF THE CAMBODIAN VOCABULARY. SIHANOUK MADE HIS DEAL WITH THE NORTH VIETNAMESE ALLOWING THEM TO USE CAMBODIAN SANCTUARIES WHICH AMOUNTED TO FORFEITING PART OF CAMBODIA'S SOVEREIGNTY. THIS WAS BITTER BUT ACCEPTABLE. IT KEPT MOST OF CAMBODIA OUT OF THE WAR FOR MANY YEARS. CAMBODIA IN

FACT BECAME A MAJOR PART OF THE WAR, A BATTLE GROUND ITSELF ONLY
AFTER AMERICAN FORCES MOVED INTO AND OUT OF THE COUNTRY LAST YEAR.
SINCE THEN THE SOUTH VIETNAMESE ARMY HAS BEEN IN AND OUT OF THERE
ON A REGULAR BASIS. CAMBODIAN ART TREASURES HAVE BEEN DESTROYED,
CAMBODIAN VILLAGES TOO. CASUALTIES HAVE MOUNTED. AN AMERICAN EM-
BASSY WAS SET UP LAST YEAR WHEN RELATIONS WERE RESTORED. IT STARTED
SMALL BUT HAS GROWN STEADILY IN MEN AND MONEY. AS A RESULT CAMBODIA
HAS BECOME LINKED TO THE US MILITARY EFFORT IN INDOCHINA AND IT IS A
MOOT QUESTION TO ASK WHETHER THE CAMBODIAN PEOPLE WERE BETTER OFF
BEFORE OR AFTER THEIR COUNTRY JOINED THE ANTI-COMMUNIST WAR EFFORT
IN INDOCHINA. LON NOL'S MOVE DISCARDING DEMOCRACY FOR THE DURATION
OF THIS INDOCHINESE WAR MAY IN FACT BE A REFRESHING BURST OF CANDOR.
HIS NEIGHBOR PRESIDENT THIEU OF SOUTH VIETNAM CONTINUES TO TALK
ABOUT DEMOCRACY AND SO DO HIS MANY SUPPORTERS IN WASHINGTON. NEV-
ERTHELESS DESPITE THE OBVIOUS EMBARRASSMENT HERE OFFICIALS SEEM MUCH
MORE INTERESTED IN POLITICAL STABILITY UNDER ANY GUISE IN ASIA THAN
THEY DO IN THE EXERCISE OF DEMOCRACY.[50]

At the same time, as seen in his narrative Decent Interval, *CIA agent
Frank Snepp comes back to Vietnam.*

By the time I returned to Saigon in October 1972 some of the old shabbiness still clung to the city like a scab. The stubby houses and hotels in the
center of town near Lam Son Square all wore the flaking gray façades
that had always betrayed their age, and the gutters even along the major
thoroughfares still reeked of urine and garbage, despite periodic rounds
by trash-sweeping trucks provided to Saigon municipal authorities under
U.S. aid programs. The traffic itself as lethal and improvisatory as ever,
and invariably at rush hour the air over the city turned gray and spongy
from the exhausts of the countless Hondas and Japanese automobiles the
Vietnamese managed to keep running despite the rising price of gas. The
last of the surviving tamarind trees along lower Tu Do Street seemed
finally to be succumbing to the pall, although wits in the local French
community continued to blame their passing on the residual effects of
U.S. military defoliants.

From what I could see and touch, there had been no improvement in
the esthetic or hygienic qualities of the city's night life. A few weeks
before, the government in a paroxysm of energy had shut down all the
junkier bars and massage parlors along Tu Do and Nguyen Hue to celebrate the shrinkage of the American market and to staunch the resulting
inflation. But like most efforts at reform in this city, this one turned out
be mere shadow play. The toughest hookers had decamped to the veranda of the colonial Continental Hotel, where Graham Greene had sat
at a corner table in the early 1950s and scrawled a first draft of *The Quiet
American,* and most of the "restaurants" that had sprung up in place of
the bars offered the same attractions, except now the girls all wore white

"waitress" smocks and offered you a salad and a hamburger of water-buffalo meat before lapsing into the usual hard sell.

For all the shabbiness, though, there was an air of accomplished and impending change about the city that perhaps only a Vietnamese could fully appreciate. The people I brushed up against in the streets or in the marketplace or in the course of business seemed more generous, less driven than before. The beggars and street urchins along Nguyen Hue Boulevard were more polite and deferential in their ancestral manner, as if they realized that the American bonanza was ending and hoped through some small act of diplomacy to keep a few of the big spenders on. And the Vietnamese GIs who still crowded into the shops and cafés on weekends were holding hands again, as they had ceased doing at the height of the American involvement only a few years before, when U.S. GIs—not knowing the custom to be an old and venerated one among Vietnamese men—had dubbed them a nation of queers.

An old Chinese merchant who had bought up one of the better massage parlors on Tu Do and turned it into a noodle stand told me with a great show of candor that it was the disappearance of the American GIs that had made all the difference, just as their arrival, he insisted, had caused the war. "Because of the riches you brought us," he said, "we were forced to acknowledge our own poverty and to compete among ourselves to change as you wanted us to do. But now that you Americans are going home, we can again feel safe and comfortable with our illusions."[51]

1972 22 October—President Nixon announces a halt to all bombing of North Vietnam above the 20th Parallel.

Four days later National Security Adviser Dr. Henry Kissinger holds a news conference.

NEWS CONFERENCE OF DR. HENRY KISSINGER,
OCTOBER 26, 1972

DR. KISSINGER: Ladies and gentlemen: We have now heard from both Vietnams, and it is obvious that as a war that has been raging for 10 years is drawing to a conclusion that this is a traumatic experience for all of the participants. The President thought that it might be helpful if I came out here and spoke to you about what we have been doing, where we stand, and to put the various allegations and charges into perspective.

First, let me talk about the situation in three parts: Where do we stand procedurally, what is the substance of the negotiations, and where do we go from here?

We believe that peace is at hand. We believe that an agreement is within sight based on the May 8 proposals of the President and some adaptations of our January 25 proposal which is just to all parties. It is inevitable that in a war of such complexity that there should be occasional difficulties in reaching a final solution, but we believe that by far the longest part of the road has been traversed and what stands in the way of an agreement now are issues that are relatively less important than those that have already been settled.[52]

In Cambodia, a U.S. embassy paper dated 5 November summarizes the American perspective of the situation in that country.

Currently there are 4 ARVN bns [battalions] operating in country and these will probably be withdrawn, thus putting a greater burden on FANK particularly in southern Takeo and Kampot provinces. Air support will probably continue although a sudden surge in North Vietnamese tactical activity near Saigon or in Vietnam in general will serve to have a sobering effect on the number of strikes afforded to Cambodia. KAF's assets are limited particularly with regard to availability of pilots and as the enemy continues to open new fronts, the airforces's effectiveness declines.

The Cambodian people are war weary. The country was already underpopulated and heavy losses est at 40,000 killed or wounded since the beginning of the war is difficult for many Khmers to accept. The possibility of a cease fire in Indochina has come as a "God send" for the Khmers, who are convinced that peace is "around the corner." This feeling may, however, be having an adverse effect on the military and could account at least in part to a declining effectiveness and lack of initiative on the battlefield. Consequently, they may be falling into the KC trap, for there is no indication that the insurgents intend to decrease their military activities in the country.

During the past six months the GKR has lost considerable terrain— some abandoned while much was lost due to mainforce enemy pressure. The important factor remains, however, that no effort has been made to regain it. FANK continues to display a shortage of aggressiveness and reacts solely to enemy initiatives. Despite an overwhelming reduction in enemy force in SE Cambodia, there has not been the slightest inclination or any interest to reopen the route between Neak Luoug and Svay Reing. Rt 2 has been cut since 25 Oct and while Takeo's provincial capital now isolated appears threatened, there has been no determined effort to reopen the road. The situation on Rt 5 becomes more pitifully embarrassing each day, while initial efforts on Rt 4 have been totally unsuccessful. Unless the 5 bns there are reinforced it is doubtful that any progress will be made. The earlier much talked about moves into the NE to retake lost territory are now only dreams of the past.

Theoretically FANK's capability has improved—better equipment, better training, and its forces outnumber the enemy's 5:1. Yet with its same capability FANK is unable to protect that territory which remains under GKR control even though it has markedly dwindled. This same scenario has repeated itself throughout much of the war, and we continue to give FANK the benefit of the doubt. It would appear that soon we'll be crediting FANK for repulsing an enemy mainforce attack on Phnom Penh, while the remaining countryside is flying the hammer and cycle [*sic*] (KC flag).

The wet season is nearly over and as for the dry season—that depends on the enemy. The outlook is far from favorable and as the KC continue to expand its operations and open new fronts, it does not apear that FANK will succeed even if it does "try harder."[53]

1972 7 November—Richard M. Nixon reelected president by a land-slide.

Poet John O'Neill describes the events of four days later.

Veterans Day, 1972

Marching through the rain, down Main,
from a cemetery in Buffalo,
Vietnam Veterans marching to end the war . . .

Before, just three years ago,
we marched through the rain
of Indochina.
We marched for other reasons,
did other things,
to other people.
These people are now dead.
So we march for them.
the people of Indochina,
the people we killed,
on Veterans day, three years ago.

One hundred veterans marching,
they say we don't represent the majority,
they are wrong.
There would have been more of us,
but it is raining,
and many have grown tired of fighting.
There are others that would have marched with us,
but they have died.[54]

After seven weeks of stalemated private peace talks between Henry Kissinger and Le Duc Tho, President Nixon on 18 December orders intensive air attacks on the Hanoi-Haiphong area "until such time as a settlement is arrived at." This air operation is called "Linebacker II," and for the first time includes B-52s, which suffer heavy losses during the first few days. Four days later the following interchanges occur at the morning Department of Defense news briefing.

Q: Has GIA LAM airfield been hit?

A: I can't talk specific targets with you.

Q: Has there been a change in the release of information on people lost over Vietnam?

A: No, you'll continue to receive information on those missing, those captured, when we place them in that status and when the SAR [Search and Rescue Operation] is complete.

Q: Was the MACV report this morning incorrect?

A: MACV's report was correct.

Q: There was a wire service story about the MACV report which said they will no longer release the number of crewmen per downed plane and it seemed to me that the enemy knows how many crewmen there are in a B-52.

A: You can make that assumption if you wish.

Q: All I want to know is has there been a change in policy?

A: We've always reported to you people that we place in the category of missing and we'll continue to do that.

Q: Why are you unable to give us information on the targets that are hit in NVN?

A: For the same reasons we've discussed here the last three days. I did provide here the types of targets that are being struck.

Q: Don't you think the enemy by now knows exactly which targets have been hit and which places?

A: We've discussed this for three days. I don't have anything better to give you today.

Q: Other than you want to withhold this information from the American public. They obviously know what you're hitting.

A: You all always say obviously, perhaps you know what they know, maybe you don't.

Q: I'll be leaving and will never know if GIA LAM was hit, particularly, since you implied it was not a target the other day. Can I assume that it's still not been targeted and not been hit?

A: I can't discuss the specific locations of things with you today. You're as aware as I am that there are newsmen resident in Hanoi for various agencies. I would think that they would probably report that if that had occurred.

Q: Why are targets not stated by you?

A: The reason is the safety and security of the crews that are still flying.

Q: Do you have any new information about air activities in NVN that you can give us?

A: I don't have anything that would add to what your colleagues have from MACV this morning. The operations do continue throughout NVN.[55]

The U.S. Air Force's summary perspective on Linebacker II is as follows:

Targeting for the Stratofortresses changed to include some of the troublesome SAM sites. In addition, nightly low-level raids by F-111 fighter-bombers now were divided between the airfields and SAM sites. Not unexpectedly, bombing the SAM sites gave the B-52s maximum exposure to the missiles. Moreover, at this very close range, radar burnthrough of ECM devices, allowing SAM operators to see through the jamming, was not altogether unlikely. One incident of a B-52 mission against a SAM site is as follows.

Captain John Mize of Shreveport, Louisiana, was on his fourth Line-backer II mission when 15 SAMs were fired at him as he released his bombs on a particularly active site. One SAM impacted the left wing of his B-52D as he executed a steep turn away from the target area. The tremendous concussion knocked out all four port engines and associated equipment. Shrapnel set one engine afire, and as red cockpit warning lights flashed, the airplane began to fall. Several thousand feet of altitude were lost before Captain Mize managed to get the big bird leveled off.

Nearly every system on the bomber was inoperative. There was no radar, ECM, or computers. Only one alternator, a radio, and the cockpit lights remained in operation. All instruments were out except the altimeter and airspeed indicator. Most of the six-man crew had received shrapnel injuries.

The B-52 was almost helpless because it no longer had the mutual protection of the other aircraft in the cell, and it had lost its self-protection equipment. The crew saw two more SAMs but they missed. Fortunately, no MIGs spotted the crippled aircraft.

After about ten minutes, the flaming engine burned itself out and the crew set about trying to nurse the aircraft back to friendly territory. Since the B-52 could not maintain altitude with only the four right wing engines operational, Captain Mize gradually descended to maintain flying airspeed. The navigators calculated that if the left wing held together, they could get to the Thailand border with only a small compromise of the 10,000 feet minimum recommended bailout altitude.

As they drew closer to the safety of Nakhon Phanom RTAFB, Thailand, the situation rapidly deteriorated. The bomb bay doors fell open, one landing gear started cycling up and down, and other electrical systems went astray. In spite of the crew's gallant efforts, it soon became obvious they would not be able to coax the rapidly descending bomber to a safe landing. Fortunately, when the bailout order was given, the B-52 was only eight miles from Nakhon Phanom. Each man ejected individually on Captain Mize's order. All ejection seats, except the navigator's which was damaged, functioned normally. When his failed, the navigator exited through the hole formed when the radar-navigator ejected. After assuring himself that everyone was safely out of the dying Superfortress, Captain Mize ejected. For his heroic efforts, he was awarded the Air Force Cross, the other crew members received the Distinguished Flying Cross. All crewmembers also received the Purple Heart.

THE FINAL THRUST

Weather in the target area during Linebacker II compounded the problem of attacking enemy defenses. Throughout December, the dominant northeast monsoon brought almost daily low clouds to the NVN delta region. Broken to overcast conditions existed below 5000 feet altitude for most of the 12-day Linebacker II campaign. Weather clear enough to permit visual bombing existed less than 12 hours total during the entire period. This thwarted most efforts to use the deadly accurate laser guided bombs and emphasized the need for an all-weather tactical bombing capability.

By 28 December, however, the bombing and revised B-52 tactics had proven so effective that bombers were no longer lost or even damaged. Compression tactics allowed more than 100 bombers to release their bombs and depart within a 15-minute period. Varying altitudes and headings avoided the previously established flight patterns. Success was such that finding enough lucrative targets began to be a problem. MIG sorties dwindled and, as more SAM sites were struck, missile firings became sporadic and ineffective. Wave after wave of bombers pounded targets with relative impunity. The bombing could have proceeded indefinitely with little likelihood of further losses.[56]

1972   30 December—President Nixon announces the cessation of bombing and the resumption of the Paris peace talks.

In Vietnam, a province adviser sums up the year in his report for December. His optimism underscores the fact, known by many province advisers, that the situation in one province of Vietnam is rarely the same as that which exists in another.

Addendum
Review of 1972

Dinh Tuong Province
December 1972

a. (U) *Overview.* The overriding fact of 1972 was the NVA invasion that dominated the last three quarters of the year. Dinh Tuong emerged from the 9-month ordeal only slightly battered, with most development programs in good shape, and relatively stronger Territorial Forces, still infused with the indomitable spirit of the Sector Commander.

The most gratifying aspect of this stout survival against the equivalent of two enemy divisions is the fact that most of the development programs continued to make progress—some made dramatic gains—despite the enemy's determined effort to kill pacification. Only three population centers (involving parts of 11 villages out of the province's 89) were disrupted, and these only temporarily. Of course, a number of other areas underwent sporadic harassment. But at most, only some 25,000 people (of 615,000) were afflicted directly by the invasion. Another noteworthy aspect of this crucial year was the maturing of the Territorial Forces (see paragraph *c* below). This is an untold story of a Vietnamization success.

b. *(C) Brief Chronology.*
Jan 72—a year ago the December HES reflected a rising perfectibility curve, with 99% of the population in ABC hamlets and 84% in AB. After the buffeting of the offensive, the percentages have laboriously climbed back up to 92.4% and 66% respectively. Dinh Tuong had 65 PF companies and 385 PF platoons (56 and 322 today). MR 4 kept faith on the cross-leveling reductions: Dinh Tuong today has 33 out-of-province RF companies deployed. Enemy-initiated incidents had jumped from 24 to 34 in December, but after an abortive high-point in mid-January, settled back to scarcely more than one a day through February and March.
Feb 72—Despite volumes of "hard" intelligence, the much-touted *Tet* and post-*Tet* offensives failed to come off—largely because of intense preemptive operatives of sector forces.
March 72—Phase III of the Accelerated Pacification Campaign was in full sway, with clearing operations deep into the "northwest passage"— the infiltration corridor from Cambodia. Enemy units were reported broken out into small elements; this is somewhat ominous, since we are saying the same thing today.
Apr 72—The enemy switched signals on the night of 6–7 April. The first onslaughts in the Cai Bo/Cai Lay corridor fizzled out after ten days, but we predicted that the big test was probably still to come.
May 72—Crucial but not decisive. The Z-15 NVA Regiment appeared in the Cai Nua area (Cai Be), determined to lock up HL-20 and Kinh 25 (then the 7th Div MSRs) and seize QL-4. Sector forces fought off the thrust for 11 days, and the Z-15 withdrew. The enemy revealed lack of initiative, but we were certain that a decisive showdown was almost inevitable.
Jun 72—The enemy made his first attempt to grab a population center, with his 14-day siege of BA Dua (Cai Lay), which failed with heavy losses. We rated the enemy's performance as mediocre, despite his numbers and firepower. The Province Chief was sparing no pains to retain the initiative, carrying the fight to the enemy at every chance.
Jul 72—Unlike the first three months, July saw fierce confrontations with NVA units across a wide swath—in Cai Be (where B-52 strikes were

used for the first time on 8 July), Cai Lay, and in Sam Giang, where a
five-battalion force besieged Vinh Kim district town. The siege was lifted
on the fourth day, with heavy losses that climaxed the enemy's last attempt to escalate the war in Dinh Tuong.

Aug 72—A period of eerie quiet, punctuated by sharp, brutal clashes,
the most serious of which was the 24th NVA Regt's 4-day drive to "liberate" Phu My (Ben Tranh).

Sep thru Dec 72—A daily agony of suspense, but no further major
enemy thrusts. Friendly spoiling operations continued throughout the
4-month period. Strong psychological pressure is being exerted by both
sides, but the GVN has a firm upper-hand. The NVA has precious little
to show for nine months of its invasion try in Dinh Tuong, abominably
costly in men and materiel, yet failing to achieve any of its objectives.
The statistics for 1972 are as follows:

	KIA	KBA	WIA	WPNS LOST/DEST/CAPT
Enemy	3,805	702	—	1,326 indiv; 195 c/s
Friendly	1,067 (176)*	—	4,396 (1,577)*	651 indiv; 12 c/s

*Booby-trap casualties

d. (U) *Development Highlights.*

(1) *Education.* The Upper Delta Community College will open on the
15th of January 1973. 830 applicants took the examination and 200 passed
in the following courses:

> English 50
> Vietnamese 50
> Physics/Chemistry   50
> Math 50

Dr. Long from the University of Saigon will be the Director. Dr. Phuoc
from the University of Phu Tho (Vocational Education) will be his assistant and Mr. Be (Principal of Nguyen Dinh Chieu High School My Tho)
will be the secretary general. MOE has allocated 200,000,000$VN
(100,000,000$VN for construction and 100,000,000$VN operations). Five
full-time professors have already been hired and seven part-time professors are on the staff. To expedite opening, the Community College will
use the new Normal School facilities.

(2) *Youth/Sports.* A total of 3,700 students have participated in gymnas-
tic courses and 400 youth cadre have attended courses in soccer, volley-
ball, table tennis and badminton.

(3) *Province/Municipal Development.* All CPDC projects except one
have been completed.

(4) *Province Maintenance Shop.* ·A year ago, eight services were sending 49 vehicles to the shop, while today, 15 services are sending 163
vehicles.

(5) *Public Health.* Five maternity/dispensaries, two aid stations have been completed and the TB clinic was repaired and upgraded. One additional sanitation hamlet was opened, a new village water system was completed and a sanitation program in Cai Lay district town was established. Vaccination of school children reached its goal of 100%.

(6) *Finance.* All 58 (out of 89) participating in the village self-sufficiency program reached their goals. Province budget attained 138% of its goal and the village budget reached 123% of its goal.

(7) *Economy.* The business community is sanguine. Mydico feedmill has opened—the largest in the Delta. My Tho now has a total of 13 gas stations with the 14th under construction. This new station will be My Tho's largest. The 13 now in operation pay 113,000$VN in salaries. Monthly profits total 6,880,000$VN. My Tho added one commercial bank in 1972, bringing the number of banks in My Tho to five (four commercial—1 government). 64 persons are employed; the banks pay over 800,000$VN in salaries per month.

(8) *Rural Credit.* As of 30 November, 48,413,000$VN had been loaned in 1972 (63,237,037$VN available). This compares very favorably to the 27,149,000$VN loaned in 1971, when there was a total of 1208 borrowers compared to 1,828 for 1972.

(9) *Rural Banks.* Despite the uncertainties of the offensive, two are on the verge of opening (Cai Lay and Cai Bo).

(10) *Public Works.* Two major bridges were opened: the cantilever Cho Gao span linking Go Cong with My Tho, and the 7-section An Huu bridge on QL-4 in Giao Duc.

e. (U) *Summary.* In 1972, Dinh Tuong was the most heavily targeted—for obvious strategic reasons—of all the Delta provinces. It not only survived Hanoi's "Easter" offensive by thwarting or blunting every enemy push, but has come through stronger than ever. This has not happened fortuitously—the history of this year, indeed, could be written in terms of what has *not* happened—thanks to countless sacrifices, aggressive friendly actions and, above all, inspired leadership. Where then, one may ask rhetorically, are the "two governments, two armies?" Not in Dinh Tuong.[57]

1972   31 December

	TOTAL	NET CHANGE
U.S. military personnel assigned in Vietnam	24,200	−132,600

U.S. casualties	YEAR	TO DATE(cumulative)
Killed in action	300	45,926
Wounded in action	1,221	303,596

Source: DOD/OASD

1973

1973 8 January—Dr. Kissinger and Le Duc Tho resume their private negotiations in Paris. **15 January**—President Nixon announces that all hostile actions against North Vietnam have ceased.

On 16 January a U.S. embassy briefing given to newsmen in Phnom Penh ends with this comment:

Since January of this year we have seen the beginning of another offensive in Cambodia. The KI [Khmer Insurgent] with VC/NVA support have put considerable pressure on the Lon Nol government and in the countryside. This is certainly associated with expectations of a cease fire in [South Vietnam]. . . .

Currently government controlled area and population are somewhat less than in 1970 but not substantially different. . . .

ENEMY FORCES
. . . Main forces or VC/NVA number some 36,000. . . . Under NVA/VC tutelage, the Khmer insurgents have increased from 3,000 in 1970 to a current estimated force of 40,000. Of these approximately 25,000 are main line combatants. The KI are now capable of presenting a significant threat to the Lon Nol government and are expected to continue the present high level of activity.

The enemy has thus sought to "Khmerize" the war. But nonetheless the final outcome depends primarily on the future actions of the VC/NVA. If they leave Cambodian soil, we believe that the Khmer armed forces have the capability to contain and ultimately to defeat the insurgent threat.[58]

In South Vietnam, because "there was not time to call a full COSVN conference," COSVN Directive 02/CT/73, dated 19 January, is adopted and circulated.

To: V6 Standing Committee and Region Party Committee Members

Absolute Secret
Flash I

DIRECTIVE
02/CT/73
Fundamental directive on policies and urgent tasks related to the political settlement and cease-fire

(Releasable to Provincial Party Committee level and above in accordance with regulations pertaining to the handling of absolute secret
materials)

This is a fundamental directive of COSVN Standing Committee dealing
with the direction of policies and substance of task activities, principally
with the necessity to *concentrate guidance in the initial period of a political
settlement and cease-fire.*

I. HISTORIC VICTORY AND NEW TURNING POINT OF OUR PEOPLE'S ANTI-U.S.
RESISTANCE FOR NATIONAL SALVATION.

Thanks to our firm attitude and the gallant fighting of our army and
people in both the North and the South, our army and people in Hanoi,
Haiphong and other provinces in the North who had defeated the adventurous strategic [air] raid launched by the American imperialists with a
view to be able to negotiate from a strong position, we have finally
compelled the Americans to accept the basic provisions of the Agreement
which had been reached in October 1972.

The achievement of a political settlement with the above-mentioned
Agreement represents a historic victory of our entire nation, a historic
defeat of the U.S. greedy aggressive imperialism. It marks a most important new turn in the advancing path of the South Viet-Nam revolution in
particular and the Viet-Nam revolution in general, and at the same time,
it bears a great international significance. . . .

*We must fully grasp the new victory and new period in order to make
outstanding efforts to win new greater victories while at the same time
anticipating new schemes and plots of the enemy with the difficulties and
complications they may create in the coming days so as to take the initiative
in dealing with and defeat the enemy in any circumstance.*

The problem facing us in the event of a settlement and cease-fire is to
bring our victory into play, seize the opportunity, while relying on the
strength of the masses and the support of our armed forces, bring into
play the legal foundations of the Agreement, concentrate guidance in
order to bring about at all costs a political movement of the masses and
turn it into a high movement of political violence which operates broadly
in all the three areas [i.e., mountainous, rural and urban areas—Ed.*]
under the slogans calling for peace, independence, democracy, rice and
clothing for the people, national concord, with the aim to largely disintegrate the puppet army and oppressive forces at the base level, divide and
weaken the puppet government at all echelons. This effort must be done
simultaneously with the building and development of our armed and political forces, the consolidation and enlargement of the liberated area and
the revolutionary administration.

Only by achieving this can we create basic conditions to guarantee the
implemention of the Agreement, maintain peace and enable the revolution to continue its march forward.

*In original translation.

II. DIRECTION OF OUR POLICIES IN THE EVENT THE AGREEMENT IS SIGNED
AND THE CEASE-FIRE GOES INTO EFFECT

1. In the face of the new situation, in order to ensure the fulfillment
of our basic mission which is to achieve the national democratic revolution in the South as a step toward peacefully unifying our country, the
direction of our immediate mission when the Agreement is signed is as
follows:

*"To mobilize the entire Party and people to bring our victory into full play
by taking part in the high political movement in the three areas using the
slogans calling for "peace, independence, democracy, rice and clothing for
the people, national concord" and demanding the implementation of the
Agreement. To disintegrate and seriously collapse the puppet army and
government, take over control of the rural area, seize power at the base level;
simultaneously, to build and develop our political and armed forces, build
and strengthen the revolutionary administration and liberated area in all
aspects, smash all enemy schemes to sabotage the Agreement, prevent large
scale conflicts, maintain peace, hold general elections as provided for in the
Agreement, bring the South Viet-Nam revolution toward the fulfillment of its
basic objectives, at the same time, maintain constant alertness and readiness
to deal with the U.S. imperialists' plot to resume hostilities.. . ."*

2. *Strategic principles and struggle guidelines [which] we must fully
grasp in the new phase.*

a. The following strategic principles must be fully grasped:

One: *We must fully grasp the objective of the national democratic
revolution and closely combine the national mission with the democratic
mission in the new situation.*

Therefore, the slogans calling for "peace, independence, democracy,
rice and clothing, national concord" are not only principal slogans to be
used in the immediate future but also strategic slogans to be used during
the whole new phase.

Two: We must fully grasp the *offensive strategy of pushing back the
enemy step by step and winning victory bit by bit before achieving complete
victory.* On the basis of persisting in the thought of unceasing and continuous revolution, we must create opportunities and grasp the opportunities in order to accelerate the development of the revolution in the new
phase.

Three: We must fully grasp the *concept of violence* in the context of the
new situation, in the political struggle phase. We must absolutely bring
into play the masses' political violence, and stand ready to surmount
fierceness and bloodshed in the course of promoting the political movement into a high tide. At the same time, we must not neglect military
violence. On the contrary, we must stand constantly ready, especially we
must unceasingly build up our three-troop-category armed forces as a
firm support for our political struggle.

Four: We must *closely associate the mission of achieving the national
democratic revolution in the South with the mission of protecting and*

building socialism in the North as a step toward the unification of our country.

Five: We must coordinate the revolutionary movement in South Viet-Nam with the revolutionary movements in Kampuchea and Laos and the Indochinese revolution in general, coordinate the struggle movement for peace, independence, democracy, improvement of living standards with the movement for peace, national liberation and socialism all over the world.

b. We must fully grasp the following guideline and method of operation.

One: We must clearly combine political struggle with armed struggle and legalistic struggle, using political struggle as the base, armed struggle as support, while bringing into full play the legalistic effects of the Agreement.

Two: We must closely combine the overt form of organization with the semi-overt and clandestine forms of organization, using the clandestine form as a base.

Three: We must clearly coordinate our offensive activities with activities to build our forces in all aspects for the purpose of creating a new position, strength and situation.

Four: We must closely coordinate the masses' struggle in the three strategic areas with the struggle of the overt organizations which are provided for in the Agreement (the Joint Military Commission, the National Council of National Reconciliation and Concord, the Prisoner Exchange Commission), using the masses' struggle as a base while bringing into full play the struggling effects of the overt organizations.

III. CONCENTRATING GUIDANCE TO STEP UP THE HIGH POLITICAL MOVEMENT IN ALL AREAS FOLLOWING THE PRINCIPAL SLOGANS

Once the Agreement is signed, the immediate central task is to promote at all costs the high political movement throughout all areas using the principal slogans. All activities must center around this central task.

The following essential things must be done properly:

1. *First of all, we must timely step up propaganda activities to create a broad movement participated in by the people of all strata to welcome peace and our national victory and demand the implementation of the Agreement. . . .*

3. *To quickly rally the masses into strong political forces and launch a high movement of revolutionary actions, widespread over all areas, operating under the form of political violence, with the support of the armed forces, and in conjunction with the exploitation of the legalistic base provided by the Agreement. . . .*

c. In applying the guideline of closely coordinated political struggle with legalistic struggle, we must consider the political struggle as a base and armed struggle as a support, while bringing into full play the legalistic effects of the Agreement. We must, according to conditions of each area, each place, each period of time, and the practical reality of each struggle, apply flexibly the three-pronged attack approach at the base level in a way suitable to the new situation. This is a delicate matter requiring that we stay away from two extreme tendencies: the tendency to utilize only the armed approach as we did during the war period and the tendency to tie ourselves in the purely legal political struggle which prevents us from bringing into play under various forms the masses' revolutionary violence. . . .

4. *Strive to build and develop political and armed forces and the revolutionary administration, consolidate and expand our liberated areas and base areas.* . . .

a. *Firmly hold the armed forces, continue to consolidate* and build the three types of troops in proper balance, bring into play the victorious stance, heighten the fighting spirit and revolutionary alertness, stand firmly on our respective area of operation, firmly maintain our new strategic deployment by protecting our base areas and liberated areas, protecting our Party, administration and people. We must bring into play our armed forces in support of the masses' struggle and improve the quality of our armed forces in conjunction with increasing their size; we must step up political education and technical and tactical training, make our troops take part in production, and civilian and military proselytizing activities; we must actively build up our reserve of food and ammunition, protect our corridors and depots and make sure that our armed forces are ready to take the initiative in any circumstance to smash the enemy's plot to resume hostilities.[59]

In Saigon, CIA agent Frank Snepp observes the developments.

Simultaneously, General Haig was sent to Saigon with a new ultimatum: If Thieu should still refuse to sign the draft accord more or less as it was written, the United States would cut off all assistance to South Vietnam and would sign a separate agreement with the North Vietnamese. Concurrently, in a personal letter to Thieu, Nixon warned that further intransigence would be "an invitation to disaster," and "would be inexcusable, above all because we will have lost a just and honorable alternative.". . .

As the talks progressed, the Administration continued to bombard Thieu with threats and promises in a relentless effort to bring him to heel. Finally, on 20 January, Nixon made it patently clear that he would conclude a separate peace with the North Vietnamese at once if Saigon refused to bend. His message to Thieu was blunt and to the point: "As I have told you, we will initial the agreement on 23 January. I must know whether you are prepared to go along with us in this cause and I must have your answer by twelve hundred Washington time 21 January 1973."

Staring total isolation in the face, Thieu capitulated.

Three days later, on schedule, Kissinger and Le Duc Tho initialed the agreement on behalf of the two other "parties"—the Saigon regime and the Communist Provisional Revolutionary Government. The next morning a white-suited Ambassador Bunker strode into the conference room on the third floor of the U.S. Embassy in Saigon and proclaimed, with tears in his eyes, "This is a great day for us all. There is to be a cease-fire." That afternoon the briefing officers at MACV flashed a cartoon onto the viewing screen they had so often used to display body counts and territorial gains. One caricatured Viet Cong soldier was shown asking another, "What is a cease-fire, after all?" The reply: "Damned if I know."[60]

That same day an American forward air controller, callsign Rustic 09, is flying a routine mission in Cambodia directing a flight of two U.S. Air Force fighter-bombers in support of FANK forces. The airborne command post, ABCCC, a C-130 that controls air traffic, tape records not only all combat transmissions but also any receptions on each of the different radios on board. On this tape "Sam the FAC" is a Khmer army lieutenant who acts as liaison between the Americans and the Khmer ground commander. As this mission begins, Rustic 09 is describing the target area to the flight leader.

RUSTIC 09:	Ahhh—it's due west of my—due east of my smoke one river's width in a wooded area. . . . Understand you'll be using the CBU first?
LEAD FIGHTER:	If that's what you want.
RUSTIC 09:	Ahh roger—either one—whichever's more convenient for you, sir.
LEAD:	We'll use the CBU first.
RUSTIC 09:	OK—and Lead, I'll want yours on the north and two, I'll take yours on the south. And I want you to run in from south to north with a—ahh—west break.
LEAD:	Roger. South to north with a west break.
RUSTIC 09:	That's charlie [*OK*] . . . thank you. . . . *Judas!* Looks beautiful today. You've really got those guys down.
LEAD:	OK—Lead is in from the south.
RUSTIC 09:	Roger, sir, you're cleared hot.
[*Pause*]	
RUSTIC 09:	Sam, ahh—where do you want, ahh, the rest of the bombs? Are they—are the bad guys moving farther north?
SAM:	No—am moving farther east—WEST!
RUSTIC 09:	Roger . . .
#2 FIGHTER:	Two's off from the south.
RUSTIC 09:	OK. And two, I'll tell you what—instead of—go ahead and put yours on the south—and Lead, I'll take your next ones farther north. . . .
LEAD:	Roger.

RUSTIC 09:   They say you're cleared hot.

[*Unintelligible and garbled transmissions in English, Cambodian, and Vietnamese.*]

SAM: Requesting further north and west.

RUSTIC 09:   Roger, Sam. How about on the south side of the river?

SAM: [*Garbled*] many bunkers are destroyed. . . .

RUSTIC 09:   OK Lead, we'll want 'em . . . ahhh—just about another river's width to the north. The bad guys are running to the north and west out of that area, so— ahh—from that wooded—ahh—section that's almost obscured by the smoke now put it—ahh—north of that.

LEAD: How far north?

RUSTIC 09:   OK—about a river's width.

LEAD: OK.

SAM: Ahh, 09 sir, you are taking ground fires from the— where the CBU going off.

RUSTIC 09:   OK. And there's also ground fire from the areas of the CBU. . . . and Two, take time to set up.

[*Pause*]

RUSTIC 09:   And the bad guys over in that area are still angry there, so, ahh—[*unintelligible*].

LEAD: Haven't they heard the news?

RUSTIC 09:   I don't think so—the guys in the town have here. . . .

[*Unidentified*]: Some people just can't take a joke.

RUSTIC 09:   Hah.

VOICE OF PRESIDENT NIXON, which will fade in and out as the mission continues [*only those phrases that are intelligible are transcribed here*]:

                  ". . . we shall also expect other interested nations to help insure that the agreement is carried out . . ."

RUSTIC 09:   I hate to tell you this, ahhh, right now you guys, but at this moment—ahhh—his speech is on Radio Australia. ". . . As this long and difficult war ends . . ."

[*Garbled and unintelligible*]

SAM: Ahh—09—the bad guys are shooting at you from the dried up lake bed which . . .

                  ". . . your courage, by your sacrifice, you have won the precious right to determine your own future . . ."

RUSTIC 09:   Ah roger, Sam, I'll track 'em.

SAM: Ahh, 09—ahh—you are taking ground fire, sir, from west of the target area again.

RUSTIC 09:   Ah roger.

                  ". . . friends in peace as we have been allies in war."

RUSTIC 09:	Cleared hot, two—and they got, ah, ground fire from west of the target area.
	". . . let us now build a peace of reconciliation. For our part, we are prepared to make a major effort to help achieve that goal [*fades out*] so too will it be needed to build and strengthen the peace."
RUSTIC 09:	Roger, two. Beautiful.
	". . . even indirectly, now is the time for mutual restraint . . ."
RUSTIC 09:	Ahhh, there's a lot of irony today, gentlemen, and Lead, I'll take your bombs in the—ahh—wooded area, ah, let's put it in the wooded area just to the—ahh—
	". . . to all of you who are listening, the American people: Your steadfastness . . ."
RUSTIC 09:	Just to the north of where two's CBU's are in you'll see the diamond shaped pond and the first wooded area to the—ah—north of the diamond.
	". . . peace with honor possible."
SAM:	09, requesting further CBU's.
	". . . secret negotiations at the sensitive stage, . . ."
LEAD:	OK—the wooded area with the heavy ground fire—is it the same wooded area you're talking about?
RUSTIC 09:	Ahh, negative, sir, The next wooded area to the northwest and it's in the northwest side of the CBU pattern.
LEAD:	OK—and you want to hit that wooded area?
RUSTIC 09:	That's charlie, sir.
LEAD:	That's just to the—ahh—east, repeat—that wooded area just to the east of that pond.
RUSTIC 09:	Ahh, roger that—inside, inside—almost to the—almost to the north of that—ahh—diamond shaped pond. It's on the—ahh—west side of that CBU pattern.
	". . . those efforts. The important thing was not to talk about peace, but to get peace . . ."
RUSTIC 09:	And it's just a hair to the east.
LEAD:	Ahh, there's quite a bit of smoke, and I'm unable to pick it up there from the south. How about a smoke on that?
RUSTIC 09:	OK, I'll get over there and put you in a smoke.
	". . . achieved an honorable agreement, let us be proud . . ."
RUSTIC 09:	If you'll hold up there, the FAC will be in with the smoke in about—ahh—twenty seconds.

> ". . . for the 50,000,000 people of In-
> dochina. Let us be proud of the 2½
> million young Americans . . ."

RUSTIC 09:   And Two, I'll be in with the smoke shortly. . . .

> "Let us be proud of those who gave
> their lives so that the people of South
> Vietnam might live in freedom and so
> that the world might live in peace. In
> particular, I would like to say a word
> to some of the bravest people I have
> ever met—the wives, children, fami-
> lies of our prisoners of war . . ."

RUSTIC 09:   OK, two, do you see my smoke? It's halfway between
                 that diamond pond and the wooded area with the
                 structure in it. I want you to hit that wooded area
                 that's just to the—ah—northeast of my smoke.

#2 FIGHTER: Stand by one.

> ". . . so that where this generation
> knew war . . ."

#2 FIGHTER: Two has the smoke.

> ". . . next generation would know
> peace."

RUSTIC 09:   OK, sir, it's the wooded area that's just to the north-
                 east of my smoke about—ah—two and a half river
                 widths and it's north of that diamond . . .

[*All transmissions here are garbled, with English, Cambodian, and Vietnamese voices drowning out President Nixon and each other.*]

LEAD: I can't see the structure. Where is it? Ahh—in which
                 corner?

RUSTIC 09:   It's almost dead center on the north side of it. Say
                 again, Sam?

> "Yesterday, a great American who
> once occupied this office died. In his
> life, President Johnson . . ."

SAM [*excited*]: You taking very heavy ground fire, sir, northwest of
                 the target one klick.

> ". . . nothing he cared about more
> deeply than achieving a lasting peace
> in the world."

RUSTIC 09:   And Sam reports very heavy ground fire northwest of
                 the target one klick.

LEAD: Got it.

SAM: Across the pagoda, sir.

RUSTIC 09:   And it's close up to that pagoda is the reason we can't
                 get near it.

> ". . . just the day after New Year's . . ."

#2 FIGHTER: Roger.

". . . concern with bringing peace,
with making it the right kind of peace,
and I was grateful that he once again
expressed his support . . ."

RUSTIC 09:   Roger, sir.

"No one would have welcomed this
peace more than he."

RUSTIC 09:   Beautiful! OK—ahh—Two, I'll want yours—ahh—to
the—ah—right about a river's width—ahh—from
Lead's bomb.

SAM: Marvelous! Good pass—right on, right on.
                    "Let us consecrate . . ."

SAM: Hit again! Hit again!

RUSTIC 09:   Ahh—in fact—Two, go ahead and hit that same area if
you want. Ground commander wants that same area
hit.

LEAD: Cleared hot?

RUSTIC 09:   Cleared hot sir.

". . . Thank you and good evening."

RADIO AUSTRALIA   [female voice]: That was Richard Nixon from Washington, three hours ago, announcing that terms had been
agreed to for peace in Vietnam.

RUSTIC 09:   Beautiful, Two. Lead, hit about a river's width to the
north of Two's bombs. If you want, we can wait about
a minute for the smoke to clear.

RADIO AUSTRALIA: And now we begin the programme with Sonata Number . . .

RUSTIC 09:   Keep it moving north, moving north to the next
wooded area, to the next wooded area north.

LEAD: Right.

[A loud blast of symphonic music from Radio Australia.]

RUSTIC 09:   Rustic 09, Roger.[61]

ACT V

January 1973–April 1975

I'm ~~so~~ short
I left yesterday—
This is a recording

8965 Days to go
how come?
I'm Vietnamese!

—GI latrine graffiti, Saigon

Three significant chapters of the Paris Agreement are as follows.

The Vietnam Agreement and Protocols
Signed January 27, 1973

AGREEMENT ON ENDING THE WAR AND RESTORING PEACE IN VIETNAM

The Parties participating in the Paris Conference on Vietnam,

With a view to ending the war and restoring peace in Vietnam on the basis of respect for the Vietnamese people's fundamental national rights and the South Vietnamese people's right to self-determination, and to contributing to the consolidation of peace in Asia and the world,

Have agreed on the following provisions and undertake to respect and to implement them:

CHAPTER I
THE VIETNAMESE PEOPLE'S FUNDAMENTAL NATIONAL RIGHTS

Article 1
The United States and all other countries respect the independence, sovereignty, unity, and territorial integrity of Vietnam as recognized by the 1954 Geneva Agreements on Vietnam.

CHAPTER II
CESSATION OF HOSTILITIES—WITHDRAWAL OF TROOPS

Article 2
A cease-fire shall be observed throughout South Vietnam as of 2400 hours G.M.T., on January 27, 1973.

At the same hour, the United States will stop all its military activities against the territory of the Democratic Republic of Vietnam by ground, air and naval forces, wherever they may be based, and end the mining of the territorial waters, ports, harbors, and waterways of the Democratic Republic of Vietnam. The United States will remove, permanently deactivate or destroy all the mines in the territorial waters, ports, harbors, and. waterways of North Vietnam as soon as this Agreement goes into effect.

The complete cessation of hostilities mentioned in this Article shall be durable and without limit of time.

Article 3
The parties undertake to maintain the cease-fire and to ensure a lasting and stable peace.

As soon as the cease-fire goes into effect:

(a) The United States forces and those of the other foreign countries allied with the United States and the Republic of Vietnam shall remain in-place pending the implementation of the plan of troop withdrawal. The Four-Party Joint Military Commission described in Article 16 shall determine the modalities.

(b) The armed forces of the two South Vietnamese parties shall remain in-place. The Two-Party Joint Military Commission described in Article 17 shall determine the areas controlled by each party and the modalities of stationing.

(c) The regular forces of all services and arms and the irregular forces of the parties in South Vietnam shall stop all offensive activities against each other and shall strictly abide by the following stipulations:

All acts of force on the ground, in the air, and on the sea shall be prohibited;

All hostile acts, terrorism and reprisals by both sides will be banned.

Article 4
The United States will not continue its military involvement or intervene in the internal affairs of South Vietnam.

Article 5
Within sixty days of the signing of this Agreement, there will be a total withdrawal from South Vietnam of troops, military advisers, and military personnel, including technical military personnel and military personnel associated with the pacification program, armaments, munitions, and war material of the United States and those of the other foreign countries mentioned in Article 3 (a). Advisers from the above-mentioned countries to all paramilitary organizations and the police force will also be withdrawn within the same period of time.

Article 6
The dismantlement of all military bases in South Vietnam of the United States and of the other foreign countries mentioned in Article 3 (a) shall be completed within sixty days of the signing of this Agreement.

Article 7
From the enforcement of the cease-fire to the formation of the government provided for in Articles 9 (b) and 14 of this Agreement, the two South Vietnamese parties shall not accept the introduction of troops, military advisers, and military personnel including technical military personnel, armaments, munitions, and war material into South Vietnam.

The two South Vietnamese parties shall be permitted to make periodic replacement of armaments, munitions and war material which have been destroyed, damaged, worn out or used up after the cease-fire, on the basis of piece-for-piece, of the same characteristics and properties, under the supervision of the Joint Military Commission of the two South Vietnamese parties and of the International Commission of Control and Supervision. . . .

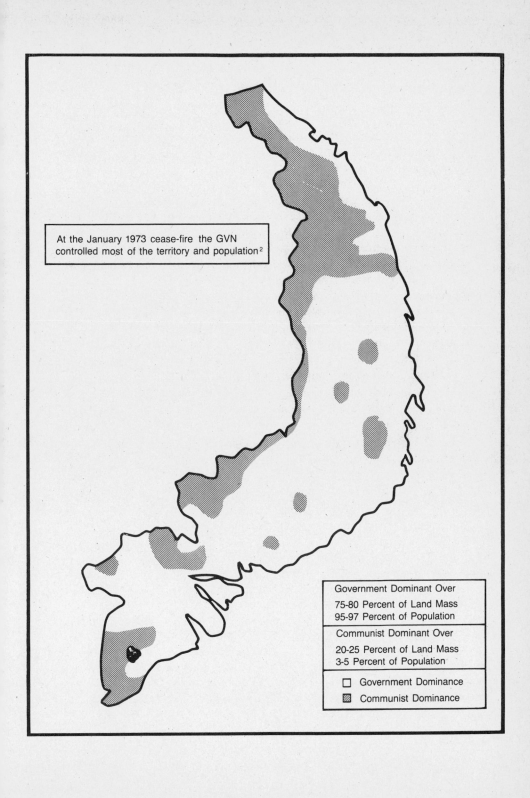

At the January 1973 cease-fire the GVN
controlled most of the territory and population[2]

Government Dominant Over

75-80 Percent of Land Mass
95-97 Percent of Population

Communist Dominant Over

20-25 Percent of Land Mass
3-5 Percent of Population

☐ Government Dominance
▨ Communist Dominance

REGARDING CAMBODIA AND LAOS

Article 20

(a) The parties participating in the Paris Conference on Vietnam shall strictly respect the 1954 Geneva Agreement on Cambodia and the 1962 Geneva Agreements on Laos, which recognized the Cambodian and the Lao peoples' fundamental national rights, i.e., the independence, sovereignty, unity, and territorial integrity of these countries. The parties shall respect the neutrality of Cambodia and Laos.

The parties participating in the Paris Conference on Vietnam undertake to refrain from using the territory of Cambodia and the territory of Laos to encroach on the sovereignty and security of one another and of other countries.

(b) Foreign countries shall put an end to, all military activities in Cambodia and Laos, totally withdraw from and refrain from reintroducing into these two countries troops, military advisers and military personnel, armaments, munitions and war material.

(c) The internal affairs of Cambodia and Laos shall be settled by the people of each of these countries without foreign interference.

(d) The problems existing between the Indochinese countries shall be settled by the Indochinese parties on the basis of respect for each other's independence, sovereignty, and territorial integrity, and non-interference in each other's internal affairs.[1]

The South Vietnamese chief of staff, General Cao Van Vien, comments on the agreement.

The Paris Agreement of January 1973 served only the immediate purposes of the United States and North Vietnam. It enabled President Nixon to keep his promise to the American people. American prisoners of war were released and reunited with their families, and all U.S. troops left South Vietnam safely and honorably. The U.S. was pleased that it had brought a "just peace" to the people of South Vietnam and terminated a long and inconclusive war, a war that divided the American people.

The Paris Agreement also offered North Vietnam favorable conditions to pursue its conquest of South Vietnam with success. No longer constrained by bombings and blockades, Hanoi devoted its efforts to reconstruction and development in order to better support its war efforts in South Vietnam. No obstacle now lay in the way of its continued infiltration through Laos and Cambodia. Hanoi simply ignored the restrictive provisions of the Paris Agreement that did not serve its purposes.

In South Vietnam, the NLF was given a legitimate national status. It now had an official government, an army, and a national territory of its own. In all respects, the NLF had become a political entity equal in power to the GVN. All the major obstructions that had prevented North Vietnam and its South Vietnamese lackeys from winning a military victory were now gone. U.S. and FWMA [Free World Military Assistance] forces had all left while nearly 300,000 NVA troops still remained on South Vietnamese soil. Never since 1954 had the Communists enjoyed such a strong political and military posture. . . .

Militarily, South Vietnam fared much worse under the Paris Agreement than the 1954 Geneva Accords in that it was compelled to define boundaries for troop regroupment areas and a time frame for it. How could that be done satisfactorily in a war without frontlines when enemy troops remained imbricated with ours throughout the country? Under such circumstances, how could a standstill cease-fire be strictly enforced since both sides could move their troops freely where and when they wanted, especially in view of Communist treachery and deceit? It was almost impossible to determine what area was under whose control; understandably enough, no side would want a smaller piece of the pie. This was especially true of contested areas to which both laid claim but in which neither side had a permanent military presence. The fact that the GVN effectively controlled a densely-populated one-third of South Vietnam's territory in no way implied that the remaining two-thirds of jungle and swampland were under Communist control. It was inacceptable to think that our border outposts were just controlling the premises of their immediate area even to the confines of their mortars' range. Likewise, the Communists also balked at the idea that their guerrilla activities were just bound within the mini-bases which lay in between villages and hamlets under GVN control. Therefore, the standstill cease-fire merely meant "grab as you can," which was exactly what had happened just before and after it went into effect, and this eventually led to bitter accusations from both sides.[3]

What General Vien refers to as the "landgrab" is shown on the map on the following page from a U.S. Army history.

1973 **27 January**—Secretary of Defense Melvin Laird announces an immediate end to the draft of American men. **28 January** —In Thailand, U.S. Support Activities Group and Seventh Air Force (USSAG/7th AF) headquarters is activated at Nakhon Phanom air base. Most command and control functions of MACV and Seventh Air Force, Saigon, are transferred. Also, Cambodian President Lon Nol declares a suspension of government military operations and calls for the North Vietnamese and Viet Cong to withdraw. In Peking, Prince Sihanouk rejects the idea of cease-fire.

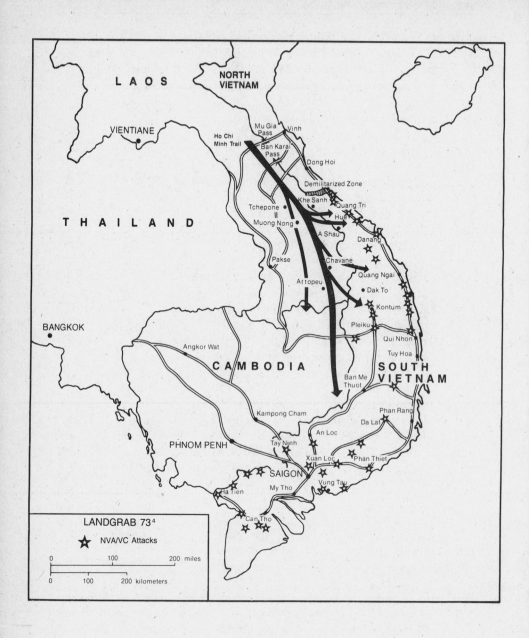

LAOS

NORTH
VIETNAM

VIENTIANE

Mu Gia
Pass

Vinh

Ho Chi
Minh Trail

Ban Karai
Pass

Dong Hoi

THAILAND

Demilitarized Zone

Tchepone

Khe Sanh

Quang Tri

Muong Nong

Hue

A Shau

Danang

Pakse

Chavane

Quang Ngai

Attopeu

Dak To

Kontum

Pleiku

Qui Nhon

BANGKOK

Tuy Hoa

Angkor Wat

CAMBODIA

SOUTH
VIETNAM

Ban Me
Thuot

Kampong Cham

Phan Rang

Da Lat

An Loc

PHNOM PENH

Tay Ninh

Xuan Loc

Phan Thiet

SAIGON

My Tho

Vung Tau

Ha Tien

Can Tho

LANDGRAB 73[4]

⭐ NVA/VC Attacks

0   100   200 miles

0   100   200 kilometers

Two days later this statement is released in Hanoi.

North Vietnamese Statement on Cambodia
January 30, 1973

[Text] At a time when all progressive mankind is displaying the highest elation and enthusiastically hailing our people's great victory won through the signing of the agreement on ending the war and restoring peace in Vietnam, in Phnom Penh, a helpless and isolated island in the middle of the impenetrable siege of the Cambodian revolution, the U.S. puppet reactionaries have not stopped uttering strange discordant allegations and vile slanders against our people. On 27 and again on 28 January, puppet president Lon Nol in messages over Phnom Penh radio distorted the spirit and letter of the 27 January 1973 Paris agreement, brazenly slandered the DRV and the PRGRSV by claiming that they have committed aggression against Cambodia, and demanded that our people put an end to this so-called aggression.

This is indeed a brazen act of changing white to black, and an evil trick designed to cover up the U.S. imperialists' aggression in that country. The American lackeys in Phnom Penh, however, have acted in vain. The actual situation in Cambodia has completely refuted their distorting allegations and vile slanders.

For a long time now the whole world has clearly known that it is the U.S. imperialists who have intervened in and invaded Cambodia and the other countries in Indochina. It was the U.S. imperialists who instigated the Lon Nol-Sirik Matak lackeys to stage the reactionary coup d'etat on 18 March 1970 against the Cambodian people in an attempt to eliminate Cambodia's independence and turn this country into a new-type U.S. colony and a springboard against the resistance of the Vietnamese and Lao peoples. The whole world knows very well that it was precisely the Lon Nol-Sirik Matak-Son Ngoc Thanh clique which let the wolf enter the house by bringing U.S.-Saigon puppet troops into Cambodia to ravage its land, causing untold misery and death to its people.[5]

On 10 February Henry Kissinger visits Hanoi to discuss implementation of the truce. The discussions are stormy.

To calm the atmosphere, Le Duc Tho offered to release twenty prisoners of war ahead of schedule, ostensibly in honor of my visit, and gave me the opportunity to pick them from the POW list. While grateful for the early release, I refused to select the names. I had no basis for making individual selections among those who had already suffered so long. (Prisoners held the longest were being released earliest in any case.) This was one promise Hanoi kept; twenty additional prisoners were released with the first group.

The North Vietnamese were at their most adamant (and obnoxious) about Laos and Cambodia. Article 20 of the Paris Agreement explicitly stipulated that "foreign countries" should end all military activities in Cambodia and Laos and totally withdraw all their forces there. In a separate written understanding, Le Duc Tho and I had agreed that Vietnamese as well as American troops were "foreign" within the meaning of this article. If words meant anything, this required immediate North Vietnamese withdrawal from Laos and Cambodia and an end to the use of Laotian and Cambodian territory for base areas, sanctuaries, or infiltration.

My conversations with Pham Van Dong had not proceeded far before it became apparent that the North Vietnamese proposed to drain Article 20 of all meaning. They took the position that the required withdrawal, unconditional on its face, would have to await not only a cease-fire in Laos and Cambodia, but also a political settlement in *both* those countries. Hanoi would withdraw only after negotiations with the new governments there. Since Communist political demands were for what amounted to Pathet Lao predominance in Laos and a total Khmer Rouge victory in Cambodia, North Vietnamese withdrawal would take place, if at all, only after it had become irrelevant and the issue had been decided in favor of the Communist side. Hanoi was proposing in effect to negotiate with itself, or at best with its Cambodian and Laotian stooges, about implementing provisions of an undertaking with us. The achievement of political settlements in Laos or Cambodia—which Le Duc Tho had in fact refused to discuss at Paris—could not possibly be made a precondition for the fulfillment of obligations that made no reference to it whatsoever and, by their plain import, were without qualification.

Hanoi's outrageous interpretation was particularly ominous for Cambodia. In Laos cease-fire negotiations were at least taking place and we had, for whatever it was worth, Hanoi's promise to bring them to a conclusion within fifteen days. But in Cambodia the Khmer Rouge refused to talk to any representative of the non-Communist side: their response to Lon Nol's unilateral proclamation of a cease-fire was a renewed military offensive. We had risked making peace in Vietnam in the absence of formal arrangements for Cambodia because the American Congress would never have tolerated any delay on account of Cambodia alone and because our experts agreed that the Khmer Rouge could not prevail by themselves. If they were deprived of North Vietnamese combat and logistical support, as the Agreement required, some form of compromise settlement was probable. But if North Vietnamese troops remained in violation of the Paris Agreement, they would almost certainly tip the balance in favor of the Khmer Rouge. Moreover, almost all our studies—the last at the end of January by the British antiguerrilla expert Sir Robert Thompson— indicated that a Communist takeover in Cambodia, by opening another enemy front and a sea route of supplies through Sihanoukville, would wreck South Vietnam's chances of survival.

In fact, we have since learned from Sihanouk's memoirs that the Khmer Rouge, considering the Paris Agreement a betrayal, had asked the North Vietnamese troops to quit Cambodia. They stayed in violation of Article 20 *and* against the wishes of both their enemies and their own allies, whom they used as an alibi in their talks with us.

Needless to say, my response to Pham Van Dong was sharp. It was all very well, I said sarcastically, to note Hanoi's fastidious regard for the sovereignty of its allies. But it was bizarre to maintain that Hanoi could not make a unilateral decision to remove troops it had introduced unilaterally, in compliance with an agreement to which it had pledged itself barely two weeks earlier. Its soldiers were not prisoners in these countries. Hanoi, having introduced its forces without the approval of the legitimate governments, could certainly withdraw them on its own.[6]

CIA agent Frank Snepp's perception of the Article 20 controversy, however, is different.

Kissinger also slipped up on the wording of the provision dealing with Laos and Cambodia. Inexplicably, he neglected to include in the text a specific deadline for the withdrawal of NVA troops from either country. In later public testimony he insisted he had reached a secret "unconditional understanding" with Le Duc Tho that ensured an immediate pullout. But the North Vietnamese denied this, claiming that the understanding had been no more than a U.S. ultimatum, which they had rejected. From their standpoint, nothing in the agreement pertaining to Laos and Cambodia was legally binding until settlements were reached there as well.

In sum, then, the peace of Paris was no peace at all. It imposed no limitation, or obligation, on either side that could not be nullified through the unanimity principle, and apart from the withdrawal of U.S. forces, all major provisions were subject to reinterpretation and further debate.

Furthermore, in his rush to complete the negotiations, Kissinger had made commitments to each of the combatants, which if known to the other—or to the American people—would have given all of them second thoughts about the wisdom and practicality of his diplomacy. On the one hand, he had assured Thieu of continued U.S. support—and had threatened to withdraw it if he did not sign the accord. On the other, he had promised Le Duc Tho that all U.S. reconnaissance flights over North Vietnam would be suspended and all American technicians withdrawn from South Vietnam within a year in return for Hanoi's acceptance of the draft. If Thieu had known of these pledges, he might well have stood his ground even longer.

Kissinger made these commitments, and kept them secret, for quite pragmatic reasons, but in doing so, he raised false hopes and expectations that could only lead both Vietnamese sides to overplay their hand in the aftermath. Like the agreement itself, the secret underpinnings were a political minefield, waiting to explode on anyone who ventured within range.[7]

1973   12 February—First American POWs released in Hanoi. **15 February**
—In Laos, as talks between the Royal Lao government and Pathet
Lao delegations continue, supporting U.S. air attacks increase as
heavy fighting continues.

*U.S. pressure of another kind, however, also affects the Laos negotiations.
Laotian General Oudone Sananikone remembers:*

Some of [the American] urgings took the form of thinly veiled threats of
cuts in American assistance. It was quite difficult for any Lao official,
who knew that resistance on his part could put the country on the ropes
very quickly, to fail to respond to the Embassy pressure.

The Pathet Lao negotiators were well aware of what was going on.
They already knew that Souvanna Phouma would agree to almost any-
thing; now they knew that the Americans were, in effect, in their corner.
Armed with these advantages, they became even more obdurate.

As the days and weeks passed, more hard issues surfaced at the conference table. Heated discussions became the norm, but each time an impasse occurred, Souvanna Phouma ordered his delegation to concede. On
the worst of these occasions, the right wing members would threaten to
resign. This put Souvanna Phouma in a difficult position which was ame-
liorated by pressure from the American Embassy. We would find that the
weekly shipments of American supplied rice for the Army would not
arrive, or that the American supplied money to pay the Army would be
delayed, or that only part of the fuel needed to run the Army's vehicles
would be delivered. Capitulation by the right wing was essential to maintain the NLA [National Lao Army]. The American military attaches
made this very clear to all senior officers of the NLA.

It pleased Souvanna Phouma to see that the right wing leadership—
which essentially was the leadership of the NLA—was being rendered
impotent by American pressure. In his view, he had suffered for too long
the opposition of the right wing during the years when American support
had contributed to their strength. He failed to understand or appreciate
that he could not have remained in office for the past 13 years without the
support of the NLA. Now his actions indicated, "I don't need you." The
result of all this was an agreement with the Pathet Lao that, as it was
implemented, turned the country over to the Communists.

The Agreement on the Restoration of Peace and Reconciliation in Laos
was signed in Vientiane on Wednesday, 21 February 1973. The cease-fire
called for in the agreement was to take effect at noon the following day.
Except for some minor skirmishes, the cease-fire was generally observed
by both sides.[8]

In late February American author James Jones arrives in Saigon.

Saigon . . . Tan Son Nhut airport. . . . The big 707s and 747s from out
of the country, touching down momentarily, looked out of place here.
Dun military fixed-wings and helicopters rested themselves in protective revetments. Tall sandbag and wire emplacements towered everywhere, their guns leaning against the sky. Outside the airport entrance,
all public buildings and military quarters were festooned with wire and
armed guards and wrapped around with sandbags. The result of the
Tet Offensive in 1968. For me it was still another memory: Honolulu,
1942.

Outside the airport you were immediately in the swarm and motor
explosion of the city, consisting mainly of myriads of Hondas, bicyclettes
and bicycles, and uncountable numbers of tiny, dented, home-painted,
blue and yellow pre-war Citroëns which served as taxis. The car that took
me into the city slowed and honked and darted among them like a broken
field runner. We passed a tall, ugly red-brick cathedral. Then a sort of
park, with trees and some Buddhist shrines and an incongruously modern, acoustical, speaker's platform, recently constructed, obviously for
band concerts—or political speeches. Under tall pleasant shade trees that
lined a filthy, dusty sidewalk the car deposited me at the crowded swarm-
ing noisy door of the Continental Palace Hotel. I was already sweating
profusely.

The lobby was a swarm of foreign newsmen. After I unpacked, I
walked the block and a half over to the *Times* office. The cease-fire had
been on a month. But there was still heavy fighting in the Central Highlands in the north around Pleiku and Kontum. Villages in the Mekong
Delta were still being hit with mortar fire every night. The first POW
exchange had gone through, though. And was still the main newsworthy
topic of talk. The Americans still had a month to go before their final
pull-out, assuming that all went well. At that precise particular moment,
nobody was assuming that. There was still an eleven o'clock curfew in
Saigon itself.

I found the curfew exciting. By ten-thirty the streets of Saigon began to
be deserted. Somewhere overhead a plane would rumble across going
North, then another, bombers heading into Tay Ninh or Bien Hoa "after
VC." An occasional faint rumble of artillery rounds going in somewhere
would come from north of the city. At five of eleven the warning siren
went off, eerie over the town, and there would be a last-minute flurry of
Hondas and a car or two. A solitary walker would pass unhurried under
the tall streetlamps on the central square with its atrocious statue. Then
emptiness again. Somewhere off on a building the siren would wind down
in a lonely way. A small whirlwind of patrolling jeeps would scurry by
like a file of bugs. The white, hot goosenecks went on burning over the
empty square. After a while one solitary jeep rolled by, checking. But the
streets were empty. Deserted. Every night that I was there, I watched this
ritual from my hotel room window, or standing in the huge double doors
downstairs in the lobby.[9]

With fighting continuing throughout South Vietnam, Frank Snepp observes the political maneuvering.

In early February, soon after the Joint Military Commission had set up its headquarters at Tan Son Nhut, the South Vietnamese and PRG delegates got together to discuss the still unresolved problem of areas of control. The South Vietnamese insisted that proprietorship be determined by the location of army units alone, while the Communists argued that since their own units never stayed in one place, the country would have to be carved up arbitrarily. The discussions ended inconclusively and thereafter each side began hunting for alternate means of staking out real estate. The Communists opted for manipulation of the Paris agreement itself. Once the prisoner exchanges got under way they were careful to schedule all pickups and deliveries in areas where they wanted to show the flag, and whenever PRG representatives gathered at the edge of the jungle to be ferried to Tan Son Nhut on American helicopters, they always managed to locate the landing zones in previously disputed territory, in hopes of conveying the impression they had been in control there all along. Their most potent weapon, however, was the Joint Military Commission itself, since one of its primary responsibilities was to delineate the territorial holdings of the two sides. Once the JMC deployed inspection teams to the field, the Communists felt, Thieu would be unable to deny them access to large parts of the country.

Thieu immediately realized what the Communists were up to and took steps to frustrate them. During the first few months of the cease-fire, whenever the PRG nominated a disputed area as the site for a prisoner exchange, he would bomb or shell the place beforehand. He also attempted to limit the movements of PRG and North Vietnamese delegates to the JMC by bottling them up at Camp Davis, their headquarters at Tan Son Nhut. In addition, to discourage them from deploying their JMC field teams, he organized anti-Communist demonstrations in a number of major cities.

In early March the PRG responded as he had wanted, refusing to cooperate any further in setting up JMC field sites. The North Vietnamese reacted less satisfactorily, however, warning the United States that unless their delegates were assured the "privileges and immunities" guaranteed under the Paris accord, they would suspend the exchange of American prisoners.

That, needless to say, had an immediate effect. Under heavy American pressure Saigon agreed to assure the safety of the two Communist delegations.

From Hanoi's standpoint these concessions came too late, however. By early March the "war of the flags" which had begun with the cease-fire had been resolved largely in Saigon's favor, and in some areas, particularly in the northernmost provinces of the country, the two opposing armies had already accepted a de facto standstill cease-fire. In view of all this, the Communists decided the JMC would no longer be of much use in their land-grabbing strategy and essentially gave up on it. At the end of the month the PRG's chief delegate, the ever-smiling General Tran Van Tra, flew off to Hanoi, never to return. He would soon take up his old post as the principal military commander at COSVN, and from there would help coordinate the cease-fire war against Saigon for the next year and a half.[10]

What Communist General Tran Van Tra will be coordinating is the COSVN policy expressed in this March directive.

1. *The Nature of the Situation, the Form of the Struggle between Us and the Enemy at this Time, the Enemy's Plots, and Facts Concerning the Possibilities for Development of the Situation after 60 Days of Implementation of the Ceasefire Agreement.*

1. Message No. 775 of 25 February 1973 made it clear that: The main feature of the situation at this time is that the Agreement to End the War and Restore Peace in Viet-Nam (VN) has been signed, and the U.S. must withdraw all its troops and must cease the bombing and shelling of our people with its fleet. However, the U.S. is, on the other hand, shielding its puppets in their not implementing the Ceasefire order and in violating the Agreement.

The situation in South Viet-Nam (SVN) is not yet stable. The instability and complexity of the situation is seen clearly in the following points: Although there is an Agreement to End the War and Restore Peace in VN, in truth in SVN there are many places where the shooting and bombing and shelling continue, and in some places more than prior to the Agreement.

Armed conflict continues without pause because of the enemy's police operations and aggression and infringement, but the scale and the methods are not what they were when the war was still going on and are concentrated in a limited number of areas. There are no B-52's, artillery, fleet, or actions by aircraft and infantry of the U.S. and satellites. . . .

We are determined to foil enemy oppression and aggression by mobilizing the masses to engage in political, armed and military-proselyting [*sic*] struggle in coordination with legality to defend the lives and property of the people, to defend the liberated areas, to defeat the enemy's plots of obstruction and destruction, and to force the enemy to implement the agreement. . . .

It must be recognized that we have the strength of the masses, the strength of all our armed forces, and now we have the legal sanction to apply to give us the cutting edge of the three strengths in all our struggles, and so we have obtained a new considerable strength for attack upon the enemy. This strength must be shown concretely in the activities of our armed forces and in the three prongs in the villages, in order to develop the new assault posture in the new situation.[11]

In Washington, as Henry Kissinger notes, the administration's concern over events in Southeast Asia is affected by additional factors.

On March 13, there was another meeting of the WSAG on this subject. The group concluded that:

> We have no intention, under any circumstances, of letting the enemy mount a big offensive this year. We will be meticulous in honoring the agreement ourselves, and we want to make public their continuing violations. There will be no press statements issued that belittle the enemy violations.
>
> The best military option appears to be a resumption of bombing the trails in Laos as soon as possible after the third tranche of POWs is released, possibly followed later by bombing of the DMZ and the area between the DMZ and the South Vietnamese lines, if necessary. The final decision will be made by the President.

But the President was in an uncharacteristically indecisive frame of mind. It was not unusual for Nixon to approach a major decision crabwise. Long recitals of the dilemmas he faced were his way of reflecting on the options. During his first term the process had led inexorably to a decision. Each successive conversation, however apparently interminable, would lead gradually, almost imperceptibly, to a sharper definition of the issues. In stages Nixon worked himself to a fever pitch emotionally so that intellectual and psychological readiness tended to coincide with the point of decision. I would often frame the issue earlier than he; but he had the better instinct for the jugular. His final decision would cut through equivocation to the heart of the matter.

But it was a different Nixon in March 1973. He approached the problem of violations in a curiously desultory fashion. He drifted. He did not home in on the decision in the single-minded, almost possessed, manner that was his hallmark. The rhetoric might be there, but accompanied this time with excuses for inaction. In retrospect we know that by March Watergate was boiling. At the end of February, he was closeted for long periods with John Dean, his White House Counsel, devising strategy for the investigations by the newly constituted Senate Select Committee chaired by Senator Sam Ervin and worried about the hearings opening in the Senate Judiciary Committee on the nomination of L. Patrick Gray as permanent director of the FBI. It was on February 27 that Dean warned Nixon the cover-up might not be contained indefinitely. Nixon was a distracted man. On March 6, for instance, he ordered a bombing strike of one day's duration on the Ho Chi Minh Trail—timed for the following weekend. The illegal bumper-to-bumper military truck traffic down the trail promised profitable targets. The next day, March 7, he canceled the order. Again he said he did not want to give the North Vietnamese a pretext for delaying the release of the next batch of American prisoners. I doubt whether this was a considered reason. Gray was in difficulties over the FBI's Watergate inquiries and was daily dragging in John Dean and the White House. The Senate Judiciary Committee was demanding that Dean appear despite the President's assertion of executive privilege. Nixon clearly did not want to add turmoil over Indochina to his mounting domestic perplexities.[12]

Some of the "activities" of COSVN's "assault posture" are observed by writer James Jones on 22 March.

This was my third general in as many weeks, and I was beginning to get used to them. They might all have their personal idiosyncrasies that had to be indulged. And might be too used to having their creature comforts taken care of for them. But those I met deserved their rank and were good solid professionals. Men who often had to carry sole responsibility for decisions that could prolong or terminate the lives of many of their fellow citizens. And who were well aware of it. As far as I was concerned they deserved the best helicopters. Especially, since I would be riding them, too.

I was arriving in the late morning, and so was missing the first day and a half of the four-day tour. But I was catching the part I wanted most, which was the trip to the north of the Delta near the fighting. Once we were airborne, the general began filling me in on what was the situation in his command.

His name was Frank Blazey. He was the only West Pointer among the four MACV Regional commanders. He was a blocky, muscled man, brave as hell and tough as nails I was told. "Windy, but tough, old devil," was the exact phrase. At first meeting, there was something a bit prissy, pedantic, something of the paternalistic schoolteacher about him. But after a while you began to get down under that.

The Delta, Blazey felt, had been changed the least by the cease-fire, of the four Regional commands. The big battles along the Cambodian border had stopped. But the Delta had been the stamping ground of the guerrillas since the days when they were called the Viet Minh, and the cease-fire had not changed that part much. They were still roaming the countryside in bands of platoon and company strength. Deftly, on a map on his knees, he showed me the basic strategies. On the southwest coast was a huge area called the U-Minh Forest, which wasn't really forest at all but a great mangrove swamp. The North Viets supplied this area by sea with men, arms, and munitions, and from there the VC—mainly North Vietnamese since 1968—carried the stuff overland along what was called the Long My Corridor, into the central Delta in Chuong Thien Province. Only last night Long My the town had been mortared again. Six rounds, eight wounded. Civilians. On 35 of the 53 nights since the cease-fire began, Long My had taken VC mortar fire. Long My was in Chuong Thien Province, forty miles from Can Tho, and Chuong Thien was the worst province in the Delta. We would be going there later. Blazey grinned.

He shifted the map on his knees. In the north the present hot spots were at Tinh Bien and Tri Ton in Chau Doc Province. At Tri Ton the North Viet Army held the slopes of the Seven Mountains, and the government troops held the tops of them and the villages at their feet. At Tinh Bien the North Viets were pushing troops against and around Nui Giai Mountain. Lately, they had begun pushing more troops in around Hong Ngu. Strategically, the idea was to open up—or reopen—an entry port down into the central Delta, that would augment the Long My Corridor in the southwest. They had had one on the Bassac River arm of the Mekong, called "The Sampan Road" by the troops, but the South Viets had closed it back in December and January.

Two weeks ago the VC in the Seven Mountains had hit a schoolyard in Tri Ton with a 75 recoilless rifle and killed a couple of teachers and half a dozen kids. This had seemed a clear-cut truce violation and the Canadians and Indonesians agreed to investigate it. The Poles and Hungarians had refused, on grounds of personal safety; which was their right; they had been doing this more and more lately, especially when the violations were clearly NVA or VC. The Canadians had shamed them into going as "Observers," if not as a full-scale "Investigation," which meant there would be no official report, but they hoped to establish a precedent for later. Since the arrival of the ICCS in Tri Ton, there had been violations four days in a row, with both 82-mm mortars and 122-mm rockets. Two people wounded on March 18th. Two wounded on the 19th. One killed, four wounded on the 20th. Two killed, fourteen wounded on the 21st, yesterday. Yesterday's rounds had gone right into the JMC compound, where, naturally, the NVA and VC contingents had never arrived. It was located across town, away from the ICCS. Even so, now of course the Poles and Hungarians were threatening to pull out and leave. Blazey grinned at me again, and folded his map. "We are getting a little tetchy about people back home who call us the evil villains out here," he said.

[After landing, we] were seated to a Vietnamese gourmet lunch in the cool HQ villa on the bank of the Mekong, when a telephone rang somewhere. A minute later a young American aide from the Consulate came rushing in excitedly, and said the North Viets had just dropped eight 122 rockets into a crowded Cambodian refugee camp at Tan Chau ten miles north on the other river. Twenty houses down. Two killed. About thirty wounded. The young vice-consul was a pretty old Vietnam hand, but he looked shocked even so. I saw Blazey's jaw tighten as he sat back down to his lunch.

Later, when I could, I asked him why. Why bombard a refugee camp that had no military targets or significance? I couldn't see any point. The reason, Blazey said, was to terrorize the people into leaving the camp. When the fighting came to their area, they left their land and came to our camps. The North Viets wanted them to go back to their land and start raising the crops the North Viets needed to supply them.[13]

1973   29 March—Last 67 reported U.S. POWs depart Hanoi and last
uniformed U.S. troops leave South Vietnam. Remaining in DAO
(Defense Attaché Office) are 50 U.S. military personnel, 1,200
DOD [Department of Defense] direct hire U.S. civilians, 5,500
DOD contract personnel, and 183 AID, CIA, and Foreign Service
personnel on U.S. ambassador's staff. **7 April**—JCCS helicopter
shot down by SAM-7 missile. Nine die.

*Now in Phnom Penh for his third tour in Southeast Asia, Assistant Air
Attaché Mark Berent starts another journal.*

Sunday—8 April (1973)
For lack of a better title I may just call this my siege book.

It was a good feeling to awaken this morning, groggy and sweaty, and
know we passed the first night of the impending attack without receiving
any inbounds.

The power is, of course, off. We are rationed to 30 liters of gas a day. I
have sent my freezer to the Embassy & just maintain the refrigerator.
Only pulling 5 amps now as opposed to 20-21 before. Am not using the
air conditioner.

Still have the car and am authorized fuel. Very nice driving in town
now since there is little powered traffic.

Had omelette at La Taverne & stopped by Sam Jackson's. Not home. . . .

Of the 30 Mekong convoy ships scheduled, only 5 or 6 went up. Some
were hit even before leaving SVN. They are very determined, the VC. . . .

09 April—Monday
Made up maps & airborne at 0430 for 0530 P/U at Phnom Penh of Maj.
Thou Savanthim.

Two ships crossed border, rest would not. Then two POL tried, both
hit 1½ KM south of border. One steamed on & joined the other two.
They pressed for PN4 around 1300G. Wonder if they made it.[14]

1973   9 April—In South Vietnam, after the third attempt in two days to
shoot down JCCS helicopters, all JCCS observation flights are suspended.

*The same day in Washington, the Defense Department's morning news
briefing contains this interchange.*

Q: I assume you still have the small military delivery group stationed in
Phnom Penh. Are they moving out of Phnom Penh to watch the deliveries to make sure things get to where they are supposed to go?

A: They're not advisors or trainers, they're there to accept the delivery of the equipment and to the best of my knowledge they don't operate outside the general area of Phnom Penh. There are other personnel attached to the embassy other than this military equipment delivery team. The attachés and other civilians in the embassy, from time to time, under the requirements that we have from the Congress, have to look into the end use of our supplies. But the people on the military equipment delivery team work primarily in Phnom Penh.

Q: Are they or any other people helping to coordinate the American air activity?

A: No.

Q: How is that worked?

A: That's kind of an all-encompassing question. We fly air control aircraft depending on what they're controlling. A Cambodian officer sometimes flies with the forward air controller and he's the one that's in direct contact with his people on the ground. Other strikes that would be pre-planned strikes, you wouldn't necessarily need a controller in touch with the ground. These operate primarily out of Thailand.

Q: Are there other places they operate out of?

A: As we've said before, from time-to-time one of the OV-10s needs to refuel at Phnom Penh, that's not a normal circumstance, but they do it if they need some gas.

Q: None of the Americans who fly those planes lives in Phnom Penh?

A: No.[15]

Colonel Berent's diary records some Cambodian highlights of April.

12 April—Tuesday

Home at 1230 to find commercial power out (gas not delivered until 1630). Had a good nap. Have to take it while you can.

Afternoon brought . . . note about "incredible fall" of Prey Svey. Found we had plenty of air. . . .

Major Kim Chandabat says soldiers gambling and generally preparing for New Year's. Probably walked out. Burnell had been there 2 hours before and saw no action. He pounded the table & said "You (to Kim) have to fight!" A little late and to the wrong person.

—News stories accredited to "hippie journalists" supposedly decried by those in the know. Funny—since most journalists in town are now very responsible.

And things are as bad as they say.

13 April—Friday

Showed up for work at 0645 with necktie, completely forgetting it was the beginning of a 3-day Khmer Buddhist New Year. . . . Worked up until noon. . . . John Wilcox stopped by at 1230—had a few beers & off to La Taverne. Sam Jackson wanted 2 M-1's, said he'd feel "safer"—already has 4 handguns. . . . Power 1000-1630.

23 April—Monday
Convoy made it up river-with only a few hits. Some small tack-on boats
lagged behind and got hit. A Nail [FAC] put a MK-82 right on the mortar
site. . . .

24 April—Tuesday
Up (awakened) 0350 by B-52. Have window rattling on tape. Very little
sleep after. . . .

Long day on the console. . . .

Off to John Moore's at 1830 . . . to meet all the generals. Spent most
of the time in conversation with MG Srey Meas. Very interested he was
in the US. Lon Non [Lon Nol's brother] was there, very mod clothes.
Almost Edwardian length coat, high (almost Mao) collar—yellow shirt,
very apparent cufflink. . . .

—then ginned up 17+ F-111 targets at [US Embassy] area. Spent a hell
of a lot of time checking and rechecking.

25 April—Wednesday
On console and duty from 0645 to 1945.

Events of the day
—arranged A[ir] A[merica] helio to take [beacon people]. . . . Gen. C.
said mission of bird was to get target info back to Phnom Penh—resolved
problem—sent MEDT man along to bring info back.

However, AA [Air America] people said they were beyond crew duty
time, so [beacon people] left in Kamphong Chom—meanwhile, (earlier,
that is) T-39 bringing them in blew tire on runway. A long haul, but
Khmer Air Force chopper brought em back at 1835.

—then shit hit fan with no FAC over Takeo since 1020 (was due to
weather and bad management). . . .

—have had electricity four days now.

—told of General Yung Noch Han getting 75 tons of ammo to push
south on Route 5—pissed it away to units other than his own. Now wants
60 tons more, while Sala Lek Pram unit—road open Phnom Penh to this
point—has no water, 4 rounds ammo & lo morale.

26 April
0245. Ten 122mm rockets hit P-Tong [Phnom Penh airport]. . . . Drove
runway. No damage.

Cambodian radio saying attack was part of conspiracy. All of morning
news broadcast was merely Khmer Rouge Ambassador to England response to Manchester Guardian article about . . . attack being isolated.

. . . *any* attack on P-Tong is major; therefore, they "closed" runway.
Too much thinking going on up there. Matt and I sat on top of Command
Post and watched F-111 and then saw bomb flashes. Wind from our
back—not much noise.

27 April—Friday
—thought it was Saturday, went to work prepared to work console.

—Old VC trick to keep people handy (civilians) & then set up real or dummy gun pit near hootches or pagoda in broad daylight, then get US to drop on it & mash civilians.

[General] Cleland wants to hit a Rx [rocket] launcher site approx 150 feet from a pagoda—set up in broad daylight, yet.

There probably are sites over there—well concealed—we mash a dummy, they fire from concealed sites at nite—result: we fired first, they were just defending themselves from . . . etc.

Cleland quote . . . 27 Apr re Takeo: "I think they can take it back if they have a carpet of bomb fragments to walk on."

Burnell quote on Takeo: It ". . . must not fall—*we* will be explaining why."[16]

1973 25 April—United States and North Vietnam publish earlier exchange of formal notes charging each other with extensive ceasefire violations.

In Washington that same day a staff report for the Senate Foreign Relations Committee is published. Entitled "U.S. Air Operations in Cambodia," it concludes as follows:

V. The Significance of U.S. Air Operations in Cambodia

When we left Washington in late March the immediate objective of U.S. policy on Cambodia appeared to be the conclusion of a cease-fire between the Phnom Penh government and the forces opposing it. That objective had been stated, in the form of an expectation, by Dr. Kissinger at his January 24 press conference and restated, in the form of a unilateral declaration, by Marshal Lon Nol on January 29.

By the time we arrived in Phnom Penh in early April, however, the prospects for an early cease-fire were non-existent. The level of fighting had increased, not diminished, since late January. Most observers on the scene considered the political deterioration within the Cambodian Government to be as serious as the more obvious deterioration in the government's military position. Indeed, we found that the immediate concern of U.S. officials was simply to find a way to insure the government's survival and it was to achieve that immediate objective that the United States had greatly increased U.S. air operations in support of Cambodian Government forces engaged by that time in fighting a predominately Cambodian adversary.

In the political sphere, it was accepted as a fact by all informed observers that the United States had, through General Alexander Haig who visited Phnom Penh while we were there, indicated to Lon Nol that U.S. economic and military support, including air support, would not be continued unless he brought certain opposition political leaders into his government and put an end to the activities of his brother, General Lon Non, so that a more "representative" government could be formed which would be better able to maintain a credible Cambodian military and negotiating posture.

By late April, when we left Southeast Asia, it was far from clear that the political and military intervention of the United States would have a decisive effect on the situation in Cambodia. It was clear, however, that the United States had become far more deeply and directly involved than ever before in the conduct of the war in Cambodia, as well as in Cambodia's internal political affairs. It was the unanimous opinion of the American military and civilian officials in Southeast Asia with whom we met, and of the Cambodians to whom we talked, that only U.S. air support had enabled the Cambodian Government's forces to survive and would permit them to continue fighting. And most observers assumed that if Lon Nol did succeed in forming a new government, as we had in effect demanded, he would then be entitled to expect continued U.S. support and that support would be as essential for the survival of the new government as it had been for that of the former government.

We found widespread doubt on the part of experienced observers in Phnom Penh that even continued American air support and a reorganization of the Lon Nol government to include opposition leaders would arrest the government's decline. It was our impression that most Cambodians felt that it was
now beyond the government's ability to do more than get out of the war and that, indeed, they had no other choice. There was, however, no indication that the Khmer insurgents (as they are now called in official U.S. terminology) and their North Vietnamese supporters were interested in a cease-fire. In fact, it was not even clear, to either American or Cambodian officials, with which individuals on the other side a cease-fire could be discussed or on what conditions the insurgents would insist.[17]

On 2 May Colonel Berent's diary comments express his perspective on some of the major issues of the continuing U.S. involvement in Cambodia.

2 May—Wednesday—Thailand
On a bus from Pattiya [sic] beach to Bangkok. Things quiet for a few days, so what with TDY troops still on board managed to get a few days off. . . .

According to [other embassy personnel], General Vogt [Commander, Seventh Air Force] very worried (incensed? angry?) about Senator Symington & Moose/Lowenstein report.* (Question: why did they reveal so much (apparently) to the press prior to turning in their report to the committee?)

*See pp. 570–71.

Gen. V feels, apparently, the spectre of Gen. La Velle [*sic*] over his head. I, however, do not feel it is quite the same thing.

Since US was giving air support to GKR, SecState had ordered the Ambassador to provide political validation for each strike request by GKR. Furthermore, there were neither any secure means of transmission between Embassy and USSAG, nor could FACs talk to anybody because Sundog Alpha (radio relay station . . . at Tay Ninh) was off the air due to the draw down.

We certainly did not "control air raids." Only a FAC controls a strike. . . .

Just read where Elliott Richardson [*sic*] is switched from SECDEF to Head of Justice Department to replace Kleindeinst [*sic*], supposedly to take over Watergate investigation. Also, I believe, prevents him from being supoened [*sic*] immediately re. Cambodia by Symington. . . .

I'm told the boys upstairs don't just plot and examine FANK and USSAG targets—that they develop their own & Cement Head, the Mad Bomber, keeps saying "Bomb this or bomb that." I certainly don't fear testifying before any committee. I believe in what we are doing, knowing full well it may not help.[18]

1973 11 May—All charges in *The Pentagon Papers* case against Daniel Ellsberg are dropped because of documented "government miscon-duct."

That same week Dr. Kissinger leaves for France.

My next meetings with Le Duc Tho registered a new reality. I went not as a representative of an America that had just demonstrated there was a penalty for treachery, but as someone with almost no cards to play.

A CHARADE WITH LE DUC THO
I set out for Paris for what turned out to be an extended series of negotia-tions with Le Duc Tho lasting (intermittently) from May 17 to June 13. The ill omens did not cease, the most extraordinary being an intelligence report I received while en route to Paris. It was a North Vietnamese account that described how the Viet Cong leaders were briefing their subordinates in the field. The report confirmed our knowledge of Hanoi's buildup, referring to a "general offensive" that was in preparation. But it was being postponed, the briefing stated, to give Watergate an opportu-nity to complete the paralysis of our Presidency and the demoralization of our South Vietnamese ally. It accurately predicted that the wounded President now lacked the authority to retaliate against North Vietnamese transgressions.

The Watergate investigations . . . have already proved that the last US Presidential election was fraudulent, and many members of the White House staff have submitted their resignations. Therefore, . . . President Nixon must also resign because he no longer has enough prestige to lead the United States. His weakened authority over the US government is now generating a favorable influence in South Vietnam for the struggle of the NLF, and will result in a new US policy in Indochina. Even if President Nixon remains in office . . . he will not dare to apply such strong measures as air strikes or bombing attacks in either North or South Vietnam, because the US Congress and the American people will violently object.[19]

With fighting in South Vietnam having reached its highest levels since the cease-fire, the United States and the DRV sign a new document, as noted in an official U.S. Army history.

June–August

The third Indochina war reached a milestone of sorts on 13 June 1973 when the four parties to the original agreement got together in Paris and issued a communique calling upon themselves to observe the provisions of the 28 January cease-fire. The communique was followed by a decline in combat activity that reached the lowest level since the brief hiatus following the LANDGRAB campaign, but this pause was also temporary. The United States then shored up its commitment to Vietnam by assigning one of its toughest, most experienced diplomats, Graham Martin, to be Ambassador in Saigon. Meanwhile, members of the Canadian delegation to the ICCS began making preparations to leave Vietnam, having announced on 29 May that they had come to supervise a cease-fire but instead were observing a war. The Canadians had had no illusions concerning the feasibility of their task. They gave it the best they could, enduring considerable hardships and dangers, and suffering casualties in the bargain.

Dr. Kissinger held a press conference in Paris in which he released the text of the joint communique to take effect at noon on 15 June. His questioners were justifiably skeptical, and Dr. Kissinger barely concealed his own doubts:

> What was signed today is an amplification and a consolidation of the original agreement. It is not a new agreement . . . it is our hope that by what has been done today a significant step has been taken in the consolidation of peace in Vietnam and Indochina. . . . the history of Indochina is replete with agreements and joint declarations. I am not naive enough to pretend to you that the mere fact of having again agreed to certain words in itself guarantees peace; but I will also say that since all parties have worked so seriously for the past three weeks, we have every hope that they will match this effort with performance and therefore there is fresh hope, and we hope a new spirit, in the implementation of the agreement, which in itself is maintained. [Department of State *Bulletin*, July 9, 1973, p. 46.]

The communique would have no lasting effect because it had no power of enforcement behind it. It contained no requirement that North Vietnam abandon its fundamental objective; neither did it promise sanctions against any party that chose to ignore its provisions. Perhaps, viewed from Saigon, it provided some reason to hope that South Vietnam could count on enough U.S. support to continue the defense of the country.[20]

As noted by another military historian, on 1 July one of the most significant pieces of legislation relative to the Southeast Asia war is passed by the U.S. Congress.

Termination of Funding for Combat Operations in SE Asia

The hue and cry raised in the United States against the continuation of U.S. air strikes in Cambodia was transformed into legislation which terminated all funding of acts of force by the United States in SE Asia on 15 August 1973. The Congress perceived that the President could, without too much difficulty, order the air forces to continue bombing, even without waiting for a more satisfactory resolution of the constitutional issues raised by the Nixon Administration's interpretations of how the Paris Agreement was being enforced. Congressional sentiment grew strong for an absolute cut-off of funds for combat operations in SE Asia; this was expressed in large majority votes in committees and in both Houses on measures dealing with war-related funds. With general agreement in Congress on *what* should be done, it remained only to determine *when* it should be done.

The debate—which was both skillful and learned—centered about selecting the appropriate amendment to the Second Supplemental Appropriations Act of 1973, with voting narrowly defeating the Eagleton amendment which would have terminated combat operations on 30 June 1973. In negotiations between the Executive Branch and the Congress, a compromise was reached with the substitution, following even more debate, of the Fulbright amendment. The new amendment allowed combat operations to continue until 15 August which, it was reasoned, would allow the Nixon Administration a reasonable period of time for pursuing negotiations with the Communists. The Second Supplemental Appropriations Act of 1973 (Public Law 93-50) with the Fulbright amendment (Section 307) was approved on 1 July 1973. The restrictive provisions of this law were attached to appropriations acts which followed the supplemental act. The Fulbright amendment (Title III, Section 307) specified:

> None of the funds herein appropriated under this Act may be expended to support directly or indirectly combat activities in or over Cambodia, Laos, North Vietnam and South Vietnam or off the shores of Cambodia, Laos, North Vietnam and South Vietnam by United States forces, and after August 15, 1973, no other funds heretofore appropriated under any Act may be expended for such purpose.

The passage of this law at the beginning of the new fiscal year was the signal for all elements of the Department of Defense to begin adjusting to the termination of combat operations.[21]

Not all funding for combat "support" operations comes from Department of Defense sources, however. In August writer Donald Kirk talks to some American civilians in Phnom Penh.

John Wayne would have dug it

Phnom Penh: August 1973
They were two American adventurers, Don Douglass and Fred Compton, and they'd come to Cambodia in search of a war. They were pilots for an odd little company named Southeast Asian Air Transport, and they flew a lumbering old DC-4 approximately four times a day to a town named Kompong Cham, some fifty miles north of here on the Mekong. That is, they flew four flights a day when the ground crews weren't working very hard and didn't load or unload the plane quite fast enough. "Godammit, tomorrow we want to make five flights," growled Douglass, a one-time Massachusetts cop who had learned how to fly in his spare time. "We get paid a certain guarantee, and then we get more if we fly over a certain number of hours," he explained. "We don't like sitting around on the ground."

Douglass and Compton belonged to what you might call the hard-hat faction of the expatriate American set. They didn't really say so, but they clearly believed in fighting Communists. They thought bombing was a good thing, and they'd signed on with Southeast Asian Air Transport not only for the pay, which was high, but for the cause. "I want to help these people," said Douglass. "They're not gonna get anywhere without air power. I could do a lot of other things, but I like following the wars. I don't like your nine-to-five Stateside routine. I want something different." One could, if one wished, condemn Douglass on a number of different grounds, ranging from ignorance to insensitivity to worse, but somehow I found him more ingenuous than anything else. And I couldn't help but laugh—perhaps reflecting my own insensitivity—when he pleasantly told me exactly what he'd *really* like to do as long as he was in Cambodia.

"They've still got one old MIG-17 in their hangar over there," he confided. "The engine's out, but they're repairing it. I ran into the general of the Cambodian air force the other night—told him I'd be glad to fly it once they got it into shape." There was, it seemed, nothing that Douglass would not do with the MIG, the last of a squadron or so bequeathed the Cambodian government by the Soviet Union before the downfall of Prince Norodom Sihanouk in 1970. "Bombing, strafing, it's a lot of fun," said Douglass. "I flew a MIG in Nigeria in 1971. They bought it from the Egyptian government. The Russians were madder than hell about it, but there was nothing they could do. It took me five days to learn how to fly it, three days on the ground and two in the air." Compton, the captain on the DC-4, had yet to fly a MIG but was eager to learn. "They'd need another guy to fly it," he said. "Don could show me how. I'm ready. I'd do anything they wanted me to do with it. I think it'd be a real kick."

I'd met Don in the bar of the Monorom Hotel the day before. Relatively new to the war, he did not yet seem to harbor the anger of most pilots and contractors, not to mention CIA and State Department and military types, regarding the press. "Hey, I fly every day to Kompong Cham," he had told me. "Come out to the airport and take a ride in my plane." So I was in the jump seat, looking over their shoulders, as we circled the town. "We go around like this because the bad guys are out there," one of them explained. "We can't come in straight and low or they might take a shot at us." I'd been reading in Cambodian government handouts all about the bad guys outside Kompong Cham. They'd long since captured the road to Phnom Penh and just a couple of days previously had seized the town of Skoun, a bunkered, bombed-out enclave at a key junction. Now they were only a few miles away. I was anxious to get into Kompong Cham to do a story about a town under siege.

The apron by the airstrip was crowded with two or three transports when we landed. The civilian planes, such as the DC-4s owned by Southeast Asian Air Transport, carried in rice and other foodstuffs and left with tobacco or raw rubber, once shipped by highway or boat to Phnom Penh. The military planes, notably a C-123 just turned over to the Cambodian air force by the United States, were hauling reinforcements for the town's defenses. Even so, one had difficulty conjuring a sense of real crisis. The few soldiers by the entrance to the airport lethargically waved almost anyone through the gate without bothering to check credentials. No bunkers were visible in the open green fields stretching beyond the road to a series of low-lying hills. "You think the enemy will attack?" I asked one of the soldiers through my interpreter, who had flown up in the same plane with me. "Our men are out there to stop them," the soldier replied, but I had the distinct sense the Khmer Rouge—"Red" Cambodian troops—could walk through the defenses like a sieve. A few mortar or rocket rounds could close the airport. Kompong Cham, population 80,000 or so, now swollen with refugees, lay like a ripe melon, ready to fall at the slightest pull.

"They can't hold it without bombing," one of the American pilots told me. "They may have to hire mercenary pilots—sign up Americans and buy some fighter planes and have them fight the war for them." The suggestion indicated the desperation of Cambodian government forces only a few days after the United States had finally ceased all bombing as a result of a rider on a congressional appropriations bill. The Khmer Rouge might not win in the first week, but they could quickly expand their control over the countryside, capturing towns and bases that had eluded them in more than three years of fighting since Sihanouk's downfall. Yet

the town, when my interpreter and I finally got there after a five-mile ride
in the early monsoon rain, did not seem to have changed much since I
had last been there, two years ago. Old French-built cars and Japanese
motor scooters and American-made military vehicles still rolled leisurely
down the broad, tree-shaded streets. The governor's mansion remained
as a symbol of power and security in the center of a gray-green-brownish
kind of park. The general, at that particular moment, was conferring with
some aides, but he was glad to talk to me.

"The enemy came from the highlands, like the water coming from
the higher to the lower region," he remarked, as the rain poured down
on the roof. "There are enemy troops, but we have stopped them in
many places. They cannot attack us." What if they hit the airfield—the
only entry for all the necessities of war and daily life now that both
the road and river routes were closed? "Around the airfield, there are
no houses or villages," said the general, with the social ease and glib-
ness that somehow seem to characterize all senior Cambodian officials,
nurtured on French colonialism and the postcolonial social milieu of
the capital. "If the enemy comes near the air field," he explained, "we
can use our air strikes," as delivered by the Cambodian air force's
newly acquired T-28s. The general was unfailingly courteous, but his
briefing was pathetically similar to dozens of conversations I have had
with Cambodian officers over the past few years. One only had to talk
to people around the town to confirm an initial impression of military
weakness and ineptitude.

"They overran three positions two miles from here last night," said a
merchant sipping thick coffee in a little café in the center of town. "We
don't think there are enough soldiers to defend us. If they keep on
attacking, the enemy will easily get into town and we will have to run
away." The coffee shop was crowded with tradesmen, clerks, bureau-
crats, and young officers. They were still there, in Kompong Cham, because they had no way to get out, no place to go, no exit. They listened
and smiled and joked about our conversation. If the town were in danger,
you couldn't tell it from the expressions on their faces. But Cambodia is
that way. You never know, when you encounter troops in the field, if
they feel they are under pressure or not unless the bullets and shells are
actually flying. And even then you can't be entirely sure. A few hundred
meters behind the front lines you are quite likely to see soldiers lolling in
hammocks or chatting and joking as if the war were a hundred miles
away. It was the same way in Kompong Cham that day—except that the
scene, if anything, was more relaxed, almost charming, as the rain gradually stopped and the sun filtered through the haze.

I'd originally thought of staying overnight in the governor's mansion, at
the invitation of the general, but by late afternoon I thought I had
gleaned about as much from Kompong Cham as my readers would care to
know. My interpreter and I found the same motorbike-taxi driver who
had met us at the airport and drove out of town on the same tranquil

road, weaving our way around occasional bicycles and bullock carts, grinning at peasant farmers who grinned back at us with open, typically Cambodian countenances. It was the end of the working day at the textile factory, and we were caught for a moment in a wave of small vehicles of varying descriptions, but the road was soon quiet again, and my interpreter asked me if I would like to see the ancient temple complex before turning down the last stretch toward the airport. "It is as old as Angkor Wat," he assured me. "Maybe you won't have another chance to see it again." The driver veered onto a mud road, past some crumbling, blackened walls, then under an arch and around a large pond. The ruins, perhaps somewhat restored but never rebuilt as completely as the temples in the Angkor region, rose mysteriously beyond thatched peasant homes. We didn't have time to stop and look as we might have wished. We wanted to reach the airstrip in time for Don and Fred's last run back to Phnom Penh. Besides, there would always be another chance, another trip. The ruins could wait.

But we were wrong. The ruins couldn't wait. Three or four days later the Khmer Rouge did what everyone except the general had anticipated. They rocketed and closed the airport. Then they advanced on the ground, overrunning the factory and the temple area and a university campus, also near the airport. They overran outpost after outpost until the Cambodian defenders, reinforced the day we were there by two fresh battalions, controlled only the center of the city and still couldn't prevent infiltrators from exploding grenades in the market and sniping at the governor's mansion. Cambodian T-28s bombed and strafed, but they could hardly replace the American F-4s and B-52s on which Cambodian commanders had always depended to postpone their final defeat. Don and Fred had to fly their DC-4 elsewhere. American military planes were airdropping supplies over the center of the city. No more easy milkruns for eager young pilots out to see the war. Nor did I hear anything about the last MIG-17 in the Cambodian air force. I assume it's still in the hangar, where it may form the nucleus of the next Cambodian air force if Prince Sihanouk returns to power.[22]

1973 10 October—Vice-President Spiro Agnew resigns because of allegations regarding his personal finances.

As has happened so often before in Laos, Cambodia, and South Vietnam, the North Vietnamese react to what they perceive as growing enemy power. CIA agent Frank Snepp sums up the North Vietnamese strategy.

As the pressure mounted, Hanoi's military leaders, General Giap and his chief of staff, General Dung, began clamoring for a response-in-kind. For the past five months NVA forces had been marking time, building their supply caches in the south and occasionally snatching territory where they could do it on the cheap. Their objective was to confront Thieu with such a threat-in-being, he would feel obliged to compromise. But clearly this tactic wasn't working. By early fall COSVN's field commanders were readily admitting to subordinates that no more than twelve percent of the population and one-fifth the land mass of South Vietnam were even accessible to them. (These points were spelled out explicitly and in some detail in COSVN Resolution 12 and a Politburo Resolution 21. Excerpts from both documents fell into CIA hands literally within a week or two of their being issued.)

Given these "realities," the hawks in the Politburo concluded a return to "revolutionary violence" was unavoidable, and General Giap, writing anonymously in the army newspaper, made this point again and again with chilling eloquence.

But against his well-wrought arguments, there were strong countervailing ones. Most compelling were the attitudes of the Soviets and the Chinese. Immediately following the Brezhnev-Nixon summit in June, Party First Secretary Le Duan had flown to Moscow and Peking, hat in hand, to ask for additional aid to carry on the war. To his surprise, he received little more than a cold shoulder. Neither the Soviets nor the Chinese were willing to promise massive new military aid, and though both agreed to increase economic assistance, they insisted on attaching all sorts of strings to ensure it was used wisely, even to the point of demanding that the North Vietnamese actually let them help supervise how the aid was applied.

None of their stipulations sat well with Hanoi, but the Politburo felt it had no choice but to accede to them. Recent flooding had very nearly wiped out the fall rice crop and the country was in dire need of immediate food imports. For the first time, moreover, the North Vietnamese were beginning to grasp the immensity of the economic problems confronting them. A property survey, undertaken at the Soviets' behest, revealed that waste, inefficiency and even corruption were far more widespread than the leadership had ever imagined, and a population census, the first since the early 1960s, carried an even greater shock: despite the war, the population of North Vietnam had grown by nearly fifty percent in the past fifteen years, thus posing far greater burdens for the economy than had been estimated.

In early October, several weeks after Le Duan returned from Moscow and Peking, the Party Central Committee convened a plenary session, the twenty-first in its history, to consider its next move. The generals argued strenuously for a step-up in the fighting, insisting that the morale and discipline of the army would more than compensate for the loss of Soviet and Chinese support. But Premier Pham Van Dong, a curious and mercurial old revolutionary with a well-honed pragmatic sense, was not so certain. Without the backing of their traditional allies, he warned, there would be nothing to keep Nixon from sending the B-52s back to Hanoi, and that would mean an end to all prospects for both victory and reconstruction.

This argument swung the debate. While reasserting their faith in "revolutionary violence," the conferees chose to peg their objectives far short of all-out warfare. Instead of striking at Saigon's army in the months ahead, they elected to target its weakest spot, its pocketbook, launching a series of hit-and-run attacks—"strategic raids" they called them—against roads, airfields and fuel storage facilities to further weaken the economy and to frighten off foreign investors.

Few of the grizzled old party members who sat through the long discussions were confident that any of this would produce immediate success, and in their directives to the field they made no effort to suggest it would, for fear of raising false expectations and undermining troop morale. The closing paragraphs of their main policy resolution explicitly cautioned troops and party members not to expect ultimate victory before 1979 at the earliest, and General Giap himself publicly acknowledged that the "struggle had become protracted and complex"—a struggle between "anti-nibbling forces and the nibblers."[23]

In Washington, another congressional amendment prohibits the State Department from using funds to support the intensifying war in Cambodia and South Vietnam.

Department of State Appropriation Authorization Act of 1973— P.L. 93–126, Section 13, October 18, 1973

Sec. 13. Notwithstanding any other provision of law, on or after August 15, 1973, no funds heretofore or hereafter appropriated may be obligated or expended to finance the involvement of United States military.[24]

In Vietnam, as Frank Snepp notes, the North Vietnamese try out their new policy.

On 6 November, only days after the plenum ended, the equivalent of a full NVA division carried out the first "strategic raid," overrunning three border outposts in Quang Duc Province northeast of Saigon, where ARVN forces had recently been conducting probes of their own. That night Le Duan and his Politburo colleagues held their breath. Would Nixon respond with B-52s? Within the next twenty-four hours they got their answer.

Quite coincidentally, the drive in Congress to limit the President's war-making authority had just come to a head, and on 7 November the House and the Senate overrode a presidential veto and passed special legislation formally setting forth the restrictions. The monumental War Powers Act made it illegal for the President to introduce American forces into "hostile" situations for more than sixty days without Congressional approval. Actually, the bill was irrelevant for Indochina, for the Cambodia bombing ban of August had already ruled out any further military involvement there for any length of time. But as confirmation of American intent, and of Nixon's political impotence, it duly impressed the North Vietnamese.

The hawks in the Politburo responded predictably, again demanding escalation, and a week later Khmer Communist forces in Cambodia launched a direct ground assault on Phnom Penh to test Lon Nol's staying power in the wake of the bombing halt.[25]

Despite the North Vietnamese/Pathet Lao/Khmer Rouge offensives, by the end of the year the U.S. Congress has effected a complete cut-off of all State and Defense Department funding for both covert and overt military support to governments at war in Indochina.

Military Procurement Authorization Act of 1973— P.L. 93–155, Section 806, November 16, 1973

Sec. 806. Notwithstanding any other provision of law, upon enactment of this Act, no funds heretofore or hereafter appropriated may be obligated or expended to finance the involvement of United States military forces in hostilities in or over or from off the shores of North Vietnam, South Vietnam, Laos, or Cambodia, unless specifically authorized hereafter by the Congress.

McGovern Amendment to Foreign Assistance Act of 1973— P.L. 93–189, Section 30, December 17, 1973

TERMINATION OF INDOCHINA WAR
Sec. 30. No funds authorized or appropriated under this or any other law may be expended to finance military or paramilitary operations by the United States in or over Vietnam, Laos, or Cambodia.[26]

1973 31 December		
	TOTAL	NET CHANGE
U.S. military personnel assigned in Vietnam	"less than 250"	−23,950
U.S. casualties	YEAR	TO DATE (cumulative)
Killed in action	237	46,163
Wounded in action	60	303,656
Source: DOD/OASD		

1974

The official U.S. Army history of this period summarizes events at the beginning of 1974.

Cease-Fire Anniversary

On the first anniversary of the Paris Agreement in early 1974, the Communists issued statements presenting their views on the cease-fire and the situation in South Vietnam. Hanoi published a "White Paper" assailing U.S. and South Vietnamese "provocations." Its charges were accompanied by the rattle and roar of thousands of trucks coursing south across the DMZ and through Laos in a mammoth "transportation offensive" started in December 1973. Thousands of tons of supplies were accumulating in the southern stockpiles, and by the cease-fire anniversary the NVA had sufficient stocks to support an offensive comparable to that of 1972 for over a year. Meanwhile, NVA engineers extended their fuel pipelines into the A Shau Valley in Thua Thien Province, and the Laotian pipeline was passing through the tri-border junction into Kontum Province. During the year following the cease-fire, the NVA increased its artillery and tank strength in the south at least four-fold.

Despite some surges of concentrated effort, such as the MR 3 air campaign of November and the aborted attempts to advance on the NVA logistical base at Duc Co, the RVNAF was unable to interfere significantly with the NVA's steady accumulation of logistical and combat strength. One major inhibiting factor was the growing density of NVA antiaircraft defending the major logistical corridors and troop concentrations. In the year following the cease-fire, the NVA added one air defense division and at least 12 regiments to the expeditionary force so that by the cease-fire anniversary 2 air defense divisions and 26 regiments were deployed in South Vietnam. Included in the force were SA-2 and SA-7 missiles and radar-controlled guns; these, in particular, forced the VNAF, which had none of the sophisticated electronic counter-measures employed by the U.S. Air Force in such a high-threat environment, to operate above effective attack altitudes.

Preparations for resuming the offensive were being made north of the DMZ in concert with the buildup in the South. The NVA strategic reserve was being reconstituted, and most of its fighting elements were being concentrated in Thanh Hoa Province between Hanoi and Vinh. Here the NVA I Corps was organized in the fall of 1973, and the 308th, 312th, and 320B Divisions, having returned from the Quang Tri front, were assigned to it. Adding to reserve strength, the major elements of the 316th Division returned to North Vietnam from northern Laos, and the 341st Division, located immediately north of the DMZ, was reorganized from its territorial status into a deployable infantry division. The sixth major element of the NVA strategic reserve, the 308B Division, was still in garrison in the Hanoi area. Compounding the already tenuous situation facing the RVNAF in Kontum and Pleiku Province, the NVA 968th Division began deploying from southern Laos into the western highlands.[27]

What the North Vietnamese plan to do is described by Frank Snepp.

As Thieu tried to adapt to the quirks and turns of American policy in the late winter and early spring of 1974, the North Vietnamese did likewise. Like Thieu, they found the Americans' renewed interest in territorial demarcation deeply unsettling—but for somewhat different reasons. Because of the meagerness of their holdings in the south, any partitioning of territory, de facto or otherwise, would have left them in a decidedly unfavorable position vis-à-vis the government. They would have preferred to ignore the proposal altogether. But they could not. With the Poles and Hungarians serving as messengers for the U.S. Embassy, pressure obviously was building toward some kind of deal, and they knew that if they were to make the best of it, they would have to grab as much territory as possible beforehand. That meant escalating the strategic-raids campaign beyond what they had intended.

Shifting course was not going to be easy, particularly since the Central Committee's Twenty-second Plenum had already set the regime on the path toward reconstruction. The hawks, however, had recently been handed new political ammunition. The Communist victories in Quang Duc in November and December had proven that NVA forces could play aggressor without provoking immediate American retaliation, and with Thieu himself now clearly on the offensive, the logic of a response in kind was almost irresistible.

In early March the party's top military experts, meeting in an old French villa at number 33 Pham Ngu Lao Street in Hanoi, decided to push the strategic raids to new limits. Not only would Communist forces continue to strike at the foundations of the South Vietnamese economy—roads, storage facilities and airfields—but from now through the summer they would also seek to regain territory lost since the cease-fire.[28]

1974   9 August—Richard M. Nixon resigns the presidency to avoid impeachment for complicity in the Watergate scandal. Gerald R. Ford becomes president.

During the next few months the pattern of North Vietnamese attacks in just one military region looks like this:

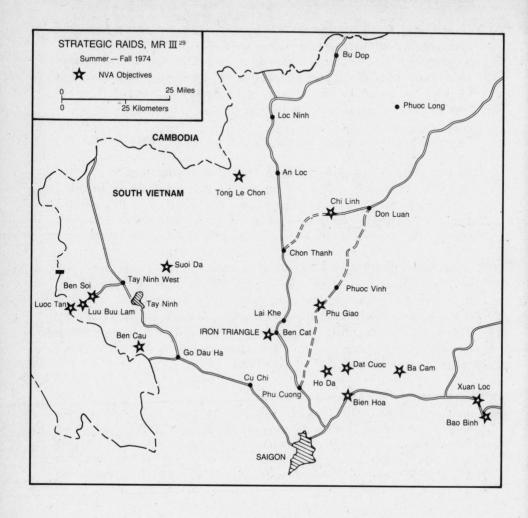

STRATEGIC RAIDS, MR III [29]
Summer — Fall 1974
★ NVA Objectives

0   25 Miles
0   25 Kilometers

CAMBODIA

SOUTH VIETNAM

Bu Dop

Phuoc Long

Loc Ninh

An Loc

Tong Le Chon

Chi Linh

Don Luan

Chon Thanh

Suoi Da

Tay Ninh West

Phuoc Vinh

Ben Soi

Tay Ninh

Lai Khe

Phu Giao

Luoc Tan

Luu Buu Lam

IRON TRIANGLE

Ben Cat

Ben Cau

Go Dau Ha

Dat Cuoc

Ba Cam

Ho Da

Cu Chi

Xuan Loc

Phu Cuong

Bien Hoa

Bao Binh

SAIGON

U.S. Army historian William E. Le Gro describes some of the North Vietnamese "step-by-step" victories as 1974 ends.

In his serialized account of the "Great Spring Victory," Senior General Van Tien Dung of the North Vietnamese Army described deliberations of the Central Military Party Committee and the General Staff as they reviewed the events of the summer campaign. He wrote of how, between April and October, from Thua Thien to Saigon, NVA forces had stepped up the offensive actions and had won great victories. The facts were, of course, that the NVA was stalemated at the extremes of this long battlefield—in Thua Thien and around Saigon—but had overrun isolated bases in the Central Highlands and succeeded at great cost in penetrating to the edge of the Quang Nam lowlands. This latter success loomed large in significance to General Dung and NVA planners:

> We paid special attention to the outcome of a battle which destroyed the district capital of Thuong Duc in the 5th Region. This was a test of strength with the best of the enemy's forces. We destroyed the enemy forces defending the Thuong Duc district capital subsector. The enemy sent in a whole division of paratroopers to launch repeated and protracted counterattacks in a bid to recapture this position, but we heavily decimated the enemy forces, firmly defending Thuong Duc and forcing the enemy to give up.

However distorted the account, the victory at Thuong Duc and the numerous, more easily won objectives in the highlands demonstrated to the satisfaction of the North Vietnamese high command that the time had arrived for an even bolder strategy. General Dung went on to relate how

> the General Staff reported to the Central Military Party Committee that the combat capability of our mobile main force troops was now altogether superior to that of the enemy's mobile regular troops, that the war had reached its final stage and that the balance of forces had changed in our favor.

General Dung believed, and the Military Committee and the General Staff agreed, that the NVA's superiority should be exploited in a new strategy. The NVA would no longer attack only to destroy the RVNAF but would combine this objective with attacks to "liberate" populated areas. It would move out of the jungles and mountains into the lowlands. NVA planners observed that, "the reduction of U.S. aid made it impossible for the puppet troops to carry out their combat plan and build up their forces" and that the South Vietnamese were "forced to fight a poor man's war," their firepower having decreased "by nearly 60 percent because of bomb and ammunition shortages" and their mobility was reduced "by half due to lack of aircraft, vehicles and fuel."

According to General Dung, the conference of the Politburo and the Central Military Committee met in October, considered the General Staff's assessments and recommendation, and unanimously agreed on the following:

1. The puppet troops were militarily, politically and economically weakening every day and our forces were quite stronger than the enemy in the south.

2. The United States was facing mounting difficulties both at home and in the world, and its potential for aiding the puppets was rapidly declining.

3. We had created a chain of mutual support, had strengthened our reserve forces and materiel and were steadily improving our strategic and political systems.

4. The movement to demand peace, improvement of the people's livelihood, democracy, national independence and Thieu's overthrow in various cities was gaining momentum.

Having assessed their own capabilities and those of RVNAF, and having concluded that the time was right for the final offensive, the conferees had to consider how the United States would react. They concluded:

After signing the Paris agreement on Vietnam and withdrawing U.S. troops from Vietnam, the United States had faced even greater difficulties and embarrassment. The internal contradictions within the U.S. administration and among U.S. political parties had intensified. The Watergate scandal had seriously affected the entire United States and precipitated the resignation of an extremely reactionary president—Nixon. The United States faced economic recession, mounting inflation, serious unemployment and an oil crisis. Also, U.S. allies were not on good terms with the United States, and countries who had to depend on the United States also sought to escape U.S. control. U.S. aid to the Saigon puppet administration was decreasing.

Comrade Le Duan drew an important conclusion that became a resolution: Having already withdrawn from the south, the United States could hardly jump back in, and no matter how it might intervene, it would be unable to save the Saigon administration from collapse.

On 17 December Duy Can Village, between Vo Xu and Tanh Linh, was overrun by the 812th NVA Regiment, and the few survivors of the 700th RF Company struggled into Tanh Linh. Although outposts still in ARVN hands, as well as Hoai Duc and Tanh Linh, were receiving heavy indirect fire, General Dong, commanding III Corps, ordered the 18th Division not try to press forward past Gia Huynh on Route 333. With his Military Region under attack from Tay Ninh to Phuoc Long, he was unwilling to risk having four of his battalions cut off and decimated. Meanwhile, the NVA blew a bridge south of Hoai Duc, occupied Vo Xu, and increased the intensity of its attack on Tanh Linh. Following a 3,000-round bombardment on 23 and 24 December, the NVA launched five successive assaults, finally overrunning the last defenses in Tanh Linh on Christmas. Hoai Duc, meanwhile, was under attack by the 274th Infantry, 6th NVA Division.

After the 274th NVA Regiment had penetrated the local defenses of Hoai Duc and had gained a foothold in the northeastern and southwestern edges of the town, the ARVN 18th Division moved the 1st and 2d

Battalions, 43d Infantry by helicopter west and north of the town respectively, and began pushing the enemy out. While two battalions of the 48th
ARVN Infantry held their positions on Route 333 north of Gia Ray, the
tired and depleted 7th Ranger Group was withdrawn to Binh Duong
Province to rest and refit. Since all available battalions of the 18th Division had been committed, the JGS moved the 4th Ranger Group from
Kontum to Long Binh where it was rested and re-equipped and made
available to General Dong as a reserve.

NVA assaults on Nui Ba Den in Tay Ninh Province continued throughout December 1974, but the tough little ARVN RF Company held on.
Meanwhile, by mid-month, an ARVN relief column eventually reached
Soui Da and found that the besieging enemy force had withdrawn. VNAF
efforts to resupply the troops on the mountain were largely unsuccessful.
Helicopters were driven off by heavy fire, and fighter-bombers were
forced to excessive altitudes by SA-7 and antiaircraft artillery. One F-5A
fighter-bomber was shot down by an SA-7 on 14 December. Finally,
without food and water and with nearly all ammunition expended, the 3d
Company, 314th RF Battalion, on 6 January picked up its wounded and
withdrew down the mountain to friendly lines.[30]

1974   31 December

	TOTAL	NET CHANGE
U.S. military personnel assigned in Vietnam	"less than 250"	0

U.S. casualties	YEAR	TO DATE (cumulative)
Killed in action	207	46,370
Wounded in action	0	303,656

Source: DOD/OASD

1975

*As 1975 begins, Song Be, capital of the Phuoc Long province, is experi-
encing its fiercest attack since May of 1965 (see pp. 205–207).*

Meanwhile, refugees poured into Song Be, and the RVNAF tried to
resupply the isolated garrison. Ten attempts were made in early January
1975 to drop supplies, but none of the bundles could be recovered by the

defenders. As least 16 enemy tanks had been destroyed in prior attacks, but on 6 January 10 more were seen approaching the city. That day General Dong sent two companies of his best troops into the battle: the 81st Airborne Rangers, whose highly trained volunteers were usually employed in commando operations. Also on 6 January, VNAF RF-5 photography disclosed seven 37-mm. antiaircraft positions around the city. It was only the first week of January and the RF-5 flying-hour allocation for the month had been nearly used up.

Very few infantry joined in the assaults on Song Be. Instead, squads of sappers followed the tanks as they rolled through the streets firing at ARVN positions, mopping up bypassed positions and establishing strong points. Most of the NVA tanks damaged or destroyed were hit by M-72 LAW and 90-mm. recoilless rifles. Often the ranges were so short that the LAW missiles failed to arm themselves and harmlessly bounced off the tank hulls. Making tank kills even more difficult, the NVA M-26 Armor Group had welded extra armor plating on the sides of the hulls, and the crews kept buttoned up so that grenades could not be dropped through the hatches.

NVA artillery was devastating, particularly after 3 January when the rate of fire increased from about 200 rounds per day to nearly 3,000. Structures, bunkers, and trenches collapsed, and casualties mounted. ARVN artillery was out of action, its guns destroyed by fire from tanks, recoilless rifles, and 130-mm. guns. Finally, on 6 January, the province chief realized that he could no longer influence the battle. With no artillery and shattered communications, under direct fire from four approaching T-54 tanks, and seriously wounded, he and what remained of his staff, withdrew from Song Be. The NVA had captured the first province capital since the cease-fire.

There were some military and civilian survivors from Song Be. Pitiful little bands of Montagnards trekked through the jungles to Quang Duc, and VNAF helicopters rescued about 200 men of the Rangers, 7th Infantry, and sector territorials in the days immediately following the collapse. The province chief never made it to safety. His wounds slowed him down and he was not seen again. A few members of the command group eventually reached the ARVN outpost of Bu Binh on Highway 14 in Quang Duc. RVNAF losses were staggering. Over 5,400 officers and men of the 7th Infantry, Airborne Rangers, and territorials were committed; less than 850 survived. Especially costly were the high losses in the Airborne Ranger Battalion—85 troopers survived—and in the 2d Battalion, 7th Infantry, fewer than 200 returned from Phuoc Long. About 3,000 civilians, Montagnards and Vietnamese, out of 30,000 or more, escaped Communist control. The few province, village, and hamlet officials who were captured were summarily executed.

Although it was the time of the dry, northeast monsoon, unseasonably heavy torrents drenched Saigon. As this writer's Vietnamese driver dolefully remarked, even the gods were weeping for Phuoc Long.[31]

1975   21 January—At a press conference, President Gerald Ford says that he can foresee "no circumstances" that could cause the United States to reenter the Vietnam War.

Set in early 1975, Bernard and Marvin Kalb's novel The Last Ambassador *presents the story of Hadden Walker, the U.S. ambassador to the republic of Vietnam. On 10 March Tony Catlett, a CIA agent assigned to the U.S. embassy in Saigon, is flying in an Air America aircraft near the town of Ban Me Thout, the scene of one of the first North Vietnamese attacks during the 1968 Tet Offensive (see pp. 332–333).*

"Over there!" Tony shouted. "To the right." Bursts of smoke—yellow, gold, orange—erupted from the ground. The plane began vibrating, shaken by artillery blasts from below.

"You see that little clump of forest off to the left?"

Tony nodded.

"Well," Jim went on, "it wasn't there yesterday. The bastards moved in during the night carrying their own trees. Damned good cover."

The forest spat out tongues of flame—big guns at work.

"What the hell is going on?" Tony called out. ARVN units shooting at each other by mistake? Crazy bastards, Tony thought. But it wouldn't be the first time. His mind instinctively produced a printout of a CIA map, back at the Embassy, with all the known NVA positions in this area. The printout showed only scattered ARVN units in the vicinity of the Darlac provincial capital of Ban Me Thuot, no NVA—*no* NVA—and if those were NVA down there, it could mean only one thing: the North Vietnamese had succeeded in outwitting Saigon and U.S. intelligence once again, infiltrating into a region where they had not yet been detected. Where they *had* been detected in any kind of strength—anything approximating the force of the artillery explosions below—was more than a hundred miles to the north, in the jungles east of Cambodia and west of the strategically situated Highlands city of Pleiku. Some unusual NVA movements had been spotted *there*. Not here.

"Can we go lower?" Tony asked, desperately hoping that, on closer inspection, the firing down there would prove to be an accidental ARVN shoot-out.

"You're my guest," replied Jim, nonchalantly. The Beech dropped from seven thousand feet to three thousand feet. The four-thousand-foot descent only made the salvos look much more threatening.

It had to be NVA, Tony thought: ARVN did not have that kind of heavy weaponry at its disposal in this sector. The big guns were laying down a barrage of fire, blasting at targets on the far approaches to Ban Me Thuot. No, there was no mistake, and given the intensity of the firing it was obvious that the NVA had moved in a lot of heavy equipment and was positioning itself for what Tony sensed would be a major attack.

The plane suddenly shuddered.

"Whoopee!" Jim shouted. "We've taken a hit."

Tony could see Jim anxiously maneuvering to retain control of the plane. For a moment, the Beech seemed to hang in midair. Jim pulled the yoke back slowly—and the plane began to climb.

"Stay cool, man," shouted Jim. "It's a war." He pointed to the wing, to a small tear in the aluminum skin. "Just a lucky hit by an NVA sharpshooter, a little memo from our 'friends' suggesting that we mind our own business."

"Let's go higher," Tony said.

"Still want to watch the show?"

"If you think it's okay."

"You're my guest."

They climbed to ten thousand feet, Jim volunteering that the higher altitude should put them out of enemy reach. "Unless of course," he added, "the Russkies or the Chicoms have shipped the NVA some new long-range stuff."

Jim piloted the plane in lazy circles in the pastel sky while Tony studied the terrain below. The continued heavy firing by the NVA confirmed his original estimate: the enemy seemed to be opening up a critical new front in an area where earlier only sporadic firefights had taken place. Why?

In the distance, Tony could see the town of Ban Me Thuot, the sleepy capital of the tribal mountain people known as the Montagnards. He remembered the place as having an exotic *National Geographic* look to it: Montagnards strolling barefoot through the dusty streets or thudding into town on the backs of elephants. In their loincloths, the Montagnards were an odd, anachronistic contrast to the Chinese shopkeepers and French coffee-tea-and-rubber planters who gave Ban Me Thuot a hint of the cosmopolitan.

Ridiculous, thought Tony, for a battle to be starting up, this late in the war, in the very place where America had first slid into the conflict—brandishing butterfly nets. Those first GIs, back in the early 'sixties, had been Special Forces soldiers—on the CIA payroll—who posed as, of all things, lepidopterists. What they were actually trying to catch were the seminomadic hill people, to train them in the art of twentieth-century killing and lead them in battle against "the other side." It was a most unlikely place to launch an "Uncle Sam Wants You" campaign, but the Montagnards—from the Rhade, Jarai, and other tribes—volunteered by the thousands. For one thing, the pay was good, more money than their civilization had ever seen; Tony remembered CIA home movies showing the Montagnards lined up on payday for piastres that had been flown in by the sackful from Saigon. But the piastres were an incidental bonus.

The Montagnards' real craving was for modern weapons with which to even the score with their old enemy, the Vietnamese. For decades, the

Vietnamese, from the height of their comparative sophistication, had looked down on the mountain people as "moi"—savages—fully deserving to be deprived of their tribal landholdings. Armed only with crossbows, the Montagnards had no real way of resisting—that is, until the "lepidopterists" arrived with their bulging arsenals. But there was a little problem. The Montagnards had to be taught to aim their newly acquired weapons at the *right* Vietnamese—those from the North and not from the South. This subtle distinction was wasted on the Montagnards; to them, a Vietnamese was a Vietnamese.

Tony scanned the erupting landscape. Wouldn't it be the ultimate irony, he thought, the last bit of crazy comedy, if some of these very U.S.-trained Montagnards—right down there, below—were now leading NVA troops over secret mountain trails and being paid for their guide services with promises? Promises that the Montagnards would be left to rule over their own lands, once Hanoi won? Tony pressed his face against the window, Nothing had changed in this fickle fuckle war since those first GIs had arrived with their nets: the U.S. was still chasing butterflies.

By now, Tony had seen enough, enough to know that he was witnessing still another intelligence failure: disastrous for the Agency, disastrous for ARVN, disastrous for the Embassy, disastrous for the U.S. One of these days, it was going to be more than a single disaster; they were going to lose the whole fucking country.

"Let's get back—fast," he shouted. "If you were a chopper, I'd ask you to land on the Embassy roof."

Jim did a U-turn and headed the plane back toward Saigon. . . .

Later, in a scene from the same novel, the defense attaché staff briefs the American ambassador.

Williams placed the pointer on the ledge beneath the map. "Let me sum it up this way, Mr. Ambassador," he said. "If Lam reinforces Ban Me Thuot, he weakens Pleiku. If he reinforces Pleiku, he weakens Ban Me Thuot. It's his dilemma. His decisions must be based on intelligence, and his intelligence is shaky."

Walker turned to Collins. "General, anything you want to add?"

"I think General Williams has given you the best picture we have," Collins said. "It's unclear, but I must say we've seen this all before: enemy activity that flares up and then disappears."

"But the NVA has not been spotted around Ban Me Thuot before," Walker interjected. "That's what worries me."

"Well, I keep thinking of the point that General Williams just made," Collins continued. "A surprise NVA appearance around Ban Me Thuot aimed, perhaps, at sucking ARVN troops into that area, prior to an attack on Pleiku. Or Kontum. Or nothing. That's what makes all this so goddamned frustrating for us. We've become military bookkeepers, checking credits and debits, without really knowing what the hell is going on. Lousy way to watch a war." He threw up his hands in disgust. "Anyway, it's all up to ARVN—these days."

For Walker, Collins's almost throwaway line pointed up the irony of the shift in the U.S. attitude toward ARVN. Once upon a time, when the GIs first began arriving in '65, the South Vietnamese military had been just about the last thing on the Pentagon's mind. In fact, ARVN was then regarded as more of a hindrance than an asset, and Americans pushed the Vietnamese soldiers aside in their headlong pursuit of the VC and the NVA. In fact, the war had become so Americanized that, if a tidal wave had floated the entire South Vietnamese population out to sea, MACV wouldn't have noticed until somebody discovered that the laundry was overdue. America would handle the "gooks." Well, it turned out that the "gooks" had handled America, and America dropped the war in ARVN's flabby lap.

Walker found himself scanning various charts on the wall dealing with ARVN: number of divisions, deployment of heavy weapons, desertion rates. It struck him once again that ARVN, representing the critical difference between Saigon's survival and collapse, had not been tested in any major battle since the final U.S. pullout in '73. What would happen when it was?

"General Collins, General Williams, I have the President's word that the emergency funds ARVN needs will be forthcoming." Walker spoke with a clinical evenness of tone, subconsciously reassuring himself as well as his military colleagues. "His word. To me personally. When the test comes—whenever, wherever, however—the South Vietnamese will have the hardware they need."

"I hope so," said Collins, without much conviction.[32]

In Washington, however, the U.S. administration's attempts to secure more "hardware" for the South Vietnamese do not succeed. As one military historian attests:

As the ring of Communist divisions tightened around Military Region 3, the flow of military assistance to Vietnam was slowed by events in Washington. Members of a House caucus on 12 March voted 189 to 49 in favor of a resolution opposing more military aid for either Cambodia or Vietnam before the end of the fiscal year. The next day, 13 March, the House Foreign Affairs Committee rejected a compromise proposal that would have provided some additional aid.

The Ford administration pressed ahead with efforts to convince Congress that additional assistance was essential to the survival of Vietnam and that the Congressional approach to this issue was the cause of the Vietnamese decision to withdraw from the highlands.

Although the decline of U.S. support was the crucial factor in the overall disaster in Vietnam, the proximate cause of the highlands debacle was the failure of the corps commander to accept an intelligence estimate and to fight the battle of Ban Me Thuot with forces available. Then, when he followed this critical mistake with two others—inadequate planning and execution of the counterattack from Phuoc An and a horribly mismanaged withdrawal down Route 7B—he started the entire nation on a downhill slide that not even the valor of thousands of loyal officers and soldiers could reverse.

The Defense and State Departments were receiving reasonably accurate daily reports from the DAO and Embassy in Saigon, but most journalists in Vietnam were having difficulty discovering what was really happening on the battlefield, and it has been argued that military assistance could not have stemmed South Vietnam's decline because the South Vietnamese lacked the will to fight. As in every war, some units performed poorly under attack, but the growing certainty that defeat was imminent, now that the United States had cut back military assistance, was at the root of the decline in combat efficiency. Yet there were countless instances of great tenacity in defense and awesome valor in combat, even in the face of overwhelming enemy firepower and numbers.[33]

1975   14 March—ARVN forces withdraw from Ban Me Thuot, leaving the city to the enemy.

A U.S. Marine Corps historian describes the events of the following few days.

WITHDRAWAL FROM THE CENTRAL HIGHLANDS

On 16 March, after determining their indefensibility, President Thieu ordered what was supposed to be an orderly withdrawal from the highlands to more defensible terrain. A lack of planning and organization turned the withdrawal into a rout. Within two hours, the road south was clogged with South Vietnamese military and civilians in vehicles and on foot. The NVA pursued the fleeing columns which moved slowly along Route 7A. By this time the South Vietnamese military units were completely disorganized and incapable of defending the retreating columns. The NVA pursued to the coast, capturing tens of thousands of refugees and tons of equipment on the way. The precipitous abandonment of the highlands set a tone of panic and defeatism which was to spread infectiously in coming days. The NVA forces moved quickly to capitalize on this situation. A few ARVN units, notably the 22nd Division in Binh Dinh Province and the 3rd Airborne Brigade in Khanh Hoa Province, resisted the Communists, but otherwise the Communist drive to the coast met little resistance.

ABANDONMENT OF THE NORTH

In MR-1 the GVN defense network broke before it was even really subjected to heavy combat. Although the Communists enjoyed many successes during early March, the heaviest blow against MR-1 defense was the movement of the ARVN Airborne Division from the area to Saigon on 12 March. The ABN Div was one of the keystones essential for a strong defense. Its loss had a severe psychological impact upon the remaining defenders. The snowball had begun to roll. After the withdrawal of the airborne troops, evacuation of the central highlands, and a series of limited but sharp enemy attacks, military morale dropped and civilian panic rose. But, while strong threats had developed in Quang Tin and Quang Ngai Provinces, the first area to break was Quang Tri Province on 19 March 1975. The Province Chief ordered Quang Tri abandoned, adding even more to the feeling of panic in the region. Nevertheless, the MR-1 commander planned to fight. These plans, however, were disrupted by the vacillation of President Thieu, who gave a series of conflicting orders first to abandon Hue in the face of heavy attacks, then to defend it. Commanders found it impossible to reverse the movement of their troops so quickly. Troops and equipment were stranded on roads already clogged by refugees, and command and control became extremely difficult. When the Communists did launch their attacks near the city panic had really set in. Efforts were made for the orderly withdrawal of some units but with only marginal success. Route QL1 was soon cut between Hue and Danang and Communist forces quickly surrounded the city. By 24 March, Quang Ngai and Quang Tin Provinces were lost and hundreds of thousands of refugees fled to what was hoped to be the Danang enclave. The snowball continued to roll. Fear stricken troops presented only token resistance to NVA forces by this time. Massive desertions were reported as GVN troops fled to Danang with their families, leaving equipment, weapons, and gear strewn along the roads. It became clear that by now even Danang was clearly indefensible. Although already too late, evacuation of Danang commenced, first by air then by sea. The air evacuation ended on 28 March when uncontrolled mobs of people crowded onto runways making air operations impossible. The last plane out, a World Airlines passenger plane, had to run over people and motorcycles to take off.[34]

With air transportation impossible, the evacuation by sea of Da Nang is described by the U.S. Navy Sealift commander.

On 28 March USNS MILLER was cleared to enter port to conduct evacuation operations. It was at that time that message reports from the PIONEER CONTENDER arrived and all concerned became aware that she was already loaded with 5000 plus refugees. The Secretary of State again requested that the Secretary of Defense utilize MSC shipping for evacuation, and concurrently provided $5 million in funds from USAID and a release from liability from claims by refugees. At this time, COMSCFE diverted SS GREEN PORT, SS AMERICAN CHALLENGER, and USNS GREENVILLE VICTORY to Danang. PIONEER CONTENDER, loaded with refugees, sailed for Cam Ranh Bay, taking with her, AB&T/MSC Rep Danang, Lee "Barry" DAVIS, some American Consulate personnel and the Danang evacuation coordinator. Some consulate personnel remained behind to continue coordination efforts on one of the tugs previously sent to Danang but the tug was required to depart essentially because her communications had broken down, and tug and barge loading operations were degraded by numerous small boats of refugee soldiers boarding. MILLER was then left to load three barges of refugees totalling approximately 7500 personnel and she departed early on 29 March for Cam Ranh Bay.

The remainder of the day in Danang brought thousands of additional refugees into the city. The tug CHITOSE MARU, badly overloaded with about 600 refugees, had a barge in tow as she departed for Nha Trang with over 2000 refugees. Additionally, numerous VNN craft and assorted small boats left loaded with refugees and personal belongings. Coordinated orderly military withdrawal was non-existent.

Early on 30 March, PIONEER COMMANDER arrived in Danang with DAO Coordinator, Mr. Ernie HEY, aboard. Because conditions were chaotic loading operations had to be conducted with ships underway. The Consul General, Mr. Al FRANCIS, had relocated to the tug OSCEOLA. PIONEER CONTENDER returned from Cam Ranh Bay for a second load of refugees. By 1800 that evening, PIONEER COMMANDER had loaded more than 8000 refugees and departed for Cam Ranh Bay. The DAO Coordinator shifted back to PIONEER CONTENDER.

The confusion ashore, reported sapper efforts directed at evacuation efforts, total chaos with respect to boats and barge loading, and armed military personnel mingled with refugees who were reported shooting VC suspects, resulted in a situation fraught with danger and risk for the safety of the vessels themselves. Accordingly, the evacuation effort at Danang was soon ordered to a halt. The tugs SAIGON 240, SHIBAURA MARU and ASIATIC STAMINA all departed Danang with barges in tow. The PIONEER CONTENDER departed with 6000 plus refugees late that evening. The SHIBAURA MARU, when she left, had three barges in tow but had been taken over by mutinous ARVN soldiers. All three of these tugs were able to rendezvous with the SS TRANSCOLORADO on 31 March and transfer their 3500 refugees.

Thus ended the evacuation of Danang. Towards the end, there were an estimated one million refugees in Danang who may have desired to be evacuated. However, the rapidly advancing North Vietnamese forces would not allow any further humanitarian evacuation, since they began firing on rescue ships when they appeared in range and subsequently refused to consider humanitarian pleas to permit continuation of the evacuation. A vast quantity of military equipment was abandoned because most RVN military forces panicked and retreated in disorder. AMERICAN CHALLENGER remained in the area off the coast to pick up stragglers, but Communist control was apparently effective, and none

appeared. All told, during this phase, the MSC evacuation effort at Danang transferred intra country approximately 34,600 refugees.[35]

*The next day Cambodia experiences a change in leadership, as Khmer
Chief of Staff General Sak Sutsakhan recalls.*

The departure of Marshal Lon Nol from Phnom Penh on 1 April 1975
was, in effect, a final gesture on the part of all concerned in our efforts to
move Cambodia toward peace. The various responsible elements in Cambodia, the National Assembly, the FANK, the leaders of Lon Nol's own
Socio-Republican Party, had begun to wonder in 1974 whether or not
Lon Nol's continued presence in Phnom Penh was perhaps an obstacle to
peace. The peace initiatives which he had made in 1973 and 1974 produced no positive results. The military situation was becoming desperate,
and the country was torn with internal political strife, as I have already
noted. All of this was insufficient, however, to move Lon Nol himself to
suggest that he go.

Finally, in January and February 1975, international opinion began to
make itself felt. The countries of Southeast Asia, particularly those of the
Association of Southeast Asian Nations (ASEAN) and Japan, all began
to make representations to our officials that they too considered that the
absence of Lon Nol might help matters. The United States was interested
as well, but appeared to prefer that the ASEAN countries take the lead
in this. U.S. Ambassador Dean never discussed this question in any way
with me, and I do not know whether Dean discussed it with anyone else
in our government.

In these circumstances, the question came to be discussed more and
more explicitly by the above-mentioned groups, leading in March to the
adoption of formal resolutions that Lon Nol leave the country on a temporary basis, while the terms of a cease-fire were worked out. In late
March, following my assumption of command, a delegation called on Lon
Nol to present the resolution; he was shocked that the country would thus
turn its back on him, and asked for a few days to consider the proposal.
During this time, Lon Nol met separately with each member of the delegation in an effort to test the degree of unity among his detractors.
Finding them both collectively and individually of one mind in support of
the resolution as submitted, Lon Nol agreed to leave, asking that those
remaining work for an honorable peace—not simply capitulate—and, failing that, continue the struggle.

The departure ceremony at the Chamcar Mon Palace was devoid of all
fanfair [*sic*] and attended by Khmer only, the diplomatic corps having not
been invited. From the grounds of Chamcar Mon, helicopters took Lon
Nol, his family and party to Pochentong, where they boarded an Air
Cambodia craft. Ambassador Dean was at Pochentong when the group
arrived. From Phnom Penh, Lon Nol traveled to the U.S. base at
Utapao, Thailand, where a plane sent by the Government of Indonesia

waited to take him to Bali. After several days in Bali, during which Lon Nol had an interview with President Suharto, the President of the Khmer Republic traveled to Hawaii to continue medical treatment for the effects of his 1971 stroke. . . .

My taking office, after the departure of Marshal Lon Nol, a departure desired by both the Khmer and the United States Embassy, gave evidence of a real effort on the part of both the Khmer Government and the United States to reach a peaceful and honorable solution to the struggle. The government called for a purge of certain key people. Although it was a little late in the game, this was carried out but not without difficulty. Everyone rejoiced, especially the civilian population from the highest placed to the most humble. It was thought, not unreasonably, that real negotiations would take place and that peace was at hand. The troops were tired of fighting, the ammunition supply was running low, supplies were increasingly difficult to deliver to the troops at the front as the battle raged around the besieged capital. People waited for a miracle which only the United States Congress could provide—a favorable vote to continue military air support. Everyone hung on the radio listening for news from the United States. Alas, the decision—a negative one—was announced soon and caused an immediate and general panic.[36]

A U.S. Air Force historian describes a major event of the next day.

On 2 April . . . a World Airways DC-8 piloted by Kenneth Healy—a flyer who had flown refugees from collapsing Nationalist Chinese cities in 1948–49 and, more recently, had been at the controls of the Boeing 727 which made the hectic last flight out of Da Nang on 29 March—unofficially inaugurated Operation Babylift. Despite having been expressly forbidden from flying any orphans out of Vietnam, on grounds that his DC-8 was a cargo jet with no individual seats, seat belts, oxygen masks, or other safety equipment installed, maverick Healy, backed by his boss, maverick Edward J. Daly, the World Airways president, who was on hand, took aboard 54 orphans in Saigon.* In addition to these orphans, who ranged in age from 8 months to 11 years, the flight carried three other children and their mothers, and 27 other adults. Most of the adults had come along as attendants for the orphans, but two were American medical doctors who had been working in Saigon, another was an American contractor, and six were Vietnamese adults without papers who had scrambled aboard at the last minute.

Daly had spent most of the previous day in a series of heated arguments with AmEmb, AID, GVN, and airport officials, seeking authorization to evacuate as many as 400 orphans. According to Daly, the

---

*MAC, as well as U.S. Army officials at Camp Presidio, reported that 58 orphans were aboard the flight. However, the senior vice-president of World Airways, Charles Patterson, who accompanied the flight from Saigon to Oakland, gave the corrected figure of 54 used in this narrative. [Footnote in original text.]

Embassy had even warned the children's orphanage not to release them. For its part, the Embassy insisted that the adoption agency concerned, Friends for All Children, had reversed its original decision to use the World Airways DC-8 flight, simply because the plane was neither heated nor pressurized.* When Daly announced that he would round up a load of orphans, with or without the cooperation of the Embassy, AID, or even adoption agencies, the U.S. Embassy commissary in Saigon refused to supply milk or other basic items for the children. Undeterred, he loaded the aircraft with milk, baby food, and diapers at his own expense.

After the plane had been stocked, the children gathered, and other preparations made, the aircraft was set to leave. As Healy began to taxi, the Tan Son Nhut air traffic controller shouted, "Don't take off! Don't take off! You have no clearance!" (Trying late to justify themselves, Vietnamese officials explained that the airfield had been closed to take-offs and landings because a Viet Cong attack was predicted.) However, as soon as the plane's wheels reached the runway, Healy gunned the four engines and was quickly airborne, bound for Yokota AB, Japan. Healy later explained his disregard for the controller's orders: "I just didn't get the message in time."

Since the flight was not chartered by the Military Airlift Command (MAC) and had no connection with the U.S. Government, it was not authorized to land at Yokota. However, with the aircraft due soon, officials at Yokota had little choice but to let it land, though they demanded that no Vietnamese deplane. Even in this, however, World Airways circumvented the rules: two babies were so dehydrated and malnourished that they had to be left behind at the Tachikawa AB hospital. The refueled DC-8 resumed its flight to Oakland International Airport, where five buses carried the children to a makeshift nursery in a truck maintenance facility at the U.S. Army's Camp Presidio in San Francisco.[37]

The next day, 3 April, President Ford opens a news conference with the following statement.

We are seeing a great human tragedy as untold numbers of Vietnamese flee the North Vietnamese onslaught. The United States has been doing—and will continue to do—its utmost to assist these people.

I have directed all available naval ships to stand off Indochina, to do whatever is necessary to assist. We have appealed to the United Nations to use its moral influence to permit these innocent people to leave, and

---

*Correspondent Peter Arnett, the only newsman who accompanied the flight, commented afterward that "Actually, the plane was warm and pressurized. The only real danger was in landing, takeoffs, and occasional turbulence. Several American adult volunteers and the plane's crew sat with babies on these occasions, and none was even bumped." (Peter Arnett (AP), "Saigon Tots Sample U.S. Delights: From Fear to Joy in 25 Hours, *Honolulu Star-Bulletin,* 3 Apr 75.) [Footnote in original text.]

we call on North Vietnam to permit the movement of refugees to the area of their choice.

While I have been in California, I have been spending many hours on the refugee problem and our humanitarian efforts. I have directed that money from a $2 million special foreign aid children's fund be made available to fly 2,000 South Vietnamese orphans to the United States as soon as possible.

I have also directed American officials in Saigon to act immediately to cut red tape and other bureaucratic obstacles preventing these children from coming to the United States.

I have directed that C-5A aircraft and other aircraft especially equipped to care for these orphans during the flight be sent to Saigon. I expect these flights to begin within the next 36 to 48 hours. These orphans will be flown to Travis Air Force Base in California, and other bases on the West Coast, and cared for in these locations.

These 2,000 Vietnamese orphans are all in the process of being adopted by American families. This is the least we can do, and we will do much, much more.[38]

Although the U.S. government appears determined to help refugees, Washington's perception of the overall situation seems confused.

By this time agencies in Washington were equally gloomy. A DIA assessment of 3 April gave South Vietnam only 30 days.

Meanwhile, a misconception was spreading in Washington that the current reverses in Vietnam did not involve much combat. In his news conference of 2 April, Secretary of Defense Schlesinger spoke of "relatively little major fighting." He repeated this view on "Face the Nation" on 6 April: "It is plain that the great offensive is a phrase that probably should be in quotation marks. What we have had here is a partial collapse of South Vietnamese Forces, so that there has been very little major fighting since the battle of Ban Me Thuot, and that was an exception in itself."

General Smith could not let that impression stand and sent a message to CINCPAC and a number of addressees in Washington attempting to correct the record:

> On the contrary, there was heavy fighting all along the coastal plain and in the foothills from south of Phu Bai to Khanh Duong in Khanh Hoa Province.
>
> In the hills south of Phu Bai, the 1st ARVN Div repelled numerous heavy two-divisional attacks and even gained some lost positions before it finally was ordered to withdraw because its northern flank was exposed.
>
> In Phu Loc District just north of Hai Van Pass on QL-1, an overpowering attack by up to two regiments of the enemy's 325th Div forced outnumbered ARVN defenders back from their positions and severed the line of communications.
>
> These attacks could not be described as "little fighting."[39]

*On board one of the U.S. Navy evacuation ships, circumstances are much
different than those experienced by Tao Kim Nam on his 1954 voyage from
Haiphong to Saigon.*

1. The following is a portion of the debriefing of 2LT Robert E. Lee,
USMC, 3d Platoon, Company B, 1st Battalion, 4th Marines who commanded the Marine security detachment onboard SS PIONEER CON-
TENDER through P.M. 7 April 1975 while this vessel was enroute to and
at PHU QUOC Island.

2. On 4 April 1975 LT LEE notified all people on the ship that Marines
were onboard. This was done by putting Marines all around the ship
before dawn. At 0800H, 4 April the platoon had a very detailed brief by
ship's officers. LT LEE was told most of the people on the forward
portion of the ship had their obvious weapons thrown overboard, however the rear portion was totally unsupervised because they were able to
climb on from the various vessels which brought them to the PIONEER
CONTENDER. To provide better security for the vessel the platoon
conducted a physical search of the refugees in the immediate vicinity of
the bridge. The search teams uncovered thirty to forty hand grenades,
fourteen .45 caliber and over twenty .38 caliber pistols. The platoon tried
to shake down the forward portion of the ship, but due to the great
number of refugees aboard this was very ineffective. While this search
was going on the Marines occupied positions on the flying bridge to cover
the search team. During the search it became evident that the refugees
did not want to go to PHU QUOC Island. An extra security watch was
set that evening because LT LEE reported there were instigators stirring
up the refugees. The night was quiet with the exception of a few gunshots
in the aft section of the ship. PIONEER CONTENDER arrived at PHU
QUOC Island at 0900, 5 April 1975. The people seemed to accept the
fact that they were going to PHU QUOC and land sure looked good to
them because of the miserable conditions aboard ship. We received a
message from SAIGON that SS PIONEER CONTENDER was last priority for disembarkation of refugees because there were three other ships
at anchor before our arrival. LT LEE and the ship's Master, Captain
FLINK, were also notified that the only landing craft available were 3
LCM's. 1200, 5 April a RVN LCM came alongside to provide food for
the refugees. A riot ensued and LT LEE was forced to fire warning shots
in the air to prevent the Marines from being trampled. The RVN craft
stated they would take 150 sick women and children ashore. At this time
LT LEE stated he observed an attitude of complete uncooperation and
indifference on the part of the RVN personnel on the vessel. The boat
crew said they wanted the sick, the women and children but started
pointing to selected men to come ashore whom they knew. This also
caused a minor riot and warning shots had to be fired in the air.

3. The equitable distribution of food was impossible due to the mass
chaos around the food distribution points. The Vietnamese in uniform

and young males who looked like they should be in uniform stole food from the issue point and the women and children. This totally unsuccessful attempt to distribute food went on until 2200 when the situation became so critical that LT LEE withdrew his troops to avoid US casualties and the use of deadly force upon the refugees. Six infants and two women were crushed to death in the chaos which broke out. The remainder of the evening was relatively quiet because of the rain although gunshots were heard both fore and aft. On 6 April at 1000 food resupply was received from USS DUBUQUE and another riot broke out. Two of LT LEE's men were knocked down and the food they were carrying taken. Warning shots were again fired to avoid injury to LT LEE's troops and he rapidly withdrew his men to avoid the use of deadly force.

4. Each day Marines escorted the crew of the PIONEER CONTENDER around the vessel filling water containers for the refugees. It took about 30–40 minutes to move from amidships to the bow to fill the containers. While the Marines were on the bow some of the Vietnamese would often cut the hose and sell water at gun point. Water resupply was a constant operation from 0600 until 0100 every day and operated both fore and aft at the same time. Water supply became a potential riot situation during the day because of the heat and LT LEE had to steadily increase his security from two to four Marines during the heat of the day. At 1500 two doctors arrived with medical supplies and four corpsmen and started a sick call. A security team search on 5 April uncovered a booby trapped cartridge belt during the weapons shakedown. LT LEE stated at this time he noticed that the refugees were becoming desperate and they started tearing wood off the cargo hold bulkheads and jumping overboard to swim ashore using the wood as a raft. All on board noticed RVN patrol boats shooting some of these swimmers but picking others up. LT LEE states he saw about 10 swimmers shot and he estimates about 30–40 of the approximately 150 who jumped were shot in the water. Sick call continued all night till about 0300 and DR. WILLIAMS and DR. OAKLAND and the other corpsmen saved many people from death and misery. The situation aboard the SS PIONEER CONTENDER could have been alleviated if it had fewer refugees. Sanitary conditions were unbearable with the refugees living in their own urine and defecation. The water situation was poor at best even with the distribution. The food situation was poor and worsened because ARVN and gangsters would steal the food from women and children as soon as they were out of sight of the Marine security personnel. Vietnamese Army and Marine officers were extensively utilized by GYSGT HERNANDEZ and LT LEE to help control the refugees and gather information. It is LT LEE's and Captain FLINK's estimate that 100 adults and 200–300 children, mostly infants, died in the past 4 days. The bodies were almost immediately discharged overboard. The Marines worked to relieve the refugees' suffering after only having an average of two to three hours sleep a night. They provided security for the crew of the PIONEER CONTENDER and it was the

Master's opinion that the vessel would have been commandeered had they not been aboard.[40]

Three days later, as noted in an official U.S. Air Force report, President Ford tries again.

Addressing a joint session of Congress on 10 April, President Gerald Ford asked for two things. The first, an emergency aid request for South Vietnam—$722 million military and $250 million economic and humanitarian—based on Ford's hope that a stable military situation could produce a political solution in Vietnam. The second was a request that Congress immediately clarify its restrictions on his use of U.S. armed forces in Southeast Asia (SEA) in case an emergency evacuation of either Vietnam or Cambodia became necessary. . . . He asked Congress to complete action not later than 19 April.

President Ford appeared to be asking Congress to acknowledge in unambiguous language that the War Powers Act gave him the authority to use troops to protect an evacuation effort. Ford was trying to meet Congress halfway, although he and his lawyers had already asserted that as Commander in Chief, he inherently had this authority without the specific approval of the Congress. Ford had set the stage a week earlier in his nationally televised news conference of 3 April when he claimed the War Powers Act gave the President "certain limited authority" to use military forces "to protect American lives," and "to that extent I will use the law." The following day, to expand his legal claims, he reported in a letter to congressional leaders, as required under the War Powers Act, that a U.S. Navy ship had entered the territorial waters of the Republic of Vietnam (RVN) on 3 April to pick up endangered Vietnamese refugees. Ford explained in his letter that his use of a Navy vessel for evacuation had been "undertaken pursuant to the President's constitutional authority as Commander in Chief and Chief Executive in the conduct of foreign relations," and pursuant to a 1973 amendment to the Foreign Assistance Act authorizing "humanitarian assistance to refugees, civilian war casualties, and other persons disadvantaged by hostilities."

President Ford's claim to such authority was promptly challenged by Senator Robert C. Byrd, the Assistant Majority Leader, who protested this "dangerous precedent." Senator Thomas F. Eagleton, who had briefly been George McGovern's Vice-Presidential running mate in 1972, joined the chorus of objectors. As the *New York Times'* Pentagon correspondent, John W. Finney, observed, however, the debate was "largely legalistic," since most Congressmen would not seriously object to the President's deciding to use Marines to rescue endangered American citizens from Saigon. A more controversial issue would be the use of U.S. troops to protect the evacuation of Vietnamese citizens. In either case, both Senators realized that an evacuation of Vietnam could prove the first test of Congress's ability to limit the war-making powers of the

President. Moreover, Senator Byrd said that if the Administration persisted in claiming inherent powers for the President's use of Marines, he was prepared to force the issue by introducing a resolution authorizing the use of military forces in an evacuation.

Senator Eagleton shared the view of many constitutional scholars that the President, as Commander in Chief, possessed an inherent right to rescue endangered Americans; however, there was "no precedent to suppport an inherent right to use United States forces to rescue foreign nationals." Hence, the President's request for a clarification of his authority "presented an important opportunity to proscribe by law the use of force for the Vietnam evacuation." Even more important, said Eagleton, "Congress had the chance to resurrect the concept, advanced by the Founding Fathers, that the Executive and Congress would participate together in decisions potentially involving war."

As this legal debate continued, the President's request for increased aid to Vietnam was in trouble too. Secretary of Defense James R. Schlesinger, appearing on 6 April on CBS-TV's "Face the Nation" to defend the request for $300 million which was pending (before Ford upped the ante to $772 million), was asked by host George Herman whether more money would "change the outcome significantly." Schlesinger replied: "Nobody knows the answer to that. That is the great imponderable about American aid. If we are to refrain from giving aid in those cases in which we do not know the outcome, then we will, through a self-fulfilling prophecy, create the fall of many countries." Even Schlesinger could not give the people or Congress any assurance that more money would help.[41]

On 12 April the U.S. Marine Corps' official daily publication, "Summary of Items of Significant Interest," begins as follows:

12 APRIL 75

1. CAMBODIA
PHNOM PENH

OPERATION EAGLE PULL WAS DIRECTED TO BE EXECUTED BY THE AMERICAN AMBASSADOR IN ORDER TO EVACUATE UNITED STATES CITIZENS THIRD COUNTRY NATIONALS AND OTHER INDIGENOUS PERSONNEL FROM PHNOM PENH BECAUSE OF THE DETERIORATED POLITICAL SITUATION. TOTAL OF 276 PERSONNEL WERE EVACUATED DURING [A FIVE-HOUR PERIOD]. A MARINE GROUND SECURITY FORCE CONSISTING OF 345 PERSONNEL WAS INSERTED FOR PROTECTION OF THE LANDING ZONE DURING THE HELICOPTER EVACUATION LIFT. EVACUEES WERE LIFTED BY TWENTY-FOUR CH-53 HELICOPTERS TO THE USS OKINAWA . . . AND THE USS HANCOCK . . . LOCATED IN THE GULF OF THAILAND. THE EVACUATION LIFT WAS COMPLETED WITHOUT ANY CASUALTIES, ALTHOUGH RECOILLESS RIFLE FIRE WAS RECEIVED DURING FINAL EXTRACTION OF THE GROUND SECURITY FORCE.[42]

Included among the rescued are the acting president of Cambodia and the U.S. Ambassador. Also, as the commander of Operation Eagle Pull notes, a large percentage of the evacuees are journalists.

Over fifty of the [276] evacuees from Phnom Penh were members of the media representatives, and as soon as they were aboard many of them desired to file press copy. . . .

The media representatives were briefed by the ARG's Public Affairs personnel on the facilities available to them on the LPH and the ground rules under which they would be allowed to file press copy. An area had been set aside for their use and stocked with typewriters and other supplies. They were encouraged to limit their initial submissions to five hundred words, and to pool their efforts where possible in order to allow all the press representatives desiring to file to do so. . . . [deleted for security reasons] The press requirements were difficult to satisfy, however the preparations made by the ARG's Public Affairs detachment provided the media representatives with adequate working space and the opportunity to file initial and follow up releases as the Task Group sailed for Thailand on the night of 12/13 April.[43]

Three days later, in Washington, Secretary of State Henry Kissinger makes a speech.

The human tragedy of Viet-Nam has never been more acute than it now is. Hundreds of thousands of South Vietnamese have sought to flee Communist control and are homeless refugees. They have our compassion, and they must also have our help. Despite commendable efforts by the South Vietnamese Government, the burden of caring for these innocent victims is beyond its capacity. The United States has already done much to assist these people, but many remain without adequate food, shelter, or medical care. The President has asked that additional efforts and additional resources be devoted to this humanitarian effort. I ask that the Congress respond generously and quickly.

The objectives of the United States in this immensely difficult situation remain as they were when the Paris agreement was signed—to end the military conflict and establish conditions which will allow a fair political solution to be achieved. We believe that despite the tragic experience to date, the Paris agreement remains a valid framework within which to proceed toward such a solution. However, today, as in 1973, battlefield conditions will affect political perceptions and the outcome of negotiations. We therefore believe that in order for a political settlement to be reached which preserves any degree of self-determination for the people of South Viet-Nam, the present military situation must be stabilized. It is for these reasons that the President has asked Congress to appropriate urgently additional funds for military assistance for Viet-Nam.

I am acutely aware of the emotions aroused in this country by our long and difficult involvement in Viet-Nam. I understand what the cost has been for this nation and why frustration and anger continue to dominate our national debate. Many will argue that we have done more than enough for the Government and the people of South Viet-Nam. I do not agree with that proposition, however, nor do I believe that to review endlessly the wisdom of our original involvement serves a useful purpose now. For despite the agony of this nation's experience in Indochina and the substantial reappraisal which has taken place concerning our proper role there, few would deny that we are still involved or that what we do— or fail to do—will still weigh heavily in the outcome. We cannot by our actions alone insure the survival of South Viet-Nam. But we can, alone, by our inaction assure its demise.

The United States has no legal obligation to the Government and the people of South Viet-Nam of which Congress is not aware. But we do have a deep moral obligation—rooted in the history of our involvement and sustained by the continuing efforts of our friends. We cannot easily set it aside. In addition to the obvious consequences for the people of Viet-Nam, our failure to act in accordance with that obligation would inevitably influence other nations' perceptions of our constancy and our determination. American credibility would not collapse, and American honor would not be destroyed. But both would be weakened, to the detriment of this nation and of the peaceful world order we have sought to build.

Mr. Chairman, as our Ambassador in Phnom Penh was about to be evacuated last week, he received a letter from a longtime friend of the United States [Gen Sirik Matak, who, with Prime Minister Long Boret, comprised two of the seven "supertraitors" condemned to death by the Cambodian Communists, declined a seat on the last plane out of Phnom Penh and subsequently paid with his life for his refusal to desert his country in her hour of defeat] who has been publicly marked for execution. Let me share that letter with you:

> DEAR EXCELLENCY AND FRIEND: I thank you very sincerely for your letter and for your offer to transport me towards freedom. I cannot, alas, leave in such a cowardly fashion. As for you, and in particular for your great country, I never believed for a moment that you would have this sentiment of abandoning a people which has chosen liberty. You have refused us your protection, and we can do nothing about it.
>
> You leave, and my wish is that you and your country will find happiness under this sky. But, mark it well that if I shall die here on the spot and in my country that I love, it is too bad, because we all are born and must die one day.

Mr. Chairman, ladies and gentlemen, I suspect that neither Ambassador [John Gunther] Dean nor I will ever be able to forget that letter or the brave man who wrote it. Let us now, as Americans, act together to assure that we receive no more letters of this kind.[44]

1975   17 April—The Senate Armed Services Committee rejects President Ford's request for additional emergency aid for South Vietnam.

In Saigon that night, CIA agent Frank Snepp holds an informal press conference of his own.

Alan Carter, the maverick USIA chief, was giving a dinner party that evening for several American journalists. The dinner was another of his rebellious little acts, since [Ambassador] Martin had outlawed all contacts with the press except those he personally approved.

I called Carter and asked if I could wangle an invitation. "No problem," he said. "But I got to warn you most of the guests probably know your agency affiliations. They'll be asking leading questions." I said that was exactly what I wanted.

The group was a perfect cross section. The electronic media had its spokesmen in Garrick Utley of NBC and Bob Simon of CBS. Keyes Beech of the *Chicago Daily News* and George McArthur of the *Los Angeles Times* were our token old-timers, both veteran war correspondents who had made a life and career of Vietnam. Fox Butterfield, patrician gadfly of the *New York Times*, who prided himself on his contacts with Polgar and the Ambassador, showed up stylishly late. So did the Embassy's most unlikely *bête noire*, Phil McComb, former speech writer for New York's conservative Senator William Buckley, who had managed to offend Martin several months before by writing a series on corruption and morale problems in the South Vietnamese army for the *Washington Post*.

Most of the guests had heard me brief before and knew me to be well informed. So they listened with more than casual interest to what I told them over dinner. After briefly detailing the balance of forces, I turned to my main topic. Without identifying my source, I emphasized that there was good evidence the Communists had decided in favor of a military solution and were determined to celebrate Ho Chi Minh's birthday in Saigon. Their planning apparently did not allow for a negotiated settlement, or even a disguised surrender. I said I was telling them all this in hopes they would get the message to Washington.

McArthur and Butterfield protested. Both had recently interviewed top Embassy officials, and they accurately played back to me what they had been told: (1) the Communists had neither the manpower nor political "assets" to absorb the country in one sweep; and (2) with some satisfactory changes in the Saigon government, they might be willing to work through the existing political structure for a while, if only to maximize their chances of attracting non-Communist aid and investment.

I acknowledged that all this made good sense in purely speculative terms, but stressed that what I had told them was not speculation but fact, a precise reflection of Hanoi's most recent guidelines.

None of the reporters filed stories on what I said. Several months later Beech apologized to me for his failure to do so. The Ambassador, he explained, had done such a "snow job" on the press corps—denying interviews, then parceling them out with exquisite timing—that no one could quite accept what other officials (aside from Polgar) were leaking to them.

Still, my performance was not an utter waste. Several of the reporters who had been at the dinner began calling me regularly to fish for additional information and to pass on observations from their own forays to the battlefront. As days passed and the Station's own agents disappeared, the intelligence they provided became an invaluable window on what was taking place only a few miles away.[45]

Not too far away, Air Marshal Ky, having been forced out of the government by President Thieu, sits at home.

Scores of big U.S. transport planes flew in past my windows every day, loaded with precious supplies—but nearly all flew back half empty, when they could have taken a far more precious cargo to safety.

Martin did try to persuade Phan Quang Dan, deputy prime minister, to allow orphans to be evacuated, but this was for propaganda, for Martin wrote in a letter to Dan that "this evacuation . . . will create a shift in American public opinion in favor of Vietnam," explaining that, once in America, the children would appear on TV and "the effect would be tremendous."

In fact Martin was hoping to persuade Congress to reverse its veto on arms aid to Vietnam, and he backed his plan up with a never-ending stream of photographs of atrocities and inspired stories calculated to wring the hearts of American people, at the same time as he was assuring all of us, "Be calm. Saigon is in no danger."

Even more incredible, at this critical moment he ordered embassy officials to compile a detailed study of the Vietnamese government information service. The man was not only stupid. He was mad.

Suddenly contacts inside the government told me on my private grapevine that Thieu was on the point of being ordered to resign. "There's no doubt about it," one told me, "all they're doing now is trying to find a formula to save everyone's face."

I knew my informant was telling the truth—but then, why didn't Martin telephone me to prepare the National Salvation Committee for action? As suspicion started to bite deeper, I suggested that we look again at our plans for a coup against Thieu. And it was because of this plan that I finally learned of Martin's double cross. Unexpectedly Timmes arrived at my house, and almost casually dropped a name that gave me the first clue.

"Is it true," he asked me, "that some of the general officers from the North—men like you—are plotting a coup?" My immediate reaction was that there must have been a leak, but before I had time to say a word, Timmes added an extraordinary sentence, a few words that absolved me from the decision of whether or not to lie.

"I mean a move against Big Minh."

I was flabbergasted. After all, Big Minh had been out of power for a long time. I blurted out, "I've heard nothing—but why Minh? He's not the president. Why should anyone make a move against a man who's not in power?"

Timmes replied, "Well, Marshal, I think I ought to tell you that if you *do* make a move against Big Minh, Washington and Hanoi will blame you for anything that happens afterward."

That was the split second when I realized that Martin had been quietly using the National Salvation Committee as a blind while he was planning to kick out Thieu, presumably to replace him with Big Minh as the man to negotiate with the Communists.

More in horror than in anger I said to Timmes, "If Big Minh becomes president, there will be a total collapse of Vietnam in twenty-four hours. Why should the Communists talk with Big Minh? He's not popular, and he never will be."

As Timmes left, I wondered if the Americans were just naïve enough to believe that Big Minh could deal with the Communists. Yet Martin was not naïve. Nor was Kissinger. Perhaps this incredible move was part of a carefully defined policy. Realizing that the end had come—though I could not believe it even then—perhaps the United States had decided to abandon us, and by putting in a man without any intellectual capabilities, to throw the last blame onto us instead of taking their share. There is no doubt that the choice of Big Minh was dictated by Martin.[46]

1975   18 April—Cambodian government collapses. Some officials flee to Thailand.

Shortly afterward, in the Kalbs' novel The Last Ambassador, *the U.S. ambassador to Saigon calls upon the South Vietnamese president at his office.*

Every chair was covered with heavy embroidered satins in brilliant reds and golds. Massive polished dark wood furniture stood on Oriental carpets. One corner was dominated by a mammoth set of elephant tusks mounted in hand-tooled silver holders. Brocaded draperies hung from the ceiling, covering walls but no windows. All of Saigon knew that, for security reasons, the room had been constructed windowless. Walker also knew—courtesy of the CIA—that one set of curtains hid a secret door to an underground tunnel that surfaced in the nearby zoo. Just in case. The room had an airless quality, always giving Walker the sense that echoes of old conversations still clung to the walls and the ceiling, trapped.

Finally, the tea was ready. The President's first words, as he poured, took the Ambassador by surprise.

"Problems in Washington?" he asked.

"Washington is not without its problems," Walker replied with a short laugh. "Neither is Hanoi, I'd venture to say." The stab at the North produced no reaction.

"What are you hearing from MR Two?"

"Not any more than you're hearing, Mr. President." Walker glanced at his watch; it had taken seven minutes to get to the point.

"I've just received a cable from Nguyen Van Hoang," the President said. Hoang was South Viet Nam's Ambassador to Washington. "Not very reassuring."

"Which means?"

"In fact," the President went on, as though Walker hadn't said a word, "Nguyen Van Hoang says more aid for South Viet Nam looks hopeless. What is more, he tells me that the antiwar movement has now attained such political strength that Washington seems ready to abandon its commitment to stand by South Viet Nam against our common enemy."

The Ambassador leaned forward in his chair; never before had he heard the President offer so blunt an assessment of U.S.–Vietnamese relations. Regardless of how close the gloomy assessment might be to the truth, Walker realized that he had to try to ease the President's anxiety.

"Your information, Mr. President," Walker began slowly, each word carefully chosen, meant to undercut Nguyen Van Hoang, "does not correspond to my own top-secret information. I am in constant communication with the President of the United States and with the Secretary of State—through various channels—and they emphasize that the U.S. commitment is unshakable, that the emergency funds for ARVN will in fact be authorized."

One small muscle twitched on the otherwise impassive face of the President of South Viet Nam. "Do you really think that your President and your Secretary will be able to stand up against Congress and public opinion?" he asked. "Do you really?"

No, I don't, Walker thought. "Yes, I do," he said.

"What about U.S. air support?" the President persisted. "You know what is now happening in the country. Don't you think Watergate grounded the B-fifty-twos?"

Yes, I do, Walker thought. "No, I don't," he said.

An ache of a smile came over the President's face. "I am glad to hear what you say," he responded wearily, "but you will excuse me if I repeat that I do not see any evidence to support that view."

It was, Walker realized, the elliptical Vietnamese way of calling him a liar—not only him but, by extension, also the President of the United States, the Secretary of State, and the U.S.A. itself. Walker's first instinct was to reiterate what he had just said, in hope that a more forceful presentation might give it the semblance of truth. But his emotions suddenly got the best of him, and he surprised himself—and the President— with an outburst of passion.

"Look, Mr. President, I speak to you directly from the heart. I am positive that the United States—despite the problems Washington is now facing—will stand by South Viet Nam and that the U.S. will not abandon a commitment just because there is noise in the streets of America. The U.S. is a superpower and will behave in the honorable way befitting a superpower."

The President kept stirring his tea.

Walker's voice escalated. "For the United States—in its dealings with the Communist world—Viet Nam is a crucial test." His eyes fixed on the President's face.

The President sipped his tea. Then, slowly and deliberately he reached into his desk and took out a writing pad and one piece of carbon paper. He inserted the carbon into the pad, picked up a pen and began writing, his hand moving swiftly across the paper. "Give me a few minutes, please, Mr. Ambassador," he said.

Walker felt he had no choice but to comply. He leaned back in his chair, his eyes fixed on the President. A rush of adjectives came to mind to describe the man bent over the desk: cautious, aloof, conspiratorial, cunning, scheming, devious. Corrupt? The President had always—predictably—denied it, but everyone knew that the key source of his power, apart from the Americans, was his toleration of corruption among the generals; the corrupt were then in his debt. And even if he didn't take any direct payoffs, it was no secret that his wife was known throughout Saigon as "Madame Moneybags," with one of the largest collections of diamonds east of the Place Vendôme. People said she never took off her diamonds, even slept with them, wore them not only on her fingers but on her toes as well—in case the family had to make a quick escape.

Walker, studying the President, reflected that the Vietnamese leader's haughty style contrasted sharply with his origins in a Central Viet Nam hamlet unmarked on any map. His mother, he was fond of telling American interviewers—but only after he had become President—carried baskets of vegetables to the village market while his father eked out a living as a farmer. He had decided that, in a country run by France, the only way up for a poor boy was to learn the language of the colonial masters; his contact with the French served to sharpen his suspicion of foreigners, but his study of their language opened doors. While he was still in his teens he joined the military—that was French, too, but there was no choice—and after the creation of an independent South Viet Nam in the mid-'fifties, he won a series of quick promotions to general. But it was his wife, the daughter of a prosperous Delta family, as ambitious as she was buxom, who encouraged him to use the stars on his collar as an entrée to the world of political power, of wealth. South Viet Nam, she told him, was not only a nation, it was also a cash box. He took her advice. When the senior generals fell to squabbling among themselves in the mid-'sixties about who should take over after the next coup, they chose him as the least dangerous. That was their fatal mistake; with the prodding of Madame President, he promptly purged his rivals. His quick rise to the top was given a veneer of legitimacy by an election in 1971 in which he was the only candidate.

Walker suppressed a smile as he recalled a true story that had made the rounds just before the presidential balloting. The future President had shared his concern with an American journalist that the world might suspect the elections of having been rigged. "Such a perception," the uniformed candidate remarked, "would be very embarrassing for South Viet Nam's image in the United States." "Well," said the journalist, "there is one way in which you could demonstrate to the world that the elections are honest, *mon général*." "How?" "*Lose!*" answered the journalist. The future President felt that would be going a bit too far. Instead, he had pulled a paratroop battalion out of MR 2 to beef up the security forces around Doc Lap.

Walker glanced at his watch. Five minutes had now gone by, and the President gave no sign that he was about to stop. He was writing quickly.

"Mr. President?" Walker ventured. The President did not even bother to look up.[47]

What the South Vietnamese president is writing is revealed to the world on 21 April.

At nightfall on 21 April, the government loudspeaker network abruptly announced that the regular curfew was being moved forward from 2100 to 2000. At almost the moment that the streets were clear, the image of Nguyen Van Thieu appeared on television screens of the country as he began to address the assembled members of the government and National Assembly at Independence Palace.

His voice "taut with emotion," President Thieu devoted most of his rambling* 90-minute speech to a scathing rebuke of the U.S. Government, saying: "The United States has not respected its promises. It is unfair. It is inhumane. It is not trustworthy. It is irresponsible." He then presented the rationale underlying his decision to step down:

> The U.S. Congress says that as long as Thieu is in power, there remains the war, Mr. Thieu is a warlord. I say that is an intention to wash its hands inhumanely. But if I leave in exchange for more aid, then I think I should leave. Today I resign to see whether, after there is no more Mr. Thieu, negotiation will be satisfactory. If the communists agree to negotiate, the

---

*It is possible that poor translations by the news services are responsible for the frequently disjointed, undramatic nature of the address as it appeared in the U.S. press. Certainly, no two direct quotations of the same part of the speech read the same. [Morita note.]

South agrees to negotiate. If so, it is lucky for the country and the entire populace.

And after Mr. Thieu leaves, if South Vietnam is immediately given sufficient aid to enable fighting by the armed forces of the Republic of Vietnam, then it is lucky for the country. My departure is worth the sacrifice. Then I would put the palms of my hands together and bow down. . . .

If the Americans do not want to support us any more, let them go, get out! No matter what we cannot accept, we are adults. We are going to continue to be insulted, because Americans will not help us. The Americans promised us—we trusted them. But you have not given us the aid you promised us. With that aid, I would not be afraid of the communists. Now my resignation will let the United States give you aid and open the way to negotiations.

Kissinger didn't see that the agreement led the South Vietnamese people to death. Everyone else sees it, but Kissinger does not see it. The superpowers have an interest between them. We have nothing to sacrifice—only this tiny land. I said at the time, we must fight. No coalition! If there is a coalition, South Vietnam cannot stand. I never thought a man like Mr. Kissinger would deliver our people to such a disastrous fate. . . ,

Today as I stand before the people, the National Assembly, I announce my resignation from the position of President. Under the constitution, Vice President Tran Van Huong will replace me as President.

Concluding his long, often tearful speech, Thieu declared:

I resign but I do not desert. From this minute I place myself at the disposal of the President and the people. I will continue to stay close to all of you in the coming task of national defense. Goodbye to you all.

At the end of his address, Thieu formally designated as his successor Vice President Tran Van Huong, a former two-term Mayor of Saigon, long-time legislator, and ex-Premier of South Vietnam. The 71-year-old Huong, asthmatic and nearly blind, spoke briefly, calling on the South Vietnamese people to unite, "because we will die if we do otherwise. If we do not help ourselves, then our hope for the assistance of others is useless." Moreover, he vowed to "fight until the troops die or the country is lost" and to "be buried with his soldiers." Then General Cao Van Vien, Chief of the Joint General Staff, took over the microphone, promising that his troops would continue fighting to "defend the homeland against communist aggressors."[48]

Air Marshal Ky watches his President's speech.

I shall never forget the moment when fifty-two-year-old Thieu told the people of Vietnam that he had been forced out of office. Two hundred friends and followers were jammed in my house to listen to the pathetic hour-long speech by the man Martin had backed, the man who had allowed the Reds to reach the outskirts of the capital. We could hear the gunfire as we listened and watched.

I was ashamed. Ashamed that any Vietnamese leader could behave as Thieu behaved in his speech. Looking at the small TV screen, at Thieu in an open-necked bush shirt, my mind flashed back to the day Johnson agreed to my request to install television in Vietnam. I felt almost sorry we had ever discussed the matter of TV as Thieu started to blame the United States for its lack of resolve. In a tirade against those who had kept him in office, he accused America of not fulfilling its obligations.

Dr. Kissinger, he said, had tricked him into signing the Paris peace agreement and had then gone back on his word by refusing to send military aid to South Vietnam. We had lost because the United States failed to re-supply the army and send aid. "You ran away and left us to do the job that you could not do. We have nothing and you want us to achieve where you failed," he accused the Americans angrily. "At the time of the peace agreement the United States agreed to replace equipment on a one-for-one basis. But the United States did not keep its word. Is America's word reliable these days?"

Then came the surprise. Thieu was succeeded by the vice president, seventy-one-year-old Tran Van Huong; dear old Huong, the ex-schoolmaster, who had given me such a handsome wedding gift of 200,000 piastres. By now his eyesight was so bad that he could hardly read. When Huong became president I could only assume that Big Minh was waiting in the wings.

Hoping to find an American senior officer and learn the latest news, I dropped by Saigon's famous *Cercle Sportif,* a tennis and swimming club near the palace dating from colonial times, but for the past decade a favorite haunt of American top brass. No longer. The change was so startling that I might have stepped twenty years back in time. No Americans and no pretty Vietnamese girls were suntanning themselves by the pool as usual. Instead the *Cercle Sportif* was French again. Martin had arranged with the French ambassador, Jean-Paul Merillon, to mediate between North and South when necessary. With this "power," the first thing the French did was to take back their beloved *Cercle Sportif.* There they were, ordering Pernod and vermouth cassis, delighted, unable to believe that the past they thought had gone forever had caught up with them.[49]

That same day, notes an air force study, the Washington debate over funding continues.

On 21 April, two days after Ford's 19 April deadline, the House Appropriations Committee voted $165 million in military aid and the same amount in humanitarian aid. They voted, after hearing U.S. Army Chief of Staff General Fred C. Weyand testify that, although communist forces had the capability to overwhelm South Vietnam, U.S. aid might deter them from doing so; the communists might decide that they would rather negotiate than suffer the heavy losses that would probably be involved in taking Saigon and achieving a total military victory. But without more U.S. aid, Weyand said, South Vietnam would "certainly fall soon."

On 23 April, by a vote of 75 to 17, the Senate passed a bill which granted the President limited authority to use American troops to protect the evacuation of U.S. citizens and South Vietnamese from Saigon. (It also established a $100 million contingency fund for humanitarian and evacuation efforts as well as $150 million for humanitarian relief to be administered through international relief agencies.) However, the bill specified that no American troops would become involved in protracted combat and U.S. troops could protect the withdrawal of Vietnamese only in areas from which Americans were also being evacuated. The next day, House and Senate conferees agreed with the Senate's position: Vietnamese could be rescued, but the American troops could not "stay any longer, stray any farther, or use any other means of combat than that essential to rescue the Americans."[50]

Shortly afterward, as seen in The Last Ambassador, *the U.S. ambassador in Saigon receives a telephone call.*

It was the Secretary of State, and Walker, the instant he put the receiver to his ear, realized this was going to be a difficult conversation. The Secretary was at his unctuous best, trying to package the bad news in a ribbon of compliments.

"The President told me just a few minutes ago to convey to you how much he admires you, how grateful, how lucky the country is to have a man of your strength of character on the spot, representing America at a critical hour," the Secretary began.

Walker's diplomatic unscrambler was already at work. That means that the emergency aid program is dead. *What else?*

"Hadden," the voice from the State Department continued, "we've known each other too long, been through too many crises together, for me to play games with you." Walker could visualize the Secretary scanning the notes from his conversation with the President. "Are you sitting down?"

What else? "I hear you fine," Walker finally said.

"Hadden, we've broken our asses with those idiots on Capitol Hill. I've tried every trick in the book, promised them a billion-dollar dam for each of their states, explained the repercussions of a disaster in Viet Nam, how it could affect the perception of U.S. power throughout the world. They are deaf, deaf, DEAF!"

A lot of words, Walker thought, a lot of big fat words. The fatter the words, the worse the news. "I've got the context, Mr. Secretary. The specifics, please."

"I'm going to give it to you straight, Hadden. First: no more aid. Not another penny. The people on the Hill see the Viet Nam stories on television every night, ARVN on the run, the NVA moving closer and closer to

Saigon, and they've decided it's all hopeless now. I'm sorry, Hadden. I know how badly you were counting on the aid. Now, second—"

Second? What was "second"? "Why don't you give me all the good news at once?" Walker said, making no effort to conceal his sarcasm.

"Look, Hadden," the Secretary answered defensively, "I've always been on your side on Viet Nam, and you know it."

"Go ahead, please."

"Second: B-fifty-two air strikes—absolutely out of the question. There would be a coast-to-coast uprising here at home if those planes ever took off again in the direction of Hanoi. *We* are out of the war."

"So South Viet Nam is simply . . . abandoned?"

"Believe me, I appreciate your agony. When I came into this office, I had the same strategy you had: to try to give Saigon enough support, and time, so that the South Vietnamese would have a chance of their own to survive and we would have a chance to extricate ourselves with at least a shred of honor. But it's always been a race—a race to come up with that aid before we were swamped by the opposition. Well, we've been . . . swamped."

"Mr. Secretary," Walker, furious, cut in, "do you remember that conversation the three of us had in the Oval Office when I was sworn in as Ambassador to South Viet Nam?"

"Yes." The impatience in the Secretary's voice came through loud and clear.

"The President gave me his word of honor that—"

"And the President meant every word of it. But, Hadden, he's boxed in. He's tried. And he's lost the fight."

"The President told me that even if it meant his own political downfall, he would get the goddamned aid before he would let South Viet Nam go down."

"Yes, I remember that conversation very well."

"And you told me the same thing."

"Yes, I remember that, too." It was the voice of a man who would prefer not to be confronted by his own past pledges. "Look, you know very well that if I had my way, you'd have the money. But both of us are stuck with a democracy and we have no choice."

"Mr. Secretary, I—"

"Wait a minute, Hadden, you haven't heard everything yet."

Third?

"There's also a third point. Now listen carefully—and try to keep the apoplexy to a minimum."

Walker held the receiver a little farther from his ear.

"I've been ordered by the President," the voice said very slowly and precisely, "to instruct you to make contact with 'the other side' to determine whether Hanoi is willing to enter negotiations looking toward the formation of a government of national reconciliation between Saigon and the Communists."

Walker resisted a strong temptation to tear the phone from the wall and hurl it through the window.

"Hadden, did you hear me?"

Walker remained silent, his knuckles white as he clenched the receiver.

"For Chrissakes, Hadden, will you let me know you're still there."

"I'm here," Walker finally said.

"Look, Hadden," the Secretary's voice picked up. "I know this is a heartbreaking assignment, especially for you. But the alternative is an America torn by riots and violence. You haven't been here. You don't know what's happening. This country is not going to get reinvolved in the war, and that leaves us with a choice of which is the lesser horror—a coalition with the Communists in Saigon or anarchy in the streets of America."

So this is it, this is what it comes to. Fifty thousand Americans dead, three hundred thousand Americans wounded, a hundred and fifty billion dollars in military aid, the U.S. ripped by years of violence on the campuses, a President driven out of office. Now this—from Washington: Sorry, Viet Nam, but I have another engagement. Let's have lunch some day. Don't call me. I'll call you.

"Why did we ever bother sending in all those troops here ten years ago?" Walker asked angrily. "Why didn't we just send in gravediggers at the very outset and they could have buried South Viet Nam in 'sixty-five, nice and simple. Been much cheaper, too. In all ways."

"Look, Hadden, cut the sarcasm. I don't feel any better about this than you do, and you're not the only one who's fighting a war. I've been fighting it on a hundred fronts myself. With the doves right here in the goddamned State Department. With Capitol Hill. With the press. With college professors. With Viet Nam veterans. Everybody wants out, out, OUT."[51]

Then Air Marshal Ky receives some visitors.

I knew it was the end from the way the Americans refused to look me in the eyes. We were at my house on Tan Son Nhut, the Saigon air base, a few miles outside the city. Though I was now a civilian I still held the rank of marshal in the air force, and was still entitled to my "married quarters." I was sitting there now, on the evening of April 27, 1975, facing Erich Von Marbod, an Assistant Secretary from the Defense Department, and two military advisers called, I think, Stevenson and Smith.

The room was plainly furnished with comfortable armchairs and tables. Its windows looked out across the busy acres of the base from which I had flown hundreds of sorties against the enemy. It was hot. The open windows did nothing to muffle the occasional mortar fire and the heavier boom of artillery, punctuated from time to time by the clang of bells or the wailing of sirens from an ambulance or fire engine.

The dark sky was stained a blotchy red, like a bad painting of a sunset.

But the sun had long since gone down, in more ways than one, for the red blotches came from fires ringing the outskirts of Saigon, funeral pyres for South Vietnam, for a cause lost, for a war lost by the world's greatest nation and its smaller comrade in arms.

Even at that moment, looking out of the window, I clung obstinately to a last fragile hope that somehow honor could be salvaged from the holocaust, that I could, metaphorically speaking, dart into the fire and drag that honor out, as one saves a prized battle flag. For weeks I had been trying to persuade the Americans to get rid of President Thieu and then back me in a last-ditch stand which, even if it did not bring victory, might as least give us the chance to argue the eventual peace terms from a position of some strength.

That was why Von Marbod was in my house. Graham Martin, the American ambassador, had already sat in the same chair, as cold and smooth as the marble slab in a mortuary.

A servant poured out more green tea and some Napoleon brandy. There was only one bottle left in the house. Then I turned to Von Marbod and said, "You know my plans. You know that I have explained to Mr. Martin how we could fight on in the Mekong Delta. I know I can organize resistance and hold out perhaps for a few last months. Will the American government support us? Not in men, but with arms. That's all we ask."

The silence never seemed to end. Then it was shattered by just one short sentence, "I'm sorry," said Von Marbod, "the answer is 'No.' "

He spoke in a flat, toneless voice, staring away from me. I wondered what the voice, devoid of any inflection, meant. Despair? Resignation? Or was it shame?

Von Marbod looked up and said quietly, "When I leave Vietnam, Marshal, you will come with me." Then he added with typical generosity, "Better get your family out right away. And don't worry. If worse comes to worst you can come and live in America."[52]

The next day, 28 April, Washington Barber, a former member of the 173rd Airborne Division who has remained in Vietnam as a businessman, is at his hotel. The main character in Stephen Harper's novel Live Till Tomorrow, *Barber is attempting to get his partner's Vietnamese wife, Moi, out of the country.*

Moi Ledger insisted that she had to go to the bank before taking a place in the growing queue for the evacuation airlift. So they missed a chance of leaving that same Sunday night. Barber was advised to take them out to Tan Son Nhut during the early evening of Monday for departure during the night or soon after daylight.

He romped with the children in the hotel suite until Moi's return just before lunch, clutching a handbag stuffed with 100 dollar bills. He asked no question, but guessed she had drawn huge bundles of piastres from the bank and bought dollars at one of the Indian bookshops known as branches of the Bank of India. The rate had gone up to an all time high of about 5000 to the dollar so the transaction must have cost her dear.

They were on the point of leaving for the airport that evening when jetplanes roared low over the rooftops. Seconds later the heavy crump of bombs shook the building. Almost simultaneously came the chatter of rifle and machine-gun fire. Barber told the Ledgers to stay put, and dashed down the stairs. People were running for cover across the square. Sentries around the Assembly Building were firing rifles in the air. A traffic policeman emptied his pistol. Bullets ricocheted like angry hornets.

Waiters from the Shelf cowered behind the broad pillars. Barber crouched behind a potted palm. The dropped grill of the hotel entrance was raised just enough to allow a three-man TV crew to pass under it and take their chance filming on the street.

Barber's immediate fear was that the outbreak was part of a general attack by communist commandos known to have infiltrated Saigon weeks before, simulating the uprising of the people which Hanoi blatantly persisted was happening. According to that thesis the flood of conquering North Vietnamese divisions—almost the entire regular army of the north was fighting in South Vietnam—were merely rushing in to aid and sustain a people's uprising.

The firing ebbed and died away. A call for calm came from a loudspeaker van recently stationed in the square to blare out patriotic music in hopes of raising some kind of morale. Soon the loudspeaker voice was ordering people to go home because the capital was placed under immediate curfew.

Tam, the moon-faced waiter, advised Barber the terrace bar was open. 'Large scotch on the rocks,' he said. 'I'll be right back.'

He returned after dashing upstairs to tell Moi and the family to relax until the new situation was sorted out, and was on his third large scotch when a pageboy called him to take his call to the American consular office.

'Stay where you are till we call you,' a brisk American voice told him. It added, 'The situation at Tan Son Nhut is confused. We hope to move people out there during the night.'

Barber called up by telephone to the Ledger family suite and advised Moi to feed the children and put them to bed for a few hours' rest.

Bond came into the hotel foyer looking hot in a dust-stained safari suit. 'Reckon you could use a drink, David.'

Bond hesitated, licked his lips, looked at his watch.

'My God I could, but it will have to be in my room. Come up there and act as barman while I take a quick shower.'

Barber poured the drinks from a bottle of PX scotch procured for Bond by an American colleague. As he towelled himself Bond said that Arvin (abbreviation for the Army of South Vietnam) was fighting stubbornly and well at Newport Bridge. They seemed to be holding it firmly. But the bridge battle, good as it was and where he had been since breakfast, was now destined to become a mere tie-on to the bombing of Saigon's last operational airport apparently by South Vietnamese air force planes. It was not clear whether they were flown by defecting pilots following the example of the pilot, forced to leave his family in married quarters at Da Nang when the communist advance overwhelmed the northern bastion, who had bombed President Thieu in his palace and then flown on to land in communist-held territory. The raid could well have been carried out by some of the many planes that had fallen intact into communist hands at numerous airfields they had captured.

'What is clear,' he said, wrapping the towel around his waist and sitting at his typewriter, 'is that the end is very near. An American final evacuation must be imminent.'

He swallowed his drink at a gulp.

'My God, what a monumental mess it all is. It's just too awesome to grasp.'

He handed Barber his empty glass.

'Fill this for me, old son. I must get words on paper.'

Barber recharged the glass with a heavy hand.

He put it on the desk where Bond was already hammering the typewriter keys.

'This should help,' he said. 'See you in the patio later.'

Bond looked up, smiled vacantly and waved.

He was already absorbed in his task, struggling with a daunting feeling of the inadequacy of words to describe the situation briefly, yet fully and accurately. But to describe it with such words as he could find he had to do, against the clock, nagged by worry that one of the greater stories of his career might never reach its destination in Fleet Street.[53]

Offshore, the U.S. naval vessels are waiting, as shown by the report of the Sealift commander.

Meanwhile the evacuation task force was in a holding area off Vung Tau on the 28th. USNS GREENVILLE VICTORY was standing by for evacuation operations as part of that task force and the Master described the fall of Vung Tau as it affected his ship.

"On the 28th at daybreak the ship anchored 3 miles south of Vung Tau sea buoy. At 1000 hours the ship received its first refugees from a local fishing boat. At 1400 received more refugees from a tug. At 1530 two more refugees came aboard from a local fishing boat. Refugees appear reluctant to come out to the ship. One of the refugees stated there are thousands who want to leave but the RVN Navy is holding the boats in shore. At approximately 1315 hours a vast armada of approximately 200 fishing boats was seen leaving a small village north of Vung Tau and being escorted in to Vung Tau harbor. No attempt by these boats to seek refuge with us. It appeared as if they were being directed to a holding area by RVN gunboats. Early evening a few more small boats from Vung Tau arrived and discharged refugees. Later in the evening much military action noted inland from Vung Tau with heavy shelling and bombing. RVN Navy vessel inside Vung Tau Harbor was observed firing at enemy positions. Refugees onboard reported that the enemy forces were only 15 miles from Vung Tau when they came aboard in the morning."[54]

In Harper's novel, that night Washington Barber observes the fighting in and near Saigon.

The night that followed was not made for sleep. The earthquaking crump of bombs, rockets and shells went on with little lull.

The roof of the ten-storey Caravelle Hotel was lined with the silhouettes of the international press and TV. Even from his lower vantage point on the Continental roof Barber was able to see much of the inferno that ringed the city closer than he had ever seen it before. There was a huge glow over towards Tan Son Nhut airfield, others in the direction of Newport Bridge and scattered areas of the suburbs. Huey helicopter gunships, identification lights bright against the backdrop of a hazy universe beyond, chuddering high above the shell trajectories, occasionally added their own ear-thumping contributions to the general din with swooshing air-to-ground missiles. Red arcs of tracer leapt up from the grounds towards them, but they seemed immune among the stars.

It looked to Barber like a repeat of the Tet offensive of 1968 when Vietcong cadres fought in the streets of the capital, winning sensational tactical victories at a crippling price in casualties.

It was American tanks and firepower, backed by crushing airpower, that eventually routed them then. This time they came with massed tanks and overwhelming firepower, intending to stay. There was only the demoralized, corrupt, leaderless army in midget sized American jungle green to stop them. Such Americans as had stayed behind as civilian experts in aviation and other complex military paraphernalia were already in full flight.

Dawn came at last, fading out livid red and yellow splashes of the night, revealing great columns of black smoke against the fresh blue of the new day, a day the world they knew ended for millions.

For the crew of one of the Huey gunships the long night of conflict was followed by their briefest day. Full daylight followed darkness in the sudden way of the tropics and Barber saw a wisp of white smoke, similar to a vapour trail break across the freshly bright sky on the far side of Tan Son Nhut. The smoke trail of the rocket reached up from earth, ending its etching line across the sky in a sudden orange fireball where the Huey gunship had been.

He gasped out loud, 'Jesus Christ.'

Then he ran downstairs, ducked under the almost closed grill at the main door and walked briskly across the front of the Assembly Building towards the Caravelle Hotel. At first light he had recognized Bond's figure among the silhouettes on the roof. Three policemen, compared with several dozen normally on duty or sleeping in hammocks slung between giant pavement plant tubs, ignored him.

He took a lift to the rooftop restaurant, regretting the risk he was taking of power failure as the doors closed shutting him in, and was delivered to the ninth floor.

Waiters were preparing tables for breakfast as he passed through the restaurant to a roof terrace garden beyond and up a circular iron staircase to the open tarmac roof around a penthouse reception and concert room.

The balcony all the way round was lined with members of the international press as though it was a press gallery on war, a function it had often in fact served over many years.

Television cameras perched on tripods, manned by crews red-eyed with want of sleep. Barber paused behind one camera to take in the panoramic view of the battlefield. The camera was panning slowly, following a plane that had just taken off from the smoke haze in the direction of Tan Son Nhut.

As he watched the plane, a jet strike bomber, the narrow stretch of blue sky between it and the hazy skyline was divided by a white trail leaping towards the plane.

It was too far away to see the tinfoil jettisoned by the pilot, just too late, picked up by the powerful camera lens. The most feared weapon of the war, the infantry Sam Seven shoulder-fired missile, exploded near enough to blow the plane to pieces.

Barber watched with gasping horror as bits of it, including a large part of a wing, fluttered almost leisurely to earth.

The whirr of a noisy camera, the only sound accompaniment to the visual drama of death in the dawn sky, ended suddenly. There was nothing left to film but empty sky.

Exclamation opened an excited buzz of conversation. Barber saw Bond among a group of correspondents hurrying towards the staircase to file a few more paragraphs to London, New York, Baltimore, Paris, Los Angeles, Frankfort, Chicago and Stockholm.

The death agony of a people's long struggle for survival outside the smothering embrace of communism commanded the world's attention briefly once more for a tragic finale.

Barber stayed on the roof. A TV cameraman was exultant over his film. 'It filled the frame,' he shouted excitedly of the plane they had just seen destroyed. 'But how the hell do we get the film out? The airport can't carry on now, no way.'

On his way down Barber paused on the iron stairway to look across a higgledy-piggledy of roofs to the wide flat roof of a modern multi-storey building close by the riverside. It was known as a CIA dormitory, and its narrow stairway made it secure against mob attack. It was now designated as an assembly point for Americans and 'third country' correspondents remaining in Saigon when the final American helicopter evacuation was called.

He noted with foreboding that a South Vietnamese warship was alongside the nearby quay with its anti-aircraft armament covering the rooftops. The odds against an unopposed helicopter evacuation were looking bad, and he had visions of American planes being forced to lay down a curtain of fire around evacuation zones. It might well be safer, even for an American veteran of the war, to stay in hiding till the communists established control. It would certainly be safe for Moi and the children . . . but would the new communist rulers ever let them join Dan Ledger in America supposing he had escaped by boat? Few of those trapped in the North after the great trek to the South in 1954 had ever joined their wives, parents and children who were among the million catholics who got out in time then. Better perhaps for them to end it quickly in a shot down helicopter than face a lifetime of separation from husband and father.

Lost in these thoughts he failed to notice that the square outside the normally heavily guarded Assembly Building was completely deserted. Not one policeman was to be seen.

He phoned the Ledger family suite from the downstairs booth. It rang several times before Moi answered in a sleepy voice.

'Moi, it's Tunny. How are things?'

He had left them trying to sleep with mattresses in the bath where they had protection of an extra wall, safe at least from flying glass.

'Tunny, hiyah. Okay I guess. The kids are sleeping. What do we do?'

'Nothing for an hour or two. Try to get some sleep. I'll call you again.'

'Thank you Tunny.'

The woman's voice was grateful. Sleep was what she needed and wanted more than anything at that moment.

Barber, who had snatched no more than about two hours in cat naps, was filled with wonder. 'What a people they are,' he muttered as he put down the phone.

He walked up to his own first-floor room to shave and shower. He was enjoying the spray of refreshing water that splashed over him when he remembered.

'My God, the radio,' he said aloud.

He left a trail of puddles across the tiles to the small rug beside the bed, and switched on a radio just as the Voice of America news broadcast began to relate the night-long battle for Saigon. It told of the planes shot down over Saigon airport, the last link with the outside world, and meetings of President Ford with the National Security Council on the question of evacuating South Vietnamese likely to be at risk as American lackeys at the hands of victorious communists.

Barber gasped at talk of evacuating 200,000 people—a figure he reckoned far beyond the bounds of possibility.

He wrapped the towel he had picked up around his waist and carried the transistor into the bathroom, perching it on the tiles around the bath while he shaved.

It had suddenly occurred to him that it was time to listen constantly to the American radio programme, still operating from Saigon, so that he would be sure not to miss the unseasonal song 'White Christmas.'

Till now the thought of that tune, conveying such contrasts climatically and in every other way with the realities of Saigon, had seemed farcical.

Now he expected to hear it any time over the next few hours.

It was the code signal for Americans and others in the know to pick up one small bag of possessions and quietly make their way to assembly points for the last pull out of Americans from Saigon.

He was not to know that the code signal had been changed because it and other details of the evacuation plan had been blown by newspapers in the 'publish and be damned' sections of the media.

The new radio signal was kept a fairly tight secret.[55]

On 29 April the U.S. evacuation fleet is offshore in the locations shown on the map on the following page.

The master of one of the navy ships describes the morning of 29 April:

"On the 29th at 0700 hours it appeared as if an attack on Vung Tau was in progress. Large splashes observed in the water along shore and several explosions observed on shore in the resort section of the city. Many rounds heard going off in the distance inland and several areas of the city were completely obscured with smoke. Started loading refugees in increasing numbers. As the refugees would come aboard they would abandon their boats and let them drift off. Enemy action still going strong at Vung Tau so for the safety of all concerned, anchorage was shifted to 6 miles off of Vung Tau. We towed four fishing boats out with us and many more followed under their own power. At the anchorage loading commenced immediately with all hands including security personnel now engaged in loading refugees. Accommodation ladders, pilot ladders and cargo nets being used to load refugees. Security personnel were screening the refugees as they came aboard and confiscating weapons. By 1600 a continuous stream of vessels and anything else that would float were alongside the vessel and the crew loading them as fast as possible. At 1720 stopped loading refugees upon orders not to exceed 6000. Had to cut boats loose and steam. During the loading, one of the abandoned boats set adrift came in contact with our propeller bending and scoring one of the blades and scoring the leading edge of another blade. After this incident security personnel were stationed on the stern with an interpreter to keep other boats away from the propeller. The security force fired into the water in front of several boats after they continued to close on the stern of the ship and at one point shots were exchanged. No injuries, boats remained clear of the ship's propeller.

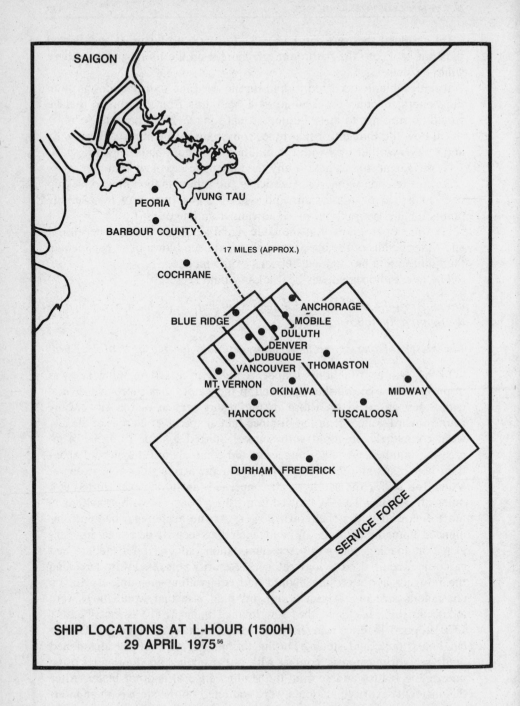

SAIGON

PEORIA

VUNG TAU

BARBOUR COUNTY

17 MILES (APPROX.)

COCHRANE

ANCHORAGE

BLUE RIDGE
MOBILE

DULUTH

DENVER

DUBUQUE

VANCOUVER
THOMASTON

MT. VERNON

OKINAWA
MIDWAY

HANCOCK
TUSCALOOSA

DURHAM FREDERICK

SERVICE FORCE

**SHIP LOCATIONS AT L-HOUR (1500H)
29 APRIL 1975**[56]

"At 1745 received orders from MSC Saigon to continue loading and to take up to 8000 refugees. Stopped the ship and shortly the boats that were following us caught up and we commenced embarking more refugees. At 1900 received orders from Saigon to load up to 10,000 refugees. At that time at least 80 boats were moored or milling alongside with hundreds streaming towards us. Refugees almost in panic stage trying to get on board. Loading refugees by cargo booms, ladders and nets. The sight was unbelievable. We requested that another ship or ships be dispatched for assistance. At least 20 or more refugees in each cargo net with 10 to 15 including women with babies in their arms and hanging on to nets. At 1920 hours at least 100 boats alongside with hundreds of more streaming toward us. Continued loading—women with small babies in their arms hanging on to cargo nets with small children hanging on to their mothers—and still they come. The situation was pitiful, unbelievable and heart rending. No assistance from other ships received. At 2000 hours we had to stop with an estimated 10,000 refugees on board and just no room for any others. 70 to 80 boats were still alongside and pleading with us to please take them and more boats still observed coming towards us. We had to cut boats loose in order to get away. It's a sight that will be impressed in everyone's memory for a long time. We did our best and yet it seemed so inadequate.

"At 2145 on 29 April a baby girl was born. Ship steaming toward MSC Holding Area. Arrived at Holding Area and anchored. Refugees overcrowded but getting settled and fairly orderly. Impressed with the large numbers of them that spoke English."[57]

At the U.S. embassy, according to a marine corps history, preparations are made for the final evacuation.

"Business as Usual" [had come] to an abrupt halt on the evening of 28 April when three A-37 aircraft bombed Tan Son Nhut Airfield between 1815 and 1830. Concurrent attacks by fire on adjacent ammunition dumps led even the most dubious observer to realize the noose on Saigon had tightened. At that time some 800–2,000 evacuees remained in the Annex awaiting fixed wing evacuation. No plan for their movement by other means existed; thus routine evacuation by fixed wing aircraft was planned for the morning of 29 April. At 0400 on that date the NVA/VC interdicted both Tan Son Nhut Airfield and the DAO Compound with high velocity artillery. The result at DAO was two Embassy Marines killed at the roadblock adjacent to gate #4 and one round in the gymnasium where evacuation processing was conducted. Fortunately, the gymnasium was empty at the time and no casualties occurred. Other rounds fell in the DAO Compound adjacent to the home of the Defense Attache and in Landing Zone 38. A tour of the area assured calm and absolutely no panic. Security had been increased and only one gate to each compound and the Annex remained open. Tan Son Nhut had numerous fires, and rounds continued to fall in that area. At first light VNAF aircraft launched from Tan Son Nhut but were quickly downed by SA-7 missiles. Security at the main gate of Tan Son Nhut, a main access to the DAO Compound, remained reliable and no large numbers of Vietnamese were accumulating around DAO.

At approximately 0900 it was announced that the Ambassador had authorized implementation of Option II. C-141 flights had been suspended, so C-130's were scheduled to conduct the lift. Evacuees began to arrive shortly thereafter by private vehicle, bus, and Air America helicopters. The first lift for C-130's was staged and departed for Tan Son Nhut. The reports concerning this flight and one more C-130 flight are contradictory, but no more than two flights departed before Tan Son Nhut was closed by RVNAF aircraft and automobiles abandoned on runways, the SA-7 missile threat, and the continuing incoming artillery. Evacuees continued to arrive at DAO while approximately 2,000 remained in the Annex. At about 1000 the Ambassador arrived at DAO and conferred with the Defense Attache. No immediate decision apparently resulted, although some 45 minutes later those in the ECC were told that Option IV, the helicopter evacuation, was to take place.

The Advance Command Element had conducted liaison with the Special Assistant for Field Operations who was responsible for NEMVAC planning and operations, and with Major KEAN USMC, who was assisting in security coordination and NEMVAC planning as well as inspection and evaluation of communications and planned HLZ's. Unfortunately, the Embassy plan for evacuation was also outdated and no valid information was available regarding numbers of evacuees, either American or Vietnamese. It literally seemed that the Vietnamese "pipeline" was wide open and no one knew how many Americans were in Saigon outside the Embassy, DAO and other government agencies. On the morning of 29 April it was anticipated that a maximum of three Air America rooftop lifts by UH-1E's and one CH-53 lift from the courtyard would remove all remaining Embassy evacuees.[58]

In Stephen Harper's novel, five of the evacuees are Washington Barber and his friend's Vietnamese family.

Shadows stretched across the embassy lawns as Barber and the Ledger family awaited their turn against the wall. Barber was designated to lead the way aboard the Jolly Green Giant threshing through the tree tops to its brief touchdown. He held Suzy over his left shoulder, carrying a suitcase containing the family valuables in the other hand. Moi held the baby and a small grip, the two boys carried their own little cases. Thic held a small suitcase. All the luggage except Barber's own hand grip had made it thus far.

The rippling air dispersed the yellow signal smoke and the chopper jolted to earth, swaying on its springs, blades whirling around, rear door already open. A figure in a flying suit ran down the slope of the dropped door and held up a thumb.

Barber began to run, then consciously dropped his pace to Vietnamese trotting speed. He stepped through the boxlike cabin to a canvas seat against the metal side right forward.

A face with grinning blue eyes called an unheard greeting from the end of a 50 mm heavy machine-gun mounted at a sliding side door. Another gunner watched the embarkation from his post at a similar weapon poking out the other side.

Thic sat next to Barber with Danny on her knees. Moi was next along with the baby and the other boy. The other seats were soon filled, and the later comers sat in rows along the floor. All were Vietnamese except Barber.

The helicopter pilot, hidden except for the backs of his legs and heels in a small upper level cockpit, increased engine power. The two gunners slipped safety catches, tensed themselves like tigers ready to spring, all concentrations directed along their gunsights waiting for the fast moving panorama of South Vietnamese gun positions soon to appear below.

The chopper rose slowly, heaving and pitching under its burden. Suddenly it seemed to slip the surly bonds of earth and soared lightly over the rooftops.

Barber, one of the few passengers able to see outside the metal box confines of the cabin, glimpsed crowds milling along Independence Avenue; tanks and guns crowded together in the grounds of the Presidential Palace; the familiar layout of the Tu Do area, almost deserted now; the My Cahn floating restaurant of hideous bomb-blast memory; the teeming quayside where they might well have been trapped and stripped of all they had; along the river a regatta of nondescript refugee boats and a few uncaring fishing boats carrying on their humble business as they had throughout many earlier twists of violent history.

For a few stark seconds he had a clear view of Newport Bridge, yesterday's marker of the communist advance. Smoke and billowing flame surrounded it on both sides, from both banks. It looked built with a toy construction set, and little objects like toy models moved across it—tanks. They were crossing from the Saigon side indicating that some units of the government army were fighting stoutly yet.

He had never seen the heart of Saigon so closely from above. In fleeting moments he made a farewell tour of many familiar landmarks, places best forgotten among them.

Soon they were flying high above a scene he had looked down upon countless times before, sitting just like this beside alert gunners in Huey helicopters, the flying jeep of the Vietcong war he had known as a soldier.

The paddyfields were green, fed by irrigation from thousands of tiny tributaries to the great rivers twisting and turning towards the earth's edges, shimmering pinkly in the last rays of a fast sinking red ball on the western horizon.

So this was what it had all been about—those early blooding 'search and destroy' sweeps through War Zone D, the slogging, costly battle to recapture Hue citadel in the bloody desperation of Tet, the costly air support of besieged Khe Sanh to prevent it becoming America's Dien Bien Phu, Waterloo of French power in the area.

This, then, was what they had died for—Tiny Tex, Big Joe, Greek Max, Busty the Pole, scores more whose names he had known, whose rations he had shared. Jim Walker, hit in the head pulling a peasant woman out of his own unit's line of fire, went home a human vegetable just for this.

Across the lacework of rivers between Saigon and the sea Barber saw billowing smoke from the direction of Vung Tau, the little port and beach resort once called Cap Saint Jacques, nearest point on the coastline to the capital. He wondered whether the man of the family sitting beside him lay rotting among the dead there, or whether he had made it to sea with his multitude of in-laws.

It was almost dark as they crossed the coast. Out at sea hundreds of lights marked small boats heading from the shore, hopefully to rendez-vous with the legendary Seventh Fleet.

Then it looked as though they were coming to a city. Lights sparkled across a wide area of ocean as a circle of giant ships came into shadowy view.

The helicopter was dropping. It fluttered across the flight deck of a giant aircraft carrier. Barber saw the glint of water close below and sud-denly figures in fluorescent jackets. Then he felt the bump as the wheels touched down.

Barber, last off the helicopter, shepherded the Ledger family across the metal deck, close under the island of metal supporting the bridge.

They joined a queue shuffling past a trestle table where each one was thoroughly searched. Weapons, knives, liquids, anything in doubt was summarily tossed over the side.

Suzy, standing holding his hand, watched with curious interest. She clutched her teddy bear tighter as a child's inflated water wings were tossed overboard. As they came to the table she began screaming, tears flooding her cheeks.

Over and over again she screeched, 'Want my Daddy, want my Daddy.'

Suzy's sobbing was subdued by exhaustion as they waited at a further table beyond the search area facing four young Americans in Navy sea-going pants and T-shirts.

They wrote down details on cyclostyled forms when able to elicit answers in English to the list of questions on the forms.

Barber stood beside Moi when his party stepped up to the table.

The fresh-faced interrogator smiled pleasantly.

'All together?'

Then, looking at Barber, 'Your family, sir?'

Barber shook his head.

'No, not my family, my responsibility. This is Mrs Ledger, Mrs Daniel O. Ledger. Her husband is my partner in a commercial company we had in Vietnam.'

The Navy youngster began writing.

'Mrs Daniel O. Ledger,' he repeated slowly as he wrote.

'Family details?'

He wrote the children's names.

'Can I see your passport, Ma'am?'

Moi opened her huge handbag, slung over her shoulder, and gasped. She slipped it from her shoulder to open it wide in front of her, searching through the contents anxiously, feverishly.

'It's gone.'

Her voice was almost a sob.

The sailor was unperturbed.

'If you find it later, please advise us.'

He added to Barber, 'Hold it, sir.'

He talked to a marine officer standing behind the table. The lieutenant, no older than the other youth, returned to the table and checked through a clip of papers.

He looked up at Barber.

'Gee, sir. Sure sorry, but we just have no bunk accommodation left, not a thing.'

Barber shrugged. 'So where do we go?'

'Guess all we can offer is deck space in the main hangar and that's mighty crowded already. We never expected so many guests aboard.'

Moi chirped up.

'Please don't worry, captain. We are happy to be here at all.'

The lieutenant smiled.

'Guess you are at that, Ma'am. It will only be for a couple of nights. We drop you at Subic for a plane to the States.'

They left the shadowy flight deck, descended two flights of metal ladders slowly with willing young sailors helping with the children and baggage, stepping into a great hall that seemed to stretch into infinity.

Its walls were bare metal, the roof girders high. Thousands of people in family groups sprawled over every yard of flooring as though at a huge picnic or crowding a holiday beach. They brushed past a long queue shuffling towards a table where young Americans in tall chefs' hats were ladling out food and handing out plastic cups of milk and cordial.

The sailor guiding them stopped at a tarpaulin-covered skeleton of a helicopter.

'Reckon this is the best berth we have left.'

He spoke apologetically.

Barber looked at it. There was just room for them to huddle together full length on the deck.

'Think nothing of it,' said Barber. 'We are much better off than many.'[59]

U.S. Navy Captain R. E. Kemble reports the circumstances of the last few hours of American military presence in South Vietnam.

It was now just after midnight [30 April], and the evacuation of the DAO Compound was completed. Average aircraft flight times were approaching ten to twelve hours, far exceeding the normal six hour maintenance inspection time. Low oil and hydraulic fluid levels now became a primary concern to flight safety. In fact, CH-53's had been grounded temporarily by CTF 76 without knowledge of the GSF Commander, who was in route back to BLUE RIDGE. During this period a decision was reached to continue the Embassy evacuation until complete, rather than wait until the following day.

Instances of hostile fire increased markedly, with pilots reporting receiving fire within five blocks of the Embassy. At 0319 a CH-53 with 53 evacuees aboard reported an SA-7 firing while outbound to the ship. At 0352 another CH-53 reported three SA-7 firings with no hits received. It had 65 evacuees aboard. At 0445 AAA fire was reported originating from the Vung Tau Peninsula. An AH-1J confirmed this report to include the use of a search-light in conjunction with that weapon.

The deteriorating weather, darkness, and poor visibility continued to make approach and takeoff from the small Embassy zones increasingly difficult. It should be noted here that the rooftop zone was marked only by a burning barrel of oil and rubbish. This, coupled with poor communication, led to confusing reports that the Embassy was on fire.

Navigation to and from the city became a difficult and dangerous task. Radar coverage was provided by control ships of the Amphibious Task Force during the feet wet portion of the flight inbound to the city. This coverage inland was reduced by a line of thunderstorms between Saigon and the ships. Once feet dry there was no radar capability for providing helicopter separation or routing. Pilots were forced to make non-controlled IFR penetrations, climbing and descending through the overcast or remaining at low altitudes where they were vulnerable to hostile fire. As previously mentioned, considerable effort had gone into planning for flight operations during reduced visibility. The pilots operated IFR, but without normal IFR control. Though not originally planned, the Cobra pilots, with the concurrence of ABCCC, assumed the roles of helicopter coordinators (Pathfinder), after dark. They provided valuable assistance to the transport helicopters in locating their respective LZ's.

THE ISSUE IS FORCED AT THE EMBASSY
Once back aboard BLUE RIDGE the Commanding General ordered the launch of more CH-53's and CH-46's in support of the Embassy evacuation. By 0215 in the morning a flow of one CH-53 and one CH-46 was started into the Embassy every ten minutes.

In hopes of terminating the Embassy evacuation as soon as possible the Commanding General relayed a message through ABCCC to the Embassy requesting a count of total evacuees. The answer was 780. He computed this would be about 20 helo loads and had this message relayed back to the Ambassador.

At 0327 a message was relayed to the Ambassador in the clear from the President of the United States that he was authorized 19 more helo lifts and that he would be on the last helo. The Ambassador acknowledged this message. Then, when it was near the end of the allocated lifts, the Commanding General instructed a helo pilot to remain in the rooftop LZ until a message to that effect had been passed to the Ambassador. The Ambassador acknowledged that message also, and was on the next helo at 0458. The last flight carrying evacuees departed the Embassy rooftop at 0509.

The next concern and, in the face of large crowds and small arms fire around the Embassy, a major problem, was extraction of the remaining Marines. This last group, under command of Major Jim KEAN, were GSF and regular Embassy guard personnel.

Major KEAN was instructed by radio to withdraw all troops into the Embassy and barricade the doors. Then he was to move up through the building until he occupied the top floor and had access to the rooftop LZ. This went pretty much according to plan, and after dodging small arms fire and having to employ riot control agents against people attempting to storm the roof, he stepped aboard the last helo for liftoff at 0753.

The last Ground Security Force Element returned aboard Task Force 76 shipping at 0825, thus terminating Operation FREQUENT WIND. In all, 978 U. S. and 1,120 other persons were lifted out of the Embassy.[60]

At the same time Washington Barber wakes up.

A marine detailed to prevent refugees wandering into working areas of the ship ignored Barber as he climbed the metal stairway to an internal veranda overlooking the hangar floor, and stepped through a hatch on to the flight deck.

Barber shaded his eyes against the brilliant sunlight as he stood between parked helicopters secured to steel rings in the deck. He felt stiff but well rested after a long sleep of exhaustion wedged against the tyre of the spare helicopter marking the Ledger family's allotment of hangar space. The frequent noise of orders from the bridge broadcast throughout the ship had not disturbed him. He had a vague recollection of an emergency call in the night, but had returned to deep slumber without fully waking. He was able to relax—the US Navy was now in charge of the Ledger family's destiny.

The deck was almost deserted of people. Tightly parked helicopters crowded every space and cranny, leaving enough open area for two helicopters to land simultaneously. He joined a marine sitting on a steel stowage bunker against metal cliffs rising up to the bridge.

'Good morning.'

'Hiyah.'

'Looks kinda peaceful today.'

'Sure does. Everybody who can is grabbing shuteye.'

'Guess so.'

The South China Sea stretched to a shimmering horizon in a carpet of azure blue, unruffled, calm as a mill pond. Barber suddenly realized they were at anchor, not steaming hard for the Philippines as he had expected.

'When do we sail?'

'Reckon even the skipper don't know that.'

The sailor, still in his teens, looked at Barber's soiled trousers and torn bush shirt.

'How was it in Saigon?'

Barber froze. Saigon had slipped completely from his mind, already like something in the distant past, something better not to think about.

His jaw tightened as he fought to maintain control over a sudden instinct to cry.

His voice came taut and unnatural.

'Kinda nasty.'

The marine sensed Barber's agony.

'Anyway, it's all over now, I guess.'[61]

1975   30 April—1024H Saigon time. President Minh announces an unconditional surrender.

A U.S. Air Force historian describes what happens next.

About 90 minutes after the surrender announcement, a small communist armored force appeared at the Independence Palace. Bui Quant Than, commander of Tank 843, a Soviet-built T-54, flattened the massive iron gate of the palace and he and two other tank commanders walked into the presidential palace where Minh, Prime Minister Vu Van Mau, and a score of aides and ministers awaited the victors' arrival. Duong Van Minh stood up and said, "The revolution has come. You have come."

Bui Quant Than, who had entered the palace with a machine gun in one hand and the National Liberation Front flag in the other, quickly made his way to the roof where he unfurled the flag and ran it up to the top of the highest pole. The hour was 1215. Saigon Radio, taken over by the PRG, proclaimed to the world that "Saigon has been totally liberated. We accept the unconditional surrender of General Duong Van Minh, President of the former government." In Paris, communist representatives of the two now-less-divided Vietnams announced that Saigon would henceforth be popularly known as Ho Chi Minh City, though its official name would remain unchanged.

Duong Van Minh and the other members of the defunct GVN were taken to the conference room on the second floor of the palace to await the arrival of a political commissar. More tanks began to arrive, the vanguard of the Western Column, which had finally eliminated resistance by an ARVN unit at Tan Son Nhut that had refused to surrender. Shortly thereafter, Bui Van Tung, political commissar of Brigade 203, entered the conference room, introduced himself to Minh, and informed him and the other members of the late government that they should consider themselves free—that "they were by no means prisoners."

To avert further unnecessary shedding of Vietnamese blood, Tung asked "Brother Minh" to deliver a second surrender order—this one aimed specifically at the armed forces. Minh was willing, but it was nevertheless two hours later before he was actually able to make the requested address. A group of students from Van Hanh University had already taken over the Radio Saigon station, but all the technicians who knew how to operate it had fled. Minh and ex-Premier Vu Van Mau were driven by jeep to the broadcasting studios but it was not until 1430 that the silence was finally broken and Minh began to read the words written for him by Tung:

> I, General Duong Van Minh, President of the Saigon government, appeal to the armed forces of the Republic of Vietnam to lay down their arms and surrender unconditionally to the forces of the National Liberation Front. Furthermore, I declare that the Saigon government is completely dissolved at all levels.

Vu Van Mau followed with these words:

> In the spirit of harmony and national reconciliation, I, Professor Vu Van Mau, Prime Minister, appeal to all levels of the population to greet this day of peace for the Vietnamese people with joy. I appeal to all employees of the administration to return to their posts and continue their work.

It was over. In the 52 days which passed since the attack on Ban Me Thuot in the Central Highlands, the NVA and Viet Cong had overwhelmed the South Vietnamese military forces. Three days before the surrender, knowing that the war was lost, South Vietnamese Senate President Tran Van Lam had commented on the situation: "We are beaten. We accept humiliation; but it is better to be beaten by your brothers than by strangers. I hope the winners think of the South Vietnamese as their brothers." That hope, at least, remained for the people of South Vietnam—the hope that the victors would still consider as brothers their enemies of so many years.[62]

In the United States, having served in Vietnam for two and a half years as a member of the International Volunteer Services, poet John Balaban writes his perspective on the war's end.

April 30, 1975
(for Bui Ngoc Huong)

The evening Nixon called his last troops off,
the church bells tolled across our states.
We leaned on farmhouse porch pilings, our eyes
wandering the lightning bug meadow thick with mist,
and counted tinny peals clanking out
through oaks around the church belltower.
You asked, "Is it peace, or only a bell ringing?"

This night the war has finally ended.
My wife and I sit on a littered park bench
sorting out our shared and separate lives
in the dark, in silence, before a quiet pond
where ducks tug slimy papers and bits of soggy bread.
City lights have reddened the bellies of fumed clouds
Like trip flares scorching skies over a city at war.

In whooshing traffic at the park's lit edge,
red brake lights streak to sudden halts:
a ski-masked man staggers through lanes,
maced by a girl he tried to mug.
As he crashes to curb under mercury lamps,
a man snakes towards him, wetting lips,
twirling the root of his tongue like a dial.

Some kids have burnt a bum on Brooklyn Bridge.
Screaming out of sleep, he flares the causeway.
And the war returns like figures in a dream.
In Vietnam, pagodas chime their bells.
"A Clear Mind spreads like the wind.
By the Lo waterfalls, free and high,
you wash away the dust of life."[63]

Almost unnoticed by the rest of the world, however, Laos, too, is taken
over by the Communists. General Oudone Sananikone, then Royal Lao
government chief of staff, remembers:

As the last days of April approached, Vietnam teetered on the brink of
defeat. Seeing the handwriting on the wall, some of us began preparing to
leave because we knew that we could not survive when the Pathet Lao
took over. Many other senior officers and civilian officials, however, took
a different course, one designed and promoted by the Pathet Lao. These
men made contact with the Pathet Lao who promised them safety and
brotherhood in the new regime to come.

Vietnam fell to the Communists on 30 April and the following day
regular Pathet Lao formations began marching into Vientiane and our

other cities. There was no opposition; no force was used by either side. All we could do was observe and report.

On 8 May, with the city crowded with Pathet Lao in uniform and in civilian clothes, a great demonstration was held against the police and leadership of the NLA. When Souvanna found out about it, he said he would order the demonstration stopped. But there were no powers competent to enforce Souvanna's order and the group in charge of the demonstration had already said that they would reject any such order. More than half of the demonstrators were armed Pathet Lao and any police or Army attempt to disperse the crowds would have led to a battle and, in light of the large force the Pathet Lao had concentrated in Vientiane, to a Pathet Lao armed seizure of power.

There was no course for Sisouk Na Champassak and me but to resign from the government. This we did and on 11 May I left my country for the last time.

Two weeks after our departure, the Pathet Lao convened a seminar at Fifth Region headquarters near Vientiane. All senior NLA commanders and staff officers who had not already left the country were ordered to attend. The ostensible purpose was to proceed with integrating the armed forces. After a few days of meeting, however, all ranking officers were taken to the Vientiane airport and flown to prison camps in the Pathet Lao zone. Every director and deputy minister remaining in the Defense Ministry disappeared into the Communist zone. This even included the Commander-in-Chief, General Bounpone Makthepharak. Also included were every general staff chief, the commanders of Military Regions I and III, and every technical service chief. So much for the leadership of the NLA and so much for the promises of the Pathet Lao.[64]

Frank Snepp, too, has a perspective on the end of the Vietnam War.

Most Americans tried to forget about Vietnam altogether. The amnesia was understandable. After all the bloodshed and bitterness of the war, who could be blamed for wanting to put it out of mind?

Yet there was also, behind the silence and public indifference, a bit of official conjuring. Those who had made cease-fire policy in Vietnam wanted us to forget how it had ended—or at least to remember only what best suited their versions of the truth.

The cover-up and the cosmeticizing of events began almost immediately. Meeting with newsmen in the final hours of the airlift, Kissinger insisted that there had been a chance for a negotiated settlement up until 27 April, whereupon, he maintained, the North Vietnamese had shifted course and opted for a military solution. He did not choose to acknowledge that the intelligence told a different story. Nor was he candid enough to admit that the Soviets, with the help of the Hungarians, Poles and the French, had played him and so many others for fools. By his lights (as he put it later, in another press conference) the Soviets had played "a moderately constructive role in enabling us to understand the possibilities there were for the evacuation, both of Americans and South Vietnamese, and the possibilities that might exist for a political solution."

While still on board the USS *Blueridge,* Polgar gave an elaborate press briefing of his own which essentially corroborated Kissinger's story. There was in fact only one significant difference between their separate accounts. Polgar could not resist taking verbal swipes at the Ambassador, intimating that Martin had never appreciated the gravity of the military situation, as he had. This was true, of course, as far as it went. But what Polgar failed to mention was that he himself had contributed mightily to Martin and Kissinger's second illusion: the notion that there was a chance for a Vichy-type peace.

Once the Administration had established its own slant on reality, Kissinger acted promptly to forestall contradictions. He cabled Martin on shipboard, ordering him to say nothing to the press. He also made it clear to former President Thieu in Taiwan that he could expect no entry visa to the United States (where his daughter was in school) until after the American presidential elections.

In the meantime, other Vietnamese notables were given a devastating lesson in humility. Shortly after arriving in Guam several of the defeated ARVN generals were brought together in one of the old metal barracks. An exhausted General Toan, the former MR 3 commander, was pushed into the meeting in a wheelchair, and General Truong, the defender of Danang, was suffering from such an acute case of conjunctivitis he could not find his way to a chair. Moments later an American naval officer marched in and demanded that the generals remove their uniforms. "Can't we at least keep our shoulder stars?" one of them asked. "No," the American replied. "You have no army, no country any more." It was as if the Republic of Vietnam had never existed at all.[65]

It was in May 1941 that Ho Chi Minh announced the formation of the Vietnam Doc Lap Dong Minh, and it is now, in May 1975, that Laos, Cambodia, and Vietnam are all under Communist rule. The following poem by Alan Dugan best expresses the intention of this book, Vietnam Voices.

Notes toward a Spring Offensive

I will begin again in May, describing weather, how
the wind swept up the dust and pigeons suddenly. Then
the rain began to fall on this and that, the regular
ablutions. The soldiers marched, the cowards wept,
and all were wetted down and winded, crushed.
Soldiers turn the dew to mud. Shivering uncontrollably
because the mild wind blew through wet fatigues,
they fell down in the mud, their pieces fouled,

and groveled in the wilderness, regardless. Some died, and how
I will not tell, since I should speak of weather. Afterwards
the clouds were stripped out of the sky. Palpably fresh,
suckingly sweet like bitten peaches, sparkling like oh,
a peeling tangerine, the air was warmed by light again,
and those who could rise rose like crushed chives from the mud
and stank and thought to dry. The cowards wept
and some got well again, profane with flowers, all was well,
and I have finished now in May. I have described
one circle of a day and those beneath it, but not why.[66]

EPILOGUE
1975–1982

America Lost Her Virginity
in Vietnam

(And she caught the clap, too.)

That's Nothing—So Did I.

I did Too,
BUT NOW I WATCH who
I Go ouT with.

So Should America.

—GI latrine graffiti, Saigon

1975   **13–15 May**—U.S.S. *Mayaguez* captured by the Cambodian Navy. President Ford orders air and sea attacks. U.S. crew freed, but announced U.S. losses are 5 killed, 16 missing, 70–80 wounded. **30 June**—USAAG/7AF headquarters deactivated in Thailand. **2 July**—North and South Vietnam declared officially reunited. Hanoi is the national capital. Saigon renamed Ho Chi Minh City.

North Vietnamese General Van Tien Dung, chief of staff of the Vietnam People's Army, reflects:

In the process of many years of resistance against the U.S. imperialists, we surprised them many times. After signing the Paris Agreement, Kissinger told us that America had been surprised twice. The first time was when they attacked Highway 9 in southern Laos in 1971; they did not expect that we could dispatch troops there so quickly or that our antiaircraft defenses there would be so strong. The second time was in 1972, when they did not expect that we would send tanks so far south as An Loc. Yet it was not just at An Loc. In 1972 we attacked on a number of other fronts of the southern battlefield with tanks, too. And those two were not the Americans' only surprises. The Tet Mau Than offensive was also a surprise to the Americans, causing them great casualties and forcing them to change their strategy. The North's victory over the B-52 strategic bombers was another surprise: the United States intended to destroy us, but instead we dealt them a heavy defeat. That was a victory that greatly strengthened our delegation at the conference table in Paris. And in our 1975 general offensive and uprising, the enemy received many big surprises. But the biggest surprise for the Americans was the U.S. imperialists' leap into Vietnam itself. That was their fundamental surprise and their strategic error.

The U.S. imperialists were always obstinate, and they would have to bear the consequences of their errors. Right after the signing of the Paris Agreement on Vietnam, and again in June 1973, we told Kissinger frankly that it was America that had seriously violated the Paris Agreement on Vietnam, continuing its neocolonial war of aggression. It was completely unreasonable for the United States to violate the agreement intentionally and cynically and yet demand that we respect the agreement. We made it clear we would never sit with folded arms and watch them violate the agreement. We would not let them do whatever they pleased, or retreat into a passive defense. We reserved for ourselves the right to freedom of action in the face of U.S. violation of the agreement.

This was something we had warned the Americans about long ago. But the United States and their crew of lackeys singlemindedly continued their systematic efforts to destroy the agreement, and continually stepped up the war and increased their operations of terror and repression against the people of the South. In order to protect the fruits of the revolution and smash their encroaching operations, our only recourse was revolutionary violence, relying on our military forces and political forces, resolutely counterattacking and attacking the enemy, in order to proceed to the total liberation of the South.

Lenin once taught that the thing to be most avoided is, once victorious, becoming intoxicated by that victory. Once intoxicated it is easy to become self-satisfied and lose vigilance. The U.S. imperialists have been defeated in Vietnam, but their dark schemes have not ended. Along with the forces of reaction, they have constantly sought means to destroy the fruits of our revolution. They have constantly interfered most viciously, and engaged in the most savage destruction. So we must raise our vigilance and build a mighty national defense, a powerful army ready for battle and always with a high will to win, in order to protect our Fatherland.

Moreover, we must absolutely avoid all thoughts of our personal importance or position. As Le Duan has said, this victory belongs to our party, to our great President Ho Chi Minh, to our people and all our heroic fighters, and to the martyrs who sacrificed their lives for the Fatherland. This victory is one of the whole country; it does not belong to any one person or unit or locality. The strength of this total victory is the strength of the whole country; it does not belong to any one person or unit or locality. The strength of this total victory is the strength of the whole country, of every person and every family, the strength of the spirit of patriotism and of socialist idealism.

Le Duc Tho also gave a very profound analysis of Vietnam's unique military arts, especially the art of the campaign in this final battle. I then presented a report summing up the Ho Chi Minh campaign. Clearly the whole party, army, and people had given us a great many unique experiences which, after we put them all together, would enrich Vietnamese military science many times over and help us develop our martial arts. They would help us build a revolutionary, modern standing army which could protect the independence, long-lasting peace, and socialist construction of the Fatherland, and which would be prepared to fulfill the internationalist responsibilities of a revolutionary army, of a true Marxist-Leninist party, our ever-victorious Vietnam Workers Party.

The total all-around victory of the General Offensive and Uprising of Spring 1975 was the greatest and most illustrious victory in our nation's 4,000-year history of building and preserving the country, opening a new age full of promise for our Fatherland. This victory, in the spirit of our history and of the times, was extremely fast. Was it because the U.S. imperialists had mistakenly or accidentally abandoned an ambitious war that they had to accept consequences which would in the long run be harmful to them in many ways? Was it because the heads of the Saigon army and administration had accidentally committed errors that their imposing war machine with its army of over a million built up over twenty years suffered destruction, dissolution, and great defeat in less than two months? No, it was not that. The defeat of the enemy had been inescapable, and it was we ourselves who had caused their defeat. Our strategy and tactics, the field positions and methods of attack we used, forced the enemy into a dilemma where either way they had to lose, and there was no way they could turn the circumstances around.

The strategic resolve of the Political Bureau was from the first to liberate the South, the sooner the better. They concluded that if the Americans came in again, we would still attack with determination, strike even harder, and win greater victory. We had prepared sufficient forces and had plans and measures ready to mete out still heavier blows to the Americans. The United States had mobilized gigantic forces for many years to carry on their invasion of our land, but in the end they were pitifully defeated and had to pull out. If they had returned, what hope would they have of reversing the positions? And one thing certain was that they would have brought upon themselves greater and more shameful defeats. The United States did not give more aid in weapons and dollars to the puppets not because they had no more forces, not because they made a mistake, but primarily because in the face of the strength of our attack, in the situation they faced at home and abroad, they were well aware that no matter how much aid they gave to their protégés, they could not save that crew of flunkies. No matter how much more the United States had supplied to the quislings in weapons and munitions in 1975, they would certainly still have collapsed, and our troops would have confiscated all the more war booty.[1]

From another perspective, however, this episode from Steve Smith's novel American Boys *presents in microcosm an attitude that so many Americans will always remember about their combat experience in Southeast Asia.*

Weird, the thoughts that floated through his head, the variety of moods he floated through. Sometimes he found himself tallying lists of wrongs in his mind, petitioning Senators like some earnest political theorist on the evils of the war, its total lack of respect for human beings. Before, he had thought mainly of himself, of not wanting to be in a position where he did stupid or unnecessary things. He didn't want to be killed, nor did he want to kill for sport.

Sport was where his speculations led him. The war was sport, the helicopters a new offense the coach needed to test, Vietnam a place to test it, where, even if it failed, the old plays could be used again to assure triumph.

The country was a field that no one would regret chewing up; the people were insignificant—bush-league players whose loss would be felt by no one. And the coaches had their own eager young players who swallowed without question the platitudes about the importance of the game.

At times he drifted into the role of spectator, viewing events as if they could only be part of a movie or a television comedy, not real things in which he participated. Yesterday twenty people from a hamlet were nearly blown to bits by two jettisoned rocket pods that had been dynamited in a ditch by a demolition team. The pods had been rigged with a short fuse, the demolition helicopter pulled pitch, and the people ran furiously for the ditch. Luckily the pods blew before they got there.

Chambers thumped his flight helmet with the palm of his hand, trying to drive from his head the spastic images of the scurrying frantic people, trying to stifle his disdain for the peasants' lust over the tiniest bauble of American trash. He imagined them, long after the war was over, worshiping before some smashed rusty aircraft hulk as though it were Buddha himself.

"Still smokin', sir," Eastman said as the chopper skimmed a ridge and floated out above a small valley. A hamlet, discovered yesterday by the rifle platoon, smoldered on the valley floor. No one had been there when the rifles arrived, but one hooch had been full of rice, so the entire hamlet was grenaded and burned. The roofs of all the hooches were gone, some walls completely demolished while others gaped with large holes made by the boots of the infantrymen. Jungle surrounded the hamlet on all four sides.

The man stood directly in the center of the charred, smoking buildings. In black pajamas, his black hair plastered to his head, he stared at the ship for a moment before raising the thirty-caliber rifle he held in his right hand.

"God, shoot him!" Sanders screamed, pulling down the infinity sight. McCutcheon's machine gun went off as Sanders began firing grenades. The tracers hit to the left of the man, while the grenades exploded fifty yards behind him, knocking down the walls of a roofless hooch.

Chambers couldn't take his eyes off him. The man stood his ground, squeezing off rounds as the helpless ship flew over him.

"Four-five, this is Red. Get that man!"

"Got him in sight, Red."

They banked to the right as the other gunship let go with rockets and machine guns. The man whirled, ducked behind a wall, then sprinted to the southern edge of the hamlet, disappearing, a black flash in the green. For a moment Chambers expected the ship to crash, but they apparently hadn't been hit.

"Okay, Four-five," Sanders said. "Let's saturate those trees with everything we've got."

"Roger that, Red."

Each ship made three more runs, expending its entire load of bullets, rockets, and grenades. Sanders called back to the base, and another team was on its way. Artillery would be called in in the meantime.

At ten o'clock Chambers' team of two helicopters went out again—to the same hamlet. The man had made brief appearances for each of the two teams that had since been there, squeezing off a few rounds before darting into the bushes. His aim was as bad as the Americans', and so far no one had been hit.

Eastman circled the hamlet while Sanders pumped a steady stream of grenades into the jungle. Chambers fired, but managed to get most of his bullets inside the tree line, into the thick grass that separated hamlet from jungle. Webster's ship followed theirs, dumping its rockets a pair at a time, lighting up the dark greenery with the tracers from six machine guns.

"I reckon that took care of him, Four-five," Sanders said.

"Hope so, Red. Grenades lookin' good."

Their ammunition spent, the ships rose and circled lazily, waiting for the new team.

"God damn it, sir!" Eastman said. "There the bastard is again."

Chambers whirled as the black-pajamaed body detached itself from the jungle cover and stood up next to a wall that seemed to be part of nothing.

"Holy Christ!" Sanders said. "And we're out of fuckin' ammo."

The man's barrel flashed three times, then he held his weapon in the air before turning and scurrying back among the trees.

"Let me go after him, sir," McCutcheon said.

"Forget that. I'm gonna get the whole rifle platoon out here to chase his sorry ass."

The new team arrived, and they flew back to the field base. The officers hurried away to the operations tent as Chambers began reloading.

At chow the talk was only of the man. He had earned everyone's respect, was almost a hero, but one who had to be killed. He seemed to excite the imagination like some Jesse James or Billy the Kid whose daring caused envy and admiration in those whose great satisfaction would be to kill him. For Chambers the man assumed heroic proportions. He hoped he was indestructible.

McCutcheon was the last crewman to chow. He'd been up to operations and heard all the plans. The hamlet was being bombarded with artillery once again, with napalm to follow before the rifle platoon went in. "We're gonna bring some smoke on that fucker, boy."

Chambers' ship went out again at one thirty. In the jungle just outside the hamlet deep holes smoldered from napalm at the four points of the compass. Smaller holes and twisted vegetation appeared randomly about the rubbled hooches. The rifle platoon had been on the ground forty-five minutes, had been fired on twice, the man appearing each time at the opposite end of the hamlet from where they were. No one had been hit.

Chambers' last mission of the day covered the extraction of the rifles at five thirty. They still had not found the harassing mosquito of a man. Chambers watched as the angry troops piled on the lift ships. A perfect opportunity for the man to spring from the bushes and kill three or four. But he didn't. The lift birds rose, speeding toward the field base while the gunships went round once again. The hamlet was completely leveled, the surrounding jungle a tangled mess. Once again they fired all their bullets and grenades, and the trail ship dropped its entire load. They circled a last time, then headed up and away. The B-52's would saturate the area tonight. Chambers looked back as the man, standing again in the center of the hamlet, raised his rifle and fired a parting shot. Chambers stuck his hand out the door, thumb up.

As the ship flew back to the field base, he began to tally up. No lives had been lost, no men wounded, no helicopters shot down. His ship had fired at least six hundred grenades. He didn't know how much they cost. Even at five bucks a throw that was three thousand dollars. Add ten thousand machine-gun rounds at twelve cents each, and you were up to forty-two hundred dollars. Throw in gas and oil and salaries and wear and tear, and they'd easily used up five thousand dollars' worth today. He chuckled as he continued playing his game. Webster's ship had fired fifty-six rockets at sixty bucks apiece for thirty-three hundred and sixty dollars. Probably twenty thousand rounds from the machine guns for twenty-four hundred dollars. Add grenades, gas, and the rest of it, and you had a good sixty-five hundred. So eleven thousand five hundred between them. Add the other three pairs of gunships like Webster's, and you got a combined total, conservative estimate, of fifty thousand five hundred dollars, not counting postage and handling. The B-52's would surely push it over a hundred—making the man worth more than Willie Mays—and yet he knew, come morning, the man would be dancing on his pile of rubble after expending probably four dollars' worth of thirty-caliber shells. Even the dumb gorilla, watching the show from his grandstand seat, would be forced to turn away in disbelief and run deeper and deeper into the jungle, as far as he could go.[2]

1977   27 July—With the world press refused access to Cambodia, the U.S. State Department announces that approximately 1.2 million people have been killed by the new Khmer Rouge regime. **25 December**—Vietnamese/Cambodian armed clashes become full-scale border war.

Poet and former marine William D. Ehrhart expresses the general attitude of many Vietnam veterans.

A Relative Thing

We are the ones you sent to fight a war
you didn't know a thing about.

It didn't take us long to realize
the only land that we controlled
was covered by the bottoms of our boots.

When the newsmen said that naval ships
had shelled a VC staging point,
we saw a breastless woman
and her stillborn child.

We laughed at old men stumbling
in the dust in frenzied terror
to avoid our three-ton trucks.

We fought outnumbered in Hue City
while the ARVN soldiers looted bodies
in the safety of the rear.
The cookies from the wives of Local 104
did not soften our awareness.

We have seen the pacified supporters
of the Saigon government
sitting in their jampacked cardboard towns
their wasted hands placed limply in their laps,
their empty bellies waiting for the rice
some district chief has sold
for profit to the Vietcong.

We have been Democracy on Zippo raids,
burning hooches to the ground,
driving eager amtracs through a farmer's fields.

We are the ones who have to live
with the memory that we were the instruments
of your pigeon-breasted fantasies.
We are inextricable accomplices
in this travesty of dreams:
but we are not alone.

We are the ones you sent to fight a war
you did not know a thing about—
those of us who lived
have tried to tell you what went wrong.
Now you think you do not have to listen.

Just because we will not fit
into the uniforms of photographs

of you at twenty-one
does not mean you can disown us.

We are your sons, America,
and you cannot change that.
When you awake
we will still be here.[3]

1978   4 December—Vietnam Radio announces formation of Kampuchean Front for National Salvation, whose objective is to overthrow
Cambodian Khmer Rouge president Pol Pot.

Micheal Clodfelter, former artilleryman with the 101st Airborne Division,
remembers his Vietnam War.

I was a regular kid, and like all other kids in all other times and places, I
had one foot in the backyard and the other in fantasyland. Where my
friends' fantasies might include batting a ball out of Yankee Stadium or
driving a race car past the checkered flag at Indianapolis, my fantasies
were those of combat. I was going to be the greatest war hero in history. I
was going to wear a general's star by the time I was thirty and make the
victories of the Duke of Marlborough, Frederick the Great, and Napoleon pale next to mine. Every kid knows that the world is going to be his
atop a silver platter; mine was going to come mounted atop a tank tread.

It was not that my dream was so weird or unique. In a way it was the
dream of every American boy, maybe of every boy everywhere. My goals
were glory, fame, status, just as they were for those who would use a bat
or a pigskin or a race car or, for those more practical among us, a
briefcase or a test tube, to achieve those aims. The one difference—and
the big difference—was that the tools of my trade would be rifles and
machine guns, not stick shifts or Louisville Sluggers.

But even in this respect I was not such an oddity. Playing soldier is at
least as universal a boyhood game as playing fireman. But most boys
grew out of their G.I. Joe phase by their teens, became more interested
in girls, basketball games and hot rods than in generals, battles and tanks.
But I didn't grow out of that phase, for to me, it was not some mere
phase but a fascination.

In the summer of 1964, at the age of seventeen, I enlisted in the United
States Army. After boot camp, AIT, and airborne training, I was assigned to an artillery unit in the 101st Airborne Division. In July 1965,
thanks to the Domino Theory and LBJ, I found myself in the middle of a
Southeast Asian jungle and at the threshold of what I was certain would
be the fulfillment of my special destiny. It turned out to be both less and
more than what I had expected. It was all an agony and an ordeal. I

wanted it to end every moment I was there, and yet I wanted it to never end. I wanted it to be all over with and forgotten, and yet I wanted it to last forever and I knew that I would never be able to forget it. I wanted to go home and leave it all behind me, and yet I knew that at least a part of me would never go home and that when I did go I would take a lot of it home with me. And I realized, in some intuitive secret room within myself, that this strange, alien, deadly place had somehow become my real home and that for a long time all else would seem strange and foreign and unreal for me. Vietnam and its war had worked its insidious magic on me. The "real world," the one back home on the other side of the Pacific Ocean, had become a fantasy world—one that so many of my instincts of old urged me to try to reclaim, but one that a new, stronger and darker instinct pulled me away from with an all-encompassing lack of logic.

There was no doubt that they had tricked us, deceived us—them with their John Wayne charging up Mount Suribachi, with their Gary Cooper-as-Sergeant York rounding up half the German Army and sharpshooting to death the other half. Have you ever seen a two-hour-long war movie that shows for an hour and fifty-nine minutes a soldier climbing a muddy mountain under the weight of a sixty-pound pack and 110-degree heat, and for only the last minute scenes of combat? That was the way the war was for us, mud mixed with sweat, sprinkled with lice, and all added to a generous portion of boredom to make a bitter recipe, a hateful dish that a pinch of the spice of combat could do little to make more palatable. We had imagined a movie; we had envisioned a feast. What we got was a reality removed from all other realities; what we got was a garbage pail.

The Vietnam War from my level, from the slit-trench and spider hole view of the hundreds of thousands of grunts on both sides, was really two wars. First there was the war that the newspapers reported, that Walter Cronkite broadcast on the evening news, that the officers in Saigon with their pointers and maps, their starched khakis and starched minds, lied about daily at the Five O'Clock Follies in the new dialect of Pentagonese, that long-haired college students protested against and hardhat hardheads paraded for. That was the war of battles and skirmishes, of firefights and ambushes, of air raids and gunship sorties. But the other war, the war that the soldiers of Vietnam were much more familiar with, the war that was rarely reported, that held little interest, that could hardly stir protests against or rallies in support of—that was the real war. This was the war of heat and rain and mud and dust, of heat exhaustion and sunstroke, of malaria and jungle rot, of sandbags and sixty-pound packs, of waiting and boredom. This was the war that was fought every day with the enemy all around, but an enemy armed with stingers and bacteria, with humidity and harshness, with thorns and with thunder.

The war against the toil and the terrain, against the sense of hopelessness and exile, was an every-day conflict, but the war of men pitted against men, of rifles blazing and bullets cracking, was much more infrequent. At first, when I was in the artillery, it seemed as if the shooting war, the one made phony-familiar to me through movies and television and G.I. Joe comic books, was a fairy tale. Because my view of arms and armies was almost exclusively of our side, the side with such power and military muscle, because nearly all I saw were American uniforms and American guns and tanks and planes in the midst of a small, un-threatening-appearing race of Orientals, it seemed that it was a game, just another military exercise, more maneuvers out on the firing range. The rare moments of action were filtered through my consciousness as fragments of a dream, quickly shattered when dull drudgerous reality resumed its nearly constant reign.

Later, after I had transferred to the infantry and became a grunt and my encounters with the enemy became much more frequent and much more intense, the fairy tale became more like a horror story and the dreams degenerated into nightmares. But even then there was still a sense of unreality about it all. Marches and monotony were still more the routine than contact and combat. Even after months in the bush a part of me was still surprised when the enemy did materialize and combat com-menced its narcotic dance of terror and temptation. And it remained that way to the end. The enemy and the war he brought us was a phantom and a fantasy—a fantasy that could and did kill, but never really took on substance and form. Maybe that was why, though at times in the cauldron of combat terror held sway over all my senses, I did not live with the day-to-day dread that the circumstances probably warranted; I did not walk with the weight of a sure sense of my own mortality. For if the war was a fantasy to me—or at least to that part of the mind that throws up such defenses to deal with the intimacy of death—then surely a fantasy was incapable of killing me.

The enemy was real though, however enigmatic he may have been. That was a big part of the problem—just trying to figure out exactly who the hell was the enemy. We were not unique in military annals in having to deal with the guerrilla; not even in American military history. Gero-nimo's Apaches, Aguinaldo's Filipinos, and Sandino's Nicaraguans had all given American troops a taste, and always a bitter taste, of insurgency warfare. And American conventional forces, like conventional forces everywhere, had been unable to fight the guerrilla clear and clean. But those events of the past were all minor affairs, while this was guerrilla war on a grand scale, a dozen dirty little wars merged into one, one of the great wars of the century but fought on the level of Geronimo's Apache campaigns.

Killing the enemy was not the problem; it was identifying him. Killing him was easy once you found him and identified him. In fact, sometimes it was much easier to do the killing first and the identifying afterwards. Where no answers were possible, no questions were necessary. For many G.I.s the equation became simple; they bored right through all the com-plexities and tagged all Vietnamese as the enemy, every damn one of

them. . . . K
enemy. If th
Solve the pr
and helmet
brigades li
punji sta
pajamas,
smiles o
and saf
 Chri
Wayn
all bl
and
still
en
be
b

652

until we started seeing and becoming a pa
cunning and courage. And then, slowly,
rode down a crippled confidence, as ca
condescension in our attitude toward
clouded over, and refocused. Whe
see the enemy anywhere, now
now; the Vietnamese were the
namese. The killing became
 As the value of Vietnam
did the realization start t
of very little importanc
that winning victories
of the men who m
to generals and a
how much its
tion around
been assem
the milit
way. B
othe
Yo

maybe
little surprise ac
next morning.

 It wasn't that way all the time a
reaches of "Eye" Corps, where the Marines
with the NVA, up around Khe Sanh and in Hue, and
Valley and on Hill 875 in II Corps, soldiers and leathernecks foun
enemy in the big battalions and in the big battles. It was hell, but it was a
hell made familiar and recognizable by history and myth. But the enemy
we encountered for the most part, in the paddy fields and hamlets of Phu
Yen Province, though no harder to destroy—probably much easier than
the better trained and better armed North Vietnamese regulars—were
much more difficult to define. Those of us fighting the guerrillas were
thrown into a hell far different than those men fighting the big battalions
and the big battles. It was a hell worse in many ways, worse for our souls
and spirits anyway, not because the fires were any hotter, but because the
smoke was so much thicker.

 Sometimes the enemy seemed so much made of the monsoon mist that
we even doubted that he really existed. We arrived in the country expecting to encounter uniformed communist hordes, but found instead this
strange small people wearing peasant garb and those inscrutable smiles.
We wondered about all this ordnance hurled about, all the napalm, the
750-pound bombs and High Explosive artillery shells; found it hard to
believe that these weak, undernourished-looking peasants could really
present a threat and a danger to all our battalions of big, husky, heavily
armed G.I.s. It seemed a laughable country and a laughable war—until
we started running into the explosive evidence of the enemy's existence,

t of the red results of their
s fear mounted frustration and
ousness started taking over from
the Vietnamese, our vision blurred,
e before we had found it difficult to
e saw him everywhere. It was simple
Viet Cong, the Viet Cong were the Viet-
o much easier now.

ese life went down in your estimation, so too
sink in that your body and your life was really
e to the men and the machines who ran the war;
was their prime concern, not safeguarding the lives
st win the victories for them; that your life had a value
rmies and nations and causes only in relation to what or
acrifice can bring. Somehow, you've carried the wild no-
hat all this firepower, all these arms and ammunition, have
bled not so much to take enemy lives as to protect yours, that
ry machine's topmost priority is to lead you safely from harm's
ut sooner or later you are made conscious of the truth. Like any
machine, the green machine is impersonal to your life and death.
u are only another piece of equipment, like a tank or the M-16 you
arry, and your loss would be counted and calculated only in those terms.
The machine would not care that a man had died, only that another part
of its inventory had been lost and would require replacement, like the
destroyed tank. And like the totaled tank, the Army would simply put in
another order at another factory—a boot camp, where your replacement
was being tooled and trained on a different kind of assembly line. It was
just exactly as hard and as heartless as that and it was a heavy thing to
accept—though accept it we all inevitably did.

So what it all came down to was that my world became the war, that
my extended family became Charlie Company of the Second Battalion of
the 502nd Airborne Infantry of the First Brigade of the 101st Airborne
Division, and that my immediate family became the men of the Second
"Hard Core" Squad of the First Platoon. At the head of that immediate
family, my surrogate father in the Nam, was our squad leader, Staff
Sergeant Heywood "Bud" Welch. The sergeant was short in stature, but
you really had to squint hard to notice that. Everything else about the
man was tall, including his tales. Welch would recount his exploits and
there wasn't a man among us who believed half of what he claimed, but
neither was there a man who doubted that the half that was maybe not
yet true he would eventually make true. The sergeant was only twenty-
two years old, but all of us were convinced that he had lived and would
always live forever. Welch could make a brave man bolder and inspire
confidence in a coward. We would have followed him anywhere—and,
unfortunately, we did. We would have taken on half the NVA with him
as our head and heart. Instead we took on an unarmed old man. We

could have been heroes, but the war never, or rarely, gave us the chance. So Welch helped make us into the next best thing this war could offer—we became killers.

There was another kind of man in the platoon, a man we all were sure was a world removed from men like Welch—but a man who turned out to be only the darker side of our indomitable squad leader, and a side toward which the sergeant increasingly inclined. The man's name was Moses Atticus Tate, a West Virginia mountain boy and a homicidal maniac. We tried putting Tate into a separate category. He wasn't like the rest of us, we said, not even like those of us who, under the burdens and blows we had to take, sometimes gave in to the temptation to cruelty. He enjoyed the killing; he reveled in it. He was the company crazy, the regulation madman; the one kill-happy psychotic that every unit seemed plagued with, as if required by some demonic T.O.&E. (Table of Organization and Equipment) chart: so many riflemen, so many machine gunners, so many noncoms, and one bad-ass, blood-craving killer.

But Tate was in all of us and in each of us. Tate was all of us distilled down and down into some dark devil brew at the bottom. Tate was each of us stripped layer by layer of all that muddied veneer of civilized, socially-acceptable behavior, stripped clean down to the core where that mean biting thing lived that existed only to snarl and snap and draw blood. We hated him because what he had done we could do, because what he had become we could also become. Maybe one more month in Nam, one more buddy blown apart by a booby trap, maybe then the Tate would come out in all of us.

It all came apart in the monsoon October of 1966 as we were conducting Operation Seward in the rice paddy valley north of Tuy Hoa in Phu Yen Province on the central coast. We had been out several days and all we had to show for our sweat and exertion were robes of mud and waves of frustration. It had been a month now since any "Hard Core" glory had come the way of the Second Squad and the body count itch was making life miserable for all the corpse counters all the way up to battalion C.O. Finally, the First Squad scored, wasting an unarmed straggler, and the body count competition intensified. Tate, who had been in on the kill, taunted us so unmercifully on our lack of scalps that several members of the Second Squad, their "Hard Core" honor at stake, resolved to count coup and even the score even if it required wasting a slopehead who became VC only after he was dead.

After another sodden, miserable night, Welch saddled up his seven-man Hard Core Squad and led a patrol down from out hilltop NDP (Night Defensive Position) into the paddy valley below. Passing through the mud and muck of a nearby hamlet, we rousted out a gray-goateed old man and his betel-nut-chewing wife from a hootch at the south end of the village. Our squad leader and point man interrogated the old man, who responded, in a voice cracked with age and apprehension, with a litany of "No VC here! No VC! No VC here!"

Leaving the frightened old man behind, we moved on toward the last houses in the hamlet. There we got our chance and blew it. Three potential marks on the body count ballet were lounging on the front porch of a bamboo bungalo, their weapons stacked to form a neat little teepee off to the side. A volley away from eternity, the yawning communists were just nestling into their dreams of a Vietnamese workers' paradise when one of them caught sight of our stalking point man and yelped an alert. The slippery slopes nipped out under an M-16 broadside and, though the sergeant and his point man both claimed hits, we found no wet red wreckage purpling the muddy ground to validate their scores.

The Charlies had escaped; an easy score had slipped from our black-muzzled clutches. One of the Hard Core hardasses had promised to bring back to Tate evidence of a kill in the form of the victim's ears. Now we had nothing to show for our effort and nothing to throw into the face of Tate's taunts. But all was not lost; our honor could still be salvaged. The old man with gray cat's whiskers still remained, and his ears, except for the scales of age, were as good as those attached to the skulls of the three nimble Victor Charlies who had escaped. Tate could have his ears, Welch could chalk up a body count, and the squad could maintain its reputation for ferocity. All it required was murder.

Welch and two of his Cossacks stomped back to the old man's hootch and hustled him outside. The rest of us took up defensive positions in a vegetable garden surrounding the hootch. I waited in dread and anticipation, and the humid breaths I sucked in burned as if I were inhaling the alien atmosphere of a distant planet. I crouched down in a corner of that garden in hell, protecting my comrades-in-arms as they wrestled the old man to his execution block. I tried to keep my eyes fixed on the paddies and thatched huts before me, but that beast's lust for blood within me clawed at my face to turn me back and behold my comrades' shame and my own shame—to stare in horror and gaze in rapture at this monster war had conjured up.

I couldn't quite believe that it would really happen. I tried telling myself that the executioners would stay the axe; that in the final moment of reckoning they would show that their bluster was nothing more than bluff and bravado carried almost too far.

But it was too late now for the killers to draw back and consider the act that they were about to commit, though doubt and hesitation rose like suffocating, sulfurous fumes among those who were about to draw blood. One of the paratroopers pointed his M-79 grenade launcher at the doomed peasant, whose eyes spoke the silent language of the already-dead. Hesitation locked the trooper in a sweating embrace, filled the garden with its strangling tension, seemed to stop the very rotation of the earth and the passage of time. The old man stood motionless on the cliff's edge of death, a squeeze on the trigger away from a red-metaled Nirvana.

My mind bolted, like the recoil of a bombarding howitzer. I arose from my morass of sweat and dread to scream out words of protest . . . words that I should have loosened at the first insane moments of this horror. A shot reared, drowning out my frantic shout of protest in its louder scream. I would, in effect, still be shouting those unheeded words of protest in dozens of anti-war marches for years after I left Nam. I am still screaming them out today . . . too late, far too late. That unheard scream will echo through my soul forever.

The dozen steel pellets from a M-79 buckshot round crashed into the bowed, black-shirted back of the gray victim. He crumpled, as if a condor's claw had ripped out his aged spine in one vicious swoop. The old man's back was shattered into a bloody pulp, his severed red vertebrae whipping like the tentacles of an octopus.

But the old man did not die quickly. Standing over their twitching victim, the slayers shuffled uneasily, waiting for the old man to die and remove a throbbing thorn from their consciences.

One Hard Core trooper complained to the grenadier who had fired the buckshot round, "Man, you'd better trade that '79 in for a fuckin' slingshot. Can't you even waste a fuckin' old man? Whadaya need? A motherfuckin' howitzer?"

The grenadier replied, "Shit, you know how fuckin' hard it is to kill these slopes. If you're in so much pain over his suffering, why don't you finish the old fucker off?"

The other man's expression wrinkled into a portrait of reluctance, but his Hard Core creed demanded that he fight off any show of squeamishness. He swallowed whatever compassion was left to him and reaffirmed his fraudulent pride with a clattering volley of automatic rifle fire into the stricken figure laying at his feet.

But still the old man, awash in a thickening red gravy in the center of the garden and at the dead center of our souls, clung to life. Not until the same rifleman thrust the muzzle of his M-16 against the old man's skull to crash a leaden fist into his brain did the life that had lingered in agony flee the heap of bullet-ravaged flesh and bones. The old man was at last dead; the Second Squad could report back to the platoon leader the attainment of a body count.

The grenadier turned away to escape the shame that was corroding his conscience, but the rifleman grabbed his arm and reminded him, "Man, are you going to forget why we zapped that old fucker?"

"What's to forget?" asked the grenadier impatiently.

"The ears, man, the mother fuckin' ears," answered the rifleman. "Them cats in First Squad are expectin' some Hard Core trophies."

"Oh yeah, the ears," muttered the grenadier. "The god damn ears."

The grenadier kneeled down to collect his bounty. He went to work with his bayonet and soon the ears were off to decorate the elastic camouflage cover band on his steel pot, like some obscene plume atop a Roman legionnaire's helmet.

As the squad prepared to retire to the platoon HQ laden with its spoils of war, rifle shots popped in the tops of the banana trees shadowing the scene of our atrocity. The Charlies who had fled the hamlet must have returned, but we had already earned an easier body count and so we did not linger. The squad hastily retraced its steps out of the tiny peasant burg to rejoin the platoon. Upon reaching the platoon position, the grenadier proudly displayed his trophies, still dripping blood, to a much impressed Tate. We had joined his ranks.

I did not join in the ensuing celebration for our success. I was appalled; appalled at what my comrades had done and at what I had failed to do. I determined that if ever I should find myself in a position of leadership— and my promotion to sergeant was due in a few weeks—at the head of a patrol, a fire team, a squad, whatever, I would exert whatever authority I might have to prevent another such incident, a recurrence of barbarity. It was all I could do to make amends; a weak resolution in the face of such strong savagery. It was too late to help the old man. I could never have pointed my M-16 at my comrades to warn them off. They would have known and I would have known that there was no way that I could have squeezed the trigger, no way would I have harmed one of my comrades to save the life of an old gook. I owned nothing in the world anymore of value other than the good will and loyalty of these men; I would have let the whole gook race die before I forfeited it. Reporting the incident, turning them in, was simply no alternative. I never considered it; it did not exist as an option. Not in my world. Without these men I would die, if not in body then surely in spirit. It was that simple. My dependence upon the men of my squad, of my platoon, their dependence upon me and each other, was total. I did not want to become an outcast from the only family that really mattered to me now. Malingering, cowardice, cruelty, nothing would earn my comrades' contempt more than disloyalty. Somewhere in me, something told me that there existed a loyalty greater than that I gave and received from the men of the First Platoon; a loyalty to truth and justice and conscience. And later it was all so obvious; but much later, after I had left this country, this war, this platoon. But back then, truth and justice and morality were only words, words that could not save me from death or madness or that slow sinking into a morass of fear and isolation. There was but one loyalty in Nam that counted and it was, without exception, colored olive drab.

Fifteen years later I still have trouble dealing with that old man. He confronts me sometimes in my dreams, his face always ill-defined, cloudy, because I've forgotten just what he looked like after all these years. But I haven't forgotten his final expression, the one frozen on his face and in my soul, the one that he carried with him out of this world of the living when that M-79 buckshot round shattered his back.

But the old man's image comes and goes, just as the guilt comes and goes. Sometimes I have to remind myself of it; sometimes I have to hide from myself because I can't get away from it. That's because part of me, the part that made me question the war, that made me turn against the war, that made me work against the war, that part of me finds me guilty, an accessory to the crime of murder, guilty through inaction, through acquiescence, through acceptance. But another part of me, the part that loved the thought of war, that even kept a little bit of that love for the experience of war, that part excuses my act of non-action, buries the guilt, tells me it's all understandable and forgivable, given the circumstances of war, given the savagery of war, given the strange but special loyalties of war.

Back then, when it happened, something bright and burning inside me flickered and went out, leaving not even a warm cinder, leaving only a pile of cold cold ashes.

I went home four months later. It was not a happy homecoming. I suppose I would have come out of any war disillusioned. Even when fought for the most glorious cause, even when resulting in the most magnificent victory, war can never be the creature of dash and daring, of adventure and admiration, that young minds might imagine. And to the misfortune of our egos and aspirations—though probably ultimately to the good fortune of our souls—the only war offered our generation was Vietnam, surely the most disillusioning war ever fought by Americans. Had it been World War II or Korea maybe we could have salvaged some scrap of our former favorable opinion of war; maybe we could have looked back as middle aged vets sitting in VFW clubs and recalled some higher purpose to our sacrifices and proposed a toast to the good fight, to "our war." But ours was not WWII or Korea; ours was Vietnam, and it would have required a far greater leap from reality—and a dishonest one at that—than that of our adolescent fantasies, now that our opinion was no longer based on ignorance, for us to bless a war that could bear no blessing.

Though separated geographically, the war stayed with me down through all the following years. In all that time, in all those years while I was either fighting in the Vietnam War or against it, I often found it difficult, if not almost inconceivable, to imagine that any American, or at least any American of my generation, could look upon the war as trivial to their own lives, as something outside of and as far removed from their own private and personal existences as, say, the chaos in the Congo in the early 60s was. I could not fathom how Vietnam could be anything to all Americans but the central concern of their lives; how it could be anything less than the dark sun around which we were all in unbreakable orbit as its doomed and somehow hopeless satellites. But I had to face the fact, the appalling fact, that to the vast majority of Americans, even those of my age, families and homes and careers, and even cars, cocaine, connections and the next piece of ass, were greater concerns than all that muck and madness in Southeast Asia. Vietnam and its war touched and tainted millions of Americans in one way or another, but it left greater millions untouched. For all that the war affected them, most of the children of the '60s might just as well have been children of the '50s. Most of my family, friends and acquaintances did not serve in the war or in the war against the war. For most of my family, friends and acquaintances, the war had an impact upon them similar to that made by a pebble dropped into the depths of the ocean.

But for me and for most of the men who fought there, the war was everything. It had been the worst experience of my life and it had been the best. I never wanted out of any place so bad as I wanted out of Vietnam. But after I left I felt an immediate and overwhelming sense of loss for Vietnam and its war. After all these years, this nostalgia, this strange yearning to return to it all, still persists, still haunts me. Looking at it in terms of good or bad is all wrong. It was simply the most awesome experience of my life and will probably remain so to the end of my years. It is a mountain range rising up abruptly and sharply from the more or less level plains that make up the topography of the rest of my life. These are heights desolate and depressing, more like the mountains of the moon than some snow-capped range, magic and majestic. They are there, undeniable and unscalable, and though time and fading memory may erode them to foothills, they will never entirely disappear from my life's landscape until the gray glacier of death wears everything down to dust.[4]

1979   8 January—Vietnamese and Kampuchean Front forces capture Phnom Penh. Pol Pot escapes, vowing "guerrilla war." **18 February–6 March**—The People's Republic of China's invasion of northern Vietnam is strongly resisted by Vietnamese forces using more modern American equipment and aircraft. After withdrawal, China admits to 20,000 casualties. **21 February**—Vietnam signs peace treaty with new Kampuchean government and declares that its army will remain in Cambodia as "advisers."

The following article, entitled "Letter to my Daughter," is written by David Halberstam, winner of the Pulitzer Prize for his reporting of the Vietnam War. This letter could also have been written for Cathy Gigante, whose narrative begins this book (see pp. 1–3).

Julia,
It is now 20 years, but I remember it as if it were yesterday, the ride in from Tan Son Nhut Airport, driving through the semi-rural outskirts of Saigon, sensing the rare combination of energy and beauty, yet aware as well of the dark shadow over the land, for there were already troops everywhere. Never as in that moment had life seemed so real to me, never had I felt so connected to a particular moment; it was as if, and I know this will sound odd and possibly arrogant to you, I had finally arrived at the place where I was always destined to go.

I believed in the cause that was at stake and in the men who were fighting it; like many in my generation, I had been touched by John Kennedy's inaugural speech and had felt stirred by his words about the long twilight struggle ahead and the great adventure we might all be part of. And here I was, fresh from more than a year of reporting in the Congo, finally, after many requests to my foreign editor, a part of it. Sometimes in those early months, in talking about what the Americans were doing in Vietnam, I, like others there, slipped unconsciously into the pronoun "we." That we were there to help another country against encroachment from within was the line, and I did not dissent. No one, it seemed to me, said it better than a friend of mine named Clarence Hornbuckle, a Special Forces sergeant with whom I spent a week near the Laotian border in the Central Highlands. On his beret was the Special Forces motto, "De Oppresso Liber," or, translated from the Latin, "To Free the Oppressed." "I figure it means 'give the little bleepers a break,' " Hornbuckle said.

Someday I hope you will understand how important those moments were for me; more, I want you to understand the importance of *remembering,* of holding onto and even cherishing a part of what you have been as, more and more, events are thrust upon you. For all too often in this world, and I think with increasing force, the present seeks to obliterate the past—something I hope you will not lightly accept. So let me begin.

I have odd and bittersweet memories of those days, of living in my dreams in the midst of an escalating war. Dreams are fine both for people and for nations. We need them for sustenance and for incentive, but they are dangerous as well, for they may turn into myth, diverting us from what we are and what we might be into what we think we are. If anything, in those days, I loved my assignment too much. There is, in all young reporters—and I was 28 at the time—a certain romanticism. And in reporters of my generation in the early days of Vietnam, that was heightened into something more complicated: the journalist in search of self as the Hemingway hero. We were testing ourselves without ever really admitting that we were testing ourselves. It was a bad time in Vietnam, not as bad as it was eventually to become, but it was, in addition to all the danger and hardship, an oddly exhilarating time for me, at least in the beginning. There is in here a contradiction that every journalist should ponder, and I reflect on it still: What of us as human beings, if we are at our best in times of such misery?

The war was very near by. A suburban war, if you will. At first, because the U.S. command tried to keep us away from battle by limiting access to helicopters, we simply took taxis to the war. We would rent them in Saigon—huge beaten-up American gas-guzzlers driven by men whose real calling was clearly Le Mans—and we would roar through the countryside to witness whatever battles we could (though never returning at night). Then a man named Ivan Slavich came to the country, and he soon became a friend. He commanded the first company of armed helicopters in American history. Ivan was absolutely fearless; if he was not the bravest man I ever met, he was certainly one of the two or three. Irreverent, joyous, unorthodox, he was the kind of man the Army loves in wartime and fears in peacetime. He feared neither the enemy, nor his superiors, nor above all the Army bureaucracy. Despite pressure from superior officers, he used to take us on his gunships and into battle whenever we wanted. This enraged the Public Information officers, whose job in those early days it was to control us and keep us away from battle and, at the very least, keep an eye on us while we worked. Once, I remember, an Army major, a PIO, showed up unannounced and uninvited to go on a mission. It was clear he was there, among other things, to spy on us.

"Who the hell are you?" Ivan asked him. The major gave his name. "Did I ask you to come on this mission?" Ivan asked. The major said no. "Then get the hell off that helicopter—this is my company and I'll damn well take who I want with me, and I don't need any spies," he said. Sometimes a call would come from him at night and he would simply say, "I think you want to have breakfast with me tomorrow." That meant getting up at 3 a.m. and going off to Tan Son Nhut. They served huge breakfasts in Ivan's mess, but I could never eat anything. Maybe sip the coffee if I was lucky.

We would take off at about 5. Ivan's men flew ships called Hueys, and when a Huey changed direction in the air, somehow it always sounded like machine-gun fire, and I would always freeze. This amused Slavich greatly; he told me the secret of my success as a war correspondent was that I was scared only at the wrong times. I still remember the sheer beauty of flying over the Mekong Delta as the dawn came up; I have never before, and never since, seen anything lovelier. I remember as well odd fragments of battle, of coming in on a tree line, taking fire, and the pilot of one of the Hueys letting go with his rocket pods at the hut where the fire was coming from. The hut simply disappeared. "Left those SOBs with a headache." he said as we turned for another pass. At night we went out for drinks with the pilots from that company, a lot of drinks, and we would often end the evening singing. There were two songs I remember. In one the men, who loved their commander, in the last stanza simply chanted his name, "Ivan Slavich! Ivan Slavich!"; in the other, the last line went like this: "Better days are coming, by-and-by/ Bleep-bleep."

I loved those moments, and sometimes in Vietnam, if I am to tell you the truth, it was as if we were watching movies of ourselves in which we were the stars; it had that kind of unreal intoxicating feeling. For in those days we lived on the very edge of life and death, and that heightened every experience. Did I like Ivan Slavich? In truth, in those days I loved him. For at moments like this, nothing is ordinary. Those days produced a rare camaraderie—that of men who have been in battle together—and the intensity of that camaraderie, these many years later, still defies any rational explanation. It is a bond so strong, so immediate, that it wipes away, at least momentarily, all the normal barriers of class, politics and race. Nothing in terms of friendship need precede it, nothing need follow it. It exists of itself, nothing more asked, nothing more required.

I'm sure any psychologist would be fascinated, for it is something short of sexual, oddly pure and spiritual. In those moments, everything is so intense, everything is so completely shared, and everyone is so dependent upon everyone else, that it defies all other relationships. Marriage has its own special bonds, but they are bonds of love and family, set (with any luck) for a long time at a gentle plateau; in contrast, combat is primal, and it is about one thing and one thing alone—the desire to live one more day.

In those days I adopted and was adopted by the American advisory team working with the Vietnamese Seventh Division. It was head-quartered in the most highly contested area of Vietnam, and it was just a short drive from Saigon. In addition, the senior adviser, Lt. Col. John Vann, was, if not the most talented American officer in the country (which many thought he was), certainly the most driven and the most fiery.

When we first met, he was still optimistic, but I watched him change as the war slipped away and as his advice was scattered in the wind. He took me in hand, taught me about the war and made sure that I went out in the field with his best captains; they were, he said, the best of a genera-tion of American officers, and he was right. If there were ever young men who seemed a direct extension of the Kennedy inaugural speech—"we will pay any price, bear any burden"—which had so stirred me just two years earlier, it was these officers in My Tho. On my first operation I went out with Capt. Ken Good.

Vann gave Good instructions that under no circumstances was he to lose me. Good was impressive, gentle, fair and strong. The next time, I went out with another captain, Jim Torrence. To this day, I cannot look at a Robert Redford film without thinking of Torrence, for he not only looked like Redford but he also seemed, like the basic Redford character, to embody all of America's best values; no one, meeting him, watching him in the field, could doubt his intelligence, his strength and his kind-ness. I was in awe of him and later wrote and published a small novel in which one character was in no small part based on him.

The Vietnamese have little hair on their bodies, and what hair they do have is dark; they were fascinated by Torrence, for his powerful forearms were covered by blond hair the color of corn silk. They regarded him, quite properly, as a visiting American god. I remember once, when his Ranger company was under fire near a tree line and everyone was duck-ing down, Torrence stood up, checked his position as casually as a com-muter checking a train schedule, and then beckoned his people forward. Later, I asked him how he could be so cool under fire. "Oh," he said, "I might have been more nervous if that stuff was incoming, but most of it was our own. Anyone got hit by that, he was going to get hit from behind."

Sometimes, after a day or two in the field, we would go out for dinner together. I remember one evening at a Vietnamese restaurant in My Tho where, at Vann's orders and for reasons I cannot properly explain— perhaps the Catch 22 quality of the war was beginning to catch up with us—we had to eat with chopsticks with the opposite hand. "Everything else here is assbackwards." he said. It was his way of proving that every- thing in Vietnam was in some way reversed, that day was night and right was wrong and, worse, wrong was right.

That night the talk, as it often did, came around to the other side, the Vietcong. There was always, when field officers spoke, a grudging admi- ration for them, for the excellence of their leadership, the bravery of their ordinary soldiers, and the careful way they exploited their limited re- sources. In contrast to the Arvin, the South Vietnamese troops, who were worthy soldiers but often poorly led, the Vietcong were seen as admirable adversaries. Both Vann and Torrence began to talk about how they would like to serve as advisers to the VC for a month or so. It was an interesting note, and I was to hear it repeated frequently in Vietnam. There was nothing political about it; this was simply one brave soldier's way of saying he admired the ability and courage of his foe. But, as I pondered it more and I learned more, the implications of it became greater, and they were inevitably political. Why was the other side braver than our side? Why was its field leadership so strikingly superior? Could this mean that we were on the wrong side?

Those dinners with Vann and the other officers turned darker and more bitter as 1963 progressed. Ken Good had been killed at a battle called Ap Bac, and the Vietnamese commanders had deliberately chosen to let the Vietcong escape. Vann was enraged and became even more outspoken, as gradually so did other officers in other sections of the country. For the war was not being won, as the Saigon command boasted; in truth it was not even being fought, and it was therefore being lost. The Vietcong were winning without any real resistance. The American expertise was being wasted.

The American officers were taking the maximum risk, they were giving their best advice, but their advice was not being listened to. That became a chorus among field officers up to the rank of colonel, and my friend Vann became the most outspoken and, as his superiors in Saigon refused to listen to him, the most bitter. His job, they told him, was to keep his mouth shut and get along. As he continued to challenge the optimism, he was almost relieved of his command. When he tried, on his return to Washington, to talk to superiors, he was threatened with a court-martial. No wonder he had made us eat with chopsticks with our opposite hands.

When something like this happens, there is only one thing for a re- porter with any conscience to do. He has to follow his information and his instincts, and I began to write pessimistically about what was happening. It was not what I wanted to write but it was, in conscience, the only thing I could write.

Later it was said by some critics of the press corps that what we did was trendy—that is, tailored to fashion—and it is true that by the late '60s, there were more journalists who opposed the war than favored it. But in those early days it was very lonely indeed, going against the main currents of American opinion and your own preconceptions and beliefs. It was the beginning of an odd and complicated reevaluation, not just of policy but of self, that I began in those days. I had wanted our side to win, I believed in our values, but we were not winning. If our values were not working, were they in fact the values we thought they were? For we saw ourselves as egalitarian, democratic, anxious to help the Vietnamese against the Communists; but the peasants saw us as rich and white, the friends and principal bankers of the French, who had been their colonial rulers and who had fought them during the bitter eight-year war for independence. Our sense of who we were was completely reversed from theirs.

My friend Bernard Fall, the distinguished French historian-journalist, once said: "The Americans are walking in the same footsteps as the French although dreaming different dreams." That change in my attitude, of course, came slowly and reluctantly. Reporters, more than most people, are fond of writing about their loss of innocence, and I have a few friends who have lost their innocence three or four times. Still, I lost my innocence in Vietnam. Ideals of egalitarianism, I decided, were not easily exported, and often the people in Washington most eager to export them were in fact those who most clearly failed to live up to them at home.

I also, for my troubles, became the enemy of not just the American Mission in Saigon but sometimes, it seemed, the entire government in Washington. In ancient times, messengers who brought the king news he did not want to hear were executed for their trouble; now, in modern times, we simply attack reporters. So it was for me. Because I was the reporter for *The New York Times,* the most influential of the country's newspapers, I became the main target of all the people who had a vested interest in making the war effort look better than it actually did. I was attacked for being left-wing, which I was not; attacked for cowardice, though I had been on some 50 missions by then; attacked even for my manhood and my patriotism. Nor was it just ambassadors and generals and magazines and newspapers. Soon it was two Presidents as well. President Kennedy, whose vision of our national responsibility had so challenged me, asked the publisher of *The Times* to pull me out of Saigon. Lyndon Johnson was more blunt. I, like my colleague and friend Neil Sheehan, was a traitor to my country, he told reporters.

There was not very much fun in this. I do not think you go into this profession to be liked or to be popular, but I think the totality of the hostility and the systematic distortion of what we were doing rankled. In an odd way, the pressure from the top, from Kennedy or from the generals, never bothered me too much. I had never believed a reporter should seek approval from politicians or high officials. But I was going through a highly personal interior debate which was far more complicated. For I bore one special burden, Julia, made up of your grandfather's own patriotism and love of country and his own high personal courage. He, a son of immigrants who I suspect believed more strongly in American values than many older American families, had served in World War I as a combat medic and in World War II as a combat surgeon.

By 1963 he had been dead 13 years, but his shadow, indeed his myth, loomed large over me. I wondered often in those days about what he might think about my reporting and decided finally that he, more than anyone else, had taught me to be true to myself, to stand up for what I thought was right, no matter if I had to stand alone. Besides, I remembered, and it cheered me immensely, he was a patriot but not a jingoist; he had hated the bombast of "The Star-Spangled Banner" and had always believed that the national anthem should instead be "America, the Beautiful." Remembering that, I felt better.

There was, however, one charge against me which rankled greatly at the time, and I think it is worth detailing for you because it may help explain some of the changes I went through. A well-known journalist from Washington named Marguerite Higgins, who was very much a voice of the Pentagon, came out to Saigon for a brief tour. She soon went around telling other reporters what she had been told by a Marine general in Washington. Halberstam, she said, quoting the general, had been shown a photo of a bunch of Vietcong bodies, and he had burst into tears. Tears were for women, of course, and not only had I wept, but I had wept for the other side.

I was stunned: the story was completely untrue and it was, I feared—for I was young and vulnerable—potentially damaging. After all, manhood was particularly important among war correspondents, and the ideal of the Hemingway hero, though fading a bit, was still important. Hemingway heroes did not cry. I was indignant and protested angrily among my colleagues, all of whom had already shared countless missions with me. A few weeks later, the very same Marine general appeared in Saigon, and when I saw him on the airport tarmac, I went roaring after him, confronted him, put my finger in his face and started shouting at him.

"Listen," I said, and I can still hear the anger in my voice, "I know what you've been saying to reporters in Washington about me crying over seeing a bunch of bodies, and it's crap, do you hear me, crap! I've been on more than 50 missions in this country and I've seen a lot of bodies and I don't cry and you better damn well get that right!"

The general was completely stunned by this—he had no idea that his words might come back at him and that he would be faced down by some demented journalist. He mumbled something about this not being a war for GI Joe reporting. "I don't want any more of your Pentagon briefing crap," I said and walked away.

I was, for a time, immensely proud of myself, as if I had passed some secret test, and my friends were both pleased and amused. But, about a year later, your godfather, Jack Langguth, who succeeded me in Saigon, put the story in better context for *The Times*. He wrote about the same incident, saying it was a symbol of a changing America, and nothing was expediting the change more than the war itself.

Though the story was not true, he wrote, perhaps it ought to have been true, not just of me but of others. Perhaps we all should have cried more over the sight of bodies from both sides. Future generations of Americans, rather than looking down on someone who, seeing bodies, has cried, might respect him all the more. I think he was right. I think he saw the truth of that incident far more clearly than I did, and I see Vietnam now as not just a story but as part of a personal journey.

I do not think I was alone in what I went through in those years. I think I was simply a part of a great national interior debate taking place throughout the country; we were reexamining not just America in Vietnam, but America itself. If we doubted that we were in the right war, or even on the right side, it did not mean that we loved our country any less. If anything, knowing America's faults and imperfections, perhaps I love it more than your grandfather and great-grandfather, for perhaps I love it more wisely. During all those years, I kept on my desk a small quote from Albert Camus which he had written during France's war in Algeria: "I should like to be able to love my country and love justice."

I have thought long and hard about Vietnam over the last 20 years, for something like this does not lightly leave you, and I have decided that the true innocents are not those—as Washington would have it—who are afraid to use force and thus do not understand the real world, but in fact those who still think that in this day and age we can impose our values and our will upon peasants by force. And your godfather was right: I wish in fact that someone had shown me a photo of Vietcong bodies and I had cried.

• *Sgt. Clarence E. Hornbuckle was killed in action on June 6, 1968, in South Vietnam.*
• *John Vann, by then one of the highest-ranking civilians in South Vietnam, was killed near Kontum in 1972.*
• *Capt. Kenneth N. Good was killed at the battle of Ap Bac on Jan. 2, 1963.*
• *Lt. Col. James E. Torrence was killed in action on May 18, 1971, in South Vietnam.*
• *Bernard Fall, the most distinguished historian of the war, was killed near Hue on Feb. 21, 1967.*[5]

On 22 June, 1982, the following news item appears in the American press.

Navy Ships Fired On By 'Vietnam' Vessel: Bullet Hits Destroyer

ASSOCIATED PRESS, Washington—Three U.S. Navy ships, including a destroyer which figured in the 1964 Tonkin Gulf incident, were fired on

Sunday night "by a vessel believed to belong to the Socialist Republic of Vietnam" while in international waters, the Navy said Tuesday.

Only one .30-caliber round penetrated the destroyer Turner Joy, no one was injured and "no appreciable damage was done," said Lt. Cmdr. Tom Jurkowsky, the Navy spokesman.

This was the first shooting incident involving the U.S. Navy in Southeast Asian waters since the Cambodian seizure of the freighter Mayaguez in May 1975, officials said.

The Navy, which did not announce the incident but acknowledged it in response to questions, said the episode occurred as four Navy ships were sailing about 70 miles off the southern tip of Vietnam en route from Thailand to the U.S. naval base at Subic Bay in the Philippines.

Jurkowsky said the U.S. ships did nothing that could be described as provocative and that they were about 20 miles from the nearest Vietnamese territory, Con Son Island.

One of the U.S. ships, the guided missile destroyer Lynde McCormick, fired back with .50-caliber machine-gun fire "intentionally directed over" what appeared to be a Vietnamese vessel, Jurkowsky said.

No other shots were fired, the Navy spokesman said.

Accompanying the Turner Joy and the McCormick were the cruiser Sterett and the guided missile destroyer Benjamin Stoddert.

The Turner Joy has a special place in U.S. history because it was sailing through the Gulf of Tonkin off North Vietnam in the summer of 1964 when, according to the Navy, it was fired on by North Vietnamese patrol craft. That incident led to the first U.S. bombing of North Vietnam and is regarded as a critical event leading to deep U.S. involvement in the Vietnam war.

According to Jurkowsky, this is what happened Sunday:

At about 9:30 p.m. local time, the Turner Joy was sent by the task group commander to investigate "what proved to be a fishing boat flashing a light."

As the destroyer drew near, Jurkowsky said, the boat fired two sets of red flares across the Turner Joy's bow and then promptly opened fire with a machine gun at a range of about half a mile.

After the Turner Joy was hit by a single round, the McCormick was ordered to identify the ship which had opened fire on the Joy.

As the McCormick approached, the fishing vessel opened fire on the guided missile destroyer, but Jurkowsky said it missed.

It was then that the McCormick returned fire, but aimed high.

Asked why the McCormick did not try to hit the fishing boat, Jurkowsky said the deliberate miss was considered to be "the minimum use of force necessary to induce the fishing vessel to cease firing."

The Navy spokesman said the fishing boat stopped shooting.

The U.S. Navy ships remained on the scene "to identify the fishing vessel more precisely in daylight," Jurkowsky said.

At 5:45 a.m. Monday, the cruiser Sterett sailed toward one of two small fishing boats and a junk. When the cruiser was about 3,000 yards away, the Navy spokesman said, one small boat fired small arms in front of the cruiser's bow.

At the same time, the McCormick circled the larger boat which had fired on it during the night, but there was no more shooting, Jurkowsky said.

The Navy vessels made two more "investigatory passes," Jurkowsky said, and on one of these passes a Vietnamese flag "was seen to be hauled down aboard one small boat."

The U.S. Navy said the Vietnamese claim jurisdiction over waters out to 12 miles from land and an additional 12-mile security area. Jurkowsky said the United States recognizes a 3-mile limit from shore as territorial waters.[6]

Two weeks later, the following events occur.

Sihanouk embraces foes

ARANYAPRATHET, Thailand (AP)—Prince Norodom Sihanouk, visiting his former Communist captors inside Cambodia today, denounced a Vietnamese plan to withdraw some forces from Cambodia as "propaganda," Thai army officers at this frontier town said.

Sihanouk, head of a new rebel coalition fighting the Vietnamese in Cambodia, embraced top Khmer Rouge leaders, men who once held him captive and who had engineered a bloody revolution in his country. He then shared an elaborate luncheon with them that included French champagne.

Sihanouk and Khmer Rouge leader Khieu Samphan later rode off together into the jungle on the back of an elephant, according to newsmen accompanying the prince. It was not known whether Sihanouk would return to Thailand later today.[7]

At the same time, a song at the top of the record charts expresses what millions of Americans, regardless of their reasons for doing so, feel about the Vietnam War.

STILL IN SAIGON
by Dan Daley, performed by the Charlie Daniels Band on *Windows*.

Got on a plane to Frisco
And got off in Viet Nam
Walked into a different world
The past forever gone

I could have gone to Canada
Or I could have stayed in school
But I was brought up differently
I couldn't break the rules

Thirteen months and fifteen days
The last ones were the worst
One minute I'd kneel down and pray
And the next I'd stand and curse

No place to run to
Where I did not feel that war
When I got home I stayed alone
And checked behind each door

Cause I'm

> Still in Saigon
> Still in Saigon
> Still in Saigon
> In my mind

The ground at home
Was covered with snow
And I was covered with sweat
My younger brother calls me a killer
And my daddy calls me a vet

Everybody says I'm someone else
That I'm sick and there's no cure
Damned if I know who I am
There was only one place I was sure
When I was

> Still in Saigon
> Still in Saigon
> Still in Saigon
> In my mind

Every summer when it rains
I smell the jungle
I hear the planes
I can't tell no one
I feel ashamed
Afraid some day
I'll go insane

That's been ten long years ago
And time has gone on by
But now and then I catch myself
Eyes searching through the sky

All the sounds of long ago
Will be forever in my head
Mingled with the wounded's cries
And the silence of the dead

> Still in Saigon
> Still in Saigon
> Still in Saigon
> In my mind[8]

In the United States, the reactions of a group of Americans exemplify the varied perspectives of the Vietnam War still held by so many. Bill Tremblay is a poet and former antiwar activist.

Evening with Novelists at Crown Point Estates

We are seated before the fieldstone fireplace in the carpets soft
as lamb's wool. Our host plays the tape.* In it a Forward Air
   Controller
with an Oklahoma drawl directs a bombing strike somewhere in
   Cambodia
as the bomber pilots break in with complaints of taking heavy fire from
a pagoda they are not authorized to respond to while Nixon's speech
declaring an end to hostilities in Southeast Asia is being piped into
their cockpits from Radio Australia. The pilots are hip to the ironic
situation. But they speak excited as boys putting a stubble-field to
the torch with the permission of their fathers.

One of the guests stands up, calling the host a psychotic, a sadist
who enjoys reliving the kill. He can't stay another minute under the
same roof with such a monster, such a moral cretin.

The host protests. True, he's a veteran but the tape is evidence he
would have used if Nixon hadn't been driven from the White House by

*See pp. 544–548.

Water-
gate. Besides, he says, everything he could ever say about a theory of
fiction is embodied on that tape. Facts no longer exist. The record is
simply a fabric of conflicting fictions which are believed in absolutely
because not to believe them would mean that everything we've
    done we've
done wrongly. That is our morality, the necessity to stick to our fictions
because the consequences would be more than we could bear without
    them.

It's obscene to maintain that you would have released this tape, the
guest replies. You wouldn't have had the guts! I suppose you have to
believe that, the host answers, smiling. The angry guest storms out the
door.

We understand them both.

The guest has been living in Europe for seven years. He hasn't been
in this atmosphere. He still believes that, like Neruda, he can show his
hands to the generals & say, "I am not part of this crime." Everything
to him is simple as an Inquisition.

We can relate to our host's passion for complicated narrative
    techniques,
his vision of blizzards obliterating all the trails of blood. We see
through the fiction of innocent, non-complicitous lives; perhaps to have
been born is itself the fundamental crime. A taste for the theology of
the Counter-Reformation is rekindling here; Goya's pictures are
    enjoying a wide-
spread revival.

The party goes on.[9]

NOTES

PROLOGUE

1. *Samisdat* pamphlet, undated, pp. 40–42. By permission of Merritt Clifton.
2. *United States–Vietnam Relations: 1945–67* [*The Pentagon Papers*], 10 (Washington, D.C.: U.S. Government Printing Office, 1971), pp. 144–49. Hereafter cited as *Gov't PP.*
3. *Gov't PP,* 10, p. 190.
4. *U.S.–Vietnam Relations, The Senator Gravel Ed.,* 1 (Boston: Beacon Press, 1971–72) p. 361. Hereafter cited as *Gravel.*
5. Robert Payne, *Red Storm Over Asia* (New York: Macmillan, 1951), pp. 1–3, 202–203.
6. Graham Greene, *The Quiet American* (New York: Viking, 1956), Penguin ed., 1980, pp. 17–18, 23–25, 176, 173, 11, 30–32.
7. *Gravel,* 1, pp. 384–90.
8. Edward Geary Lansdale, *In the Midst of Wars* (New York: Harper & Row, 1972), pp. 109–113.
9. *Gravel,* 1, pp. 487, 497.
10. Desmond Meiring, *The Brinkman* (Boston: Houghton Mifflin, 1965), pp. 57–61.
11. Gravel, 1, pp. 574–75.
12. Gareth Porter, *Vietnam: The Definitive Documentation of Human Decisions,* 2 vols. (Staffordville, N.Y.: Earl M. Coleman Enterprises, 1979), pp. 633–34, 635–36. Hereafter cited as Porter, *Vietnam.*
13. Lansdale, *Wars,* pp. 146–49.
14. *Background Information Relating to Southeast Asia and Vietnam,* 7th ed. rev. (Washington, D.C.: U.S. Government Printing Office, 1975), pp. 217–19. Hereafter cited as *Background.*
15. Lansdale, *Wars,* pp. 164–65.
16. Jean Larteguy, *Yellow Fever,* trans. Xan Fielding (New York: E.P. Dutton, 1965), pp. 19–20.
17. M.J. Bosse, *The Journey of Tao Kim Nam* (New York: Doubleday, 1959), pp. 16–18, 19–20.
18. *Gov't PP,* 10, pp. 703–704.
19. *Gov't PP,* 10, V. B. 3., p. 737.
20. *Gravel,* 1, pp. 575–77.
21. Bosse, *Nam,* pp. 227, 229–31.
22. *Gravel,* 1, pp. 576–79.
23. William J. Lederer and Eugene Burdick, *The Ugly American* (New York: W.W. Norton, 1958), pp. 181–84.
24. Lansdale, *Wars,* pp. 252–55.
25. Larteguy, *Yellow Fever,* pp. 195–96, 197, 199–200.
26. Lansdale, *Wars,* pp. 282–85, 289–91, 306–309.
27. Larteguy, *Yellow Fever,* pp. 308, 316–19, 361.
28. *Gov't PP,* pp. 969–70.

ACT I

1. Lansdale, *Wars,* p. 313.
2. Porter, *Vietnam,* 1, pp. 697–98, NSC 5519.
3. Porter, *Vietnam,* 1, pp. 711–12.
4. Porter, *Vietnam,* 2, pp. 1–2.
5. Lansdale, *Wars,* pp. 332–33.
6. Lansdale, *Wars,* pp. 345–47.
7. *Gov't PP,* 2, IV. A. 5. Tab 1, pp. 31–32.
8. Porter, *Vietnam,* 2, pp. 22–23, NSC 5612 1.
9. Quoted in *Comrade Mao Tse-tung on* "Imperialism and All Reactionaries Are Paper Tigers" (Peking: Foreign Languages Press, 1958), pp. 24–26.
10. Porter, *Vietnam,* 2, trans. Gareth Porter, pp. 38–41.
11. *Gov't PP,* 2, IV. A. 5. Tab 3, pp. 33–35.
12. *Gov't PP,* 10, pp. 1190–95.
13. *Gov't PP,* 10, p. 1202.
14. *Hearings before the Subcommittee on State Department Organization and Public Affairs of the Committee on Foreign Relations,* United States Senate, July 30 and 31 and December 7 and 8, 1959 (Washington, D.C.: U.S. Government Printing Office, 1959, 1960), pp. 103, 170–71.
15. Benjamin F. Schemmer, *The Raid* (New York: Harper & Row, 1976), pp. 78–79.
16. Porter, *Vietnam,* 2, pp. 53–56.
17. Porter, *Vietnam,* 2, pp. 61–62, trans. Major Van Elliott.
18. William Colby, *Honorable Men: My Life in the CIA* (New York: Simon & Schuster, 1978), pp. 162–64.
19. *Gov't PP,* 2, IV. A. 5. Tab 3, p. 61.
20. Colby, *Honorable Men,* pp. 165–69, 171–72.
21. *Gov't PP,* 2, IV. A. 5. Tab 4, pp. 66–77.
22. *The Royal Lao Army and U.S. Army Advice and Support,* Indochina Monographs (Washington, D.C.: U.S. Army Center of Military History, 1981), pp. 74–78. Hereafter cited as *Royal Lao Army.*
23. "Memorandum of a Conference on January 19, 1961," *Gov't PP,* 10, pp. 1362–63.
24. *Gravel,* 1, pp. 339–40.
25. Arthur Schlesinger, *A Thousand Days* (Boston: Houghton Mifflin, 1965), pp. 282–85.
26. Colby, *Honorable Men,* p. 172.
27. *Gov't PP,* 11, pp. 230–31.
28. *Gov't PP,* 11, p. 328.
29. Porter, *Vietnam,* 2, pp. 122–23.
30. Smith Hempstone, *A Tract of Time* (Boston: Houghton Mifflin, 1966), pp. 21–25.
31. *Gov't PP,* 11, pp. 406–409.
32. *Gov't PP,* 11, p. 425.
33. Hempstone, *Tract,* pp. 93–96.
34. *Gov't PP,* 2, IV. A. 5., Tab 3, p. 62.
35. Pamela Sanders, *Miranda* (Boston: Little, Brown, 1978), pp. 169–70, 195–97, 216–17.
36. Richard Tregaskis, *Vietnam Diary* (New York: Holt, Rinehart and Winston, 1963), pp. 9–16.

37. Letter to John Clark Pratt. Reprinted by permission.

38. James Crumley, *One to Count Cadence* (New York: Random House, 1969), pp. 256–58, 266–72.

39. Kenneth Babbs, Esq., manuscript journal, "Vietnam Vignettes," 1962. Reprinted by permission.

40. Major J. M. Yingling and others, *United States Marine Corps Activities in Vietnam, 1954–63,* II (Washington, D.C.: HQ G-3, HQUSMC, n.d.), pp. 190–93. Declassified at USMC archives, June 21, 1976.

41. Roger Hilsman, *To Move a Nation* (Garden City, N.Y.: Doubleday, 1967), pp. 446–49, 456–59.

42. *Gov't PP,* 12, pp. 523–24.

43. Charles Larson, *The Chinese Game* (Philadelphia: J.B. Lippincott, 1969), pp. 186–87.

44. Nguyen Cao Ky, *Twenty Years and Twenty Days* (New York: Stein and Day, 1976), pp. 34–35. Later retitled *Why We Lost the Vietnam War.*

45. Robin Moore, *The Green Berets* (New York: Crown, 1965), pp. 174–75.

46. Ky, *Twenty Years,* pp. 35–36.

47. *Gravel,* 2, pp. 734–35.

48. *Gravel,* 2, p. 735.

49. *Gravel,* 2, pp. 738–39.

50. *Public Papers of the Presidents, Kennedy, 1963,* p. 673. Cited in *Gravel,* 2, p. 828.

51. *Gov't PP,* 11, pp. 554–59 (*passim*).

52. *Gravel,* 2, pp. 770–73.

53. Sheehan, Neil, *The Pentagon Papers as Published by The New York Times* (New York: Bantam, 1971), pp. 217–13. Hereafter cited as *NYT PP.*

54. *NYT PP,* p. 219.

55. *NYT PP,* pp. 224–26.

56. *NYT PP,* pp. 226–29.

57. *Gravel,* 2, pp. 792–93.

58. Thomas Fleming, *Officers' Wives* (Garden City, N.Y.: Doubleday, 1981), pp. 437–48, 440–45.

59. Fleming, *Wives,* pp. 450–53.

60. Ky, *Twenty Years,* pp. 41–42.

ACT II

1. Declassified document quoted in Porter, *Vietnam,* 2, p. 234.

2. Barbara Garson, *MacBird* (New York: Grove Press, 1967), pp. 54–55.

3. *Viet-Nam Documents and Research Notes,* Document No. 96, July 1971.

4. *Gravel,* 3, pp. 150–51.

5. Jim G. Lucas, *Dateline: Vietnam* (New York: Award House, 1966), pp. 41–44.

6. Anonymous. Courtesy of Mark Berent.

7. *Gravel,* 3, p. 160.

8. *Gravel,* 3, p. 511.

9. Moore, *Berets,* pp. 192–95.

10. Foreign Broadcast Information Service (FBIS), Far East, 3 August 1964. Cited in Porter, *Vietnam,* 2, pp. 301–2.

11. *Gravel,* 5, pp. 323–29.

12. *Congressional Record, Senate* (August 5, 1964).

13. Department of State *Bulletin* (August 24, 1964).

14. *NYT PP,* pp. 289–91.

15. *Gravel,* 3, pp. 537–38.

16. *Gov't PP,* 12, VI. B., p. 111.

17. *Gravel,* 3, pp. 576–77.

18. *Gravel,* 3, pp. 666–67.

19. Lucas, *Dateline,* pp. 152–53.

20. Bo Hathaway, *A World of Hurt* (New York: Taplinger, 1981), pp. 192–94.

21. Dick Shea, *Vietnam Simply* (Coronado, Calif.: The Pro Tem Publishers, 1967), unpaginated.

22. *Gravel,* 3, pp. 686–87.

23. Shea, *Vietnam,* n.p.

24. *Gravel,* 3, p. 686.

25. Robert Bly, ed., *A Poetry Reading Against the War in Vietnam* (Madison, Minn.: The Sixties Press, 1966), pp. 28–29.

26. *Gravel,* 3, pp. 271–72.

27. Major A. J. C. Lavalle, ed., *The Tale of Two Bridges and the Battle for the Skies over North Vietnam,* U.S.A.F. Southeast Asia Monograph Series, Volume I (Washington, D.C.: U.S. Government Printing Office, 1976), p. 4. Hereafter cited as USAF *Tale.*

28. Porter, *Vietnam,* 2, pp. 363–64.

29. *Gravel,* 3, p. 423.

30. Shea, *Vietnam,* n.p.

31. *Gravel,* 3, p. 426.

32. *Gravel,* 3, p. 695.

33. *Gravel,* 3, p. 465.

34. USAF *Tale,* pp. 31–38.

35. Office of Air Force History, Bolling AFB, Washington, D.C. Project CHECO microfilm. Document declassified, June, 1982.

36. USAF *Tale,* pp. 39–40.

37. Quoted in M. S. Aroni, *The Minority of One,* VII, 6 (June, 1965).

38. Department of State *Bulletin,* April 26, 1965, p. 607.

39. Walter Lowenfels, ed., *Where Is Vietnam? American Poets Respond* (Garden City, N.Y.: Doubleday, 1967), p. 138.

40. *Gov't PP,* 12, IV. B., p. 136.

41. Lowenfels, *Vietnam?* p. 130.

42. Interview, Captain (U.S.A.F.) John S. Lynch, May, 1965, Republic of Vietnam. Office of USAF History, Bolling Air Force Base, Washington, D.C. Project CHECO microfilm.

43. *Gov't PP,* 12, IV. B., p. 119.

44. Jack Shulimson and Major (U.S.M.C.) Charles M. Johnson, *U.S. Marines in Vietnam: The Landing and the Buildup, 1965* (Washington, D.C.: HQUSMC, 1978), p. 57.

45. *Gravel,* 4, pp. 615–16.

46. *Gravel,* 2, pp. 516–17, 530–31.

47. Working draft, *U.S. Marines in Vietnam . . . 1965,* Office of Marine Corps History, Washington Navy Yard, Washington, D.C.

48. *New York Times* (August 4, 1965), p. 2, col. 4.

49. *Diary,* Office of Air Force History, Bolling Air Force Base, Washington, D.C., Project CHECO microfilm. Used with author's permission.

50. *NYT PP*, pp. 489–90.

51. Used with author's permission. In possession of the editor.

52. *Gravel*, 2, pp. 545–48.

53. "Harrison E. Salisbury's Trip to North Vietnam," Hearing before the Committee on Foreign Relations, United States Senate, February 2, 1967 (Washington, D.C.: U.S. Government Printing Office, 1967), p. 24.

54. Bill Adler, ed., *Letters From Vietnam* (New York: E. P. Dutton, 1967), pp. 205–11 (*passim*).

55. Elaine Shepard, *The Doom Pussy* (New York: Trident Press, 1967), pp. 93–94, 102–103.

56. Quoted in Porter, *Vietnam*, 2, pp. 418–19.

57. Sexton, *Diary*, n.p.

58. Adler, *Letters From Vietnam*, pp. 151–2.

59. Sexton, *Diary*, n.p.

60. Document provided by the Pentagon.

61. Air Force microfiche RO 39, #10 of 12, pp. 2–5 of transcript.

62. "Giving to Johnson What Is Johnson's," Introduction to *A Poetry Reading Against the Vietnam War* (Madison, Minn.: The Sixties Press, 1966), pp. 5–7.

63. Bly, *Reading*, pp. 16–17.

64. USAF *Tale*, pp. 52–55.

65. Anonymous. Reprinted often without attribution.

66. *Gov't PP*, 6, C. 2, pp. 24–26.

67. Wallace, *Diary*, n.p.

68. Working paper, no classification. HQ 7/13 AF, Udorn RTAFB, Thailand, 7 November 1966, Office of Air Force History, Bolling Air Force Base, Washington, D.C., Project CHECO microfilm.

69. Pentagon debriefing, n.d., pp. 23–24.

70. *Gravel*, 2, pp. 595–97.

71. David Kraslow and Stuart H. Loory, *The Secret Search for Peace in Vietnam* (New York: Vintage Books, 1968), pp. 40–41.

72. Anonymous. Various versions exist in individual unit songbooks.

73. Alan Clark, *The Lion Heart* (New York: William Morrow, 1969), pp. 65–66.

74. Steven Smith, *American Boys* (New York: G.P. Putnam's, 1975), pp. 406–409.

75. Clark, *Lion Heart*, pp. 112–14.

76. *Gov't PP*, 13, IV. B., pp. 45–46.

77. Reproduced in *Senate Republican Policy Committee Report—The War in Vietnam*. Congressional Record, Senate, May 9, 1967.

78. USAF *Tale*, pp. 57–59.

79. William Westmoreland, *A Soldier Reports* (Garden City, N.Y.: Doubleday, 1976), pp. 215–16.

80. Derek Maitland, *The Only War We've Got* (New York: William Morrow, 1970), pp. 132–35.

81. Larry Heinemann, *Close Quarters* (New York: Farrar, Straus, and Giroux, 1977), pp. 17–22.

82. "Hanoi in My Time," *Washington Quarterly* (Spring 1981) pp. 5–9.

83. Robert Roth, *Sand in the Wind* (Boston: Little, Brown, 1973), pp. 3–5.

84. Holograph transcription, no classification, Office of Air Force History, Bolling AFB, Washington, D.C., Project CHECO microfilm.

85. Heinemann, *Close Quarters,* pp. 105–11.

86. James Trowbridge, *Easy Victories* (Boston: Houghton Mifflin, 1973), pp. 14–17, 22–23.

87. *Letters to Dorothy Weik* (ms.). By permission of the author.

88. Trowbridge, *Victories,* pp. 49–51.

89. *Gravel,* 2, pp. 508–509.

90. Colvin, "Hanoi," n.p.

91. John Cassidy, *A Station in the Delta* (New York: Scribners, 1979), pp. 6–8.

92. *Letters,* as dated.

93. William Pelfrey, *The Big V* (New York: Liveright, 1972), pp. 13–19.

94. *Letters,* as dated.

95. Michael Herr, *Dispatches* (New York: Alfred A. Knopf, 1977), pp. 89–91.

96. Department of State *Bulletin,* December 11, 1967, pp. 786–88.

97. William Eastlake, *The Bamboo Bed* (New York: Simon & Schuster, 1969), pp. 247–48.

98. Trowbridge, *Victories,* pp. 88–93.

99. Quang Tri Senior Advisor, *I Corps MACCORDS Provincial Report,* December, 1967, pp. 1, 4.

100. *Gravel,* 2, pp. 505–506.

101. Trowbridge, *Victories,* pp. 106–107.

102. Heinemann, *Close Quarters,* pp. 228–34, 247–49.

103. *USMC in Vietnam,* p. 97.

104. Office of Air Force History, Bolling AFB, Washington, D.C., Project CHECO microfilm. Declassified under GP-4 (12 years).

105. Cassidy, *Station,* pp. 270–74.

106. Hugh Atkinson, *The Most Savage Animal* (London: Rupert Hart-Davis, 1972), pp. 145–47.

107. Office of Air Force History, Bolling AFB, Washington, D.C., Project CHECO microfilm. Declassified under GP-4 (12 years); also by Secretary of the Army.

ACT III

1. Ltc. (RVNA) Pham Van Son and others, *The Viet Cong TET Offensive (1968),* trans. J5/JGS Translation Board (Saigon: P + P Center, RVNAF, July 1, 1969), pp. 30–31. Hereafter cited as RVNAF, *TET.*

2. Map based on drawing in RVNAF, *TET,* p. 21.

3. Fleming, *Officers' Wives,* pp. 522–24.

4. RVNAF, *TET,* pp. 327–28.

5. *Letters,* as dated.

6. Michael Herr, *Dispatches* (New York: Knopf, 1977), pp. 76–77.

7. RVNAF *TET,* pp. 273–74, 276–77.

8. Gustav Hasford, *The Short-Timers* (New York: Harper & Row, 1979), pp. 106–107.

9. *Letters,* as dated.

10. Declassified JCS Memo, 12 February 1968, Porter, *Vietnam,* 2, pp. 498–500.

11. *Letters,* as dated.

12. *The Gulf of Tonkin Incidents,* Hearings before the Committee on Foreign

Relations, U.S. Senate, 20 February 1968 (Washington, D.C.: U.S. Government Printing Office, 1968), pp. 20–21, 22–25.

13. W.D. Ehrhart, *The Awkward Silence* (Stafford, Va.: Northwoods Press, 1980), p. 22.

14. *Letters,* as dated.

15. Herr, *Dispatches,* pp. 118–21.

16. Cassidy, *Delta,* pp. 324–27.

17. Lao Dong Party Central Committee, *Forty Years of Party Activity.* Hanoi: Nhan Dang, 12–19 January, 1970. *Viet-Nam Documents and Research Notes,* Saigon, March, 1970, pp. 88–89.

18. Letter to Deputy for CORDS, 3 March 1968, *MACCORDS Provincial Reports* for February, 1968 (Washington, D.C.: Center for Military History).

19. Loan photo: reproduced courtesy of Wide World Photos.

20. Jan Barry and W.D. Ehrhart, eds., *Demilitarized Zones.* (Perkasie, Pa.: East River Anthology, 1976), pp. 122–23.

21. *Gravel,* 4, p. 576.

22. Arthur J. Dommen, *Conflict in Laos,* rev. ed. (New York: Praeger, 1971), pp. 294–95.

23. Arthur Everett and others, *Calley* (New York: Dell, 1971), pp. 51–56, 72–73. Hereafter cited as *Calley.*

24. Ehrhart, *The Awkward Silence,* p. 14.

25. Declassified document, Porter, *Vietnam,* 2, pp. 510–11.

26. Department of State *Bulletin* (April 15, 1968), pp. 481–86.

27. *Vietnam Intelligence Summary,* 30 Mar–5 Apr 68 (Saigon: 7AF, Tan Son Nhut AB). Project CHECO microfilm. Document declassified 1 May 82.

28. USMC *Vietnam,* p. 104.

29. *Letters,* as dated.

30. Herr, *Dispatches,* pp. 154–57.

31. William Huggett, *Body Count* (New York: Putnam's, 1973), pp. 73–75.

32. Jerome Klinkowitz and John Somer, eds., *Writing Under Fire* (New York: Delta, 1978), p. 211. Hereafter cited as *Writing Under Fire.*

33. Tim O'Brien, *If I Die in a Combat Zone* (New York: Delacorte, 1973), pp. 25–27, 29–31.

34. *Writing Under Fire,* pp. 213–14.

35. *Writing Under Fire,* pp. 219–20.

36. *Writing Under Fire,* p. 224.

37. Barry and Ehrhart, *Demilitarized Zones,* p. 73.

38. Quoted in Henry Kissinger, *The White House Years* (Boston: Little, Brown, 1979), p. 241. Hereafter cited as HAK, *White House.*

39. *Congressional Record,* May 10, 1972, pp. E4977–E4981. Porter, *Vietnam,* 2, pp. 522–29.

40. Msg., (C) Commander, 3rd Btn, 9th Marines to Commanding General, 3rd Marine Division, Subject: "Combat Operations After Action Report," 25 March 1969 (Washington, D.C.: USMC Archives). Document declassified, GP-4 (12 years).

41. Courtesy of Mark Berent.

42. Msg., (C) CINCPACAF to [various addressees], 15 Feb 69, Subject: "UPI Article—Souvanna Phouma." Declassified 6 May 82.

43. James Webb, *Fields of Fire* (Englewood Cliffs, N.J.: Prentice-Hall, 1978), pp. 49–52.

44. Anonymous parody, courtesy of Mark Berent.

45. Letter from Major (U.S.A.F.) Mark Berent, as dated. By permission of author.

46. HAK, *White House,* p. 247.

47. Msg., CO7AF to [various addressees], 27 Mar 69, Project CHECO microfilm. Document declassified 6 Mar 82.

48. O'Brien, *Combat Zone,* pp. 118–24.

49. Courtesy of F.T. Kiley.

50. *Background Information Relating to Southeast Asia and Vietnam,* 7th Ed. Rev. (Washington, D.C.: U.S. Government Printing Office, 1975), pp. 345, 346–47. Hereafter cited as *Background.*

51. *Betrayal, Samisdat #24,* no. 4 (1980) pp. 22–24.

52. Lao Dong Party, *Activity,* n.p. Translation courtesy of Historical Records Branch, Center for Military History, Washington, D.C.

53. *Background,* p. 573.

54. *Background,* p. 377.

55. Quoted in Porter, *Vietnam,* 2, pp. 535–36.

56. HAK, *White House,* p. 310.

57. HAK, *White House,* pp. 271, 276.

58. Webb, *Fields of Fire,* pp. 341–43.

59. *Background,* p. 377.

60. Quoted in *Calley,* pp. 96–97.

61. Courtesy of Mark Berent.

62. Reproduced in HAK, *White House,* pp. 1480–82.

63. Reproduced in HAK, *White House,* p. 1482.

64. Paul Hoffman, *Moratorium: An American Protest* (New York: Tower Publications, 1970), pp. 34–38.

65. Reproduced in Hoffman, *Moratorium,* pp. 65–67.

66. Hoffman, *Moratorium,* pp. 174–75, 177–82, 188–91.

67. "Briefing on Vietnam," *Hearings before the Committee on Foreign Relations,* United States Senate, November 18, 19, 1969 (Washington, D.C.: U.S. Government Printing Office, 1969), pp. 98–99, 114.

68. Tape #26, Tracks 2 and 1. Vietnam War Literature Collection, Colorado State University. By permission of Colonel Preyss.

69. *Background,* p. 574.

70. JJR 1516 011470 (Saigon: 26 Jan 1970), Project CHECO microfilm. Document declassified 18 June 72.

71. Briefing notes, HQ7AF (Saigon: 15 Jan 70). Project CHECO microfilm. Document declassified 6 May 82.

72. HAK, *White House,* pp. 440, 444–45.

73. DOCO Contribution to Commander's End of Tour Report HQ7/13AF, Udorn RTAFB, Thailand, 1 Mar 70. Project CHECO microfilm. Document declassified under GP-4 (12 years).

74. *Background,* pp. 404–406.

75. HAK, *White House,* pp. 463–64.

76. John Clark Pratt, *The Laotian Fragments* (New York: Viking, 1974), pp. 223–26.

77. Project CHECO microfilm. Document declassified 6 May 82.

78. Donald Kirk, *Tell It to the Dead* (Chicago: Nelson-Hall, 1975), pp. 133–37.

79. Telex, Acting JCS Chairman Westmoreland to CINCPAC and COMUS-

MACV, 22 Apr 70. Reproduced in Porter, *Vietnam*, 2, pp. 390–92.

80. *Background*, pp. 411–13, 415.

81. HAK, *White House*, p. 511.

82. Document declassified by secretary of the army, May 1982.

83. *Writing Under Fire*. pp. 196–208.

ACT IV

1. HAK, *White House*, pp. 511–12.

2. Webb, *Fields of Fire*, pp. 404–10.

3. Walter McDonald, *Burning the Fence* (Lubbock, Texas: Texas Tech Press, 1981), p. 32.

4. Barry and Ehrhart, *Demilitarized Zones*, p. 155.

5. *Background*, pp. 418–19.

6. Msg., 7AF [Saigon] to All Commanders, Subject: "Air Operations in Steel Tiger," 10 Jun 70, Project CHECO microfilm. Document declassified 6 May 82.

7. By permission of the author.

8. *Background*, pp. 436–38.

9. Jay Boyer, *As Far Away as China*. Unpublished, pp. 77–84. Copy in Vietnam War Literature Collection, Colorado State University. By permission of the author.

10. No classification on document. Courtesy of Mark Berent.

11. Address, "Developing Vietnamese Military Science, 2 Sep 70, Saigon, *Viet-Nam Documents and Research Notes*, number 87, December, 1970, pp. 1, 3, 32.

12. *Background*, p. 574.

13. *Harper's* 248 (June 1974), p. 72. By permission of Mrs. Kingsley. Hereafter cited as *Harper's*.

14. *Viet-Nam Documents and Research Notes*, number 99 (Saigon: October 1971), quoted in Porter, *Vietnam*, 2, pp. 550–55.

15. *Harper's*, pp. 73–74.

16. Webb, *Fields of Fire*, pp. 373–78.

17. *Harper's*, pp. 76–78.

18. Charles Durden, *No Bugles, No Drums* (New York: Viking, 1976), pp. 132–37.

19. *Harper's*, p. 78.

20. Department of State *Bulletin*, April 12th, 1971, pp. 499–500.

21. *Harper's*, p. 78.

22. Fred Kiley and Tony Dater, eds., *Listen, the War* (Colorado Springs, Colo.: U.S.A.F. Academy Association of Graduates, 1973), pp. 2–3.

23. *Royal Lao Army*, p. 134–5.

24. Msg., 7AF [Saigon] to COMUSMACV, 18 May 71, Project CHECO microfilm. Document declassified 6 May 1982.

25. Kirk, *Tell It to the Dead*, pp. 48–51.

26. By permission of the author.

27. Msg., 8TFW (UBON) to 7AF (TSN), 4 Aug 71. Project CHECO microfilm. Document declassified 6 May 82.

28. Courtesy of Mark Berent.

29. Russell L. Meerdink, Province Advisor, Memo, JCS, Washington, 1 Sep 71, pp. 22–26. Document declassified by GP-4 (12 years).

30. Boyer, *China,* pp. 104–14.

31. Letter, 7 Oct '71. Courtesy of Mark Berent.

32. C.D.B. Bryan, *Friendly Fire* (New York: Putnam's, 1976), pp. 341–42, 346–48.

33. By permission of the author.

34. Anonymous. Courtesy of John Sutten.

35. *Commander's Digest,* Department of Defense (Washington, D.C.: April 6, 1972), p. 3.

36. Walter McDonald, *Waiting for the End,* unpublished. This chapter printed as a separate story in *Sam Houston Literary Review,* I, i (April, 1976), pp. 45–48.

37. Col. (U.S.A.F.) John A. Doglione and others, *Airpower and the 1972 Spring Offensive,* USAF Southeast Asia Monograph Series, II (Washington, D.C.: Office of Air Force History, n.d.), pp. 4–9.

38. Doglione, *Airpower,* pp. 31, 34, 35–43.

39. Major (U.S.A.F.) Paul T. Ringenbach and Captain (U.S.A.F.) Peter J. Melly, *The Battle For An Loc* (HQ PACAF, Project CHECO Report, 31 January 1973), pp. 16–17. Document declassified by secretary of the air force. Hereafter referred to as CHECO *An Loc.*

40. Doglione, *Airpower,* p. 43.

41. CHECO *An Loc,* pp. 24–27.

42. *Background,* pp. 646–47.

43. *Background,* p. 647.

44. USAF *Tale,* pp. 84, 79–81, 85.

45. CHECO *An Loc,* pp. 42–44, 46.

46. USAF *Tale,* pp. 85–86.

47. Hearing, Armed Services Subcommittee, House of Representatives (Washington, D.C.: U.S. Government Printing Office, 1972), pp. 6, 7, 38–9, 46.

48. CHECO *An Loc,* pp. 52–53.

49. Ron Kovic, *Born On the Fourth of July* (New York: McGraw-Hill, 1976), pp. 176–80, 182–84.

50. (U) "News Releases, Cambodia." Department of State Message to Southeast Asia Embassies, n.d.

51. Frank Snepp, *Decent Interval* (New York: Random House, 1977), pp. 6–7.

52. Department of State *Bulletin,* November 13th, 1972, p. 549.

53. Working paper (U), "Cambodia: An Overview of the War," n.d. Courtesy of Mark Berent.

54. Barry and Ehrhart, *Demilitarized Zones,* p. 71.

55. Telegram, Department of State to [SEA Embassies], "Briefing: Department of Defense" (22 December 1972).

56. USAF *Tale,* pp. 186–87.

57. John D. Evans, Senior Advisor, "Addendum," JCS Memo, IV Corps MACCORDS Provincial Reports (n.d.), pp. 26–29. Office of Military History, Washington, D.C., pp. 1–4. Document declassified 31 Dec 78.

58. Overview of the Military Situation in the Khmer Republic" (U.S. Embassy, Phnom Penh, 16 January 1973). Courtesy of Mark Berent.

59. *Viet-Nam Documents and Research Notes,* number 113, June 1973.

60. Snepp, *Interval,* p. 29.

61. Courtesy of Mark Berent. By permission of Rick Scaling, Rustic 09.

ACT V

1. *Background*, pp. 516–18, p. 522.
2. Map redrawn from Claude G. Morita, (S) *USSAG/7AF in Thailand (1973–1975): Policy Changes and the Military Role* (HQ PACAF: Project CHECO, Report 27 January 1979), Fig. 1. Hereafter cited as Morita, *USSAG/7AF*.
3. *Reflections on the Vietnam War* (Washington, D.C.: U.S. Army Center of Military History, 1980), pp. 116–18.
4. Map redrawn from Colonel (U.S.A.) William E. Le Gro, *Vietnam from Cease-fire to Capitulation* (Washington, D.C.: U.S. Army Center of Military History, 1981), p. 22. Hereafter cited as Le Gro, *Vietnam*.
5. *Background*, pp. 653–54.
6. Henry Kissinger, *Years of Upheaval* (Boston: Little, Brown, 1982), pp. 34–35. Cited hereafter as HAK, *Upheaval*.
7. Snepp, *Interval*, p. 50.
8. *Royal Lao Army*, pp. 150–51.
9. James Jones, *Viet Journal* (New York: Delacorte, 1974), pp. 23–25.
10. Snepp, *Interval*, pp. 59–60.
11. *Viet-Nam Documents and Research Notes*, number 115, September, 1973, pp. 4–10; 11–13. Quoted by Porter, *Vietnam*, 2, pp. 430–33.
12. HAK, *Upheaval*, pp. 318–19.
13. Jones, *Journal*, pp. 203–207.
14. By permission of the author.
15. Department of State telegram, Subject: "DOD Newsbriefing, 10 Apr 73" (Washington, D.C.: 11 April 1973).
16. By permission of the author.
17. James G. Lowenstein and Richard M. Moose, *U.S. Air Operations in Cambodia, April 1973*, A Staff Report for the Committee on Foreign Relations, United States Senate (Washington, D.C.: U.S. Government Printing Office, 1973), pp. 8–9.
18. By permission of the author.
19. HAK, *Upheaval*, p. 327.
20. Le Gro, *Vietnam*, pp. 51–52.
21. Morita, (S) *USSAG/7AF*, pp. 61–63. These pages are unclassified.
22. Kirk, *Dead*, pp. 94–99.
23. Snepp, *Interval*, pp. 92–93.
24. *Background*, p. 577.
25. Snepp, *Interval*, p. 93.
26. *Background*, p. 577.
27. Le Gro, *Vietnam*, p. 78.
28. Snepp, *Interval*, p. 107.
29. Map redrawn from Le Gro, *Vietnam*, p. 97.
30. Le Gro, *Vietnam*, pp. 135–36.
31. Le Gro, *Vietnam*, pp. 138–39.
32. Bernard Kalb and Marvin Kalb, *The Last Ambassador* (Boston: Little, Brown, 1981), pp. 18–21, 60–61.
33. Le Gro, *Vietnam*, p. 170.
34. Brigadier General (U.S.M.C.) Richard E. Carey and others, *Operation Frequent Wind* (HQ 9th MAB, U.S.M.C.: 5 August 1975), pp. 3–5, U.S.M.C. Archives, Washington, D.C.

35. Captain (U.S.N.) R. E. Kemble, Report to Commander, Military Sealift Command, Subject: "Vietnam Sealift Evacuation History," 24 July 75, pp. 2–3, Naval Historical Center, Washington, D.C. Hereafter cited as Kemble, *Report.*

36. *The Khmer Republic at War and the Final Collapse* (Washington, D.C.: U.S. Army Center of Military History, 1980), pp. 158–62.

37. Report, (S) *The Fall and Evacuation of South Vietnam* (HQ PACAF: Project CHECO Report, 30 April 1978), pp. 61–63. All pages quoted are unclassified. Hereafter cited as CHECO, *Fall.*

38. CHECO, *Fall,* p. 61.

39. Le Gro, *Vietnam,* p. 117.

40. Report, *Evacuation Operations Conducted in Cambodia, and Republic of Vietnam, March–April, 1975,* to Commander Seventh Fleet, 28 May 1975, pp. III—F-2 to III—F-4, Naval Historical Center, Washington, D.C. Document declassified 5 May 1982. Hereafter cited as Report, *Evacuations.*

41. CHECO, *Fall,* pp. 108–110.

42. HQ U.S.M.C. (Washington, D.C.: 12 April 75), p. 1. Document declassified 31 Dec 81. U.S.M.C. Archives, Washington, D.C.

43. Report, *Evacuations,* pp. 2–34 to 2–35.

44. CHECO, *Fall,* pp. 110–12.

45. Snepp, *Interval,* pp. 369–70.

46. Ky, *Twenty Years,* pp. 220–21.

47. Kalb, *Ambassador,* pp. 104–107.

48. Morita, *USSAG/7AF,* pp. 44–45.

49. Ky, *Twenty Years,* pp. 221–23.

50. CHECO, *Fall,* p. 112.

51. Kalbs, *Ambassador,* pp. 160–63.

52. Ky, *Twenty Years,* pp. 7–8.

53. Stephen Harper, *Live till Tomorrow* (London: Collins, 1977), pp. 68–71.

54. Kemble, *Report,* p. 13.

55. Harper, *Live,* pp. 71–75.

56. Map redrawn from Carey, *Frequent Wind,* p. 78.

57. Kemble, *Report,* pp. 14–15.

58. Carey, *Frequent Wind,* pp. 54–55.

59. Harper, *Live,* pp. 98–102.

60. Kemble, *Report,* pp. 94–96.

61. Harper, *Live,* pp. 102–103.

62. CHECO, *Fall,* pp. 52–53.

63. John Balaban, *Blue Mountain* (Greensboro, N.C.: Unicorn Press, 1979), p. 43.

64. *Royal Lao Army,* pp. 168, 175.

65. Snepp, *Interval,* pp. 572–73.

66. In Lowenfels, ed., *Where Is Vietnam?* (Garden City, N.Y.: Anchor, 1967), p. 30.

EPILOGUE

1. General Van Tien Dung, *Our Great Spring Victory* (New York: Monthly Review Press, 1977), pp. 257–61.

2. Steven Phillip Smith, *American Boys* (New York: Putnam's, 1975), pp. 354–58.

3. Ehrhart, *The Awkward Silence,* pp. 27–28.

4. Micheal Clodfelter, untitled work. Ms. in possesion of JCP. By permission of the author.

5. *Parade,* May 2, 1982.

6. *The Denver Post,* June 23, 1982.

7. The Fort Collins *Coloradoan,* July 8, 1982.

8. Reprinted by permission of Dreena Music, a division of RBR Communications, Inc. © 1981 Dreena Music, a division of RBR Communications, Inc. and Dan Daley Music.

9. Ms. poem, written after a party at JCP's house. By permission of the author.

BIBLIOGRAPHY

SPECIAL COLLECTIONS OF DOCUMENTS AND PRIMARY MATERIALS

UNITED STATES GOVERNMENT

Air Force: Two major document repositories exist, the first at the Office of Air Force History, Bolling Air Force Base, Washington, D.C., the second at the Alfred F. Simpson Historical Research Center, Maxwell Air Force Base, Montgomery, Alabama. Each location contains millions of microfilmed and hard copy documents, reports, letters, and messages. Although many items are now unclassified, individuals proposing in-depth research should apply for an access security clearance to the Magazine and Book Division, Office of Public Affairs (AFOP-MB), Office of the Secretary of the Air Force, Washington, D.C., 20330.

Army: The Historical Records Branch, Center of Military History, Washington, D.C., 20314, holds most of the pertinent documentation of the U.S. army's role in the Vietnam War. Most documents are in hard copy. Access to still classified material is extremely difficult because many documents hastily retrieved during the evacuation have not been catalogued as of 1984.

Marine Corps: The Archives Section, Marine Corps Historical Center, Washington Navy Yard, Washington, D.C. 20371, is the most compact and accessible U.S. military repository. Most of the U.S.M.C. materials have been declassified. In addition, on permanent display is the largest extant collection of Vietnam War paintings and drawings.

Navy: There are limited research possibilities at the Operational Archives Branch, Naval Historical Center, Washington Navy Yard, Washington, D.C. 20374. Even with a security clearance, one cannot examine materials without first asking for them.

Defense Department and Central Intelligence Agency: Although each of these organizations maintains a Historical Branch, scholarly access is virtually impossible. Researchers will be referred to the military agencies mentioned above.

(NOTE: Because of extremely limited space, researchers not on official U.S. government business are requested to make advance arrangements for access to any of the military archives.)

UNIVERSITY LIBRARIES

Colorado State University, Fort Collins, Colorado 80523. The Vietnam War Literature Collection of fiction, poetry, and drama depicting Americans at war in Indochina is the most extensive in the world. Access is by prior arrangement.

Cornell University Libraries, Ithaca, New York 14853. Two collections: Archives of Vietnam War Veterans and the John M. Echols Collection on Southeast Asia. The latter general collection is the largest extant and includes all genres and subjects published *in* and *about* Vietnam in all languages of the world.

Indo-China Project, Center for International Policy, 120 Maryland Ave. N.E., Washington, D.C. 20002. Documentation on Vietnam-related issues dated primarily after 1978.

Southeast Asia Resource Center, P.O. Box 4000D, Berkeley, California 94704. Transcripts of interviews, manuscripts, news clippings, dating primarily from 1971. Good documentation on Vietnam–Kampuchea (Cambodia) conflict, 1978–79.

University of Rochester, Vietnam War Collection, Rush Rhees Library, Rochester, New York 14627. Collections of letters written by veterans and others associated with the Vietnam War.

PUBLISHED BIBLIOGRAPHIES

Chen, John J. M. *Vietnam: A Comprehensive Bibliography.* Metuchen, N.J.: Scarecrow Press, 1973.

Clifton, Merritt, and others. *Those Who Were There.* Paradise, Calif.: Dustbooks, 1984. Annotated bibliography of poetry, fiction, and memoirs by Vietnam veterans. Many of the entries are written by the original authors.

Colonnese, Tom, and Jerry Hogan. "Vietnam War Literature, 1958–1979; A First Checklist." *Bulletin of Bibliography* (January–March, 1981). Lists some criticism and journalism as well as fiction, poetry, and drama.

Leitenberg, Milton, and Richard Dean Burns. *The Vietnam Conflict.* Santa Barbara, Calif.: ABC-CLIO, 1973.

Newman, John. *Vietnam War Literature.* Metuchen, N.J.: Scarecrow Press, 1982. Comprehensive, *annotated* bibliography of more than 250 novels, short stories, poetry collections, and plays about Americans fighting in Vietnam.

Smith, Myron J. *Air War: Southeast Asia,* 1961–73. Metuchen, N.J.: Scarecrow Press, 1979. Articles and studies. Also contains a listing of pertinent U.S. government 16 mm. films.

The Vietnam Era: A Guide to Teaching Resources. Washington: The Indochina Curriculum Group, 1978.

SERIES AND MULTIVOLUME PUBLICATIONS

The Pentagon Papers

Sheehan, Neil, and others. *The Pentagon Papers as Published by The New York Times.* New York: Bantam, 1971. A selection of documents interspersed with evaluative and chronological commentaries.

United States–Vietnam Relations: 1945–67. 12 volumes. Washington: U.S. Government Printing Office, 1971. The largest compilation, poorly indexed; some documents are difficult to read.

U.S.–Vietnam Relations, The Senator Gravel edition. 5 volumes. Boston: Beacon Press, 1971–72. Reprint of selections from the above, with some additional materials not officially approved for release. Index in volume 5. (NOTE: In order to consult all the documents that comprise *The Pentagon Papers,* one must examine *all three* of these versions. Each edition contains materials not present in the other two. Also, there are no similar compilations available by 1984 for the conduct of the war *after* 1967).

United States Air Force *Southeast Asia Monograph Series.* Montgomery, Ala.: The Airpower Research Institute, Maxwell Air Force Base, 1976 ff. A continuing series of monographs written from the U.S. Air Force's perspective about operations and tactics of the war. Information and titles may be obtained from the Office of Air Force History (above).

United States Army *Indochina Monographs.* Washington: The Center of Military History, 1980 ff. Ongoing series of monographs written by former senior officers of the Cambodian, Laotian, and South Vietnamese military forces. Interesting retrospectives on tactics, policies, and events.

The U.S. Marines in Vietnam. 9 volumes (proposed). Washington: History and Museums Division, HQ USMC. The first two volumes, 1954–64, 1965, have been published.

The Vietnam Experience. 14 volumes. Boston: Boston Publishing Company, Inc. Proposed complete history of the Vietnam War. First three volumes (to 1965) published by 1982. Competent general survey.

SELECTED INDIVIDUAL WORKS

Novels

Alexander, David. *When the Buffalo Fight.* Richmond, Victoria, Aus.: Hutchinson, 1980.

Anderson, Robert A. *Cooks and Bakers.* New York: Avon, 1982.

Anderson, William C. *The Gooney Bird.* New York: Crown Publishers, 1968.

Atkinson, Hugh. *The Most Savage Animal.* London: Rupert Hart-Davis, 1972.

Baber, Asa. *The Land of a Million Elephants.* New York: William Morrow and Company, 1970.

Bausch, Robert, *On the Way Home.* New York: St. Martin's Press, 1982.

Becker, Stephen. *Dog Tags.* New York: Berkley Publishing Corp. 1973.

Blacker, Irwin P. *Search and Destroy.* New York: Random House, 1966.

Boatman, Alan. *Comrades in Arms.* New York: Harper & Row, 1974.

Bosse, M. J. *The Incident at Naha.* New York: Simon & Schuster, 1972.

———. *The Journey of Tao Kim Nam.* Garden City, N.Y.: Doubleday & Co., 1959.

Boulle, Pierre. *Ears of the Jungle.* New York: Vanguard Press, 1972.

Briley, John. *The Traitors.* New York: G. P. Putnam's Sons, 1969.

Brooke, Dinah. *Games of Love and War.* London: Jonathan Cape Ltd., 1976.

Brossard, Chandler. *Wake Up. We're Almost There.* New York: Richard W. Baron, 1971.

Browne, Corrine. *Body Shop.* New York: Stein and Day, 1973.

Bunting, Josiah. *The Lionheads.* New York: George Braziller, 1972. Popular Library, 1972.

Buonanno, C. *Beyond the Flag.* New York: Tower Publications. 1981.

Burke, Martyn. *The Laughing War.* New York: Playboy Paperbacks, 1981.

Butler, Robert Olen. *The Alleys of Eden.* New York: Horizon Press, 1981.

———. *Sun Dogs.* New York: Horizon Press, 1982.

Butterworth, W. E. *Air Evac.* New York: W. W. Norton & Company, 1967.

———. *Orders to Vietnam.* Boston: Little, Brown and Company, 1968.

Cameron, Lou. *The Dragon's Spine.* New York: Avon, 1968.

Caputo, Philip. *Del Corso's Gallery.* New York: Holt, Rinehart and Winston, 1983.

Cassidy, John. *A Station in the Delta.* New York: Charles Scribner's Sons, 1979. Ballantine, 1981.

Certo, Dominic N. *The Valor of Francesco D'Amini.* New York: Manor Books, 1979.

Chandler, David. *Captain Hollister.* New York: Macmillan Publishing Co., 1973.

Chaplin, Gordon, *Joyride,* New York: Coward, McCann & Geoghegan, 1982.

Clark, Alan. *The Lion Heart.* New York: William Morrow and Company, 1969.

Coleman, Charles. *Sergeant Back Again.* New York: Harper & Row, 1980.

Collingwood, Charles. *The Defector.* New York: Harper & Row, 1970.

Corder, E. M. *The Deer Hunter.* New York: Exeter Books, 1978. Jove, 1979.

Crawford, William. *Gunship Commander.* New York: Pinnacle, 1973.

———. *The Marine.* New York, Pinnacle, 1972.

Crowther, John. *Firebase.* New York: St. Martin's Press, 1975.

Crumley, James. *One to Count Cadence.* New York: Random House, 1969.

Cunningham, Ben. *Green Eyes.* New York: Ballantine, 1976.

Davis, George. *Coming Home.* New York: Dell, 1975.

de Borchgrave, Arnaud and Robert Moss. *The Spike.* New York: Avon, 1980.

Del Vecchio, John M. *The 13th Valley.* New York: Bantam, 1982.

Derrig, Peter. *The Pride of the Green Berets.* New York: Paperback Library, 1966.

Dibner, Martin. *The Trouble with Heroes.* Garden City, N.Y.: Doubleday & Co., 1971.

Doolittle, Jerome. *The Bombing Officer.* New York: E. P. Dutton & Co., 1982.

Downs, Hunton. *The Compassionate Tiger.* New York: Popular Library, 1960.

Dunn, Mary Lois. *The Man in the Box: A Story from Vietnam.* New York: McGraw-Hill Book Company, 1968.

Durand, Loup. *The Angkor Massacre.* New York, William Morrow, 1983.

Durden, Charles. *No Bugles, No Drums.* New York: The Viking Press, 1976, Charter, 1978.

Eastlake, William. *The Bamboo Bed.* New York: Simon & Schuster, 1969.

Edgar, Ken. *As If.* Englewood Cliffs, N.J.: Prentice Hall, 1973.

Faherty, Pat. *The Fastest Truck in Vietnam.* San Francisco, Calif.: Pull/Press, 1983.

Field, Della. *Vietnam Nurse.* New York: Avon, 1966.

Fleming, Thomas. *Officers' Wives.* Garden City, N.Y.: Doubleday & Company, 1981.

Ford, Daniel. *Incident at Muc Wa.* Garden City, N.Y.: Doubleday & Company, 1967. Pyramid, 1968.

Ford, Richard. *The Ultimate Good Luck.* Boston, Mass.: Houghton Mifflin Co., 1981.

Gangemi, Kenneth. *The Interceptor Pilot.* London: Marion Boyars, 1980.

Garfield, Brian. *The Last Bridge.* New York: David McKay Company, 1966.

Giovanitti, Len. *The Man Who Won the Medal of Honor.* New York: Random House, 1973.

Graham, Gail. *Cross-fire.* New York: Pantheon Books, 1972.

Graves, Richard. *Rolling Thunder.* New York: Pocket Books, 1977.

Grey, Anthony. *Saigon.* Boston: Little, Brown and Company, 1982.

Groom, Winston. *Better Times Than These.* New York: Summit Books, 1978. Berkley, 1979.

Grossbach, Robert. *Easy and Hard Ways Out.* New York: Harper's Magazine Press, 1975.

Halberstam, David. *One Very Hot Day.* Boston: Houghton Mifflin Company, 1967. New York: Avon, 1969.

Haldeman, Joe W. *War Year.* New York: Holt, Rinehart and Winston, 1972. Pocket Books, 1978.

Harper, Stephen. *Live till Tomorrow.* London: William Collins & Co., 1977.

Hasford, Gustav. *The Short-Timers.* New York: Harper & Row, 1979. Bantam, 1980.

Hathaway, Bo. *A World of Hurt.* New York: Taplinger Publishing Company, 1981.

Heckler, John. *Safekeeping.* New York: G. P. Putnam's Sons, 1983.

Heinemann, Larry. *Close Quarters.* New York: Farrar, Straus, and Giroux, 1977.

Hempstone, Smith. *A Tract of Time.* Boston: Houghton Mifflin Company, 1966.

Hennesey, Hal. *Midnight War.* New York: Pyramid, 1967.

Hershman, Morris. *Mission to Hell.* New York: Pyramid, 1968.

Honig, Louis. *For Your Eyes Only: Read and Destroy.* Los Angeles: Charles Publishing Co., 1972. New York: Bantam, 1973.

Huggett, William Turner. *Body Count.* New York: G. P. Putnam's Sons, 1973. Dell, 1978.

Hughes, Frank. *Everyday Heroes.* Norwalk, Conn.: Tower Books, 1982.

Hunter, Evan. *Sons.* Garden City, N.Y.: Doubleday & Company, 1969.

Hynd, Noel. *Revenge.* New York: The Dial Press, 1976. Dell, 1978.

James, Allston. *Attic Light.* Santa Barbara, Calif.: Capra Press, 1979.

Joss, John. *Sierra Sierra.* New York: William Morrow and Company, 1978.

Just, Ward. *In the City of Fear.* New York: The Viking Press, 1982.

———. *Stringer.* Boston: Little, Brown and Company, 1974.

Kaiko, Takeshi. *Into A Black Sun.* New York: Kodansha International, 1980.

Kalb, Bernard, and Marvin Kalb. *The Last Ambassador.* Boston: Little, Brown and Company, 1981.

Karl, S.W. *The Last Shall Be First.* New York: Manor Books, 1978.

Kauffman, Joel. *The Weight.* Scottsdale, Penn.: Herald Press, 1983.

Kempley, Walter. *The Invaders.* New York: Dell, 1979.

Kinary, Philip. *The Monk and The Marines.* New York: Bantam, 1974.

Kirkwood, James. *Some Kind of Hero.* New York: Thomas Y. Crowell Company, 1975. New American Library, 1976.

Klose, Kevin, and Philip A. McCombs. *The Typhoon Shipments.* New York: W. W. Norton & Company, 1974.

Kolpacoff, Victor. *The Prisoners of Quai Dong.* New York: New American Library, 1967.

Krueger, Carl. *Wings of the Tiger.* New York: Frederick Fell, 1966.

Larson, Charles. *The Chinese Game*. Philadelphia: J. B. Lippincott Company, 1969.

Larteguy, Jean. *Yellow Fever*. New York: E.P Dutton, 1965.

Lederer, William J., and Eugene Burdick. *Sarkhan*. New York: McGraw-Hill Book Company, 1965. Also published as *The Deceptive American*.

———. *The Ugly American*. New York: W. W. Norton & Company, 1958.

Lee, Larry. *American Eagle: The Story of A Navajo Vietnam Veteran*. Madrid, N.M.: Packrat Press, 1977.

Littell, Robert. *Sweet Reason*. Boston: Houghton Mifflin Company, 1974. New York: Popular Library, 1976.

Little, Loyd. *Parthian Shot*. New York: The Viking Press, 1975.

Louang, Phou. *The Men of Company 97*. Hanoi: Neo Lao Haksat Publications, 1971.

McCarry, Charles. *The Tears of Autumn*. New York: Saturday Review Press, 1975.

McMahon, Thomas P. *Jink*. New York: Simon and Schuster, 1971.

McQuinn, Donald E. *Targets*. New York: Macmillan Publishing Co., 1980.

Magnuson, Teodore. *A Small Gust of Wind*. New York: Bobbs-Merrill, 1980.

Mailer, Norman. *Why Are We in Vietnam?* New York: G. P. Putnam's Sons, 1967.

Maitland, Derek. *The Only War We've Got*. New York: William Morrow and Company, 1970.

Martin, Ian Kennedy. *Rekill*. New York: G. P. Putnam's Sons, 1977.

Mason, Robert. *Chickenhawk*. New York: The Viking Press, 1983. Penguin, 1984.

Meiring, Desmond. *The Brinkman*. Boston, Mass.: Houghton Mifflin Co., 1965.

Meyer, Nicholas. *Target Practice*. New York: Pinnacle Books, 1974.

Meyer, Ted. *Body Count*. New York: Exposition Press, 1982.

Miller, Kenn. *Tiger the Lurp Dog*. Boston, Mass.: Little Brown and Co., 1983.

Moore, Gene D. *The Killing at Ngo Tho*. New York: W. W. Norton & Company, 1967.

Moore, Robin. *The Country Team*. New York: Crown, 1967.

———. *The Green Berets*. New York: Crown Publishers, 1965. Avon, 1966.

Moore, Robin, with June Collins. *The Khaki Mafia*. New York: Crown Publishers, 1971.

Moore, Robin, and Henry Rothblatt. *Court Martial*. Garden City, N.Y.: Doubleday & Company, 1971.

Morris, Jim. *Strawberry Soldier*. New York: Ace, 1972.

Myrer, Anton. *Once an Eagle*. New York: Holt, Rinehart and Winston, 1968. Berkley, 1977.

Nagel, William. *The Odd Angry Shot*. Sydney: Angus and Robertson, 1979.

Nahum, Lucien. *Shadow 81*. London: New English Library, 1976.

Naparsteck, M.J. *A Hero's Welcome*. New York: Norden Publications, 1981.

———. *War Song*. New York: Lesiure Books, 1980.

Nelson, Charles. *The Boy Who Picked the Bullets Up*. New York: William Morrow and Company, 1981.

Newhafer, Richard. *No More Bugles in the Sky*. New York: New American Library, 1966.

O'Brien, Tim. *Going After Cacciato*. New York: Delacorte Press, 1978. Delta, 1979.

Parker, Gilbert L. *Falcons Three*. New York: Vantage Press, 1978.

Pelfrey, William. *The Big V*. New York: Liveright, 1972.

Petrakis, Harry Mark. *In The Land of Morning*. New York: David McKay Co., 1973.

Pollock, J.C. *Misson M.I.A*. New York: Crown Publishers, 1982.

Pollock, Lawrence. *Xin Loi (Sorry About That) Doc!* New York: Vantage Press, 1971.

Porter, John B. *If I Make My Bed in Hell*. Waco, Texas: World Books, 1969.

Powell, Hollis C. *The River Rat*. Smithtown, N.Y.: Exposition Press, 1982.

Pratt, John Clark. *The Laotian Fragments*. New York: The Viking Press, 1974.

Proud, Franklin M. and Alfred F. Eberhardt. *Tiger in the Mountains*. New York: St. Martin's Press, 1976.

Riggan, Rob. *Free Fire Zone*. New York: W.W. Norton, 1984.

Rivers, Gayle, and James Judson. *The Five Fingers*. Garden City, N.Y.: Doubleday & Company, 1978. New York: Bantam, 1979.

Roth, Robert. *Sand in the Wind*. Boston: Little, Brown and Company, 1973. New York: Pinnacle, 1974.

Rowe, John. *Count Your Dead*. Sydney: Angus and Robertson, 1968.

Rubin, Jonathan. *The Barking Deer*. New York: George Braziller, 1974.

Sadler, Barry. *The Moi*. Nashville, Tenn.: Aurora Publishers, 1977.

Sanders, Pamela. *Miranda*. Boston: Little, Brown and Company, 1978.

Scofield, Jonathan. *Junglefire*. New York: Dell, 1982.

Sellers, Con. *Where Have All the Flowers Gone?* New York: Pyramid Books, 1982.

Shaplen, Robert. *A Forest of Tigers*. London: Andre Deutsch Ltd., 1958.

Silver, Joan, and Linda Gottlieb. *Limbo*. New York: The Viking Press, 1972.

Sloan, James Park. *War Games*. Boston: Houghton Mifflin Company, 1971.

Smith, Steven Phillip. *American Boys*. New York: G. P. Putnam's Sons, 1975.

Sparrow, Gerald. *Java Weed*. London: Triton Books, 1968.

Spetz, Steven N. *Rat Pack Six*. New York: Fawcett, 1969.

Stone, Robert. *Dog Soldiers*. Boston: Houghton Mifflin Company, 1973. New York: Ballantine, 1975.

Stone, Scott C. S. *The Coasts of War*. New York: Pyramid, 1966.

Tauber, Peter. *The Last Best Hope*. New York: Harcourt Brace Jovanovich, 1977.

Taylor, Thomas. *A-18*. New York: Crown Publishers, 1967.

———. *A Piece of This Country*. New York: W. W. Norton & Company, 1970.

Teed, Jack H. *The Killing Zone*. New York: Zebra, 1983.

Theroux, Joseph. *Black Coconuts, Brown Magic*. Garden City, N.Y.: Doubleday & Co., 1983.

Thorpe, Stephen J. *Walking Wounded*. Garden City, N.Y.: Doubleday & Co., 1983.

Tiede, Tom. *Coward*. New York: Trident Press, 1968.

Trowbridge, James. *Easy Victories*. Boston: Houghton Mifflin Company, 1973.

Tully, Andrew. *The Time of the Hawk*. New York: William Morrow and Company, 1967.

Vaughn, Robert. *The Valkyrie Mandate*. New York: Simon & Schuster, 1974.

Vaughn, Robert, and Monroe Lynch. *Brandywine's War*. New York: Bartholomew House, Ltd., 1971.

Walsh, Patricia. *Forever Sad the Hearts*. New York: Avon, 1982.

Webb, James. *A Country Such As This.* Garden City, N.Y.: Doubleday & Co., 1983.

———. *Fields of Fire.* Englewood Cliffs, N.J.: Prentice-Hall, 1978. New York: Bantam, 1979.

West, Morris. *The Ambassador.* New York: William Morrow and Company, 1965.

Whittington, Harry. *Doomsday Mission.* New York: Banner, 1967.

Williams, Alan. *The Tale of the Lazy Dog.* London: Anthony Bland, 1970.

Williams, John A. *Captain Blackman.* Garden City, N.Y.: Doubleday & Company, 1972.

Wilson, William. *The LBJ Brigade.* New York: Pyramid, 1966.

Winn, David. *Gangland.* New York: Alfred A. Knopf, 1982.

Wolfe, Michael. *The Two-Star Pigeon.* New York: Harper & Row, 1975.

Woods, William Crawford. *The Killing Zone.* New York: Harper's Magazine Press, 1970.

Wright, Stephen. *Meditations in Green.* New York: Charles Scribner's Sons, 1983.

Short-Story Collections

Chung, Ly Qui (ed.). *Between Two Fires.* New York: Praeger Publishers, 1970.

Duncan, Maj. H. G. *Brown Side Out.* San Diego, Calif.: James H. Gregory, 1983.

The Fire Blazes. Hanoi: Foreign Languages Publishing House, 1965.

Henschel, Lee (ed.). *Short Stories of Vietnam.* Guthrie, Minn.: Guthrie Publishing Co., 1982.

Karlin, Wayne, and others (eds.). *Free Fire Zone.* New York: McGraw-Hill Book Company, 1973.

Klinkowitz, Jerome, and John Somer (eds.). *Writing Under Fire.* New York: Delta, 1978.

Mayer, Tom. *The Weary Falcon.* Boston: Houghton Mifflin Company, 1971.

Suddick, Tom. *A Few Good Men.* Samisdat, 4:1 (1974).

Tri-Quarterly, 45 (Spring 1979).

Poetry Collections

Baker, Richard E. *Shell Burst Pond.* Tacoma, Wash.: Rapier Press, 1980.

Balaban, John. *After Our War.* Pittsburgh: University of Pittsburgh Press, 1974.

———. *Vietnam Poems.* Oxford, England: Carcanet Press, 1970.

———. *Blue Mountain.* Greensboro, N.C.: Unicorn Press, 1982.

Barry, Jan, and W. D. Ehrhart (eds.). *Demilitarized Zones.* Perkasie, Pa.: East River Anthology, 1976.

Berkhoudt, John C. *Vietnam: A Year Before the "Peace."* New York: Carlton Press, 1975.

Berry, D. C. *saigon cemetery.* Athens, Ga.: University of Georgia Press, 1972.

Bly, Robert, and David Ray (eds.). *A Poetry Reading Against the Vietnam War.* Madison, Minn.: The Sixties Press, 1966.

Cantwell, James M. *Highway Number One.* Smithtown, N.Y.: Exposition Press, 1983.

Casey, Michael. *Obscenities.* New Haven, Conn.: Yale University Press, 1972.

Clover, Timothy. *The Leaves of My Trees, Still Green.* Chicago: Adams Press, 1970.

Connell, Robert. *Firewinds; Poems on the Vietnam War*. Sydney: The Wentworth Press, 1968.

Curry, Richard. *Crossing Over: A Vietnam Journal*. Cambridge, Mass: Applewood Press, 1980.

Di Prima, Diane (ed.). *War Poems*. New York: The Poet's Press, 1968.

Eastlake, William. *A Child's Garden of Verses for the Revolution*. New York: Grove Press, 1970.

Ehrhart, W. D. *The Awkward Silence*. Stafford, Va.: Northwoods Press, 1980.

———. *A Generation of Peace*. New York: New Voices Publishing Company, 1975.

———. *A Generation of Peace*. Samisdat, 14:3, 54th release, 1977.

———. *Matters of the Heart*. Easthampton, Mass.: Adastra Press, 1981.

———. *The Samisdat Poems of W. D. Ehrhart*. Samisdat, 24:1, 93rd release, 1980.

———. *To Those Who Have Gone Home Tired: New and Selected Poems*. New York: Thunder's Mouth Press, 1984.

Floyd, Bryan Alec. *The Long War Dead*. New York: Avon, 1976.

Gray, Nigel. *Aftermath*. Lancaster, England: Lancaster University Students' Union, n.d.

Gray, Nigel (ed.). *Phoenix Country*. Fireweed, 6 (September 1976).

Hanh, Thieh Nhat. *The Cry of Vietnam*. Santa Barbara, Calif.: Unicorn Press, 1968.

Hollis, Jocelyn. *Vietnam Poems; The War Poems of Today*. New York: American Poetry Press, 1979.

———. *Vietnam Poems II: A New Collection*. Upper Darby, Pa.: American Poetry Press, 1983.

Johnson, G. P. *I Was Fighting for Peace, but, Lord, There Was Much More*. Hicksville, N.Y.: Exposition Press, 1979.

Kiley, Fred, and Tony Dater (eds.). *Listen, the War*. Colorado Springs, Colo.: The Air Force Academy Association of Graduates, 1973.

Kilmer, Forest L. (ed.). *Boondock Bards*. San Francisco: Pacific Stars and Stripes, 1968.

Layne, McAvoy. *How Audie Murphy Died in Vietnam*. Garden City, N.Y.: Anchor Books, 1973.

Lowenfels, Walter (ed.). *Where Is Vietnam?* Garden City, N.Y.: Anchor Books, 1967.

McCarthy, Gerald. *War Story*. Trumansburg, N.Y.: The Crossing Press, 1977.

McDonald, Walter. *Caliban in Blue and Other Poems*. Lubbock, Texas: Texas Tech Press, 1976.

———. *Burning the Fence*. Lubbock, Texas: Texas Tech Press, 1981.

Martin, Earl E. *A Poet Goes to War*. Bozeman, Mont.: Big Sky Books, 1970.

Oldham, Perry. *Vinh Long*. Meadows of Dan, Va.: Northwoods Press, 1976.

Rottmann, Larry, Jan Barry, and Basil T. Paquet (eds.). *Winning Hearts and Minds*. Brooklyn, N.Y.: 1st Casualty Press, 1972.

Scott, L. E. *Time Came Hunting Time*. Cammeray, Australia: Saturday Centre Books, 1978.

Shea, Dick. *Vietnam Simply*. Coronado, Calif.: The Pro Tem Publishers, 1967.

Topham, J. (ed.). *Poems of the Vietnam War*. New York: American Poetry Press, 1980.

Drama

Balk, H. Wesley. *The Dramatization of 365 Days*. Minneapolis: University of Minnesota Press, 1972.

Berry, David. *G.R. Point*. New York: Dramatists' Play Service, 1979.

Cole, Tom. *Medal of Honor Rag*. New York: Dramatists' Play Service, 1981.

Garson, Barbara. *MacBird*. New York: Grove Press, 1967.

Gray, Amlin. *How I Got That Story*. New York: Dramatists' Play Service, 1981.

Kustow, Michael, and others (eds.). *The Book of US*. London: Calder and Boyars, 1968. Indianapolis: Bobbs-Merrill Company, 1968.

Rabe, David. *The Basic Training of Pavlo Hummel/Sticks and Bones*. New York: The Viking Press, 1973. Penguin, 1978.

Ribman, Ronald. *The Final War of Ollie Winter*. New York: CBS Television Network, 1967.

Terry, Megan. *Viet Rock*. New York: Simon & Schuster, 1967.

General Nonfiction

Acheson, Dean. *Present at the Creation*. New York: W. W. Norton & Company, 1969.

Adams, Nina S., and Alfred W. McCoy (eds.). *Laos: War and Revolution*. New York: Harper & Row, 1970.

Adler, Bill (ed.). *Letters from Vietnam*. New York: E. P. Dutton & Co., 1967.

Amter, Joseph A. *Vietnam Verdict: A Citizen's History*. New York: Continuum, 1982.

Archer, Jules. *Riot! A History of Mob Action in the United States*. New York: E.P. Dutton & Co., 1974. Hawthorn, 1974.

Arlen, Michael J. *Living Room War*. New York: The Viking Press, 1969.

Ashmore, Harry S., and William C. Baggs. *Mission to Hanoi*. New York: Harper & Row, 1972.

Asinof, Eliot. *Craig and Joan: Two Lives for Peace*. New York: The Viking Press, 1971.

Austin, Anthony. *The President's War*. Philadelphia: J. B. Lippincott Company, 1971.

Baker, Mark. *Nam*. New York: William Morrow and Company, 1981.

Barnet, Richard. *Intervention and Revolution: The United States in the Third World*. New York: World, 1968.

———. *The Roots of War*. New York: Atheneum, 1972.

Berman, Larry. *Planning A Tragedy: The Americanization of the War in Vietnam*. New York: W. W. Norton & Company, 1982.

Bernstein, Carl, and Woodward, Bob. *All the President's Men*. New York: Simon & Schuster, 1974.

———. *The Final Days*. New York: Avon, 1976.

Bloodworth, Dennis. *An Eye for the Dragon: Southeast Asia Observed: 1954–1970*. New York: Farrar, Straus, and Giroux, 1970.

Boettiger, John R. (Comp.). *Vietnam and American Foreign Policy*. Boston: D. C. Heath, 1968.

"Bombing in Cambodia," Hearings Before the Committee on Armed Services, U.S. Senate, 93rd Congress, First Session, July/August 1973.

Braestrup, Peter. *Big Story: How the American Press and Television Reported and Interpreted the Crisis of Tet 1968 in Vietnam and Washington.* 2 vols. Boulder, Colo.: Westview Press, 1976.

Brandon, Henry. *Anatomy of Error: The Inside Story of the Asian War on the Potomac, 1954–69.* Boston: Gambit, 1969.

Branfman, Fred (ed.). *Voices from the Plain of Jars.* New York: Harper & Row, 1972.

Brodie, Bernard. *War and Politics.* New York: Macmillan Publishing Co., 1973.

Brown, Weldon. *The Last Chopper: The Denouement of the American Role in Vietnam 1963–1975.* Port Washington, N.Y.: Kennikat Press, 1976.

Bryan, C. D. B. *Friendly Fire.* New York: G. P. Putnam's Sons, 1976.

Burchett, Wilfred. *Grasshoppers and Elephants: Why Vietnam Fell.* New York: Urizen Books, 1977.

Buttinger, Joseph. *A Dragon Defiant: A Short History of Vietnam.* New York: Praeger Publishers, 1972.

———. *The Smaller Dragon: A Political History of Vietnam.* New York: Praeger Publishers, 1958.

———. *Vietnam: A Dragon Embattled.* 2 vols. New York: Praeger Publishers, 1967.

———. *Vietnam: The Unforgettable Tragedy.* New York: Horizon Press, 1977.

Cairns, James F. *The Eagle and the Lotus: Western Intervention in Vietnam, 1847–1971.* Melbourne, Australia: Lansdowne Press, 1971.

Caldwell, Malcolm, and Lek Tan. *Cambodia in the Southeast Asian War.* New York: Monthly Review Press, 1973.

Center for Strategic Studies. *Economic Impact of the Vietnam War.* Washington: Georgetown University Press, 1967.

Chester, Lewis, and others. *An American Melodrama.* New York: The Viking Press, 1969.

Chomsky, Noam. *American Power and the New Mandarins.* New York: Pantheon Books, 1969.

———. *At War with Asia: Essays on Indochina.* New York: Pantheon Books, 1970.

Christian, George. *The President Steps Down: A Personal Memoir of the Transfer of Power.* New York: Macmillan Publishing Co., 1970.

Cohen, Warren. *Dean Rusk.* New York: Cooper Square Publishers, 1980.

Colby, William. *Honorable Men: My Life in the CIA.* New York: Simon & Schuster, 1978.

Collins, Colonel John M. *The Vietnam War in Perspective.* Washington: Strategic Research Group, The National War College, 1972.

Commission on the Causes and Prevention of Violence. *Rights in Concord: The Response to the Counter-Inaugural Protest Activities in Washington, D.C.* Washington: U.S. Government Printing Office, 1969.

Committee of Concerned Asian Scholars. *The Indochina Story.* New York: Bantam, 1970.

Cooper, Chester L. *The Lost Crusade.* New York: Dodd, Mead, 1970.

Corson, William R. *The Betrayal.* New York: W. W. Norton & Company, 1968.

Cortright, David. *Soldiers in Revolt: The American Military Today.* Garden City, N.Y.: Doubleday, Anchor Press, 1975.

Crowell, Joan. *Fort Dix Stockade: Riot and Demonstration.* New York: Links Books, 1974.

Dawson, Alan. *55 Days: The Fall of South Vietnam.* Englewood Cliffs, N.J.: Prentice-Hall, 1977.

Dellums Committee Hearings on War Crimes in Vietnam: An Inquiry into Command Responsibility in Southeast Asia. Edited by the Citizens Committee of Inquiry. New York: Vintage Books, 1972.

Denton, Jeremiah A. *When Hell Was In Session.* New York: Reader's Digest Press, 1976.

Dommen, Arthur J. *Conflict in Laos: The Politics of Neutralization.* Rev. ed. New York: Praeger Publishers, 1971.

Draper, Theodore. *Abuse of Power.* New York: The Viking Press, 1967.

Drury, Allen, and Fred Maroon. *Courage and Hesitation.* Garden City, N.Y.: Doubleday & Company, 1971.

Dung, General Van Tien. *Our Great Spring Victory.* New York: Monthly Review Press, 1977.

Ellsberg, Daniel. *Papers on the War.* New York: Simon & Schuster, 1972.

Emerson, Gloria. *Winners and Losers: Battles, Retreats, Gains, Losses and Ruins from the Vietnam War.* New York: Harcourt Brace Jovanovich, 1976.

Everett, Arthur and others (eds.). *Calley.* New York: Dell, 1971.

Fair, Charles. *From the Jaws of Victory.* New York: W. W. Norton & Company, 1972.

Fairlie, Henry. *The Kennedy Promise.* Garden City, N.Y.: Doubleday & Company, 1973.

Fall, Bernard. *Anatomy of a Crisis: The Laotian Crisis of 1960–61.* Garden City, N.Y.: Doubleday & Company, 1969.

———. *Hell in a Very Small Place: The Siege of Dien Bien Phu.* Philadelphia: J. B. Lippincott Company, 1966.

———. *Last Reflections on a War.* Garden City, N.Y.: Doubleday & Company, 1967.

———. *Street Without Joy: Indochina At War, 1946–54.* Harrisburg, Pa.: Stackpole, 1961, 1963.

———. *The Two Vietnams: A Political and Military Analysis.* New York: Praeger Publishers, 1967.

———. *Vietnam Witness, 1953–1966.* New York: Praeger Publishers, 1966.

Fanning, Louis. *Betrayal in Vietnam.* New Rochelle, N.Y.: Arlington House, 1976.

Fifield, Russell H. *Americans in Southeast Asia: The Roots of Commitment.* New York: Thomas Y. Crowell, 1973.

Fishel, Wesley (ed.). *Vietnam: Anatomy of a Conflict.* Itasca, Ill.: F. E. Peacock, 1968.

FitzGerald, Frances. *Fire in the Lake.* Boston: Little, Brown and Company, 1972.

Fulbright, J. William. *The Arrogance of Power.* New York: Random House, 1967. Vintage, 1967.

———. *The Crippled Giant: American Foreign Policy and Its Domestic Consequences.* New York: Random House, 1972.

———. ed. *Vietnam Hearings.* New York: Random House, 1966.

Furgurson, Ernest B. *Westmoreland, the Inevitable General.* Boston: Little, Brown and Company, 1968.

Galloway, John. *The Gulf of Tonkin Resolution.* Rutherford, N. J.: Fairleigh Dickinson University Press, 1970.

Gallucci, Robert. *Neither Peace Nor Honor: The Politics of American Military Policy in Viet-Nam.* Baltimore: Johns Hopkins University Press, 1975.

Gavin, James. *Crisis Now*. New York: Random House, 1968.

Gelb, Leslie H., and Richard K. Betts. *The Irony of Vietnam: The System Worked*. Washington: Brookings Institute, 1979.

George, Alexander. *Presidential Decisionmaking in Foreign Policy: The Effective Use of Information and Advice*. Boulder, Colo.: Westview Press, 1979.

Gettleman, Marvin, and others (eds.). *Conflict in Indochina: A Reader on the Widening War in Laos and Cambodia*. New York: Random House, 1970.

Gettleman, Marvin (ed.). *Vietnam: History, Documents, and Opinions on a Major World Crisis*. New York: New American Library, 1970.

Geyelin, Philip L. *Lyndon B. Johnson and the World*. New York: Praeger Publishers, 1966.

Giap, Gen. Vo Nguyen. *Big Victory, Great Task*. New York: Praeger Publishers, 1967.

Goldman, Eric F. *The Tragedy of Lyndon Johnson*. New York: Dell, 1969.

Goodwin, Richard N. *Triumph or Tragedy: Reflections on Vietnam*. New York: Random House, 1966.

Goulden, Joseph C. *Truth Is the First Casualty*. Chicago: Rand McNally, 1969.

Graff, Henry F. *The Tuesday Cabinet: Deliberation and Decision on Peace and War under Lyndon B. Johnson*. Englewood Cliffs, N.J.: Prentice-Hall, 1970.

Halberstam, David. *The Best and the Brightest*. New York: Random House, 1972.

——. *The Making of a Quagmire*. New York: Random House, 1965.

Hammer, Richard. *One Morning in the War: The Tragedy at Son My*. New York: Coward, McCann and Geoghegan, 1970.

Harvey, Frank. *Air War—Vietnam*. New York: Bantam, 1967.

Heath, G. Louis. *Mutiny Does Not Happen Lightly: The Literature of the American Resistance to the Vietnam War*. Metuchen, N.J.: Scarecrow Press, 1976.

Herbert, Anthony. *Soldier*. New York: Holt, Rinehart and Winston, 1973.

Herr, Michael. *Dispatches*. New York: Alfred A. Knopf, 1978.

Herring, George C. *America's Longest War*. New York: John Wiley & Sons, 1979.

Hildebrand, George, and Gareth Porter. *Cambodia: Starvation and Revolution*. New York: Monthly Review Press, 1976.

Hilsman, Roger, *To Move a Nation: The Politics of Foreign Policy in the Administration of JFK*. Garden City, N.Y.: Doubleday & Company, 1967.

Hoffman, Paul. *Moratorium: An American Protest*. New York: Tower Publications, 1970.

Honey, P. J. *Communism in North Vietnam*. Cambridge, Mass.: M.I.T. Press, 1963.

Hoopes, Townsend. *The Limits of Intervention*. New York: David McKay Company, 1970.

Horne, A. D. (ed.). *The Wounded Generation*. Englewood Cliffs, N. J.: Prentice-Hall, 1981.

Hubbell, John G. *P.O.P.* New York: Reader's Digest Press, 1976.

Humphrey, Hubert H. *The Education of a Public Man*. Garden City, N.Y.: Doubleday & Company, 1976.

Huyen, N. Khac. *Vision Accomplished: The Enigma of Ho Chi Minh*. New York: Macmillan Publishing Co., 1971.

Janis, Irving L. *Victims of Groupthink*. Boston: Houghton Mifflin Company, 1972.

Johnson, Haynes B., and Bernard M. Gwertzman. *Fulbright: The Dissenter*. Garden City, N.Y.: Doubleday & Company, 1968.

Johnson, Lady Bird. *A White House Diary*. New York: Holt, Rinehart and Winston, 1970.

Johnson, Lyndon B. *The Vantage Point: Perspectives of the Presidency*. New York: Holt, Rinehart and Winston, 1971.

Joiner, Charles A. *The Politics of Massacre: Political Processes in South Vietnam*. Philadelphia: Temple University Press, 1974.

Joint Hearings Before the Committee on Foreign Relations and the Committee on Armed Services, U.S. Senate, Eighty-eighth Congress, Second Session, August 6, 1964.

Jones, James. *Viet Journal*. New York: Delacorte Press, 1974.

Just, Ward. *Military Men*. New York: Alfred A. Knopf, 1970.

Kahin, George, and John Lewis. *The United States in Vietnam*. New York: Dell, 1969.

Kalb, Marvin, and Elie Abel. *Roots of Involvement: The United States in Asia, 1784–1971*. New York: W. W. Norton & Company, 1971.

Kalb, Marvin, and Bernard Kalb. *Kissinger*. New York: Dell, 1975.

Karnow, Stanley. *Vietnam: A History*. New York: The Viking Press, 1983. Penguin, 1984.

Kasinsky, Renee. *Refugees from Militarism: Draft-Age Americans in Canada*. New Brunswick, N.J.: Transaction Books, 1976.

Kattenburg, Paul. *The Vietnam Trauma in American Foreign Policy, 1945–75*. New Brunswick, N.J.: Transaction Books, 1980.

Kaufman, William W. *The McNamara Strategy*. New York: Harper & Row, 1965.

Kearns, Doris. *Lyndon Johnson and the American Dream*. New York: Harper & Row, 1976.

Kendrick, Alexander. *The Wound Within: America in the Vietnam Years, 1945–1974*. Boston: Little Brown and Company, 1974.

Kerry, John, and the Vietnam Veterans Against the War. *The New Soldier*. New York: Macmillan Publishing Co., 1971.

Kiley, Frederick T. *The Vietnam PW Experience*. Washington: U.S. Government Printing Office, 1985 (forthcoming).

Kinnard, Douglas. *The War Managers*. Hanover, N.H.: University Press of New England, 1977.

Kirk, Donald. *Tell It to the Dead*. Chicago: Nelson-Hall, 1975.

———. *Wider War: The Struggle for Cambodia, Thailand and Laos*. New York: Praeger Publishers, 1971.

Kissinger, Henry A. *A World Restored: The Politics of Conservatism in a Revolutionary Age*. New York: Grossett & Dunlap, 1964.

———. *White House Years*. Boston: Little, Brown and Company, 1979.

———. *Years of Upheaval*. Boston: Little, Brown and Company, 1982.

Knightley, Phillip. *The First Casualty*. New York: Harcourt Brace Jovanovich, 1975.

Kovic, Ron. *Born on the Fourth of July*. New York: McGraw-Hill Book Company 1976.

Kraslow, David, and Stuart H. Loory. *The Secret Search for Peace in Vietnam*. New York: Random House, 1968.

Krause, Patricia A. (ed.). *Anatomy of an Undeclared War: Congressional Conference on the Pentagon Papers*. New York: International Universities Press, 1972.

Ky, Nguyen Cao. *Twenty Years and Twenty Days* [*Why We Lost The Vietnam War*]. New York: Stein and Day, 1976.

Lacouture, Jean. *Ho Chi Minh*. New York: Random House, 1968.

————. *Vietnam: Between Two Truces*. New York: Vintage, 1966.

Lake, Anthony (ed.). *The Vietnam Legacy: The War, American Society, and the Future of American Foreign Policy*. New York: New York University Press, 1976.

Lansdale, Edward Geary J. *In the Midst of Wars*. New York: Harper & Row, 1972.

Lewy, Guenter. *America in Vietnam*. New York: Oxford University Press, 1978.

Lifton, Robert J. *Home From the War: Vietnam Veterans, Neither Victims Nor Executioners*. New York: Simon & Schuster, 1973.

Littauer, Raphael, and Norman Uphoft (eds.). *The Air War in Indochina*. Boston: Beacon Press, 1972.

Lodge, Henry Cabot. *The Storm Has Many Eyes: A Personal Narrative*. New York: W. W. Norton & Company, 1973.

Lucas, Jim G. *Dateline: Vietnam*. New York: Award House, 1966.

Lynd, Staughton, and Thomas Hayden. *The Other Side*. New York: New American Library, 1966.

Maclear, Michael. *The Ten Thousand Day War*. New York: St. Martin's Press, 1981.

Marchetti, Victor, and John D. Marks. *The CIA and the Cult of Intelligence*. New York: Alfred A. Knopf, 1974.

May, Ernest. *Lessons of the Past: The Use and Misuse of History in American Policy*. New York: Oxford University Press, 1973.

May, Ernest, and Janet Fraser (eds.). *Campaign '72: The Managers Speak*. Cambridge, Mass.: Harvard University Press, 1973.

McCoy, Alfred W. *The Politics of Heroin in Southeast Asia*. New York: Harper & Row, 1972.

Mecklin, John. *Mission in Torment: An Intimate Account of the U.S. Role in Vietnam*. Garden City, N.Y.: Doubleday & Company, 1965.

Michener, James. *Kent State: What Happened and Why*. New York: Random House, 1971.

Milberg, Major Warren H. *The Future Applicability of the Phoenix Program*. Alexandria, Va.: Defense Documentation Center, Cameron Station, May 1974.

Miller, William. *Martin Luther King*. New York: David McKay Company, 1968. Weybright, 1968.

Millet, Allan (ed.). *A Short History of the Vietnam War*. Bloomington, Ind.: Indiana University Press, 1978.

Miroff, Bruce. *Pragmatic Illusions*. New York: David McKay Company, 1976.

Montgomery, John. *The Politics of Foreign Aid*. New York: Praeger Publishers, 1962.

Morris, Roger, *Uncertain Greatness: Henry Kissinger and American Foreign Policy*. New York: Harper & Row, 1977.

Mueller, John E. *War, Presidents and Public Opinion*. New York: John Wiley & Sons, 1973.

Mulligan, James A. *The Hanoi Commitment*. Virginia Beach, Va.: RIF Marketing, 1981.

Neary, Jon. *Julian Bond*. New York: William Morrow and Company, 1971.

Nhat-Hanh, Thich. *Vietnam: Lotus in a Sea of Fire*. New York: Hill & Wang, 1967.

Nighswonger, William. *Rural Pacification in Vietnam*. New York: Praeger Publishers, 1967.

Nixon, Richard. *RN: The Memoirs of Richard Nixon.* New York: Grosset & Dunlap, 1978.

————. *The Real War.* New York: Warner, 1980.

O'Ballance, Edgar. *The Wars in Vietnam 1954–1973.* New York: Hippocrene Books, 1975.

O'Brien, Tim. *If I Die in a Combat Zone.* New York: Delacorte Press, 1973.

O'Neill, Robert J. *The Strategy of General Giap Since 1964.* Canberra: Australian National University Press, 1969.

Official History of the United States Air Force in Southeast Asia. Washington: U.S. Government Printing Office, 1977.

Paolucci, Henry. *War, Peace, and the Presidency.* New York: McGraw-Hill Book Company, 1968.

Patti, Archimedes L. A. *Why Viet Nam: Prelude to America's Albatross.* Berkeley, Calif.: University of California Press, 1980.

Payne, Robert. *Red Storm Over Asia.* New York: Macmillan Publishing Co., 1951.

Pettit, Clyde E. *The Experts.* Secaucus, N.J.: Lyle Stuart, 1975.

Pike, Douglas. *VietCong: The Organization and Techniques of the National Liberation Front of South Vietnam.* Cambridge, Mass.: M.I.T. Press, 1966.

————. *War, Peace, and the Viet Cong.* Cambridge, Mass.: M.I.T. Press, 1969.

Podhoretz, Norman. *Why We Were in Vietnam.* New York: Simon & Schuster, 1982.

Ponchaud, François. *Cambodia: Year Zero.* New York: Holt, Rinehart and Winston, 1977.

Porter, Gareth. *A Peace Denied: The United States, Vietnam, and the Paris Agreement.* Bloomington, Ind.: Indiana University Press, 1975.

————. (ed.). *Vietnam: The Definitive Documentation of Human Decisions.* 2 vols. Stanfordville, N.Y.: Earl M. Coleman Enterprises, 1979.

Powers, Thomas. *The War at Home: Vietnam and the American People, 1964–1968.* New York: Grossman, 1973.

Prouty, Fletcher. *The Secret Team: The CIA and Its Allies in Control of the United States and the World.* New York: Ballantine, 1972.

Purifoy, Lewis McCarroll. *Harry Truman's China Policy: McCarthyism and the Diplomacy of Hysteria, 1947–1951.* New York: New Viewpoints, 1976.

Randle, Robert F. *Geneva 1954: The Settlement of the Indochinese War.* Princeton, N.J.: Princeton University Press, 1969.

Raskin, Marcus G., and Bernard Fall (eds.). *The Vietnam Reader: Articles and Documents on American Foreign Policy and the Vietnam Crisis.* Rev. ed. New York: Vintage Books, 1967.

Reich, Dale E. *Good Soldiers Don't Go to Heaven.* Whitewater, Wis.: Garden of Eden Press, 1979.

Report of the Committee on the Judiciary on the Impeachment of Richard M. Nixon, President of the United States, 93rd Congress, August 20, 1974.

Roberts, Charles W. *LBJ's Inner Circle.* New York: Delacorte Press, 1965.

Roherty, James. *Decisions of Robert S. McNamara: A Study of the Role of the Secretary of Defense.* Coral Gables, Fla.: University of Miami Press, 1970.

Rostow, Walt W. *The Diffusion of Power: An Essay in Recent History.* New York: Macmillan Publishing Co., 1972.

Rowan, Stephen A. (ed.). *They Wouldn't Let Us Die.* Middle Village, N.Y.: Jonathan David, 1973.

Rutledge, Howard, and Phillis Rutledge. *In the Presence of Mine Enemies*. Old Tappan, N.J.: Fleming H. Revell, 1973.

Safire, William. *Before the Fall*. Garden City, N.Y.: Doubleday & Company, 1975.

Salisbury, Harrison E. *Behind the Lines: Hanoi, December 23, 1966–January 7, 1967*. New York: Harper & Row, 1967.

Santoli, Al (ed.) *Everything We Had*. New York: Oxford University Press, 1978.

Schandler, Herbert. *The Unmaking of the President: Lyndon Johnson and Vietnam*. Princeton, N.J.: Princeton University Press, 1977.

Schell, Jonathan. *The Time of Illusion*. New York: Alfred A. Knopf, 1976.

Schemmer, Benjamin F. *The Raid*. New York: Harper & Row, 1976.

Schlesinger, Arthur M., Jr. *A Thousand Days*. Boston: Houghton Mifflin Company, 1965.

———. *The Bitter Heritage: Vietnam and American Democracy*. Boston: Houghton Mifflin Company, 1967.

———. *The Imperial Presidency*. Boston: Houghton Mifflin Company, 1966.

———. *Robert Kennedy and His Times*. New York: Ballantine, 1981.

Schoenbrun, David. *Vietnam: How We Got In, How to Get Out*. New York: Atheneum, 1968.

Schurmann, Franz, and others. *The Politics of Escalation in Vietnam*. Boston: Beacon Press, 1966.

Scott, Peter Dale. *The War Conspiracy: The Secret Road to the Second Indochina War*. Indianapolis: Bobbs-Merrill, 1972.

Shadegg, Stephen C. *Winning's a Lot More Fun*. Toronto: The Macmillan Company, 1969.

Sharp, Admiral U.S. Grant. *Report on the War in Vietnam: Section I, Report on Air and Naval Campaigns Against North Vietnam and Pacific Command-Wide Support of the War, June 1964–July 1968*. Washington: U.S. Government Printing Office, 1969.

———. *Strategy for Defeat: Vietnam in Retrospect*. San Rafael, Calif.: Presidio Press, 1978.

Shawcross, William. *Sideshow: Kissinger, Nixon and the Destruction of Cambodia*. New York: Simon & Schuster, 1979.

Shepard, Elaine. *The Doom Pussy*. New York: Trident Press, 1967.

Sherrill, Robert. *The Accidental President*. New York: Pyramid, 1968.

Sidey, Hugh. *A Very Personal Presidency: LBJ in the White House*. New York: Atheneum, 1968.

Sihanouk, Norodom. *My War With the CIA: The Memoirs of Prince Norodom Sihanouk*. New York: Pantheon, 1973.

Skolnick, Jerome H. *The Politics of Protest: A Report, Submitted by Jerome H. Skolnick*. New York: Simon & Schuster, 1969.

Snepp, Frank. *Decent Interval*. New York: Random House, 1977.

Sorenson, Theodore. *Decision-Making in the White House*. New York: Columbia University Press, 1963.

Stavins, Ralph, and others. *Washington Plans an Aggressive War*. New York: Vintage, 1971.

Stevens, Robert Warren. *Vain Hopes, Grim Realities: The Economic Consequences of the Vietnam War*. New York: New Viewpoints, 1976.

Stevenson, Charles. *The End of Nowhere: American Policy Toward Laos Since 1965*. Boston: Beacon Press, 1972.

Stoessinger, John. *Crusaders and Pragmatists*. New York: W. W. Norton & Company, 1979.

Stratton, Richard. *Prisoner at War*. Garden City, N.Y.: Doubleday & Company, 1978.

Sullivan, Cornelius D. and others, eds. *The Vietnam War: Its Conduct and Higher Direction*. Washington: Center for Strategic Studies, Georgetown University, 1968.

Szulc, Tad. *The Illusion of Peace: Foreign Policy in the Nixon Years*. New York: The Viking Press, 1978.

Taylor, Charles. *Snow Job: Canada, the United States and Vietnam*. Toronto: Anasi, 1974.

Taylor, Clyde (ed.). *Vietnam and Black America: An Anthology of Protest and Resistance*. Garden City, N.Y.: Doubleday, Anchor, 1973.

Taylor, Maxwell D. *Swords and Plowshares*. New York: W. W. Norton & Company, 1972.

———. *The Uncertain Trumpet*. New York: Harper & Row, 1959.

Taylor, Telford. *Nuremberg and Vietnam: An American Tragedy*. Chicago: Quadrangle Books, 1970.

Terzani, Tiziano. *Giai Phong! The Fall and Liberation of Saigon*. New York: St. Martin's Press, 1976.

Thompson, James Clay. *Rolling Thunder*. Chapel Hill, N.C.: University of North Carolina Press, 1980.

Thompson, Sir Robert G. K. *No Exit from Vietnam*. London: Chatto & Windus, 1969.

Thompson, W. Scott, and Donaldson Frizzel (eds.). *The Lessons of Vietnam*. New York: Crane, Russak, 1977.

Toye, Hugh. *Laos: Buffer State or Battleground?* London: Oxford University Press, 1968.

Tregaskis, Richard. *Vietnam Diary*. New York: Holt, Rinehart and Winston, 1963.

Trewhitt, Henry L. *McNamara: His Ordeal in the Pentagon*. New York: Harper & Row, 1971.

Ungar, Sanford J. *The Papers and the Papers: An Account of the Legal and Political Battle over the Pentagon Papers*. New York: E. P. Dutton & Co., 1972.

U.S. Commission on the Organization of the Government for the Conduct of Foreign Policy. *Commission on the Organization of the Government for the Conduct of Foreign Policy*. June, 1975. Summary and vols. 1–7. Washington: U.S. Government Printing Office, 1975.

U.S. Congress, Senate, *Background Information Relating to Southeast Asia and Vietnam*. 6th rev. ed. Washington: U.S. Government Printing Office, June 1970.

———, Committee on Appropriations. *Supplemental Defense Appropriations Bill, 1967*. H. R. 13546, Senate Report no. 1074, 89th Cong., 2d sess., March 17, 1966.

———, Committee on Armed Service. *Air War Against North Vietnam*. Hearings before the Preparedness Investigating Subcommittee, 90th Cong., 1st sess., 1967.

———, Committee on Foreign Relations. *The Vietnam Conflict: The Substance and the Shadow. Report of Senator Mike Mansfield and Others*. 89th Cong., 2d sess., Committee Print, January 6, 1966.

————, *Conflicts Between United States Capabilities and Foreign Commitments.* Hearings, 90th Cong., 1st sess., with Lt. Gen. James M. Gavin, U.S. Army, ret., February 21, 1967.

————, *U.S. Involvement in the Overthrow of Diem, 1963.* Staff study based on the Pentagon Papers. Washington: U.S. Government Printing Office, July 20, 1972.

U.S. Department of Defense. *United States-GVN Relations.* 12 vols. Washington: U.S. Government Printing Office, 1972.

U.S. Department of State. *Aggression from the North: The Record of North Vietnam's Campaign to Conquer South Vietnam.* Publication 7339, February 1965.

U.S. Military Assistance Command, Vietnam. *1967 Wrap-up: A Year of Progress.* Saigon: U.S. Military Assistance Command, Vietnam, 1968.

U.S. President. *Public Papers of the Presidents of the United States: Lyndon B. Johnson, 1965.* 2 vols. Washington: U.S. Government Printing Office, 1966.

————. *Public Papers of the Presidents of the United States: Lyndon B. Johnson, 1967.* 2 vols. Washington: U.S. Government Printing Office, 1968.

————. *Public Papers of the Presidents of the United States: Lyndon B. Johnson, 1968–69.* 2 vols. Washington: U.S. Government Printing Office, 1970.

United States Department of Defense. *A Pocket Guide to Vietnam.* Washington: U.S. Government Printing Office, 1966.

Valenti, Jack. *A Very Human President.* New York: W. W. Norton & Company, 1975.

Vietnam Veterans Against the War. *The Winter Soldier Investigation: An Inquiry into American War Crimes.* Boston: Beacon Press, 1972.

Walton, Richard. *The Remnants of Power.* New York: Coward, McCann, 1968.

Warner, Denis. *Certain Victory: How Hanoi Won the War.* Kansas City, Mo.: Andrews and McMeel, 1978.

West, Richard. *Sketches from Vietnam.* London: Jonathan Cape, 1968.

Westmoreland, General William C. *A Soldier Reports.* Garden City, N.Y.: Doubleday & Company, 1976.

————. *Report on the War in Vietnam: Section II, Report on Operations in South Vietnam, January 1964–June 1968.* Washington: U.S. Government Printing Office, 1969.

Whalen, Richard J. *Catch a Falling Flag.* Boston: Houghton Mifflin Company, 1972.

White, Ralph K. *Nobody Wanted War: Misperceptions in Vietnam and Other Wars.* Garden City, N.Y.: Doubleday & Company, 1968.

White, Theodore, *The Making of the President 1964.* New York: Atheneum, 1965.

————. *The Making of the President 1968.* New York: Atheneum, 1969.

————. *The Making of the President 1972.* New York: Atheneum, 1973.

Wicker, Tom. *JFK and LBJ: The Influence of Personality upon Politics.* Baltimore: Penguin, 1972.

Williams, Roger Neville. *The New Exiles: American War Resisters in Canada.* New York: Liveright, 1971.

Windchy, Eugene C. *Tonkin Gulf.* Garden City, N.Y.: Doubleday & Company, 1971.

Wittner, Lawrence. *Cold War America: From Hiroshima to Watergate.* New York: Praeger Publishers, 1974.

Woodstone, Norma Sue. *Up Against the War*. New York: Tower Publications, 1970.

Yezzo, Dominick. *A G.I.'s Diary*. New York: Franklin Watts, 1974.

Zagoria, Donald S. *Vietnam Triangle: Moscow, Peking, Hanoi*. New York: Pegasus, 1967.

Zinn, Howard, *Vietnam: The Logic of Withdrawal*. Boston: Beacon Press, 1967.

THE VOICES

Grateful acknowledgment is made to the following for permission to reprint copyrighted material:

The Associated Press: "Navy Ships Fired On" from the June 23, 1982, issue of *The Denver Post;* and "Sihanouk Embraces Foes" from the July 8, 1982, issue of *The Fort Collins Coloradoan.*

Kenneth Babbs, Esq.: Manuscript journal, "Vietnam Vignettes," 1962. Copyright © 1984 by Kenneth Babbs.

John Balaban and Unicorn Press: Poem, "April 30, 1975," by John Balaban from *Blue Mountain.* Copyright © 1982 by John Balaban, published by Unicorn Press, P.O. Box 3307, Greensboro, North Carolina 27402.

Bantam Books Inc.: Selection from *The Short Timers* by Gustav Hasford. Copyright © 1979 by Gustav Hasford. First published by Harper & Row, Publishers, Inc. All rights reserved.

Mark Berent: Excerpts from letters, journals, diaries, and memorabilia. Copyright © 1984 by Mark Berent.

Robert Bly: "Giving to Johnson What Is Johnson's," Introduction to *A Poetry Reading Against the Vietnam War,* edited by Robert Bly and David Ray, published by the Sixties Press, 1966. Robert Bly's translation of "On the War in Vietnam" by Goran Sonnevi, from *A Poetry Reading Against the Vietnam War.*

M. J. Bosse: Selections from *The Journey of Tao Kim Nam* by M. J. Bosse. Copyright © 1959 by M. J. Bosse. All rights reserved.

Jay Boyer: Selections from *As Far Away as China* (unpublished) by Jay Boyer. Copyright © 1984 by Jay Boyer. All rights reserved.

Merritt Clifton: "When I Was Young" by Cathy Gigante from a *Samisdat* pamphlet, and "Betrayal" by Merritt Clifton from *Samisdat,* 24, No. 4, 1980.

Micheal D. Clodfelter: Memoir/essay by Micheal D. Clodfelter. Copyright © 1984 by Micheal D. Clodfelter.

Earl M. Coleman: Gareth Porter translations from *Vietnam: The Definitive Documentation of Human Decisions,* edited by Gareth Porter. Copyright © 1979 by Earl M. Coleman Enterprises, Inc.

William Collins & Sons Ltd. and *Stephen Harper:* Selections from *Live Till Tomorrow* by Stephen Harper. Copyright © 1977 by Stephen Harper.

Delacorte Press/Seymour Lawrence: Selections from *If I Die in a Combat Zone: Box Me Up and Ship Me Home* by Tim O'Brien. Copyright © 1973 by Tim O'Brien.

Delacorte Press and *Robert Gluckman:* Selections from *Viet Journal* by James Jones. Copyright © 1974 by James Jones.

Dell Publishing Co., Inc.: Selections from *Calley* by the Associated Press. Copyright © 1971 by the Associated Press.

Doubleday & Company, Inc.: Selections from *A Soldier Reports* by William C. Westmoreland. Copyright © 1976 by William C. Westmoreland.

Doubleday & Company, Inc., and *The Lantz Office, Inc.:* A selection from *To Move a Nation* by Roger Hilsman. Copyright © 1964, 1967 by Roger Hilsman.

Doubleday & Company, Inc., and *W. H. Allen Ltd.:* Selections from *The Officers' Wives* by Thomas Fleming. Copyright © 1981 by Thomas Fleming.

Richard B. Doyle: Entries from the personal diary of Richard B. Doyle. Copyright © 1984 by Richard B. Doyle.

Dreena Music, a division of RBR Communications, Inc.: The lyrics of the song "Still in Saigon" by Dan Daley. Copyright © 1981 by Dreena Music, a division of RBR Communications Inc., and Dan Daley Music.

Alan Dugan: Poem, "Notes Toward a Spring Offensive," from *Collected Poems* by Alan Dugan. Copyright © 1961 by Alan Dugan. Yale University Press, 1973.

Charles Durden: A selection from *No Bugles, No Drums* by Charles Durden. Published by Viking Penguin Inc. Copyright © 1976 by Charles Durden.

E. P. Dutton, Inc.: A selection from *Letters from Vietnam,* edited by Bill Adler. Copyright © 1969 by Bill Adler.

Jean Ebbert: "MIA?" by Jean Ebbert from *Listen: The War,* edited by Fred Kiley and Tony Dater (Colorado Springs: Air Force Academy Association of Graduates, 1973).

W. D. Ehrhart: "Coming Home," "Guerrilla War," and "A Relative Thing," from *The Awkward Silence* by W. D. Ehrhart. Copyright © 1980 by W. D. Ehrhart, published by Northwoods Press.

W. D. Ehrhart and Jan Barry: Selections from *Demilitarized Zones: Veterans after Vietnam,* edited by Jan Barry and W. D. Ehrhart, 1976, East River Anthology.

Farrar, Straus and Giroux, Inc., and *Curtis Brown Associates, Ltd.:* Selections from *Close Quarters* by Larry Heinemann. Copyright © 1974, 1975, 1976, 1977 by Larry Heinemann.

Roy G. Francis: Address given to the Hartford High School, Hartford, Wisconsin, June, 1970. Copyright © 1970 by Roy G. Francis.

David Halberstam: "Letter to My Daughter" by David Halberstam. Copyright © 1982 by David Halberstam. This selection appeared originally in the May 2, 1982, issue of *Parade.*

Harper & Row, Publishers, Inc., and *Brandt & Brandt Literary Agents, Inc.:* Selections from *In the Midst of Wars* by Edward Geary Lansdale. Copyright © 1972 by Edward Geary Lansdale.

Harper & Row, Publishers, Inc., and *JCA Literary Agency:* A selection from *The Chinese Game* by Charles Larson, published by J. B. Lippincott. Copyright © 1969 by Charles Larson.

Harper & Row Publishers, Inc., and *Benjamin Schemmer:* A selection from *The Raid* by Benjamin Schemmer. Copyright © 1976 by Benjamin Schemmer and Armed Forces Journal International.

Paul Hoffman: Selections from *Moratorium: An American Protest* by Paul Hoffman. Copyright © 1970 by Paul Hoffman.

Holt, Rinehart and Winston, Publishers, and *Paul Reynolds, Inc.:* Selections from *Vietnam Diary* by Richard Tregaskis. Copyright © 1963 by Richard Tregaskis.

Houghton Mifflin Company and *Andre Deutsch Ltd.:* A selection from *A Thousand Days* by Arthur M. Schlesinger, Jr. Copyright © 1965 by Arthur M. Schlesinger, Jr.

Houghton Mifflin Company and *Smith Hempstone:* Selections from *A Tract of Time* by Smith Hempstone. Copyright © 1966 by Smith Hempstone.

Houghton Mifflin Company and *the author's agent, Blassingame, McCauley & Wood:* Selections from *Easy Victories* by James Trowbridge. Copyright © 1973 by James Trowbridge.

Sam Houston Literary Review: "The Track" by Walter MacDonald from Sam Houston Literary Review I, No. 1, April 1976.

International Creative Management: "On the Perimeter" by Robert Chatain, from *Writing Under Fire* edited by Jerome Klinkowitz and John Somer, Dell, 1978. Copyright © 1971 by New American Review. From *The Only War We've Got* by Derek Maitland. Copyright © 1970 by Derek Maitland. Published by William Morrow. From *MacBird* by Barbara Garson. Copyright © 1967 by Barbara Garson. Published by Grove Press.

Kayak: Poem, "On A Clear Day," by Clemens Starck, from *Kayak 4.* Copyright © 1965 by Kayak.

Mrs. Fred Kingsley: Selections from "Letters Home" by Thomas Kingsley, which appeared in the June 1974 issue of *Harper's.*

Donald Kirk: Selections from *Tell It to the Dead* by Donald Kirk. Copyright © 1975 by Donald Kirk. Published by Nelson-Hall.

Bertha Klausner International Literary Agency, Inc.: A selection from *Red Storm Over Asia* by Robert Payne. Copyright © 1951 by Robert Payne. Published by Macmillan.

Alfred A. Knopf, Inc., and *Russell and Volkening:* Selections from *Dispatches* by Michael Herr. Copyright © 1977 by Michael Herr.